DESIGN GUIDE
TO THE 1991
UNIFORM BUILDING CODE

by

Alfred Goldberg, P.E., H.A.I.A.
CONSULTING ENGINEER

Third Edition

JOHN WILEY & SONS, INC.
New York • Chichester • Brisbane • Toronto • Singapore

Acknowledgements

Acknowledgement is gratefully made for the use of certain documents, as follows:

REPRODUCTION FROM THE UNIFORM BUILDING CODE, 1991 EDITION, COPYRIGHT © 1991, WITH PERMISSION OF THE PUBLISHER, THE INTERNATIONAL CONFERENCE OF BUILDING OFFICIALS.

"THE USE OF THE MATERIAL IN FIGURE 8-4 WAS ORIGINALLY PUBLISHED IN FIRE TECHNOLOGY MAY 1979 ON PAGE 109 AND IS PROVIDED WITH PERMISSION OF THE COPYRIGHT OWNER, THE NATIONAL FIRE PROTECTION ASSOCIATION.

"THE USE OF THE MATERIAL IN FIGURE 8-8 WAS ORIGINALLY PUBLISHED IN THE CARBOLINE SPECIFIERS' GUIDE IN 1978 AND IS PROVIDED WITH PERMISSION OF THE CARBOLINE CORPORATION.

"THE USE OF THE MATERIAL IN FIGURES 8-12, AND 8-13 WAS ORIGINALLY PUBLISHED IN THE 1984 BUILDING CONSTRUCTION DIRECTORY AND IS PROVIDED WITH PERMISSION OF THE PUBLISHER AND COPYRIGHT OWNER, UNDERWRITERS LABORATORIES INC."

Library of Congress Catalog Card Number 90-86363

ISBN 0-471-30391-7

This book is dedicated to my wife, Marilyn, whose inspiration and confidence sustain me and to my grandson Joe, from whom I gain the optimism that makes all things possible.

PREFACE TO THIRD EDITION

This third edition of the Design Guide incorporates the code changes of particular concern to the designer that were adopted in the past three years and that are a part of the 1991 Uniform Building Code.

The prior editions of the Guide have been very well received and accepted by designers and building officials as well as others associated with the building construction industry. Of personal satisfaction has been the acceptance and use of the Guide as a teaching tool by college and university staffs and by building officials. The Guide is increasingly being used both in the training of design professionals and in the preparatory studies for licensing contractors and other design professionals.

We have expanded some portions of the Guide in answer to requests from users. We have placed much of the technical backup material and discussions into Technical Appendices so that the main text relates primarily to the code provisions. To separate the author's opinion from the generally accepted understanding of provisions of the code, we have set these off by enclosing them in boxes.

We have placed asterisks in the Table of Code References to flag those parts of the Design Guide that were amended in the past three years. Flagged changes of particular importance are:

- New accessibility requirements all occupancies
- Protection of penetrations of fire-resistive assemblies
- Provisions for the elimination of parapets on exterior walls adjacent to property lines
- Provisions for a new residential division covering congregate housing
- Smoke detector requirements for all bedrooms
- Two-hour enclosures for stairways in four story buildings
- Low-level exit signs in Group R, Division 1 Occupancy hotel and motel exit corridors
- Vertical spread of flame barrier requirements
- Permission of Group A, Division 3 Occupancy over a garage as a separate building (as for Group B, Division 2 and R, Division 1 Occupancies)
- Design criteria for vehicle barriers in parking structures

My appreciation once again to Milton Ortega for his assistance in the drawings and cover design and to Sue Arnold for editing. A special thanks to John Raeber for his comments on my discussion of the new Chapter 31 accessibility provisions in Article 10.

Alfred Goldberg
Mill Valley, California
April 21, 1991

About the Author

Alfred Goldberg is a consulting engineer specializing in building codes, standards and construction. He received his Bachelor of Civil Engineering degree at City College of New York in 1945. Mr. Goldberg is an Honorary member of the American Institute of Architects and a Fellow of the American Society of Civil Engineers. He is a licensed Civil Engineer and Fire Prevention Engineer in the State of California.

In 1960 he was appointed as the Assistant Superintendent of the Bureau of Building Inspection of the City and County of San Francisco. In l968 he became Superintendent of that agency. During his years of activity in the Bureau of Building Inspection he was responsible for development of all code changes to the San Francisco Building Code. He completed three major code rewrites and transformed the format of the code to that of the UBC.

His 30 years of experience in the field of codes and standards has included participation in numerous national, state and local committees and organizations in that field. He served as a member of the General Design and Fire and Life Safety Committees of the International Conference of Building Officials, Chairman of the Ad Hoc committee that developed the high rise life safety provisions used in all model codes, Chairman of the American Society of Civil Engineers' national code committee, Chairman of the Task Group on Nonstructural Elements for the ATC-3 seismic recommendations, member of Underwriters Laboratories Inc. Fire Council,and a member of ASTM Committees E-5 on Fire Testing and E-6 on Building Construction.

He has written papers on various subjects of interest to the Building Official and has been a guest lecturer at the University of California at Berkeley and the University of Hawaii in Honolulu as well as at Bay Area AIA state licensing seminars. His present activities include participation in the ICBO code committees and in the San Francisco Chamber of Commerce code committee relating to the city and state codes.

He actively participates as a member of Underwriters Laboratories Fire Council and the American Society for Testing and Materials.

In 1976 Mr. Goldberg retired to private practice. He presently maintains a consulting practice through his office in Mill Valley, California.

TABLE OF CONTENTS

TABLE OF CONTENTS cont.

TABLE OF CONTENTS cont.

APPENDICES

TABLE OF CONTENTS cont.

TECHNICAL APPENDICES

TABLE OF CODE REFERENCES

* Notes that Section or Table was amended or added since 1988 UBC.

TABLE OF CODE REFERENCES cont.

TABLE OF CODE REFERENCES cont.

TABLE OF CODE REFERENCES cont.

TABLE OF CODE REFERENCES cont.

TABLE OF CODE REFERENCES cont.

TABLE OF CODE REFERENCES cont.

TABLE OF FIGURES

TABLE OF FIGURES cont.

TABLE OF FIGURES cont.

TABLE OF FIGURES cont.

TABLE OF FIGURES cont.

ARTICLE 1
BACKGROUND FOR THE READER

a) Presentation of Material in this Guide

This Guide is based on the 1991 Uniform Building Code (UBC).

The 1991 code text of a provision is followed by a discussion of the provision.

When only a portion of the UBC section's text is given in this Guide, the symbol ► ■■■ ◄ follows the code text to indicate that additional code text is not shown.

When a discussion is of a general nature and does not require the actual code text for reference therein, the symbol ► □□□ ◄ immediately follows the code section number and title.

Although the author has permission to reprint code provisions from the UBC, it should be clearly understood that the discussions of the code's intent and the interpretations of the provisions are solely those of the author. They do not necessarily have the support or backing of the International Conference of Building Officials (ICBO).

Certain of the technical material that was in the body of the previous editions of the Guide have been relocated into the Technical Appendix portion at the end of this Guide.

The purpose of the UBC is to protect the public by regulating the construction, alteration and maintenance of structures. The UBC establishes certain minimum criteria that define the code intent. The criteria set forth for accomplishing the code's goals are stated in specific language, because codes are legal ordinances adopted by government and are ultimately enforced by the courts. However, the code language is meant not to exact a specific method of meeting the code but to establish the code intent.

The emphasis in the discussions of the code provisions is on providing the reader with an explanation of the intent behind the provision. In some instances, historical precedent is used to establish this intent. In other instances, the established intent is represented as the author's opinion. In these latter situations, the opinion may be at variance with an ICBO position or may cover an item for which there is no formal opinion. When this is the case, the rationale for the opinion is provided so that the reader can formulate an independent judgment on the matter.

The modern approach to codes is to strive for performance rather than specificity. The reader is advised that there may be several different ways to meet a particular provision. Where it will help in clarifying a provision, sketches and diagrams are provided in this Guide. A description or diagram should not be viewed as the only solution but rather one of several possible solutions. Careful attention should be given to the reasoning provided in the interpretations, because understanding that reasoning can lead to other solutions to problems involving the particular provision.

The building code should not be used as one would use a dictionary or encyclopedia. The various provisions do not function alone, but together comprise part of a regulatory outline of public safety philosophy. Although many designers and others tend to use the code as a catalog of isolated requirements, doing so limits the design flexibility essential to many projects. Therefore, understanding the intent of the code provisions as a whole is a critical initial step in the process of properly applying the code.

The approach used in this Guide does not offer a section-by-section explanation of the UBC or an examination of set problems and their solutions in meeting a specific code provision. Instead it provides:

- overviews of the intent of the major design provisions,
- the background to the concepts involved where relevant to the explanation,
- examples of the types of solutions the designer might consider in meeting that intent.

When a particular provision of the UBC is discussed, the discussion also covers:

- the less obvious implications of the provision,
- how the provision ties in with the code concept being expressed.

The code changes adopted in the three years since the 1988 edition of the UBC, which are of importance to the designer, have been noted in the Table of Code References by an asterisk at section citation. The Guide text reflects whether this is a new provision or, where the section was amended, the effect of the change.

The reader should understand, in regard to Articles 3 through 10 of this Guide, that each Article presents an integrated discussion of the provisions of the particular chapter(s) of the UBC being reviewed. The discussion will provide the philosophy or intent of the code as represented by that chapter of the code.

An illustration of how one could relate to the code intent, instead of only the specific requirement, may help clarify the concept.

> **Example:** The code might require two buildings on the same lot to be separated from one another by 20 feet if both buildings are to have operable plain glass windows instead of fixed wired-glass fire windows. The intent is to prevent fire from spreading rapidly from one building to another, i.e., concern with the prevention of conflagration.
>
> It may be that only one building needs to have operable windows. The facing wall of the other building could have:
>
> - no openings in it
> - openings with fixed wired-glass windows.
>
> The distance between the buildings could be reduced to as little as 10 feet. For a detailed discussion on this matter, see Figures 5-9 and 5-10 and the analysis in Article 5 re: Section 504 (c).
>
> Another possible way of satisfying the code might be to equip both buildings with fire sprinkler systems not otherwise required by the code. These systems, along with an adequate water supply, can be accepted by the enforcement official as an alternative method of meeting the intent of the code in preventing conflagration by suppression of fire. That acceptance would allow a closer spacing of the buildings. The acceptance of alternative methods of construction will be discussed in more detail with regard to the provisions of Section 105.

Essentially, there are different ways to satisfy the code's intent. Knowledge and understanding of that intent provides the designer with the ability to choose a solution that will both meet the code and best serve the design.

Many building code requirements relate to the prevention of conflagration and the providing of structures in which the occupants are protected against the hazards of fire and panic. Besides the siting requirements for conflagration control, the building code also regulates the type of construction permitted based on the degree of life and property hazard a proposed use may present to the occupants and the structure.

There are many subjects addressed by the UBC; this Guide deals with the primary concerns of fire and panic. We will be examining these areas of concern through the following provisions of the code:

- Occupancy
- Height of building
- Areas of occupancy
- Separation between buildings and other properties
- Fire-resistive requirements
- Exiting

These subjects, contained in Chapters 5, 17, 33 and 43 of the UBC, will be given detailed discussion in Articles 5, 6, 7 and 8, respectively, of this Guide.

Requests for additional coverage of certain code provisions together with increasing numbers of code changes to other portions of the code that affect life safety and the designer have resulted in additions to the Guide. The Guide has been expanded in regard to the other Chapters of the UBC in Articles 9 of this Guide, which covers Chapters 7, 9, 12, 18 and 20, and Article 10, which covers Chapters 25, 31, 32, 37, 38, 52 and Appendix Chapter 31.

The structural, general construction and other provisions of the UBC will be discussed only as they relate to aspects of the design process that involve the primary concerns of fire and panic.

b) Model Building Codes in the United States

The background to codes in the United States, and to the model codes in particular, may assist the designer in understanding the development of the UBC provisions and the processes involved in amending that code.

The regulation of building construction in the United States is generally handled through a building permit process. This process establishes minimum construction criteria to protect life and property. These criteria are contained in various documents, primarily the building code. Other documents are supplemental to the building code and usually are used to establish the criteria for electrical, plumbing, mechanical, fire prevention, and elevator construction in buildings.

Building codes are normally enforced at the lowest level of government, i.e., the city or town. When enacted into law, these codes are legal documents in the same manner as are traffic laws and the multitude of other laws at the local or state level. In some instances, the building code enforced in a jurisdiction is one adopted by the state legislature and required to be enforced by the local government. The enforcement official may have any of a variety of titles ranging from building inspector to manager of a public safety department.

There has been a longstanding trend to reduce the number of differences among the various codes. The main method for doing this has been through the use of "model codes." A model code is a document developed by knowledgeable people in the field of that code's activity. It is reviewed and amended by a body of enforcement officials on an annual basis to keep it reasonably current with construction and design technology and materials.

The "model code" serves the same purpose as a model house: that of a complete and functional structure one views when planning to buy a new home. The model represents the home a buyer may wish to purchase rather than having an architect or builder develop drawings and then build a home to those specifications.

A "model code" is a complete document that can be adopted into law, by reference, without the jurisdiction having to write it. The term "by reference" means that a law or ordinance enacted by the legislative body need only refer to the name and edition of the code and need not print the code in its entirety.

The three model codes in general use in the United States are:

1. The Uniform Building Code (UBC) published by the International Conference of Building Officials (ICBO). This is the most widely used model building code in the United States. It is used by over 1200 jurisdictions in all parts of the country, and is almost the exclusive code west of the Mississippi. In some states it is the state code.

2. The Basic National Building Code published by Building Officials and Code Administrators International (BOCA). It is used primarily in the northeastern part of the country.

3. The Standard Building Code, published by the Southern Building Code Congress International (SBCCI). It is used almost exclusively in the southeastern part of the country.

A jurisdiction, which may be a town, city or state, adopts the code into law. That adoption may include amendments to portions of the code or simply be the code as written, since the code's form permits direct adoption. The jurisdiction also adopts into law the companion codes needed to provide a full range of regulations for construction. Except for the electrical code, these companion code documents are published by each of the model code bodies. The model electrical code most in use in this country is the National Electrical Code published by the National Fire Protection Association.

In addition to the codes in effect in a jurisdiction, state and federal laws also apply to building construction. Some but not all of these other laws may be enforced by the local enforcement official. These other laws include:

- OSHA regulations,
- environmental regulations,
- planning and zoning laws,
- energy conservation,
- security,
- handicapped and
- other special laws too numerous to list.

With the passage in 1990 of the Americans with Disabilities Act (ADA), the federal government has in effect mandated substantial changes in the model codes as they relate to handicapped provisions.

The addition of Chapter 31 and Appendix Chapter 31 to the code has been a major step toward meeting the ADA requirements. However, at the time of the availability of the 1991 UBC, the ADA regulations mandated by that legislation was not available. Therefore a potential inconsistency may occur. Future supplements to this Guide will update this important matter.

In the author's opinion, the designer and the enforcement official should insist on the adoption of both the Chapter 31 and the Appendix Chapter 31 simultaneously in order to avoid impacting existing buildings by the new egress requirements of Chapter 31. See the more detailed discussions in Article 10 of this Guide.

This Guide does not deal with most of these other laws and regulations, except to point out that they exist and vary from jurisdiction to jurisdiction. The impact of the "accessibility" provisions of Chapter 31 on the exiting requirements in Chapter 33 will be discussed in Part 7 of this Guide.

Codes are ordinances adopted by local or state governments and are generally enforced at the local level. Enforcement involves a permit of one type or another, issued to the owner or his agent, by the local jurisdiction. The process by which the permit is issued involves one or more of the codes in effect in that jurisdiction.

The permit process may vary from one jurisdiction to another, but all have a basic similarity that warrants understanding by anyone who must use the process. The details of the typical permit process are discussed in the Appendix A1. The designer should be familiar with the procedure in the jurisdiction under consideration and coordinate the design with both the codes and local officials.

NOTES

ARTICLE 1A
THE DESIGNER AND THE LOCAL OFFICIALS

a) The Relationship of the Designer to the Enforcement Official

An important relationship to understand is that between the designer and the government official who will review the design for code compliance and building permit issuance. The designer sets the parameters that determine the review process. The designer has control over all phases of the design and therefore over which provisions of the code will apply.

The designer decides:

- the location of the building on the site,
- the type of construction to be used,
- the layout of the interior of the building,
- the occupancy type,
- the relationships between different occupancies within the building, and
- all the other elements of a design.

The function of the building official is to review and verify the designer's decisions. That review will determine the compliance of the submitted documents with the various code requirements pertaining to:

- the type of construction, and
- the site location and occupancy relationships.

The official's review is a verification of the code compliance of the designer's documents. The official is not charged with the responsibility for the design of the building. The official is charged with the responsibility of determining or verifying that all proposed construction meets the local code or its intent.

A designer may decide that a particular building and its use should be classified as a Hazardous Occupancy — a Group H, Division 2 or 3 (H-2 or H-3) Occupancy, rather than a Business Occupancy — Group B, Division 2 (B-2) Occupancy. The permit documents must be reviewed by the building official under the H-2 or H-3 Occupancy provisions (provided the designer's selected occupancy reflects the "most restrictive" use the actual construction and use warrant).

On the other hand, if the occupancy chosen by the designer is "less restrictive" than that reflecting the true use or occupancy proposed for the building, the building official can and must require that the proper occupancy be used. For example, assume that the designer has designated a use to be B-2 when in fact it should be the more restrictive H-2. The building official will require that all documents reflect the H-2 Occupancy. The official will then review those documents using the H-2 requirements of the code.

The official cannot require compliance with code provisions that relate to other occupancy classifications unless the designer has chosen an occupancy less restrictive than the correct one for the intended use.

The terms "more restrictive" and "less restrictive" must be defined to enable the designer and the officials to evaluate design decisions on a common basis. Using the provisions of Table Nos. 5-C and 5-D, the restrictiveness can be established based on the allowable areas and heights permitted for a particular use or occupancy in the same type of construction.

For example, a comparison, using Table No. 5-C, of a Type III One-hour building with an H-2 Occupancy to the same building with a B-2 Occupancy reveals a difference in their allowable areas:

H-2 Occupancy = 5,600 square feet
B-2 Occupancy = 18,000 square feet

Similarly, referring to Table No. 5-D, the number of stories allowed are:

H-2 Occupancy = one story
B-2 Occupancy = four stories

These comparisons readily show that the code is "more restrictive" regarding the H-2 Occupancy than it is for the B-2 Occupancy.

The same general concept holds true for the type of building construction proposed by the designer, for example, Type I versus Type V One-hour. This concept is contained in Sections 502 and 1701, which will be discussed further in Articles 5 and 6, respectively, of this Guide.

b) The Preliminary Plan Check

To obtain a permit with a minimum of delay or problem, the designer should use techniques that are encouraged by local building officials. They want to facilitate the issuance of permits, a task that can be accomplished most easily when the submitted documents comply with the code.

Within a particular jurisdiction, some form of preliminary plan check procedure is usually provided and made available by the staff of the local agencies. This procedure is recommended to be used at the earliest conceptual stage of the design when there are sufficient details developed to show the following:

- the general overall size of the building,
- the arrangement of the occupancies within the structure and
- the arrangement of the exits.

The purpose of the preliminary plan check meeting with the local officials during the early schematic design phase is:

- to familiarize them with what you intend to do and
- to determine their concerns with the design and to have them indicate potential problem areas.

An early meeting is necessary to avoid substantial redesign later and to reduce excess work in coordinating the several design disciplines if changes are found necessary. The meeting should be arranged by the principal design professional with the building official of the jurisdiction. A request should be made to have the fire department represented at the meeting, so that any items involving their responsibilities or concerns can be addressed at the same time.

The design professional should bring along with him others who can add technical information and facilitate understanding at the meeting. Extra copies of the design drawings should be made available for both the building official and fire official.

During the discussion it will be the responsibility of the design professional to keep notes or minutes of the discussion. This is an extremely important step, since the results of the meeting will form the basis of the detailed design and because it will be the only recorded summary. If no such summary of the meeting is made and no copy sent to the jurisdiction for confirmation, there will be no record of the meeting ever having taken place or of any conclusions having been reached. *Do not assume that a representative of the jurisdiction will make notes of the meeting.*

Note that there may actually be a series of preliminary plan check meetings, especially as more detailed information is developed or revisions are made as a result of prior meetings or owner needs.

Again, it is imperative to document the discussions and conclusions of all such meetings. At the end of each meeting, the designer should indicate that he will send the officials copies of his understanding of the discussions' outcomes for review and concurrence, so that he can confidently proceed with the drawings.

At such meetings, alternatives to be evaluated should be presented and explained by the design professional. To provide design flexibility, the designer should seek acceptance of as many alternatives as necessary. At the meeting, the building official may make a decision based on some provision of the code or an interpretation thereof. The decision may prevent an alternative from being accepted. When this happens, the designer should note the section of the code involved for later verification and, if necessary, redesign to comply.

The designer is responsible for:

- initiating the request for acceptance of an alternative to the code requirements and
- providing the documentation for demonstrating the equivalence of the alternative to the code.

The designer must demonstrate, per Section 105, the obvious equivalence or superiority of the design to the code requirements.

c) Summarizing the Meetings—The Confirmation Letter

After the meeting with the officials, the design professional should send a copy of the notes or minutes to both the building official and the fire marshal (or the head of the fire code enforcement agency in the jurisdiction if that agency had a representative at the meeting).

It is suggested that courtesy copies be sent to all actual attendees at the meeting, together with any drawings discussed at the meeting if these were not previously left with them.

The agreements and conclusions reached at the meeting should be summarized in the confirmation letter. To expedite review of the letter, citations of the relevant code sections that were discussed should be provided therein. Doing this will also create a detailed record of the areas discussed and the compliance sought and received.

Similarly, the designer should document an understanding of any unaccepted design or concept along with the relevant sections of the code pertaining to that disapproval. If the designer believes that the interpretation of these sections was incorrect, this would be a good time to request reconsideration of the item. In Appendix A3, an example of such a letter is provided.

If an alternative design or system was discussed and accepted, the confirmation letter should provide the rationale behind the request and its acceptance to make clear in the record that the code was met as a result of the alternative presented.

The cover letter for these notes should request written confirmation that the summary meets the attendee's understanding of the discussions.

Do not use either of the following approaches in the confirmation letter, because they may result in problems:

"Unless I hear from you within days, I will presume that you concur with my summary."

"Please sign at the bottom of this letter indicating you accept the summary."

The designer should not assume anything; the designer alone has the responsibility to create a written record in the jurisdiction's files. To expect that such a record of the meeting will be created by simply mailing or delivering a letter to the local jurisdiction is presumptuous. The letter could be lost or misrouted.

If no record exists in the files, the meeting is assumed never to have occurred. The officials cannot be bound to the agreements that may have been reached. By the time the final design drawings are completed, the individuals who attended the meeting may no longer be in the same responsible positions and their successors may know nothing about their oral agreements.

Therefore, the designer should request *written* confirmation. Make sure the letter was received. If there is no response after a reasonable time, the designer should write a follow-up letter indicating when the original letter was sent and enclose a copy of it therewith. The designer should emphasize the desire for an early written reply; he is entitled to one. If no reply is received after a month, the building official should be contacted personally by phone and reminded of the meeting and the need for an immediate reply.

The reason for waiting a reasonable time before calling is to avoid giving the official the impression of being harassed. The building official has a great many other jobs to deal with, the designer's being only one of them. By proceeding at a reasonable pace in awaiting the response, the designer is in a position to suggest that the official look into the matter as a possible internal communications breakdown.

The preliminary plan check phase is the time for all parties to become familiar with the building in question. Both applicant and official must become knowledgeable in the particular project, and this is best done with all parties present. Written records must be kept.

The value of this procedure for all concerned cannot be overemphasized. A successful preliminary plan check will expedite the future building permit review. It will reduce the impact and number of code problems that may arise during the actual plan check for permit issuance, because most will have been corrected in the earlier plan check stages. Finally, it will usually mean an earlier start of construction.

ARTICLE 2
UNIFORM BUILDING CODE OVERVIEW

This Article outlines the Uniform Building Code (UBC) development process and the main elements affecting the design of buildings. This Article generally familiarizes the reader with the code and its philosophy in major areas, so that the detailed provisions can be understood in their proper context. The main design provisions of the UBC will be reviewed in greater detail in Articles 3 through 10 of this Guide.

a) The Code Amendment and Adoptive Procedures

The Uniform Building Code is the product of the International Conference of Building Officials (ICBO), the largest of the three model building code organizations. The code is amended annually at ICBO's Annual Business Meeting with the amendments issued as supplements in the year following that meeting. Every third year the code is published as a complete new edition.

The most recent code available at the time of writing this Guide is the 1991 edition. Unless otherwise stated, all references to Sections or Chapters in this Guide are to those in the 1991 Uniform Building Code. Certain provisions of that edition are new and of particular concern to the designer. They will be emphasized where they appear in the discussion herein.

The code may be adopted locally or on a statewide basis. The adoption may be by ordinance or by a legislative act depending on whether the state has, by law, preempted the field of building codes. In the latter case, a local jurisdiction enforces the state-adopted version of the UBC rather than adopting its own version.

In most jurisdictions, the UBC is adopted with few amendments except in the administrative part of the code. The adoptive process is the same as for any other legislation involving hearings and a vote by the legislative body of the jurisdiction. The code is usually enforced by an official and staff members of the local governmental department or agency legally charged with building code enforcement. In this Guide, the head of the enforcement agency will be referred to as the building official.

The adoptive ordinance may include the appendix provisions of the code. Unless the ordinance so specifies, the appendix has not been adopted, since to do so requires a specific act on the part of the jurisdiction.

Section 103 paragraph 4

> **Wherever in this code reference is made to the appendix, the provisions in the appendix shall not apply unless specifically adopted.**

Because the adoptive process is time consuming, the jurisdiction may not choose, as a general practice, to adopt the supplements that are issued each year. However, the building official can either:

- consider the provisions in a supplement as equivalent to the code in effect in the jurisdiction by using the provisions of Section 105 or
- recommend to the legislative body the adoption of all or part of the supplement.

b) Organization of the Code

The UBC is organized into ten Parts, a listing of the companion Standards and the Appendix. Each Part is designed as a broad umbrella covering several chapters of similar subject matter. For example, Part I contains Chapters 1 through 3, under the designation "Administrative." These chapters cover:

- the title, scope and purpose of the code
- the code enforcement and administration
- the permit and inspection requirements

The other main Parts of the code are:

Part II Chapter 4 - Definitions of terms used in the code.

Part III Chapters 5 through 12 - Occupancy Requirements.

(Note: There are no Chapters 13 through 16 at present.)

Part IV Chapters 17 through 22—Requirements Based on the Different Types of Construction.

Part V Chapters 23 through 28 - The Engineering Design Requirements.

Part VI Chapters 29 through 40 - Detailed construction requirements including the provisions for exit design.

(*There is no Chapter 41 at present.*)

Part VII Chapters 42 through 43—The Fire-Resistive Design Provisions.

Parts VIII through X contain a number of chapters relating to public space regulations, the construction of wall and ceiling coverings, and special subjects including glazing, plastic light-transmitting materials and enclosed malls.

The chapters primarily used in the design of a building include:

Chapter 5— Occupancy Classification and Requirements.

Chapter 17—Types of Building Construction Classification and Requirements.

Chapter 33—Exit Requirements.

Chapter 43—Fire-Resistive Construction Requirements.

The designer must understand the entire code as it affects a particular project. However, for preliminary design purposes the main code considerations are Chapters 5, 17, 33 and 43. This Guide will concentrate primarily on these Chapters. Other chapters and sections of the UBC will be discussed to a lesser degree.

c) Occupancy Classifications

The occupancy classification is one of the primary regulatory criteria in the code. A building is assigned a classification based on its proposed use or occupancy. Other key code criteria include:

- the type of construction to be used for the building and

- the height and areas of the proposed building.

The various Occupancy Classifications are listed and defined in Table No. 5-A. They are divided into seven major classes or Occupancy Groups:

A — Assembly
B — Business
E — Educational
H — Hazardous
I — Institutional
M — Miscellaneous
R — Residential

These Occupancy Groups are further subdivided into categories called Divisions. The Divisions distinguish specific subtypes of the occupancy from one another. For example, Group R, Division 1 refers to an occupancy having a large number of dwelling units (three or more), and Division 3 refers to a single or two-family dwelling. There is no Division 2 at present.

NOTE: The above examples of these Divisions have been chosen by the author merely as a means of highlighting their differences. The reader is referred to Table No. 5-A and Chapters 6 through 12 for the more complete, detailed descriptions of each occupancy.

Although a considerable number of occupancies are listed in the code, they do not represent the large range of occupancies possible. Section 501 of the code provides the building official with the means for classifying a use that does not fit any specific code description with the one it most nearly resembles, the criteria being based on life safety and fire hazard.

This code provision does not preclude the designer electing a "higher" hazard (more restrictive) classification for the building's use. The building official, in reviewing the permit documents, may bring this higher than necessary classification to the designer's attention. The building official would be overstepping legal authority if the designer's choice was not honored. Though one cannot predict the action of an individual official, it is likely that most building officials will recognize the validity of this concept.

By applying the method established in Tables No. 5-C and 5-D, the occupancy class, together with the type of building construction, is used to determine the allowable floor area and permitted number of stories. This method will be discussed in detail in Chapter 5.

When there is more than one occupancy in a structure, the relationship of these occupancies within the building is a code concern because the hazards of fire, explosion or panic in one occupancy can endanger another. To reduce the dangers the code requires that different occupancies be separated from each other by the level of fire-resistive construction determined in Table No. 5-B.

A final regulatory concern based on occupancy is the relationship of a building, housing one or more occupancies, to the adjacent property line. The setback and fire-resistive requirements of the exterior walls, which vary depending on proximity to the property line, are contained in Table No. 5-A and the Section–03 provisions of Chapters 9, 18, 19, 20 and 21.

d) Types of Construction

Five general types of building construction are defined by the code and are designated by the roman numerals I through V. All but Type IV are divided into two or more subtypes, each based upon the degree of fire resistance required for the building elements. The types of construction are described in detail in Chapters 18 through 22. The required level of fire resistance of the building elements for each type is provided in Table No. 17-A.

The construction types range, in the degree of requisite fire protection, from unprotected wood frame buildings (Type V-N) such as the typical home, to the fire-resistive type (Type I) such as the high-rise buildings found in downtown areas of major cities. As the fire resistance of a building increases, so does the allowable floor area and the number of stories permitted by the code, as shown in Table Nos. 5-C and 5-D.

A designation **"N"** following the roman numeral designation for the type of construction means that minimum construction provisions do not require any general level of fire resistance. However, the "N" type building may have individual fire-resistive requirements for certain building elements based on:

- Table No. 17-A,
- proximity to a property line,
- required occupancy separations,
- stairway and shaft enclosures and
- area separation walls.

A designation of "One-hour" following the type of construction means that the building has fire-resistive construction of at least a one-hour rating for all elements as required in Table No. 17-A. In general, these elements in a building include:

- floors,
- roof,
- columns,
- beams,
- exterior walls,
- bearing walls,
- shaft enclosures.

The general concept behind establishing the various types of construction involves compartition of the fire hazard. As a building becomes larger in either floor area or height, its elements require a higher degree of fire resistance. The public is thereby afforded a degree of safety from fire in one part of the building by the fire-resistive compartments formed by the building's walls and floors. In the same sense, the building itself forms a compartment to confine a fire and prevent it from spreading from one building to another. This will be discussed in greater detail in Article 6.

Chapters 18 through 22

The provisions in Chapters 18 through 22 address the specific construction requirements for the five general types of construction. These are used in conjunction with the provisions in Chapter 17 and in particular, Table No. 17-A. In Article 6 we discuss the different types of construction and the rationale behind Table No. 17-A.

In Chapters 18 through 22, the intent is to set out the philosophy of that building construction type insofar as the types of materials that are permitted for the building envelope and specific portions within the building.

Thus, the "01" and "02" sections of each Chapter provide the accepted types of materials that may be used for the structural elements of that building. It further states which of the building's structural elements may be combustible. For Type I and II all the structural elements must be noncombustible; only certain nonload-bearing walls may be combustible.

It is important to recognize that the requirements of the Sections 1801 and 1901 do not prevent the use of interior finishes or combustible insulation on or within the building elements as permitted in Sections 1712 and 1713.

The "03" sections provide, for the various types of construction, the permitted exterior wall constructions insofar as fire-resistive ratings and materials permitted. In particular one should note that for Type III and IV buildings, where Table No. 17-A requires four-hour fire-resistive rating, these ratings may be substantially reduced based on distance to adjacent property lines. Furthermore, these sections permit certain combustible materials where noncombustibility is essentially otherwise required.

In using the "03" provisions, the designer should first check the subsection (b) requirements for the opening protection requirements that generally determine the permissible wall construction per the Exceptions in subsection (a). This reversal of normal code reading will facilitate the designer in determining the applicable requirements. See Figure 2-1 for an example of how the "03" provisions apply for a Type III building.

The "03" sections are comparable to the Table No. 5-A provisions that apply only to Type II-one hour, II-N and V buildings.

For additional explanatory material on the detailed application of the "03" provisions, see Article 5 of this Guide.

The "04" and "05" provisions provide for the types of materials permitted for the stair and roof construction respectively.

The special high-rise provisions of 1807 and 1907 are discussed generally in Article 9 of this Guide.

In preparing the preliminary design, designers must inter-relate two

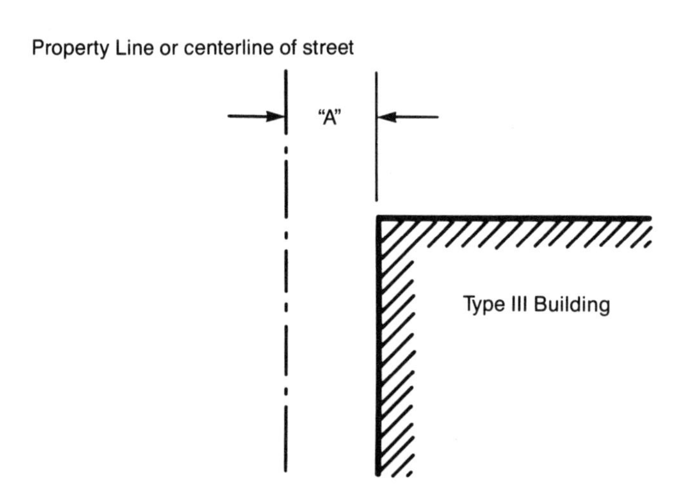

Distance from Property Line "a"	Occupancy Group/Div.	Exterior Wall Fire Rating	Openings Permitted in Exterior Wall Protected	Openings Permitted in Exterior Wall Unprotected
>3′	B-4, R or M	4-hour	No openings permitted	
>5′	A, E, I, B/1, 2, 3	4-hour	No openings permitted No openings permitted	
>20′	All Occupancies except H & I Nonbearing	2-hour	3/4-hour	NA
>20′	All Occupancies Bearing	4-hour	3/4-hour	NA
≤20′	All Occupancies except H & I Nonbearing	1-hour	NA	X
≤20′	B/2, R	2-hour	NA	X
≤40′	All Occupancies Nonbearing	Unrated	NA	X

REFERENCE: SECTION 2003

FIGURE 2-1 LOCATION ON PROPERTY, TYPE III BUILDING, EXTERIOR WALL REQUIREMENTS

critical code criteria with the space requirements of their clients:

- the occupancy class and
- the type of construction.

These criteria are under designers' control in the design process and are their responsibility when it comes to deciding what best applies to a particular building.

e) Exiting

The main panic control provisions in the building are the exiting requirements in Chapter 33. The purpose of these exits is to provide a means for the public to reach a protected area and progress to the outside of the building in a reasonably short period of time. This aim is accomplished by limiting the distance a person must travel before reaching a fire-resistive enclosure, i.e., a corridor or stairway.

The width of these protected segments of the exit path is based on the following:

- occupancy class served,
- occupant load factor per square foot for that occupancy,
- size of the occupancy served,
- minimum width permitted by the code and
- minimum width in lineal feet for the occupancy served based on the calculated occupant load of the occupancy.

The relationship of width to numbers of people is based on studies of the movement of large numbers of people in confined spaces.

Having entered the fire-protected exit system, the occupant must remain protected until reaching the exterior of the building. The code establishes the fire-resistive requirements for the walls, floors and ceilings of these enclosures and the doors and windows opening into or adjacent to them.

The arrangement of the exit ways is another critical element of the preliminary design. The exit ways should be given detailed study by the designer in that stage of the design. The preliminary plan check meeting with the local officials will usually lead to consideration of that item before others. The exit arrangement involves:

- the length of travel (travel distance) on a floor to reach a stairway or other higher level exit facility and
- the concept of requiring access to at least two exits separated from one another.

The Chapter 33 exit provisions will be discussed in greater detail in Article 7 of this Guide.

f) Fire Resistance

The fire-resistive requirements of buildings are defined in Table No. 17-A according to the types of building construction. Details of how the hourly fire-resistive ratings can be obtained for the various building elements are provided in Chapter 43. That chapter contains three tables that provide descriptions of assemblies with the required hourly rating. These assemblies have all been prequalified by the code as complying with the fire test standards set forth in Chapter 43. There are numerous other assemblies that can also qualify for use but either are proprietary or for other valid reasons have not been placed in the tables.

The ICBO Evaluation Reports also furnish listings of assemblies deemed by that organization's Evaluation Committee as satisfying the equivalency requirements of Section 105. It is important to understand the difference between the tables in Chapter 43 and an Evaluation Report. The listings in the code are legally a part of the code, and must be accepted and are binding on the building official. On the other hand, an Evaluation Report is just that: an evaluation that may or may not be accepted by a building official.

A building official has to make a specific acceptance or approval of an Evaluation Report for it to be used in a jurisdiction.

The listings in the Gypsum Association's "Fire Resistance Design Manual" have been accepted by the UBC (see Footnote No. 1 of the three Chapter 43 tables). Therefore, the designer has available many ways of satisfying the code fire resistance requirements without making necessary an extended review by the officials.

The designer may propose assemblies not described in one of the references noted. Any assembly can be submitted for review and approval by the official. However, the designer is cautioned that a job undertaken to obtain such acceptance may become time consuming and require more information and expertise than the designer is able to provide. Due to the demands involved in the process, it is best left to the manufacturer and his technical staff to pursue such approvals.

The use of generally referenced assemblies will speed up the permit review.

The code intends that the support elements of fire-resistive construction have at least the same or greater fire resistance rating than the element being supported. Although this is not stated in Chapters 17 or 43, this intent is clearly stated in Section 503 (b) relating to occupancy separations.

Where the occupancy separation is horizontal, structural members supporting the separation shall be protected by equivalent fire-resistive construction.

This limitation of the support continuity to horizontal occupancy separations does not provide a consistency that is requisite to the code.

> In the author's opinion, to achieve both a consistency in the code and the development of designs that provide logical fire resistance to a building, the general principle previously stated should be used: *A fire-resistive element shall be supported by elements of the same or greater fire resistance.*

For an example of these occupancy separation wall fire rating requirements, see Figures 2-2 and 2-3.

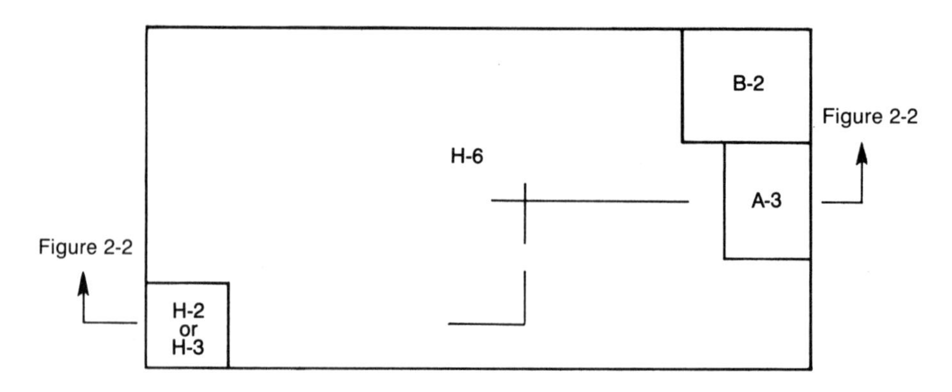

PLAN 1st FLOOR

ASSUME
Type II One-Hour Building
Two Story
First Floor as Shown
Second Floor all H-6 and B-2

Occupancy Separation Requirements

Second Floor	B-2/H-6	1-Hour
Between Second/ & First Floor	B-2/H-2	2-Hour
	B-2/H-3	1-Hour
	H-6/A-3	3-Hour
First Floor	H-6/H-2	2-Hour
	H-6/H-3	1-Hour
	H-6/A-3	3-Hour

Because the building is Type II One-hour, separation requirements are readily met.

The B-2/H-2 and H-6/H-2 two-hour requirements mean that the floor of the second floor and its supports for the segment over the H-2 Occupancy must have two-hour fire resistance to the ground. The three-hour requirement between the H-6/A-3 Occupancies similarly must have three-hour rated supports to the ground.

REFERENCE: SECTION 503 (d), TABLE NO. 5-B

FIGURE 2-2 FIRE-RESISTIVE SEPARATION WALLS

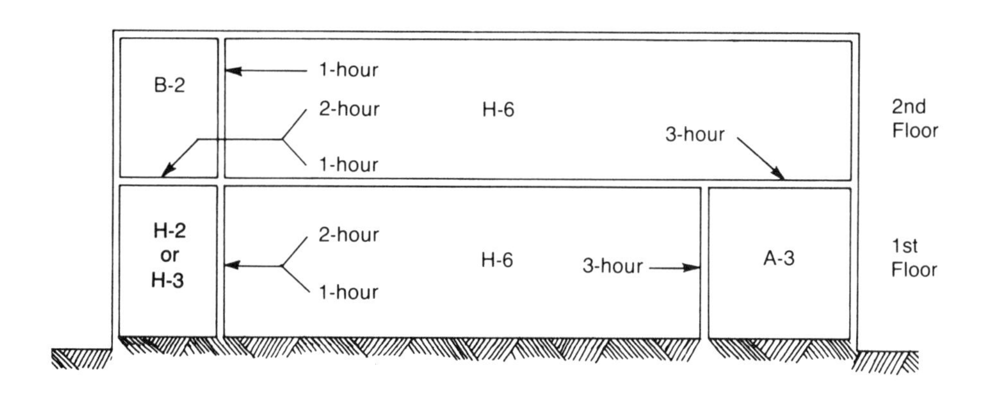

Occupancy Separations per Table No. 5-B

1st Floor	H-6/H-2	2-hour	1½-hour
	H-6/H-2	1-hour	1-hour
	H-6/A-3	3-hour	3-hour
	B-2/A-3	N	N
2nd Floor	H-6/B-2	1-hour	1-hour
Between 1st Floor & 2nd Floor	Depending on Location of Occupancies on each floor		
	H-6/H-2, H-3, A-3, B-2	Same as First Floor	
	Floor B-2/A-3, H-6, H-2, H-3	Same as First Floor except B-2/H-2 = 2-hour	1½-hour
		B-2/H-3 = 1-hour	1-hour

N - No fire rating required

NOTE: Where the second floor separations are required to have fire-resistive ratings greater than one-hour, the wall/floor construction involved must have the same higher rating for all support members down to the ground. See Figure 2-2.

REFERENCE: SECTION 503 (b), TABLE NO. 5-B

FIGURE 2-3 FIRE-RESISTIVE SEPARATION SUPPORTS

NOTES

ARTICLE 3
ADMINISTRATIVE PROVISIONS OF THE UBC

The Administrative provisions of the UBC are contained in Chapters 1, 2 and 3, certain sections of which, being of particular interest to the designer, are discussed in this Article. These sections are reprinted, followed by an analysis and discussion.

CHAPTER 1
TITLE, SCOPE AND GENERAL

This chapter defines the overall philosophy of the code as it pertains to public welfare and safety. It sets the parameters for changes of use or occupancy, alterations, maintenance, approval of new materials and methods of construction and, in special cases, variances.

Purpose

Sec. 102. The purpose of this code is to provide minimum standards to safeguard life or limb, health, property and public welfare by regulating and controlling the design, construction, quality of materials, use and occupancy, location and maintenance of all buildings and structures within this jurisdiction and certain equipment specifically regulated herein.

The purpose of this code is not to create or otherwise establish or designate any particular class or group of persons who will or should be especially protected or benefited by the terms of this code.

The code establishes the minimum criteria for the protection of the public and of property. Although the code's primary emphasis is on life safety, property, to a lesser degree, is also a concern. The code provides the minimum requirements, representing the least one is required to do; it is not and should not be considered a handbook for design. There are many construction concerns, of building owners or occupants, not addressed by the code; these are the responsibility of the design professionals involved in the process.

The code is a legal document, usually adopted by ordinance in the local jurisdiction. All its provisions, therefore, have legal implications and are not simply a collection of minimum standards. An example of the enacting ordinance can be found on Page xxii of the UBC.

The Section 102 Purpose mentions maintenance of structures. This is an important matter that will be discussed later in Section 104 (d); for the time being it is sufficient to note that the code's legal requirements apply for the life of the building.

Scope

Sec. 103. The provisions of this code shall apply to the construction, alteration, moving, demolition, repair and use of any building or structure within this jurisdiction, except work located primarily in a public way, public utility towers and poles, mechanical equipment not specifically regulated in this code, and hydraulic flood control structures.

Additions, alterations, repairs and changes of use or occupancy in all buildings and structures shall comply with the provisions for new buildings and structures except as otherwise provided in Sections 104, 307 and 502 of this code.

Where, in any specific case, different sections of this code specify different materials, methods of construction or other requirements, the most restrictive shall govern. Where there is a conflict between a general requirement and a specific requirement, the specific requirement shall be applicable.

Wherever in this code reference is made to the appendix, the provisions in the appendix shall not apply unless specifically adopted.

Section 103 states that the code governs all construction of buildings in the jurisdiction, whether new or alteration work. That is, the same code requirements as they relate to new buildings will apply to alteration work done on an existing building and to the part of the building in which the change of occupancy occurs.

The third paragraph of this section establishes the relationship of the code's general provisions to its specific ones. For example, a general requirement such as that for a Type V One-hour building requires that such a building be constructed as one-hour fire-resistive throughout as stated in Section 2201.

However, there are special provisions that either increase or decrease that one-hour general standard:

- An occupancy separation may require a two-hour fire rating per Section 503 (d).
- Within a dwelling unit in an apartment house, the nonbearing walls may be of nonfire-rated construction per Section 1705 (b)2.

Application to Existing Buildings and Structures

Sec. 104. (a) General. Buildings and structures to which additions, alterations or repairs are made shall comply with all the requirements of this code for new facilities except as specifically provided in this section. See Section 1210 for provisions requiring installation of smoke detectors in existing Group R, Division 3 Occupancies.

This provision restates the basic requirement that the alteration work must meet the new construction regulations except as specifically stated otherwise in the section.

A reference to Section 1210 is provided as that section contains the only retroactive provision in the code. The smoke detector requirement in Section 1210 (a)2 is triggered when any work proposed to be done in an existing dwelling (R-3 Occupancy) has a permit valuation "in excess of $1000." In all other respects, the code, unless the Appendix Chapter 1 or 31 are specifically adopted in the jurisdiction, is not retroactive.

Although the UBC is not a retroactive document except as noted, many states and some jurisdictions have legislated portions of the UBC as being retroactive. The designer should determine early in the preliminary design phase whether the Appendix Chapter 1 or other retroactive provisions are in effect in that locality. See Article 12 for further discussion of this important subject.

Sec. 104.

(b) Additions, Alterations or Repairs. Additions, alterations or repairs may be made to any building or structure without requiring the existing building or structure to comply with all the requirements of this code, provided the addition, alteration or repair conforms to that required for a new building or structure. Additions, alterations or repairs shall not be made to an existing building or structure which would cause the existing building or structure to become unsafe. An unsafe condition shall be deemed to have been created if an addition or alteration will cause the existing building or structure to be structurally unsafe or overloaded; will not provide adequate egress in compliance with the provisions of this code or will obstruct existing exits; will create a fire hazard; will reduce required fire resistance or will otherwise create conditions dangerous to human life. Any building so altered, which involves a change in use or occupancy, shall not exceed the height, number of stories and area permitted for new buildings. Any building plus new additions shall not exceed the height, number of stories and area specified for new buildings. Addition or alterations shall not be made to an existing building or structure when such building or structure is not in full compliance with the provisions of this code except when such addition or alteration will result in the existing building or structure being no more hazardous based on life safety, fire safety and sanitation, than before such addition or alterations are undertaken. [See also Section 911 (c) for Group H, Division 6 Occupancies.]

Alterations or repairs to an existing building or structure which are nonstructural and do not adversely affect any structural member or any part of the building or structure having required fire resistance may be made with the same materials of which the building or structure is constructed. The installation or replacement of glass shall be as required for new installations.

This section is a further restatement of the principle that the alteration work meet the present code requirements. The entire existing building in which the work is to be done need not be brought into compliance with the present code.

A further latitude is afforded in this section for proposed construction work that neither involves a structural element nor adversely affects the structural capacity or fire resistance of the building. In such instances the materials for the new work may be the same as those previously in place. The new work, in this case, need not conform to the present code.

It should be understood that the provision in the last paragraph of Section 104 (b) does not permit the use of the same material with which the building was originally constructed if that original material and construction failed to comply with the earlier code.

Sec. 104

(c) Existing Installations. Buildings in existence at the time of the adoption of this code may have their existing use or occupancy continued, if such use or occupancy was legal at the time of the adoption of this code, provided such continued use is not dangerous to life.

Any change in the use or occupancy of any existing building or structure shall comply with the provisions of Sections 307 and 502 of this code.

For existing buildings, see Appendix Chapter 1.

Existing installations are covered by this section as remaining legal uses. So long as an existing use or occupancy in the building was permitted by the code in effect at the time the use or occupancy was installed, it can remain. Thus, new code provisions do not have retroactive application to an existing use.

The reference to Appendix Chapter 1 applies only in those jurisdictions that have specifically adopted the Appendix provision in their enacting ordinance or where the state has adopted it or other specific retroactive requirements. See Article 12 for detailed discussion of what code applies to existing buildings.

Sec. 104

(d) Maintenance. All buildings and structures, both existing and new, and all parts thereof, shall be maintained in a safe and sanitary condition. All devices or safeguards which are required by this code shall be maintained in conformance with the code edition under which installed. The owner or his designated agent shall be responsible for the maintenance of buildings and structures. To determine compliance with this subsection, the building official may cause any structure to be reinspected.

The UBC's purpose includes maintenance. Section 104 (d) requires the owner to be responsible for maintaining the building. In particular, all safeguards and devices required by the code in effect at the time of the construction or alteration of the facility must be maintained in conformance with that code.

Under this code provision, the owner has the responsibility of continuing to maintain the building henceforth in compliance with the earlier code.

In this section the term "safeguards and devices" includes, in part, fire-resistive assemblies, fire doors, sprinklers and detectors.

When alterations or additions are contemplated for an existing building, the designer has the responsibility of determining whether the building is in compliance with the maintenance provision. The designer should ascertain that either:

- the original construction complied with the code then in effect, or
- the work now contemplated will satisfy both the original code and the present one as it effects the new work.

The designer is often faced with the situation in which a major alteration is contemplated for an old building. The second sentence of Section 104 (d) clearly indicates that the building must conform at least to the code in effect at the time of original construction. All too often the designer assumes that the construction in place was compliant with the code and then proceeds to duplicate that construction.

The designer has the responsibility to determine whether compliance existed, so that the owner can be notified to correct the preexisting violations and thus have the structure comply with both the prior and the present code.

The alteration work must meet the present code. If only the new work was done, the existing deficiencies not checked and corrected, and an incident occurred, the possible ensuing litigation could cite the present designer for failing to correct obvious preexisting deficiencies. For this reason, any alteration work should be preceded by a check of the area of the proposed work for potential non-complying construction.

In the author's opinion the designer should undertake certain necessary protective steps when dealing with existing buildings. Although not professing to be an attorney, this author believes that the designer may incur legal liability for the failure to identify and correct a prior violation if:

- the designer does not determine that the building was in compliance with the code at the time of original construction and
- in the new work encounters construction that does not conform to that earlier code and fails to advise the owner.

The designer should contact either an attorney or professional liability insurance carrier to provide for this contingency. A suggested approach, for consideration, is outlined hereafter.

The designer should specify in the service contract documents that the designer be held harmless by the owner for all pre-existing code violations. In the absence of a hold-harmless provision, the designer should notify the owner in writing of any code violation findings, recommending that they be corrected. If the owner does not want to correct the violations then the owner takes full responsibility for the violations and all claims and legal costs that may subsequently be incurred by the designer regarding those violations.

There have been cases in which the alteration designer has been brought into a suit for just such a failing, even though the designer's work may have been code complying. To avoid such a situation, the designer should review both the records of the original construction and the requirements that were then applicable. This information can be obtained from the building inspection agency's files and should be checked by the designer.

Alternate Materials and Methods of Construction

Sec. 105. The provisions of this code are not intended to prevent the use of any material or method of construction not specifically prescribed by this code, provided any alternate has been approved and its use authorized by the building official.

The building official may approve any such alternate, provided he finds that the proposed design is satisfactory and complies with the provisions of this code and that the material, method or work offered is, for the purpose intended,

at least the equivalent of that prescribed in this code in suitability, strength, effectiveness, fire resistance, durability, safety and sanitation.

The building official shall require that sufficient evidence or proof be submitted to substantiate any claims that may be made regarding its use. The details of any action granting approval of an alternate shall be recorded and entered in the files of the code enforcement agency.

Section 105 permits the development of alternative arrangements and constructions other than those specifically cited in the code. The burden of demonstrating the equivalence of the proposed alternative system is placed on the person desiring the alternative's acceptance. The second paragraph establishes the criteria for the building official's evaluation of the suggested equivalence.

To use this section, the designer or owner has to be assured that the enforcement official is both willing and capable of reviewing the alternative. The official can use the ICBO conference headquarters staff to assist him in the evaluation. The staff is not usually available to a designer or owner for such review. The ICBO policy is that its staff will respond only to a building official's request.

Another method of obtaining the acceptance of new materials is to proceed through the Evaluation Committee of the conference. This involved process is usually the province of the manufacturer and should not be undertaken by the designer. The procedure will not be detailed in this Guide.

If the local official is willing to evaluate the request or to refer it to ICBO staff, the designer or owner should fully prepare the case for the alternate design so that its obvious equivalence to the code is demonstrated. The request should be documented and a written response requested so that a clear record is made of the process and the acceptance.

The purpose of this section is to provide the code with flexibility that permits innovation and ingenuity. This flexibility enables the designer to develop a design that fits the needs of the owner and meets the code's intent, if not its precise letter. This concept is at the heart of modern codes and code enforcement.

Modifications

Sec. 106. Whenever there are practical difficulties involved in carrying out the provisions of this code, the building official may grant modifications for individual cases, provided he shall first find that a special individual reason

makes the strict letter of this code impractical and that the modification is in conformity with the intent and purpose of this code and that such modification does not lessen any fire protection requirements or any degree of structural integrity. The details of any action granting modifications shall be recorded and entered in the files of the code enforcement agency.

This section provides the building official with the authority to allow modifications of or variances from code compliance when practical problems prevent strict code compliance. The use of this provision places great responsibility on the official. To use the latitude afforded, the official has to find that:

- there are unusual circumstances to warrant consideration of the matter and
- the modification does not lessen the fire protection or structural integrity.

These criteria are substantial and must be justified in writing for permanent retention in the code agency's records.

> It is the author's opinion that all parties consider the use of this provision with care and avoid its use unless absolutely necessary. Its use and the resultant waiving of code provisions may place the parties involved in legally exposed positions. A strong, well-documented case must be prepared whenever the provision is used, so that the designer and the official can fully substantiate the modification.

CHAPTER 2
ORGANIZATION AND ENFORCEMENT

This chapter establishes the legal authority of the building official. It defines unsafe buildings and the means of dealing with them.

Sec. 202. (a) General. The building official is hereby authorized and directed to enforce all the provisions of this code. For such purposes, he shall have the powers of a law enforcement officer.

The building official shall have the power to render interpretations of this code and to adopt and enforce rules and regulations supplemental to this code as he may deem necessary in order to clarify the application of the provisions of this code. Such interpretations, rules and regulations shall be in conformity with the intent and purpose of this code.

This section establishes the authority of the building official as the enforcement officer for the code. Because the official is directed to enforce the code, the official has no option whether or not to enforce the code.

The second paragraph is new to the code. It allows the official to develop interpretations, rules and regulations to implement the enforcement process by helping to clarify the provisions of the code. It is most important that these interpretations, rules and regulations be put in writing, even when there is only one project to which a particular determination applies.

The official and the designers must work together to develop interpretations, rulings or regulations to assure that the intent of the code is not sacrificed. It would be prudent for the building official to use the criteria in Section 105 in making an interpretation, ruling or regulation.

When they will have broad application to many projects, they should be available to the designers and the public. The building official should use the locally available methods for distributing these documents to those interested in the code. Some resources are the local chapters of the American Institute of Architects, the local builders' exchange or similar builder or contractor organization, the local newspaper and other public access media.

The reason given for this change was that administrative policies must be established for the building official to carry out the assigned function properly. The authority to promulgate rules and regulations was partially intended to cover that area of the enforcement activity.

The authority extended by the second paragraph is couched in language reflecting the requirement that the official must clarify the code within the intent of the code. Thus, this authority is not to be used in place of Section 106 or to authorize a departure from the code, but is the authority to make reasonable application of the code provisions to a particular project within the overall intent of the code. The criteria in Section 105 are good touch-points in developing an interpretation.

An important provision of the UBC, contained in Section 204, provides for the establishment of a Board of Appeals, which can review new construction methods and materials and which has the authority to interpret the code. This provision conceives of a board made up of individuals knowledgeable in building construction. Unfortunately, many jurisdictions either do not have such appeals boards, or their respective legislative bodies assume the role of an Appeals board without the members possessing the requisite construction knowledge. In either instance the intent is lost.

Jurisdictions having such boards have found them to provide an excellent means of bringing the professionals and others in the construction industry into the code process. The resulting interchange benefits both the public and private sector. It makes available to the official the expertise that often is needed to evaluate complex new products or systems. Organizations of architects, engineers and contractors are usually willing to recommend qualified members to serve on the board. It is advised that the appointments be based on these recommendations rather than on politics.

The right of appeal to a qualified technical board strengthens the code and the enforcement process.

CHAPTER 3
PERMITS AND INSPECTIONS

Sec. 301. (a) Permits Required. Except as specified in Subsection (b) of this section, no building or structure shall be erected, constructed, enlarged, altered, repaired, moved, improved, removed, converted or demolished unless a separate permit for each building or structure has been obtained from the building official.

The intent of this section is to require a building permit when virtually any construction work in a building is to be done. Specific items exempt from permits are listed in Section 301 (b). Except for low (5'-9") partitions and painting, almost any work in an occupancy requires a building permit.

The less obvious intention of this section is to establish a record for the operation of the facility in compliance with the code. Were some untoward event to occur, the owner would be in a poor legal position if it were found he had been allowing work to be done without a permit. Whether or not that work was code compliant would not be the issue. The owner would be a scofflaw and presumed to be in the wrong. The burden would then rest on the owner to prove innocence. The owner would have a self-made credibility problem.

One benefit of obtaining permits is the assistance local officials can provide the designer or owner in meeting the intent, though not necessarily the letter, of the code. If contact is not opened with them via permits, this assistance will be unavailable. In most instances, given the opportunity, the officials are cooperative, knowledgeable and will provide assistance in solving problems.

Application for Permit

Sec. 302. (a) Application. To obtain a permit, the applicant shall first file an application therefore in writing on a form furnished by the code enforcement agency for that purpose. Every such application shall:

1. Identify and describe the work to be covered by the permit for which application is made.
2. Describe the land on which the proposed work is to be done by legal description, street address or similar description that will readily identify and definitely locate the proposed building or work.
3. Indicate the use or occupancy for which the proposed work is intended.
4. Be accompanied by plans, diagrams, computations and specifications and other data as required in Subsection (b) of this section.
5. State the valuation of any new building or structure or any addition, remodeling or alteration to an existing building.
6. Be signed by permittee, or his authorized agent.
7. Give such other data and information as may be required by the building official.

Section 302 (a) lists the several items required on a building permit application. The designer should be particularly concerned with Item 3. The proposed use should be carefully and properly identified, preferably by the code designation for the occupancy or occupancies in the building. The reason for carefully and fully describing the use(s) is that in the future the decision of whether a change of occupancy may be allowed in an alteration or new tenancy will in great part be based on the original use(s) entered in the permit records.

Sec. 302.

(d) Information on Plans and Specifications. Plans and specifications shall be drawn to scale upon substantial paper or cloth and shall be of sufficient clarity to indicate the location, nature and extent of the work proposed and show in detail that it will conform to the provisions of this code and all relevant laws, ordinances, rules and regulations.

Plans for buildings more than two stories in height of other than Group R, Division 3 and M Occupancies shall indicate how required structural and fire-resistive integrity will be maintained where a penetration will be made for electrical, mechanical, plumbing and communication conduits, pipes and similar systems.

The designer should be sure that the plans comply to this section. Items often overlooked in regard to the first paragraph are:

1. All fire-resistive assembly details must fully cover the requirements for the project. These include details for:
- walls,
- floor-ceiling and roof-ceiling assemblies,
- area separation walls including the foundation and roof intersections and proximity to openings,
- occupancy separations and their supporting elements and
- structural members and the method of protecting them including materials, attachments and other conditions associated with their use.

2. In the second paragraph, the code requires that the plans indicate how the fire-resistive and structural integrity is maintained where certain penetrations are made. The designer should consider the following:
- utility lines and how they are brought to and from each floor. Included in these items are telephone, waste and vent lines, electrical and duct systems, computer and other services.
- poke-thru, and how it is to be avoided. See Article 8 for further discussion of this subject.

3. Weather tightness is not specifically regulated in this section. It is implied by the phrase in the first paragraph:

"the work proposed will conform to the provisions of this code..."

See discussion of Section 1707 in Article 6 for the minimal code provisions on this subject. The only other reference in the code to weather protection is in Section 3201, second paragraph.

The designer should be sure the weather tightness details are sufficient and drawn to a large enough scale to be clear to the contractor. This is an area in which the designer, not the official, carries the prime and almost total responsibility. Included in this subject area are flashings for the roof, windows and doors, exterior intersections and penetrations.

Permits Issuance

Sec. 303 (a) Issuance. The application, plans, specifications, computations and other data filed by an applicant for permit shall be reviewed by the building official. Such plans may be reviewed by other departments of this jurisdiction to verify compliance with any applicable laws under their jurisdiction. If the building official finds that the work described in an application for a permit and the plans, specifications and other data filed therewith conform to

the requirements of this code and other pertinent laws and ordinances, and that the fees specified in Section 304 have been paid, he shall issue a permit therefore to the applicant.

When the building official issues the permit where plans are required, he shall endorse in writing or stamp the plans and specifications "APPROVED." Such approved plans and specifications shall not be changed, modified or altered without authorizations from the building official, and all work regulated by this code shall be done in accordance with the approved plans.

► ■■■ ◄

This section sets forth the requirements for issuing a permit after review of the drawings and related submissions in conformity with the laws in the jurisdiction. The new provision contained at the end of the second paragraph relieves the building official of the responsibility for enforcing the entire contents of the approved plans.

The enforcement official will be responsible only for those contents of the approved plans that are regulated by the code. As a result, the designer and the owner can no longer rely on the enforcement agency to back up their intentions with regard to noncode-regulated items shown on drawings.

Among the typical noncode-regulated items usually found on the drawings are:

- Decorative items such as paint, wall papering and other coverings not subject to Chapter 42 regulation
- Nonfire-rated windows and doors
- Methods of flashing and waterproofing
- Floor coverings
- Types of hardware other than those regulated by Chapter 33 and 43

The designer and the owner must provide for the enforcement of items on the approved plans hereafter.

Sec. 303.

(c) Validity of Permit. The issuance or granting of a permit or approval of plans, specifications and computations shall not be construed to be a permit for, or an approval of, any violation of any of the provisions of this code or of any other ordinance of the jurisdiction. Permits presuming to give authority to violate or cancel the provisions of this code or of other ordinances of the jurisdiction shall not be valid.

The issuance of a permit based upon plans, specifications and other data

shall not prevent the building official from thereafter requiring the correction of errors in said plans, specifications and other data, or from preventing building operations being carried on thereunder when in violation of this code or of any other ordinances of this jurisdiction.

Notwithstanding the previous discussion regarding the value of a permit to the owner, important caveats exist with regard to what the permit does or does not grant the owner. The substance of this subsection can be stated as follows:

The issuance of a permit or the issuance of a final completion for the building does not legalize noncompliance if:

- there are elements in the design that do not comply with the code or
- the construction does not follow the design or code requirements.

This section emphasizes the need for honest communication among the designer, the owner and the local officials. Do not presume that getting past the building official or obtaining the permit closes the matter. There have been numerous successful suits against the owners and the design professionals based on code violations in a building for which a building permit and Certificate of Occupancy had been issued.

The jurisdiction has covered itself in this section. The responsibility of being in legal compliance with the code remains with the designer and owner. In some states, the statute of limitations for latent defects, such as code violations, begins at the point when the violations are discovered and not from the date of permit issuance. The design professional and the owner are bound by law to follow the code and will be looked to at some future time for recompense if corrections need to be made.

The second sentence in the first paragraph extends the statement relating to a permit not authorizing any violation of the code to include any other ordinance of the locality. This extension of the intent of the paragraph has been necessitated by the increasing amount of litigation involving the codes and ordinances of the localities.

The reason presented for the expansion of the intent contained the following language that clearly indicates that permits, inspections and Certificates of Occupancy will not legalize the violation of the code or any other ordinance:

"the issuance of an inspection approval of a Certificate of Occupancy does not imply, nor is intended to imply, that violations which may surface after the fact have been sanctioned or approved."

For no other reason than that stated in this section, the permit process must be an open interchange of ideas and knowledge. Documentation should be presented at the conclusion of the discussions for equivalence on which the permit will subsequently be issued. The written record of the decisions will provide testimony in the future of why and how code equivalence was established. Such equivalence, however, should be obvious and not the result of the parties ignoring the problem.

Sec. 305.

(e) Required Inspections. Reinforcing steel or structural framework of any part of any building or structure shall not be covered or concealed without first obtaining the approval of the building official.

The building official, upon notification, shall make the following inspections and shall either approve that portion of the construction as completed or shall notify the permit holder or his agent wherein the same fails to comply with this code:

1. FOUNDATION INSPECTION: To be made after excavations for footings are completed and any required reinforcing steel is in place. For concrete foundations, any required forms shall be in place prior to inspection. All materials for the foundation shall be on the job, except where concrete is ready mixed in accordance with UBC Standard No. 26-13, the concrete need not be on the job. Where the foundation is to be constructed of approved treated wood, additional inspections may be required by the building official.

2. CONCRETE SLAB OR UNDER-FLOOR INSPECTION: To be made after all in-slab or under-floor building service equipment, conduit, piping accessories and other ancillary equipment items are in place but before any concrete is poured or floor sheathing installed, including the subfloor.

3. FRAME INSPECTION: To be made after the roof, all framing, fire blocking and bracing are in place and all pipes, chimneys and vents are complete and the rough electrical, plumbing, and heating wires, pipes, and ducts are approved.

4. LATH and/or GYPSUM BOARD INSPECTION: To be made after all lathing and gypsum board, interior and exterior, is in place but before any plastering is applied or before gypsum board joints and fasteners are taped and finished.

5. FINAL INSPECTION: To be made after finish grading and the building is completed and ready for occupancy.

The required inspections in this section are usually overrated by most people. They assume that the building inspector who visits the job site will reveal and note for correction any deficiencies that may exist.

The required inspections are only minimal inspections. They relate to specific areas of the work and do not represent an inspection of all work that has been done. Ideally, these inspections are made as the code lists them. Unfortunately, due to the workload of the inspectors, for the most part only some of the work will be seen at a time when all the elements needing verification are visible.

For example, consider a three-story wood-frame office building with the framing completed and the wallboard installation in progress. When will the inspector be called? If the wallboard is up and cannot be taped until the inspector sees all the fasteners and their spacings, then the wallboard subcontractor will be unable to phase the job efficiently. Therefore, the wallboard will probably be installed with the taping to proceed sequentially. The inspector will only see a portion of the fasteners at the time of the "called" inspection.

In many jobs the dates found for the particular inspection clearance are the same for 30 to 50 buildings. It is impossible for all of these buildings to have been inspected at the same time and for the wallboard in none of them to have been taped previous to that inspection!

The purpose of this discussion is to point out that the designer should not rely completely on the building inspector for assurance that the construction by the contractor has adhered to the designer's drawings. The designer has a responsibility to determine whether or not the design is being properly followed, because any future non-compliance noted may come back to haunt all parties.

If deviations from the design are sought by the contractor, the designer should be aware that the design may be compromised. Although the inspectors are legally responsible for seeing that the approved drawings are followed, their workload usually prohibits them from adequately doing so. In such instances it is up to the designer to ascertain compliance.

This process will no doubt be costly in time and effort to the designer. If the designer does not want to be held responsible, the designer can, at best, formally advise the jurisdiction and the owner of the fact that the designer is not responsible for the construction and that field changes will not be reviewed or approved by the designer.

As a result, the jurisdiction will be required to place responsibility on the owner for designating a design professional who will be responsible for any changes proposed. Unless a design professional is designated by the owner, *there should be no changes permitted from the original approved drawings.* If a design professional is named, that person should be required to take on the full responsibility for the original design and the construction phase so as to avoid divided responsibility for the building.

Certificate of Occupancy

Sec. 307. (a) Use or Occupancy. No building or structure shall be used or occupied, and no change in the existing occupancy classification of a building or structure or portion thereof shall be made until the building official has issued a Certificate of Occupancy therefore as provided herein.

EXCEPTION: Group R, Division 3, and M Occupancies.

Issuance of a Certificate of Occupancy shall not be construed as an approval of a violation of the provisions of this code or of other ordinances of the jurisdiction. Certificates presuming to give authority to violate or cancel the provisions of this code or of other ordinances of the jurisdiction shall not be valid.

In many situations alterations are made within a building that result in a change of occupancy from the previous legal use to a new one. This may involve a complete change in the use of a structure, the change of one office or the extension of one area's use into space previously used for other occupancies.

Note, however, that the addition of the second paragraph to this section reiterates the similar provisions in Section 303 (c); i.e., that a Certificate of Occupancy may be issued for buildings that may contain code violations. The issuance of such a certificate in no way validates, cancels or sanctions the violation. When discovered, the code violations will require correction to the requirements of the code in effect at the time of original construction.

In all these instances, and in any other of a similar nature, the obtaining of a Certificate of Occupancy (CO) at the conclusion of the permit work is as much a safeguard for the designer and the owner as is the filing for the building permit. The CO represents the final step by the jurisdiction in determining legal compliance. Although the caveat previously stated regarding Section 303 (c) still applies, the CO can establish a reasonably safe position for the designer and the owner in that they have complied with the code.

NOTES

ARTICLE 4
DEFINITIONS, ABBREVIATIONS AND GLOSSARY

CHAPTER 4.
DEFINITIONS AND ABBREVIATIONS

Certain specialized terms used in the code either are not in the 1981 edition of Webster's New Third International Dictionary of the English Language, to which the UBC refers for generally accepted definitions, or have meanings different from those found in that dictionary. Chapter 4 provides the code's intended meanings for such terms.

However, there are additional specialized terms not defined anywhere in the code. To understand these terms, the reader must either rely on general construction knowledge or infer meanings from the context of the provisions. This Guide provides definitions for some of these terms where they appear in this review of the code.

The designer should clarify with the enforcement official any term encountered that is either ambiguous or otherwise lacking adequate definition.

In our review of Chapter 4 we will address only selected terms of special importance to the designer.

Sec. 402. ADDITION is an extension or increase in floor area or height of a building or structure.

This term forms one subgroup of the activities generally included in the overall term "alteration." It involves the vertical or horizontal extension of a building. All work has to be in compliance with the current UBC.

ALTER OR ALTERATION is any change, addition or modification in construction or occupancy.

This is the general term for any work on an existing building. The code requirements for such work are set forth in Section 104 (b).

APARTMENT HOUSE is any building or portion thereof which contains three or more dwelling units and, for the purposes of this code, shall include residential condominiums.

This definition, together with that of a dwelling, establishes the two classes of residential occupancies, namely:

- the multi-family Group R, Division 1 Occupancy and
- the single- or two-family dwelling, Group R, Division 3 Occupancy.

There is no Group R, Division 2 Occupancy at present.

The designer should understand the distinctions between the two residential occupancy divisions and also the code requirements that regulate these differences.

A frequently encountered problem is that of determining which type of occupancy is involved in a project. What may look like a group of single-family dwellings, may be either:

- a series of one- or two-family dwellings or
- an apartment house.

Such situations often arise with townhouse construction, which could be in the form of side-by-side, one- or two-family row houses. These could be separated into Group R, Division 3 segments, with each pair of units bounded by property line walls. An alternative method of segmentation would be the use of area separation walls to define the pairs of dwelling units.

Without either of these means of separation, the building would be defined as multi-family because there would be three or more dwelling units within the building. The building would be defined as an apartment house, R-1.

This confusion arises from the real estate industry's desire to sell property. The terms used by the realtor or the developer do not precisely fit into the categories the code establishes for residential uses. The designer and enforcement officials are confronted with such terms as "townhouse," "condominium" and "garden apartment." Any of these uses could be defined as a Group R, Division 1 Occupancy.

Residential condominiums come in a variety of dwelling unit arrangements. The building official and designer must ignore the promotional hype of the developer and determine the occupancy classification from the configuration and based on the code's criteria.

In Figure 4-1, for example, four townhouse condominium arrangements are shown.

Detail A is a typical townhouse-configured apartment house, two or three stories in height.

Detail B is the same townhouse arrangement, but because it is an Group R, Division 1 Occupancy (apartment house) condominium, it is shown with property lines between the units.

Detail C is also the same townhouse arrangement, but this time the pairs of dwelling units are separated from each other by area separation walls creating Group R, Division 3 Occupancy buildings. The units still have property lines between them to define the condominium ownership limits.

Detail D shows a typical single-family row house arrangement. For this example it is part of a condominium, and unless the dwelling units are constructed as for Group R, Division 3 Occupancy, it may be a Group R, Division 1 Occupancy building. The Group R, Division 3 Occupancy requirements, which must be in the Caveats, Covenants and Regulations (CC&Rs) that govern the condominium, must include:

- Two one-hour walls, one on each side of the property line between each unit.
- Access to each owner for future repair of the property line walls
- Title to the shared foundation if this is present
- Proper roof-ceiling construction to avoid a parapet at the property line where a parapet is required
- Noncontinuous side walls and roof construction
- Separate utilities for each unit without common lines crossing the property lines

Furthermore, the CC&Rs must clearly place on each owner the responsibility for the maintenance of that unit's building envelope. Otherwise, as in most condominiums, the enclosing envelope (exterior walls, tenant walls, roof, etc.) form a single building entity that may be a Group R, Division 1 Occupancy building and not a series of Group R, Division 3 Occupancy buildings.

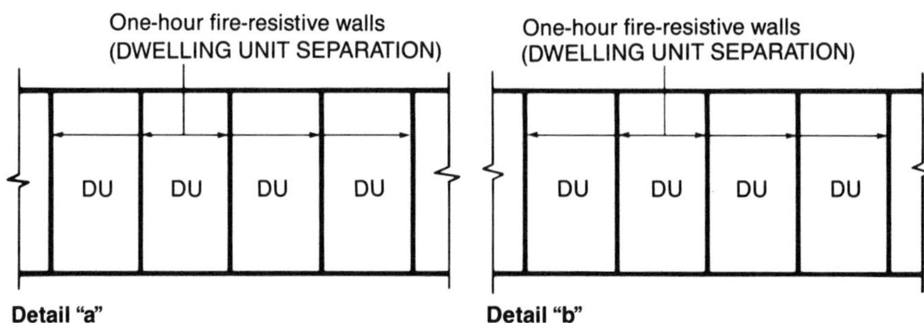

Detail "a"

PLAN VIEW

APARTMENT BUILDING
Group R, Division 1 Occupancy

ONE BUILDING

ONE-HOUR TENANT WALLS BETWEEN DWELLING UNITS (DU) Per Section 1202 (b)

Detail "b"

PLAN VIEW

TOWN HOUSES (CONDOS)
Group R, Division 1 Occupancy

ONE BUILDING

ONE-HOUR TENANT WALLS BETWEEN DWELLING UNITS (DU) Per Section 1202 (b)

Two-hour fire-resistive area separation walls

One-hour fire-resistive walls (DWELLING UNIT SEPARATION)

DU DU DU DU

Two one-hour walls on separate or jointly owned foundation

DU DU DU DU

Detail "c"

PLAN VIEW

TOWNHOUSES (CONDOS)
Group R, Division 3 Occupancy

MULTIPLE BUILDINGS WITH AREA SEPARATION WALLS BETWEEN PAIRS OF DWELLING UNITS

ONE-HOUR TENANT WALLS BETWEEN ALTERNATE DWELLING UNITS (DU) Per Section 1202 (b)

Detail "d"

PLAN VIEW

TOWNHOUSES AS Group R, Division 3 Occupancy

ROW HOUSING

TWO ONE-HOUR WALLS

ONE EACH SIDE OF PROPERTY LINES

REFERENCE: SECTION 402, 1202 (b)

FIGURE 4-1 APARTMENT HOUSE DEFINITION – COMPARISON OF ARRANGEMENTS, TOWNHOUSES, CONDOMINIUMS & GROUP R, DIVISION 3 OCCUPANCY

The designer should not be confused as to what type of occupancy is involved and should be prepared to discuss this subject with the owner. All parties should be aware of the code requirements applicable to each residential occupancy and type of construction and of the means by which the occupancy classification may be changed.

A designer who applies for a building permit and uses terms such as "townhouse" in place of R-1 or R-3 designations is creating a problem for both the designer and the official. The building official should determine whether the designer fully understands the code and how it may be applied to the proposed structure and use.

Several important exiting and fire protection requirements apply to a multi-family Group R, Division 1 Occupancy structure, including the allowable areas and heights of such structures. Therefore, in the design process it is important that the designer use code-recognized terminology and phraseology. Doing so leads to proper design decisions and will avoid having to adapt the building to the code later when the building official brings the problems to the designer's attention.

The term "condominium" was added to the 1985 UBC. The definition of an apartment house was also amended to include a condominium when there are three or more condominium dwelling units in the building.

At the time this code change was adopted, another change proposing to add the term "townhouse" was denied inclusion in the R-1 apartment house definition because townhouse construction was considered by many building officials to be row housing containing either a single- or two-family dwelling and by others to be an apartment house.

When a building contains three or more dwelling units connected without either property line or area separation walls between groups of two units, by definition it is an apartment house.

In some jurisdictions the building official has encountered only townhouses built as true row housing of one- or two-dwelling units and has not seen them in groups of three or more, as would constitute apartment houses.

It is probable that as more problems are experienced by building officials with the townhouse concept, construction and the misapplication of occupancy requirements, the term "townhouse" will be added to the apartment house definition.

APPROVED, as to materials and types of construction, refers to approval by the building official as the result of investigation and tests conducted by him, or by reason of accepted principles or tests by recognized authorities, technical or scientific organizations.

Throughout the code there are occasions when a material or method of construction is accepted "when approved." The term "approved" requires the application of the criteria in Section 105. Section 105 provides the basic concept of acceptance of alternative methods and materials and the evaluation to be made by the enforcement official. It provides latitude to the official to accept variations of design and materials other than those set forth in the code.

The building official can use any of the following means for granting approval:

1. The Evaluation Reports promulgated by ICBO.
2. The building official can request the ICBO staff to assist him in review of designs that may be too complex or novel for him to evaluate on his own.
3. If the jurisdiction has a technical review body such as the Board of Appeals described in Section 204, said body can assist the building official.

All these approaches are aimed at making the code flexible and receptive to new materials and designs.

ASSEMBLY BUILDING is a building or portion of a building used for the gathering together of 50 or more persons for such purposes as deliberation, education, instruction, worship, entertainment, amusement, drinking or dining or awaiting transportation.

An assembly occupancy or building is one with an occupant load of 50 or more. This occupant load cut-off is a distinction that places the building in either:

- a Group A Occupancy when the occupant load is 50 or more or
- a Group B, Division 2 Occupancy when the occupant load is less than 50.

The occupant load is determined by the floor area of the building or the space in the building and not by the actual number of occupants that will use the facility. This is discussed more fully in Article 7 of this Guide (Chapter 33).

Thus a room or space with a 49-person maximum occupant load will have an area of either:

- less than 750 square feet, where there are tables and seats or
- less than 375 square feet where there are no tables, such as in a bar.

When these areas are exceeded, the designer will have an A Occupancy, not a B-2 Occupancy.

Group A Occupancies are rigorously regulated and often subject to state law enforced by state and local fire marshals. Examples of uses considered to be Assembly-type occupancies, besides restaurants, bars and theaters, include:

Conference rooms
Libraries
Gymnasiums
Churches
Bus, railroad and airport facilities
Museums
Bowling alleys

ATRIUM is an opening through two or more floor levels other than enclosed stairways, elevators, hoistways, escalators, plumbing, electrical, air-conditioning or other equipment, which is closed at the top and not defined as a mall. For the purpose of defining an atrium, balconies within an assembly occupancy or mezzanines complying with Section 1717 shall not be considered floor levels.

The designer should be aware that an atrium is subject to code requirements only when the opening exceeds two stories in height. It is possible for a two-story building with an opening between the two stories not to be subject to the atrium provisions. This is true because the atrium provisions apply only to openings that go through two or more floors, i.e., connect three or more levels.

The designer should avoid using the term "atrium" unless the space truly meets the definition of an atrium. This will avoid considerable difficulty and the imposition of restrictive provisions that should not apply to non-atrium spaces.

AUTOMATIC, as applied to fire protection devices, is a device or system providing an emergency function without the necessity of human intervention and activated as a result of a predetermined temperature rise, rate of rise of temperature or increase in the level of combustion products such as is incorporated in an automatic sprinkler system, automatic fire door, etc.

In the code this term is well defined. It appears at different points throughout the code, often in conjunction with another term, "self-closing," relating to fire door operation.

Although it may appear that an automatic closing door would be preferable, in the parlance of the fire protection field an automatic door is one that is normally found in the open position. It is the normal position of the door that may be of concern in a specific situation, and not the means of activating the closing device.

Thus, a self-closing door is one that is normally found in a closed position. It will self-close after each opening through the presence of a door closer and the absence of a hold-open device. In many situations, the preference may be for the self-closing feature in order to provide a better smoke barrier.

Sec. 403. BALCONY is that portion of the seating space of an assembly room, the lowest part of which is raised 4 feet or more above the level of the main floor and shall include the area providing access to the seating area or serving only as a foyer.

This definition of balcony is only a partial one. The term is also applied in the code to non-assembly uses as well. For instance, residential and office balconies may be recreational or serve purposes other than assembly uses. Thus, the definition given here, referring to a public assembly such as a theater, is not one exclusively so used in the body of the code. The dictionary definition also applies.

BASEMENT is any floor level below the first story in a building, except that a floor level in a building having only one floor level shall be classified as a basement unless such floor level qualifies as a first story as defined herein.

Determining whether a level is a basement requires more than simply reading the definition. It requires recourse to other definitions including those of "grade" and "story." Once it is found that a definition is applicable to the level in question, other sections of the code are affected. For example, an area defined as a basement is not, as specified in Section 505 (d), to be included as part of the total allowable area calculation.

The definition of story states that the determination of whether a level is to be a story is based on the relationship of the level to adjacent grade. Once a level is determined to be a basement, it could not be a story and would not be counted in the allowable floor area calculation.

According to the definition of story, if a finished floor is less than six feet above adjacent grade, that level would be considered the first floor of the building; by the code definition of "basement," the area below would be a basement. The determination of grade would have to satisfy the criteria of Section 408.

The purpose of the code provisions cited above is to reduce the overall height of a building and to count only those levels that are mainly above ground.

The height limits are based on the difficulty the average fire department faces in fighting fires when it is necessary to reach, with hose streams and ladder, the upper levels of tall, minimally fire-resistant buildings.

This discussion points out the considerable degree of interrelationship that exists between code concepts, requirements and definitions. The designer can greatly benefit from understanding the intent of the code and the relationships permitted or required to exist in order to make a provision operative.

BUILDING is any structure used or intended for supporting or sheltering any use or occupancy.

This is the basic definition of what constitutes a building. It is all-inclusive and encompasses every type of structure and any use or occupancy.

The designer or owner should assume in all instances that any structure contemplated is a building and is thus subject to the building code regulations.

BUILDING, EXISTING, is a building erected prior to the adopting of this code, or one for which a legal building permit has been issued.

There is considerable distinction between whether a design applies to a building not yet constructed or to one already in existence. If the building is in existence, no code requirements will apply until alteration work is contemplated, as long as:

- the use is determined to be the same as originally intended in the building permit for its construction
- the use is found to be in compliance with any subsequent building permit covering the change in use or occupancy. No code requirements will apply until alteration work is contemplated. This subject was discussed earlier in relation to Section 104 in Article 3. The key point to remember is the importance of the building permit that establishes the legal status of the building.
- the jurisdiction has not adopted the Appendix Chapter 1 or there are no locally or state-mandated retroactive regulations. See Article 12.

Sec. 404.
CONDOMINIUM, RESIDENTIAL. See "Apartment House."

The term "condominium" was added for the first time to the 1985 UBC. The cross-reference to "apartment house" was used to avoid any misunderstanding or misapplication of the code when this form of unit ownership is involved in a building. When three or more condominium dwelling units are in the building, it is an R-1 apartment house.

It should be noted that legally a condominium owner does not own a portion of the structure but really owns a portion of the airspace within the structure that defines the dwelling unit. The unit owner shares the ownership of the building's common areas with the other owners. These common areas include the actual structure as well as all the spaces that are in common use. All the walls, floors and roofs are actually owned by the condominium association. The condominium owner is merely a shareholder in that association.

The term added is "residential condominium." There are also commercial condominiums. These latter condominiums are B-2 Occupancies. Therefore the qualification of the term included in the code is necessary to differentiate the R-1 from the B-2 condominiums.

Sec. 405.
DRAFT STOP is a material, device or construction installed to restrict the

movement of air within open spaces of concealed areas of building components such as crawl spaces, floor-ceiling assemblies, roof-ceiling assemblies and attics.

This definition relates to the requirements of the new provisions primarily found in Section 1706 and Chapter 43.

The definition of draft stop henceforth will differentiate between materials that are to limit air movement and those for fire stops that are to resist passage of flame, heat and hot gases. The provisions in Section 2516 (f) that relate to "Fire Blocks and Draft Stops" avoid the semantics problems previously experienced when fire stops meant two different things.

DWELLING is any building or portion thereof which contains not more than two dwelling units.

This is one definition for a Group R, Division 3 Occupancy. The designer should be sure that an R-3 is constructed and not an R-1 without its required safeguards.

Sec. 407.

FAMILY is an individual or two or more persons related by blood or marriage or a group of not more than five persons (excluding servants) who need not be related by blood or marriage living together in a dwelling unit.

This definition is a carry-over from the one- and two-family dwelling definition previously used for the Group R, Division 3 Occupancy concept. It is now more accurate to refer to a Group R, Division 3 Occupancy as one containing one or two dwelling units.

FIRE RETARDANT-TREATED WOOD is any wood product impregnated with chemicals by a pressure process or other means during manufacture, and which, when tested in accordance with U.B.C. Standard No. 42-1 for a period of 30 minutes, shall have a flame spread of not over 25 and show no evidence of progressive combustion. In addition, the flame front shall not progress more than 10 1/2 feet beyond the centerline of the burner at any time during the test. Materials which may be exposed to the weather shall pass the accelerated weathering test and be identified as Exterior type, in accordance with U.B.C. Standard No. 25-28. Where material is not directly subject to rainfall but exposed to high humidity conditions, it shall be subject to the hygroscopic test and identified as Interior Type A in accordance with U.B.C. Standard No. 25-28.

All materials shall bear identification showing the fire performance rating thereof. Such identification shall be issued by an approved agency having a service for inspection of materials at the factory.

A general misinterpretation of the definition of fire retardant treated wood is that it means fireproof wood. This is not the case: the fire retardant chemicals merely reduce the rate by which flame-spread travels over the surface of the wood.

For a better understanding of flame-spread and fire resistance, refer to the discussions in Article 8 of this Guide.

The BTU fuel content of fire retardant wood and untreated wood is essentially the same.

FLOOR AREA is the area included within the surrounding exterior walls of a building or portion thereof, exclusive of vent shafts and courts. The floor area of a building, or portion thereof, not provided with surrounding exterior walls shall be the usable area under the horizontal projection of the roof or floor above.

The floor area of a building is of great importance to the owner and the designer since it is a key determinant of the type of construction that has to be used for the building. This will be discussed in detail in Article 5 in relation to Sections 502, 505 and 506 and Table No. 5-C. The floor area definition requires the measurement of the area to include everything within the exterior walls except for vent shafts and courts.

There is a difference of opinion among building officials whether the exterior wall thickness is to be included or excluded from the computation. That is, is the measurement to be made from the outside of the exterior wall or from the inside? Early in the design stage, the designer should determine the prevailing method in the jurisdiction and confirm it in writing if it is an important consideration in the particular building.

The area calculation is a gross figure. Items such as elevators, stairways and utility or mechanical shafts are not to be deducted. Where there is an overhang covering a portion of the floor area without enclosing walls, as might be found in a loading dock or a balcony, the floor area must be calculated to the outside edge of the overhang. (See Figure 4-2.)

The floor area calculation is of such importance that the designer should establish this figure early in the preliminary discussions with the local enforcement agency.

Sec. 408.
GARAGE is a building or portion thereof in which a motor vehicle containing

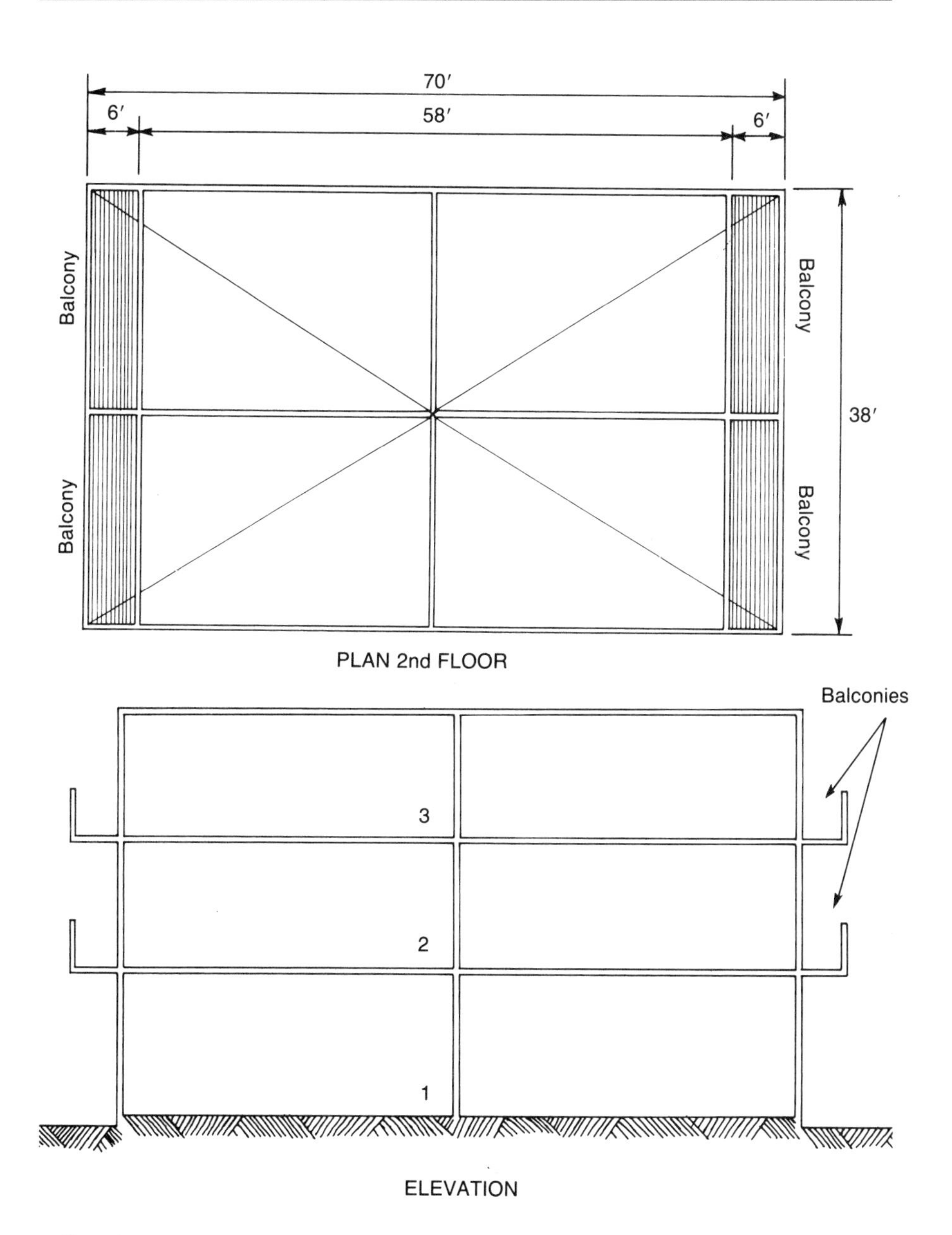

Floor Area of 1st and 2nd Floors is shown by diagonal lines, i.e., 70 × 38 = 2660 square feet.
Floor Area of 3rd floor = 58 × 38 = 2204 square feet, since the 3rd floor balcony is not covered by a roof.

REFERENCE: SECTION 407

FIGURE 4-2 FLOOR AREA CALCULATION WITH BALCONY

flammable or combustible liquids or gas in its tank, is stored, repaired or kept.
GARAGE, PRIVATE, is a building or a portion of a building, not more than 1000 square feet in area, in which only motor vehicles used by the tenants of the building or buildings on the premises are stored or kept. (See Section 1101.)
GARAGE, PUBLIC, is any garage other than a private garage.

There are several definitions, and three different classifications, of garages. The least restrictive definition refers to a garage in conjunction with a dwelling or a small office building: a private garage. It is classified as a Group M Occupancy.

When the garage is larger, or if it is in a larger building or serves occupants other than those in the building, it is called a public garage. This garage is classified as a Group B, Division 1 Occupancy.

The third class of garage is a repair garage classed as a Group H, Division 4 Occupancy.

The reason for the three different garage classes is illustrated in Table No. 5-C. In a Type III-N building, a Group B, Division 1 Occupancy allows a floor area of 12,000 square feet. In a similar building, a Group H, Division 4 Occupancy limits the floor area to 7,500 square feet. The smaller allowable area is due to the presence of repair equipment, including torches and flammable liquids (oil and gasoline) which may permeate the area when repairs are made.

On the other hand, the Group M private garage is limited to 1,000 square feet with a maximum of 3,000 square feet in any one building. The provisions in Chapter 11 enable the private garage to reach the maximum of 3,000 square feet in the building provided each 1,000 square foot area is separated from another by a one-hour area separation wall.

GRADE (Adjacent Ground Elevation) is the lowest point of elevation of the finished surface of the ground, paving or sidewalk within the area between the building and the property line or, when the property line is more than 5 feet from the building, between the building and a line 5 feet from the building.

This definition requires that the elevation of the ground surface to be used be either:

- the level between the building and the property line or
- where the property line is more than five feet from the building, the lowest point within a distance of five feet from the building.

The code intent is to establish what would be a natural ground line and to prevent someone from piling soil up against the foundation of the building and claiming that it represents the grade. By requiring the measurement to be the lowest elevation within five feet of the building, the code establishes a five-foot width to represent grade and not simply a mound of earth against the foundation. A retaining wall can be used to establish this five-foot level width.

The determination of the grade level is important to the designer for several reasons, including the qualification of a level as a basement and the measurement of the allowable overall height of the building. (See Figure 4-3.)

Sec. 409

HEIGHT OF BUILDING is the vertical distance above a reference datum measured to the highest point of the coping of a flat roof or to the deck line of a mansard roof or to the average height of the highest gable of a pitched or hipped roof. The reference datum shall be selected by either of the following, whichever yields a greater height of building:

1. **The elevation of the highest adjoining sidewalk or ground surface within a five-foot horizontal distance of the exterior wall of the building when such sidewalk or ground surface is not more than 10 feet above lowest grade.**
2. **An elevation 10 feet higher than the lowest grade when the sidewalk or ground surface described in Item 1 above is more than 10 feet above lowest grade.**

The height of a stepped or terraced building is the maximum height of any segment of the building.

Height of building discussed in this definition relates to the provisions in Chapter 5 for considering the maximum height for a given type of construction and number of stories in a building. See Figure 4-4.

Height and stories are interdependent in Table No. 5-D wherein the limitations for the height in feet and the number of stories are established. The provisions for measuring the height require reference to the ground surface. The five-foot horizontal width in Item 1 is comparable to the five-foot width measurement for determining grade.

The concern with the method of height measurement is based on the fire and panic hazards presented by taller structures or those with more levels of occupancy. Many times the misinterpretation or misapplication of the height and story measurement has been the result of a desire to avoid the added exit and fire protection requirements that apply

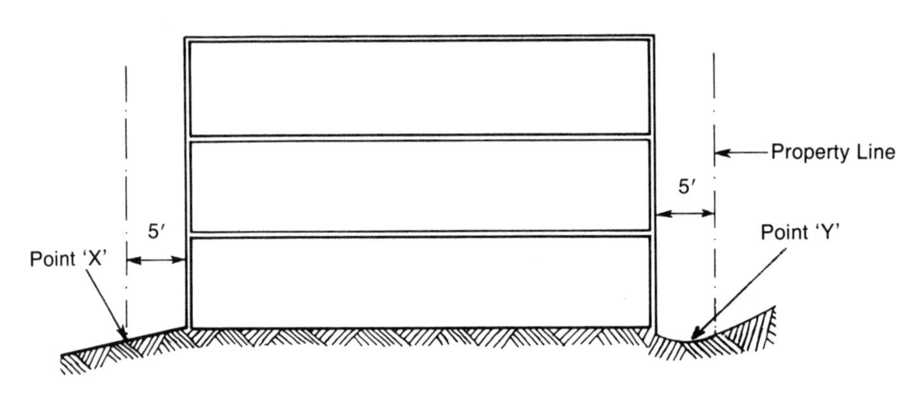

ELEVATION 'A'

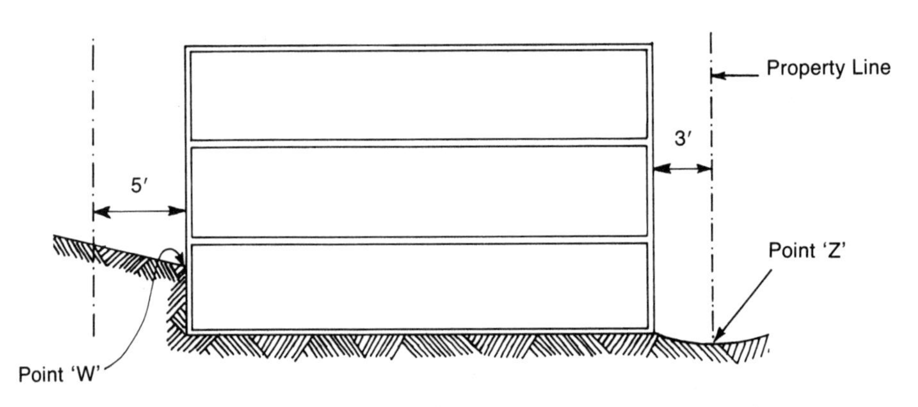

ELEVATION 'B'

The "lowest" grade elevation to be used in connection with the definition of "story" are, for the 2 examples above:

Elevation A
Points 'X' and 'Y' show how to determine the lowest point within 5′ of the building.

Elevation B
Points 'W' and 'Z'; Point 'Z' is the grade at the property line which is used when that line is less than 5′ from the building.
Points 'W' is the grade used when it is the lowest point within 5′ of the building.

REFERENCE: SECTION 408

FIGURE 4-3 GRADE DETERMINATION

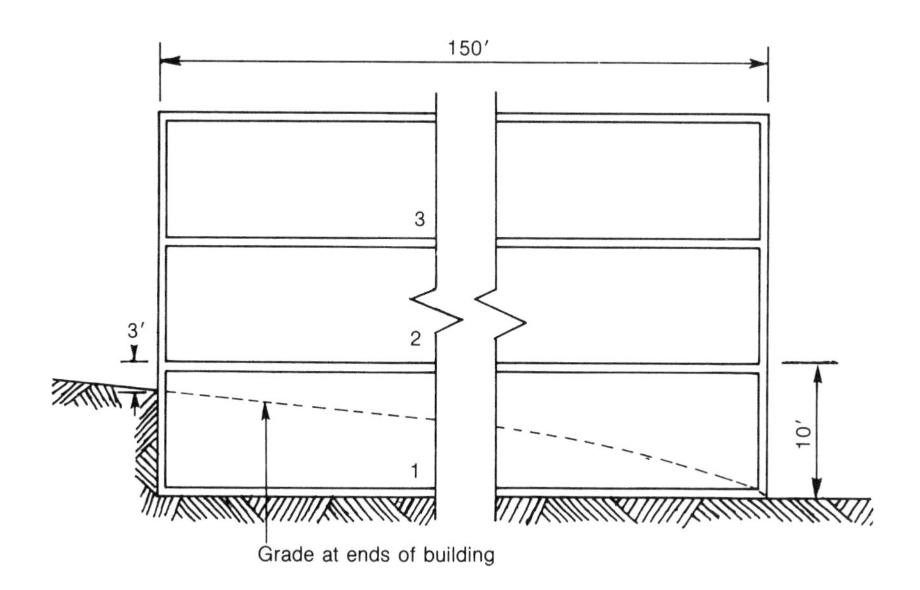

Level 1 is a story if the floor of the level above is more than 6′ above grade for more than 50% of the total perimeter of the building or more than 12′ above grade at any point.

Grade is the level of the lowest point of the adjacent ground finished surface within 5′ of the building or if the property line is less than 5′ from the building, the elevation along that property line. See Figure 4-2.

In the example above, assuming the building to be 150′ × 300′, and the 6′ elevation of the 2nd level of one end is 90 feet back from the 10′ high side and at the other end is 75 feet back from the 10′ high side, the percentage of the perimeter that is more than 6′ above grade is:

$$\frac{300 + 90 + 75}{300 + 300 + 150 + 150} = \frac{465}{900}$$

$$\text{Percentage} > 6' = 52\%$$

Therefore, Level 1 is a story.

REFERENCE: SECTIONS 403, 408, 420

FIGURE 4-4 RELATIONSHIP OF GRADE FOR STORY DETERMINATION

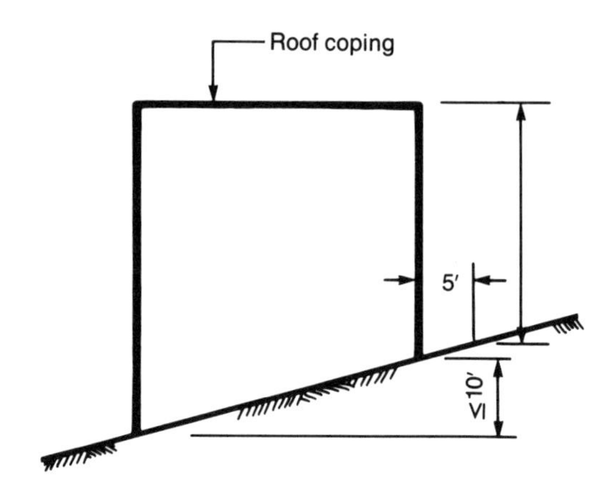

CASE 1

GROUND @ UPPER WALL
MORE THAN 10 FEET ABOVE GRADE
OF GROUND @ LOWER WALL OF BUILDING

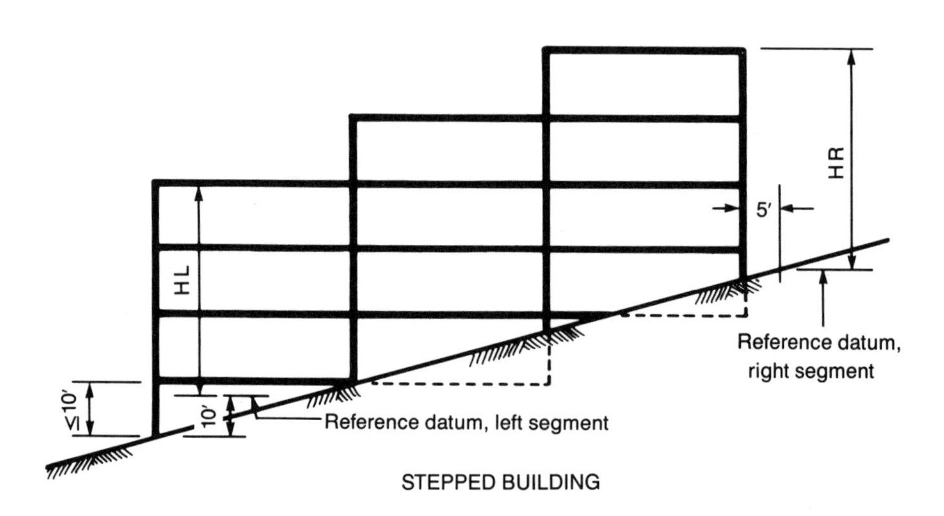

STEPPED BUILDING

REFERENCE: SECTION 409

FIGURE 4-5 HEIGHT OF BUILDING MEASUREMENT

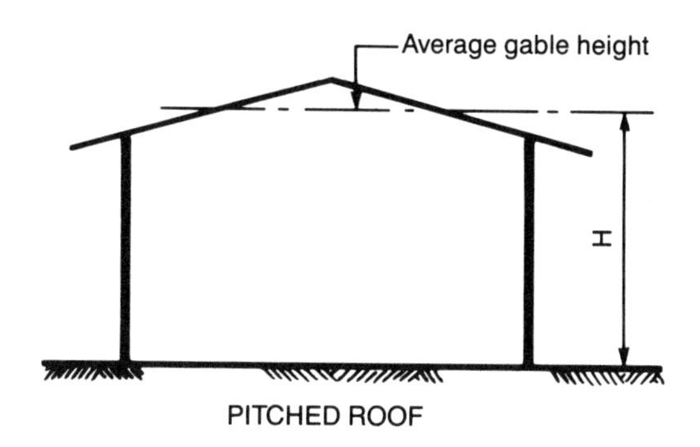

PITCHED ROOF

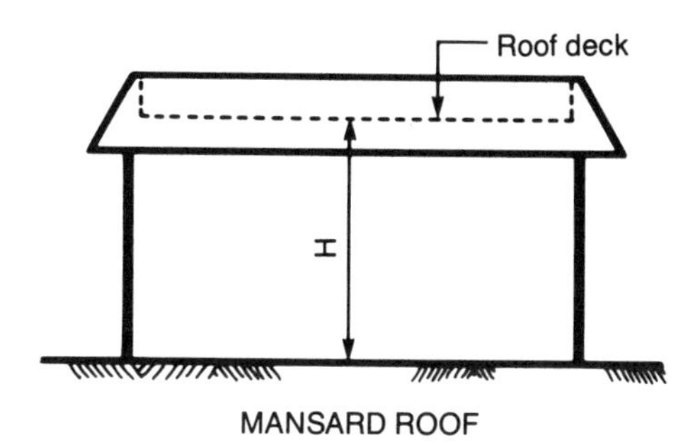

MANSARD ROOF

H = Height of Building

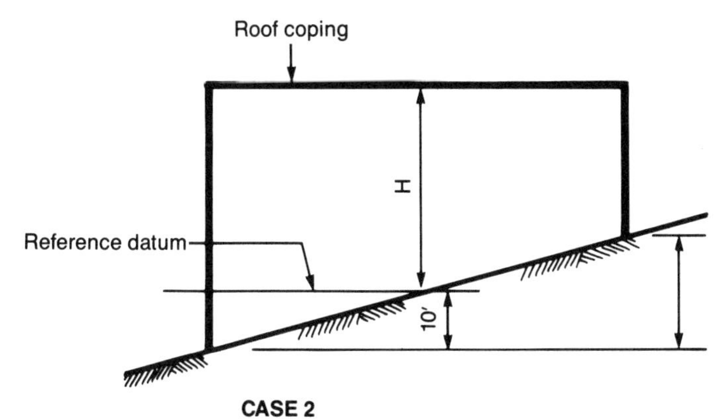

CASE 2

GRADE OF GROUND @ UPPER WALL
10 FEET OR LESS ABOVE GRADE
OF GROUND @ LOWER WALL OF BUILDING

when a building is three or more stories in height.

The designer is cautioned that any error in this part of the design can produce considerable repercussions; hence, the designer should use a conservative approach to the height measurement.

HOTEL is any building containing six or more guest rooms intended or designed to be used, or which are used, rented or hired out to be occupied, or which are occupied for sleeping purposes by guests.

The hotel is another sub-group of the R-1 Occupancy, multi-family usage. The controlling criterion is the number of guest rooms rather than dwelling units (as is used in the apartment house definition).

Sec. 414.

MECHANICAL CODE is the Uniform Mechanical Code promulgated jointly by the International Conference of Building Officials and the International Association of Plumbing and Mechanical Officials, as adopted by this jurisdiction.

One of the codes referenced in the UBC provisions is the Mechanical Code, in particular the Uniform Mechanical Code (UMC). It is adopted by a jurisdiction in a similar manner as is the UBC.

MEMBRANE PENETRATION FIRE STOP is a material, device or construction installed to resist, for a prescribed time period, the passage of flame, heat and hot gases through openings in a protective membrane in order to accomadate cables, cable trays, conduits, tubing or similar items.

This definition relate to the requirements of the new penetration provisions primarily found in Chapter 43.

MEZZANINE OR MEZZANINE FLOOR is an intermediate floor placed within a room.

The construction provisions for mezzanines are contained in Section 1717. The key determinant in whether a level qualifies as a mezzanine is stated in Item 3 of Section 1717, which reads:

3. The aggregate area of mezzanines within a room shall not exceed one third the area of the room in which it is located. Intermediate floor levels that are 6 or more feet above grade shall be considered a story when the area of such level exceeds one third the area of the room in which it is located.

Sec. 415.

NONCOMBUSTIBLE as applied to building construction material means a material which, in the form in which it is used, is either one of the following:

1. **Material of which no part will ignite and burn when subjected to fire. Any material conforming to U.B.C. Standard No. 4-1 shall be considered noncombustible within the meaning of this section.**
2. **Material having a structural base of noncombustible material as defined in Item No. 1 above, with a surfacing material not over 1/8 inch thick which has a flame-spread rating of 50 or less.**

"Noncombustible" does not apply to surface finish materials. Material required to be noncombustible for reduced clearances to flues, heating appliances or other sources of high temperature shall refer to material conforming to Item No. 1. No material shall be classed as noncombustible which is subject to increase in combustibility or flame-spread rating, beyond the limits herein established, through the effects of age, moisture or other atmospheric condition.

Flame-spread rating as used herein refers to rating obtained according to tests conducted as specified in U.B.C. Standard No. 42-1.

The term "noncombustible" is used to define the basic burning characteristic of a material. It is not a term applicable to interior finish materials but rather applies to components of the building and to fire-resistive assemblies.

The primary requirement for a material to be classed as noncombustible is that it meets the UBC Standard No. 4-1, which is derived from the national standard ASTM E-136. This standard requires that the test specimen not raise the temperature of the test furnace by more than 54^{0}F after the test sample is inserted into the preheated furnace. The initial test furnace temperature is 1382^{0}F.

Therefore, the material has to have a high resistance to ignition or a low BTU content in order to maintain the temperature at or below the permissible limit. Another test criteria is that, after 30 seconds exposure in the furnace, the test sample does not flame.

The purpose of requiring a material to be noncombustible is to prevent it from contributing to a fire as would a combustible material. This requirement serves as a means of reducing the available fire load in an area.

Examples of some of the common building materials regarding their combustiblity are:

	NonCombustible	Combustible
Chipboard, with or without FR treatment		X
Fiberglass or mineral insulation	X	
if paperbacked		X
Gypsum wallboard, all	X	
Plastics, with or without FR treatment		X
Plywood, regular or FR treated		X
Steel studs and other members	X	
Plaster	X	
Wood studs and other members		X
Wood stud, FR treated		X

FR = fire retardant

The term "incombustible" is often used synonymously with noncombustible.

Sec. 416.
OCCUPANCY is the purpose for which a building, or part thereof, is used or intended to be used.

The term "occupancy" encompasses one of the main criteria in the design of a building. The occupancy of a building is, by code, to be assigned by the building official per Chapter 5. Regardless of the use that may be proposed for the building, the building official has to assign it to a general occupancy class: the one which it most nearly resembles.

The occupancy or use may vary from time to time. However, whenever the occupancy or use changes from one occupancy group or division to another, as defined in Chapter 5, the code requires a building permit be obtained to legalize that change of occupancy. There is no such requirement when the change is within the same occupancy division, such as a grocery store changing to a barber shop, both being Group B Division 2 Occupancies. (See the discussion of Section 503 in Article 3.)

OWNER is any person, agent, firm or corporation having a legal or equitable interest in the property.

This term includes more than one might think on first reading the definition. The phrase "having a legal or equitable interest" refers also to a lessee or tenant of the property. Once a building or portion thereof is leased, the improvements to the premises often are made by the tenant or lessee; in fact, most lease agreements stipulate that this be the case.

The code often refers to the responsibilities of the building permit applicants. Because any action regarding a permit involves the legal status of a building, it can readily be seen that the applicant for the permit has the power to affect this status.

In the leasing agreements between owners and tenants, the lessee is usually required to comply with local codes and ordinances. Usually there is no provision in the lease covering the possible affect that a tenant applied-for building permit might have on the owner's investment.

For example, assume that a tenant files for a permit. To lower the cost of the intended work, the tenant may request that the building type of construction be changed from Type I to Type V One-hour. That change, along with the subsequent work, will result in a legal change in the city's records for that building. Any future use of the building could involve substantial expense to the owner. These changes can occur without the owner being aware of them until much later.

The owner might also be unaware of a change in the building's occupancy classification. A tenant could apply for a permit, indicate a less hazardous occupancy will be involved than previously, and thereby change the occupancy of the building from that previously recorded to the new use. The tenant may have arranged this change in occupancy in order to reduce the code requirements applicable to his proposed alteration. In the future the owner may find that, if the building's original occupancy classification were to be reestablished, it would have to conform to the requirements for that occupancy in the most recent building code. This could prove to be costly. [See Sections 104 (c), 307 (c) and 502.]

The tenant or lessee is accepted, in the code and by the local jurisdiction, as acting for the owner. The tenant or lessee, in proposing to make improvements to the building or changes in the occupancy classification thereof, should be required to provide the owner with written notification of that intention. The tenant would thus be subject to future liability as a result of having taken action without first advising the owner.

Sec. 417.

PENETRATION FIRE STOP is a through-penetration fire stop or membrane penetration fire stop.

PROTECTIVE MEMBRANE is a surface material which forms the required outer layer or layers of a fire-resistive assembly containing concealed spaces.

These definitions relate to the requirements of the new penetration provisions primarily found in Chapter 43.

Sec. 419.

REPAIR is the reconstruction or renewal of any part of an existing building for the purpose of its maintenance.

The code regards repair work as an "alteration." All repairs, except for minor ones such as filling holes in walls, require a building permit per Section 301. Before doing repair work, it is best to determine whether that jurisdiction requires a permit for that class of repair work.

Sec. 420.

SHAFT is an interior space, enclosed by walls or construction, extending through one or more stories or basements which connects openings on successive floors, or floors and roof, to accomadate elevators, dumbwaiters, mechanical equipment or similar devices or to transmit light or ventilation air.

SHAFT ENCLOSURE is the walls or construction forming the boundaries of a shaft.

These definitions relate to the requirements of the new provisions primarily found in Section 1706 and Chapter 43.

SMOKE DETECTOR is an approved listed device that senses visible or invisible particles of combustion.

There are two general categories of smoke detectors, the ionization type and the photoelectric type. A smoke detector containing both means of detection provides maximum protection. Each detection means has a different reaction time in response to varying fire and smoke conditions.

In Section 1210 (c), the code stipulates that when alterations of $1,000 or more are done in single- or two-family dwelling unit occupancies (R-3 Occupancies), a smoke detector must be installed. Some jurisdictions also require that smoke detectors be provided upon changes in ownership.

STORY is that portion of a building included between the upper surface of any floor and the upper surface of the floor next above, except that the topmost story shall be that portion of a building included between the upper surface of the topmost floor and the ceiling or roof above. If the finished floor level directly above a usable or unused under-floor space is more than 6 feet above grade as defined herein for more than 50 percent of the total perimeter or is more than 12 feet above grade as defined at any point, such usable or unused under-floor space shall be considered as a story.

The most important part of this definition lies in the second sentence. Together with the definitions of "grade" and "basement," this provision determines whether there is an extra level included in the count of the floor area and in the overall number of stories in a building. This, in turn, will affect the choice of the building construction type. (See Figure 4-4.)

STREET is any thoroughfare or public way not less than 16 feet in width which has been dedicated or deeded to the public for public use.

A "public way" is one form of frontage or separation and is thus acceptable in determining whether the allowable floor area may be increased. [See Section 506 (a).] Because at least one building line may front on a street, the requirements of Table No. 5-A will apply to that line.

This allowance is usually not a problem unless the street or public way is narrow. In such a situation, the application of Section 504 (a) and Table No. 5-A could result in a requirement for protection of the wall and/or openings on that part of the building.

Sec. 421.
THROUGH-PENETRATION FIRE STOP is a material, device or construction installed to resist, for a prescribed time period, the passage of flame, heat and hot gases through openings in a protective membrane in order to accomadate cables, cable trays, conduits, tubing or similar items.

This definitions relate to the requirements of the new penetration provisions primarily found in Chapter 43.

Sec. 422. U.B.C. STANDARDS is the Uniform Building Code Standards promulgated by the International Conference of Building Officials, as adopted by this jurisdiction. (See Chapter 60.)

Throughout the code there are references made to the "U.B.C. Standard X-X." These standards are contained in a separate document titled "Uniform Building Code Standards" which is reprinted every three years concurrent with the triennial reprinting of the UBC.

The standards are listed in Chapter 60 of the UBC with the source document identified. With some exceptions, the bulk of the UBC Standards are derived from existing national standards. Appropriate editing makes them enforceable as legal documents.

The numbering system of the UBC Standards is such that the first number corresponds to that of the primary chapter to which the standard relates. The second number is sequentially assigned. Thus, UBC Standard 43-1 is the first standard cited in Chapter 43. A check of the Chapter 60 provisions reveals that Standard 43-1 is derived fromsource document ASTM E-119, the American Society for Testing and Materials, Standard Methods for Fire Tests of Building Construction and Materials.

The standards are as much a part of the code as is any section or chapter contained therein, as is specifically stated in Section 6001:

The U.B.C. Standards which are referred to in various parts of this code shall be the Uniform Building Code Standards, 1991 Edition, and are hereby declared to be a part of this code.

Sec. 424.
Walls
Exterior Wall is any wall or element of a wall, or any member or group of members, which defines the exterior boundaries or courts of a building and which has a slope of 60 degrees or greater with the horizontal plane.

The definition of "exterior wall" should be noted. An A-frame building with a slope of more than 60 would be a wall; however, a surface of less than 60, as might be found in a mansard, could be considered a roof.

WEATHER-EXPOSED SURFACES are all surfaces of walls, ceilings, floors, roofs, soffits and similar surfaces exposed to the weather, excepting the following:

1. **Ceilings and roof soffits enclosed by walls or by beams which extend a minimum of 12 inches below such ceiling or roof soffits.**
2. **Walls or portions of walls within an unenclosed area, when located a horizontal distance from an exterior opening equal to twice the height of the opening.**
3. **Ceiling and roof soffits beyond a horizontal distance of 10 feet from the outer edge of the ceiling or roof soffits.**

For illustrations of the provisions of this definition, see Figure 4-6.

The three criteria in the above definition may not be sufficient because topography and climatic conditions vary. The designer should be aware that he could be liable for failing to take into account these conditions should they cause the deterioration of the surfaces or the materials they cover. The designer is responsible for the design and should know the site conditions to which the surfaces will be subjected.

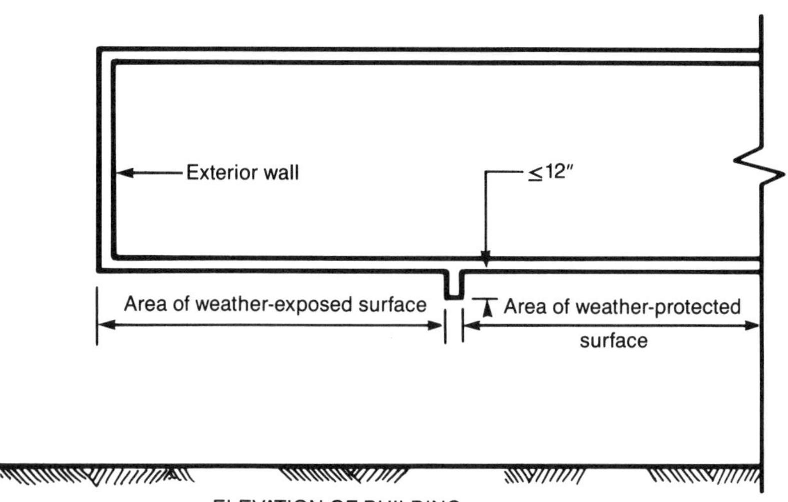

ELEVATION OF BUILDING
WITH UNENCLOSED EXTERIOR OPENING
EXCEPTION 1
SECTION 424 WEATHER-PROTECTED SURFACES

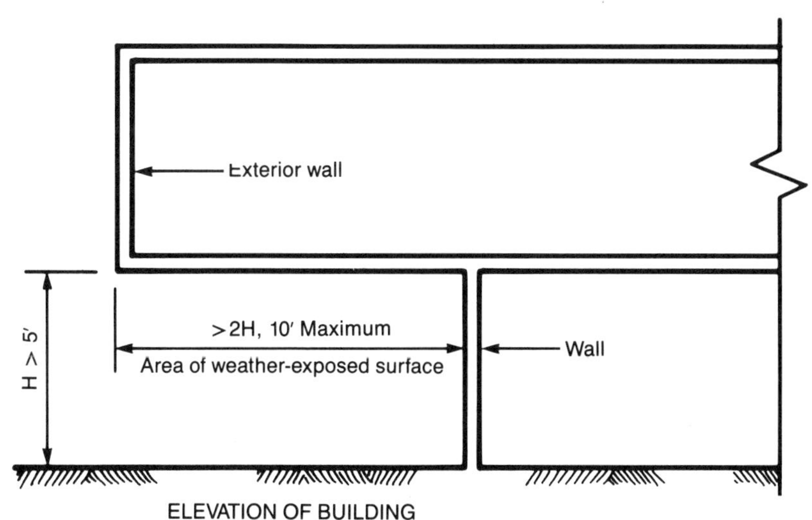

ELEVATION OF BUILDING
WITH UNENCLOSED EXTERIOR OPENING
EXCEPTION 2 AND 3
SECTION 424 WEATHER-PROTECTED SURFACES

NOTE: When 2H = 10′, regardless of the height of the opening, any surface more than 10′ from the outer edge is considered as a weather-protected surface.

REFERENCE: SECTION 424

FIGURE 4-6 DEFINITION OF WEATHER-EXPOSED SURFACE ILLUSTRATED

Sec. 426.

YARD is an open, unoccupied space, other than a court, unobstructed from the ground to the sky, except where specifically provided by this code, on the lot on which a building is situated.

A yard is another of the specific frontages or separations that may be used in determining whether the allowable area may be increased per Section 506 (a). For most occupancies, the parking lot around a building can be considered a yard.

The main characteristic of a yard is that it is open to the sky from the ground level up. Section 702 (b) provides that the definition of ground level need not mean the actual ground but may mean the top of a slab on which the structures are built.

GLOSSARY OF TERMS

The following are terms that are used in this Guide but that have special meanings not usually found in the dictionary. These terms are supplementary to the definitions in the Uniform Building Code:

ADA. Federal law "Americans with Disabilities Act"

ANSI. American National Standards Institute.

ASTM. The American Society for Testing and Materials.

ENFORCMEMENT AUTHORITY OR OFFICIAL. The enforcement authority referred to in this Guide is the building inspection agency that enforces the building code in its locality and the fire service enforcement official (usually the fire marshal) or the fire prevention agency of the fire department which is charged with enforcing the fire code.

ICBO. The International Conference of Building Officials is the organization that publishes several model codes including the Uniform Building, Fire, and Mechanical Codes.

JURISDICTION. This term is used as a blanket reference to the legal governmental entity that enacts and enforces the code. It includes any level of government from town, city, county, or state. It has the legal power and responsibility to adopt the laws and to prosecute violations thereof. (See also the definition in the UBC.)

MAINTENANCE. This term has two slightly different meanings, one relevant to the UBC and another, broader term used in the UFC. As used in the UBC, it refers to the maintaining, by the owner of the building, of all devices and safeguards in conformance with the requirements in effect when the building was constructed.

The UFC, on the other hand, is concerned with the overall maintenance of the safety features including the materials in use within the building and its exit paths. Thus the building, once it has been built, is subject to periodic fire service inspections performed to assure that the use and occupancy has not been made more hazardous than intended under the original building permit, and that exits as well as other safety features are operational.

In short, one builds under the requirements of the building code and one maintains and operates under those of the fire code.

NFPA. The National Fire Protection Association.

OFFICIAL. As used herein, this term refers to one of the enforcement officials, usually the building official.

UBC. Uniform Building Code.

UFAS. Uniform Federal Accessibility Standards

UFC. Uniform Fire Code.

ULI. Underwriters Laboratories, Inc.

NOTES

ARTICLE 5
THE OCCUPANCY PROVISIONS OF CHAPTER 5

As mentioned in Article 2, Chapter 5 provides the occupancy requirements for the design of a building. The pertinent sections of Chapter 5 are discussed in this Guide in the same sequence as they appear in the UBC. Each analysis and discussion is preceded by all or a portion of the code text.

Occupancy Classified

Sec. 501. Every building, whether existing or hereafter erected, shall be classified by the building official, according to its use or the character of its occupancy, as a building of Group A, B, E, H, I, M or R as defined in Chapters 6, 7, 8, 9, 10, 11 and 12. (See Table No. 5-A.)

Any occupancy not mentioned specifically or about which there is any question shall be classified by the building official and included in the group which its use most nearly resembles, based on the existing or proposed life and fire hazard.

This section charges the building official with two responsibilities:

1) to designate the occupancy classification for an existing or proposed use in a building.
2) if a use does not fit into one of the existing occupancy Groups or Divisions listed in Table No. 5-A, to place the use in the Group and Division it most nearly resembles, based on life and/or fire hazard that would exist with that use.

Early in the design process, the designer should ascertain the categories for uses that do not fit into predefined groups. The categorizing is done to avoid problems resulting from a difference of opinion with the building official. If the official does not agree with the designer's choice of the classification, he could place the use in an entirely different and possibly more restrictive classification. Such an action could necessitate the redesign of the proposed structure or of the alterations planned for an existing building.

Change of Use

Sec. 502. No change shall be made in the character of occupancies or use of any building which would place the building in a different division of the same group of occupancy or in a different group of occupancies, unless such building is made to comply with the requirements of this code for such division or group of occupancy.

EXCEPTION: The character of the occupancy of existing buildings may be

changed subject to the approval of the building official, and the building may be occupied for purposes in other groups without conforming to all the requirements of this code for those groups, provided the new or proposed use is less hazardous, based on life and fire risk, than the existing use.

No change in the character of occupancy of a building shall be made without a Certificate of Occupancy, as required in Section 307 of this code. The building official may issue a Certificate of Occupancy pursuant to the intent of the above exception without certifying that the building complies with all provisions of this code.

This section requires that when a change in building use occurs, the building must be brought up to the requirements applicable to the new use under the provisions of the current code. It must be understood that many changes do not involve what the code defines as a change in use. For example, a change in a building's original use from a grocery store to a bank or an office is not considered a change in use Because all these uses are classified under Group B Division 2 Occupancy. (See Table No. 5-A.)

The change in use provisions apply only when the new use belongs to another occupancy group or another division of the original occupancy group.

In the author's opinion, and contrary to an ICBO interpretation, a change in the character of an occupancy *within the same occupancy division does not constitute* a change of occupancy under the provisions of Section 502.

Section 502 also states that it is the code's intent to allow a change in the occupancy or use in an existing building without requiring full compliance with the code. The code stipulates in the Exception, however, that for such an allowance the proposed use must be "less hazardous" than the previous one. In the Article 1 discussion in this Guide, it is recommended that Tables No. 5-C and 5-D be used to determine whether one use is more or less hazardous than another.

The designer should note that according to the last sentence of the second paragraph cited above, the issuance of a Certificate of Occupancy (CO) for an existing building does not require the building official to certify that the entire building meets the code. Clearly, the intent of the code is to have the official determine the relative hazard of the proposed use and then to require only those code provisions be met that relate to an increased hazard of the proposed use.

The latitude expressed in this section places a judgmental responsibility on the official to evaluate the existing building and determine whether the proposed use is more or less hazardous than the previous use. Thus, Section 502 permits the determination of the life and fire hazards of a proposed use on basis more realistic than one of invoking the literal provisions of the code.

Mixed Occupancy.

Sec. 503 (a) General. When a building is used for more than one occupancy purpose, each part of the building comprising a distinct "Occupancy," as described in Chapters 5 through 12, shall be separated from any other occupancy as specified in Section 503 (d).

EXCEPTIONS: 1. Where an approved spray booth constructed in accordance with the Fire Code is installed, such booth need not be separated from other Group H Occupancies or from Group B Occupancies.

2. The following occupancies need not be separated from the uses to which they are accessory:

A. Assembly rooms having a floor area of not over 750 square feet.

B. Administrative and clerical offices and similar rooms which do not exceed 25 percent of the floor area of the major use when not related to Group H, Division 2 and Group H, Division 3 Occupancies.

C. Gift shops, administrative offices and similar rooms in Group R, Division 1 Occupancies not exceeding 10 percent of the floor area of the major use.

D. The kitchen serving the dining area of which it is a part.

3. An occupancy separation need not be provided between a Group R, Division 3 Occupancy and a carport having no enclosed uses above, provided the carport is entirely open on two or more sides.

4. A Group B, Division 1 Occupancy used exclusively for the parking or storage of private or pleasure-type motor vehicles need not be separated from a Group B, Division 3 Occupancy open parking garage as defined in Section 709.

When a building houses more than one occupancy, each portion of the building shall conform to the requirements for the occupancy housed therein.

An occupancy shall not be located above the story or height set forth in Table No. 5-D, except as provided in Section 507. When a mixed occupancy building contains a Group H, Division 6 Occupancy, the portion containing the Group H, Division 6 Occupancy shall not exceed three stories nor 55 feet in height.

The mixed occupancy provisions that were previously contained in Section 503 (a) second and third paragraphs of prior editions of the code have been transferred to a new Section 505 (c).

i. **General**

Most buildings contain one or more occupancie in addition to the main occupancy or use. An office building, Group B, Division 2 Occupancy, often contains parking facilities (B-1), a canteen or cafeteria (A-2.1 or A-3), and conference or meeting rooms (A-2.1 or A-3). These other uses within the office building are not unusual and represent a mixed occupancy regulated by this section.

This section requires that when there are different occupancies in a building, they must be separated from each other by fire-resistive construction in accordance with Section 503 (d). It further limits the location of each particular occupancy, vertically within a building, to no higher than the number of stories and height stated in Table No. 5-D.

In Exception 3 reference is made to a carport. The code does not have a definition of a carport or what differentiates it from a garage. This exception provides such a definition; i.e., a carport is a facility that is open on at least two sides used for storing an automobile or similar vehicles.

It is important that the designer be aware of this characteristic of a carport to avoid inadvertently considering a space with only one open side as a carport.

ii. **Mixed Occupancy and Effect of Change in Type of Construction.**

In certain circumstances, a change proposed for a portion of a building warrants a reexamination of the building. The results can be surprising. For example, assume there is a one-story Type III-N building (typical tilt-up warehouse) of Group B, Division 2 Occupancy with an area of 110,000 square feet, sprinklers and side yards of 60 feet or more all around. With these qualifications, the B-2 Occupancy is permitted to use the unlimited area provisions of Section 506 (b).

Assume there is now a proposal to use 27,000 square feet of the building for Group H, Division 6 Occupancy (semiconductor facility). The code does not permit an H-6 Occupancy to have the unlimited area benefits. It is therefore necessary to reassess the building under the provisions of Section 503, Table No. 5-A together with the separation and sprinkler credits allowed. (See Figure 5-1.)

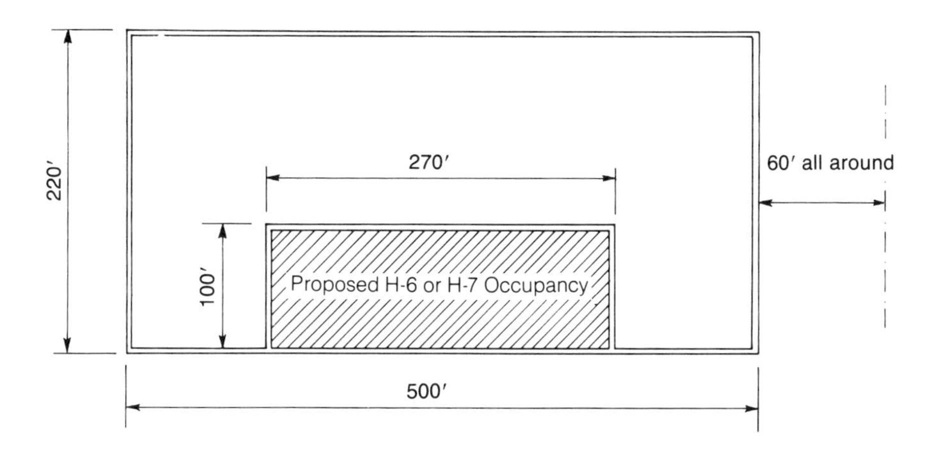

This example relies on material to be discussed later in the Guide. However, it does meet the change of occupancy intent of Section 502.

Section 502 requires a change in use meet the requirements for the new use or occupancy. However, the type of construction requirements must similarly be satisfied. Thus Table No. 5-C provisions apply.

This example illustrates a possible means for satisfying the code by downgrading the building's type of construction from Type III-N to Type V One-hour and the benefit that could derive.

ASSUME:
Type III-N Building, One Story
B-2 Occupancy, 110,000 S.F.
Fully sprinklered, 60-foot separations all around
Building with only B-2 is permitted unlimited area

a) B-2 and H-6 in Type III-N, 4 separations and sprinklered
   B-2 and H-6 allowable area – 1 story building = 12,000 × 2 × 3 = 72,000 S.F., since building overall area = 110,000 S.F., it exceeds allowable area.
b) If Type III-N were changed to Type V one-hour,
   H-6 and B-2 allowable area = 18,000 × 2 × 3 = 84,000 S.F.; 83,000 S.F. desired.
   Use one area separation between B-2 and H-6, two-hour construction.
   H-6 allowable area = 14,000 × 3 = 42,000 S.F., the 27,000 S.F. desired is O.K.

Thus, by reducing the construction type and adding one area separation wall of two-hour construction (which need not have a parapet), this proposed mixed occupancy building meets the code.

REFERENCE: SECTIONS 502, 503 (a), 506 (b) AND TABLE NO. 5-C

FIGURE 5-1 CHANGE IN USE/CHANGE IN BUILDING CONSTRUCTION TYPE

The B-2 Occupancy will now occupy an area of 13,000 square feet of the building with the H-6 Occupancy at 27,000 square feet.

Per Table No. 5-C, a B-2 use in a Type III-N building is allowed:

A basic floor area of .... 12,000 square feet
The separations on four sides permit a
100% increase .... 24,000 square feet
The one story building is allowed sprinkler
credit of 300%, or a total allowable for
the B-2 .... 72,000 square feet

Because the B-2 and H-6 are both allowed the same basic floor areas in Table No. 5-C, for the floor area determinations the building can be considered as if it were a single type of occupancy.

The B-2 and H-6 areas aggregate 110,000 square feet. Type III-N construction cannot be used because the building exceeds the code allowables.

If the fire resistance in the building is increased to Type III One-hour:

The basic allowable area increases to. .... 18,000 square feet
The separations then allow .... 36,000 square feet
The sprinkler credits (300%) raise
the allowable area to .... 108,000 square feet

Because the overall size of the building is 110,000 square feet, increasing the fire resistance to Type III One-hour is still not sufficient.

A solution to the problem created in this example may be to add an area separation wall to either the Type III-N or III One-hour construction. Such a wall must be of four-hour construction. Because the roof of either of these two types of construction will be of either nonrated or one-hour combustible construction, the area separation wall must penetrate the roof and form a parapet above the roof. The alternative to a parapet does not apply when a four-hour area separation wall is involved. The construction of such an area separation wall and parapet is costly and may not be acceptable to the building owner because it precludes future flexibility.

Another alternative for the designer to consider is to downgrade the original building's construction type from Type III-N to Type V and to add one-hour fire resistance throughout.

If the Type V One-hour building with the B-2 occupancy has three separations as shown in Figure 5-1:

The basic allowable area is .... 14,000 square feet
Separation increase (100%) .... 28,000 square feet
Sprinkler increase (300%) .... 84,000 square feet

Therefore, the total allowable size for the B-2 is 84,000 square feet.

If the same building contains the H-6 occupancy as shown in Figure 5-1 with only one area separation:

The basic allowable area is .... 14,000 square feet
Sprinkler increase (300%) .... 42,000 square feet

Total allowable area of the H-6 is 42,000 square feet. Thus, the allowable area for the H-6 occupancy exceeds the 28,000 square feet of H-6 space needed.

The downgrading of type of construction and the addition of the one-hour fire resistance enables these two occupancies to meet the code in a Type V One-hour building that could be permitted to be up to 126,000 square feet in size (84,000 + 42,000 = 126,000).

Furthermore, using this design is more feasible than attempting to accomplish the same results in a Type III building due to:

- the lesser fire rating required of the area separation wall (two-hour) for Type V buildings, and
- the termination at the roof of the area separation wall by use of Section 505 (f) Exception 3 for the parapet alternative permitted in the Type V building.

The designer should explain the options to the owner before proposing to downgrade the construction of a building. As shown in this example, there are some advantages that may be worth exploring with the owner before deciding on a course of action.

The Exceptions in Section 503 (a) recognize that there are inherent ancillary or auxiliary uses in addition to the primary use or occupancy. These include:

- offices in connection with public garages, for example, where the parking fees are paid and the record of the vehicle location is kept. These offices are normally small rooms.
- administrative offices for principals in schools. These Group B, Division 2 Occupancies need not be separated from the Group E Occupancy, provided they do not have excessive floor areas. Similarly for B-2 uses in hotel lobbies or the administrative offices in hotels.

The 25 percent limitation is the code's means of recognizing the relationship the related activities have to the major use.

In the author's opinion, the general rule to use is that the auxillary space should:

- be less hazardous, as evaluated from the Table No. 5-C allowables and
- involve a larger occupant load factor from Table No. 33-A, i.e., 100 square feet/person vs. 20 square feet/person.

Sec. 503

(b) Forms of Occupancy Separations. Occupancy separations shall be vertical or horizontal or both or, when necessary, of such other form as may be required to afford a complete separation between the various occupancy divisions in the building.

Where the occupancy separation is horizontal, structural members supporting the separation shall be protected by equivalent fire-resistive construction.

The various occupancies within a mixed occupancy building can generally exist located in almost any spatial relationship to one another. The occupancy separation may be vertical or horizontal or a combination of both. (See Figure 5-2.)

The supports for an occupancy separation are required to have at least the same fire-resistive rating as that of the member being supported. (See Figure 5-3.)

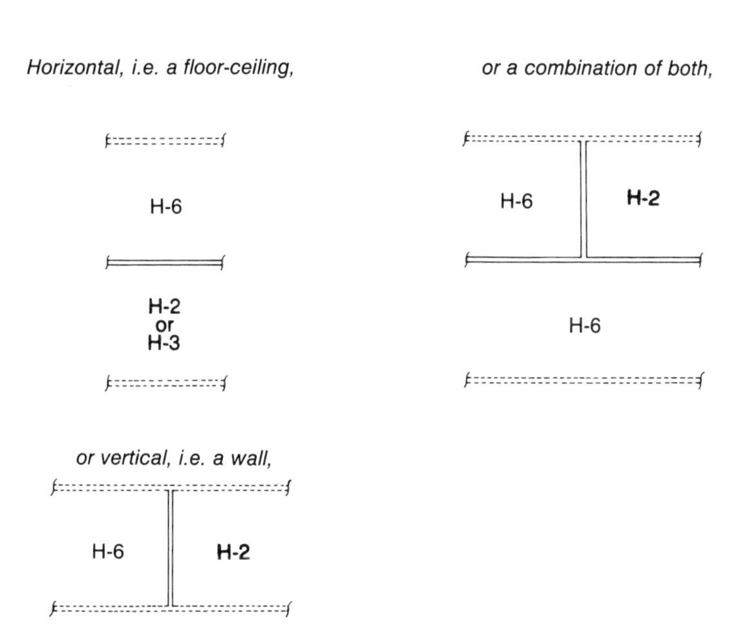

An occupancy separation may occur either in the horizontal or vertical plane. In some instances there will be both a vertical and horizontal component to the separation. Note that in addition to the fire-resistive rating of the wall or floor as required in Section 503 (c) and Table No. 5-B, there are specific limits set in Section 503 (c) for openings in the separation. These limits include the fire-resistive rating for the opening protection as well as percentage limits for the amount of opening permitted in a given surface.

REFERENCE: SECTION 503 (b)

FIGURE 5-2 FORMS OF OCCUPANCY SEPARATION

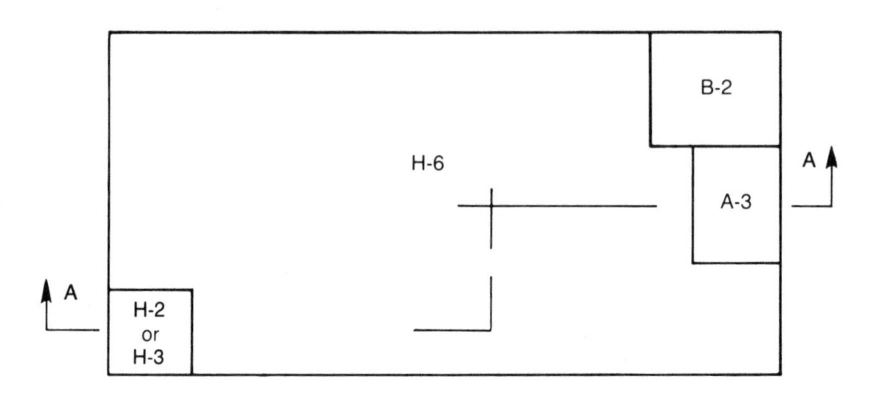

PLAN 1st FLOOR

OCCUPANCY SEPARATIONS PER TABLE NO. 5-B

		Wall Requirement	Opening Protection
On 1st Floor	B-2/A-3	N	N
	H-6/A-3	3-hour	3-hour
	H-6/B-2	1-hour	1-hour
	H-6/H-2	2-hour	1½-hour
	H-6/H-3	1-hour	1-hour
Between 1st and 2nd Floor	B-2/A-3	N	N
	B-2/H-2	2-hour	1½-hour
	B-2/H-3	1-hour	1-hour
	H-6/A-3	3-hour	3-hour
	H-6/H-2	2-hour	1½-hour
	H-6/H-3	1-hour	1-hour
On 2nd Floor	H-6/B-2	1-hour	1-hour

N = No fire rating required

In this figure, the hourly rating of the various occupancy separations are tagged on the sectional view.

The table indicates the several fire resistive ratings for the various occupancy separation in accordance with Table No. 5-B. Also shown are the corresponding opening protection in accordance with the provisions of Section 503 (c).

Since the building is of Type II one-hour fire-resistive construction, the one-hour requirements are met. The B-2/H-2 and H-6/H-2 two-hour requirement mandates the floor of the second story and its supports for the segment over the H-2 occupancy must have two-hour fire resistance to the ground. The three-hour occupancy separation of the second floor over the A-3 Occupancy and its supports similarly must have that rating carried to the ground.

REFERENCE: SECTION 503 (b), 503 (c) TABLE NO. 5-B

FIGURE 5-3 OCCUPANCY SEPARATION REQUIREMENTS

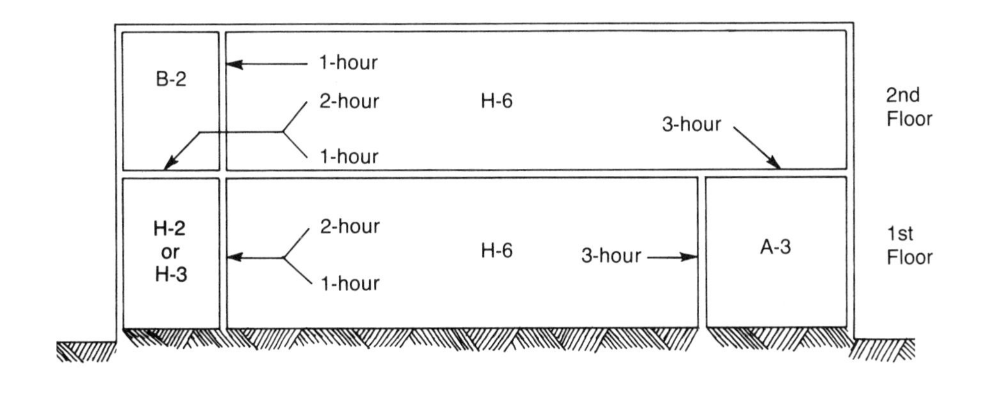

SECTION A-A

ASSUME:
Type II One-hour Building
2 Story
1st Floor as Shown
2nd Floor all H-6 and B-2

Assume the occupancy separation is a wall requiring a two-hour rating by Table No. 5-B, such as between an H-2 and a B-2 Occupancy. See Figure 5-3. That wall is supported by a floor system that rests in turn on a bearing wall directly beneath the two-hour wall. The lower wall separates H-3 and B-2 Occupancy areas located directly below the respective H-2 and B-2 Occupancies.

Because the lower wall need only have a one-hour rating by Table No. 5-B (H-3/B-2 in the matrix) and because the floor between the H-2 and H-3 Occupancies similarly need only be one-hour rated, both the floor system and the upper wall could fail in just over one hour from a fire located in the H-3 area. Were this to happen, the two-hour wall between the H-2 and B-2 areas would collapse because the supporting wall below it would have failed. Fire, therefore, would attack the upper level B-2 Occupancy and expose it to the hazards of the H-2 Occupancy in one hour, instead of the two hours intended by the code.

Sec. 503

(c) Types of Occupancy Separations. Occupancy separations shall be classed as "four-hour fire-resistive," "three-hour fire-resistive," "two-hour fire-resistive," and "one-hour fire-resistive." (See U.B.C. Standard No. 43-7 for fire dampers in air ducts piercing occupancy separations.)

1. A "four-hour fire-resistive occupancy separation" shall have no openings therein and shall be of not less than four-hour fire-resistive construction.

2. A "three-hour fire-resistive occupancy separation" shall be of not less than three-hour fire-resistive construction. All openings in walls forming such separation shall be protected by a fire assembly having a three-hour fire-protection rating. The total width of all openings in any three-hour fire-resistive occupancy separation wall in any one story shall not exceed 25 percent of the length of the wall in that story and no single opening shall have an area greater than 120 square feet.

All openings in floors forming a "three-hour fire-resistive occupancy separation" shall be protected by vertical enclosures extending above and below such openings. The walls of such vertical enclosures shall be of not less than two-hour fire-resistive construction and all openings therein shall be protected by a fire assembly having a one and one-half-hour fire-protection rating.

3. A "two-hour fire-resistive occupancy separation" shall be of not less than two-hour fire-resistive construction. All openings in such separation shall be protected by a fire assembly having a one and one-half-hour fire-protection rating.

4. A "one-hour fire-resistive occupancy separation" shall be of not less than one-hour fire-resistive construction. All openings in such separation shall be protected by a fire assembly having a one-hour fire-protection rating.

The fire rating of an occupancy separation is determined through the use of Table No. 5-B. Once the fire-resistive time period is determined, the fire rating and construction limitations for openings in that separation can be located in Section 503 (c).

The fire-resistive construction requirements for the elements of the occupancy separation are listed in Chapter 43. The construction requirements for fire assemblies for opening protection in the occupancy separation are found in Section 4306. (See Figure 5-3.)

It is important to note that where a four-hour occupancy separation is required, no openings are allowed in the occupancy separation.

TABLE OF OCCUPANCY SEPARATION PROVISIONS

RATING	OPENING PROTECTION REQUIREMENT	
	HORIZONTAL	VERTICAL
4-hour	No openings allowed	No openings allowed
3-hour	3-hour Aggregate width max. 25%	2-hour vertical enclosure w/1 1/2 hour opening protection
2-hour	1 1/2 hour	1 1/2 hour
1-hour	1 hour	1 hour

Sec. 503

(d) Fire Ratings for Occupancy Separations. Occupancy separations shall be provided between the various groups and divisions of occupancies as set forth in Table No. 5-B.

EXCEPTION: 1. A three-hour occupancy separation may be used between a Group A, Division 1 or a Group I Occupancy and a Group B, Division 1 Occupancy used exclusively for the parking or storage of private or pleasure-type motor vehicles and provided no repair or fueling is done. A two-hour occupancy separation may be used between a Group A, Division 2, 2.1, 3 or E or I Occupancy and a Group B, Division 1 Occupancy that is used exclusively for the parking or storage of private or pleasure-type motor vehicles provided no repair or fueling is done.

2. Unless required by Section 702 (a), the three-hour occupancy separation between Group R, Division 1 Occupancy and a Group B, Division 1 Occupancy used only for the parking or storage of private or pleasure-type vehicles with no repair or fueling may be reduced to two hours. Such occupancy separation may be further reduced to one hour where the area of such Group B, Division 8 Occupancy does not exceed 3,000 square feet.

3. In the one-hour occupancy separation between a Group R, Division 3 and M Occupancy, the separation may be limited to the installation of materials approved for one-hour fire-resistive construction on the garage side and a self-closing, tight-fitting solid wood door 1 3/8 inches in thickness

or a self-closing tight-fitting door having a fire-protection rating of not less than 20 minutes when tested in accordance with Part II of U.B.C. Standard No. 43-2 will be permitted in lieu of a one-hour fire assembly. Fire dampers need not be installed in air ducts passing through the wall, floor or ceiling separating a Group R, Division 3 Occupancy from a Group M Occupancy, provided such ducts within the Group M Occupancy are constructed of steel having a thickness not less than 0.019 inch (No. 26 galvanized sheet gauge) and having no openings into the Group M Occupancy.

When two different occupancies are adjacent to each other, either horizontally or vertically, a fire-resistive occupancy separation is usually required. The Table No. 5-B matrix provides the required fire-resistive time rating for the occupancy separation.

The constructions required to meet the time period are found in Table Nos. 43-B and 43-C. These tables list various constructions and their respective fire-resistive time values. As stated in Article 2(f) of this Guide, other listings and means of obtaining acceptance of assemblies are available to be used.

The occupancy separation must completely separate the two different occupancies.

- If the occupancies are side by side, the separation takes the form of a wall.
- If one occupancy is below the other, the separation involves a floor-ceiling assembly. See Figure 5-2.

In either case, the supporting structure for the occupancy separation must have a fire-resistive rating at least equal to that of the occupancy separation as was stated in the discussion of Section 503 (b) in this Guide. (See Figure 5-3.)

Exceptions 2 and 3 of this section relate to the garages in residential buildings. It should be clearly understood that Exception 2 relates to Group M-type garages and not to all public garages, (Group B, Division 1). That limitation is indicated by the 3,000 square foot area allowed.

This is consistent with both the Section 1102 and Table No. 5-B provisions that allow Group R, Division 1 buildings to contain Group M garages with a reduction in the fire-resistive separation. This reduction is warranted due to the limitation of:

- the overall size of the garage and

- the type of vehicles, the ones allowed being passenger cars generally owned by tenants of the building.

In Exception 3, the code refers to the garage attached to a single- or two-family dwelling. The requirement for the separation between garage and dwelling considers the general nonfire-resistive construction of the building and requires only that the garage side surface be covered with a type of material used to make a fire-resistive assembly, for example, 5/8-inch Type X wallboard and a 1 3/8-inch solid core door with closer.

This required protection applies not only to the ceiling in the case of a room above the garage but also to:

- walls providing the support of the ceiling, because a fire in the garage would attack both the ceiling and walls. If the walls were unprotected, a failure of the wall would cause a breach of the protection formed by the ceiling.
- piping, tubing and ductwork that penetrate the required separation. These elements are required to be fire-stopped so that a fire cannot bypass the surface of the membrane.

Exception 3 was clarified to permit a tested and labeled smoke and draft stop door meeting the UBC Standard No. 43-2 test requirements for use in this location without regard to the door's thickness or material of construction.

The prior code text appeared to have precluded the acceptance of a tested door that met the performance requirements in lieu of an untested door of stated thickness. The door that meets the UBC Standard No. 43-2 requirements will be a gasketed door satisfying the tight-fitting provision.

Table No. 5-B

In Table No. 5-B the requirement for a one-hour occupancy separation between Group B, Division 2, 3 and 4 Occupancies and a Group R, Division 3 Occupancy is more restrictive than the occupancy separation between Group R, Division 3 and a Group M Occupancy.

In the case of a Group R, Division 3 building with a dwelling unit being used for an office or business purpose (Group B, Division 2 use) as now required in Table No. 5-B, there must be an occupancy separation between the two occupancies. Per Section 503 (d) Exception 3 and Table No. 5-B, the code does not require a full one-hour occupancy separation, however, between the Group R, Division 3 and a Group M garage occupancy. Per Section 503 (d) Exception 3, the separation and the supporting structure need only have the covering of a one-hour assembly. Openings therein may have a solid-core door with closer instead of a one-hour fire assembly.

The Group B, Division 2 Occupancy must be separated from both the Group M and the Group R, Division 3 Occupancies by one-hour fire-resistive construction. As shown in Figure 5-4, the entire horizontal separation and its supporting structure must be of at least one-hour fire-resistive construction. Per Section 503 (b), the horizontal occupancy separation must be supported by one-hour fire-resistive construction. These more restrictive provisions take precedence over the Exceptions for the Group R, Division 3 Occupancy.

Location on Property
Sec. 504

► □□□ ◄

Section 504 contains the siting requirements applicable to individual buildings.

Sec. 504

(b) Fire Resistance of Walls. Exterior walls shall have fire resistance and opening protection as set forth in Table No. 5-A, Part III, and in accordance with such additional provisions as are set forth in Part IV and Part VII. Distance shall be measured at right angles from the property line. The above provisions shall not apply to walls at right angles to the property line.

Projection beyond the exterior wall shall not extend beyond:

1. **A point one-third the distance to the property line from an assumed vertical plane located where fire-resistive protection of openings is first required due to location on the property; or**
2. **More than 12 inches into areas where openings are prohibited.**

Where openings in exterior walls are required to be protected due to distance from property line, the sum of the area of such openings shall not exceed 50 percent of the total area of the wall in each story.

The requirements of Section 504 (b) relate to the proximity of the building to adjacent property lines. The intent is to avoid the hazard of conflagration — fire spreading from one property to the next.

The required fire resistance of an exterior wall is dependent on the distance that wall is from the adjacent property line and on the use or

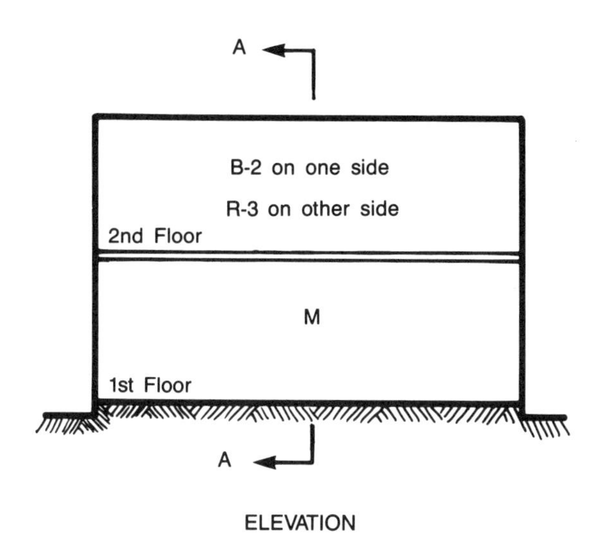

ELEVATION

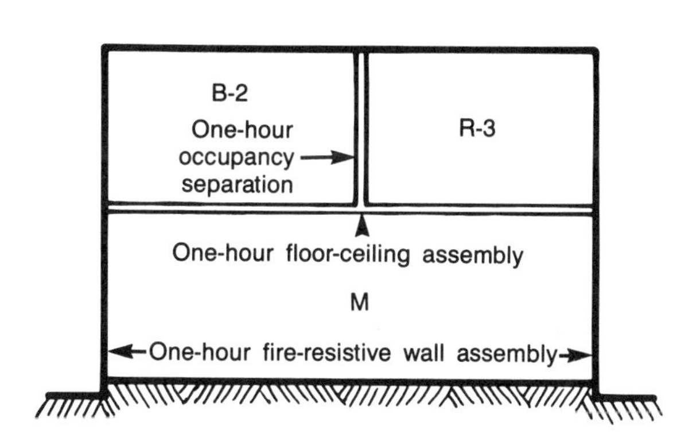

SECTION A-A

In Section A-A, the floor-ceiling occupancy separation between the Group B-2 and the M occupancies has to be one-hour fire rated construction. Similarly, there must be a one-hour occupancy separation wall between the B-2 and R-3 Occupancies per Table No. 5-B.

The supports for the floor-ceiling assembly, per Section 503 (b) must be one-hour construction. This requirement is more restrictive than the Group R-3/M separation requirement. Thus, the entire floor-ceiling assembly over this garage arrangement and its supporting walls must have at least one-hour construction.

REFERENCES: SECTIONS 503 (b), 1202 (b) and TABLE NO. 5-B

FIGURE 5-4 OCCUPANCY SEPARATION REQUIREMENTS, GROUP R, DIVISION 3 & GROUP B, DIVISION 2 AND M OCCUPANCIES

occupancy of the building in question. The farther away, the lesser the degree of required fire protection.

The fire-resistive time ratings required are set forth in Table No. 5-A for buildings of Type II One-Hour, II-N and V construction. The wall and opening protection requirements for buildings of Type I, II-FR, III and IV construction are outlined in Sections 1803, 1903, 2003 and 2803—the 03 sections referred to hereinafter.

For most occupancies, the Table No. 5-A provisions require the exterior wall to be firerated when the wall is less than 10 feet from the property line. If the wall is more than 10 feet from the property line, it may have unprotected openings (i.e., plain glass windows). For other occupancies, however, the specific provisions vary from these general 10-foot distances.

There are instances when the "fixed" property line of a lot can be "moved" to accommodate the exterior wall fire protection requirements for a building.

1. The adjacent property is permanently and legally declared open space (cannot be built on), such as railroad rights-of-way, green belts or parks, streets and alleys.
2. A permanent deed restriction, acceptable to the enforcement authority, declaring that a specific width of the space on the other property is to be kept free of buildings or structures, based on rulings made by the enforcement authority to meet code requirements of the jurisdiction. When such deed restrictions require that any changes in the restrictions must have the approval of the enforcement authority, there is assurance that public concern is protected.

This method of determining the exterior wall construction requirements has been used many times, but it does require individual approval by the enforcement authority. The text of the deed restriction must provide clear and permanent assurance of the equivalence of the movement of the property line involved. (See Figures 5-5 and 5-6.) Note that any change in the location of the moved property line will require a reassessment of the effect on the two buildings.

The eave projection provision of Section 1710 of the prior code has been transferred to the second paragraph of this section. It limits the

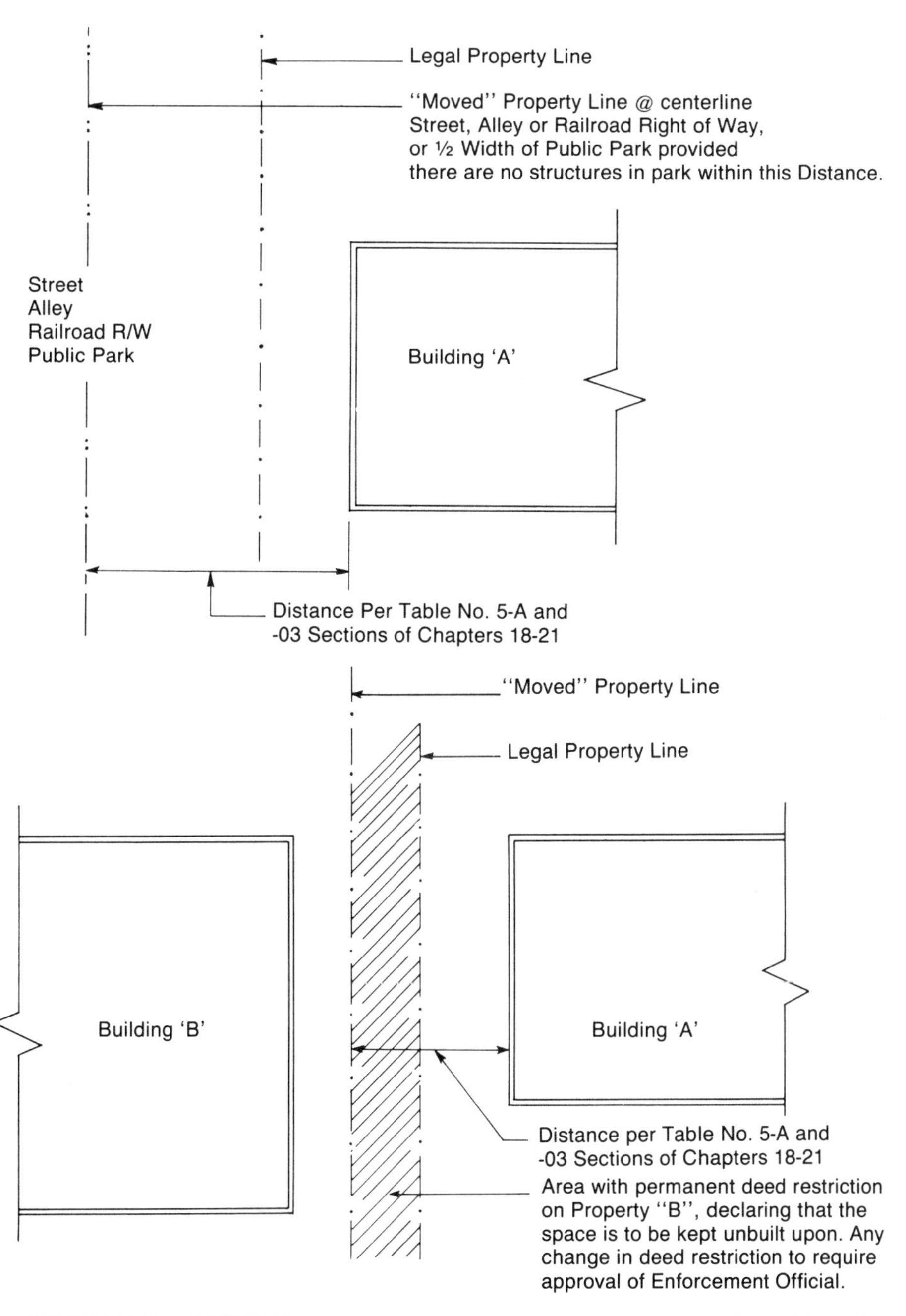

REFERENCE: SECTION 504 (b), 1803, 1903, 2003, 2103 and 2203, Table No. 5-A.

FIGURE 5-5 EXTERIOR WALL REQUIREMENTS—ADJUSTMENT OF PROPERTY LINE

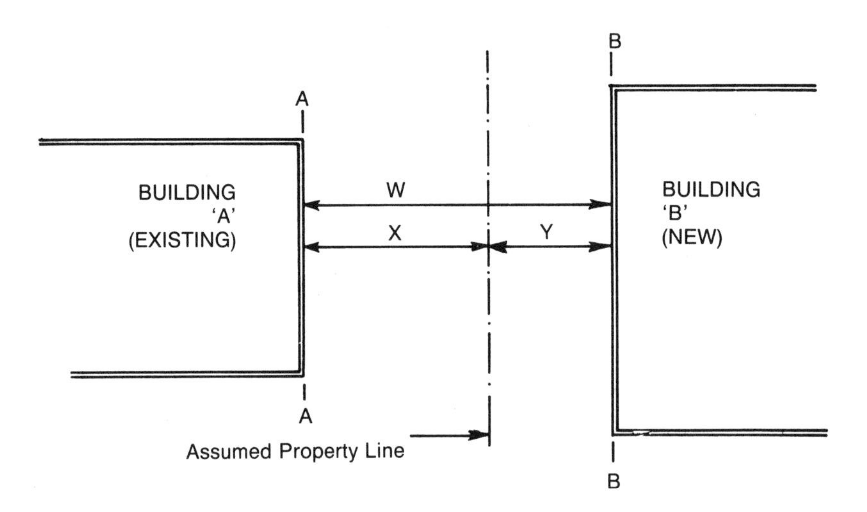

Property line may be located at any distance from the two buildings, depending on the most advantageous distances to the designer.

Distances X + Y = W.

The respective distances X and Y will be based on the provisions of Table No. 5-A and the -03 sections Chapters 18-21. There are a large number of variables which will permit the width "W" to vary from about 0′ to 40′ depending on the types of construction and occupancies involved in each building. See also Section 903.

Example: Building A = Type V One-hour, Group B-2 Occupancy
Building B = Type III-N, Group B-2 Occupancy

To illustrate the large number of possibilities the designer may have in any particular instance, the following example is used. For illustrative purposes the "X" and "Y" dimensions have been assigned letter designations. Thus, a combination of 'C+G' is the "X" designated 'C' dimension of 20′ and the "Y" designated 'G' dimension of 20′ with a total width of 40′. Similarly the combination of 'C+P' has a "Y" dimension of 1″ resulting in a total dimension of 20′ - 1″, which is noted as 20′+.

For each different occupancy and combination of occupancies there will be a different set of dimensions possible. The designer can readily develop similar tables of variables for any particular project.

FIGURE 5-6 EXTERIOR WALL—PROPERTY LINE RELATIONSHIP, BUILDING ON SAME PROPERTY

Property Line

Existing Bldg. 'A' Type V One-Hr, B-2 WALL 'A-A'				New Bldg. 'B' Type III-N, B-2 WALL 'B-B'			
"X" Comb.	Fire-Resistant Rating	Opening Protection	Setback from PL	"Y" Comb.	Setback from PL	Fire-Resistant Rating	Opening Protection
C	N	N.O.	20′+	G	20′+	N	N.O.
D	N	N	20′+	H	20′+	N	N
E	1-Hr.	N.O.	1″±	J	10′+	1-Hr.	N.O.
F	1-Hr.	¾ Hr.	5′+	K	10′+	1-Hr.	¾ Hr.
				L	5′+	2-Hr.	N.O.
				M	5′+	2-Hr.	¾ Hr.
				P	1″±	4-Hr.	N.O.

Comb. = Assigned reference combination for X or Y
N.O. = No Openings
N = No Rating Required

TOTAL COMBINATION OF POSSIBILITIES

Comb.	X	Y	W	Comb.	X	Y	W
C+G	20′+	20′+	40′+	E+G	1″±	20′+	20′+
+H	"	"	"	+H	"	"	"
+J	"	10′+	30′+	+J	"	10′+	10′+
+K	"	"	"	+K	"	"	"
+L	"	5′+	25′+	+L	"	5′+	5′+
+M	"	"	25′+	+M	"	"	"
+P	"	1″±	20′+	+P	"	1″±	2″±
D+G	"	20′+	40′+	F+G	5′	20′+	25′+
+H	"	"	"	+H	"	"	"
+J	"	10′+	30′+	+J	"	10′+	15′+
+K	"	"	"	+K	"	"	"
+L	"	5′+	25′+	+L	"	5′+	10′+
+M	"	"	"	+M	"	"	"
+P	"	1″±	20′+	+P	"	1″±	5′+

REFERENCE: SECTION 504 (b), 2003 (a), (b) and Table No. 5-A

projection where openings in the exterior wall are prohibited to not more than 12 inches. See Case A and B of Figure 5-7.

In using these two criteria, the first provision involves the establishment of an assumed vertical plane parallel to the property line and at a distance equal to the dimension in Table No. 5-A or the -03 sections of Chapters 18 through 22, at which opening protection is first required.

For example, for a Group B, Division 2 Occupancy in a Type V building, Table No. 5-A requires protection of openings when the exterior wall is five feet from the property line. Item 1, therefore, allows a projection of 20 inches (60/3 = 20). Thus, this criterion would allow the edge of the roof overhang to be within 40 inches (3 feet 4 inches) of the property line. However, openings are prohibited in Table No. 5-A when the exterior wall is within five feet of the property line. Item 2 of this section limits the projection in such instances to not more than 12 inches. Because this is more restrictive, Item 2 controls, and the projection therefore cannot exceed 12 inches.

With the exterior wall when openings are prohibited within three feet of the property line, the effect of either provision will be the same.

The benefit of Item 1 occurs when the building is located a greater distance than the minimum for prohibited openings. Using our example building and locating the exterior wall eight feet from the property line, we get the following permissible projection:

The assumed vertical plane of when opening protection is first required from Table No. 5-A is 10 feet from the property line. Because the exterior wall of the building is eight feet from the property line, Item 1 allows 10/3 or 3 feet 4 inches projection from the assumed plane. As shown in Case C of Figure 5-7, this allows the projection to be 3 feet 4 inches from the exterior wall toward the property line.

If the exterior wall of the building was located 12 feet from the property line, the projection allowed would again be 3 feet 4 inches (10/3) and the overall projection could be 5 feet 4 inches. This is the 3 feet 4 inches plus the greater setback of 2 feet 0 inches for the building's exterior wall. See Case D of Figure 5-7.

Sec. 504

(c) Buildings on the Same Property. For the purposes of determining the required wall and opening protection and roof-covering requirements, build-

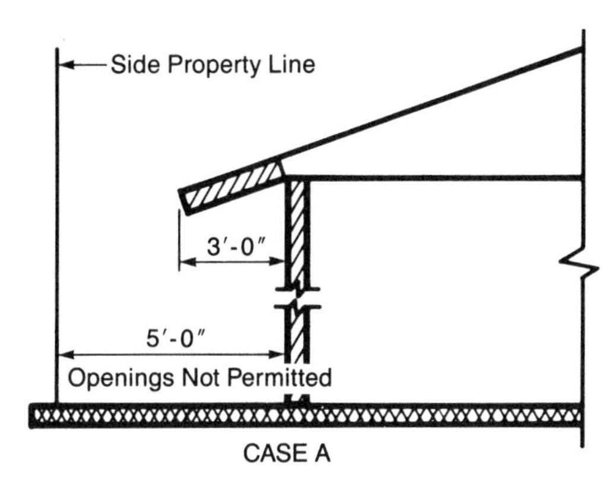

CASE A

ASSUME: 3′-0″ Eave desired

VERIFY: Is eave code complying?

Type V Building, Group R, Div.1 Occupancy

Distance to property for unprotected openings = 5′-0″ (60″)

1/3 x 60″ = 20″

Maximum eave projection may not exceed 20″. However, as eave projects into space where openings are not permitted, maximum projection is 12″. Eave must be reduced to 12″.

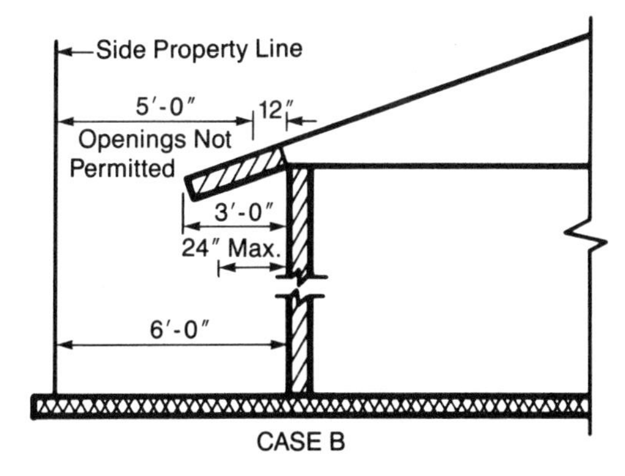

CASE B

ASSUME: 3′-0″ Eave desired

VERIFY: Is eave code complying?

Type V Building, Group R, Div. 1 Occupancy

Distance to property for unprotected openings = 5′-0″ (60″)

1/3 x 60″ = 20″

Maximum eave projection may not exceed 20″. However, as eave projects into space where openings are not permitted, maximum projection is 12″. Eave must be cut back to 24″ from exterior wall.

REFERENCE: SECTION 504 (b)

FIGURE 5-7 PROJECTION BEYOND EXTERIOR WALL (EAVE)

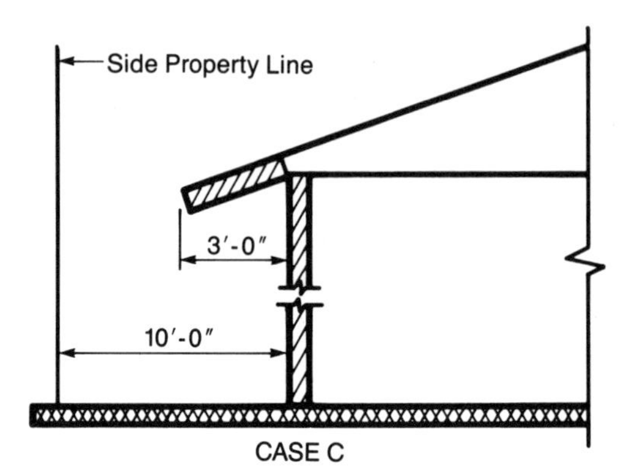

ASSUME: 3′-0″ Eave desired

VERIFY: Is eave code complying?

Type V Building, Group B, Div. 2 Occupancy

Openings not permitted within 5′-0″ of property line.

Distance to property line for unprotected openings is 10′-0″.

As maximum setback of exterior wall is 10′, the maximum eave projection may be 3′-4″; (10′/3). Therefore, the 3′-0″ eave projection is OK.

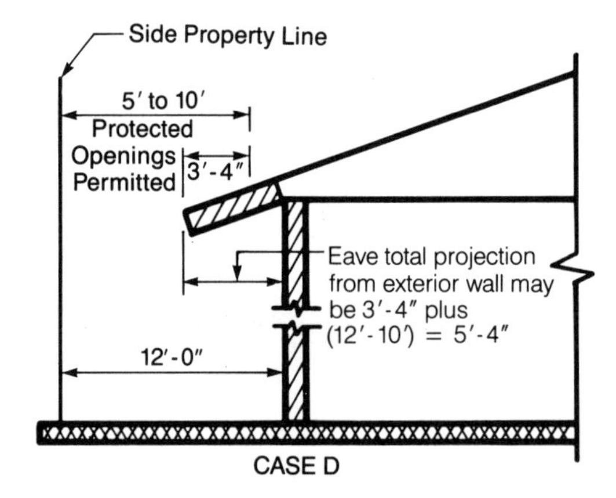

ASSUME: Type V Building, Group B, Div. 2 Occupancy

DETERMINE: Maximum permitted eave projection

10′/3 = 3′-4″

However, as the exterior wall is 12′ from the property line, the total eave projection may be 3′-4″ + 2′ = 5′-4″.

> **ings on the same property and court walls of buildings over one story in height shall be assumed to have a property line between them.**
>
> **EXCEPTION: In court walls where opening protection is required such protection may be omitted, provided (1) not more than two levels open into the court, (2) the aggregate area of the building including the court is within the allowable area and (3) the building is not classified as a Group I Occupancy.**
>
> **When a new building is to be erected on the same property with an existing building, the location of the assumed property line with the relation to the existing building shall be such that the exterior wall and opening protection of the existing building meet the criteria as set forth in Table No. 5-A and Part IV.**
>
> **EXCEPTION: Two or more buildings on the same property may be considered as portions of one building if the aggregate area of such buildings is within the limits specified in Section 505 for a single building.**
>
> **When the buildings so considered house different occupancies or are of different types of construction, the area shall be that allowed for the most restricted occupancy or construction.**

In Section 504 (c), the requirements relate to the proximity of one building to another on the same property or site.

The designer should be aware that the requirements of Sections 504 (b) and (c) must not be intermixed or misapplied.

The property line of the lot to which the Section 504 (b) provisions apply is fixed on the record and not "movable." As stated in the discussion of that section, that property line can be "moved" on paper for fire protection considerations. That line lies between separate properties and buildings.

On the other hand, the assumed property line in the first paragraph of Section 504 (c), applies to multiple buildings on the same property.

The more restrictive provisions are mandatory in their application to the building's relationship to the fixed property line of an adjacent property and not to the building line of an adjacent structure on the same property. The provisions of Section 504 (c) permit the designer, not the enforcement official, to locate the "movable assumed" property line between two buildings on the same lot. (See Figure 5-5.)

For conditions whereby the "fixed" property line may be "moved," see the discussion in Section 504 (b).

Except for the wall requirements relating to a court, in no instance are the exterior wall requirements ever applicable to a wall or occupancy within a building as it relates to another wall or occupancy within the same building. The exterior wall requirements apply only to a wall as it relates to another building or property line of an adjacent property.

The key provision in this section, stated in the second paragraph, allows the placement of a theoretical property line between the buildings on the same property. This flexibility permits the designer to determine the exterior wall construction that best suits his design. The designer can make use of the existing construction of the adjacent building to assist him in that design.

For example, assume the existing building is a Type V One- hour warehouse with nonbearing concrete walls and no openings near the new building, as shown in Figure 5-6.

In the examples listed in Figure 5-6, the new building, Type III-N, can be located in relation to the assumed property line as if the line were a real property line.

For siting of a new Group B, Division 2 building, where the wall of the existing building has a four-hour rating, the property line can be assumed to lie at the face of the wall; where the wall has a two-hour rating, the property line can be assumed to be five feet from that wall; where the wall has a one-hour rating, the property line can be assumed to be 20 feet from the wall.

NOTE: If the existing building has walls at least 7.5 inches thick, then per Table No. 43-B Item 34 the wall has a four-hour fire-resistance rating; if at least 5.5 inches thick, it has a two- hour rating; if at least 4 inches thick, it has a one-hour rating.

Other variations of siting are possible, and are limited only by the imagination of the designer and the physical conditions present.

Allowable Floor Areas.

Sec. 505 (b) Areas of Buildings Over One Story. The total combined floor area for multistory buildings may be twice that permitted by Table No. 5-C for one-story buildings, and the floor area of any single story shall not exceed that permitted for a one-story building.

The basic allowable floor area for a one story building is provided in Table No. 5-C. When there is a multistoried building, the aggregate basic allowable area is not to exceed two times the Table No. 5-C values. Thus, if there is a two-story building, each story can have the area permitted in Table No. 5-C. When the building contains more than two stories, the maximum area of any one story is still limited to the value in Table No. 5-C; however, the sum of the areas of all stories still must not exceed two times the Table No. 5-C value.

Therefore, in a three-story building with equal floor areas on each floor, and notwithstanding any allowable area increases for separations or sprinklers, each floor cannot have more than two times the basic allowable floor area per Table No. 5-C divided by three. If the basic allowable are for a Type V one-hour building with a Group B, Division 2 Occupancy is 14,000 square feet, a three-story Group B, Division 2 Occupancy building can have three stories of 14,000 x 2/3 = 9,333 square feet per story. If the building had four stories, the maximum allowable area per floor would be 7,000 square feet. (See Figure 5-8.)

Sec. 505 (c)

The provisions previously located in Section 503 (a) 2nd and 3rd paragraphs have been transferred to new Section 505 (c).

> **Sec. 505 (c) Allowable Floor Area of Mixed Occupancies. When a building houses more than one occupancy, the area of the building shall be such that the sum of the ratios of the actual area for each separate occupancy divided by the allowable area for each separate occupancy shall not exceed one.**
>
> **Where minor accessory uses do not occupy more than 10 percent of the area of any floor of a building, nor more than the basic allowable area permitted in the occupancy by Table No. 5-C for such minor use, for the purpose of determining allowable area the major use of the building shall determine the occupancy classification, provided the uses are separated as specified in Section 503 (d).**

Section 505 (c) establishes two general criteria or rules. These are:

1. The Unity Rule. This is contained in the first paragraph of the section. Its application is to buildings when the minor uses exceed 10 percent of the floor area of the floor of the building on which the minor uses are located. The sum of the ratios of the various actual floor areas for each use, divided by the allowable area for that use, cannot exceed one (1). (See Equation 5-1.)

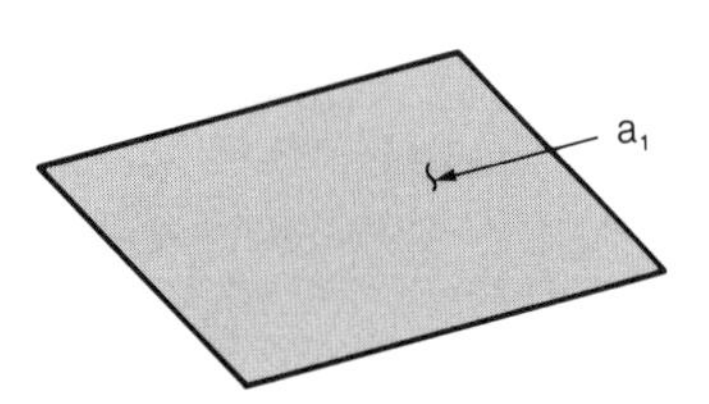

Basic Floor Area
One Story Building
Maximum a_1 = Value per Table No. 5-C
= 14,000 s.f. maximum

EXAMPLE 1

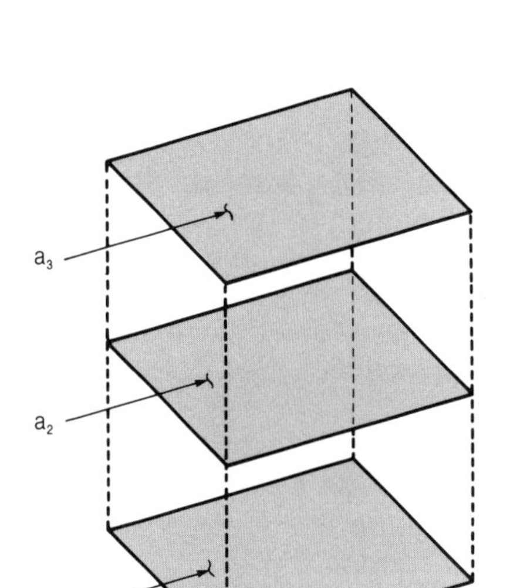

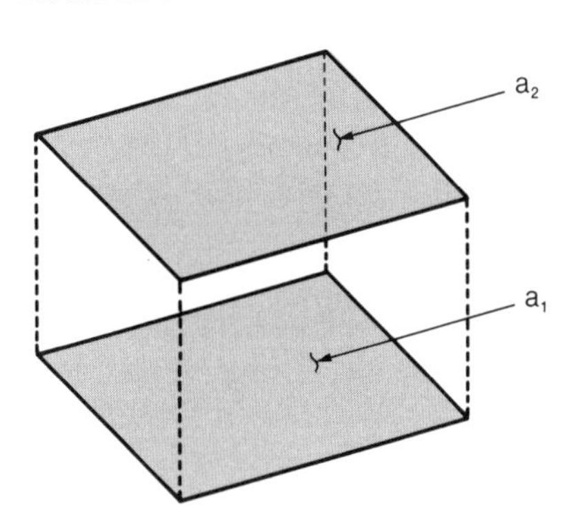

Multistoried Building
$a_1 + a_2 + a_3 = > 2 \times a_1$
$= > 2 \times$ value per Table No. 5-C

EXAMPLE 3

Two Story Building
Maximum area building = $2 \times a_1$
= $2 \times$ value in Table No. 5-C

EXAMPLE 2

For any number of storied building
$a_1 + a_2 + a_3 + a_n = > 2 \times a_1$
where a_1 = value from Table No. 5-C

Assume a Type V One-hour Building, Group B, Division 2 Occupancy with each floor of the same area
To obtain the maximum size of each floor
In Example 1: a_1 = 14,000 s.f. maximum
In Example 2: $a_1 + a_2$ = 14,000 s.f. maximum each
In Example 3: $a_1 + a_2 + a_3$ = 14,000 x 2/3 = 9,333 s.f.
If there were six stories in the building, the maximum floor area per floor
= 14,000 s.f. x 2/6 = 4,667 s.f. each

REFERENCE: SECTION 505 (c)

FIGURE 5-8 ALLOWABLE AREA CALCULATIONS WITHOUT AREA INCREASES OR SEPARATIONS OR SPRINKLERS

$$\frac{a_1}{A_1} + \frac{a_2}{A_2} + \ldots \frac{a_n}{A_n} =< 1.0 \quad (5.1)$$

Where:

a_1 = Area of one use
a_2 = Area of a second use
a_n = Area of any other use
A_a = Maximum allowable area of first use per Table No. 5-C and allowable increases
A_2 = Maximum allowable area of second use per Table No. 5-C or infinity if Section 506 (b) applies
A_n = Maximum allowable area of any other use per Table No. 5-C and allowable increases

2. The 10% Rule. This is contained in the second paragraph of this section. Always check if the aggregate of the minor uses on any floor is equal to or less than 10 percent of the floor area of that floor. In conjunction with this rule is a key stipulation that the basic allowable area of the minor uses cannot exceed that permitted in Table No. 5-C. See Figures 5-9 and 5-10 for examples of calculations of these two criteria..

Because of the importance of this section of the code, the author provides a detailed analysis of the intent of these criteria and the rationale that must be used in Technical Appendix TA-1.

Sec. 504 (f). Area Separation Walls. Each portion of a building separated by one or more area separation walls which comply with the provisions of this subsection may be considered a separate building. The extent and location of such area separation walls shall provide a complete separation.

When an area separation wall also separates occupancies that are required to be separated by an occupancy separation, the most restrictive requirements of each separation shall apply.

1. Area separation walls shall be not less than four-hour fire-resistive construction in Types I, II-F.R., III and IV buildings and two-hour fire-resistive construction in Types II One-hour, II-N or V buildings. The total width of all openings in such walls shall not exceed 25 percent of the length of the wall in each story. All openings shall be protected by a fire assembly having a three-hour fire-protection rating in four-hour fire-resistive walls and one and one-half-hour fire-protection rating in two-hour fire-resistive walls.

► ■■■ ◄

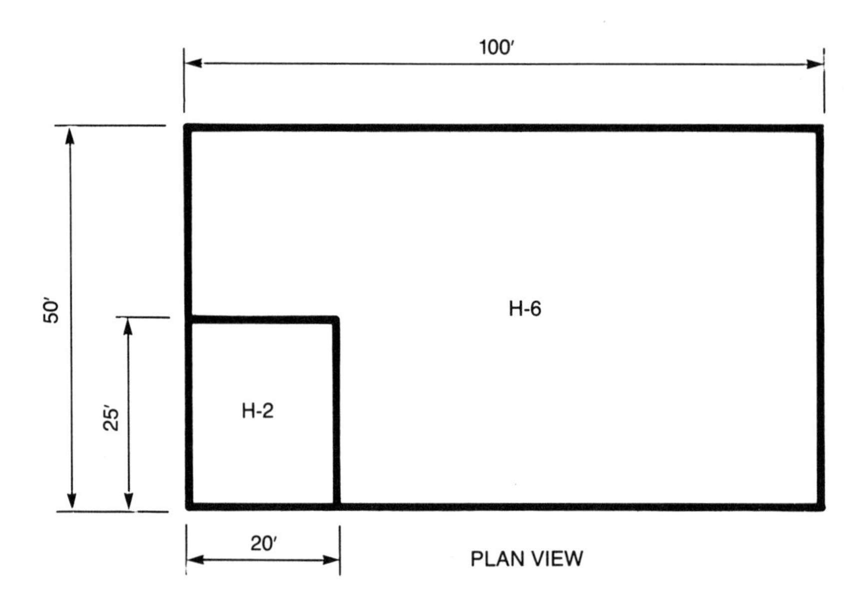

One-hour Occupancy Separation
Per Table No. 5-B

Given: Type V-N Building, one story

Group H, Div. 6 space = 4,500 s.f.; consider as area a_1
Group H, Div. 2 space = 500 s.f.; consider as area a_2

Allowable areas per Table 5-C are:
Group H, Div. 6 8,000 s.f.; consider as allowable area A_1
Group H, Div. 2 2,500 s.f., consider as allowable area A_2

Check for Unity Rule

$$\frac{a_1}{A_1} + \frac{a_2}{A_2} = \leq 1.0$$

$$\frac{4{,}500}{8{,}000} + \frac{500}{2{,}500} = .56 + .2 = .76 < 1.0 \quad \text{OK}$$

Check for 10% Rule

Minor use (H-2) is less than 10% of the floor area and less than the Table No. 5-C basic allowable area. Building is therefore a Group H, Div. 6 occupancy with the Group H, Div 2 occupancy as a minor use.

REFERENCE: SECTION 505 (c)

FIGURE 5-9 MIXED OCCUPANCY CALCULATION OF ACCEPTABILITY—TWO OCCUPANCIES

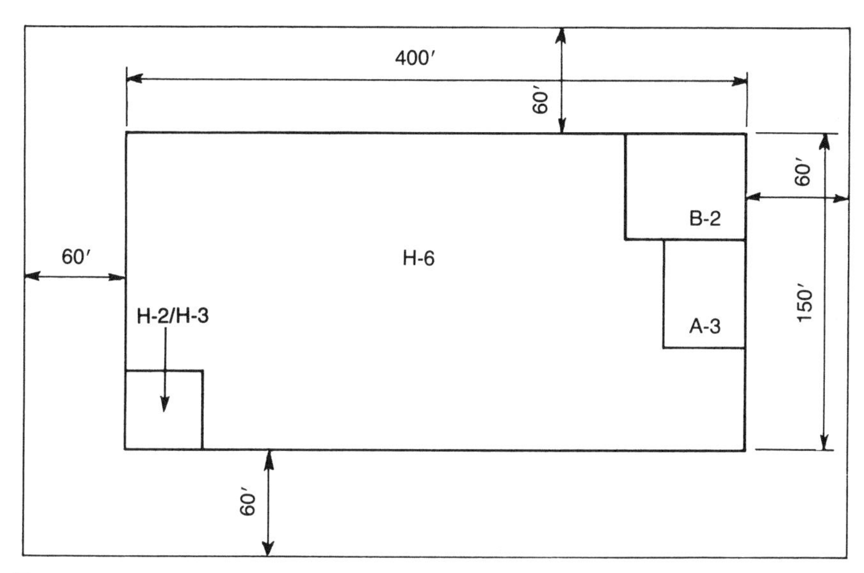

Given:
Type II 1-Hour, 2 Story Building – 60,000 s.f. overall
Fully Sprinklered; 60′ clear all around building (4 separations)

Group H-6 space	=	50,000 s.f.
Group H-2/H-3 space	=	1,500 s.f.
Group B-2 space	=	5,500 s.f.
Group A-3 space	=	3,000 s.f.
		60,000 s.f.

(Note: Arrangement of Occupancies within building shown schematically only.)

Allowable Areas

	Basic Allowable (Table No. 5-C)		Sprinkler Increase		Separation Increase*		Gross Allowable Area
H-6	18,000	×	2	×	2	=	72,000
H-2/H-3	5,600	×	-	×	2	=	11,200
B-2	18,000	×	2	×	2	=	72,000
A-3	13,500	×	2	×	2	=	54,000

*Separation increase for 60′ all around = (60 – 20) × 2.5% = 100%

Mixed Occupancy Calculation Per Sec. 503 (a)

$$\frac{\text{Actual Area}}{\text{Allowable Area}} \leq 1.0$$

H-6, H-2/H-3, B-2, A-3

$$\frac{50{,}000}{72{,}000} + \frac{1{,}500}{11{,}200} + \frac{5{,}500}{72{,}000} + \frac{3{,}000}{54{,}000} \leq 1.0$$

$0.69 + 0.13 + 0.08 + 0.06 = 0.96 < 1.0$ O.K.

REFERENCE: SECTION 505 (c)

FIGURE 5-10 MIXED OCCUPANCY EXAMPLE

3. Area separation walls shall extend from the foundation to a point at least 30 inches above the roof.

EXCEPTIONS: 1. Area separation walls may terminate at the underside of the roof sheathing, deck or slab, provided the roof-ceiling assembly is of at least two-hour fire-resistive construction.

2. Two-hour separation walls may terminate at the underside of the roof sheathing, deck or slap, provided:

A. Where the roof-ceiling framing elements are parallel to the walls, such framing and elements supporting such framing shall be of not less than one-hour fire-resistive construction for a width of not less than 5 feet on each side of the wall.

B. Where roof-ceiling framing elements are perpendicular to the wall, the entire span of such framing and elements supporting such framing shall be of not less than one-hour fire-resistive construction.

C. Openings in the roof shall not be located within 5 feet of the area separation wall.

D. The entire building shall be provided with not less than a Class B roof covering as specified in Table No. 32-A.

3. Two-hour area separation walls may terminate at the underside of noncombustible roof sheathing, deck or slab of roofs of noncombustible construction provided:

A. Openings in the roof are not located within 5 feet of the area separation wall.

B. The entire roof is provided with not less than a Class B roof covering as specified in Table No. 32-A.

4. Parapets of area separation walls shall have noncombustible faces for the uppermost 18 inches, including counterflashing and coping materials.

The use of area separation walls (ASWs) permits a structure to be considered as divided into separate buildings. An illustration of how an area separation wall is installed in a two-story Group R, Division 1 Occupancy building is shown in Figure 5-11 both with and without a parapet. The parapet requirements and the conditions to be met if a parapet is to be omitted are contained in this section.

Each subdivided area can have the maximum allowable areas per Table No. 5-C for its occupancy and construction type.

The second sentence in the first paragraph requires that the choice of the location and the extent of the ASW must achieve a complete separation of the structure. This provision will enable the enforcement official to assure that the ASW is located where it is effective in creating the intended separation.

The new second paragraph combines the requirements of occupancy separation and ASW. This is a new interpretation of the code, although some enforcement officials may have made similar interpretations

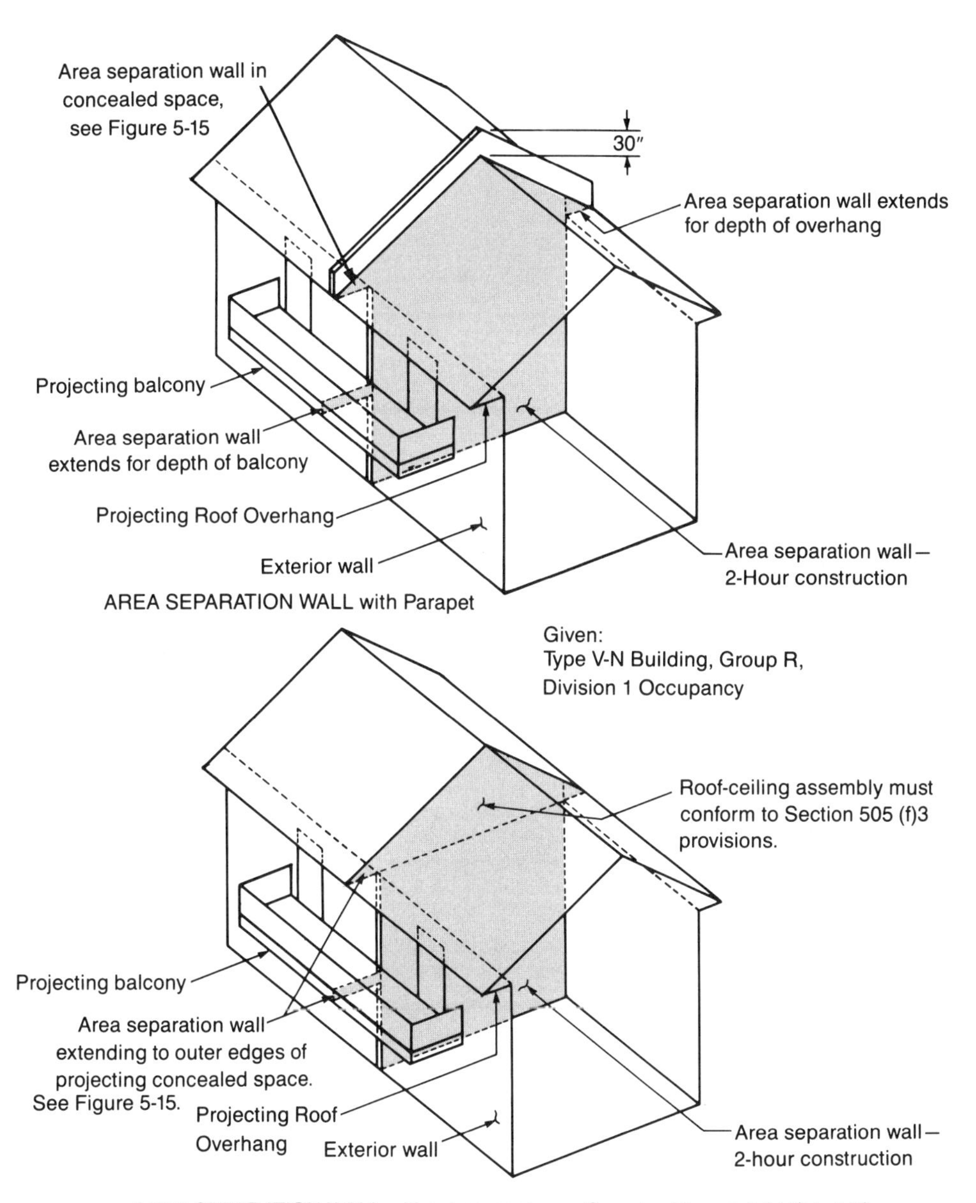

AREA SEPARATION WALL without parapet See also Figures 5-14 thru 5-16.

NOTE: Under projections (i.e. roof overhang or balcony), unless the wall at right angles to the ASW is of one-hour fire-resistive construction for a length at least equal to the depth of the projection on each side of the ASW, the ASW must extend to the edge of the projection.

REFERENCE: SECTION 505 (f)

FIGURE 5-11 AREA SEPARATION WALL EXAMPLE WITH & WITHOUT PARAPET GROUP R, DIVISION 1 BUILDING

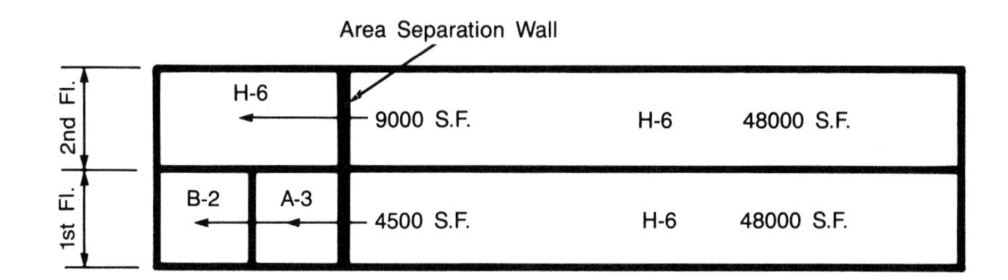

ELEVATION

GIVEN: Type II-N Building
Two Story, Sprinklered
Group A Div. 3, Group B, Div. 2 and Group H, Div. 6 Occupancy on First Floor
Group H, Div. 6 Occupancy on Second Floor
ASSUME: Area separation wall required due to maximum allowable area calculated per sec. 503(a) exceeds unity.

The walls between the Group A, Division 3 Occupancy and the Group H, Division 6 Occupancy on the first floor and the Group B, Division 2 Occupancy and the Group H, Division 6 Occupancy on the second floor serve as both an area separation wall and an occupancy separation wall. This is in accordance with the provisions of Sec. 505 (f) first paragraph, second sentence.

Per Table No. 5-B, the occupancy separation required is 3 hour. Per Sec. 505 (f)1, first paragraph, a Type II-N building may have a two-hour area separation wall.

The second paragraph of Sec. 505 (f) requires that the most restrictive provision applicable to an area separation wall and an occupancy separation wall shall apply. Therefore, the wall will have to meet the following conditions as a minimum:

a) Fire-resistive rating – 3 hour.
b) Extend from foundation to a point at least 30 inches above the roof. (Parapet to comply with area separation wall requirements.)
c) Openings to have a fire assembly with three-hour rating. (occupancy separation provisions.)
d) Maximum area of single opening limited to 120 S.F. (occupancy separation provisions.)

The Sec. 503 (b) requirements also apply to the separation between the first floor and the second floor. The Group A, Division 3 Occupancy and the Group H, Division 6 Occupancy above require a three-hour fire-resistive floor-ceiling assembly with the supports for that assembly to be of at least three-hour fire-resistive construction.

REFERENCES: SECTIONS 103, 503 (b), 505 (f) AND TABLE NO. 5-B

FIGURE 5-12 MIXED OCCUPANCY BUILDING, OCCUPANCY SEPARATION AND AREA SEPARATION WALL REQUIREMENT, TYPE II-N BUILDING

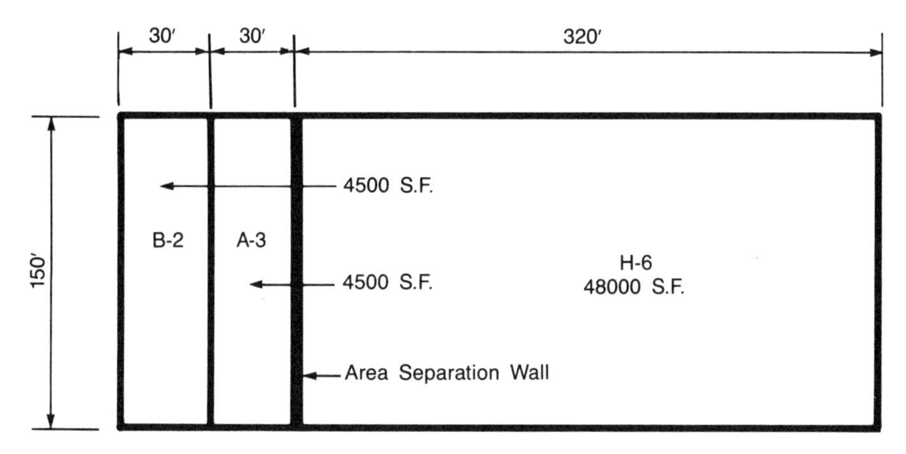

PLAN VIEW—FIRST FLOOR

of the code in the past.

The change appears to contradict the longstanding provisions in the opening paragraph,; namely, that an ASW creates separate buildings. In that concept there is no need for an occupancy separation between the "buildings."

If this new principle, as contained in this subsection, were, in fact, of long standing, then the addition of this new sentence simply repeats Section 103, second paragraph. There has been a great reluctance on the part of ICBO to repeat provisions for emphasis.

> It is therefore the author's opinion that this is not just emphasis of an accepted principle but a new provision and thus changes the ASW concept.

The *Handbook to the Uniform Building Code* discusses ASWs on pages 34 and 35. That discussion emphasizes the separate building concept and does not mention the occupancy separation aspect as applying. We must conclude that up to this time the separate building concept was the intent of the code and this new change reverses that concept.

In Figure 5-12, the several specific requirements governing the construction of the ASW are shown and listed. The provisions in Exception 2 of Section 505 (f)3 apply based on the two-hour ASW criteria.

> In the author's opinion, there is an inconsistency in invoking the ASW and occupancy separation requirements under the two examples shown in Figure 5-13.

That figure demonstrates, in Plan View B, that with an unrated building on each side of a property line, only one-hour fire-resistive walls are required alongside the property line: one on each side.

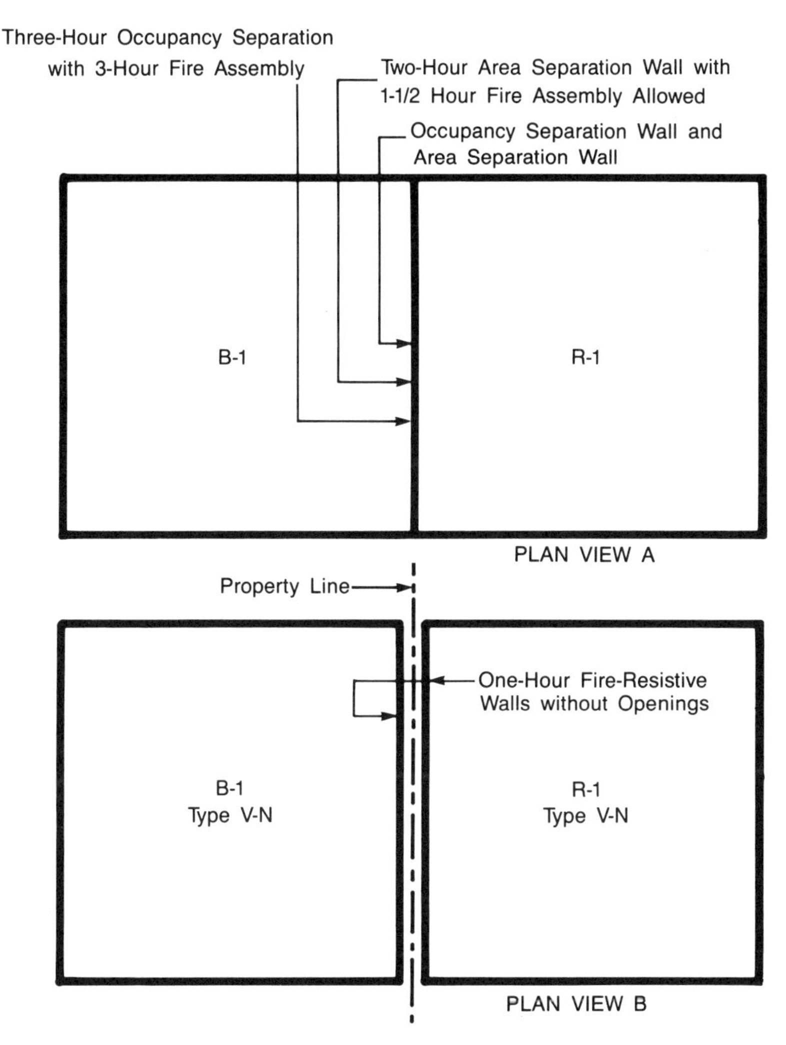

ASSUME: Building Type V-N with Group B, Division 1 Occupancy and Group R, Division 1 Occupancy (See Note).

NOTE: This is an illustration of how the Section 505 (f) first and second paragraph apply to two different but comparable situations.

In Plan View A, where a single building is involved, both the area separation wall and occupancy separation wall requirements apply.

In Plan View B, where the individual occupancies of Plan View A are in separate buildings on different properties, only one-hour fire-resistive walls are required on the property line.

REFERENCE: SECTION 505 (f)

FIGURE 5-13 COMPARISON OF AREA SEPARATION WALL/ OCCUPANCY SEPARATION WALL/PROPERTY LINE WALL REQUIREMENTS-SAME TYPE OF CONSTRUCTION & OCCUPANCIES

Therefore, there would be only a two-hour fire-resistive rating provided under that condition as against the three-hour fire-resistive rating required by Section 505 (f) for the occupancy separation of Plan View A.

The walls alongside the property line would not be permitted to have any openings; however, the ASW or occupancy separation provision in Section 505 (f) does not allow a reduction in the occupancy separation provision (three-hour rating) if there are no openings in the separation. For most conditions of mixed occupancies, the new provisions in Section 505 (f) will not cause problems. That is because the ASW requirement of two-hour construction usually exceeds the occupancy separation requirements of Table No. 5-B. However, in some special mixed occupancies, this interpretation-into-code provision may cause considerable problems.

> In the author's opinion, there has been a trend to erode the ASW provisions. In particular, changes have recently been made that violate the "separate building " concept. The fire alarm provision in Section 1211 was the first such erosion, and this is the second. All parties should be aware of this tendency to make the code unnecessarily restrictive and to downgrade the use of ASWs, an important design tool.

The fire-resistive requirements for ASWs are contained in Item 1 of the subsection as are the opening protection criteria. A four-hour ASW may have openings in the wall, whereas a four-hour occupancy separation wall is not permitted to have any openings.

Item 4 requires only the uppermost 18 inches of the parapet to have noncombustible faces. This is a companion change to the Section 1709 (b) parapet provisions. The intent behind the change is to prevent fire spread over the parapet by the surfacing material and to permit the roofing to be effectively flashed to the parapet.

Opinions differ in regard to the intent and applicable requirements for ASWs in such matters as:

- street frontage for the segments of the building created by the ASW,
- exiting through an ASW,
- utilities through the walls,
- accessibility of fire department equipment to building segments.

The designer is urged to discuss with the enforcement official the use of ASWs and should obtain written confirmation from the official of the official's understanding of that jurisdiction's regulations governing the ASWs being considered in the project.

> In the author's opinion, each segment of the building created by the ASW should have its own street frontage and access.

The computation of the allowable floor areas for each segment depends on the number of streets or yards on which any given segment of the building fronts, as provided in Section 506. (See Figures 5-14 through 5-16.)

Each segment should have its own exits. However, an ASW can be considered to provide a horizontal exit per Section 3308, thereby reducing the total number of exits. See discussion of horizontal exits in Section 509 hereinafter and Article 7 of this Guide.

ASWs are useful devices, provided one understands their limitations as well as their benefits. The ICBO staff interpretations regarding ASWs clearly limit them to vertical elements with no horizontal offsets; that is, the ASW cannot be offset laterally, using a floor/ceiling assembly as part of the area separation. (See Figure 5-17.)

The prohibition against use of an offset ASW, as shown in Figure 5-17, applies to projecting building elements such as cantilevered upper levels of a building. (See Figure 5-18 Section A-A.) Where such projections of upper level floors are desired, the projection must be eliminaed at the location of the ASW. This also applies for a bay window or the ASW must extend vertically projection. (See Figure 5-18 Elevation View.)

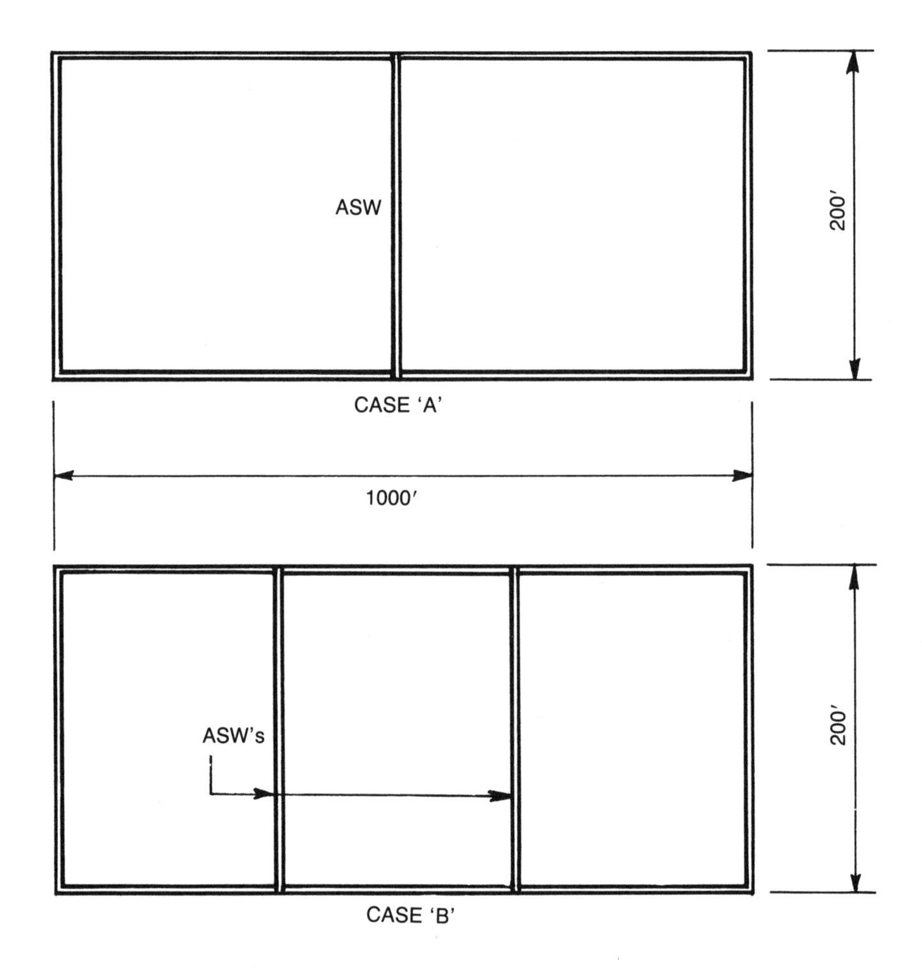

REFERENCE: SECTION 505 (f), 506 (a) and (c)

FIGURE 5-14 AREA SEPARATION WALLS FOR AREA INCREASES

ASSUME:
Type III One-Hour Building, One Story
Sprinklered, H-6 Occupancy
200,000 S.F., 40-foot separations all around

Allowable Area per Table No. 5-C	18,000
Increase for separation (40 – 20) × 5% = 100%	18,000
	36,000
Increase for Sprinklers = (300%)	108,000
	(not sufficient, proposed building over area)

Illustrative building is 200,000 sq. ft., therefore either the type of construction will have to be upgraded to Type II-F.R. or an area separation wall (ASW) installed. Since one-ASW will establish 2 separate buildings in effect; each will have only 3 sides with separations of 40′. Therefore the allowable increase for separations will be (40 – 20) × 2½% = 50%. Unless the width of the separations is increased there will have to be more ASW's in order to reach the 200,000 sq. ft. of the building. The separations can be increased up to 60′ to allow a 100% area increase (60 – 20) × 2½% = 100%

The following example of the calculations can illustrate the effect of increasing the number of ASW's in a one-story building (assume 200,000 sq. ft. building).

Case A

One ASW - 40′ separations all around

Basic allowable area	18,000
Separation increase (40 – 20) × 2½% = 50%	9,000
	27,000
Sprinkler increase - 300% - 1 Story	81,000

Total allowable area w/one ASW = 2 × 81,000 = 162,000 S.F. (not sufficient)

Case B

Two ASW's - 40′ separation all around	3 sides	2 sides
Basic allowable area	18,000	18,000
Separation increase -		
3 sides = 50%	9,000	
2 sides = (40 – 20) × 1¼% = 25%		4,500
	27,000	22,500
Sprinkler increase 300% - 1 Story	81,000	67,500

Total allowable area 2 × 3 sides + 1 × 2 sides
= 162,000 + 67,500 = 239,500 OK exceeds 200,000 S.F. proposed

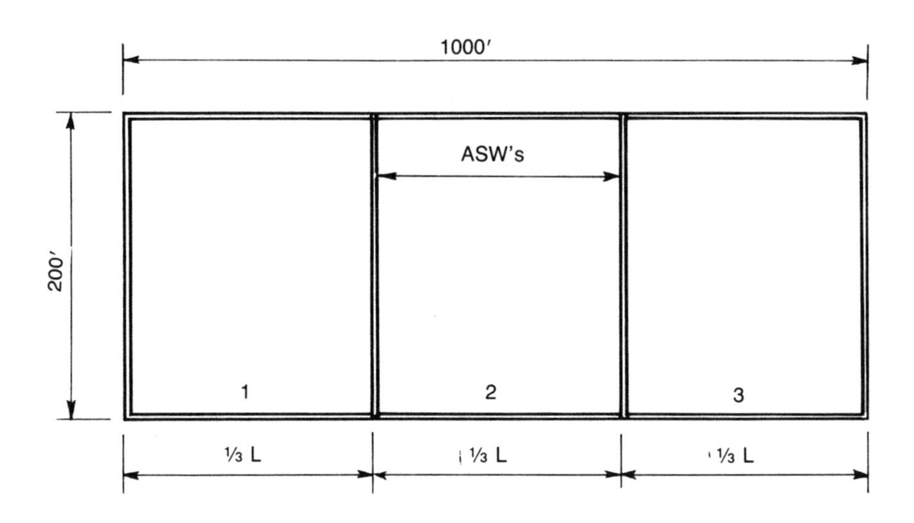

ASSUME:
Type III 1-Hour Building
B-2 Occupancy; 200,000 S.F.
2 stories, 40′ yards all around (parking lot)

For all Segments

Basic Allowable Area	18,000	18,000
For Segments 1 and 3: Separation credit = (40 – 20) × 2 ½% = 50% =	9,000	
For Segment 2: Separation credit = (40 – 20) 1¼% = 25% =		4,500
Allowable: Segements 1 and 3 = 18,000 + 9,000 =	27,000	
Allowable: Sprinkler increase Segments 1 and 3 = 200% =	54,000	
For Segment 2: allowable area w/separation increase = 18,000 + 4,500 =		22,500
Allowable sprinkler increase Segment 2 = 200% =		45,000

Total building, Segments 1 + 2 + 3 = 54,000 + 45,000 + 54,000
Maximum Allowable Area = 153,000 sq. ft. NG
Another ASW is needed (total 3 ASW) = 2 × 54,000 + 2 × 45,000
+ 108,000 + 90,000 = 198,000 sq. ft.

Reduce overall size if possible to 198,000 sq. ft. or increase separation width 1′ to 41′ which will result in a 2.5% increase in the 3 separation credits (450 sq. ft. each) and a 5% (2 × 2.5) increase in the sprinkler credits (900 sq. ft. each) for total allowable increase of 2,700 sq. ft., 198,000 + 2,700 = 200,700 sq. ft., OK each story.

REFERENCE: SECTION 505 (f), 506 (a) AND 506 (c)

FIGURE 5-15 AREA SEPARATION WALLS—SEPARATION CREDITS TWO STORY EXAMPLE

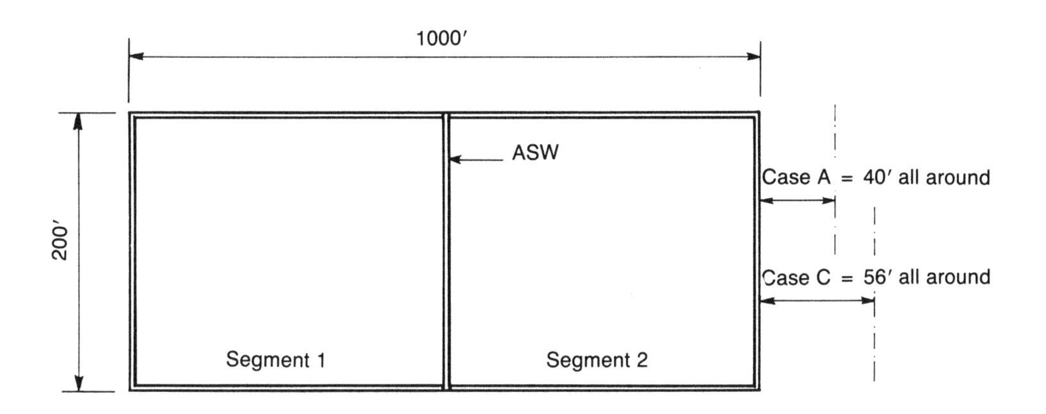

NOTE: Building same as Figure 5-9 Case A.

Case C

Another way to increase the allowable area other than by using the second area separation wall (ASW) is to increase the width of the separation. If we use one ASW and increase the separation width to 56′ all around:

Basic Allowable area for segment	18,000
Separation increase (56 – 20) × 2½% = 90% × 18,000 =	16,200
(3 sides per segment)	34,200
Sprinkler increase 300% - (1 Story Building)	102,600 per segment
Total allowable area-building = 2 × 102,600 =	205,200 OK

REFERENCE: SECTION 505 (f), 506 (a) AND 506 (c)

FIGURE 5-16 AREA SEPARATION WALL AND INCREASE IN SEPARATION WIDTH

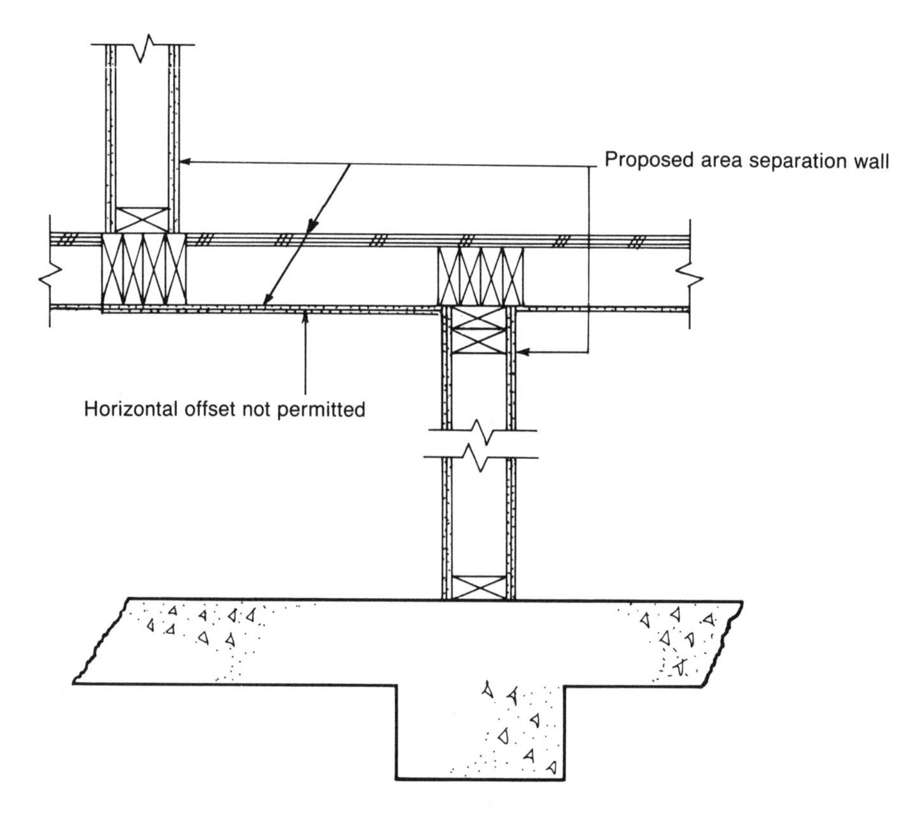

REFERENCE: SECTION 505 (f)

FIGURE 5-17 AREA SEPARATION WALL WITH HORIZONTAL OFFSET

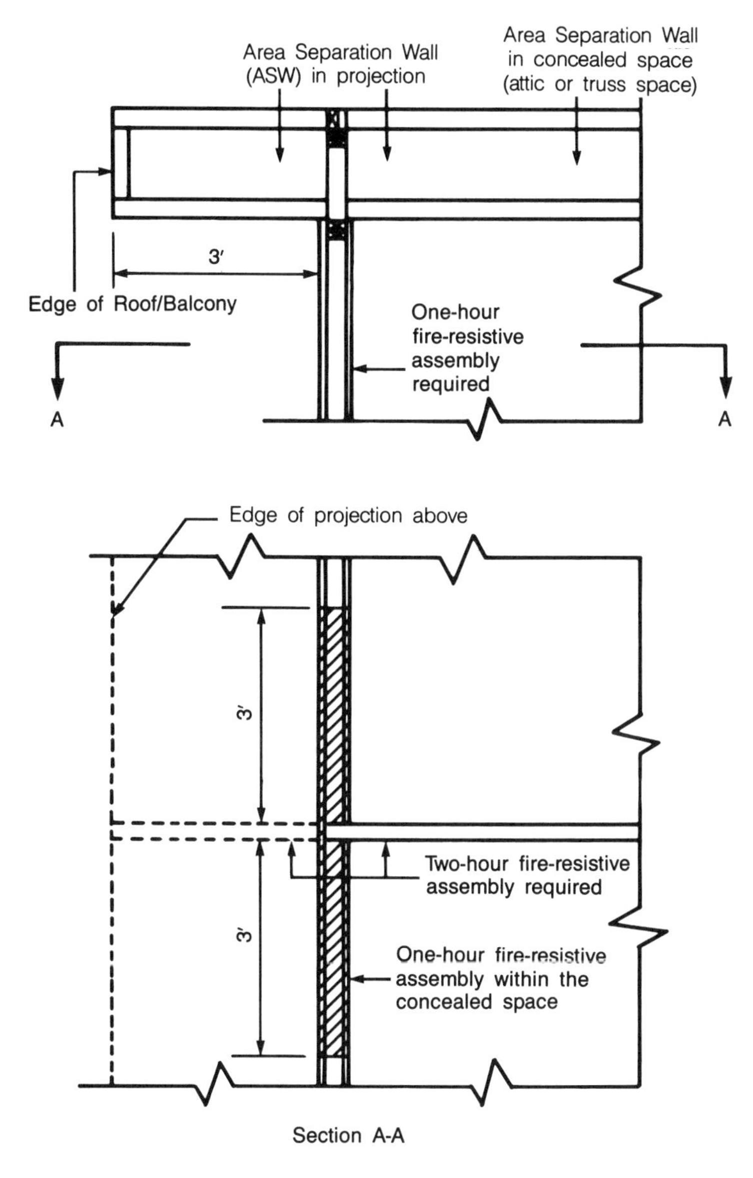

Section A-A

NOTE: The one-hour fire-resistive assembly within the concealed space may be omitted when the entire length of the projecting element is constructed as a one hour fire-resisistive assembly.

REFERENCE: SECTION 505 (f)2, ICBO INTERPRETATION MANUAL

FIGURE 5-18 AREA SEPARATION WALL—ROOF/CEILING SUPPORT REQUIREMENTS; "N" BUILDING, NO PARAPET

Of equal importance to where and how to design an ASW are the methods allowed by the code for the roof termination of the ASW. The basic requirement is that the ASW penetrate the roof, terminating in a parapet above the roof.

However, Exception 3 refers to those situations when an ASW may terminate at the underside of the roof sheathing. (Item 5 contains similar provisions for roofs of buildings of different heights.)

These Exceptions apply only to ASWs of two-hour fire-resistive construction. The designer should understand that, where a parapet cannot be constructed due to conditions beyond the control of the client, the designer must look to the types of building construction that will allow the use of a two-hour and not a four-hour ASW.

In Item 3, for omission of a parapet, the entire roof must have roof covering as specified in Table No. 32-A. The intent is to reduce the spread of fire across both the roof covering and the ASW and to restore the effectiveness of the ASW where the Item 3 provision is used. When the roof is required to be of noncombustible construction, the intent is that the noncombustibility encompass the entire roof including the framing and decking.

When an ASW terminates at the underside of the roof sheathing, the method of framing the roof supports determines how much of that roof-ceiling must comply with a one-hour fire-resistive rating: (See Figure 5-19.)

- When the supporting members are at right angles to the ASW, one-hour construction is required for the entire span of the roof-ceiling assembly.
- When the supporting members are parallel to the ASW, the one-hour construction is required only for a minimum of five feet on each side of the ASW.

> In the author's opinion, the support elements for the roof-ceiling assembly, other than the ASW itself, must in turn also be supported by not less than one-hour fire-resistive construction. When this support condition occurs on an upper floor of a building, the same degree of fire protection must be used for all applicable construction down to the ground or to such point where it rests on a level of at least one-hour fire-resistive protection.

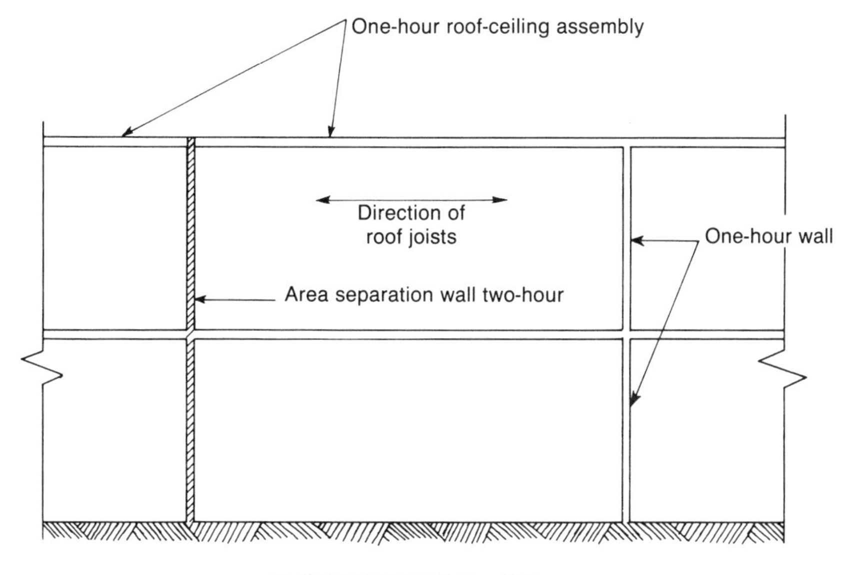

Where joists, adjacent to area separation wall (ASW) are parallel to the ASW, the roof-ceiling assembly need only be one-hour fire-resistive for distance of 5 feet from the ASW. However the support walls and other members for that one-hour roof-ceiling segment will also require at least one-hour fire-resistance to the ground.

The above requirement also applies to roof trusses. Note that where the joists or trusses are parallel to the ASW and there is no parapet, the walls supporting the ends of the joists or trusses within five feet of the ASW must also be of at least one-hour fire-resistive construction down to the ground.

REFERENCE: SECTION 505 (f)3

FIGURE 5-19 AREA SEPARATION WALL AT PROJECTING ELEMENTS

This is similar to the requirements for occupancy separations discussed in Section 503 (b) and shown in Figure 5-3.

This concept is of importance particularly in a building that may otherwise be of nonfire-resistive construction. It requires that the far end of the roof system span be supported all the way down to the foundation by minimum one-hour fire-resistive construction. The designer should take care to note that this requirement is often overlooked when using an ASW. The fire-resistive construction for these roof-ceiling support elements should be designed as complete fire-resistive assemblies and not simply as protection for the side of the wall facing the ASW. (See Figure 5-20.)

Two prerequisites have been added to the permissible termination of the two-hour ASWs at the underside of noncombustible roofs:

1. No openings in the roof within five feet of the ASW are allowed.
2. Roof covering of the entire building must be at least Class B.

These provisions are identical to the provisions for combustible roofs in Exception 2 Items C and D. The purpose of this change is to exclude the roof covering from the noncombustible limitation of the general provision and at the same time restrict the roof covering to at least Class B fire-retardant roofing.

Because many Class B roof coverings contain combustible components, the latter provision allows such roof coverings to be used in conjunction with the noncombustible roof construction and to qualify for termination of the ASW at the underside of said roof.

The designer is advised to trace the support elements for the roof-ceiling framing down to the ground, because in some buildings these support elements are not vertically aligned. The actual support elements to which the one-hour fire resistance apply may include walls, floor-ceiling assemblies and possibly beams and columns.

As previously noted, when the roof support framing is parallel to the wall, the framing need only be protected with one-hour construction for a distance of five feet on both sides of the ASW. There is no method through which that fire-resistive rating can be achieved by placing wallboard directly under the roof sheathing or metal or 5/8-inch Type

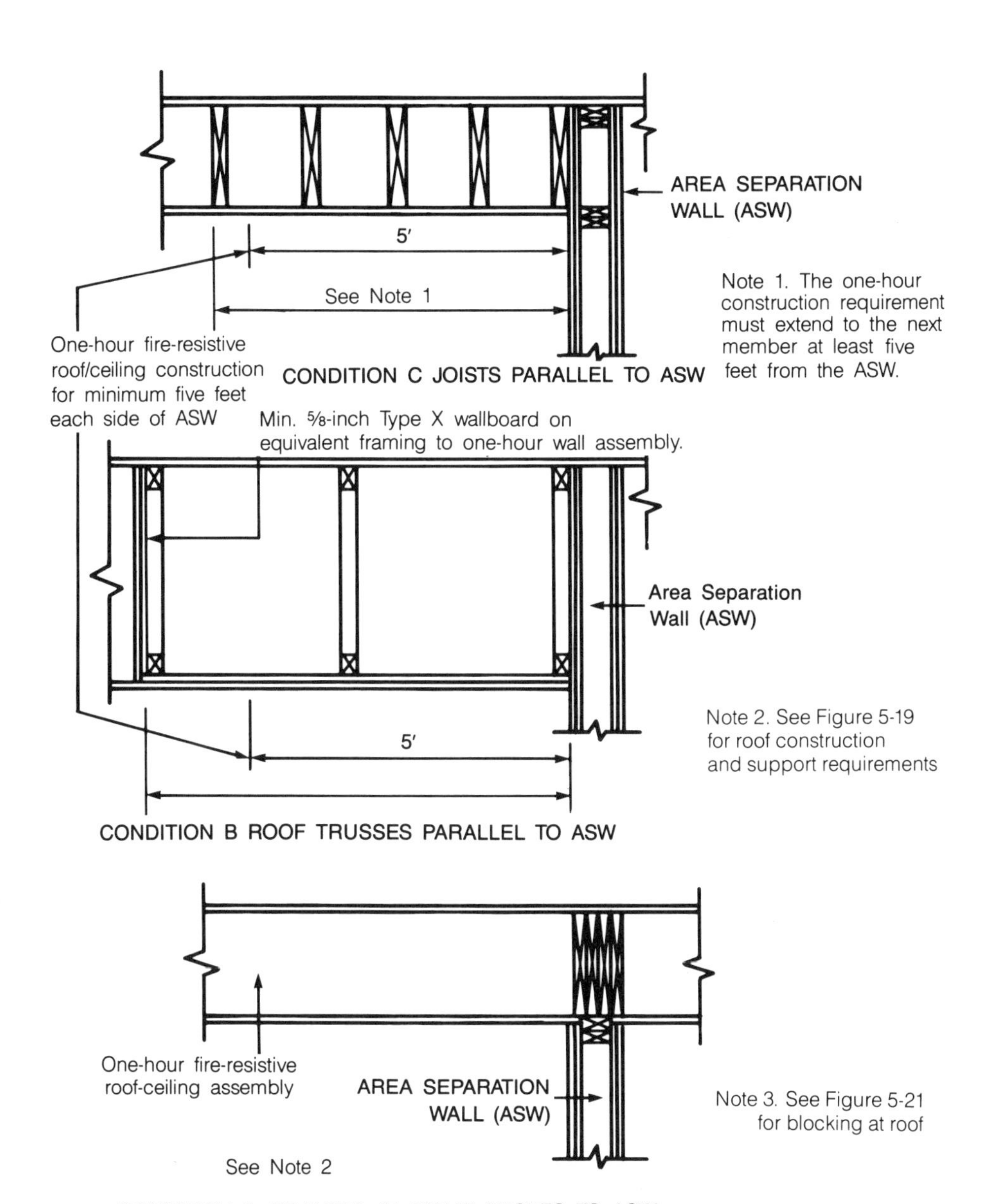

REFERENCE: SECTION 505 (f)3, APPLICATION/INTERPRETATION MANUAL, PAGE 24

FIGURE 5-20 ROOF-CEILING PROTECTION AREA SEPARATION WALL, BASED ON DIRECTION OF FRAMING

X wallboard above the roof sheathing. Unfortunately, such constructions have been frequently used by designers, apparently on the advice of someone who has misunderstood the intent of the code or who is unaware of the type of construction that qualifies as a one-hour assembly.

As is discussed in Article 8 of this Guide, a fire-resistive roof-ceiling assembly consists of two elements separated by an air space. The ceiling of the room or space under the roof framing is one part of the fire-resistive membrane of the assembly.

In warehouses, due to the type and spacing of the roof framing used, it is unlikely that only a five-foot strip of the framing, adjacent to the ASW and supporting the roof sheathing, would need the one-hour protection. In most residential and office building construction, to keep the plane of the ceiling flat, the entire roof-ceiling probably must be of one-hour construction for the length of its span within the room adjacent to the ASW.

It should be noted that the ASW must continue to the underside of the roof sheathing. Therefore, the wall extension, in the space above the ceiling membrane, must be equivalent to the two-hour ASW. This can be accomplished by any of the following methods:

1. continuing the two-hour wall above the ceiling line
2. in wood construction, solid blocking with a minimum of four layers of 2x material for the full height of the intervening space
3. in steel construction, installing several layers of wallboard in the space

(See Figure 5-21.)

On the drawings, these ASW details should be fully delineated, so that in discussions with the building official they can be reviewed and accepted as equivalent to the code-accepted construction. Examples of intermediate floor intersection details are shown in Figure 5-22.

When an ASW extends below the first floor, usually in a crawl space or basement area and to the foundation, it must be of the same fire-resistive rating as required for the main segments of the ASW. (See Figure 5-23.)

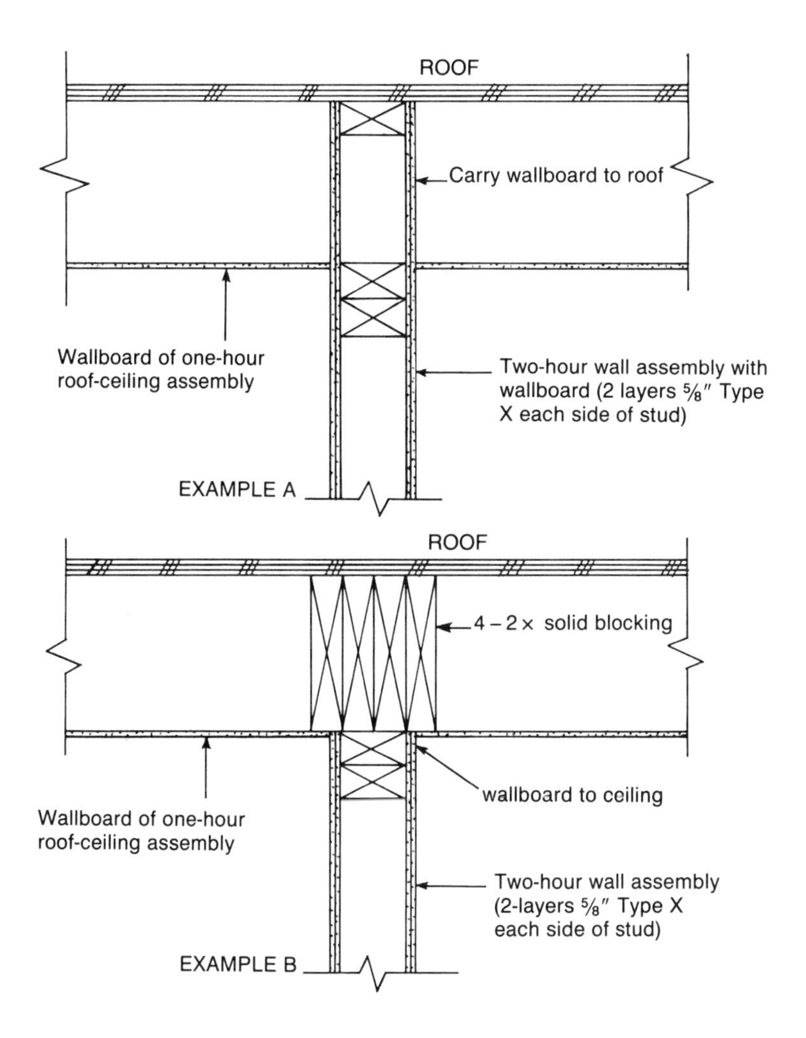

REFERENCE: UBC APPLICATIONS/INTERPRETATION MANUAL, PAGE 24

FIGURE 5-21 AREA SEPARATION WALL – ROOF/CEILING (NO PARAPET) TYPICAL CONSTRUCTION

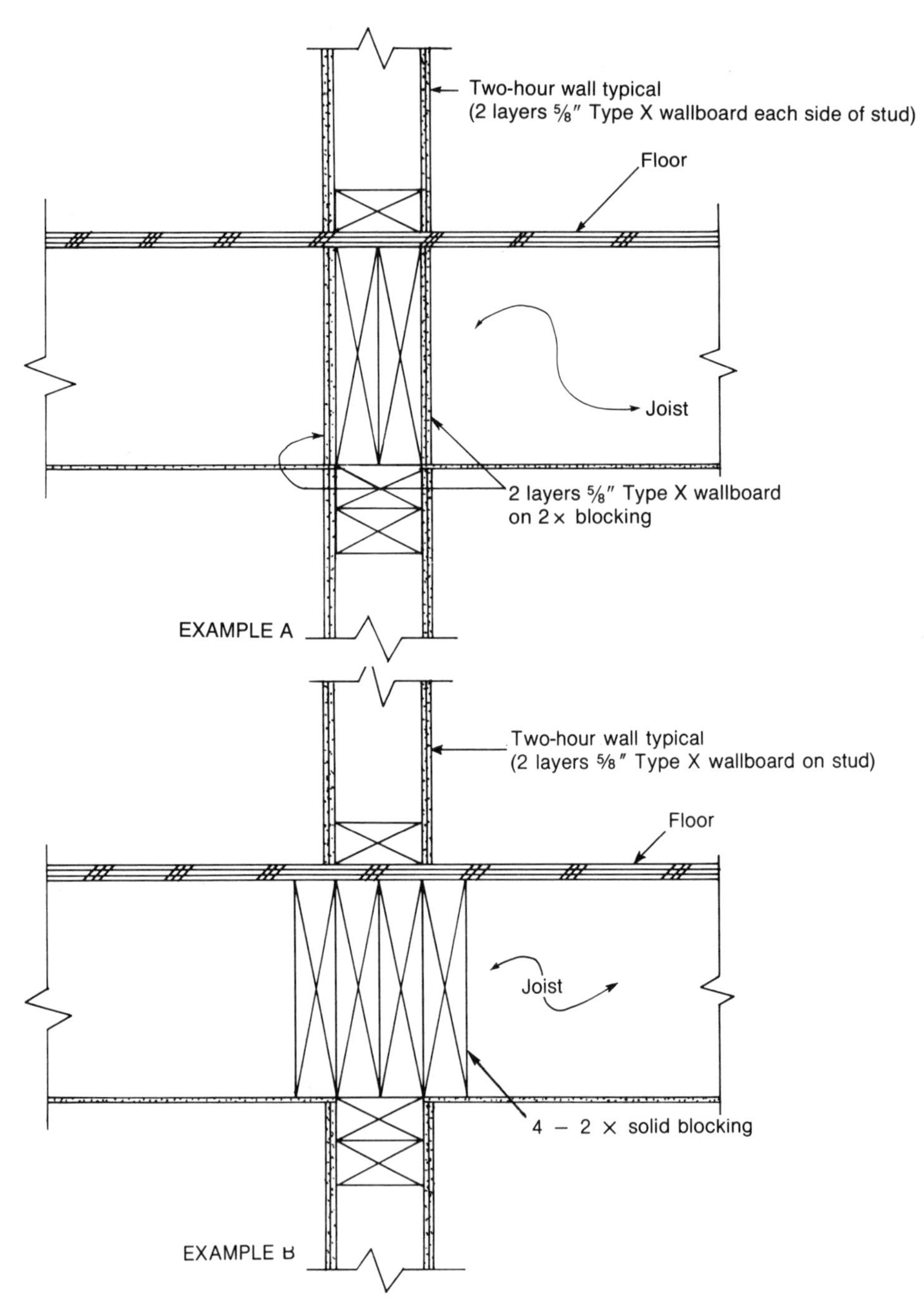

REFERENCE: UBC APPLICATIONS/INTERPRETATION MANUAL, PAGE 24

FIGURE 5-22 AREA SEPARATION WALL—INTERMEDIATE FLOOR DETAILS

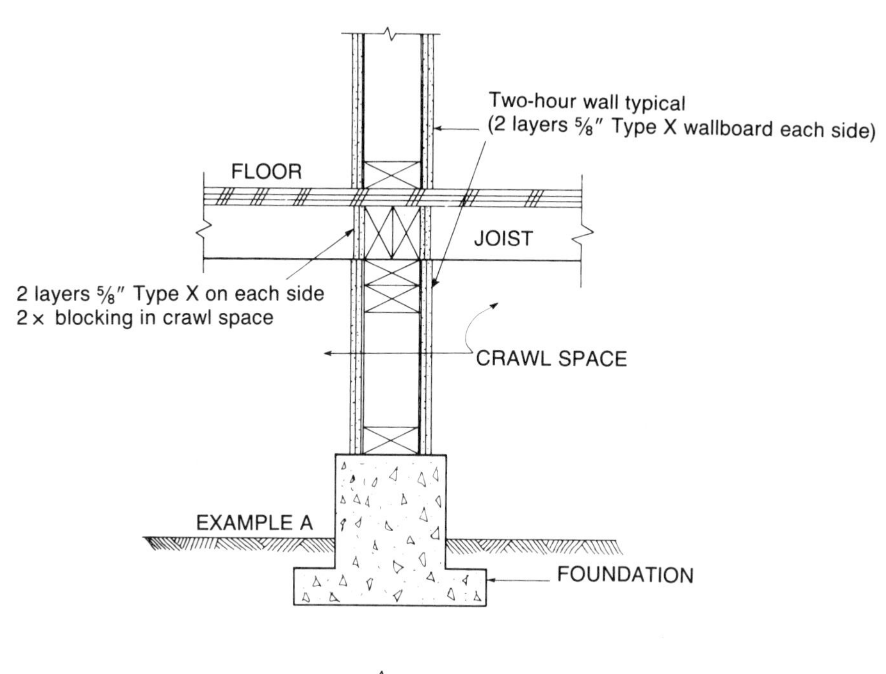

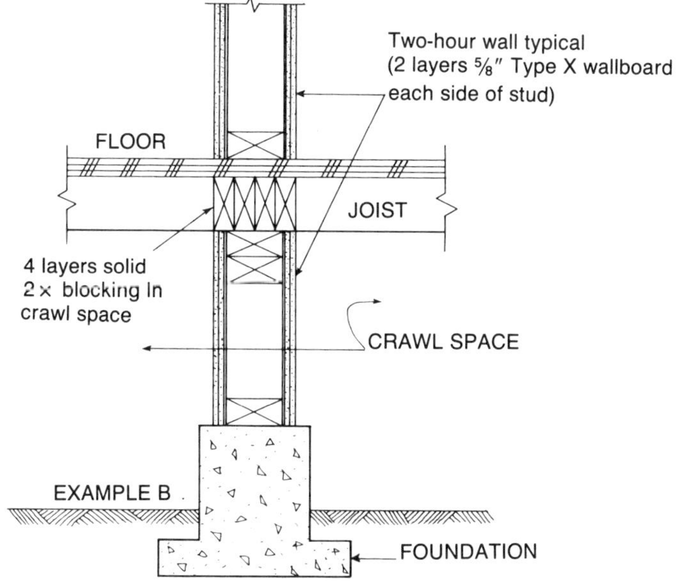

REFERENCE: UBC APPLICATION/INTERPRETATIONS MANUAL

FIGURE 5-23 AREA SEPARATION WALL—FOUNDATION DETAILS

Other projecting elements such as roof overhangs, balconies and similar architectural projections are covered in Section 505 (f)2. When there are concealed spaces in the projecting element, such as are created by joists or trusses, the ASW must extend through the projection to the outer edge of the projection. (See Figure 5-18.)

There are exceptions to extending the ASW in the concealed space of the projection. The essential requirements for use of these exceptions are:

The projection must be a one-hour fire-resistive assembly for a distance on each side of the ASW equal to the depth of the projection. Thus, in Section A-A, with a three-foot roof overhang the one-hour construction must extend at least three feet on each side of the ASW. See Plan View.

- Openings in the exterior wall below the projection and within a distance of the ASW equal to the depth of the projection must be protected by fire assemblies with at least three-quarter hour fire resistance rating.
- The protection of the exterior wall below the projection must continue down to the foundation to avoid a premature failure of the wall section directly below the projection.
- When the concealed space in the projection contains openings parallel to the exterior wall, as would be the case if trusses were involved or where architectural treatment frames an open concealed area, the one-hour protection for the projection must be carried up, within the concealed space, to the point of termination of the one-hour projection construction. If the entire length of the projection was constructed with a one-hour fire-resistive rating, this internal cutoff within the concealed space is not required. See Plan View.

Separation walls are of such importance that the designer must be assured that the contractor carries out the intent of the code requirements. The designer's drawings should fully detail the ASWs so that the contractor does not confuse the ASWs with other walls of the building. They are not the same. ASWs have the validity and importance of an exterior wall located at a property line and hence, except for protected openings, must be constructed in an unbreached manner.

Site visits by the designer are essential to assure that the ASWs are constructed properly. An improperly constructed ASW will be difficult or impossible to correct without great expense and can jeopardize the validity of that building's entire occupancy.

The author has found more violations of ASWs, knowingly or unknowingly committed, than any other element of building design.

Allowable Area Increases.

Sec. 506 (a) General. The floor areas specified in Section 505 may be increased by one of the following:

1. **Separation on two sides. Where public space or yards more than 20 feet in width extend along and adjoin two sides of the building, floor areas may be increased at a rate of 1 1/4 percent for each foot by which the minimum width exceeds 20 feet, but the increase shall not exceed 50 percent.**
2. **Separation on three sides. Where public space or yards more than 20 feet in width extend along and adjoin three sides of the building, floor areas may be increased at a rate of 2 1/2 percent for each foot by which the minimum width exceeds 20 feet, but the increase shall not exceed 100 percent.**
3. **Separation on all sides. Where public space or yards more than 20 feet in width extend on all sides of a building and adjoin the entire perimeter, floor areas may be increased at a rate of 5 percent for each foot by which the minimum width exceeds 20 feet. Such increases shall not exceed 100 percent, except that greater increases shall be permitted for the following occupancies:**

► ■■■ ◄

The basic floor area for a given occupancy and type of construction is indicated in Table No. 5-C. This area may be increased depending on the number of streets, yards or equivalent open spaces that bound the building.

The code's intent is to permit a building to have larger allowable areas when wide separations exist:

- between it and the property lines or
- between it and other buildings on the site.

The increases are based on the amount of separation in excess of a 20-foot minimum. Where there are several separations of differing widths around the building, the minimum width is used in the calculations. The separation must extend for the entire length of the building.

The percentages used to calculate the increase are based on:

- the number of frontages and
- the minimum width of separation in excess of 20 feet for the frontages involved.

Number of Separations	Maximum Percentage Increase	Percentage Permitted	Minimum Distance for Max.
1	0	0	—
2	1.25	50	60
3	2.5	100	60
4	5.0	100	40

Note: Distance calculation based on total separation is as follows:

Allowable = % Increase X (total width of separation-20 feet)

In some instances, the designer might do better to use the larger separations and eliminate a smaller one, thereby obtaining a greater percentage increase than otherwise. For instance, assume a building has three separations of 60 feet and one of 30 feet.

Either:

a) four separations can be used, with a 30-foot width used in the calculations or
b) three separations with a 60-foot width could be used.

Thus:

a) four separations: 5% (30-20) = 50% increase allowed.
b) three separations: 2.5% (60-20) = 100% increase allowed.

The effect of using the larger separations on a multi-storied building would be to increase the allowable area for the building as a whole. The percentage increase applies to the overall allowable for the building per Section 505 (b) which is two times the basic area per Table No. 5-C. Thus, for a multi-storied building, two times the separation percentage increase is also permitted. An example of these calculations is shown accompanying Figure 5-24.

Where there are different occupancies in the building, the basic area

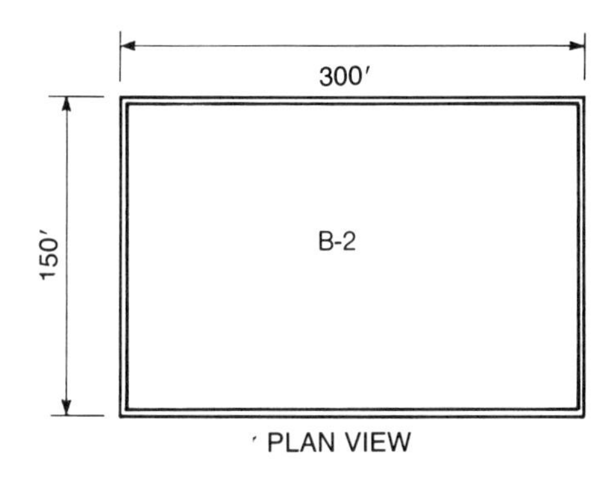

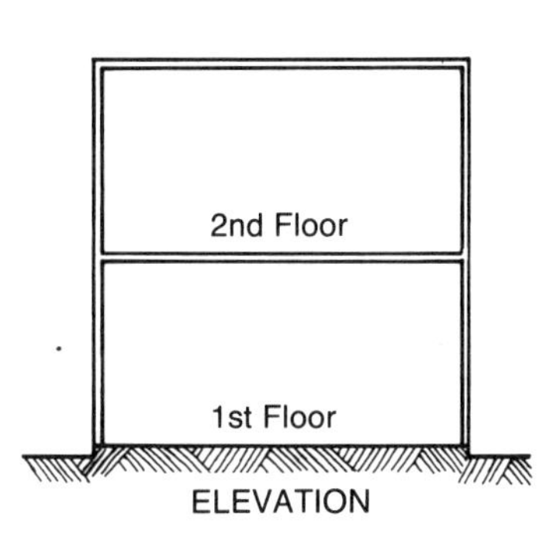

ASSUME:
Type III-N Building
B-2 Occupancy, Sprinklered
2 story, 40′ separations all around (4 sides)
Each story = 45,000 S.F., Gross area = 90,000 S.F.

Allowable area per Table No. 5-C =	12,000
Increase for separations (4) = (40 – 20) × 5% = 100%	12,000
	24,000
Increase for sprinklers (2 Story Bldg.) = 200% =	48,000
Total allowable area in building = 2 × 48,000 =	96,000

Each story is allowed the 48,000 sq. ft. area
Actual area = 45,000 sq. ft. per story O.K.

NOTE: The 96,000 sq. ft. total allowable area is also the maximum area allowed for a B-2 Occupancy in a Type III-N building *regardless* of the number of additional stories. Therefore, a 3 story B-2 Type III building can have only 48,000 sq. ft. max/story and 96,000 sq. ft. maximum for the entire building.

REFERENCE: SECTION 505 (b), 506 (a) and (c)

FIGURE 5-24 ALLOWABLE AREA CALCULATIONS – MULTI-STORIED BUILDING

is computed based on the Section 505 (c) calculations. When there are ASWs in the building, each of the segmented areas has the percentage increase computed based on that area's frontages, without regard to the frontages of the building as a whole.

It must be noted that the provisions of these increases only apply to separations in the form of streets, yards and public ways. Parking lots are considered yards.

The definition of these terms are taken from Chapter 4:

> **STREET is any thoroughfare or public way not less than 86 feet in width which has been dedicated or deeded to the public for public use.**
>
> **YARD is an open, unoccupied space, other than a court, unobstructed from the ground to the sky, except where specifically provided by this code, on the lot on which a building is situated.**

In calculating the area increases, a court is not considered to be a yard and thus does not qualify as a separation. The definition of yard clearly precludes a court from being considered as a yard. As stated in Section 506 (a), only public way, streets or yards qualify as separations.

In the author's opinion, the concept of the increases includes an unstated prerequisite for qualifying a space for the frontage: The ability for the fire service to access the building for fire fighting.

An acceptable space would provide fire service access as well as have the required width and extent of separation to qualify for the area increase. In keeping with this concept of access, parking lots and their driveways that meet the minimum width and open to the sky requirements are usually accepted as yards thereby meeting the separation requirements.

On the other hand, if the yard to be used for separation credits is a storage yard or other such obstructed use with limited access by the fire service, then it fails to satisfy the access criteria and also presents a greater fire hazard than does a parking lot. Thus, a storage yard or other obstructed space, in the author's opinion, should not be credited for separation area increases.

Sec.506

(b) Unlimited Area. The area of any one- or two-story building of Group B and Group H, Division 5 Occupancies shall not be limited, if the building is provided with an approved automatic sprinkler system throughout, as specified in Chapter 38, and entirely surrounded and adjoined by public space, streets or yards not less than 60 feet in width.

The area of a group B, Division 4 Occupancy in a one-story Type II, Type III One-hour or Type IV building shall not be limited if the building is entirely surrounded and adjoined by public space, streets or yards not less than 60 feet in width.

Section 506 (b) permits an unlimited area building to be built of any type of construction, including Type V-N, provided the building is:

- a one- or two-story structure,
- used for Group B or H, Division 5 occupancies,
- fully sprinklered and
- is entirely surrounded and adjoined by public space, streets or yards not less than 60 feet in width.

This section is probably the most liberal provision in the code. It permits shopping centers, markets, warehouses and factories to use their parking areas, usually required for their day-to-day operation, together with standard sprinkler protection in lieu of all built-in fire protection. See the Technical Appendix TA-1 discussion for additional detailed commentary on the unlimited area building with mixed occupancies.

The designer should be aware of both the benefits and liabilities to the owner in making use of these provisions. The large cost savings possible when not using fire-resistive construction are offset to a degree by a total reliance on the sprinkler system to protect the property.

The designer should consider increasing the reliability of the sprinkler system by:

- requiring all shut-off valves and the waterflow detectors to be supervised by a central station and not simply relying on locks to keep the valves open.
- providing a second source of water either by connection to another main or by providing on-site water storage.

The supervision alone will raise the reliability level of sprinkler performance to 99.9+ percent.

Sec. 506

(c) Automatic Sprinkler Systems. The areas specified in Table No. 5-C and Section 505(b) may be tripled in one-story buildings and doubled in buildings of more than one story if the building is provided with an approved automatic sprinkler system throughout. The area increases permitted in this subsection may be compounded with that specified in paragraphs 1, 2 or 3 of Subsection (a) of this section. The increases permitted in this subsection shall not apply when automatic sprinkler systems are installed under the following provisions:

1. **Section 507 for an increase in allowable number of stories.**
2. **Section 3802 (f) for Group H, Divisions 1, 2 and 3 Occupancies.**
3. **Substitution for one-hour fire-resistive construction pursuant to Section 508.**
4. **Section 1715, Atria.**

This section provides another method for increasing the allowable area of a building: the installation of a complete fire sprinkler system in the building. The area increases allowed with the sprinklers is either three times or two times the basic allowable area depending on whether the building is a single or multi-storied structure, respectively.

Section 506 (c) is *not* applicable when sprinklers are required for any of the four provisions specifically listed in this section.

1. The designer may compound the sprinkler increase with that from separations in Section 506 (a), but cannot compound the sprinkler increase with both area increases and increase in the number of stories per Section 507.
2. When a sprinkler installation is required in Section 3802 (f) for Group H-1, H-2 and H-3 Occupancies.
3. When the sprinklers are used as a substitute for the structural fire resistance of a one-hour building per Section 508.
4. When a sprinkler installation is required in Section 1785 for atria.

The area increases for sprinklers may be compounded with the percentage increases obtained based on Section 506 (a) separations.

Examples of the method used to compound sprinkler credits and the separation credits for street, yard or public space are shown in Figures 5-14 through 5-16.

In short, separation and sprinkler credits can be added together but sprinklers credits alone cannot be used to gain both area and height increases.With the exception of those described in Section 3802 (f), all the required fire sprinkler installations cited in Chapter 38 can be used for the sprinkler credits as specified in Chapter 5, provided the entire building is sprinklered. Therefore, the designer may use sprinkler credits to obtain area increases even when the sprinklers are required by a provision of Chapter 38.

Maximum Height of Buildings and Increases

Sec. 507. The maximum height and number of stories of every building shall be dependent upon the character of the occupancy and the type of construction and shall not exceed the limits set forth in Table No. 5-D, except as provided in this section and as specified in Section 503(a) for mixed occupancy buildings.

► ■■■ ◄

The story limits set forth in Table No. 5-D may be increased by one story if the building is provided with an approved automatic sprinkler system throughout. The increase in the number of stories for automatic sprinkler systems shall not apply when the automatic sprinkler systems throughout are installed under the following provisions:

1. **Section 3802(f) for Group H, Divisions 1, 2, 3, 6 and 7 Occupancies.**
2. **Section 506, for an increase in allowable area.**
3. **Substitution for one-hour five-resistive construction pursuant to Section 508.**
4. **Section 1715, Atria.**
5. **Section 3802 (g) for Group I, Division 1 Occupancies used for hospitals or nursing homes in Type II One-hour, Type III One-hour, Type IV or Type V One-hour construction.**

This section provides the requirements for the number of stories and overall height in feet for each type of construction and occupancy. The matrix in Table No. 5-D contains these limitations.

The increase permitted in the number of stories, under the condition that fire sprinklers are installed, is not permitted for the three provisions cited.

Sprinklers may be used to increase, by one story, the number of stories allowed in a building. For example, a Type V One-hour building of Group R, Division 1 per Table No. 5-D is limited to three stories. If fully sprinklered, the same building type and occupancy can be four stories.

Where there is more than one occupancy in the building, and these occupancies are located on different floors, the maximum level a particular occupancy may be in the building is regulated by the Table No. 5-D provisions.

For example, consider a building that is proposed to have a Group B, Division 2 Occupancy on the first and second floors, an A-3 Occupancy on the third floor, and a Group R, Division 1 Occupancy on the top floor. The overall height of the building is 4 stories. The designer would like to use a building of either one-hour or Type IV construction.

In this example, checking Table No. 5-D, we note that the limits for a Type II One-hour, III One-hour and IV for the three occupancies are:

B-2 ... 4 stories
A-3 ... 2 stories
R-1 ... 4 stories

A Type V One-hour building would allow the B-2 and R-1 Occupancies no higher than the third story.

The A-3 Occupancy cannot be located on the third floor in any of these four types of buildings because the maximum height permitted for that use is two stories. Thus the proposed arrangement is not allowed.

If the A-3 use were to be located on the second floor and the B-2 Occupancy in a basement and first floor, the mixed uses would be allowed on the levels desired in any of these types of construction except for the Type V One-hour.

Another solution could be to provide sprinklers for the entire building. Doing this would allow the various occupancies to be located one floor higher than that shown in Table No. 5-D.

Thus, the building could be constructed as Type V One-hour with the arrangement of the occupancies as originally intended. The A-3 use could be on the third floor and the R-1 Occupancy on the fourth floor.

Fire-Resistive Substitution

Sec. 508. When an approved automatic sprinkler system is not required throughout a building by other sections of this code, it may be used in a building of Type II One-hour, Type III One-hour and Type V One-hour construction to substitute for the one-hour fire-resistive construction. Such substitution shall not waive or reduce required fire-resistive construction for:

1. **Occupancy separations [Section 503 (c)].**
2. **Exterior wall protection due to proximity of property lines [Section 504 (b)].**
3. **Area separations [Section 505 (f)].**
4. **Dwelling unit separations [Section 1202 (b)].**

5. **Shaft enclosures (Section 1706).**
6. **Corridors [Section 3305 (g) and (h)].**
7. **Stair enclosures (Section 3309).**
8. **Exit passageways [Section 3312 (a)].**
9. **Type of construction separation (Section 1701).**
10. **Boiler, central heating plant or hot-water supply boiler room enclosures.**

Although not immediately apparent, this section has been substantially changed from the prior edition of the code. It has returned to the original intent of the provision. The substitution of fire sprinklers for structural fire-resistive construction is permitted for buildings in which *only one-hour fire-resistive construction throughout* is required by the code. These types of buildings are Type II One-hour, Type III One-hour and V One-hour. The section does not therefore apply to any other type of building or to any building not required to be of one-hour fire-resistive construction throughout.

Certain specific limitations to this substitution in the three types of building are listed. In addition, the substitution is not permitted when sprinklers throughout are required by other provisions of the code. Thus, for example, the substitution would not be permitted in Group H Occupancy buildings or in three-(or more) story Group R, Division 1 Occupancy buildings.

In the author's opinion, the change to this section provides the opportunity for enforcement officials to permit the use of sprinklers as an alternative for certain other code provisions or limitations. For example, in a Group B, Division 2 Occupancy, Type V One-hour building, the designer may be willing to provide the one-hour fire-resistive construction, but may want to increase the percentage of protected glazing in an exit corridor.

The designer may offer to provide closely spaced fire sprinklers on both sides of the wired glass area. By using Section 105, the enforcement official can accept increased glazing area and fire sprinklers as providing equivalent or greater protection to the corridor and not be in violation of this section.

The provisions of this section do not limit the use of sprinklers in lieu of one-hour fire-resistive construction in Type I or Type II-FR buildings for elements of those buildings. For example, If the designer offered to fully sprinkler a floor of a building that otherwise did not require sprinklers, the enforcement official could permit a wall required for a one-hour occupancy separation to be of unrated construction.

This change provides opportunities for designers and enforcement officials to reach innovative solutions to design problems without sacrificing safety.

Pedestrian Walkways
Sec. 509

(a) General. A pedestrian walkway shall be considered a building when determining the roof covering permitted by Table No. 32-A.. Pedestrian walkways connecting separate buildings need not be considered as buildings and need not be considered in the determination of the allowable floor area of the connected buildings when the pedestrian walkway complies with the provisions of this section.

(g) Required Exits. Pedestrian walkways at other than grade shall not be used as required exits. Pedestrian walkways at grade level used as required exits shall provide an unobstructed means of egress to a public way and shall have a minimum width in accordance with Section 3303(b).

EXCEPTION: Pedestrian walkways conforming to the requirements of a horizontal exit may be used as a required exit.

This section regulates the connections between buildings, including those that may be on different properties. The provisions include ground level connections, such as covered arcades, and elevated connections or bridges. The “skyways” in Minneapolis are examples of the latter type.

The intent of this section is to permit such facilities, but not to include them in the floor area calculations for the buildings to which they are attached, and to require the necessary construction to protect buildings and users of the walkways.

The Exception in the provisions in Section 509 (g) allows the use of a passageway between buildings, i.e., a connecting bridge, to be used as an exit way provided it conforms to the requirements for a horizontal exit.

This type of construction, where two or more buildings are interconnected via bridges, has increasingly been used as a design tool. All too often, however, the designer and the building official have failed to realize that additional protection is required when the bridge is used as an exit way. Section 509 (g) makes a clear statement of what has logically been the legal requirement for such use.

The key construction requirements for the horizontal exit are contained in Sections 3308 (b) and 3308 (b), which read in part:

> **Sec. 3301 (b)**
> **HORIZONTAL EXIT is an exit from one building into another building on approximately the same level, or through or around a wall constructed as required for a two-hour occupancy separation and which completely divides a floor into two or more separate areas so as to establish an area of refuge affording safety from fire or smoke coming from the area from which escape is made.**
>
> **Sec. 3308 (b)**
> **(b) (Horizontal Exit) Openings. All openings in the two-hour fire-resistive wall which provides a horizontal exit shall be protected by a fire assembly having a fire- protection rating of not less than one and one-half hours.**

The two-hour requirement of Section 3308 (b) is comparable to that for an ASW (ASW) in a Type II-N or one-hour, Type V-N or one-hour building.

Imagine a building with an ASW: See Figure 5-25 Detail (a.) One part of the building is moved away from the other a distance of 10 feet, at the location of the ASW. See Figure 5-25 Detail (b.) An extension of the corridor in one segment of the building can be added across the separation. This corridor extension forms a connecting passageway across the separation. The segments separated by the ASW are considered as separate buildings by Section 505 (f).

This passageway must serve as an exit way, because there are not two exits in each building on either side of the ASW. As can readily be seen in Figure 5-25, each building need only have one exit stairway when a horizontal exit (i.e., the passageway) can provide the second exit for each building.

There remains to be determined, however, the method of restoring the two-hour requirement for the horizontal exit or ASW and of determining the construction required for the passageway or bridge.

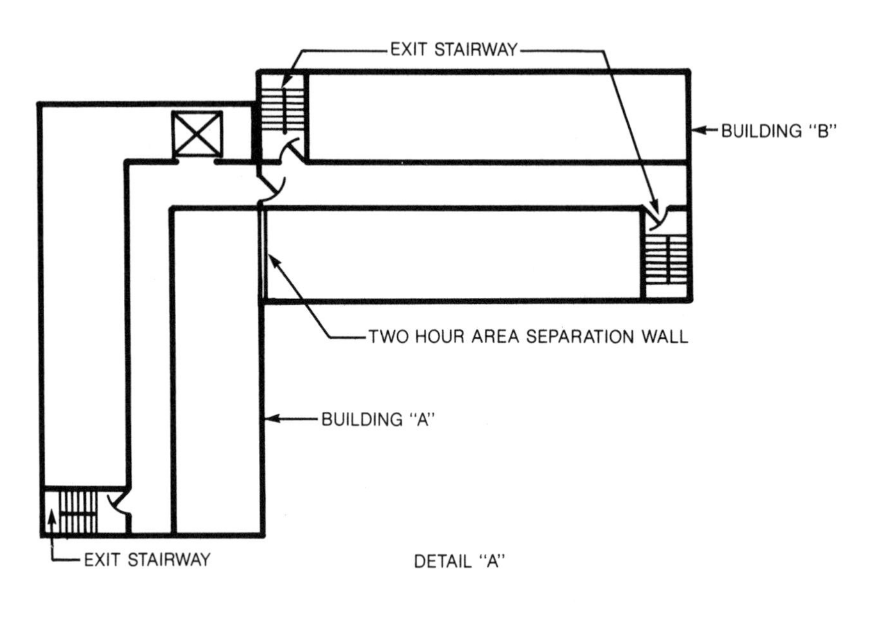

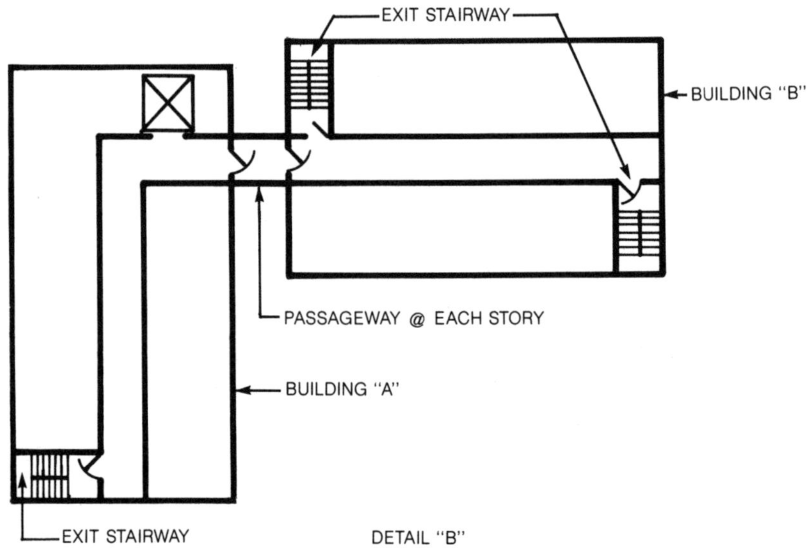

ASSUME: 2-THREE STORY, TYPE V ONE-HOUR BUILDINGS EACH WITH GROUP R, DIVISION 1 OCCUPANCY. BUILDING "A" HAS ONE EXIT STAIRWAY. BUILDING "B" HAS TWO EXIT STAIRWAYS. PASSAGEWAY BETWEEN BUILDINGS TO PROVIDE SECOND EXIT FOR BUILDING "A". AREA OF EACH BUILDING EQUALS MAXIMUM ALLOWABLE.

REFERENCES: SECTIONS 509, 3301(b) and 3308

FIGURE 5-25 PASSAGEWAY BETWEEN BUILDINGS USED AS EXIT WAY

In the author's opinion, the key requirements are to:

1. protect the connection (passageway) for two hours from a fire in either building at the ends of the passageway.
2. protect all openings adjacent to the connecting passageway in a similar manner as for openings adjacent to exterior stairways [Section 3306 (l)]. For this case, however, all openings including those at the same level and those below and all within 10 feet of the passageway must be protected for at least one and one-half hours.
3. construct the passageway for at least one-hour fire resistance.

The author's reasons for these requirements, listed in the same numerical order as presented above, are:

1. The horizontal exit serves two functions:
   a) It provides an exit path for the occupants away from the fire source and provides them with a haven until the fire is suppressed.
   b) It allows the fire service to reach the floor level of the fire via the unaffected building segment and to have a firefighting platform from which to work.
2. This recommendation for protection maintains the integrity of the fire service access and the protection of the haven.
3. The passageway must be provided with fire-resistive protection from radiant energy exposure, both after the failure of the fire assemblies that provide the opening protection and for some time thereafter.

NOTE: When either building has an occupant load of 50 or more on a floor, the doors to the exit path passageway must swing in the direction of exit travel. This may necessitate a pair of doors at each end. One door in each pair must swing in the opposite direction to satisfy this code provision.

Sanitation
Sec. 510

Access to other Features.
Sec. 511 .

Section 510 provide the minimum sanitation requirements. This section and Section 511 refer to the new Chapter 31 provisions which consolidate the prior code provisions for access to the handicapped and expand the overall requirements. The designer and enforcement official should review the comments in Article 1 an 11 of this guide relating to the impact of the Chapter 31 provisions and the American with Disabilities Act.

The UBC handicap provisions are generally based on the ANSI standards which form the basis of most nationally adopted provisions. However, local government may have enacted more restrictive provisions. See the general comments in Article 1.

Premises Identification

Sec. 513. Approved numbers of addresses shall be provided for all new buildings in such a position as to be plainly visible and legible from the street or road fronting the property.

This provision may seem to be an odd requirement to be placed in a building code. However, to provide emergency services, the fire department must be able to identify the location of the building.

Often when an alarm is phoned in and an address given, the fire in question may not be visible from the fire department's approach side of the building. The only means of identifying the location of the fire is the building address. It is for such emergency reasons that the code mandates that the address be visibly located.

TABLE NO. 5-A WALL AND OPENING PROTECTION OF OCCUPANCIES BASED ON LOCATION ON PROPERTY TYPE II ONE-HOUR, II-N AND V CONSTRUCTION

The designer should make careful note of the full title of this table. All too often it is assumed to cover all requirements for exterior wall and opening protection.

Table No. 5-A covers only two of the five classes of building construction, namely Type II One-hour and II-N and both Type V buildings. All other requirements for exterior walls are contained in the "03" sections of the code, i.e., 1803, 1903, 2003 and 2803.

In the preliminary plan check, the siting of the building on the property should be one of the first subjects of discussion with the building official to ensure that the exterior wall code provisions are satisfied.

TABLE NO. 5-A—WALL AND OPENING PROTECTION OF OCCUPANCIES BASED ON LOCATION ON PROPERTY

TYPES II ONE-HOUR, II-N AND V CONSTRUCTION: For exterior wall and opening protection of Types II One-hour, II-N and V buildings, see table below. Exceptions to limitations for Types II One-hour, II-N and Type V construction, as provided in Sections 709, 1903 and 2203 apply. For Types I, II-F.R., III and IV construction, see Sections 1803, 1903, 2003, and 2103.

GROUP	DESCRIPTION OF OCCUPANCY	FIRE RESISTANCE OF EXTERIOR WALLS	OPENINGS IN EXTERIOR WALLS[3]
A See also Section 602	1—Any assembly building with a stage and an occupant load of 1000 or more in the building	Not applicable (See Sections 602 and 603)	
	2—Any building or portion of a building having an assembly room with an occupant load of less than 1000 and a stage 2.1—Any building or portion of a building having an assembly room with an occupant load of 300 or more without a stage, including such building used for educational purposes and not classed as a Group E or Group B, Division 2 Occupancy	2 hours less than 5 feet, 1 hour less than 20 feet	Not permitted less than 5 feet Protected less than 10 feet
	3—Any building or portion of a building having an assembly room with an occupant load of less than 300 without a stage, including such buildings used for educational purposes and not classed as a Group E or Group B, Division 2 Occupancy	2 hours less than 5 feet, 1 hour less than 40 feet	Not permitted less than 5 feet Protected less than 10 feet
	4—Stadiums, reviewing stands and amusement park structures not included within other Group A Occupancies	1 hour less than 10 feet	Protected less than 10 feet
B See also Section 702	1—Gasoline service stations, garages where no repair work is done except exchange of parts and maintenance requiring no open flame, welding or use of Class I, II or III-A liquids, parking garages other than open parking garages 2—Drinking and dining establishments having an occupant load of less than 50, wholesale and retail stores, office buildings, printing plants, police and fire stations, factories and workshops using material not highly flammable or combustible, storage and sales rooms for combustible goods, paint stores without bulk handling Buildings or portions of buildings having rooms used for educational purposes, beyond the 12th grade, with less than 50 occupants in any room	1 hour less than 20 feet	Not permitted less than 5 feet Protected less than 10 feet

[3] Openings shall be protected by a fire assembly having at least a three-fourths hour fire-protection rating.

(Continued)

TABLE NO. 5-A—Continued
TYPES II ONE-HOUR, II-N AND V ONLY

GROUP	DESCRIPTION OF OCCUPANCY	FIRE RESISTANCE OF EXTERIOR WALLS	OPENINGS IN EXTERIOR WALLS
B (Cont.)	3—Aircraft hangars where no repair work is done except exchange of parts and maintenance requiring no open flame, welding, or the use of highly flammable liquids Open parking garages (For requirements, See Section 709.) Helistop	1 hour less than 20 feet	Not permitted less than 5 feet Protected less than 20 feet
	4—Ice plants, power plants, pumping plants, cold storage and creameries Factories and workshops using noncombustible and nonexplosive materials Storage and sales rooms of noncombustible and nonexplosive materials	1 hour less than 5 feet	Not permitted less than 5 feet
E See also Section 802	1—Any building used for educational purposes through the 12th grade by 50 or more persons for more than 12 hours per week or four hours in any one day 2—Any building used for educational purposes through the 12th grade by less than 50 persons for more than 12 hours per week or four hours in any one day 3—Any building used for day-care purposes for more than six children	2 hours less than 5 feet, 1 hour less than 10 feet[1]	Not permitted less than 5 feet Protected less than 10 feet[1]
H See also Sections 902 and 903	1—Storage, handling, use or sale of hazardous and highly flammable or explosive materials other than flammable liquids [See also Section 901 (a), Division 1.]	See Chapter 9 and the Fire Code	
	2—Storage, handling, use or sale of Classes I, II and III-A liquids; dry cleaning plants using Class I, II or III-A liquids; paint stores with bulk handling; paint shops and spray-painting rooms and shops [See also Section 901 (a), Division 2.] 3—Woodworking establishments, planing mills, box factories, buffing rooms for tire-rebuilding plants and picking rooms; shops, factories or warehouses where loose combustible fibers or dust are manufactured, processed, generated or stored; and pin-refinishing rooms 4—Repair garages not classified as a Group B, Division 1 Occupancy	4 hours less than 5 feet, 2 hours less than 10 feet, 1 hour less than 20 feet	Not permitted less than 5 feet Protected less than 20 feet

[1]Group E, Divisions 2 and 3 Occupancies having an occupant load of not more than 20 may have exterior wall and opening protection as required for Group R, Division 3 Occupancies.

H (Cont.)	5— Aircraft repair hangars and Helistops.	1 hour less than 60 feet	Protected less than 60 feet
	6/7 See Table No. 9-C	4 hours less than 5 feet, 2 hours less than 10 feet, 1 hour less than 20 feet	Not permitted less than 5 feet, protected less than 20 feet
I See also Section 1002	1—Nurseries for the full-time care of children under the age of six (each accommodating more than five persons) Hospitals, sanitariums, nursing homes with nonambulatory patients and similar buildings (each accommodating more than five persons)	2 hours less than 5 feet, 1 hour elsewhere	Not permitted less than 5 feet Protected less than 10 feet
	2—Nursing homes for ambulatory patients, homes for children six years of age or over (each accommodating more than five persons)	1 hour	
	3—Mental hospitals, mental sanitariums, jails, prisons, reformatories and buildings where personal liberties of inmates are similarly restrained	2 hours less than 5 feet, 1 hour elsewhere	Not permitted less than 5 feet, protected less than 10 feet
M[2]	1—Private garages, carports, sheds and agricultural buildings (See also Section 1101, Division 1.)	1 hour less than 3 feet (or may be protected on the exterior with materials approved for 1-hour fire-resistive construction)	Not permitted less than 3 feet
	2—Fences over 6 feet high, tanks and towers	Not regulated for fire resistance	
R See also Section 1202	1—Hotels and apartment houses Convents and monasteries (each accommodating more than 10 persons)	1 hour less than 5 feet	Not permitted less than 5 feet
	3—Dwellings and lodging houses	1 hour less than 3 feet	Not permitted less than 3 feet

[2]For agricultural buildings, see Appendix Chapter 11.

NOTES: (1) See Section 504 for types of walls affected and requirements covering percentage of openings permitted in exterior walls.
(2) For additional restrictions, see chapters under Occupancy and Types of Construction.
(3) For walls facing streets, yards and public ways, see Part IV.

TABLE NO. 5-B — REQUIRED SEPARATION IN BUILDINGS OF MIXED OCCUPANCY (In Hours)

	A-1	A-2	A-2.1	A-3	A-4	B-1	B-2	B-3[4]	B-4	E	H-1	H-2	H-3	H-4-5	H-6-7[1]	I	M[2]	R-1	R-3
A-1		N	N	N	N	4	3	3	3	N	Not Permitted in Mixed Occupancies. See Chapter 9.	4	4	4	4	3	1	1	1
A-2	N		N	N	N	3	1	1	1	N		4	4	4	4	3	1	1	1
A-2.1	N	N		N	N	3	1	1	1	N		4	4	4	4	3	1	1	1
A-3	N	N	N		N	3	N	1	1	N		4	4	4	3	2	1	1	1
A-4	N	N	N	N		3	1	1	1	N		4	4	4	4	3	1	1	1
B-1	4	3	3	3	3		1	1	1	3		1	1	1	1	4	1	3[3]	1
B-2	3	1	1	N	1	1		1	1	1		1	1	1	1	2	1	1	N
B-3[4]	3	1	1	1	1	1	1		1	1		1	1	1	1	3	1	1	N
B-4	3	1	1	N	1	1	1	1		1		1	1	1	1	4	N	1	N
E	N	N	N	N	N	4	1	1	1			4	4	4	3	1	1	1	1
H-1	Not Permitted in Mixed Occupancies. See Chapter 9																		
H-2	4	4	4	4	4	1	1	1	1	4			1	1	1	4	1	3	3
H-3	4	4	4	4	4	1	1	1	1	4		1		1	1	4	1	3	3
H-4-5	4	4	4	4	4	1	1	1	1	4		1	1		1	4	1	3	3
H-6-7[1]	4	4	4	3	4	1	1	1	1	3		1	1	1		4	3	4	4
I	3	3	3	3	3	4	2	4	4	1		4	4	4	4		1	1	1
M[2]	1	1	1	1	1	1	1	1	N	1		1	1	1	3	1		1	1
R-1	1	1	1	1	1	3[3]	1	1	1	1		3	3	3	4	1	1		N
R-3	1	1	1	1	1	1	N	N	N	1		3	3	3	4	1	1	N	

Note: For detailed requirements and exceptions, see Section 503.

[1] For special provisions for highly toxic materials, see Fire Code.

[2] For agricultural buildings, see also Appendix Chapter 11.

[3] For reduction in fire-resistive rating, see Section 503(d).

[4] Open parking garages are excluded, except as provided in Section 702(a).

TABLE NO. 5-C—BASIC ALLOWABLE FLOOR AREA FOR BUILDINGS ONE STORY IN HEIGHT[1]

(In Square Feet)

OCCUPANCY	TYPES OF CONSTRUCTION								
	I	II			III		IV	V	
	F.R.	F.R.	ONE-HOUR	N	ONE-HOUR	N	H.T.	ONE-HOUR	N
A-1	Unlimited	29,900	Not Permitted						
A) 2-2.1	Unlimited	29,900	13,500	Not Permitted	13,500	Not Permitted	13,500	10,500	Not Permitted
A)3-4[2]	Unlimited	29,900	13,500	9,100	13,500	9,100	13,500	10,500	6,000
B)1-2-3[3]	Unlimited	39,900	18,000	12,000	18,000	12,000	18,000	14,000	8,000
B-4	Unlimited	59,900	27,000	18,000	27,000	18,000	27,000	21,000	12,000
E[2]	Unlimited	45,200	20,200	13,500	20,200	13,500	20,200	15,700	9,100
H-1	15,000	12,400	5,600	3,700	Not Permitted				
H-2[4]	15,000	12,400	5,600	3,700	5,600	3,700	5,600	4,400	2,500
H-3-4-5[4]	Unlimited	24,800	11,200	7,500	11,200	7,500	11,200	8,800	5,100
H-6	Unlimited	39,900	18,000	12,000	18,000	12,000	18,000	14,000	8,000
I) 1-2	Unlimited	15,100	6,800	Not Permitted[8]	6,800	Not Permitted	6,800	5,200	Not Permitted
I-3	Unlimited	15,100	Not Permitted[5]						
M[6]	See Chapter 11								
R-1	Unlimited	29,900	13,500	9,100[7]	13,500	9,100[7]	13,500	10,500	6,000[7]
R-3	Unlimited								

[1]For multistory buildings, see Section 505 (b).
[2]For limitations and exceptions, see Section 502 (a).
[3]For open parking garages, see Section 709.
[4]See Section 903.
[5]See Section 1002 (b)
[6]For agricultural buildings, see also Appendix Chapter 11.
[7]For limitations and exceptions, see Section 1202 (b).
[8]In hospitals and nursing homes, see Section 1002 (a) for exceptions.

N—No requirements for fire resistance
F.R.—Fire resistive
H.T.—Heavy Timber

TABLE NO. 5-D—MAXIMUM HEIGHT OF BUILDINGS

OCCUPANCY	TYPES OF CONSTRUCTION								
	I	II			III		IV	V	
	F.R.	F.R.	ONE-HOUR	N	ONE-HOUR	N	H.T.	ONE-HOUR	N
	MAXIMUM HEIGHT IN FEET								
	Unlimited	160	65	55	65	55	65	50	40
	MAXIMUM HEIGHT IN STORIES								
A-1	Unlimited	4	Not Permitted						
A) 2-2.1	Unlimited	4	2	Not Permitted	2	Not Permitted	2	2	Not Permitted
A)3-4[1]	Unlimited	12	2	1	2	1	2	2	1
B)1-2-3[2]	Unlimited	12	4	2	4	2	4	3	2
B-4	Unlimited	12	4	2	4	2	4	3	2
E[3]	Unlimited	4	2[2]	1	2[2]	1	2[2]	2[2]	1
H-1[7]	1	1	1	1	Not Permitted				
H-2[7]	Unlimited	2	1	1	1	1	1	1	1
H-3-4-5[7]	Unlimited	5	2	1	2	1	2	2	1
H-6-7	3	3	3	2	3	2	3	3	1
I-1[7]	Unlimited	3	1	Not Permitted	1	Not Permitted	1	1	Not Permitted
I-2[8]	Unlimited	3	2	Not Permitted	2	Not Permitted	2	2	Not Permitted
I-3	Unlimited	2	Not Permitted[4]						
M[5]	See Chapter 11								
R-1	Unlimited	12	4	2[6]	4	2[6]	4	3	2[6]
R-3	Unlimited	3	3	3	3	3	3	3	3

[1]For limitations and exceptions, see Section 602 (a).
[2]For open parking garages, see Section 709.
[3]See Section 802 (c).
[4]See Section 1002 (b).
[5]For agricultural buildings, see also Appendix Chapter 11.
[6]For limitations and exceptions, see Section 1202 (b).
[7]See Section 1002 (a) for exceptions to number of stories in hospitals and nursing homes.
[8]See Section 902.

N—No requirements for fire resistance
F.R.—Fire resistive
H.T.—Heavy Timber

ARTICLE 6
THE TYPE OF CONSTRUCTION PROVISIONS OF CHAPTER 17

CHAPTER 17
CLASSIFICATION OF ALL BUILDINGS BY TYPES OF CONSTRUCTION AND GENERAL REQUIREMENTS

Chapter 17 contains the requirements relating to the type of construction for buildings. Included are the fire-resistive requirements of the building elements(the structural framing, roofs, shaft enclosures, and bearing walls), insulation and weather protection.

The main fire-resistive construction requirements are described in Section 1701 and Table No. 17-A. The remainder of Chapter 17 covers:

- specific fire-resistive requirements,
- clarifying details for certain fire-resistive requirements,
- miscellaneous provisions for other aspects of the building construction that do not readily belong in another Chapter.

The concept contained in Table No. 17-A, used in the model codes for the majority of buildings, is compartition. Compartition is defined as the dividing of a space into compartments. As discussed in Article 5 of this Guide in regard to the provisions of Chapter 5, control of conflagration from building lot to building lot is achieved through compartition of the building site according to the exterior wall and setback requirements for each building.

Within a building, the compartition is primarily created by:

- the floor system,
- the stair and shaft enclosures and
- the protection of the structural load bearing members (columns, beams, walls).

These building elements prevent both fire spread from floor to floor, and the type of collapse which would break down the compartment formed by the floor system.

A fire is confined to a floor by these fire-resistive compartments. Floors with corridors serving different tenants or occupants generally have fire-rated walls. These walls further subdivide a floor into smaller compartments.

Within a tenant space, be it an apartment or an office, there are no specific requirements for compartition since these would:

- be difficult to maintain,
- hamper operations within the space and
- not afford more than token safety in the event of fire due to inability to enforce the door closer, width of aisles, height of partitions and similar enforceability factors.

The less restrictive tenant provisions are contained in the Exceptions to Section 1705 for the partitioning and nonload-bearing walls within apartments and offices.

The compartition concept also includes regulating the materials of construction and their combustibility for the compartment envelope, based on the building's type of construction. The materials in the envelope should not provide potential fire loading in a Type I building. In a Type V building, however, they are permitted to be combustible and could contribute to the fire load once the protective membrane on the structural element (the stud) has been breached.

The Chapter 17 provisions cover a wide range of construction requirements for buildings. The primary emphasis of this Article of the Guide is on the fire-resistive provisions: other items in Chapter 17 such as weather protection, solar collectors and guardrails will be discussed to a limited degree.

The materials and fire-resistive requirements in Table No. 17-A are related to the occupancies in the buildings, as discussed in Article 5 of this Guide. This inter-relationship must be recognized because the mandated requirements in Table No. 17-A and Section 505 (e) may influence the designer's decision.

For example, assume the building under design consideration is required to have an area separation wall, but that a fire-resistive rating is not required for its roof. Unless a parapet is constructed, the roof-ceiling assembly and its supporting structure must have at least a one-hour fire rating. For this to be achieved, the entire building may have to be upgraded to at least a one-hour fire-resistive rating. See Figure 5-19.

General

Sec. 1701. The requirements of Part IV are for the various types of construction and represent varying degrees of public safety and resistance to fire. Every building shall be classified by the building official into one of the types of construction set forth in Table No. 17-A. Any building which does not entirely conform to a type of construction set forth in Table No. 17-A shall be classified by a building official into a type having an equal or lesser degree of fire resistance.

A building or portion thereof shall not be required to conform to the details of a type of construction higher than that type which meets the minimum requirements based on occupancy (Part III) even though certain features of such building actually conform to a higher type of construction.

Where specific materials, types of construction or fire-resistive protection are required, such requirements shall be the minimum requirements and any materials, types of construction or fire-resistive protection which will afford equal or greater public safety or resistance to fire, as specified in this code, may be used.

Portions of buildings separated as specified in Section 505 (e) may be considered a separate building for classification of types of construction. When there is no such separation, the area of the entire building shall not exceed the least area permitted for the types of construction involved.

This section provides for the building official to determine the type of construction classification for a building. The classification is to be made based on the construction requirements for the particular type as set forth in Table No. 17-A. If the designer desires the building to be classified into a lesser type of fire-resistive construction, the building official can do so. The official must determine that, for the proposed building size and occupancy, Chapter 5 of the code permits a type of construction of equal or lesser fire resistance than that assigned to the building in Table No. 17-A. The evaluation of the "equal or lesser degree of fire resistance" is based on the proposed fire resistance of the building elements.

For example, if the proposed construction, as shown on the drawings, meets the type of construction known as Type II-FR, the designer could request that the building be classified as Type II One-hour, Type V One-hour or Type V-N. If such a lower type of construction is chosen by the designer, the height and area limitations of that class of construction, per Chapter 5, would govern.

The other provisions of this section:

- repeat the concept stated in Section 105, i.e. acceptance of equivalent construction to that required in Table No. 17-A and
- permit the use of area separation walls per Section 505 (e) so that each segment may be constructed as if it were a separate building, provided each segment created by the area separation walls meets the requirements for its particular type of construction.

Usable Space Under Floors

Sec. 1703. Usable space under the first story shall be enclosed except in Groups R, Division 3 and M Occupancies and such enclosure when constructed of metal or wood shall be protected on the side of the usable space as required for one-hour fire-resistive construction. Doors shall be self-closing, of non-combustible construction or solid wood core, not less than 1 3/4 inches in thickness.

This section permits the omission of certain fire protection for unusable space under the first floor. The designer is cautioned to consider this provision together with the definition of "story" and be sure that the design provides a reasonable level of code compliance. These two code provisions, Section 1703 and the story definition, present a conflict.

If the space below the first floor meets the following criteria, i.e., if the height above grade exceeds:

- 6 feet average for more than 50 percent of the perimeter, or
- 12 feet at any point,

by definition that space is a story.

In the author's opinion, whether the space is usable or not, the space usable or not, the space should be protected in the same manner as the rest of the building. A fire in that space could cause collapse of the building unless the surfaces enclosing the space are protected.

The term "usable space" is often a transient concept; that is, the space may be unused today and used tomorrow. The designer should be aware of this possibility and the tendency of individuals to use all available space. The designer should consider providing the built-in protection.

The conflict between what the code allows and what, logically, should be done has concerned many building and fire officials. However, at present there exists no code change proposal that would resolve the conflict.

Vertical Fire Spread at Exterior Walls

Sec. 1704. (a) General. The provisions of this section are intended to restrict the passage of smoke, flame and hot gases from one floor to another at exterior walls. See Section 4305 for floor penetrations.

(b) Interior. Where fire-resistive floor or floor-ceiling assemblies are required, voids created at the intersection of the exterior wall assemblies and such floor assemblies shall be sealed with an approved material. Such material shall be securely installed and capable of preventing the passage of flame and hot gases sufficient to ignite cotton waste when subject to U.B.C. Standard No. 43-1 time-temperature fire conditions under a minimum positive pressure differential of 0.01 inches of water column for the time period at least equal to the fire-resistance rating of the floor assembly.

(c) Exterior. Where openings in an exterior wall are above and within 5 feet laterally of an opening in the story below, such openings shall be separated by an approved flame barrier extending 30 inches beyond the exterior wall in the plane of the floor or by approved vertical flame barriers not less than 3 feet high measured vertically above the top of the lower opening. Flame barriers shall have a fire resistance of not less than three-fourths hour.

EXCEPTIONS: 1. Flame barriers are not required in buildings equipped with an approved automatic sprinkler system throughout.

2. This subsection shall not apply to buildings two stories or less in height.

These exterior wall provisions apply to all buildings more than two stories in height and are not sprinklered. Therefore, the requirements do not apply to:

- high-rise buildings complying with Section 1807
- Group R, Division 1 Occupancy buildings complying with Section 3802 (h)
- Group H, Division 2, 3, 6 and 7 Occupancy buildings
- any other building that is sprinklered throughout, regardless of the reason therefore

The primary concerns of the new provisions are:

- to seal the floor-exterior wall intersection and
- to provide flame barriers at the exterior wall to restrict floor-

to-floor fire spread on the exterior wall surface

Section 1704 (b) addresses the first concern by requiring that voids at the building exterior wall and floor be filled with approved materials. These are commonly referred to as fire safing by manufacturers.

Section 1704 (c) addresses the second concern regarding openings in the exterior wall that are above and within five feet of an opening in the floor below. (See Figure 6-1.) The hazard of the spread of fire can be reduced by providing either a three-quarter-hour fire-resistive flame barrier in the form of a three-foot-high spandrel or a 30-inch wide "eyebrow."

This is the first time fractional hourly ratings have been permitted for wall assemblies. No three-quarter-hour fire-resistive wall assemblies are presently listed in the UBC or have Evaluation Reports.

It is the author's opinion that until such time as these Evaluation Reports are made available, the designer should use one-hour fire-resistive assemblies.

The spandrel or eyebrow requirement is the result of the major fire losses in Los Angeles and Las Vegas that had substantial degree of fire spread via the exterior wall openings.

Exceptions to Table No. 17-A

Sec. 1705. (a) General. The provisions of this section are exceptions to the construction requirements of Table No. 17-A, Chapters 5 through 12 and 18 through 22.

(b) Fixed Partitions. 1. Stores and offices. Interior nonload-bearing partitions dividing portions of stores, offices or similar places occupied by one tenant only and which do not establish a corridor serving an occupant load that would require it to be of fire-resistive construction under the provisions of Section 3305 (g) may be constructed of:

A. Noncombustible materials.

B. Fire-retardant treated wood.

C. One-hour fire-resistive construction.

D. Wood panels or similar light construction up to three fourths the height of the room in which placed; when more than three fourths the height of the room, such partitions shall have not less than the upper one fourth of the partition constructed in glass.

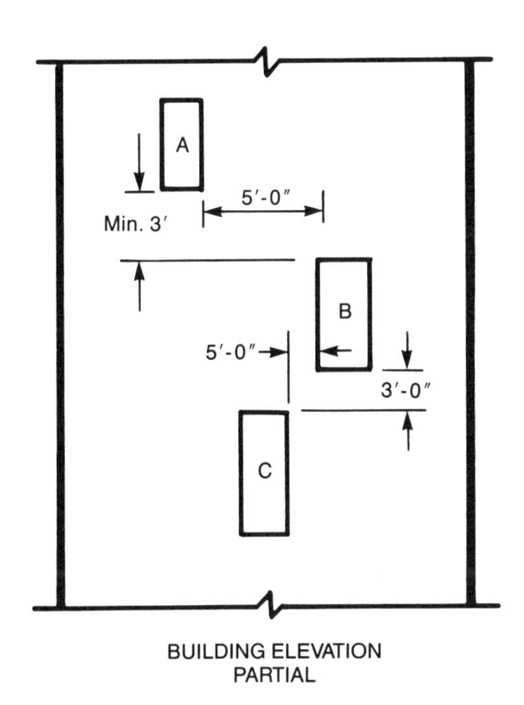

BUILDING ELEVATION
PARTIAL

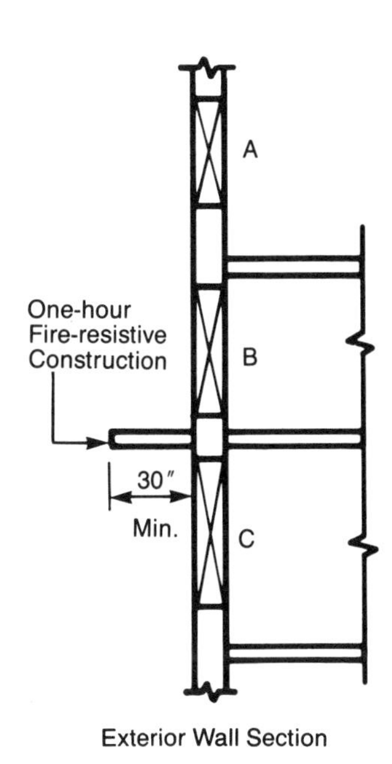

Exterior Wall Section

GIVEN:

Building is Not Sprinklered
Window A is more than 5′ laterally from window B.
Window C is either less than 5′ laterally from window B, or is less than 3′ below window B or both conditions apply.

If window A were less than 5′ from window B, and there were room for a 3′ high one-hour spandrel between windows A and B, that would meet Section 1704 (c) requirements. Otherwise, window A as shown does not require any special protection because it is more than 5′ from window B.

Window C does not have sufficient room for a 3′ height of one-hour spandrel. It is less than 5′ from window B, therefore a one-hour "eyebrow" must be provided. The "eyebrow" must project at least 30 " from the exterior wall.

REFERENCE: SECTION 1704 (c)

FIGURE 6-1 VERTICAL FLAME SPREAD AT EXTERIOR WALLS – FLAME BARRIER

2. Hotels and apartments. Interior nonload-bearing partitions within individual dwelling units in apartment houses and guest rooms or suites in hotels when such dwelling units, guest rooms or suites are separated from each other and from corridors by not less than one-hour fire-resistive construction may be constructed of:

A. Noncombustible materials or fire-retardant treated wood in buildings of any type of construction; or

B. Combustible framing with noncombustible materials applied to the framing in buildings of Type III or V construction.

Openings to such corridors shall be equipped with doors conforming to Section 3305 (h) regardless of the occupant load served.

For use of plastics in partitions, see Section 5210.

The exceptions outlined in this section were discussed earlier. The designer should also note the provisions of Section 3305 (g) for consideration along with Section 1705 (b) relating to nonload-bearing interior partitions in offices and stores.

Where there are sprinklers provided on an entire floor, the occupant load may be as great as 100 before fire-rated corridor walls are required within a tenancy. Where the partitions are less than 5 feet 9 inches high, the occupant load criteria does not apply. In fact, there is no maximum occupant load in such an office facility. (See the extensive discussion, in Article 7 of this Guide, regarding the Chapter 33 exit corridor requirements.)

NOTE: See comments at the end of Section 1705 (e) discussion.

Sec. 1705.

(d) Walls Fronting on Streets or Yards. Regardless of fire-resistive requirements for exterior walls, certain elements of the walls fronting on streets or yards having a width of 40 feet may be constructed as follows:

1. **Bulkheads below show windows, show-window frames, aprons and show-cases may be of combustible materials, provided the height of such construction does not exceed 15 feet above grade.**
2. **Wood veneer of boards not less than 1-inch nominal thickness or exterior-type panels not less than 3/8-inch nominal thickness may be applied to walls, provided the veneer does not exceed 15 feet above grade and further provided such veneer shall be placed either directly against noncombustible surfaces or furred out from such surfaces not to exceed 1 5/8 inches with all concealed spaces fire blocked as provided in Section 2516 (f). Where boards, panels and furring as described above comply with Section 407 as fire-retardant treated wood suitable for exterior exposure, the height above grade may be increased to 35 feet.**

See the discussion regarding Section 2516 (f).

Sec. 1705

(e) Trim. Trim, picture molds, chair rails, baseboard, handrails and show-window backing may be of wood. Unprotected wood doors and windows may be used except where openings are required to be fire protected.

Foam plastic trim covering not more than 10 percent of the wall or ceiling area may be used, provided such trim:

(1) has a density of no less than 20 pounds per cubic foot,

(2) has a maximum thickness of 1/2-inch and a maximum width of 4 inches and

(3) has a flame-spread rating no greater than 75.

Materials used for interior finish of walls and ceilings, including wainscoting, shall be as specified in Chapter 42.

The designer should be aware that these code provisions for foam plastic trim can be misapplied. During construction, the determination of these percentages will be made by field personnel whose decision may differ from that of the designer as represented in his drawings. The materials can then be used in actual constructions that are outside the control of the designer *unless* the designer, through field observations, becomes actively involved in the construction phase.

Technically, in cases of litigation, the designer may truly have no responsibility for any misapplication or for extension beyond the allowed percentages. However, the litigation process would probably involve the designer in some capacity. Because of this possibility, the designer should consider avoiding use of materials that rely on "bookkeeping" controls, unless the designer has the authority during the construction phase to prevent misuse of this code section.

> In the author's opinion, foam plastic materials present a serious hazard potential of generating considerable quantities of smoke in the event of a fire. This potential hazard therefore warrants the designer to carefully evaluate the use of these materials.

NOTE:

In the following comments regarding Section 1705 (b) Item 2 and Section 1705 (e), this Guide offers conservative recommendations that should result in lesser likelihood of field errors and, hence, a safer building. When the designer is confident that the field work will be properly controlled, the use of these code provisions is warranted.

To avoid misapplication of materials, the designer should consider whether his involvement in the project, after the design phase is completed, will allow adequate field control of the construction. These cautions are presented based on the author's findings, during investigations conducted as part of litigation, of many field errors. It is unlikely that the level of field supervision or materials control on a large project will be adequate enough to avoid these field errors. It is best that such avoidance begin during the design process.

When considering the use of Section 1705 (b) Item 2 for Group R, Division 1 Occupancy, it is important to anticipate the possible results from the use of nonrated construction within the dwelling units. For example, assume that a designer proposes to have the load-bearing elements in the Group R, Division 1 Occupancy building covered with 5/8-inch Type X wallboard and the interior nonload-bearing partitions covered with 1/2-inch standard (nonfire-rated) wallboard. There is a strong possibility that when the carpenters install the wallboard, they may mix the materials and use whatever is on hand at that particular location.

Unfortunately this has repeatedly been the case. Nonrated construction has been found installed in locations that were to have fire-rated construction. The designer should consider whether to accept the probability of misapplication or, for the nominal additional cost involved, use only the 5/8-inch Type X wallboard in the building. Doing this would avoid the possibility of misapplication by the workman of the required wallboard.

Since the code requirements set only the minimum acceptable standard, good practice to avoid field errors would be to design to a higher-than-minimum level.

Shaft Enclosures

Sec. 1706 (a) General. Openings through floors shall be enclosed in a shaft enclosure of fire-resistive construction having the time period set forth in Table No. 17-A for "Shaft Enclosures" except as permitted in Subsection 1706 (c), (e) and (f). See occupancy chapters for special provisions.

(b) Extent of Enclosures. Shaft enclosures shall extend from the lowest floor opening through successive floor openings and shall be enclosed at the top and bottom.

EXCEPTIONS: 1. Shafts extending through or to the underside of the roof

sheathing, deck or slab need not be enclosed at the top.

2. Noncombustible ducts, vents of chimneys used to convey vapors, dusts or combustion products may penetrate the enclosure at the bottom.

3. Shafts need not be enclosed at the bottom when protected by fire dampers conforming to U.B.C. Standard No. 43-7, installed at the lowest floor level within the shaft enclosure.

Shaft enclosures shall be constructed to continuously maintain the required fire-resistive integrity.

(c) Special Provisions. In other than Group I Occupancies, openings which penetrate only one adjacent floor and are not connected with openings communicating with other stories or basement and which are not concealed within the building construction need not be enclosed.

Exit enclosures shall conform to the applicable provisions in Sections 3309 and 3310. See Section 706 for exception in Group B, Division 4 Occupancies and Section 709 (j) for open parking garages.

In one- and two-story buildings of other than Group I Occupancies, gas vents, ducts, piping and factory-built chimneys which extend through not more than two floors need not be enclosed, provided the openings around the penetrations are fire stopped at each floor.

EXCEPTION: BW gas vents installed in accordance with their listing.

Gas vents and factory-built chimneys shall be protected as required by the Mechanical Code.

Walls containing gas vents or noncombustible piping which pass through three floors or less need not provide the fire-resistance rating specified in Table No. 17-A for "Shaft Enclosures," provided the annular space around the vents or piping is filled at each floor or ceiling with noncombustible materials.

EXCEPTION: BW gas vents installed in accordance with their listing.

Openings made through a floor for penetrations such as cables, cable trays, conduit, pipes or tubing which are protected with approved through-penetration fire stops to provide the same degree of fire-resistance as the floor construction need not be enclosed. For floor-ceiling assemblies see Section 4305.

(d) Protection of Openings. Openings into a shaft enclosure shall be protected by self-closing or automatic-closing fire assembly conforming to Section 4306 and having a fire-protection rating of one-hour for openings through one-hour walls and one and one-half hours through two-hour walls.

EXCEPTIONS: 1. Openings to the exterior may be unprotected when permitted by Table No. 5-A or Sections 1803 (b), 1903 (b), 2003 (b) and 2103 (b).

2. Openings protected by through-penetration fire stops to provide the same degree of fire resistance as the shaft enclosure. See Sections 4304 and 4305.

(e) Rubbish and Linen Chute Termination Rooms. In other than Group R, Division 3 Occupancies, rubbish and linen chutes shall terminate in rooms separated from the remainder of the building by an occupancy separation having the same degree of fire resistance as required for the shaft enclosure, but not less than one-hour. Openings into chutes and chute termination rooms shall not be located in exit corridors or stairways. For sprinklers, see Section 3802 (b).

(f) Chute & Dumbwaiter Shafts. In buildings of Type V buildings, chutes and dumbwaiter shafts with a cross-sectional area of not more than 9 square feet may be either of approved fire-resistive wall construction or may have the inside layers of the approved fire-resistive assembly replaced by a lining of not

less than 0.19-inch (26-gauge) galvanized sheet metal with all joints locklapped. All openings into any such enclosure shall be protected by not less than a self-closing solid wood door 1-3/8 inch thick or equivalent.

Section 1706 has been extensively revised, primarily editorially, with some material transferred to the occupancy chapters (Sections 706 and 906) and other material deleted and replaced by provisions in Chapter 43 as part the requirements relating to penetrations of fire-resistive wall, floor-ceiling and shaft wall assemblies.

This section provides the exceptions to the general requirement of Table No. 17-A that shafts be enclosed with walls of fire-resistive construction.

The provisions of Section 1706 are comparable to the provisions in Section 3306 dealing with stairways. Both sets of provisions require the enclosures except when the openings are through only two adjacent floors.

Subsection (f) describes small shafts, less than nine square feet in cross-sectional area, in Type V buildings only, which may have lesser construction than would be required for a fire-resistive wall assembly. (See Figure 6-2.)

The intent of this Item is to facilitate the construction of small cross-sectional area shafts, the interiors of which workers cannot finish as required for fire-resistive assemblies.

The requirements for elevator shafts are also located in Chapter 51.

Construction Joints

Sec. 1707. Construction joints, such as those used to accommodate wind, seismic or expansion movements, installed in fire-resistive walls required to have protected openings or in floors, shall be protected with an approved material or construction assembly designed to provide the same degree of fire resistance as the floor or wall in which it is installed when tested in accordance with U.B.C. Standard No. 43-1. See Section 4302 (b).

Such material or construction assembly shall be securely installed in or on the joint for its entire length so as not to dislodge, loosen or otherwise impair its ability to accommodate expected building movements and to resist the spread of fire and hot gases.

This is a new section and is part of the requirements relating to penetrations of fire-resistive wall, floor-ceiling and shaft wall assemblies. It is the result of experiences in fires such as at McCormick Place in

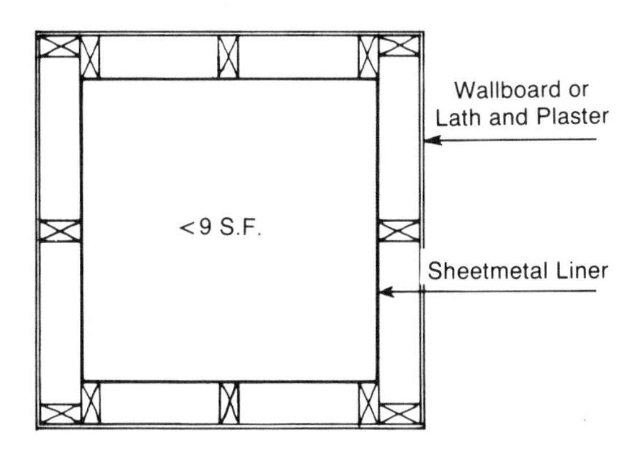

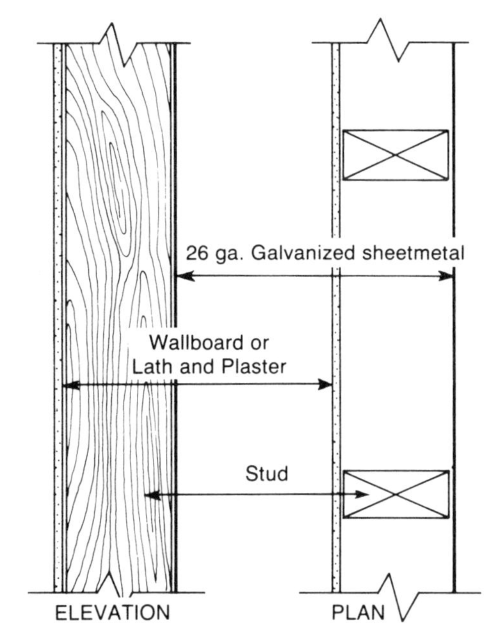

SMALL SHAFTS < 9 S.F.

NOTE: Openings to have metal or metal-clad doors, jambs, casings or frames

REFERENCE: SECTION 1706 (f)

FIGURE 6-2 SMALL SHAFT WALL CONSTRUCTION—TYPE V BUILDINGS

Chicago and the MGM Grand Hotel in Las Vegas. In both instances the spread of fire, smoke and hot gases was facilitated by expansion, wind or seismic joints in fire-resistive assemblies.

The common method of providing for these joints disregards the fire-resistance requirement and usually simply uses a sliding joint cover as shown in Figure 6-3. Such a joint cannot provide the required fire resistance of the floor or wall assembly, because the materials will buckle, open or melt out.

Some examples of fire-resistive methods for providing for such movements and retaining the fire resistance of the assembly are shown in Figure 6-4.

The designer should be aware that there are numerous configurations of methods for maintaining the fire-resistive integrity for openings through fire-resistive assemblies. Many can be adapted from the assemblies used for protecting pipe penetrations as shown in Figures 8-13 and 8-14. Other systems are in the Underwriters Laboratories, Inc. *Building Materials Directory*.

When a material is to be used to provide both watertightness and fire resistance, it is important that the material be compressible so that, as shown in Detail (D) of Figure 6-4, it will permit the movement of the joint and still stay in place. The gap must be designed to provide for the amount of movement expected and must be based on the compressibility of the material inserted within the space to avoid binding.

Where the fire resistance is to be provided by either a material that bridged the gap, as in Detail (C) of Figure 6-4, or on the intumescent action of the material such as the intumescent tapes shown in Details (A) and (B) of Figure 6-4, the amount of fire-resistive material will be determined by:

- the amount of the expanded material required to provide the degree of fire resistance needed and
- the amount of expanded material needed to close off the gap. See Details (A) and (B) of Figure 6-4.

The enforcement official should be aware that the great variety of conditions the designer may have in a building will require the official to apply judgment when evaluating the system the designer chooses.

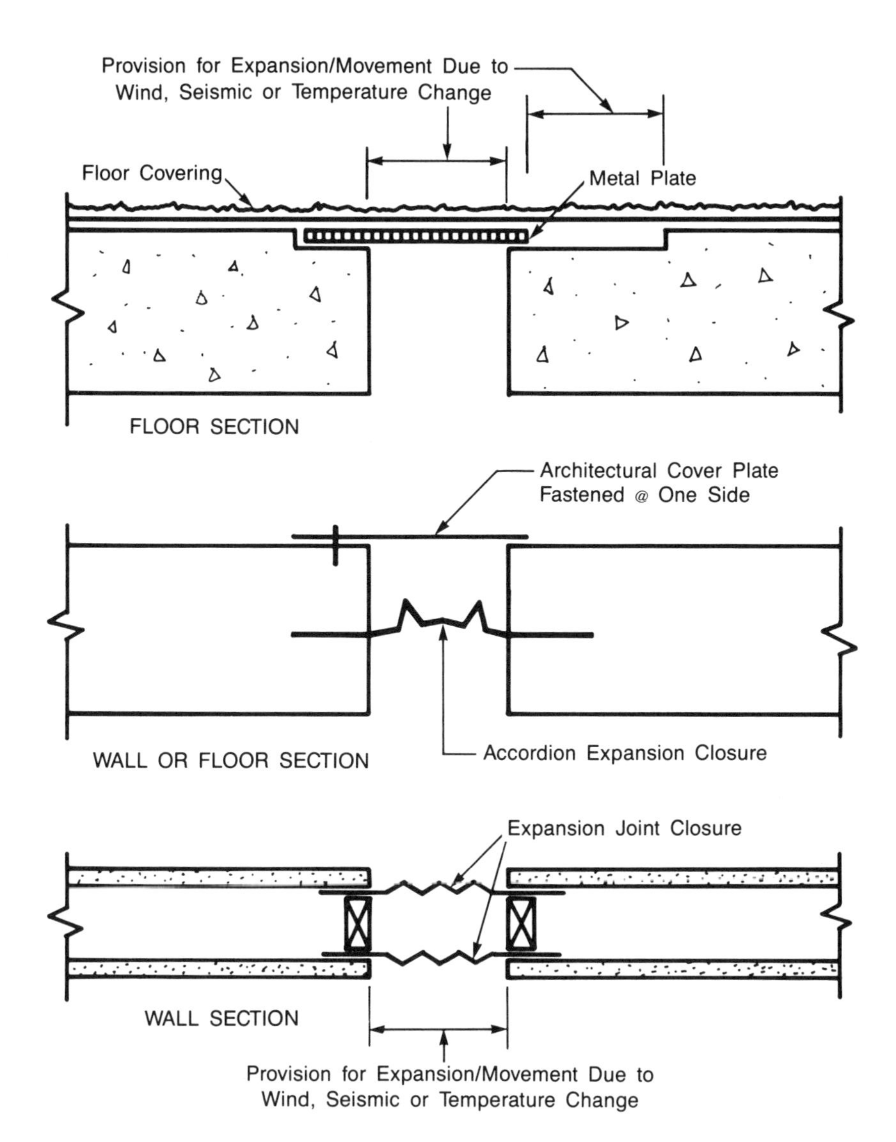

TYPICAL UNPROTECTED JOINTS IN FIRE-RESISTIVE ASSEMBLIES

REFERENCE: SECTION 1707

FIGURE 6-3 TYPICAL UNPROTECTED JOINTS IN FIRE-RESISTIVE ASSEMBLIES FOR WIND, SEISMIC OR EXPANSION MOVEMENTS—NOT ACCEPTABLE

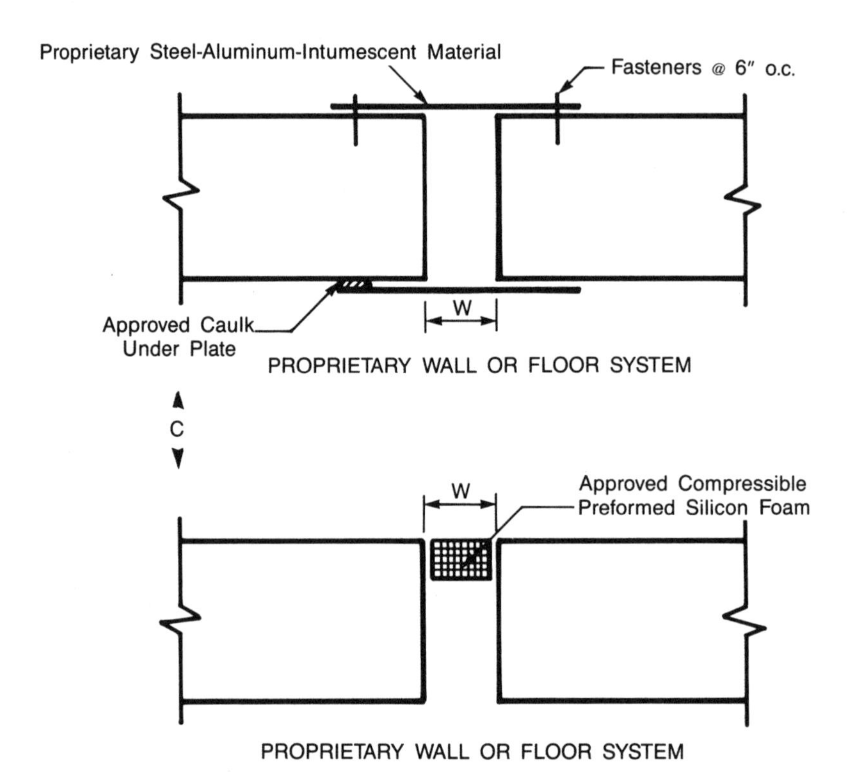

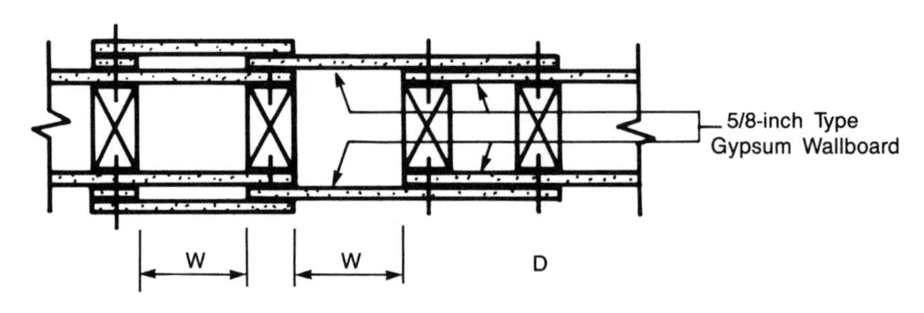

GYPSUM WALLBOARD WALL ASSEMBLY (TYPICAL)

$$W = \text{Width of Gap} = \frac{\text{Amount of Expansion/Movement Required}}{\text{Compressibility Coeficient of Compressible Gasket}}$$

REFERENCE: SECTION 1707, ULI BUILDING MATERIALS DIRECTORY

FIGURE 6-4 TYPICAL METHODS OF PROTECTING JOINTS IN TO PROVIDE FOR WIND, SEISMIC OR EXPANSION MOVEMENT

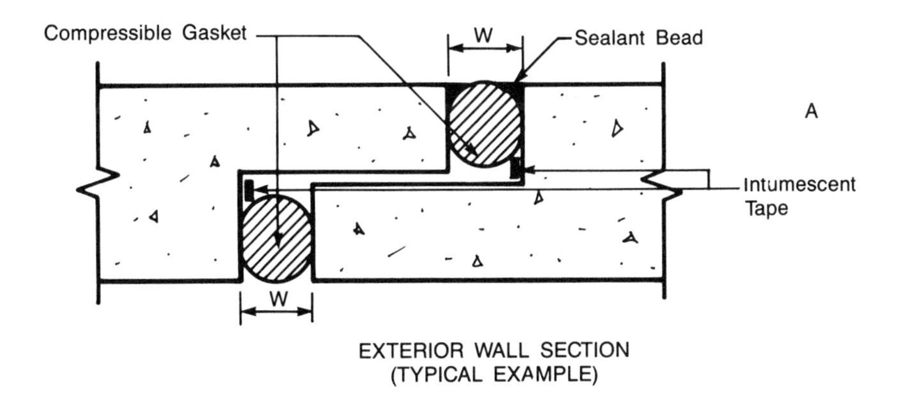

EXTERIOR WALL SECTION
(TYPICAL EXAMPLE)

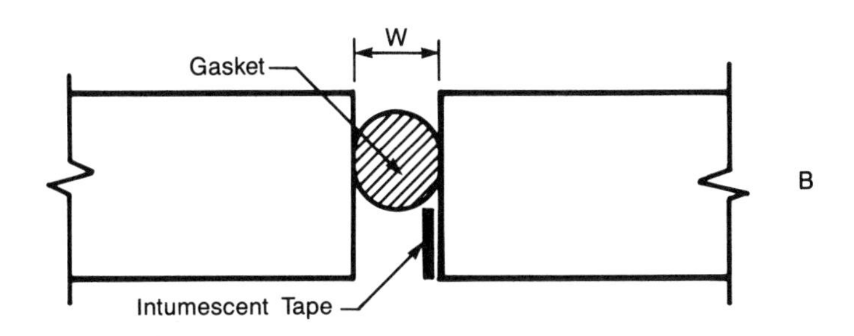

That judgment should be based on requiring that the system is a listed one and one that has comparable applicability to the materials on the project. In other words, a system designed for solid concrete or masonry should not be used for a gypsum wallboard cavity wall or floor-ceiling assembly unless permitted to do so by the approved listing.

The use of intumescent materials is a relatively new innovation in the field of fire protection. It is the direct result of the concern over the penetrations, the subject of the Chapter 43 code changes discussed in Article 8 of this Guide.

An intumescent material, as used in connection with fire-resistive assemblies, is a material that will, on exposure to high temperature, foam up to create a fire-resistant barrier. The barrier acts in much the same way that char does for wood or foamed insulation does in clothing and as a building insulation. The materials come in various forms, including tapes, foam boards and paste format. The most common materials are manufactured by such firms as Minnesota Mining and Dupont. The materials are listed in the Underwriters Laboratories, Inc. *Building Materials Directory.*

Use of intumescent materials must be based on:

- the width of the gap required for the movement anticipated,
- the thickness of intumescent material required at ambient temperature to close that gap,
- the fire-resistive time period for the wall or floor element,
- the compatible of the intumescent material with the materials to which it is attached

In many instances the intumescent material needs a substantial backing material against which to expand. Thus, an intumescent material recommended for use in concrete or masonry, with wide surfaces against which to act, should not be used in a 5/8-inch Type X gypsum wallboard gap without some other devices provided to assure the presence of sufficient resistance to allow the intumescent material to expand under heat.

Weather Protection.
Sec. 1708.

► □□□ ◄

The provisions contained in this section are minimal. The designer should not rely on them to provide adequate or proper weather protection for all buildings. These provisions require far less than what is necessary to provide full weather protection to the building and particularly to the parts of the building that are subject to decay. It is up to the designer to design the weather protection details.

These designs should be based on:

- an evaluation of the materials to be used,
- the construction and arrangement of the various building elements and
- the method by which wind pressures are handled so that water build-up and by-passing the weather resistant membranes are avoided.

In many instances, minimum quality building paper cannot adequately resist early deterioration when moisture is present on its exterior side. The use of inadequate materials together with heat build-up in areas subject to high temperatures for long periods of time, or to intense weather exposures, will result in failure. The designer should carefully consider the materials proposed for the job so that he will choose ones that are long-lasting and effective.

A designer should never rely solely on the construction practices of the contractor's personnel or on those of a subcontractor. Such reliance has often been found to result in the considerable decay of building elements over a short period of time. Moreover, these conditions bring about the initiation of litigation which may result in substantial costs for corrections.

The designer is urged to use three-dimensional drawings and perspective to thoroughly demonstrate in the design how the prevention of water infiltration is to be achieved. Reliance on partial or incomplete details and the repetitive use of old details without careful consideration of how they apply to the new project has resulted in numerous instances of leakage.

Section 1708 does not cover the following areas of design:

- Windows and sliding doors, where reliance on the industry standard is insufficient for the location. Windows designed for 25 mph winds and placed in locations subject to 50, 60 or

70 mph exposure, constitutes a misapplication of the industry's standards. This misapplication can result in buildings that have high levels of leakage, frequent litigation and costly repairs. These areas fall within the designer's responsibility: he is to determine the compatibility of materials and assemblies.

- Windows and doors that are selected on a cost basis only and are fabricated as knock-down-type assemblies. These have open corners and low cost joint sealants. In a relatively short time, due to heat, ultra-violet rays and general movement of the completed building, they usually fail. The designer should carefully select the proper window and after having done so, should take care that the contractor does not substitute it with a more economical type of window, one with a potentially poor performance.
- In high wind areas, the size and number of the weep holes required to permit adequate weepage. These requirements should be determined by the designer as well as the amount of the water table provided.
- Installation of sliding doors on level decks. Generally, this type of installation can be expected to cause problems unless an adequate water table is provided and all flashing details are well thought through. This problem will be particularly serious when these windows and decks are stacked one above another. If a leak occurs, its origin would be more difficult to locate since the defect could be at any level above the outlet of the leak.

The design details for the situations described are frequently shown only by a two-dimensional drawing. The designer may not be aware of the need for three-dimensional detailing. As a result, the contractor could fail to complete the flashing of a three-dimensional joint. It is the designer's responsibility to provide adequate details for the contractor to follow; it is the contractor's responsibility to question a condition that may lead to improper construction.

In many situations concerning weather protection, relying on the code proves to be inadequate. Reliance on generally accepted practices within the field similarly proves inadequate. At this point the professional training, background, knowledge and experience of the designer comes into play. For assemblies designed to provide weather protection, it is the designer's responsibility to choose the materials, indicate their interrelationship and describe their mode of installation. The designer must *fully detail* how this weather protection is to be accomplished.

Members Carrying Masonry or Concrete

Sec. 1709. All members carrying masonry or concrete walls in buildings over one story in height shall be fire protected with not less than one-hour fire protection or the fire-resistive requirement of the wall, whichever is greater.

Exception: Fire protection may be omitted from the bottom flange of lintels spanning not over 6 feet, shelf angles, or plates that are not a part of the structural frame.

This section requires that supporting members for masonry or concrete walls have at least one-hour fire resistance. This is aimed at both wood and unprotected steel members in particular. The language was changed to reflect the concept outlined in Article 5 of this Guide regarding support elements. If the wall is required to have a fire-resistive rating greater than one hour, the support member must have at least that higher rating as well. (See Figure 6-5.)

Thus, if a wall is required to be of two-hour or four-hour construction, as may be the case with an occupancy separation wall or an exterior building wall near a property line, all the support elements for that wall must be of at least the same rating down to the ground. Previously, the code provision had only the one-hour minimum requirement.

Under prior codes, a designer could err in providing only a one-hour fire-resistive support for a two-hour or four-hour concrete or masonry wall. In the event of a fire in such a situation lasting just over one hour, the wall could collapse at a much earlier time than its own required fire rating, after the support element failed.

The designer should be aware that whenever a rating is required, regardless of whether it is for an area separation wall, occupancy separation, or if a structural element is involved, the support for that construction must have equivalent or greater fire resistance than the supported item. This degree of fire resistance for the support must be carried down to the ground, so that the support member will not fail sooner than the time period required of the supported element.

The designer should clearly understand this concept of tracking the support system. Tracking should become a standard procedure during the design and contract document preparation stages.

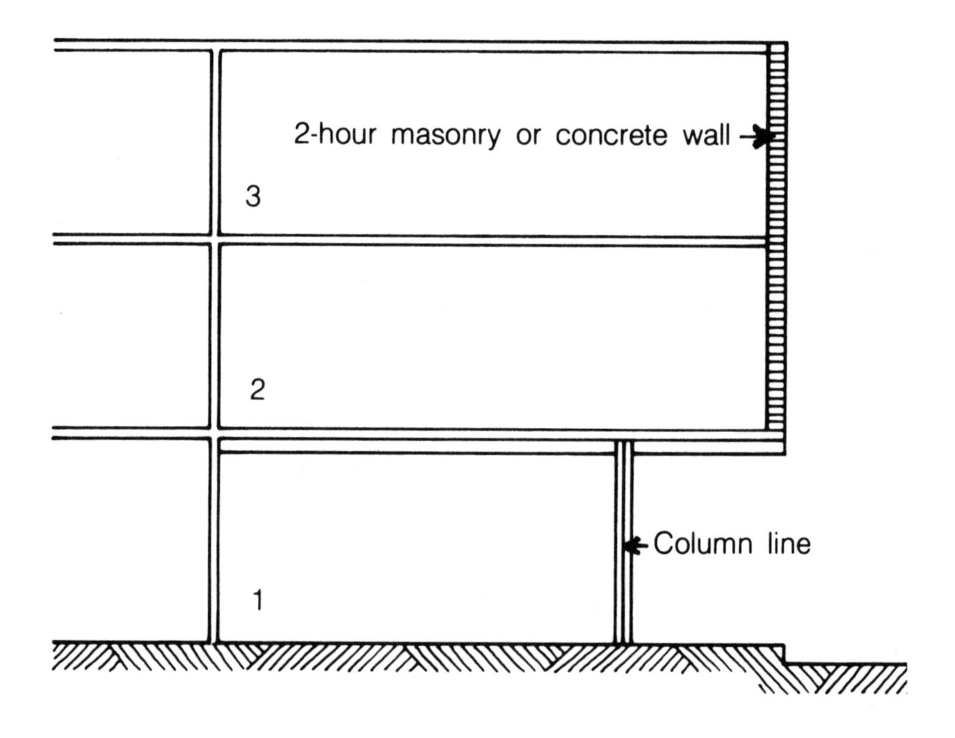

ASSUME:
TYPE III-1 HOUR, 2-HOUR MASONRY OR CONCRETE EXTERIOR WALL
Floor-ceiling assembly of 2nd floor = >2 hour

Columns on 1st floor supporting 2-Hour masonry or concrete wall = >2-hour

REFERENCE: SECTION 1708

FIGURE 6-5 FIRE RATING FOR MEMBERS SUPPORTING RATED MASONRY OR CONCRETE WALLS

Parapet

Sec. 1710. (a) General. Parapets shall be provided on all exterior walls of buildings.

EXCEPTIONS: A parapet need not be provided on an exterior wall when any of the following conditions exist:

1. The wall is not required to be of fire-resistive construction.
2. The wall, due to location on property, may have unprotected openings.
3. The building has an area of not more than 1000 square feet on any floor.
4. Walls which terminate at roofs of not less than two-hour fire-resistive construction or roofs constructed entirely of noncombustible materials.
5. One-hour fire-resistive exterior walls may terminate at the underside of the roof sheathing, deck or slab, provided:
    a. Where the roof-ceiling elements are parallel to the walls, such framing and the elements supporting such framing shall be of not less than one-hour fire-resistive construction for a width of 5 feet on the interior side of the wall for Group M and R Occupancies and 10 feet for all other occupancies.
    b. Where roof-ceiling framing elements are perpendicular to the wall, the entire span of such framing and elements supporting such framing shall be of not less than one-hour fire-resistive construction.
    c. Openings in the roof shall not be within 5 feet of the one-hour fire-resistive exterior wall for Group M and R Occupancies and 10 feet for all other occupancies.
    d. The entire building shall be provided with not less than a Class B roof covering.

The parapet requirements for all buildings are contained in this section. The exceptions generally cover a substantial number of buildings including most single-family dwellings. Exception 5 is an attempt to reduce the construction costs and problems associated with parapet construction. The Exception does this without sacrificing the fire containment intent of the parapet provision.

The provisions of Exception 5 are somewhat similar to the provisions of Section 505 (e)3 for the omission of parapets on area separation walls. However, because the concern is to assure that fire does not spread readily across a property line, the criteria for omitting the parapet are more restrictive than for the area separation wall.

A parapet can be omitted under Exception 5 only when the exterior wall is of not more than one-hour fire-resistive construction. Thus, the Exception does not apply to a building unless the exterior wall is permitted to be so constructed per Table No. 5-A. In some instances this would apply only when the buildings were set back as much as 40 feet from the property line.

Example: Group A (Public Assembly), Division 2.1 Occupancy.

Another requisite is that the roof covering must be at least Class B roofing. This requirement takes precedence over the other permissive roofing provisions of the code and the locality. Thus, a Class C or an unrated roof would not be permitted where the Exception 5 provisions apply. This requirement was made a part of the Exception so that the top surface of the roof-ceiling assembly would not readily be ignited from either:

- an exterior fire brand falling on the roof or
- from a fire inside the building extending up through a skylight some distance from the exterior wall

A Class B roof has substantially slower flame-spreading characteristics and uses larger brands in the tests required to obtain its rating than does a Class C roof. An unrated roofing material provides virtually no such protection.

If Exception 5 is to apply, a "special purpose roof" per Section 3204 (e) is not allowed. The roofs must be at least Class B.

The one-hour fire-resistive roof-ceiling assembly requirements in Exception 5 are substantially more restrictive than those in Section 505 (e)3 for area separation walls, except for Group M and R Occupancies, where they are comparable. The major differences for all occupancies, except Group M and R Occupancies, are:

1. The one-hour fire-resistive construction for the roof-ceiling assembly and the supports for the roof-ceiling assembly is to extend 10 feet from the exterior wall for framing parallel to that exterior wall.
2. The one-hour fire-resistive construction is to extend for the entire span of the framing elements that are perpendicular to the exterior wall. The supports for the roof-ceiling assembly are also to be of not less than one-hour fire-resistive construction.
3. Openings in the roof-ceiling assemblies for skylights are not to be within 10 feet of the exterior wall.

As with the supports for the roof-ceiling assembly adjacent to an area separation wall, the one-hour fire-resistive construction applies to the amount of roof-ceiling assembly involved based on the direction of the framing. See Figures 5-19 and 5-20.

The openings in the roof are permitted based on the distance of the opening to the exterior wall on which the parapet is to be omitted. The intent of this provision was based on the assumption that the building was on, or immediately adjacent to, the property line as shown in Figure 6-7.

However, as seen in Table No. 5-A, many occupancies require a one-hour wall without openings or with protected openings, when the exterior wall is 10 feet or more from the property line. In such instances, the roof openings will be at least 20 feet from the property line: the distance the exterior wall is from the property line plus the 10 feet the opening is set back from the exterior wall as required in Item 5 (c).

> In the author's opinion, the intent of the roof opening provision was translated into an excessively restrictive provision for locating the roof openings. The location of the openings should be predicated on the distance to the property line in a manner similar to that in Sections 5206 Item 2 and 5207 Item 7.

(b) Construction. Parapets shall have the same degree of fire resistance required for the wall upon which they are erected and on any side adjacent to a roof surface shall have noncombustible faces for the uppermost 18 inches, including counterflashing and coping materials. The height of the parapet shall be not less than 30 inches above the point where the roof surface and the wall intersect. Where the roof slopes toward a parapet at slopes greater than 2:12, the parapet shall extend to the same height as any portion of the roof that is within the distance where protection of wall openings would be required, but in no case shall the height be less than 30 inches.

This section requires that a parapet have the same degree of fire resistance as the wall on which it is erected. As the walls can be area separation walls, the parapets that surmount them must have either one-hour, two-hour or four-hour construction.

Section 505 (e) Item 4 and Section 1709 (b) require that the noncombustible surface of the parapet need only be provided for the upper 18 inches on both sides when above an area separation wall and on the roof side for other parapets. The intent of this provision is to prevent,

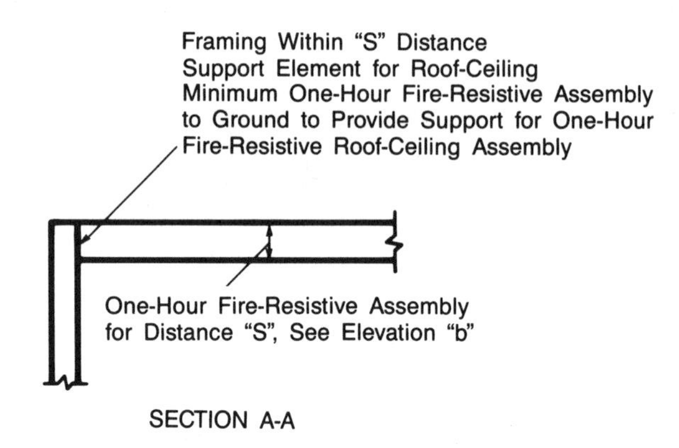

SECTION A-A

S = 5 feet for Group M and R Occupancies
= 10 feet for All Other Occupancies

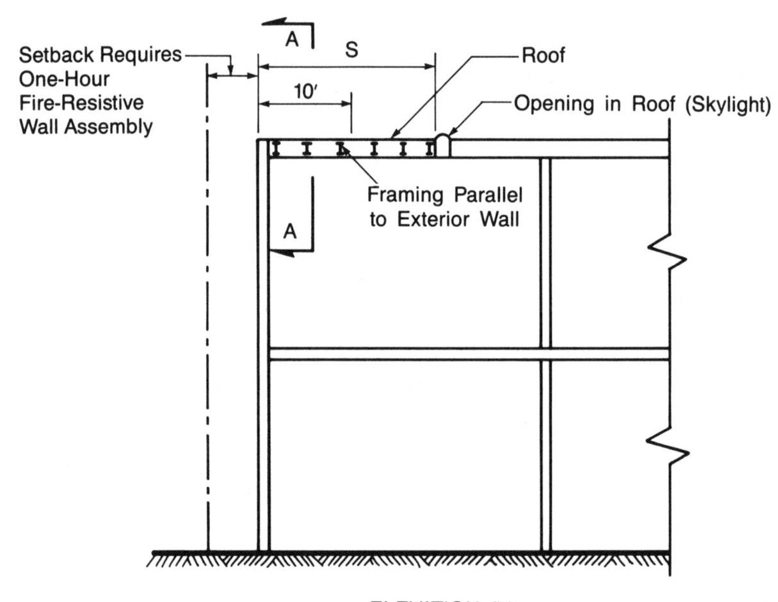

ELEVATION (b)

NOTE: Parapet may be omitted only when exterior wall is of one-hour fire-resistive construction.

REFERENCE: SECTION 1709 (a) EXCEPTION 5 AND TABLE NO. 5-A

FIGURE 6-6 OMISSION OF PARAPETS AT EXTERIOR WALLS INCLUDING AT PROPERTY LINES FOR BUILDINGS WITH ONE-HOUR FIRE-RESISTIVE EXTERIOR WALL ASSEMBLIES

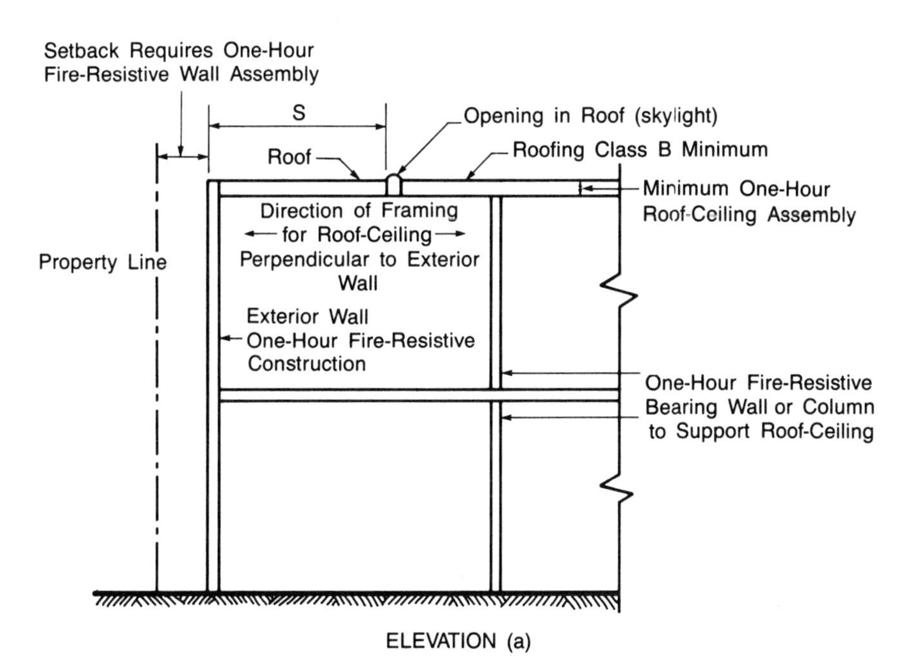
Setback Requires One-Hour
Fire-Resistive Wall Assembly
S
Opening in Roof (skylight)
Roofing Class B Minimum
Roof
Minimum One-Hour
Roof-Ceiling Assembly
Direction of Framing
for Roof-Ceiling
Perpendicular to Exterior
Wall
Property Line
Exterior Wall
One-Hour Fire-Resistive
Construction
One-Hour Fire-Resistive
Bearing Wall or Column
to Support Roof-Ceiling

ELEVATION (a)

through use of noncombustible surfacing materials, the spread of fire from one side of the area separation wall to the other and to require the roof covering to be effectively flashed. (See Figure 6-7.)

Guardrails and Vehicle Barriers

Sec. 1712. (a) Guardrails. Unenclosed floor and roof openings, open and glazed sides of stairways, landings and ramps, balconies or porches, which are more than 30 inches above grade or floor below and roofs used for other than service of the building shall be protected by a guardrail.

EXCEPTION: Guardrails need not be provided at the following locations:

1. On the loading side of loading docks.

2. On the auditorium side of a stage or enclosed platform.

3. Along vehicle service pits not accessible to the public.

The top of guardrails shall be not less than 42 inches in height.

EXCEPTIONS: 1. The top of guardrails for Group R, Division 3 and Group M, Division 1 Occupancies and interior guardrails within individual dwelling units, Group R, Division 3 congregate residences and guest rooms of Group R, Division 1 Occupancies may be 36 inches in height.

2. The top of guardrails on a balcony immediately in front of the first row of fixed seats and which are not at the end of an aisle may be 26 inches in height.

3. The top of guardrails for stairways, exclusive of their landings, may have a height as specified in Section 3306 (j) for handrails.

Open guardrails shall have intermediate rails or an ornamental pattern such that a sphere greater than 4 inches in diameter cannot pass through.

EXCEPTIONS: 1. The open space between the intermediate rails or ornamental pattern of guardrails in areas of commercial and industrial-type occupancies which are not accessible to the public may be such that a sphere 12 inches in diameter cannot pass through.

2. The triangular openings formed by the riser, thread and bottom element of a guardrail at the open side of a stairway may be of such size that a sphere 6 inches in diameter cannot pass through.

(b) Vehicle Barriers. In all parking garages where any parking area is located more than 5 feet above the adjacent grade, vehicle barriers shall be provided.

EXCEPTION: Parking garages of Group M, Division 1 Occupancies.

Vehicle barriers shall comply with the following:

1. The vehicle barrier shall be designed to resist a minimum horizontal load of 6,000 pounds. The horizontal force shall be applied over a one-foot-square area at a height of 18 inches above the parking surface. The force shall be distributed through the vehicle barrier into the structural frame.

2. The vehicle barrier shall have a minimum vertical dimension of 12 inches and shall be centered at 18 inches above the parking surface.

Section 1712 regulates guardrails and vehicular barriers. The section has been revised and expanded in its scope. The guardrails and barriers referred to in this section are only those that are part of a building or structure. Furthermore, although not stated in the code, numerous exceptions are traditionally applied in addition to those cited in the section.

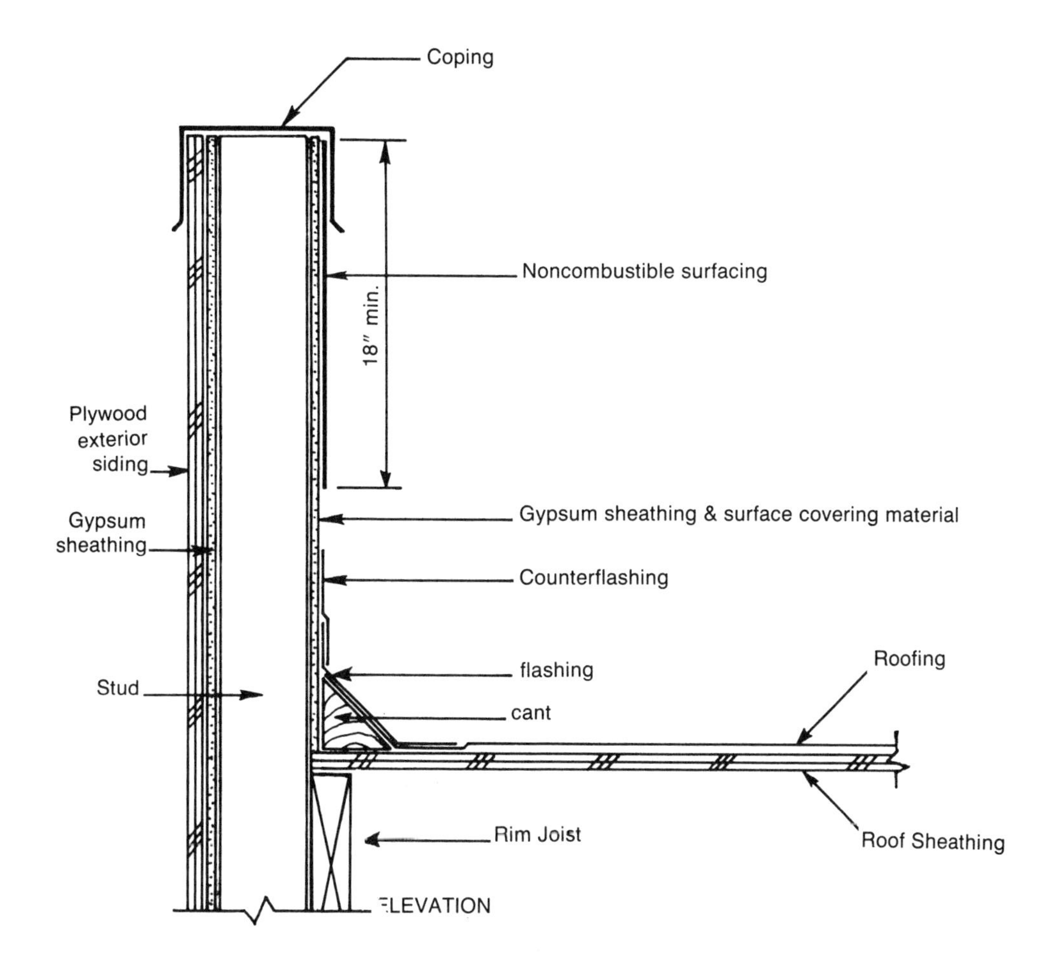

NOTES: 1. Coping can be part of non-combustible surfacing.
2. Where parapet is part of an area separation wall, the noncombustible surface must be on both sides of the parapet.

REFERENCE: SECTION 1709 (b)
SECTION 506 (e) Item 4

FIGURE 6-7 PARAPET CONSTRUCTION DETAILS

In the author's opinion, some additional exceptions should include:

- play structures such as slides, jungle gyms, diving platforms, etc.
- walks and ramps outside the building or structure
- stairs and walls in gardens not within a building
- show windows
- trap doors in stages and other locations
- attic access openings

The previous requirements of this section were designated as subsection (a) with the third paragraph of that subsection amended to require that a sphere greater than four inches must not pass through the intermediate rails or pattern. This reduction in the spacings permitted from the six-inch sphere was predicated on considerable data obtained by the American Academy of Pediatrics on the physiognomy of young children.

A second Exception was added to this paragraph to permit the triangular space formed on a stairway by the bottom rail of a guardrail, the riser and the tread. (See Figure 6-8.) This Exception permits the size of the opening to prevent passage of a six-inch sphere.

Although the code provisions refer to rails and ornamental patterns, there is no prohibition of the use of tempered glass or other solid or partially solid materials in constructing the guardrails.

Section 1712 contains regulations for vehicle barriers in garages for those parking levels more than five feet above grade. Group M, Division 1 garages are exempted from these requirements.

In prior codes, the requirement for vehicle barriers was contained in Section 709 (c), where the provisions were inadequate and ambiguous. The use of the phrase "Adequate curbs and guardrails shall be provided at every opening" provided no performance standard for determining the adequacy of the design. This sentence was deleted when Section 1712 (b) was added.

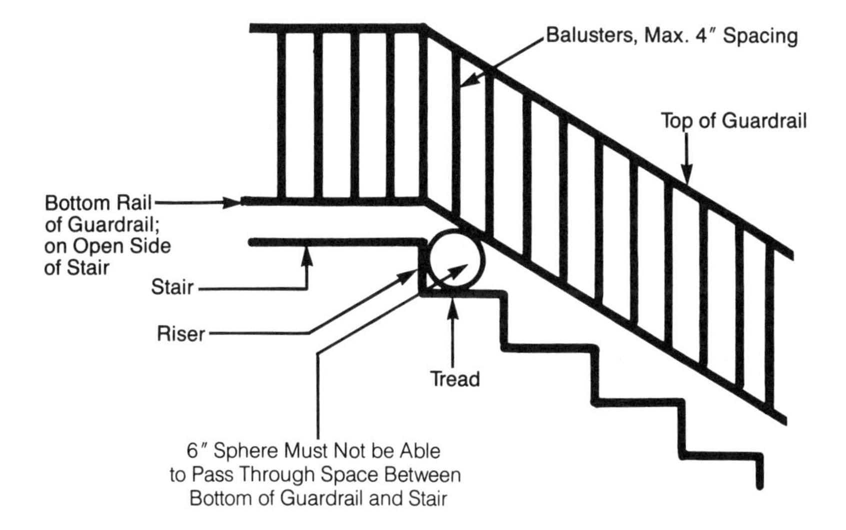

REFERENCE: SECTION 1711 EXCEPTION 3

FIGURE 6-8 GUARDRAIL, OPENING BETWEEN BOTTOM RAIL AND STAIR

The design force provision assumes a one-square-foot area of impacting force on the guardrail, i.e., 6,000 pounds on one square foot of guardrail. With this loading, the designer can design a vehicle barrier that will perform properly.

The barrier design may be a part of the guardrail or an independent element. In either design, the code requires that the forces be carried down to the structural framing. This provision mandates a properly thought out design carried to the support framing. (See Figure 6-9.)

The minimum design elements of the barrier are set forth in the code provision; however, the design can incorporate these minimums within a design that serves the function of the barrier and satisfies the building design parameters of the project.

The barrier provision is the result of accidents and deaths resulting from barrier failures and recommendations of national groups in the parking garage field.

Foam Plastic Insulation.

Sec. 1713 (a) General. The provisions of this section shall govern the requirements and uses of foam plastic in buildings and structures. For trim, see Section 1705 (e).

Except where otherwise noted in this section, all foam plastics used in building construction shall have a flame-spread rating of not more than 75 and shall have a smoke-developed rating of not more than 450 when tested in the maximum thickness intended for use in accordance with U.B.C. Standard No. 42-1. All packages and containers of foam plastic and foam plastic ingredients shall bear the label of an approved agency showing either the flame-spread rating and smoke-developed rating of the product at the thickness tested or the use for which the product has been listed. The interior of the building shall be separated from the foam plastic by an approved thermal barrier having an index of 15 when tested in accordance with U.B.C. Standard No. 17-3. The thermal barrier shall be installed in such a manner that it will remain in place for the time of its index classification based upon approved diversified tests.

Section 1713 (a) relates to the fire hazard of foam plastic materials that do not have proper coverings. The provisions regulate the foam plastic and the covering materials. The flamespread value of the foam plastic must not exceed 75 when tested by the Tunnel Test. (See Article 8 of this Guide.)

The covering material, called a thermal barrier, to be placed over the foam plastic is to be tested by a different standard, the UBC Standard 17-3. This test standard subjects a small-scale version of a wall to fire,

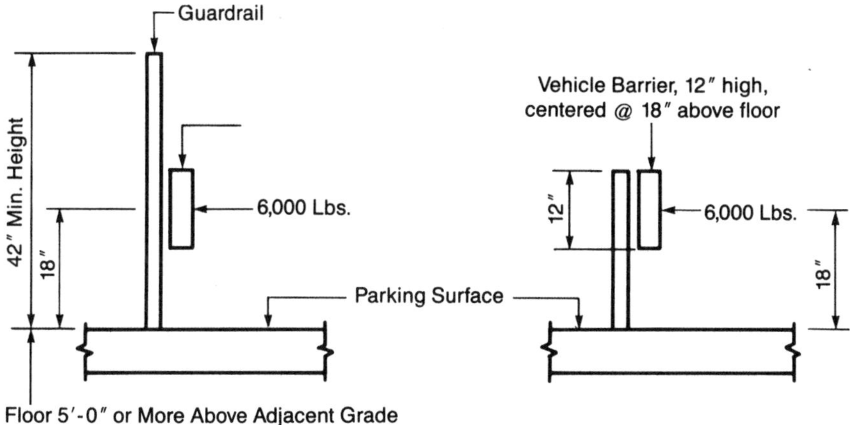

When the parking surface is more than 5′-0″ above adjacent grade, there must be a vehicle barrier provided. The barrier can be either on the guardrail at the edge of the parking surface or can be a separate element.

The barrier must be capable of resisting a horizontal force of 6,000 pounds applied at 18″ above the parking surface over a one square foot area of the barrier.

REFERENCE: SECTION 1711 (b)

FIGURE 6-9 VEHICLE BARRIER – MINIMUM DESIGN CRITERIA

employing the time-temperature values of UBC Standard 43-1. The time period in minutes for the thermocouples behind the covering material and a calcium silicate board to reach a specific end point temperature becomes the index value for the covering. To meet this section of the code, the covering, or thermal barrier, must have an index of 15 minutes or more.

The combination of the foam plastic and thermal barrier is then to be tested by approved diversified tests, to demonstrate that the thermal barrier will remain in place for the same time as its index rating, i.e., 15 minutes. This is the time period during which the surface covering is to remain in place thereby shielding the foam plastic material. (See Figure 6-10.)

Fire tests have shown that when foam plastic materials without thermal barriers are used as surfaces of interior walls, an interaction occurs between the surfacing materials on the adjacent walls and ceilings at the corners or intersections. A severe fire condition can rapidly develop because of this interaction. It is therefore necessary to shield the foam plastic from the fire for a period of time sufficient to develop the required rating and thereby provide at least minimum protection

Insulation

Sec. 1714. (a) General. Thermal and acoustical insulation located on or within floor-ceiling and roof-ceiling assemblies, crawl spaces, walls, partitions and insulation on pipes and tubing shall comply with this section. Duct insulation and insulation in plenums shall conform to the requirements of the Uniform Mechanical Code.

EXCEPTION: Roof insulation shall comply with Section 3204.

(b) Insulation and Covering on Pipe and Tubing. Insulation and covering on pipe and tubing shall have a flame-spread rating not to exceed 25 and a smoke density not to exceed 450 when tested in accordance with U.B.C. Standard No. 42-1.

EXCEPTION: Foam plastic insulation shall comply with Section 1712.

(c) Insulation. All insulation materials including facings, such as vapor barriers or breather papers installed within floor-ceiling assemblies, roof-ceiling assemblies, walls, crawl spaces or attics shall have a flame-spread rating not to exceed 25 and a smoke density not to exceed 450 when tested in accordance with U.B.C. Standard No. 42-1.

EXCEPTIONS: 1. Foam plastic insulation shall comply with Section 1712.

2. When such materials are installed in concealed spaces of Types III, IV and V construction, the flame-spread and smoke-developed limitations do not apply to facings, provided that the facing is installed in substantial contact with the unexposed surface of the ceiling, floor or wall finish.

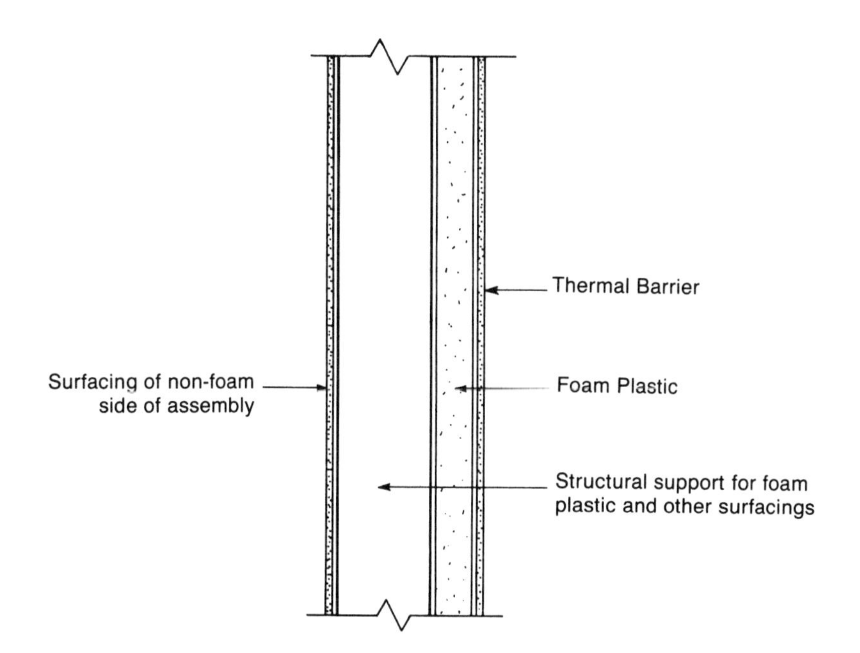

REFERENCE: SECTION 1712 (a)

FIGURE 6-10 FOAM PLASTIC THERMAL BARRIER

Section 1714 regulates thermal or acoustical insulation in general. Its primary requirement is that the flame spread not exceed 25 and smoke density not exceed 450.

Duct insulation and plenum linings are subject to more rigorous criteria in the UMC. These UMC criteria limit the flame spread to 25 and smoke density to 50.

Atria

Sec. 1716. a) General. Buildings of other than Group H Occupancy with automatic sprinkler protection throughout may have atria complying with the provisions of this section. Such atria shall have a minimum opening area and dimension as set forth in Table No. 17-B.

The designer should note that an atrium exists only when the opening is through two or more floors and not when through a single floor. Floor penetrations are permitted through a single floor for shafts, stairs and escalators, without special requirements, by the provisions in Sections 1706 and 3309. (See Figure 6-11.)

The requirements for atria are:

- an automatic sprinkler system throughout the building,
- a smoke control system so that the building does not get smoke-logged and
- compliance with the provisions of Section 1807 (the high rise life safety requirements) for:
  a) Stand-by power
  b) Handling of the smoke control system within the occupied spaces of the building.

Exit balconies may be open to the atrium without any separation between the balcony and the atrium space provided the balconies:

- are sprinklered,
- have smoke-tight doors into the tenant spaces, either self-closing or automatic-closing by a smoke detector-operated release device.

The minimum spatial criteria for the atrium is set forth in Table No. 17-B and is dependent on the height of the atrium in stories. These minimum limits are required in order to provide a sufficiently large volume for dissipation of smoke to be handled by the smoke control

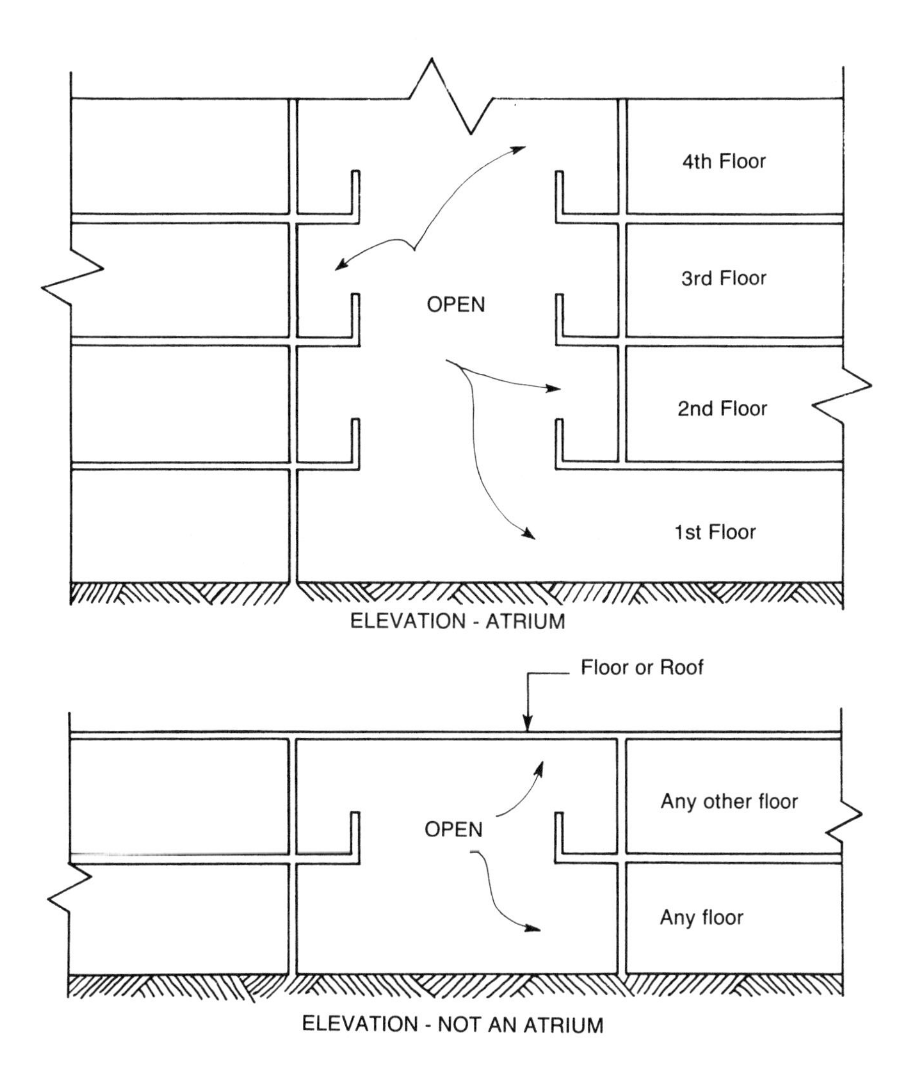

REFERENCE: SECTION 1715

FIGURE 6-11 ATRIUM, DEFINITION

system. The combustibility of the atrium furnishings is regulated under the Fire Code. The designer should discuss these regulations with the fire service to assure that the combustible loading and smoke generation limits of the furnishings are not exceeded. The atrium smoke control provisions are detailed and specialized and will not be discussed in detail in this Guide.

Sec. 1716 (b) Smoke-control system

► ■■■ ◄

In Item 4 of this section, the third sentence reads:

> **Actuation of the exhaust and supply system shall follow immediately after actuation of the second smoke detector.**

This requirement for two detector activation is to reduce false alarms. The triggering of the smoke control system depends essentially on smoke detectors placed throughout the atrium.

The required locations of detectors is in Item 8 of this section. This provides for better understanding of the code intent as to the required locations of smoke detectors.

Item 8 of Section 1716 (b) reads as follows:

> **8. Smoke detector locations. Smoke detectors which will automatically operate the atrium smoke-control system shall be accessible for maintenance, testing and servicing and shall be installed in the following locations:**
>
> **A. When integral-type detectors are used they shall be installed:**
>
> **i. At the atrium ceiling, spaced in accordance with their listing.**
>
> **ii. On the underside of projections spaced in accordance with their listing.**
>
> **iii. Around the perimeter of the atrium opening on all floors open to the atrium. These detectors shall be spaced no more than 30 feet on center and be located within 15 feet of the atrium opening.**
>
> **B. When projected beam-type smoke detection is used, it shall be installed and spaced in accordance with its listing.**

The development of projection beam-type detectors to cover large open spaces has been incorporated into the atrium detection provisions as an alternate to certain of the traditional detectors. Both the "integral-type" and "projection beam-type" detectors can be used in any installation, provided they are installed in accordance with their listings.

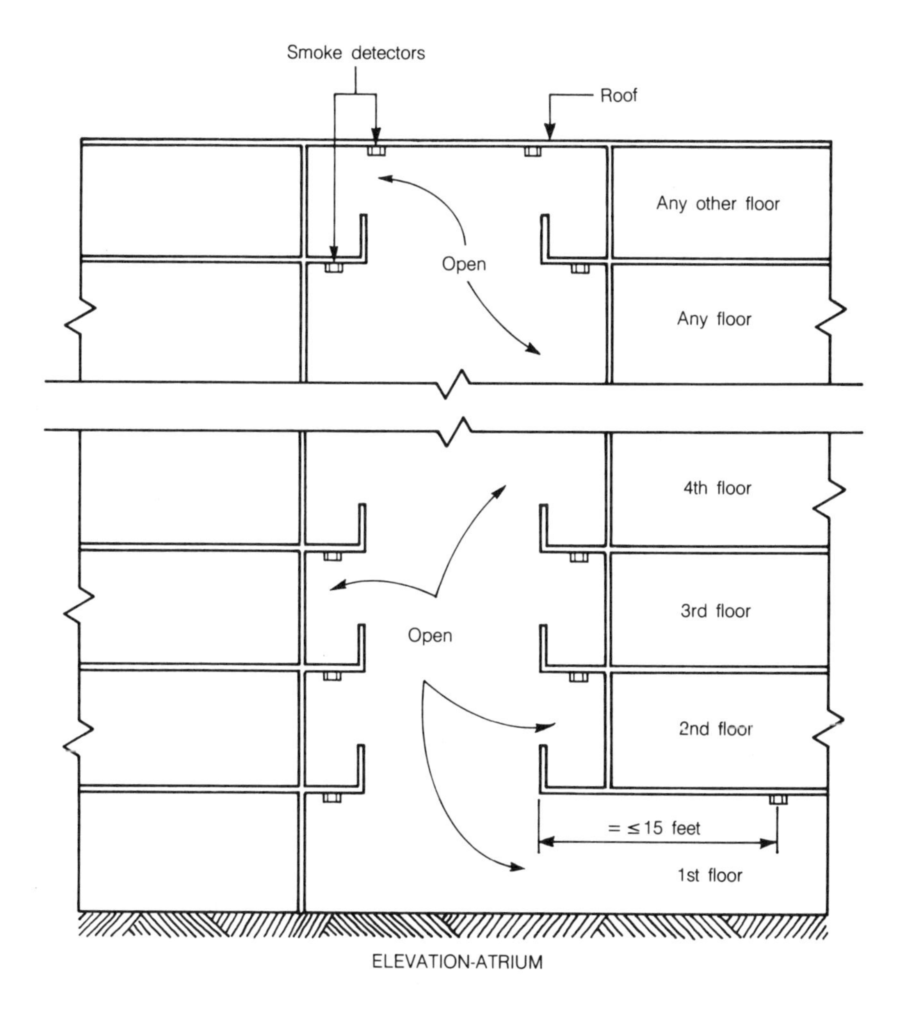

REFERENCE: SECTION 1715 (b)

FIGURE 6-12 ATRIUM, SMOKE DETECTOR LOCATIONS

Although the provisions of Section 1716 (b)8Aii for the integral-type detector installation do not define "projections" as applied to this section, prior editions of the code did contain such clarifying information.

It is the author's opinion that such clarification would apply to this edition of the code as well, as follows:

> Because corridors are usually required to be at least 44 inches in width, they should be subject to this provision. On the other hand, minor projections less than 36 inches in width, such as those provided for architectural reasons, should not be not subject to the smoke detector requirements.

Section 1716 (b)8Aiii requires integral-type detectors at the lowest level and any other level where the entire floor is open to the atrium. The smoke detectors on these levels are required to be placed at not more than a 30-foot spacing and not simply in accordance with their listing. The first row of detectors must be not more than 15 feet back from the edge of the atrium opening.

(See Figure 6-12 for illustrations of these specific requirements.)

Sec. 1716

c) Enclosure of Atria. Atria shall be separated from adjacent spaces by not less than one-hour fire-resistive construction.

EXCEPTION: 1. The separation between atria and tenants spaces that are not guest rooms, congregate residence, or dwelling units be omitted at three floor levels.

2. Open exit balconies are permitted within the atrium.

Openings in the atrium enclosure other than fixed glazing shall be protected by smoke- and draft-control assemblies conforming to Section 3305 (h).

EXCEPTION: Other tight-fitting doors which are maintained automatic closing, in accordance with Section 4306 (b), by actuation of a smoke detector, or self-closing may be used when protected as required for glazed openings in Exception 2 below.

Fixed glazed openings in the atrium enclosure shall be equipped with fire windows having a fire-resistive rating of not less than three-fourths hour and the total area of such openings shall not exceed 25 percent of the area of the common wall between the atrium and the room into which the opening is provided.

EXCEPTIONS: 1. In Group R, Division I Occupancies, openings may be unprotected when the floor area of each guest room, congregate residence, or dwelling unit does not exceed 1000 square feet and each room or unit has an approved exit not entering the atrium.

2. Guest rooms, dwelling units, congregate residences and tenant spaces may be separated from the atrium by approved fixed wired glass set in steel frames. In lieu thereof, tempered or laminated glass or listed glass block may be used subject to the following:

A. The tempered or laminated glass shall be protected by a sprinkler system equipped with listed quick-response sprinklers. The sprinkler system shall completely wet the entire surface of the glass wall when actuated. Where there are walking surfaces on both sides of the glass, both sides of the glass shall be so protected.

B. The glass shall be in a gasketed frame so installed that the glazing system may deflect without breaking (loading) the glass before the sprinkler system operates.

C. The glass block wall assembly shall be installed in accordance with its listing for a three-fourths-hour fire-resistive rating and Section 2407 (i)5.

D. Obstructions such as curtain rods, drapery traverse rods, curtains, drapes or similar materials, shall not be installed between the sprinkler and the glass.

Section 1716 (c) provides the requirement for the atrium enclosure walls. The key provision in the Exception to the first paragraph permits use of open exit balconies facing the atrium. The third paragraph permits the use of glazed walls fronting directly onto the atrium. The requirements for the glazing are stated with the details of the permitted construction.

Plain glass is allowed, in the Exception to the third paragraph, for Group R, Division 1 Occupancies with specific limitations.

The use of quick-response sprinklers is required by the present code to protect the plain glass, provided the heads are listed. Prior codes had a temperature designation for the sprinkler heads adjacent to the atrium glazing. The availability and preferability of the listed quick-response sprinkler heads take precedent over the temperature characteristic.

Thus, the deletion of the temperature designation in favor of the quick-response characteristic results from an improved performance requirement. The listed requirement is defined in Section 412. The new heads must have been tested by an accredited independent agency.

This reflects the increasing emphasis on the use of the new generation of sprinkler heads. Prior to the development of the quick-response heads, the usual method for obtaining fast action from a sprinkler head was to require a lower temperature actuation mechanism.

The new sprinkler head is constructed in such a way that it reduces the heat sink lag time and thereby accelerates the action of the release mechanism. These heads are listed and manufactured by several sprinkler companies.

The allowance of plain glass is a less-restrictive provision that recognizes the suites now popular in atrium construction. The code allows guest rooms, dwelling units and tenant spaces to face directly on the atrium, provided the openings are protected by any of the following: (See Figure 6-13.)

- Fixed wired glass set in steel frames,
- Tempered glass set in steel frames,
- Laminated glass set in steel frames.

When any of the glazing cited above is used, the criteria governing the glazing as described in Items A, B and C of Exception 2 apply.

The last paragraph of Section 1716 (c) permits the omission of the otherwise required opening protection on not more than three floor levels, provided all other floors have the required protection. This provision is consistent with the covered mall provisions in Chapter 56.

Mezzanines

Sec. 1717. A mezzanine need not be counted as a story for determining the allowable number of stories when constructed in accordance with the following:

1. The construction of a mezzanine shall be consistent with the requirements for the type of construction in which the mezzanine is located, but the fire-resistive time period need not exceed one hour for unenclosed mezzanines constructed. The clear height above and below the mezzanine floor construction shall be not less than 7 feet.

2. There shall be not more than two levels of mezzanines in a room. However, there is no limitation on the number of mezzanines within a room.

3. The aggregate area of mezzanines within a room shall not exceed one third the area of the room in which it is located.

4. All portions of a mezzanine shall be open and unobstructed to the room in which it is located, except for columns and posts and protective walls or railings not more than 42 inches in height.

EXCEPTIONS: 1. Partitioning may be installed if either of the following conditions exist:

A. The aggregate area of the enclosed space does not exceed 10 percent

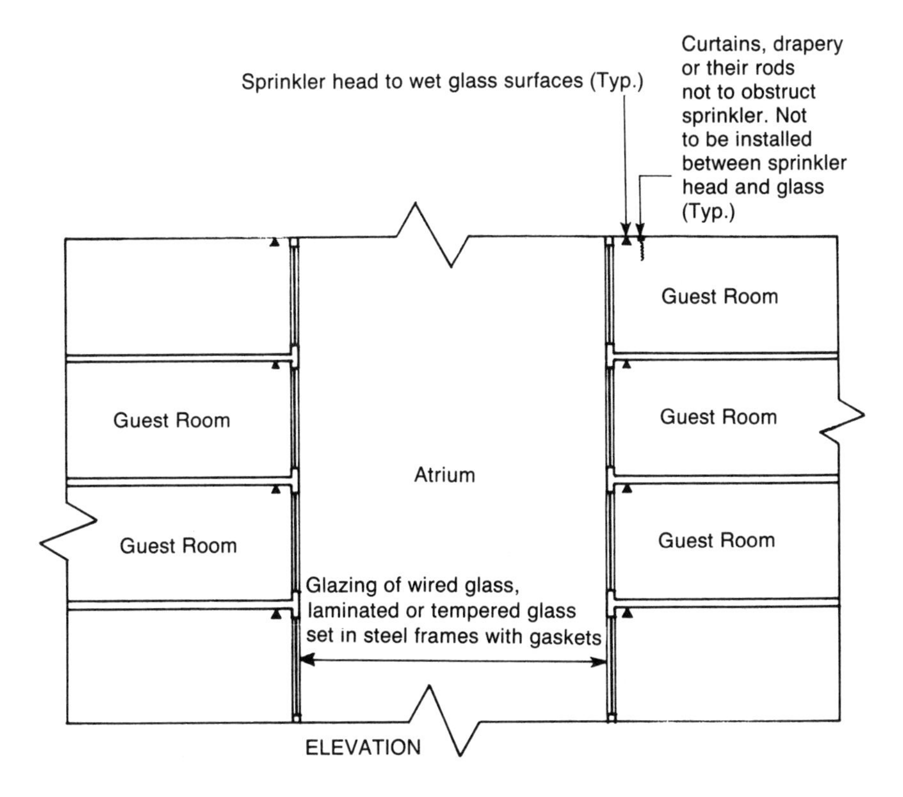

REFERENCE: SECTION 1715 (c) EXCEPTION 2

FIGURE 6-13 ATRIUM AND ADJACENT ROOMS

of the mezzanine area.
B. The occupant load of the enclosed space does not exceed 10.
2. Mezzanines having two or more exits need not open into the story in which they are located, provided at least one of the exits gives direct access to a protected exit corridor, an exit court, enclosed exit stairway, exterior exit, exterior exit balcony or exit passageway.
3. In industry facilities, mezzanines used for control equipment may be glazed on all sides.
5. Two exits shall be provided from a mezzanine when two exits are required by Table No. 33-A.
6. If any required exit enters the room below, the occupant load of the mezzanine shall be added to the occupant load of the room in which it is located.

The provisions for mezzanines are grouped together into this section. The basic criterion for a mezzanine is that it not occupy more than one-third the floor area of the room in which it is located. If this limitation is met, the mezzanine cannot be considered as constituting a story of the building. Thus, the mezzanine level avoids being added to the other stories of the building in determining compliance with Table No. 5-D.

A mezzanine generally is unenclosed on the side facing the room below. However, this requirement is not mandatory if the provisions of subsection 4 Exception 2 are met. This Exception requires that there be two exits from an enclosed mezzanine with at least one exit providing direct access to an enclosed stairway, protected exit corridor (i.e., one-hour corridor) or similar protected exit enclosure.

When the mezzanine is used only for the control equipment of an industrial operation, as in a B-2 factory, the mezzanine can be enclosed with glazing on all sides without having to meet the exit provisions just cited. (See Figures 6-14 and 6-15.) The other provisions of the section require:

- The mezzanine area must be added to that of the floor below for determination of occupant load. The occupant load of the mezzanine is to be added to that of the floor into which it exits. Thus, a mezzanine's occupant load will be added to that of the floor below it. If there are two exits required, as in Exception 2 above, one-half the mezzanine occupant load will exit as stated and the other may go to the floor below it and be added to that floor's occupant load.
- The construction of the mezzanine must be comparable to that of the building in which it is located, with the further

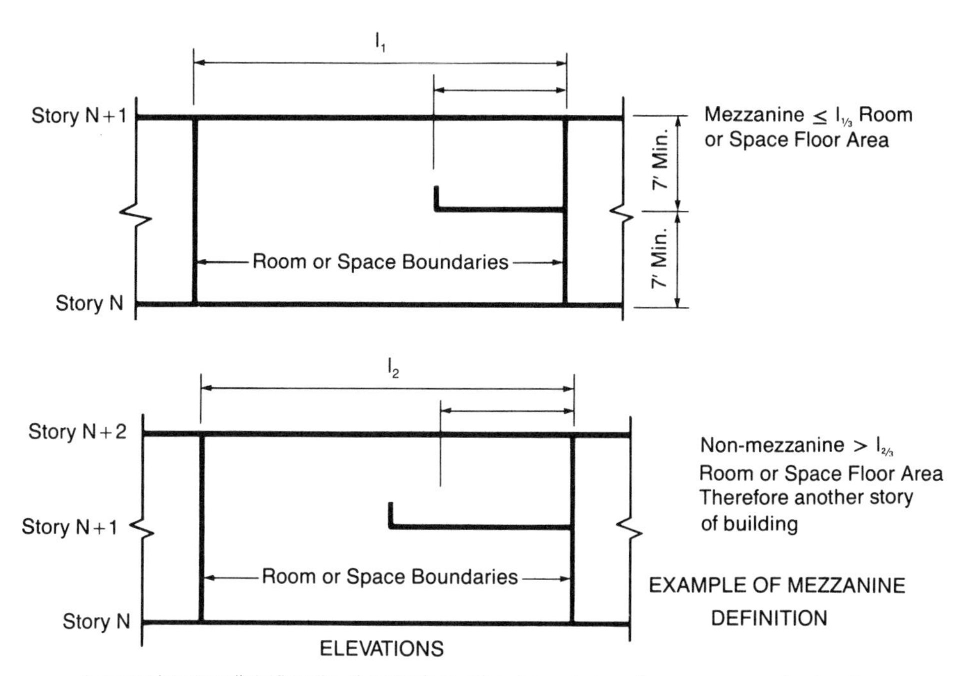

Assume intermediate floor level extends to other boundaries of room or space in elevations

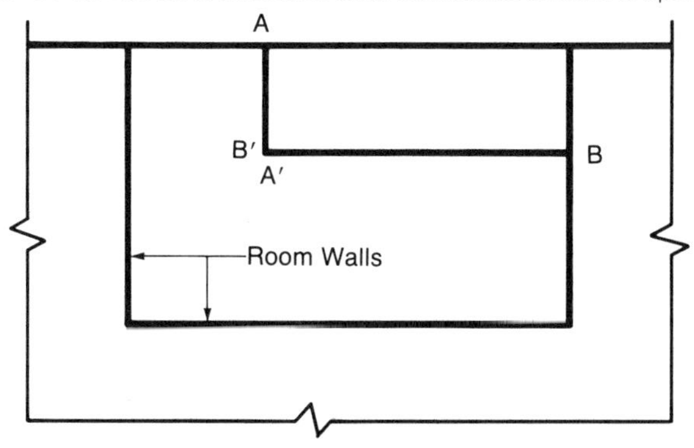

AA′ and BB′ essentially unenclosed

LIMITATIONS FOR UNENCLOSED MEZZANINES

1. Total of mezzanine areas in a room or space shall not exceed ⅓ the floor area of that room or space.
2. Construction of the mezzanine shall be the same as for the room or space in which it is located. Fire-resistive construction need not exceed one-hour.
3. Ceiling clear height above and below mezzanine to be 7 feet minimum.
4. Open sides may have columns, posts and 42″ high wall or railing.
5. Two exits required per Table No. 33-A when mezzanine area exceeds 2,000 square feet.

REFERENCE: SECTION 414, 1717

FIGURE 6-14 MEZZANINE – UNENCLOSED

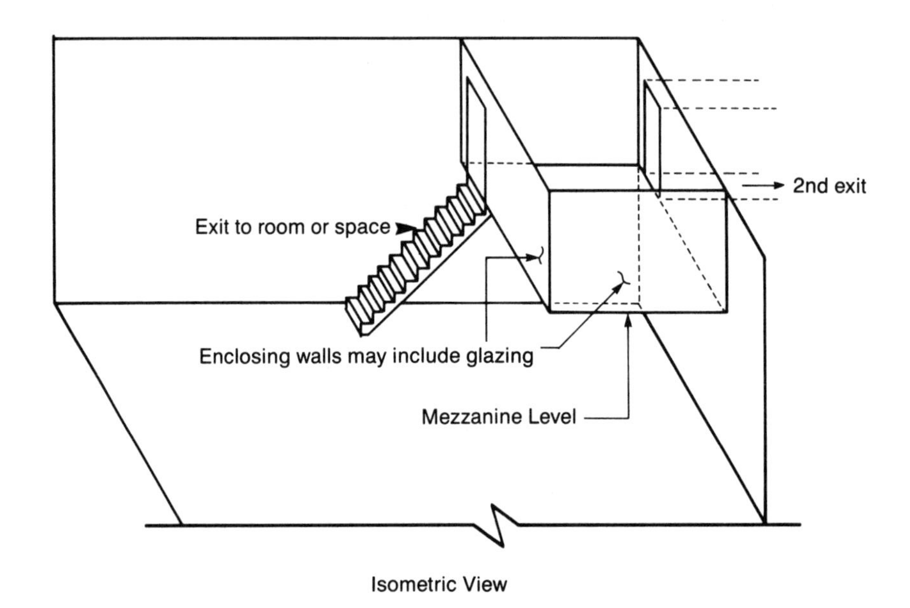

Isometric View

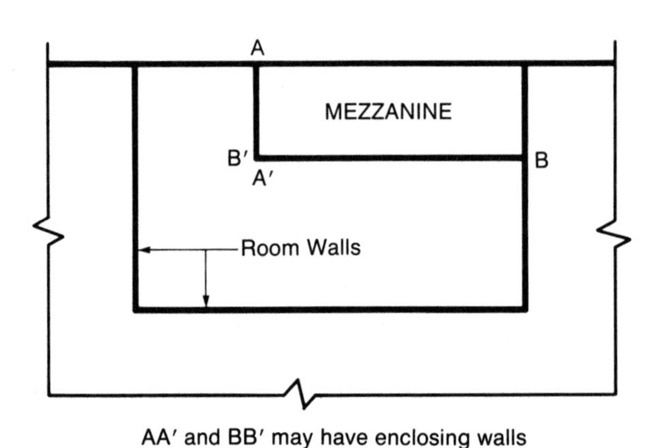

AA′ and BB′ may have enclosing walls

LIMITATIONS FOR ENCLOSED MEZZANINES

1. See Figure 6-14, Items 1-3: these items also apply to enclosed mezzanines.
2. Every enclosed mezzanine must have two exits. One exit must go directly to a protected exit corridor, enclosed exit stairway, exterior exit balcony, exit court, exterior exit or exit passageway

REFERENCE: SECTION 414, 1717

FIGURE 6-15 MEZZANINE – ENCLOSED

limitation that the fire-resistive rating of the mezzanine need not exceed one hour.
- There must be two exits for any mezzanine when required by Table No. 33-A provisions or when the mezzanine area is greater than 2,000 square feet. The more restrictive criteria shall govern. If the mezzanine is enclosed, the provision cited in subsection 4 Exception 2 takes precedence over this provision.

TABLE NO. 17-A.
TYPES OF CONSTRUCTION-FIRE RESISTIVE REQUIREMENTS

This table is used with the provisions of:

- Sections 503 (d) and 505 (c) for occupancy separation and area separation walls, respectively.
- Section 3305 (g) for corridors.
- Section 3309 for stairways.

The table provides the overall construction requirements of the basic building elements and systems.

Chapter 5 addresses the two main fire concerns of the code provisions:

1. prevention of a conflagration spreading from building to building
2. prevention of fire spread within a building to avoid either collapse of the structure or fire moving from floor to floor

The details for achieving the degree of fire resistance indicated in the table are outlined in Chapter 43. There are, in addition, other reference documents including the Evaluation Reports of ICBO, the Underwriters Laboratories Inc. *Fire Resistance Directory* and the Gypsum Association *Fire Resistance Manual,* to name a few of the most common sources.

The concepts of fire protection, allowable areas and heights are represented in the hourly ratings in this table. An examination of the elements of the table is of assistance in visualizing this code approach. For an analysis of this table and the types of construction therein, see Technical Appendix TA-2.

Table No.17-A has had stairway construction added as a building element. Although the item appears to simply be a listing of the cross-references to the Chapters 18 through 22 provisions, the intent is to clarify the fire protection requirements particularly for Type V one-hour buildings.

Stairways in Type V one-hour buildings may have exposed wood stair treads, risers and stringers. The enclosure provisions of Section 3309 (b) apply to the separation requirements of the stairway from the rest of the building. Section 3306 (m) first paragraph allows a stairway to be in accordance with Part IV of the code; Part IV includes Chapters 17 through 22.

Thus, the stairway construction provision of Table No 17-A is consistent with the Chapter 33 provisions and provides cross-references for the stairway construction requirements only insofar as the materials and riser/tread/stringer construction are concerned. The stairway enclosure and occupancy separation requirements, when applicable, would still apply per Chapters 33 and 5 respectively.

Footnote 1 of Table No. 17-A was amended to read as shown below. Footnote 3 was added, reading as shown below. As part of the change relating to adding Footnote 3, the prior reference to "Section 1706" for "Shaft Enclosures" under Type V 1-Hr. and V-N columns were deleted.

Footnotes:

[1] Structural frame elements in an exterior wall that is located where openings are not permitted or where protection of openings is required, shall be protected against external fire exposure as required for exterior bearing walls or the structural frame, whichever is greater.

[3] For special provisions, see Subsections 1706 (c), (e) and (f).

The text in Footnote 1 was revised for clarity of intent.

The text relates to the fire-resistance of the exterior structural frame for fire exposure from the adjacent property. Thus, the structural frame requires a higher fire-resistance rating when it is close to the property line. This intent is accomplished by using two criteria: the distances at which openings are not permitted or when openings are to be fire protected and the rating of an exterior bearing wall in Table No. 17-A.

The method for determining the exterior structural frame rating is illustrated for Type I and II buildings in Figures 6-16 and 6-17, for Group B, Division 2 Occupancy. Similar rationale can apply to other occupancies and types of construction.

Type of Construction Analysis, see TA-2.

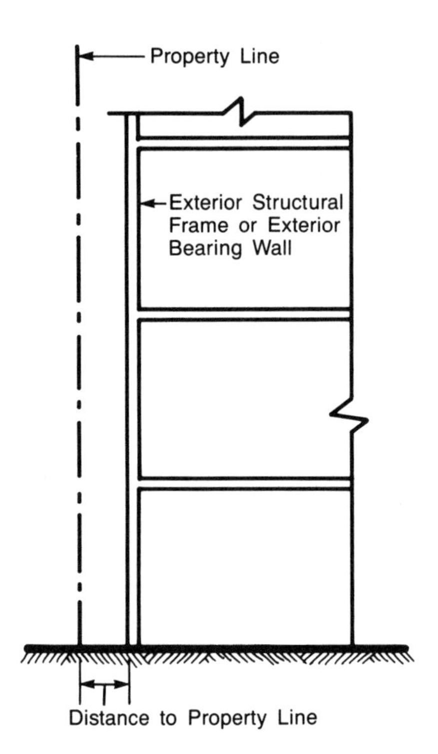

GIVEN: Type II-FR Building
Group B, Division 2 Occupancy

When the exterior wall is located so that, per Table No. 5-A or the -03 (b) sections of Chapters 18 through 21, openings are either not permitted or require protection, the structural frame must be protected for the time period cited in Table No. 17-A for the exterior bearing walls or for the "structural frame" requirements, whichever is the higher hourly rating.

Thus, for a Type I or II-FR building within 20 feet of the property line, the structural frame must be protected for four-hours. When the exterior wall is more than 20 feet from the property line, the structural frame need only be protected for two-hours. See Sections 1803 (b) and 1903 (b) and Table No. 17-A.

For those building types covered by Table No. 5-A, i.e., Types II One-hour, II-N and V One-hour or V-N, the Table No. 5-A criteria in the right hand columns will control. For example, for a Type V-N Group R, Division 3 Occupancy building, with an exterior wall within 3 feet of the property line, a structural frame on the exterior wall facing that property line requires a one-hour fire-resistive rating in accordance with the requirements in the third column of Table No. 5-A

REFERENCE: TABLE NO. 17-A FOOTNOTE 1 AND THE -O3 (b) SECTIONS OF CHAPTERS 18 THROUGH 21

FIGURE 6-16 FIRE-RESISTIVE RATING FOR STRUCTURAL FRAME EXTERIOR WALL

See Figure 6-16 for Elevation and general discussion.

ASSUME: Group B, Division 2 Occupancy.

	1	2	3	4
		TYPE		
	I	II	II-1-Hr.	II-N
Distance to property line	HOURLY RATING, STRUCTURAL FRAME			
<20′	4[a]	4[a]		
20′ or >	3[b]	2[b]		
<10′			1[c]	1[e]
10′ or ≤20′			1[d]	1[f]
>20″			1[d]	N[g]

The hourly ratings shown above for the structural frame are derived as follows for the examples shown above:

Column 1 & 2 – a From Table No. 17-A and Sections 1803 (b) and 1903 (b), based on the distance of the exterior wall to the property line being less than 20 feet and the rating in the Table for "exterior bearing wall."

b From Table No. 17-A and Sections 1803 (b) and 1903 (b) based on the distance of the exterior wall to the property line being 20' or more, i.e., openings are permitted, and the rating in the Table for the "structural frame" applies.

Column 3 – c & e From Table No. 5-A based on the distance to the property line of less than 10′, the Table No. 17-A one-hour exterior bearing wall/structural frames rating applies.

Column 4 – d & f From Table No. 5-A based on the distance of the exterior wall to the property line of between 10′ and not more than 20 feet, and the Table No. 17-A rating for "exterior bearing wall/structural frame" are both one-hour.

g From Table Nos. 5-A and 17-A based on the distance of the exterior wall from the property line being more than 20 feet and where no opening protection is required. The wall can be of unrated (N) construction.

REFERENCE: TABLES NO. 5-A AND 17-A, SECTIONS -03 OF CHAPTERS 18-21

FIGURE 6-17 EXAMPLES OF STRUCTURAL FRAME REQUIREMENTS @ EXTERIOR WALL. TYPE I AND II BUILDINGS WITH GROUP B, DIVISION 2 OCCUPANCY

TABLE NO. 17-A—TYPES OF CONSTRUCTION—FIRE-RESISTIVE REQUIREMENTS
(In Hours)
For Details see Chapters under Occupancy and Types of Construcion and for Exceptions see Section 1705.

BUILDING ELEMENT	TYPE I	TYPE II			TYPE III		TYPE IV	TYPE V	
	NONCOMBUSTIBLE				COMBUSTIBLE				
	Fire-Resistive	Fire-Resistive	1-Hr.	N	1-Hr.	N	H.T.	1-Hr.	N
Exterior Bearing Walls	4 Sec. 1803 (a)	4 1903 (a)	1 1903 (a)	N	4 2003 (a)	4 2003(a)	4 2103 (a)	1	N
Interior Bearing Walls	3	2	1	N	1	N	1	1	N
Exterior Nonbearing Walls	4 Sec. 1803 (a)	4 1903 (a)	1	N	4 2003 (a)	4 2003 (a)	4 2103 (a)	1	N
Structural Frame[1]	3	2	1	N	1	N	1 or H.T.	1	N
Partitions—Permanent	1[2]	1[2]	1[2]	N	1	N	1 or H.T.	1	N
Shaft Enclosures[3]	2	2	1	1	1	1	1	1	1
Stairway Construction	Sec. 1805	1905	1905	1905	2004	2004	2104	2204	2204
Roofs-ceilings/Roofs	2 Sec. 1806	1 1906	1 1906	N	1	N	H.T.	1	N
Exterior Doors and Windows	Sec. 1803 (b)	1903 (b)	1903 (b)	1903 (b)	2003 (b)	2003 (b)	2103 (b)	2203	2203

1. Structural frame elements in an exterior wall that is located where openings are not permitted or where protection of openings is required, shall be protected against external fire exposure as required for exterior bearing walls or the structural frame, whichever is greater.
2. Fire-retardant treated wood (see Section 407) may be used in the assembly, provided fire-resistance requirements are maintained. See Sections 1801 and 1901, respectively.
3. For special provisions, see Subsections 1706 (c), (e) and (f).

ARTICLE 7
THE EXITING PROVISIONS OF CHAPTER 33

Chapter 33 Exits

OVERVIEW

Chapter 33 of the UBC contains the requirements for designing an exit system in a building which will provide escape from fire or panic. The chapter is divided into segments:

a) The basic criteria for determining the number and width of exits required.
b) The elements constituting the exit path from a room or space within the building to the outside, including doors, corridors, stairs and other exit components.
c) The requirements for large assembly-type occupancies.
d) Special exit requirements based on occupancy or use.
e) Requirements for grandstands and bleachers.

The exits for every occupancy in a building must meet the provisions of this chapter. Many buildings contain several different occupancies. The designer has to consider all the uses, present or contemplated, so that adequate numbers and widths of exits are provided.

The handicapped provisions of the prior codes have been replaced by a new Chapter 31 entitled "Accessibility." Within that chapter are egress provisions which will affect the design of exiting systems where access to the handicapped must be provided to any level of a building.

In the author's opinion, the stair width requirements of Section 3104 (b) 3 take precedence over the provisions in Section 3306 (b) in those buildings required to be accessible. Therefore, the minimum gross width of stair will henceforth be 55 inches instead of 44 inches as has long been the criteria. See Figure 7-1.

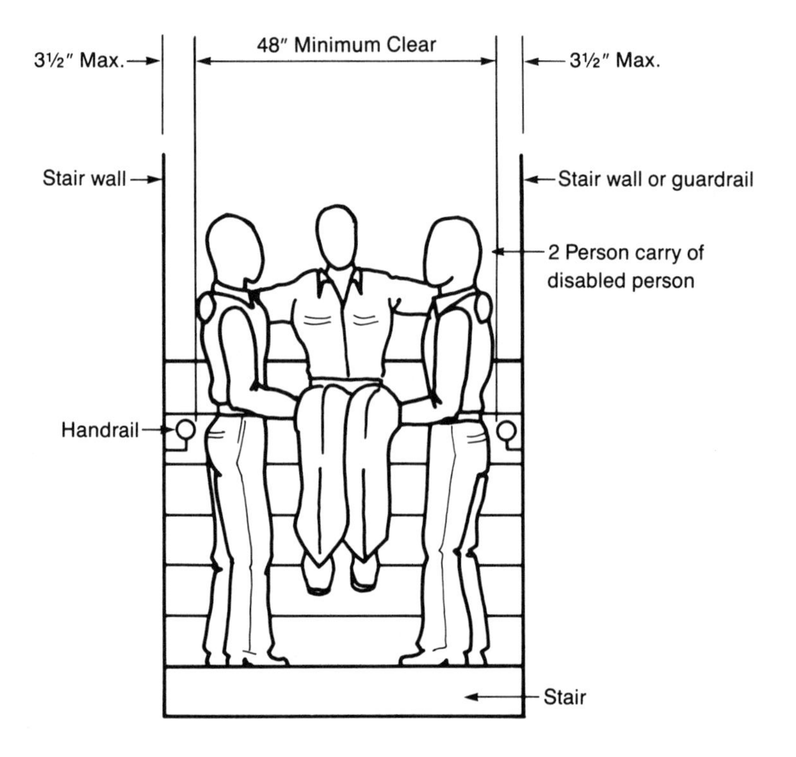

EVACUATION OF DISABLED PERSON DOWN STAIR TWO PERSON CARRY

This illustration shows the basis of the minimum clear width requirement of Section 3104 (b)3. The provisions of Section 3104 (b)3 supersede the minimum provisions of Section 3306 (b) because the minimum requirement in Section 3104 (b)3 are greater than that in Section 3306 (b). The intent of these two sections is also different. Section 3306 (b) was based on the gross width of the stairwell assuming handrails projecting not more than 3½″ from the wall. This would allow a net width between handrails of 37″ and a gross width of stairway of 44″ minimum. Section 3104 (b)3 is based on a net width between the handrails. This will result in a nominal 55″ wide stairway as the minimum.

REFERENCE: SECTION 3104 (b)3

FIGURE 7-1 MINIMUM WIDTH OF STAIRWAY BASED ON TWO PERSONS CARRYING OF DISABLED PERSON DOWN STAIRWAY

The 55 inch width is premised on a clear width between handrails of 48 inches mandated in Section 3104 (b)3 and the 7 inch handrail incursion into the stairway permitted in Section 3306 (d).

It is recommended that a cross-reference be added to Section 3306 (b) to refer back to Section 3104 (b)3 so that this important requirement is not overlooked.

The basic exiting principle is that there be at least two different exit paths from the interior of a building to the outside at ground level. The rationale of the code is that if one path is blocked or endangered by the hazard, from which one is trying to escape, then the other path will be available.

An exit path usually consists of three components or sections:

1. Travel within a room or space to a door giving access to a fire-rated, protected enclosure such as a corridor or a stairway. In the exit path of a room or space, it may be necessary to cross aisles, corridors and other rooms before gaining access to the protected enclosure. The distance to be traversed is limited by the code and will be covered in the Section 3303 (d) analysis hereinafter.
2. Travel through the protected enclosure. Where the enclosure is a corridor, as in an upper level of a building, it will connect to at least one, and usually to two, stairways. The distance one must travel within the protected corridor to reach a stairway is also regulated by the code.
3. The connection from the corridor to the exterior of the building. In the upper stories of a building this component includes the stairways and their connection to the building's exterior at ground level. This part of the exit path may be very long, as are the stairways in a high-rise building. The code does not set a maximum length of travel in a stairway. However, the fire-resistive requirements for the stairway are usually greater than those for the corridors.

These elements of an exit system are shown in Figures 7-2, 7-3 and 7-4.

The exit path for a one-story building is simple since the second and third sections of the exit path are combined. The corridor extends to the

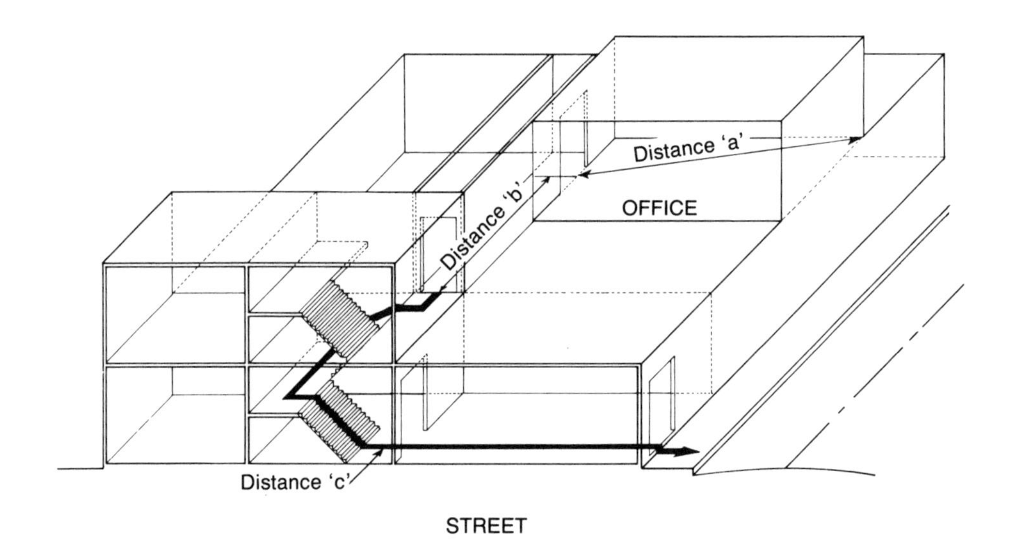

Distance 'a' is travel within a room or space to a door to exit corridor or stairway.

Distance 'b' is travel within a protected exit corridor to an exit stair. It commences at the door to the exit corridor and terminates at the exit stair doorway.

Distance 'c' is the travel within an exit stairway and exit passagweay to the street. It commences at the door to the exit stairway and terminates at the exit to the street.

In Unsprinklered Building

Distance 'a' has maximum of 100 feet.

Distance 'b' has maximum of 150 feet provided the corridor is at least one-hour construction.

Distance 'c' has no maximum length. Entire stair (except in most two story buildings) has to have minimum of one-hour construction.

REFERENCE: SECTION 3301 (b)

FIGURE 7-2 ELEMENTS OF EXIT PATH

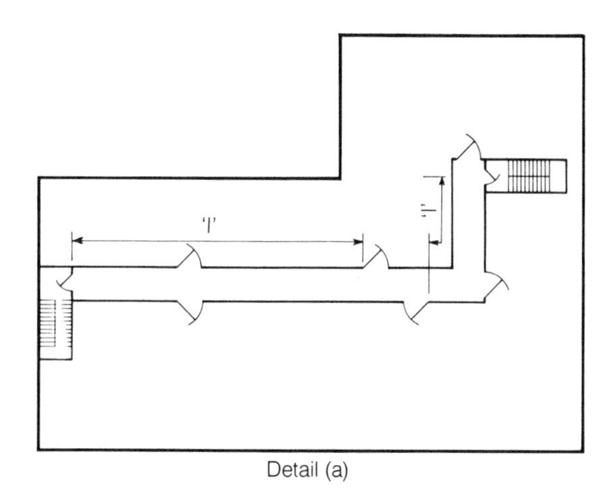

Detail (a)

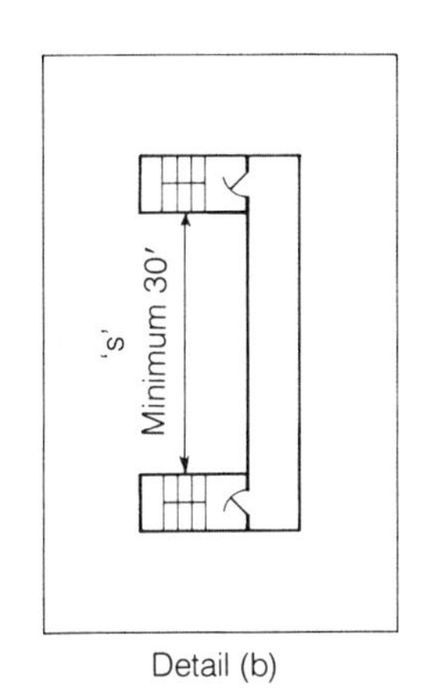

Detail (b)

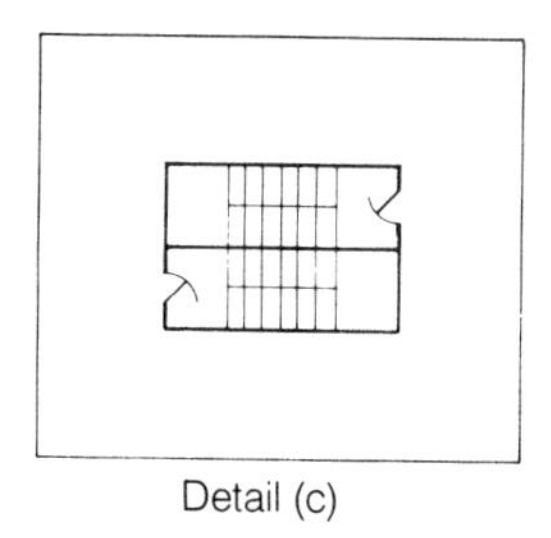
Detail (c)

Assume double loaded exit corridor, stairs at each end, with occupant load of *less than* 500 on floor. Corridor one-hour construction, then:

Maximum travel distance 'l', from any exit doorway into corridor to stair, per Sec. 3303 (c) = 150′

Minimum distance between stair enclosures, 's' = 30′

Travel distance of measurement 'l' in Detail ''a'' is between exit doors to corridor and door to stairway. Separation of the stairs 's' is measured between the walls of the stair enclosure in Detail ''b'' per to Sec. 3303 (c) Exception.

Detail 'c' illustrates a ''scissors'' stair arrangement which is not permitted. The stair walls are < 30′ apart; in fact there is zero distance due to the common wall between the stair runs.

REFERENCE: SECTION 3303 (c)

FIGURE 7-3 EXIT CORRIDOR, DISTANCE OF TRAVEL, ANY STORY OF BUILDING

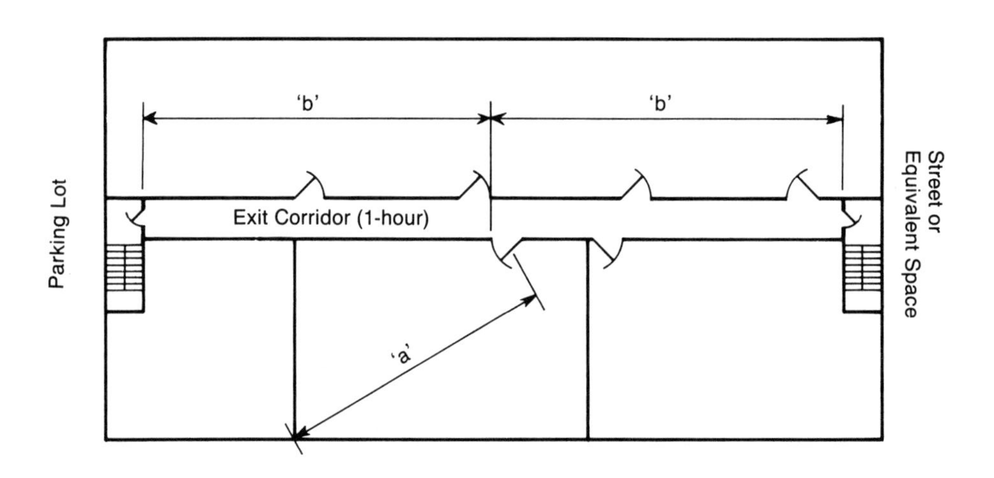

Unsprinklered	'a'	=	Travel distance within room or area (Maximum 100')*
Building	'b'	=	Travel distance within exit corridor (Maximum 150')*
Sprinklered	'a'	=	Maximum 150′
Building	'b'	=	Maximum 150′

*Where 'a' leads directly to an exit stair, horizontal exit or exit passageway:

'a' = 150′ in unsprinklered building
'a' = 200′ in sprinklered building

REFERENCE: SECTION 3303 (d)

FIGURE 7-4 EXIT TRAVEL, ANY FLOOR OF BUILDING (TYP.)

exterior wall and opens onto a street, yard or public space. It provides the exit to the exterior of the building at ground level.

In many one-story buildings, such as retail stores and banks, only the first section of the exit path exists. The room or space opens directly to the building's exterior without need of protected corridors or stairways. The distance one must travel from the most remote point in the room or space to the exterior doorway is still regulated by the code. (See Figure 7-5.)

The general requirement that there be two exit paths available has as its determinants:

- the number of people that may be in a room, space or floor
- the number of stories in the building.

If the maximum number of people or occupants of a space is small, the code does not require two paths be provided. Although this allowance may at first seem to reflect a callous disregard for people's lives, one must consider that a building code has to take into realistic account the cost/benefit involved in a requirement. It would be impractical to require a two-story building, with a 500-square-foot apartment on both floors, to provide two separate exits for each unit. On the other hand, the larger or taller the building, the greater the number of its occupants. And, as the number of occupants increases, so does the danger to them, thus warranting the two exit requirement.

If a space were used as a warehouse, the probable number of occupants would be low since the majority of the space would contain stored material. On the other hand, if a space were used as a bar, in a popular area, the number of occupants at times could be very large in relation to the relatively small area of the bar. Although one might want to challenge these seemingly arbitrary numbers established by the code, there is sufficient evidence to sustain their validity.

The term used for describing the code-required space assigned per occupant for the different occupancies is "occupant load." In Table No. 33-A it is called the "occupant load factor," but the simpler term will be used hereafter due to its general use in both the UBC and other references. The occupant load for a space is the floor area of that space divided by the occupant load factor from Table No. 33-A for the particular occupancy.

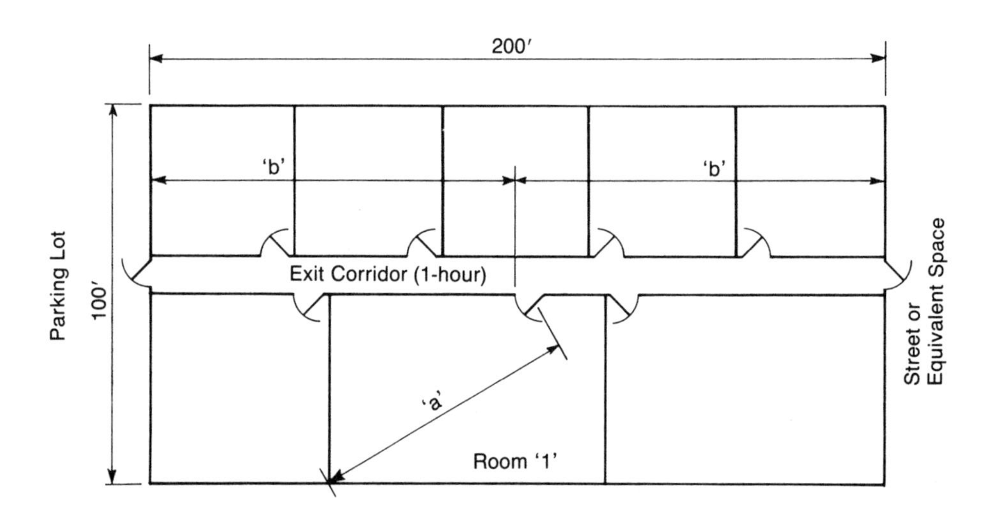

Unsprinklered Building	'a' =	Travel distance within room or area (Maximum 100′)*
	'b' =	Travel distance within exit corridor (Maximum 150′)*
Sprinklered Building	'a' =	Maximum 150′
	'b' =	Maximum 150′

*Where 'a' leads directly to horizontal exit or exterior of building:

'a' = 150′ in unsprinklered building
'a' = 200′ in sprinklered building

REFERENCE: SECTION 3303 (d)

FIGURE 7-5 EXIT TRAVEL – FIRST FLOOR

Section 3302 is entitled "Occupant Load." Table No. 33-A uses the more precise term only to avoid any assumption that there is a code requirement stating that the area per person shown in the Table is to be legally provided each occupant. Several years ago, a labor union insisted that the prior code language be interpreted as mandating the space required to be furnished each employee. That mandate was never the intent of the Table No. 33-A provisions. As previously indicated, the values and numbers are based not on the actual physical situation within any building, but, for code purposes, on probability. The values are codified so that they can be used by anyone in determining the exit details; i.e., the number and width of the exit components.

The number of occupants, for each particular use, that triggers the two exit path requirement is contained Table No. 33-A. Multiplying the Table's assigned occupant load factor for a given use by the number of occupants for that use for which two exits are required, results in the fewest allowable square feet of space for which two exits are required.

For example, consider a B-2 office occupancy. The occupant load factor is 100 and two exits are required when there are more than 50 occupants. Therefore, the allowable area will have to exceed (100 x 50 =) 5,000 square feet before two exits are required. Conversely, given the size of a space and dividing it by the occupant load factor of Table No. 33-A results in the occupant load for the area. For example, a 6,000 square foot space with a Table No. 33-A occupant load factor of 50 square feet per occupant, would have an occupant load of (6000/50 =) 120 occupants.

The above calculation applies only to one-story buildings and to spaces within any building. As previously indicated, two additional determinants apply to taller buildings. In all buildings three stories and taller, at least two exit paths must be provided, regardless of the occupant load. In most buildings two stories in height, two exits are required when the occupant load exceeds 10 on the second floor.

The same calculations are used to determine the number of exit doorways, from a room or space anywhere in a building, required to give access to a protected corridor, stairway or the exterior of a building. At least two exit doorways are required when the occupant load of the room or space equals or exceeds the number for that use according to Table No. 33-A. To assure that such doorways remain accessible in the event of fire or panic, they must be separated from each other by a distance equal to at least one-half the diagonal dimension of the space involved. (See Figures 7-6 and 7-7.)

SPECIFIC REQUIREMENTS

Sec. 3301

(b) Definitions. For the purpose of this chapter, certain terms are defined as follows:

► ■■■ ◄

EXIT is a continuous and unobstructed means of egress to a public way and shall include intervening aisles, doors, doorways, corridors, gates, exterior exit balconies, ramps, stairways, smokeproof enclosures, horizontal exits, exit passageways, exit courts and yards.

EXIT COURT is a yard or court providing access to a public way for one or more required exits.

EXIT PASSAGEWAY is an enclosed exit connecting a required exit or exit court with a public way.

HORIZONTAL EXIT is an exit from one building into another building on approximately the same level, or through or around a wall constructed as required for a two-hour occupancy separation and which completely divides a floor into two or more separate areas so as to establish an area of refuge affording safety from fire or smoke coming from the area from which escape is made.

► ■■■ ◄

PUBLIC WAY is any street, alley or similar parcel of land essentially unobstructed from the ground to the sky which is deeded, dedicated or otherwise permanently appropriated to the public for public use and having a clear width of not less than 10 feet.

► ■■■ ◄

Certain definitions have important application for the designer. The term "exit" is obviously one such term. The essential feature of an exit is a continuity or unobstructed traverse to the public way outside the building.

The exit door to the exterior of the building should provide access to the public way in compliance with the definition of exit. This means that the access should meet the criteria for access, open to the sky and available for public use.

There are many ways of attaining such access to the public way. The designer should determine early in the design phase that the proposed means satisfies the intent of the code, particularly when it does not show a clear exit path but may require traversing courts, yards or obstructed spaces.

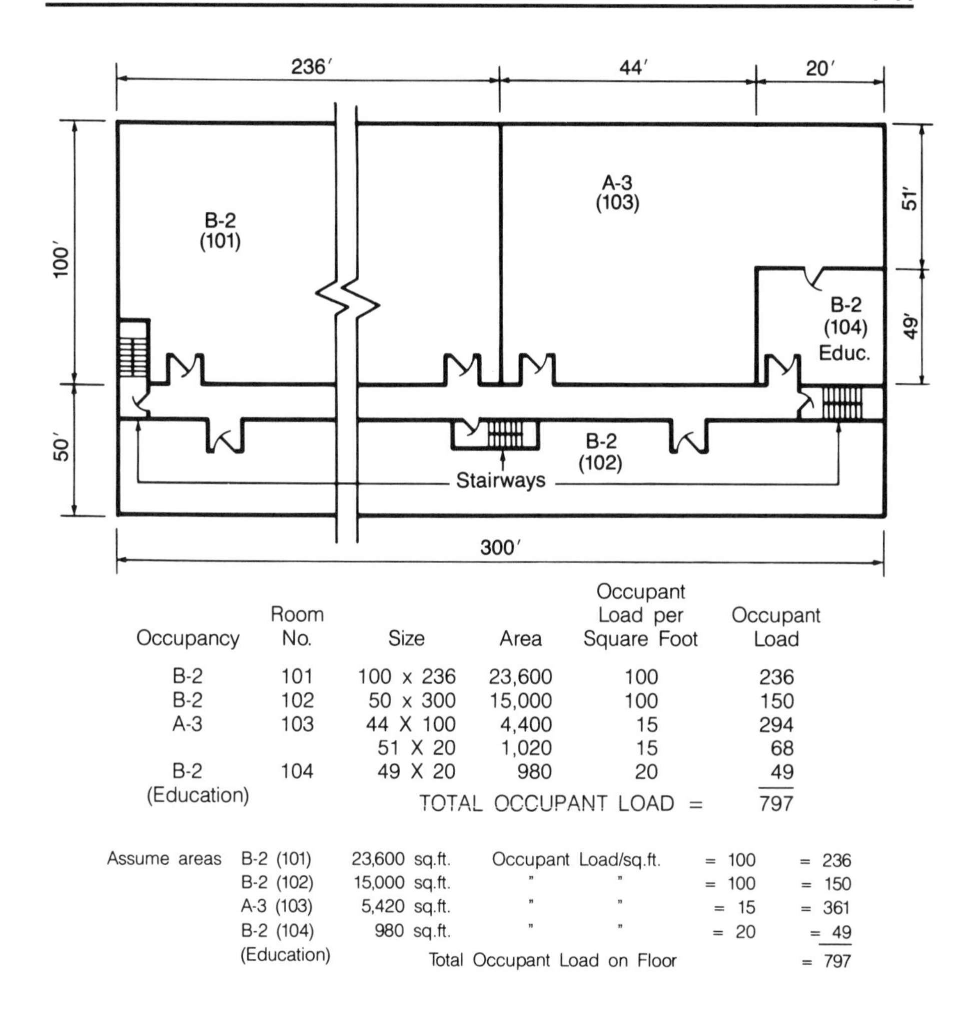

Occupancy	Room No.	Size	Area	Occupant Load per Square Foot	Occupant Load
B-2	101	100 x 236	23,600	100	236
B-2	102	50 x 300	15,000	100	150
A-3	103	44 X 100	4,400	15	294
		51 X 20	1,020	15	68
B-2 (Education)	104	49 X 20	980	20	49
		TOTAL OCCUPANT LOAD =			797

Assume areas					
	B-2 (101)	23,600 sq.ft.	Occupant Load/sq.ft.	= 100	= 236
	B-2 (102)	15,000 sq.ft.	" "	= 100	= 150
	A-3 (103)	5,420 sq.ft.	" "	= 15	= 361
	B-2 (104)	980 sq.ft.	" "	= 20	= 49
	(Education)		Total Occupant Load on Floor		= 797

Per Section 3303 (b),

width of exits required = 797/50 = 15.94′.

This width is divided by the 3 exit stairs required to give an average minimum width of 5.32′ per stair.

Per Section 3303 (a),

number of exits required = 3 (occupant load > 500).

Each exit can be 5½′ wide, (3 x 5.5 = 16.5′) or one can be 4′ wide and the others 6′ each.

It is the author's opinion that as there is a Group B-2 Educational Occupancy on this floor, the minimum width criteria of Section 3319 (e) applies. Therefore the corridors cannot be less than the width required in Section 3303 (b) plus 2 feet, but not less than 6 feet in width.

As the minimum width of the corridor required was found to be 15.94′/3, the minimum width per Section 3319 (e) must be 15.94/3 = 64″ + 24″ = 88″ rather than the 72″ minimum in Section 3319 (e).

Except for the small B-2 Educational Occupancy in room 104, all rooms require a minimum of two exits as each room has an occupant load greater than 50.

REFERENCE: SECTIONS 3303 (a) & (b), 3304 (b), 3305 (b) 3306 (b) & 3319 (e)

FIGURE 7-6 NUMBER OF EXITS—BASED ON OCCUPANT LOAD

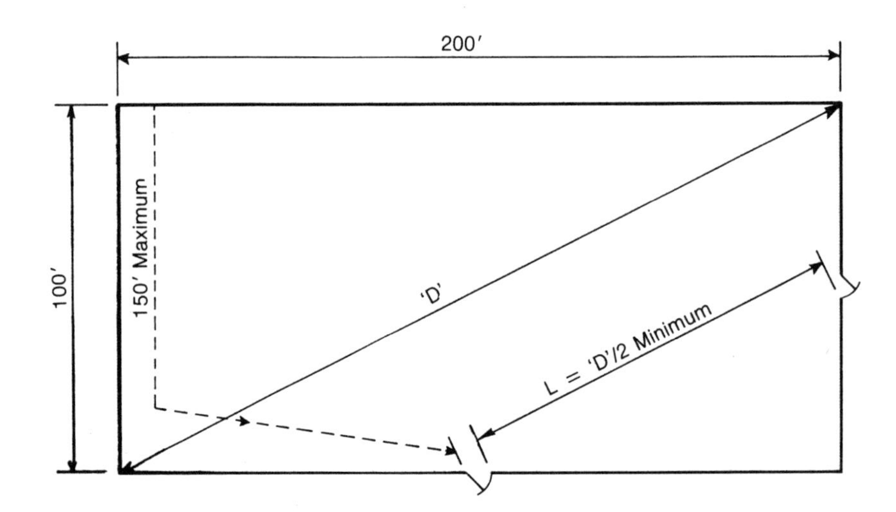

Occupant load per Table No. 33-A, for B-2 office (Item 17) =

$$200 \times 100/100 = 200 \text{ occupants}$$

2 exits required – minimum.

Diagonal dimension of area = $\sqrt{200^2 + 100^2} = \sqrt{50,000} \doteq 224' \pm$

Required minimum distance between exit doors = 112′+

While the minimum number of required exits is readily determined, the actual number of exit doors will vary dependent on the room layout.

See Figure 7-2 for measurement of travel distance within a corridor per Section 3303 (c) Exception.

REFERENCE: SECTION 3303 (c)

FIGURE 7-7 MEASUREMENT OF DISTANCE BETWEEN EXITS

Two sections of the exit path are required to provide fire-resistive protection to the occupant. These sections start at the access door to an exit corridor and extend to the stairway down through the building to the exterior. Once in the corridor enclosure or stairway, the occupant is to remain protected until the building exterior is reached.

In some instances, the fire-resistive enclosure passes by other occupancies. In the process of exiting, the occupant cannot go into and through those occupancies to get to the exterior because doing so would necessitate removing the protection the exit enclosure is required to provide. This concept of protection is specifically indicated in Section 3309 (b), where the extent of the enclosure for a stairway is delineated. (See Figures 7-8 and 7-9.)

The general objective, that of providing a continuous path of protection to the outside of the building, is basic to the code and must be thoroughly understood. It must also be understood that when the exit path from a major occupancy of the building passes through an area containing another occupancy, possibly a public assemblage or a garage area, for protection purposes the exit path retains the occupancy class designation of the main use. The provisions of Table No. 5-B occupancy separations apply to these locations.

In some instances these separation requirements may exceed the stairway enclosure rating. Therefore, if the path of travel is through a tunnel, corridor, or exit passageway from the stairway to the street, the separation may be required to have a greater hourly rating than the one- or two-hour rating of the stair enclosure. If, according to Table No. 5-B, a higher degree of protection is required for the occupancy separation between thc occupancy on the floor and the occupancy whose exit way is traversing the floor, the higher protection requirement will apply.

Horizontal exit. This is a unique concept for exiting because it provides an area of refuge rather than a means of egress to grade. The concept is such that by providing a high degree of fire-resistive separation between two segments of a building, one can pass through the separation, which could be an area separation wall, and be safe from the danger that caused the egress.

The essential characteristics of a horizontal exit are as follows:

- The separation must be of at least two-hour construction.

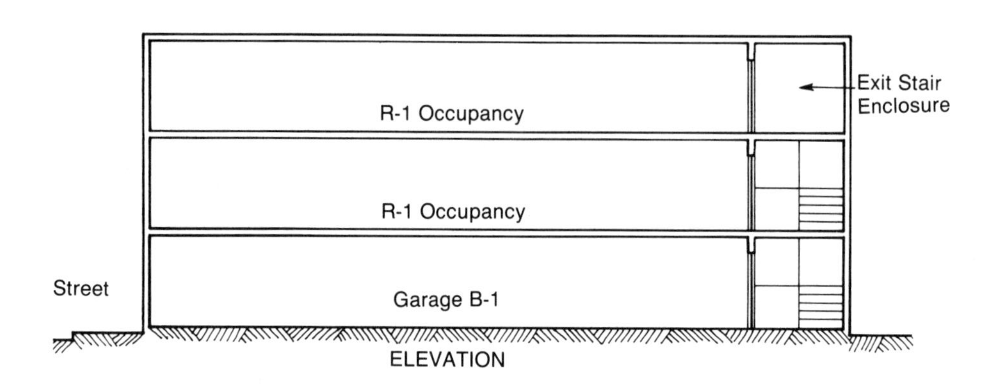

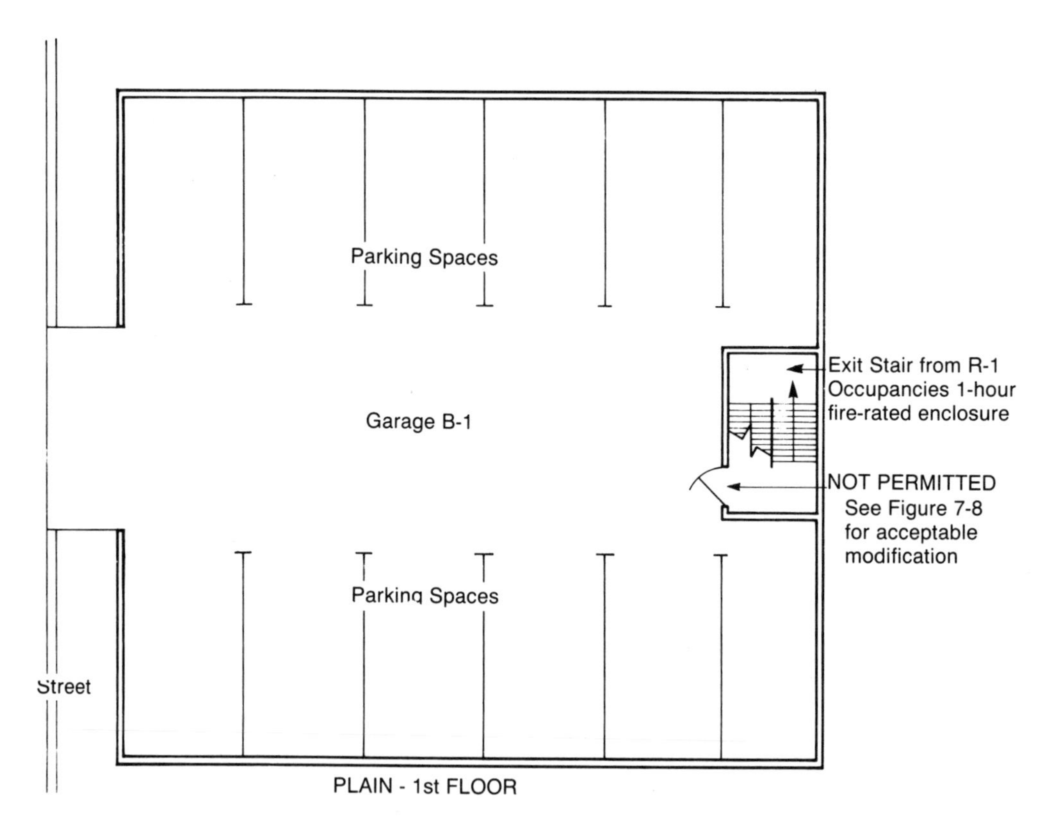

NOTE: Exit stair from upper floors with R-1 Occupancy exits through garage B-1 space without proper occupancy separation. This is a code violation.

REFERENCE: SECTION 3301, 503 AND TABLE NO. 5-B

FIGURE 7-8 ILLEGAL EXIT ENCLOSURE FROM ONE OCCUPANCY PAST ANOTHER

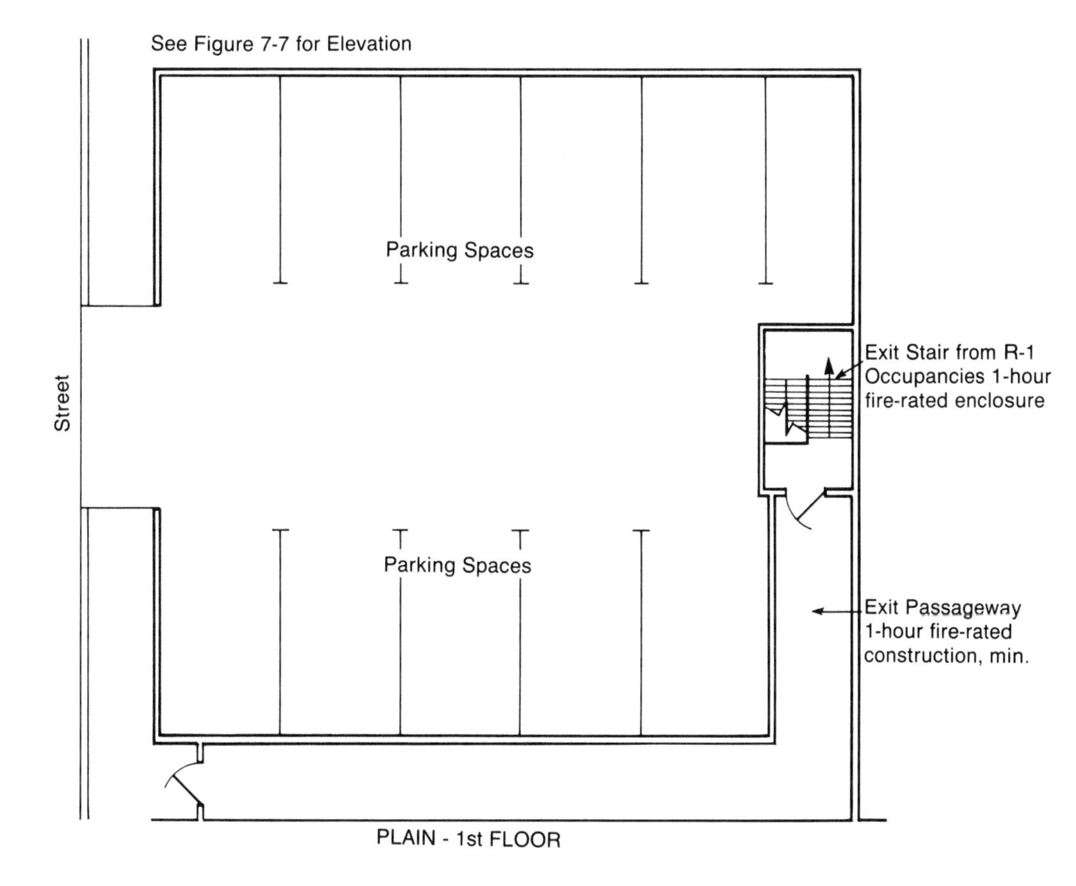

REFERENCE: SECTION 3301, 503 AND TABLE NO. 5-B

FIGURE 7-9 ACCEPTABLE EXIT ENCLOSURE FROM ONE OCCUPANCY PAST ANOTHER

- There must be no interconnection of the ductwork or utilities that would permit fire or smoke to enter the refuge area.
- It may be only used for one of the required exits.

For many buildings, using this concept enables the omission of one stairway. (See discussion in Article 5 regarding Section 509.) If a building exceeds the allowable area and an area separation wall is used, only one stairway need be provided for each segment and the horizontal exit can be used as the second exit for each segment. (See Figure 7-10.)

When the occupant load is 50 or more in each segment, the door in the area separation wall must swing in the direction of exit travel. In such instances there must be two doors in the horizontal exits, one swinging into each segment per Section 3304 (b). Each door leaf must be at least 36 inches wide, thus necessitating that the designer provide at least a 6-foot-wide corridor at the location of the horizontal exit.

As discussed in Article 5 of this Guide, the integrity of the area separation wall is dependent on its construction and details. The designer must give more detailed consideration when the area separation wall is used as part of a horizontal exit.

A frequent question that arises, primarily after an accident, is, "Where does the exit path of the code terminate?" This concern arose because of some misapplication of Chapter 33 provisions, which have erroneously been applied to areas outside the building or structure.

For example, the handrail provisions of Section 3306 (j) and 3307 (b), (c) and (g) have been applied to ramps in shopping centers where there are curb cuts for wheeling shopping carts from a store to one's car. In other instances, were there are paths containing stairs at some distance from a building, the requirements of Section 3306 (j) have been applied to the stairs.

If we look at the areas on a property, aside from the building, we find numerous areas that can have paths, stairs, ramps and other features comparable to certain Chapter 33 regulated exit elements. That similarity does not mean that the Chapter 33 provisions apply. A terraced garden would have to have some means of reaching each terraced level. The stair or ramp need not have a minimum width, rise and run of step, handrail or guardrail per Section 3306.

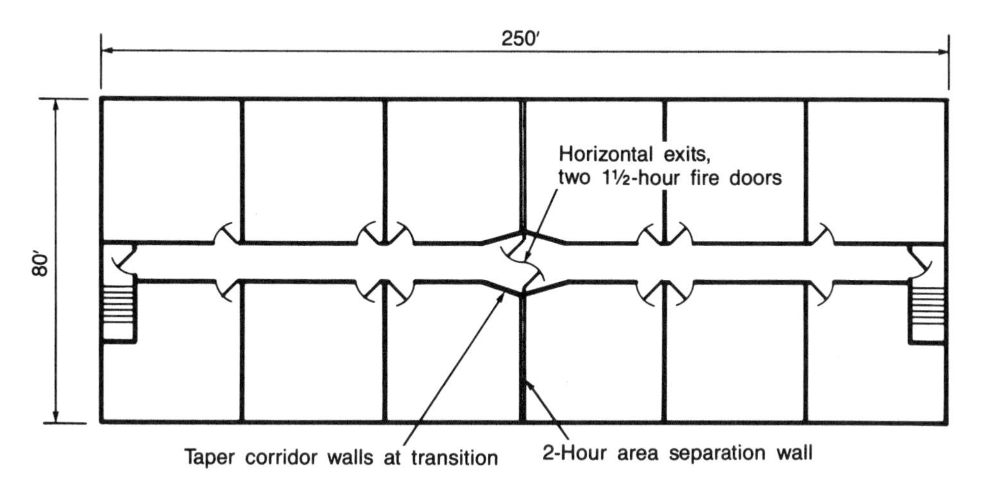

PLAN VIEW

Assume:
R-1 Occupancy, Type V One-hour Building
Three story over Type I garage

60′ separation all around

Proposed area per floor = 80 x 250 = 15,000 S.F.
Proposed Area of building – 3 x 20,000 = 60,000 S.F.

Allowable area, Type V One-hour = 10,500 S.F.
Separation, four sides, increase 100% = 10,500 S.F.

Allowable area with separation increase = 21,000 S.F.
TOTAL ALLOWABLE AREA = 21,000 X 2 = 42,000 S.F.

As the proposed area exceeds the allowable area, an area separation wall will be used.

Occupant load, ½ floor = 125 x 80/200 = 50 persons

Therefore two 1½-hour fire doors are required for the horizontal exit, each swinging in direction of exit travel.

REFERENCE: SECTIONS 505 (e), 3301 (b), 3308

FIGURE 7-10 HORIZONTAL EXIT, EXAMPLE WITH AREA SEPARATION WALL

Many cities have relatively steep streets, exceeding a slope of 1 in 8. In some cities such as San Francisco, streets of slopes of 1 in 5 are not uncommon. In these cities, there are no handrails along such streets. When the street's sidewalk is provided with a stairway, we find no handrail or minimum width of stair involved because these areas are not subject to the UBC provisions of Chapter 33. They are not part of the exit path within a building or structure. In fact, per Section 103, first paragraph, because they are primarily in the public way they are not subject to the code at all.

There is a decided difference between a mandatory code requirement applicable to a situation and a situation when the choice of construction rests with other agencies, e.g., the street department, or with the property owner. The use of an exit path within a building is predicated on that use being involved in an emergency. Outside the building, the use is generally in a nonemergency mode, with the use having the time and choice of direction and speed of traverse.

Unfortunately, there has been no clear delineation of the limitations of applicability of Chapter 33, and this has led to the problems previously described. The ICBO staff in their Interpretation Manual suggested that the path of exiting extends all the way from the building to the street, regardless of how long that path may be.

In the opinion of the author, that interpretation is excessively restrictive and is contrary to the provisions of Chapter 33. The intent of the code can readily be met by termination of the exit path reasonably close to building or structure and away from the hazard causing the exiting in the first place.

The answer to the question of the exit path termination is found in Section 102, which states in part:

> **"The purpose of this code is to provide minimum standards...controlling the design, construction,...of buildings and structures."**

In Section 3301 (a), the code specifically defines the provisions of Chapter 33 to address

> **"Every building or portion thereof..."**

Thus, the exiting provisions of Chapter 33 and the code relate only to buildings and structures.

To see how this concept applies we will look at three variations of building exiting and determine the termination of the exit path in each example.

1. Figure 7-11. Group R, Division 1 buildings with an exterior or interior exit stairway. Because the exterior exit stairway is part of the building (i.e., the building would be illegal without it), the exit path terminates at the base of the exterior stairway intersection adjacent to the street. The interior stair exit path termination point is the door to the street at grade.

In the event the termination point for the interior stairway was not a level or reasonably level area outside the building, it may be reasoned that there should be some extension of the exit path to reach such a safe open area. A garden, lawn or other open space would satisfy as that extension and would not necessitate an extensive conformance with Chapter 33 provisions for the segment outside the building. Remember that the purpose of the exit path is to escape from the hazard "within the building or structure."

2. Figure 7-12. A Group R, Division 3 dwelling within a condominium complex. All areas outside the building are "common areas" of the condominium, designated as permanent open space. The path from the front door of the unit to the private street has three steps spaced from 10 feet to 20 feet apart along the walk. The termination point of the unit's exit path is the front door, because at that point an occupant enters the public way as defined in Section 3301 (b), "a parcel of land essentially unobstructed from the ground to the sky which is deeded, dedicated or otherwise permanently appropriated to the public for public use and having a clear width of ten feet."

In this case, the entire 25-foot width meets this public way definition. Furthermore, because the exit provisions of the UBC relate only to a building or structure, the point at which the building exit leaves the building or structure must be the exit termination.

We can look at this concept and extend its application by assuming the dwelling unit to be a single-family dwelling not involved in a

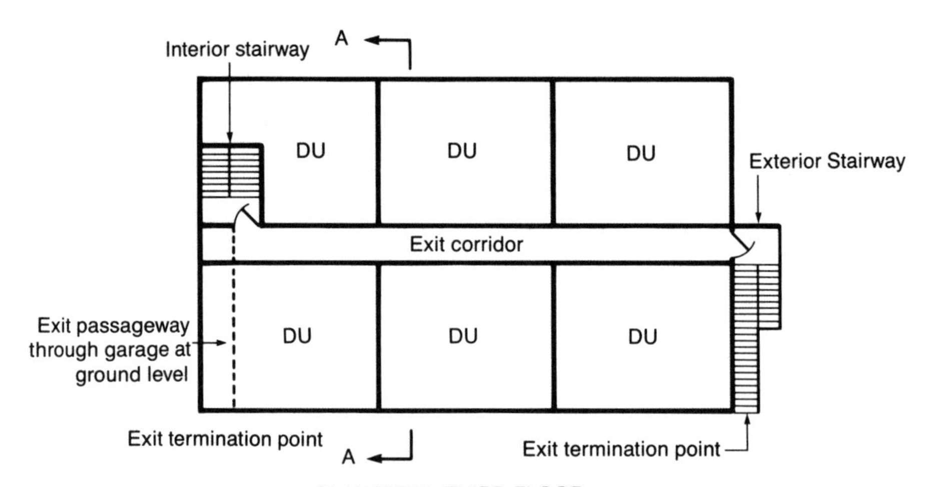

PLAN VIEW—THIRD FLOOR
Group R, Division 1 Occupancy

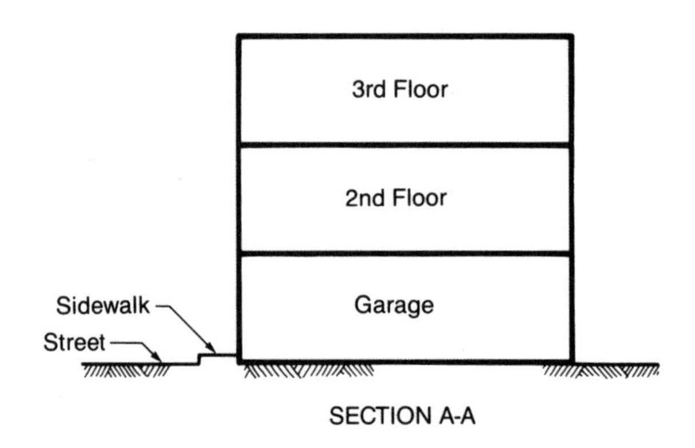

SECTION A-A

REFERENCE: SECTION 102, 3301 (a),(b)

FIGURE 7-11 EXIT TERMINATION—GROUP R, DIVISION 1 OCCUPANCY WITH EXTERIOR OR INTERIOR EXIT STAIRWAY

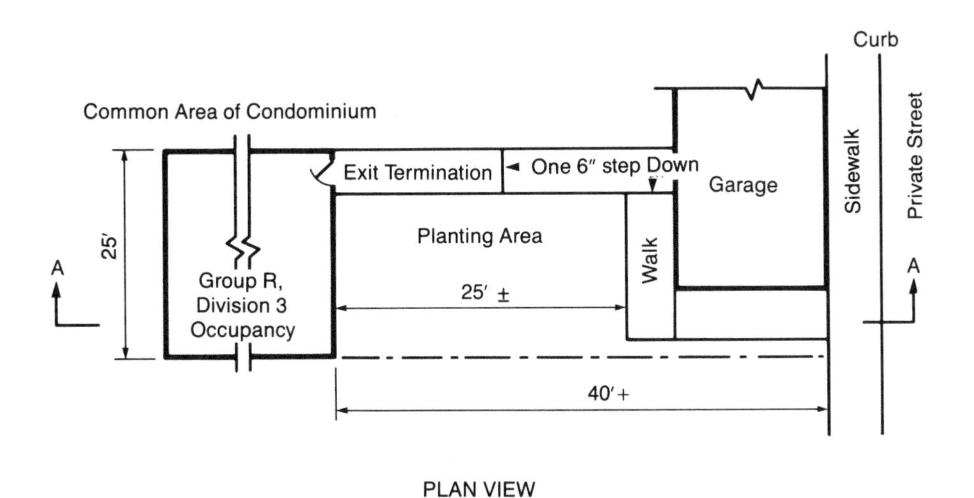

PLAN VIEW

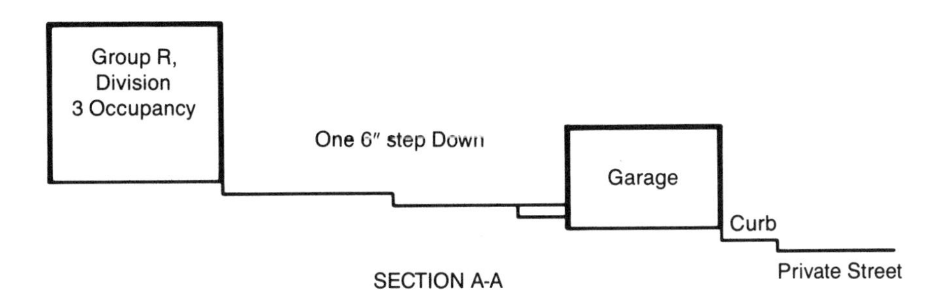

SECTION A-A

REFERENCE: SECTION 3301 (b)

FIGURE 7-12 EXIT TERMINATION—GROUP R, DIVISION 3 OCCUPANCY (CONDO)

condominium but otherwise having the similar open space represented by lawn or setback requirements of the locality. After the occupant has reached the exterior of the building, all the criteria for safety as provided by the public way definition are met. There is no need to project the exit path indefinitely to the street because safety from a hazard within the building has been attained.

3. Figure 7-13. A retail store, Group B, Division 2 Occupancy is located in a shopping center with parking lots and streets completely surrounding the center. The store has direct exiting to the center's sidewalk that surrounds the retail areas. At intervals, to facilitate shopping carts, the sidewalk curbs are ramped to the parking lot pavement. The termination of the retail store exit path is the exit door from the store to the sidewalk/parking lot because that is the point at which the store's clients and personnel leave the building or structure and because the parking lot and the sidewalk meet the public way definition of Section 3301 (b). Furthermore, once outside the store, one has escaped from the store's hazardous situation that necessitated the use of the exit path.

In each case, there are two ways to determine the exit path termination:

1. where the exit path leaves the building or structure
2. where the exit path enters a public way or equivalent open space outside the building or structure

If either criterion is met, that is the point of exit termination. Both criteria need not be satisfied.

An exception to this general rule is a stairway that empties into an exit court and then extends via an exit passageway through the building to the public way. See Figure 7-14. The exit court is not dedicated for public use; the exit path requires returning to the building via the exit passageway. Therefore, the exit stairway's entry into the exit court is not the point of the exit termination. The exit path termination is the intersection of the exit passageway and the public way or equivalent open space, i.e., the point the exit path truly leaves the building.

Sec. 3301.

(e) Building Accessibility. In addition to provisions of this chapter, exits which provide access to, or egress from, buildings for persons with disabilities shall also conform with Chapter 31.

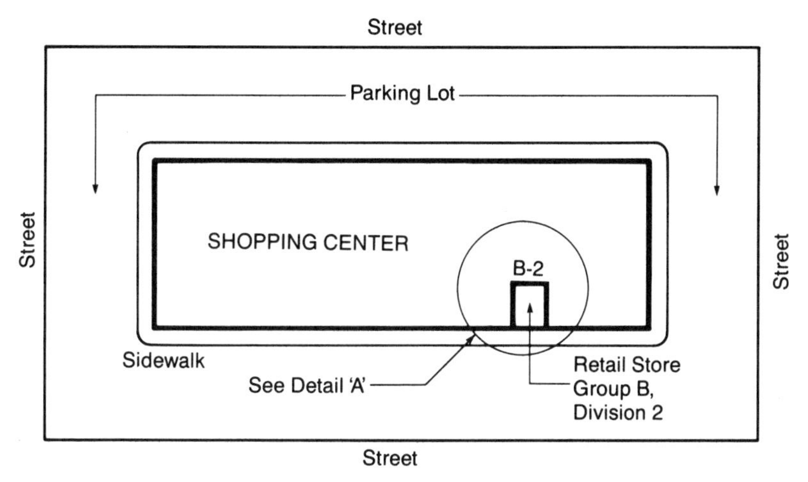

PARKING LOT SITE PLAN – SHOPPING CENTER (NTS)

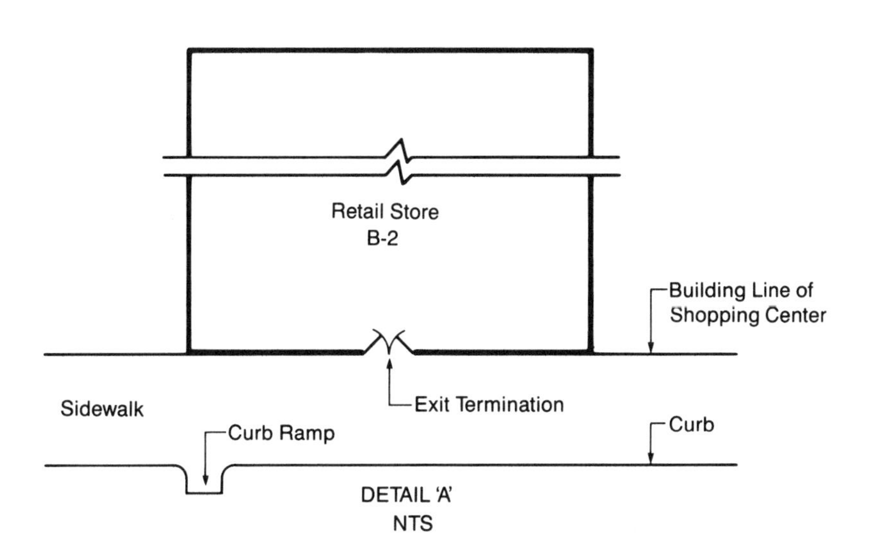

DETAIL 'A'
NTS

REFERENCE: SECTION 3101 (b)

FIGURE 7-13 EXIT TERMINATION – GROUP B, DIVISION 2 OCCUPANCY IN SHOPPING CENTER

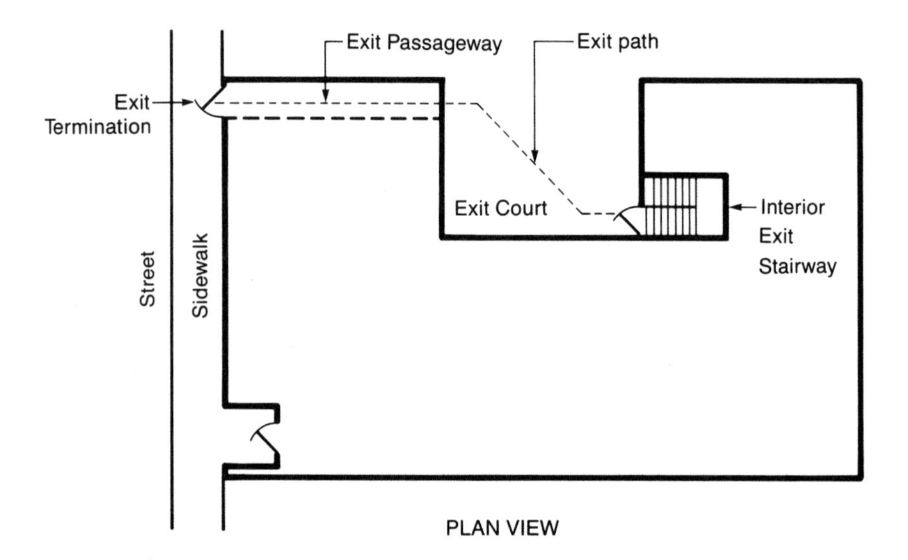

The exit path from the interior exit stairway, in the rear of the building, crosses the exit court and then follows the exit passageway under the front portion of the building. Because the exit passageway is not "unobstructed from the ground to the sky" and is not "deeded, dedicated or otherwise permanently appropriated for public use" it cannot be considered a public way. Therefore, the exit termination of this interior exit stairway is at the street sidewalk where the exit passageway opens onto the street.

REFERENCE: SECTION 3301 (b)

FIGURE 7-14 EXIT TERMINATION WITH EXIT COURT & EXIT PASSAGEWAY

With the enactment of the federal American with Disabilities Act (ADA) in 1990 and the adoption of Chapter 31 to the code, building accessibility for the handicapped has become an important consideration for virtually all buildings. Chapter 31's egress requirements are frequently more restrictive than their counterparts in this chapter. (See the discussion of Chapter 31 in Article 10 of this Guide.) Furthermore, particularly when a retrofit is involved, the provisions of Appendix Chapter 31 should be used when the requirements apply because of a proposed alteration to an existing building. If the locality does not adopt Appendix Chapter 31 provisions, the designer and enforcement official must use Chapter 31 provisions without any means for ameliorating the severe impact of such requirements on an existing building.

Sec. 3301 (f). Yards, Patios and Courts. Yards, patios courts and similar outdoor areas accessible to and usable by the building occupants shall be provided with exits as required by this chapter. The occupant load of such outdoor areas shall be assigned by the building official in accordance with their anticipated use. When outdoor areas are to be used by persons in addition to the occupants of the building, exits from the outdoor areas should be based on the sum of the occupant loads of the building and plus the outdoor areas.

EXCEPTION: 1. Outdoor areas used exclusively for service of the building may have only one exit.

2. Outdoor areas associated with Group R, Division 3 Occupancies.

This is a new provision to the code. It requires exits for outdoor areas. Unless the areas are locked off or otherwise made inaccessible and unusable by the building occupants, the provisions must apply.

This section presumes that all accessible outdoor areas will contain occupant loading. Large open areas may be dictated by the topography or easements or other sources beyond the control of the owner or the designer. The only means of minimizing the exiting provisions rests with the building official. This unfortunately places a severe burden on that official.

The reasoning given for this provision relates to Group A Occupancies, i.e., restaurants. However, the code provision is not occupancy limited.

In the author's opinion, this provision should be limited as to occupancy. The intent of the proponent and the code change committee was with regard to Group A Occupancy and Group B, Division 2 restaurant occupancy. It should not apply to all occupancies as is the present wording. The building official should recognize this and provide relief from an onerous provision of the code. In the event the building official cannot provide that relief, the owner and designer should consider physically limiting access to the outdoor space.

Occupant Load

Sec. 3302. (a) Determination of Occupant Load. In determining the occupant load, all portions of a building shall be presumed to be occupied at the same time.

EXCEPTION: Accessory use areas which ordinarily are used by persons who occupy the main areas of an occupancy shall be provided with exits as though they are completely occupied, but their occupant load need not be included in computing the total occupant load of the building.

The occupant load for buildings or areas containing two or more occupancies shall be determined by adding the occupant loads of the various use areas as computed in accordance with the applicable provisions of this section.

These paragraphs indicate the method for determining the occupant load. The overview of this chapter covered this subject. The example given in this Guide demonstrated how the Group B, Division 2 office occupant load factor was determined from Table No. 33-A.

The Exception for accessory uses does not apply to corridors, toilet facilities, storage areas and other rooms. These public areas are to be included in the occupant load determination.

The third paragraph referenced is of importance in any building with more than one occupancy. A B-2 office building, for example, will usually have within it several other uses. Each of the other areas of use will have its occupant load determined individually and the exit requirements will be initially based on the affect of each occupant load on its space. The aggregate occupant load will then be applied to the rest of the exit path. (See Figure 7-15.)

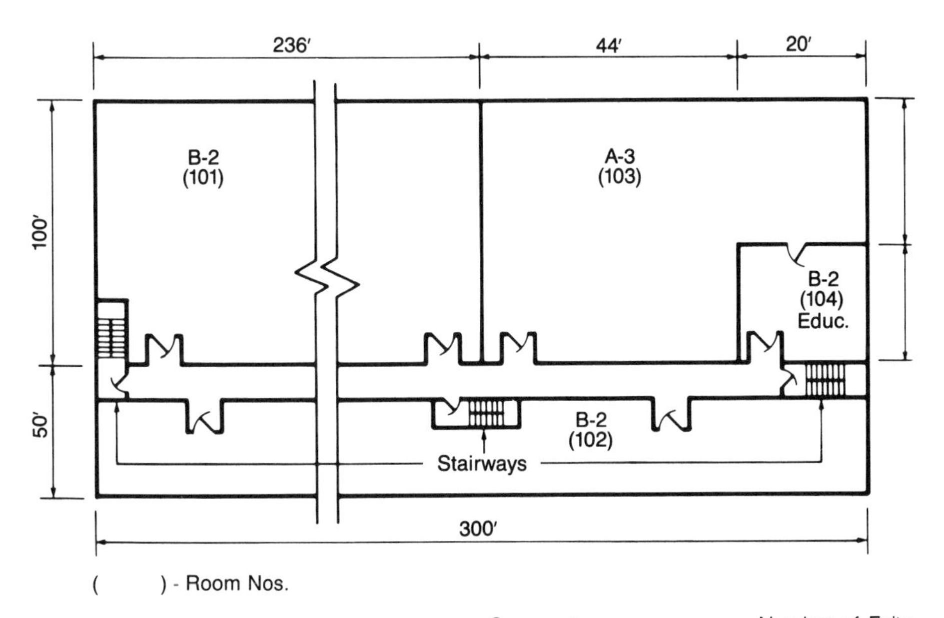

( ) - Room Nos.

Occupancy	Room No.	Size	Area	Occupant Load per Square Foot	Occupant Load	Number of Exits Required From Room or Area
B-2	101	100 x 236	23,600	100	236	2
B-2	102	50 x 300	15,000	100	150	2
A-3	103	44 X 100	4,400	15	294	2
		51 X 20	1,020	15	68	2
B-2 (Education)	104	49 X 20	980	20	49	1
		TOTAL OCCUPANT LOAD =			797	

Three exits are required per Section 3303 (a) for this floor.

REFERENCE: SECTION 3302 (a), 3303 (a) AND TABLE NO. 33-A

FIGURE 7-15 OCCUPANT LOAD CALCULATION

Exits Required

Sec. 3303. (a) Number of Exits. Every building or usable portion thereof shall have at least one exit, not less than two exits where required by Table No. 33-A and additional exits as required by this subsection.

For purposes of this section, basements and occupied roofs shall be provided with exits as required for stories.

EXCEPTION: Occupied roofs on Group R, Division 3 Occupancies may have one exit if such occupied areas are less than 500 square feet and are located no higher than immediately above the second story.

Floors complying with the provisions for mezzanines as specified in Section 1717 shall be provided with exits as specified therein.

The second story shall be provided with not less than two exits when the occupant load is ten or more. Occupants on floors above the second story and in basements shall have access to not less than two separate exits from the floor or basement.

EXCEPTIONS: 1. Two or more dwelling units on the second story may have access to only one common exit when the total occupant load served by that exit does not exceed ten.

2. Except as provided in Table No. 33-A, only one exit need be provided from the second floor or a basement within an individual dwelling unit or a Group R, Division 3 congregate residence.

3. When the third floor within an individual dwelling unit or a Group R, Division 3 congregate residence does not exceed 500 square feet, only one exit need be provided from that floor.

4. Floors and basements used exclusively for service of the building may have one exit. For the purposes of this exception, storage rooms, laundry rooms, maintenance offices and similar uses shall not be considered as providing service to the building.

5. Storage rooms, laundry rooms and maintenance offices not exceeding 300 square feet in floor area may be provided with only one exit.

6. Elevator lobbies may have one exit provided the use of such exit does not require keys, tools, special knowledge or effort.

Every story or portion thereof having an occupant load of 501 to 1000 shall have not less than three exits.

Every story or portion thereof having an occupant load of 1000 or more shall have not less than four exits.

The number of exits required from any story of a building shall be determined by using the occupant load of that story plus the percentages of the occupant loads of floors which exit into the level under consideration as follows:

1. Fifty percent of the occupant load in the first adjacent story above and the first adjacent story below, when a story below exits through the level under consideration.

2. Twenty-five percent of the occupant load in the story immediately beyond the first adjacent story.

The maximum number of exits required for any story shall be maintained until egress is provided from the structure. (See Section 3311.)

The first paragraph of Section 3303 (a) states the basic proviso, discussed earlier, that there be at least two exits provided in most buildings. The intent is that if one exit is blocked or otherwise not usable the other should be available. This requirement is invoked by the code:

- in the fourth paragraph, based on occupant load, which is determined by the area and occupancy of the floor in question and
- in the fifth paragraph, based on the height of the building.

The requirements are specific in these paragraphs and their Exceptions. The second floor of a building must have two exits when the occupant load exceeds 10, with the Exceptions for the special cases noted. For a building with a B-2 (office) occupancy, this exit requirement will apply when the floor area exceeds 1,000 square feet, and for a R-1 (multiple residential) use when the floor area exceeds 2,000 square feet.

According to Table No. 33-A, any building with an aggregate occupant load of more than 10 for the occupancies on the second floor must have two exits from the second floor. Any floor above the second must have two exits as stated in the fifth paragraph of this section. The Exceptions to the fifth paragraph are special cases for low occupant load uses.

The general rule is that regardless of the size of the floor, there must be two exits for all floors above the second.

Unusual situations can arise as a result of using only these criteria.

For example, if an R-1 building has 1,500 square feet per floor, only the third floor must have two exits. The second floor, by these criteria alone, need only have one exit. This determination is based on the occupant load of the second floor being 8 (1500/200 = 7.5 occupants or 8 in whole numbers).

However, the provisions of the ninth paragraph of this section also apply. This paragraph requires the number of exits to be determined by the occupant load on a particular floor plus one-half the occupant load from the floor directly above, when that occupant load exits into the floor in question. Thus, if the stairway from the third floor exits into the second floor, the second floor will need two exits because the total occupant load on the second floor will be (8 + 8/2) = 12. Because this number exceeds 10, the two exits are needed. (See Figure 7-16.)

If the general floor area was 1,200 square feet, the second and third

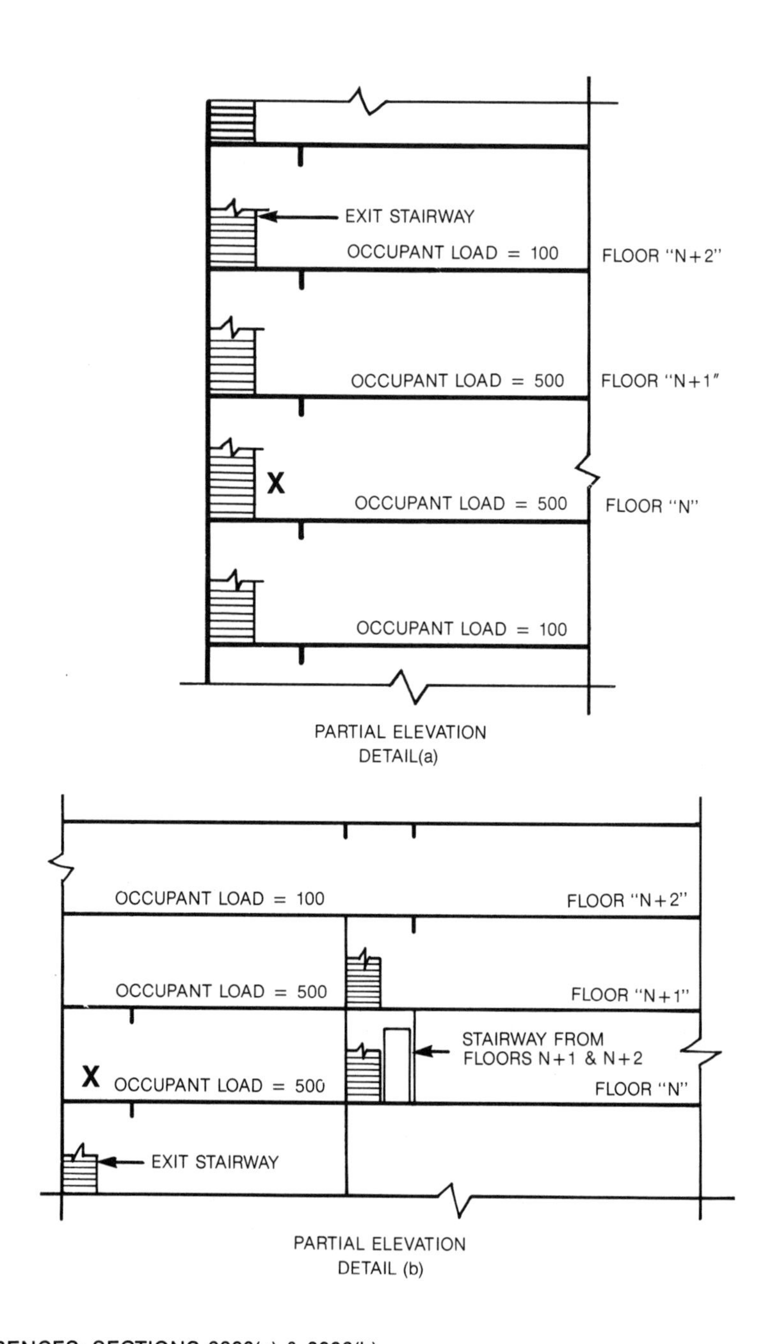

REFERENCES: SECTIONS 3303(a) & 3303(b)

FIGURE 7-16 NUMBER OF EXIT STAIRWAYS REQUIRED, COMPARISON OF 1985 AND 1991 UBC

floors would each have an occupant load of 6 (1200/200 = 6). If the stairway from the third floor exits into the second floor, the total occupant load at the second floor would be (6 + 6/2) = 9. The second floor would then require only one exit; the third floor would still require two exits because of the general exiting rule as stated in paragraph 5 of this section.

NOTE: The escape window required in Section 1204 cannot substitute for one of the required exits. Such windows are in addition to the number of exits required by the other provisions of Chapter 33.

The designer should be aware of all these criteria and their applications. If the third-floor stairway exits into the second floor, the occupant loads of both floors must be considered, even if the occupant load of the second floor alone warrants only one exit. This is a commonly overlooked exiting provision. (See Figure 7-17.)

The determination of the number of exits required for a given story is based, in part, on the number of occupants that will be on that floor plus one-half the occupant load from the adjacent floors that exit through the floor in question. If there are additional floors above these, 25 percent of the next adjacent floor's occupant load is also added if that floor exits through the floor in question. The deciding factor is whether the adjacent floors exit through or bypass the floor in question.

The aggregation of the contributing occupant load from the adjacent floors is not required for determining the number of exit stairways on a floor, unless that tributary occupant load enters the floor in question. Up to 1988, the number of exits was calculated using the occupant loads of the tributary floors and the floor in question, even if the occupant loads from adjacent floors passed only through the stairwell of the subject floor. The difference between the present and codes prior to the 1988 UBC is best illustrated by an example under each code's provisions. (See Figure 7-18.)

Figure 7-18 shows a partial vertical cross-section of an exit stairway and the adjacent exit corridors. The 1988 UBC calculation method for the number of exit stairways required was as follows (note that the occupant loads on each floor have already been calculated based on the occupancies thereon):

The determination to be made is whether there is a combination of

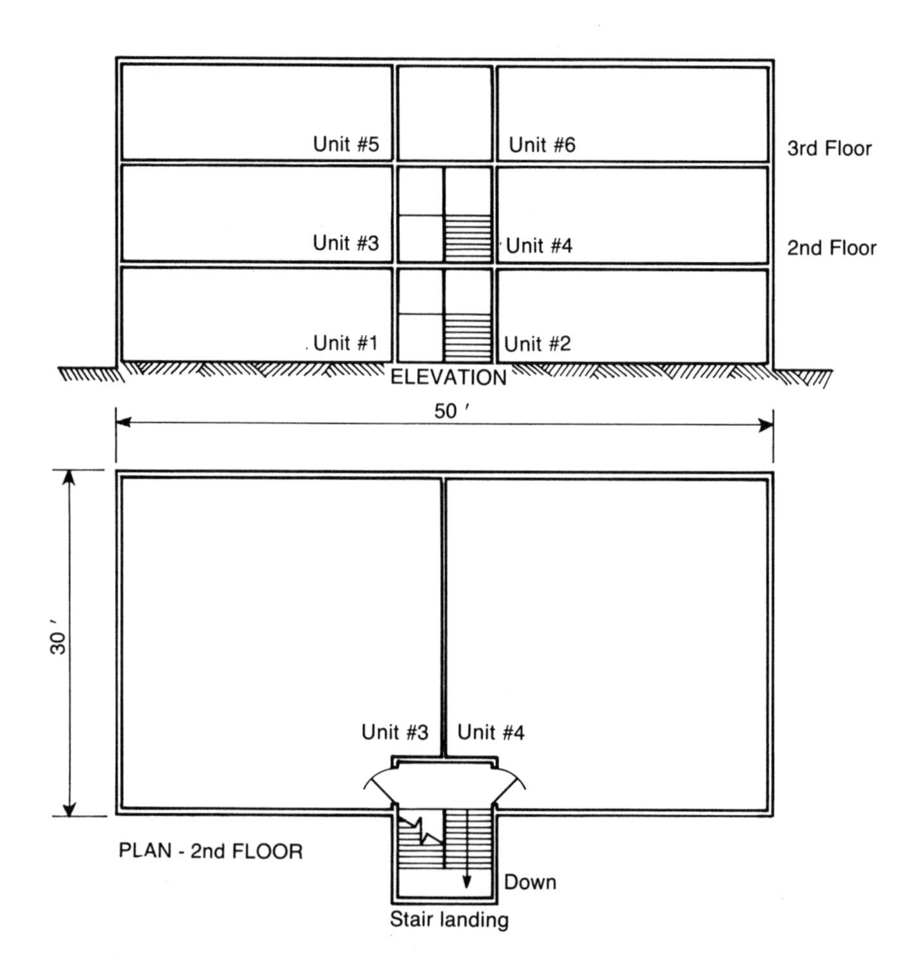

Occupant load 2nd & 3rd Floors = 30 × 50 = 1500 S.F each.

@200 S.F./person = 7.5, use 8 occupants each floor

Total occupant load at 2nd floor:

100 % of 2nd floor	=	7.5	or	8	
50 % of 3rd floor	=	3.75	or	4	
		11.25		12	occupants

REFERENCE: SECTION 3303 (a)

FIGURE 7-17 EXIT CALCULATIONS, SMALL R-1 OCCUPANCY BUILDING

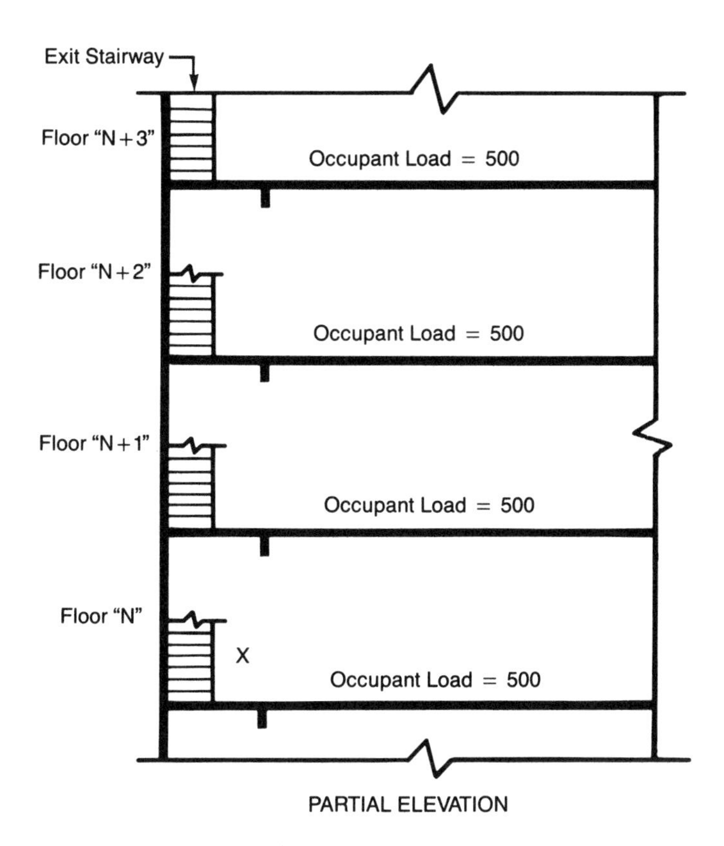

PARTIAL ELEVATION

COMPARISON OF EXIT CALCULATIONS

	1988 UBC	1991
CORRIDOR on any floor	500/50 = 10′	500 x .2 = 100″ = 9′-4″
STAIR @ "N+3" (Assume no occupant load from "N+4")	500/50 = 10′	500 x .3 = 150″ = 12′-6″
STAIR @ "N+2"	(500+250)/50 = 15′	500 x .3 = 150″ = 12′-6″
STAIR @ "N+1"	$\frac{(500+250+125)}{50}$ = 17′-6″	500 x .3 = 150″ = 12′-6″
STAIR @ "N"	= 17′-6″	500 x .3 = 150″ = 12′-6″

REFERENCE: SECTION 3303 (b)

FIGURE 7-18 EXIT WIDTH CALCULATIONS – COMPARISON OLD VS PRESENT PROVISIONS

occupant loads on a floor "N" plus its tributary occupant loads from floors "N + 1" and "N + 2" that would require a larger number of exit stairways, per the ninth paragraph of Section 3303 (a) 1988 UBC. If the aggregate occupant load exceeds 500, three exits stairways are required. Under the codes prior to 1988, the point at which the calculation is to be made is shown by the bold "X" in Figure 7-18.

The resultant calculation on floor "N" at point "X," using the 1988 UBC Section 3303 (a) ninth paragraph is:

Floor "N" occupant load 500	Contribution @ Point "X" =	500
Floor "N + 1" occupant load 500	Contribution @ Point "X" =	250
Floor "N + 2" occupant load 100	Contribution @ Point "X" =	25
	Total occupant load Point "X" =	775

Therefore, per Section 3303 (a) seventh paragraph, with an aggregate occupant load of more than 500 but not exceeding 3,000, three exits were required. The total width of the three exits was to be at least 775/50 = 15.5 linear feet.

Figure 7-16 Detail (b) shows the configuration of the adjacent floor exit ways to floor "N" for the same calculations to apply under the present UBC provisions. Note that floors "N + 1" and "N + 2" exit onto floor "N." Thus, the stairs from these adjacent floors do not continue to the ground, and the stairway from floor "N" does not necessarily extend to floors "N + 1" and "N + 2." For floor "N" three exit stairways are required, with an aggregate width of 15.5 linear feet.

Assume, however, that the Figure 7-18 applies to the building in question under the present UBC provision. In this case, the occupant load for the number of exit stairway calculations at point "X" is only that from floor "N," because the occupant loads from the adjacent floors do not exit into floor "N." Thus, the calculation of the number of stairways for floor "N" with an aggregate occupant load of 500 requires only two stairways.

The aggregate width of these exit stairways must be determined using the method in Section 3303 (b), which uses "the occupant loads of floors that exit through the level under consideration."

Because of the difference between the two terms, that of the number of exits being "the occupant loads of floors that exit into the level under consideration" and the one cited herein for the width of the exits, there must be two methods used for the calculations.

The resultant width for the two exits required in the last example is 775/50 = 15.5 linear feet, because that is the aggregate tributary load passing through point "X."

This new provision is an important one for the code, from both a practical point of view and for its effect on the intent of the code. Only the number of exits is affected. The width of the required exits still must consider the effect of "friction" the occupants from the adjacent floors create on those on the floor in question.

When there are mixed occupancies in the building, the calculation of the occupant load must be made for each floor, using the appropriate occupant load factor from Table No. 33-A for each area of the floor and building. The occupant load must be aggregated per floor and for the adjacent contributing floors in the manner described above.

As was discussed with regard to Section 3302 (a)3, the occupant load is the aggregate of the incremental percentages of occupant loads for each area and use. All parts of a floor are considered in this determination, including corridors, stairways and storage rooms. The corridors and other spaces are considered to be of the same occupancy classification as the primary occupancy of the floor.

Exits Required.

Sec. 3303. (b) Width. The total width of exits in inches shall not be less than the total occupant load served by an exit multiplied by 0.3 for stairways and 0.2 for other exits nor less than specified elsewhere in this code. Such width of exits shall be divided approximately equally among separate exits.

The maximum exit width required from any story of a building shall be maintained.

This section and four other sections, Section 3305 (b), 3306 (b), 3307 (b) and 3321 (c), have all been changed to use a new method of calculating the width of the required exit.

The prior codes used a constant divisor of 50 for the occupant load to obtain the minimum required width in feet for all elements of the exit path. For example, if the occupant load is 300, the required width is 300/50 = 6 feet. This width would apply to corridors, doorways and stairways. The only increase in width is due to the cascade effect in stairways serving several floors.

Section 3303 (b) provides two numerical constants to be multiplied by the occupant load to obtain the minimum required width of exits in inches. The factors are 0.3 for stairs and 0.2 for level or ramped exit ways. The reason for the different constants is that the speed of travel on stairways is assumed to be 50 percent slower than on level or ramped surfaces due to the forced reduction in stride on a stairway as contrasted with the full stride permitted on level or ramped surfaces.

The comparable constant multiplier under the prior code was 12 inches/50 = 0.24.

The cascade effect previously contained in the third sentence of the first paragraph of Section 3303 (b) was deleted because the factor of 0.3 for stairways is almost 30 percent more than the prior code's equivalent width factor of 0.24. Thus, the stairs are wider. Although this increased width does provide some rationale for the omission of the cascading effect, that rationale uses the increased width for both the slow-down caused by the shorter stride on a stair and for the cascade effect.

The provisions are based on the following assumptions:

- The egress flow-time for comparing level surfaces and stairways is 3.5 minutes.
- The single width required for an occupant is 22 inches.
- The number of occupants passing a given point is 100 on level or ramped surfaces.
- The number of occupants passing a given point is 75 on stairs.

These assumptions are based on empirical and theoretical conclusions. Any change in any assumption would substantially alter the resultant factor. For example, the 75-occupant figure for the stairway is up from 60 occupants previously used, increased as a result of the 7:11 stair riser-to-run ratio.

In a 44-inch-wide corridor, 44/0.2 = 220 persons would move past a given point every 3.5 minutes. Using the same 44-inch minimum width of a stairway, 44/0.3 = 147 persons would move past a point on the stairway every 3.5 minutes. Therefore, for an even exit flow, the stairway must be wider to accommodate the occupant load without considering any cascading occupant flow in the stairway.

Thus, for the 300 occupants in our example, the new provisions require a stairway width to be 300 x 0.3 = 90 inches or 7 feet 6 inches. The level or ramped surface exit way must be 300 x 0.2 = 60 inches or 5 feet wide. Under prior codes, the level and ramped surface and the stairways ignoring the cascade effect were all required to be 300/50 = 6 feet wide. See Figure 7-18 for comparisons of the calculations based on the 1988 UBC and on the present provisions.

In our example, assuming the same occupant load on all floors of the building, the cascading effect would have required a stairway width of (100 percent + 50 percent + 25 percent) = 1.75 x 300/50 = 10 feet 6 inches. Therefore, the new provisions reduce the level or ramped exit way widths by 20 percent and the stairway widths by 33 percent. The provision attempts to achieve a balance in the exiting flow, but ignores the cascade effect. (See Figure 7-18.)

A similar end result for balanced exit flow, which could provide wider exits and thus accommodate more persons, would be to use a 0.24 factor for the level or ramped surfaces from the prior code and a new 0.36 factor for stairways.

In our example, the widths would be 300 x 0.24 = 72 inches or 6 feet for level or ramped surfaces and 300 x 0.24 x 1.5 = 108 inches or 9 feet for stairways. This stairway width would be less than that calculated in the prior codes, but would provide the consistency in the exit flow that is at the heart of the code change intent.

> In the author's opinion, due to the omission of the cascading effect and other objections raised during the code hearings, this change will undergo further revision.

A comparison of the prior code and the present code provisions for the minimum exit width and for certain other occupant loads follows:

When the occupant load in a story is not more than 183, the prior code required the minimum 44-inch width.

183/50 = 3.67 feet = 44 inches

The same minimum 44-inch width under the present provisions occurs when the occupant load is 220:

44/0.2 = 220 occupants

Therefore, for all occupant loads that exceed 183 on a floor, the present provisions will result in the lesser width of exit.

The 44-inch minimum width of a stair serving only one floor would be required for 183 occupants per the prior codes. For a stairway serving two floors of equal occupant loads, because of the cascade effect, a 44-inch stair width can serve 122 occupants per floor:

122 + 122/2 = 189/50 = 3.66 feet = 44 inches

Under the present provisions, without the cascading factor the occupant load served by the 44-inch minimum requirement would permit 147 occupants on each floor of the building:

44/0.30 = 147

Therefore, the present provisions will result in a substantial lesser required exit width for stairways.

COMPARISON OF EXIT CALCULATIONS
(in inches)

OCCUPANT LOAD/FLOOR	ON A FLOOR		IN A STAIRWAY			
	1988 UBC	1991 UBC	1988 UBC			1991 UBC
			1 STORY	2 STORY	3 STORY	ANY # of STORIES
200	48	44 (min.)	48	72	84	60
300	72	60	72	108	126	90
400	96	80	96	144	168	120
500	120	100	120	180	210	150

Sec. 3303.

(c). Arrangement of Exits. If only two exits are required, they shall be placed a distance apart equal to not less than one-half of the length of the maximum overall diagonal dimension of the building or area to be served measured in a straight line between exits.

EXCEPTION: Exit separations may be measured along a direct line of travel within an exit corridor when exit enclosures are provided as a portion of the required exit and are interconnected by a one-hour fire-resistive corridor conforming to the requirements of Section 3305. Enclosure walls shall be not less than 30 feet apart at any point in a direct line of measurement.

When three or more exits are required, at least two exits shall be placed a distance apart equal to not less than one-half of the length of the maximum overall diagonal dimension of the building or area to be served measured in a straight line between exits, and additional exits shall be arranged a reasonable distance apart so that if one becomes blocked the others will be available.

When two or more exits are required, they must be separated by a distance equal to at least one-half the length of the diagonal of the area served, to assure that there will be an exit available in most circumstances. The Exception allows the separation to be measured along the corridor connecting two exit enclosures. This is the case of the typical protected exit corridor that runs between two exit stairway enclosures. (See Figure 7-19.)

There is a considerable difference in the method used to measure the distance between the exits when they are located within a room or space versus those accessed by an exit corridor. This difference limits the exposure of a person in the possible fire origination room or space and is done by requiring the separation of the exits within a room or space to be measured by the shortest means, i.e., along a straight line.

On the other hand, when there is protection provided, such as in the Exception via a protected exit corridor, the actual line of travel in the corridor can be used. This is permitted, regardless of the number of twists and turns in the corridor, so long as the minimum separation required is achieved and the maximum travel distance allowed is not exceeded.

The Exception has been clarified to limit the measurement between exits, which may be made along a corridor only when that corridor is of at least one-hour fire-resistive construction. The reference to Section 3305 deletes the previous specific citation of Section 3305 (g). This was done to reflect that the provisions of both Sections 3305 (g) and (h) apply when this Exception is used.

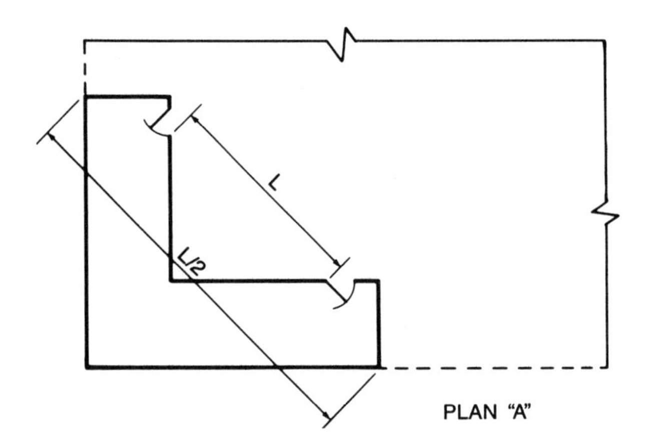

PLAN "A"
This is a common corner configuration for a building's partial floor. In all these examples only a portion of a building may be shown. The concept remains the same whether for a portion of a floor or the entire floor. The exits have to be separated by not less than one-half the length of the longest diagonal of the area served.

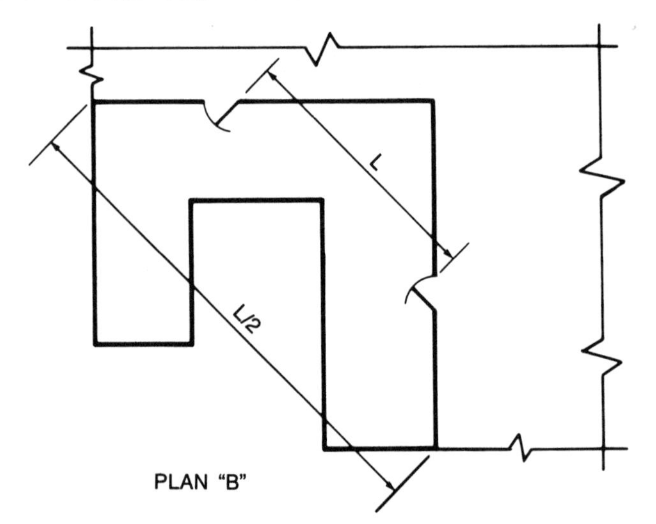

PLAN "B"
The shape of the area for which the separation of exits is to be determined can surround space outside the area under consideration. The length of the longest diagonal may extend through the outside space. Thus, the measurement is unchanged by the configuration or the presence of outside space. The method remains the same, i.e., the longest diagonal is used.

REFERENCE: SECTION 3303 (c)

FIGURE 7-19 CALCULATION OF SEPARATION OF EXITS FOR IRREGULARLY SHAPED SPACES

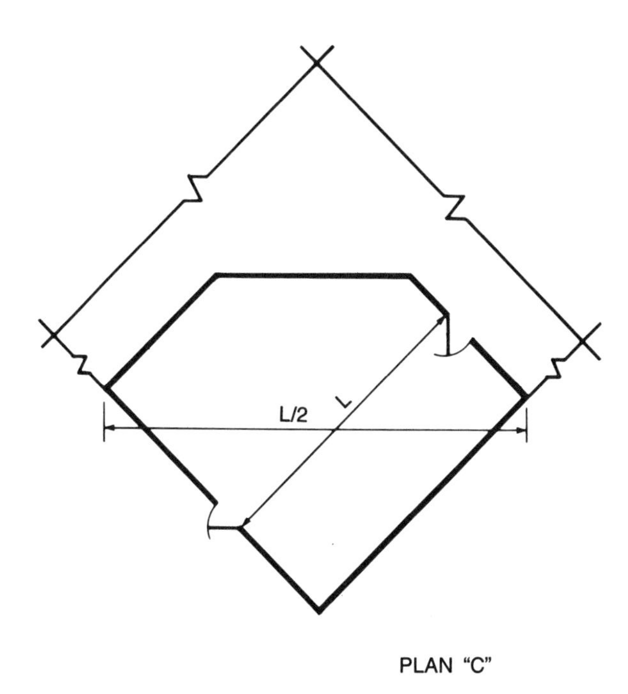

PLAN "C"

PLAN "C"
When the area served is irregular, with more than four sides, the longest diagonal must be used to determine the required separation of the exits.

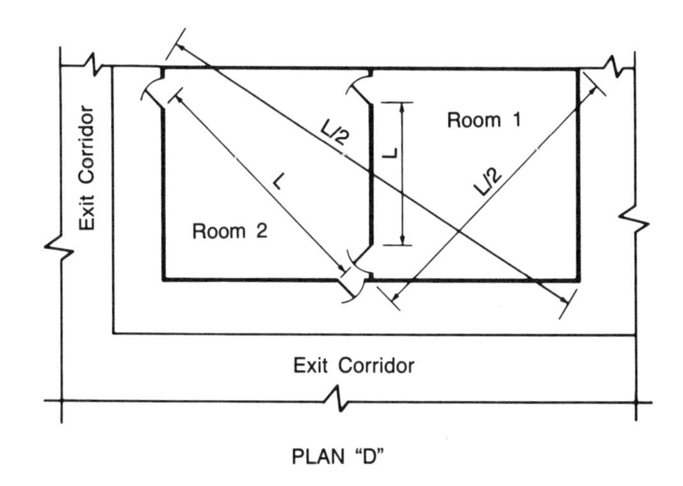

PLAN "D"

PLAN "D"
Room 1 exits into Room 2. In Room 1 the separation of exits has to use its longest diagonal of the room as the area served. The Room 2 measurement of the separation of the exits has to include the Room 1 space because it is part of the area served.

The intent of the change is to prevent the use of any Section 3305 (g) Exceptions to the one-hour fire-resistive construction requirement for the measurement along a corridor. In addition, the measurement along the corridor would not be permitted when the occupant loads stated in the first paragraph of Section 3305 (g) are not exceeded; i.e., a one-hour fire-resistive corridor is not required when the occupant load in a Group R, Division 1 Occupancy or Group I Occupancy is less than 10, or less than 30 for other occupancies. In these instances the measurement along the corridor would not be permitted unless the corridor was of one-hour fire-resistive construction even though it need not be so constructed otherwise.

In the author's opinion, the Exception is now overly restrictive because each of the Exceptions to the one-hour requirement is at least equal in life safety protection to the one-hour corridor. This change infers that the Exceptions are not valid equivalents to the one-hour requirement. If this is the case, then there is an unusual code conflict created between the two Exceptions.

The last sentence of the Exception requires that the stairway enclosures be at least 30 feet apart, thereby prohibiting the use of so-called scissor stair arrangements. Scissor stairs are two stairway enclosures that are constructed with a common wall between the enclosures. Access to one enclosure is opposite the other. When viewed from the side, the stair flights from any story cross each other, giving the appearance of open scissors. (See Figure 7-3.)

The last paragraph of this section clearly states the code's basic intent previously discussed in this Guide: redundancy in the exiting is desired so that if one is blocked, the other(s) will be available.

It is the author's opinion that when two exits are required and must be separated, the intent is based on the same concept of redundancy: attempting to separate the exits so that one incident will not eliminate both means of egress.

Real-world experiences one often encounters provide more than sufficient justification for the code writers feet concern that there be separate ways to exit a building. In modern urban areas it is not unusual for an arsonist to torch a stairway of a building as an act of anger directed toward a building's tenant or owner. Although it is possible for arsonists to place flammable liquids in more than one stairway, fortunately, they usually do so only to the stairway they associate with the object of their anger. It is for this type of situation, whether it be from arson or accident, that the separation of exits is an essential part of the code.

Sec. 3303.

(d) Distance to Exits. The maximum distance of travel from any point to an exterior exit door, horizontal exit, exit passageway or an enclosed stairway in a building not equipped with an automatic sprinkler system throughout shall not exceed 150 feet, or 200 feet in a building equipped with an automatic sprinkler system throughout. These distances may be increased by a maximum 100 feet when the increased travel distance is the last portion of the travel distance and is entirely within a one-hour fire-resistive corridor complying with Section 3305. See Section 3319 for Group E Occupancy and Section 3320 for Group H Occupancy travel distances.

See Section 3339 for Group E Occupancy and Section 3320 for Group H Occupancy travel distances.

In a one-story Group B, Division 4 Occupancy classified as a factory or warehouse and in one-story airplane hangars, the exit travel distance may be increased to 400 feet if the building is equipped with an automatic sprinkler system throughout and provided with smoke and heat ventilation as specified in Section 3206. In an open parking garage, as defined in Section 709, the exit travel distance may be increased to 250 feet which may be measured to open stairways which are permitted in accordance with Section 3309 (a).

The distance to an exit, or the travel distance (as it is generally referred to in most code discussions), may have two components and thereby exceed the commonly prescribed limitations. The general limit to travel distance is 150 feet, but can be extended to 200 feet for fully sprinklered buildings.

When the travel path includes a length of fire-protected exit corridor, the allowable travel distance may be increased by 100 feet to an aggregate of 250 feet, provided 150 feet of the travel length is in the protected corridor. Thus, the total allowable travel distances would be 100 feet within the room or space and 150 feet within the protected exit corridor for the general type of occupancy in an unsprinklered building. In a fully sprinklered building, the allowable travel distances are 150 feet in the room or area and 150 feet in the protected corridor, for a total of 300 feet. (See Figures 7-3 and 7-4.)

For Group H Occupancies, there is a special limitation of 300 feet to this bonus provision. This section now specifically requires that the last portion of the travel distance has to be within a one-hour fire-resistive corridor if the bonus provision is to be used. The intent of the code exiting concept is that one travels from one location to another to gain increased safety. Thus, the bonus distance of 100 feet must provide greater safety than the general travel distance of 150 feet, which may be unprotected.

Symbolically, Section 3303 (d) provisions can be as shown in Figure 7-20.

The use of the bonus distance, together with the general travel distance, is shown in Figures 7-21 and 7-22 for two examples. In one example the travel is within one tenant space, with the enclosed exit stairways directly accessible therein.

In the second example, the access to the enclosed exit stairway requires leaving the tenant space. In the one-tenant-space example, the travel paths are considerably variable. Therefore, only two possible paths are illustrated: one within aisles defined by furnishings and the other without such a defined path, i.e., an empty loft area.

In this example a variation would be to construct a portion of the exit path as a one-hour fire-resistive corridor. See example 1 (b) in Figure 7-21.

Sec. 3303.

(e) Exits Through Adjoining Rooms. Rooms may have one exit through an adjoining or intervening room which provides a direct, obvious and unobstructed means of travel to an exit corridor, exit enclosure or until egress is provided from the building, provided the total distance of travel does not exceed that permitted by other provisions of this code. In other than dwelling units, exits shall not pass through kitchens, store rooms, rest rooms, closets or spaces used for similar purposes.

EXCEPTIONS; 1. Rooms within dwelling units may exit through more than one intervening room.

2. Rooms with a cumulative occupant load of 10 or less may exit through more than one intervening room.

Foyers, lobbies and reception rooms constructed as required for corridors shall not be construed as intervening rooms.

One intent of this section is to allow smaller rooms adjoining a large space to exit through that space so that an exit corridor or other exiting element can be reached. This section permits offices and other rooms to exit through one other office or space to an acceptable exit facility.

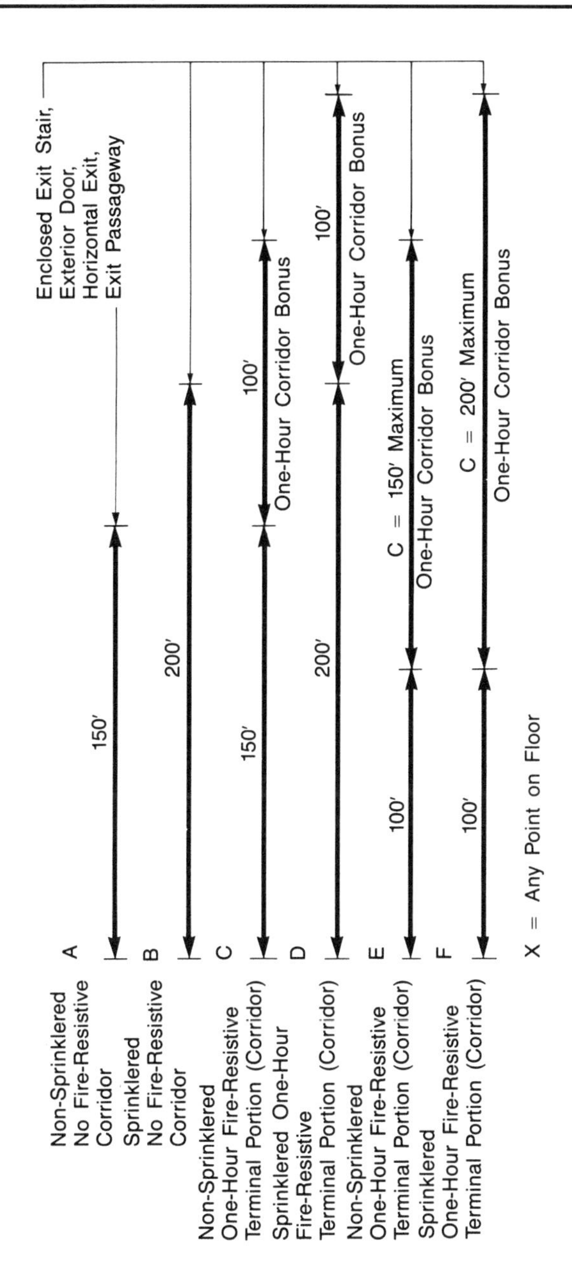

NOTE: E and F are examples of alternative arrangements of travel distances with protected and unprotected segments.

REFERENCE: SECTION 3303 (d)

FIGURE 7-20 TRAVEL DISTANCE SYMBOLICALLY ILLUSTRATED

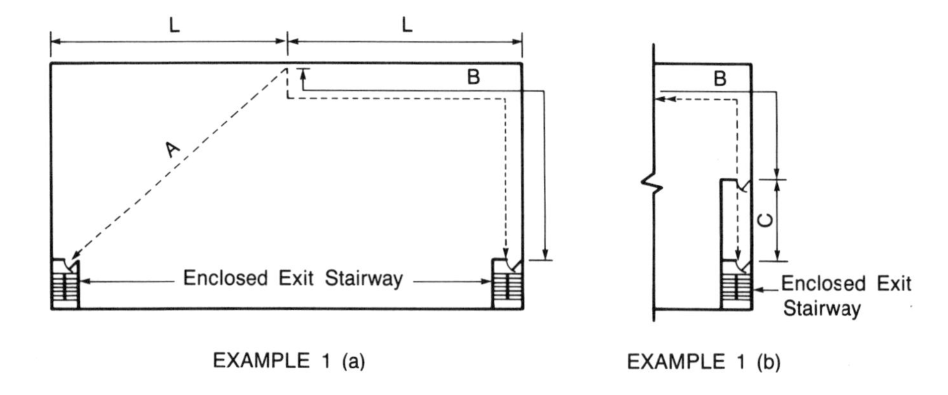

EXAMPLE 1 (a)

EXAMPLE 1 (b)

A = Travel distance assuming no obstructions, unprotected path of travel

B = Travel distance assuming desks, low partitions, etc. define specific path of travel; unprotected path of travel

C = Travel distance within one-hour fire-resistive corridor per Section 3305 (d). If A or B = 150 feet, maximum value of C = 100 feet.

Maximum travel distance, A or B = 150 feet, unsprinklered building

Maximum travel distance, A or B = 200 feet, sprinklered building

A + C, or B + C } ≤ 250 in unsprinklered building

A + C, or B + C } ≤ 300 in sprinklered building

For additional explanatory material, see Figure 7-22

REFERENCE: SECTION 3303 (d) and SECTION 3305 (h)

FIGURE 7-21 TRAVEL DISTANCE MEASUREMENTS, OPEN PLAN SPACE AND BONUS DISTANCE CONSIDERATIONS FOR ONE-HOUR FIRE-RESISTIVE CORRIDOR

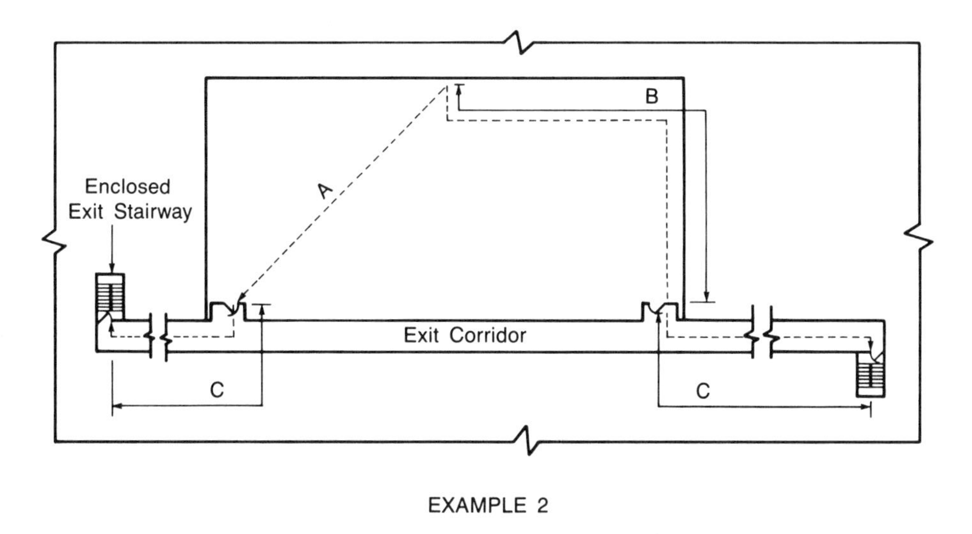

EXAMPLE 2

OPEN FLOOR PLAN—EXIT STAIRS DIRECTLY ACCESSIBLE WITHIN TENANT SPACE

TRAVEL PATH REQUIRES ENTRY INTO ONE-HOUR FIRE-RESISTIVE CORRIDOR

If A or B is less than 150 feet, C can be increased accordingly to provide the aggregate lengths that do not exceed 250 feet and 300 feet.

C must not exceed the 150 feet or 200 feet limiting factors. The reason for this goes back to the original intent of the bonus provision. That intent was to encourage the use of the fire-resistive corridors and to do so by not counting the travel distance within the room or space that exits into the corridor against the 150 feet and 200 feet limiting factor.

The distance within that room or space was not to exceed 100 feet for this intent to be used. Although the text has changed from the original, the intent has remained the same and should be applied for the use of this code provision

For additional explanatory material, see Figure 7-21

REFERENCE: SECTION 3303 (d) and SECTION 3305 (h)

FIGURE 7-22 TRAVEL DISTANCE WITH ENTRY INTO EXIT CORRIDOR OUTSIDE OF TENANCY

If the smaller room is large enough to require two exits, only one of its two exits can pass through the larger room. Only one intervening room can be crossed by this exit path from the smaller room unless permitted by Exception #2. (See Figure 7-23.)

Section 3305 (c) clearly indicates that one can go from one room through another to reach one of the cited exit facilities. It should be understood that once in an exit enclosure facility, such as a exit stairway enclosure, one cannot leave that level of protection and go through a room to reach another exit facility or leave the building. One must remain in the protected enclosure until the exterior of the building has been reached.

To reiterate what is stated in the first sentence of this section, one must be protected "until egress is provided from the building."

Doors.

Sec. 3304.

(a) General. This section shall apply to every exit door serving an area having an occupant load of 10 or more, or serving hazardous rooms or areas, except that Subsections (c), (i), (j) and (k) shall apply to all exit doors regardless of occupant load. Buildings or structures used for human occupancy shall have at least one exterior door that meets the requirements of Subsection (f). Doors and landings at doors which are located within an accessible route of travel shall also comply with Chapter 31.

Section 3304 (a) applies to exit doors for all rooms or spaces with an occupant load of 10 or more. It should be noted that only exit doors are subject to the requirements of this section. Other doors are not regulated.

For example, a B-2 Occupancy, by Table No. 33-A, has an occupant load of 100 square feet per occupant. The exit doors for a room or space that exceeds 999 square feet must comply with the provisions of Section 3304 (1000/100) = 10.

Sec. 3304.

(b) Swing and Opening Force. Exit doors shall be pivoted or side-hinged swinging type. Exit doors shall swing in the direction of exit travel when serving any hazardous area or when serving an occupant load of 50 or more. The door latch shall release when subjected to a 15-pound force, and the door shall be set in motion when subject to a 30-pound force. The door shall swing to full-open position when subjected to a 15-pound force. Forces shall be applied to the latch side. See Section 4507 for doors swinging over public property.

Double-acting doors shall not be used as exits when any of the following conditions exist:

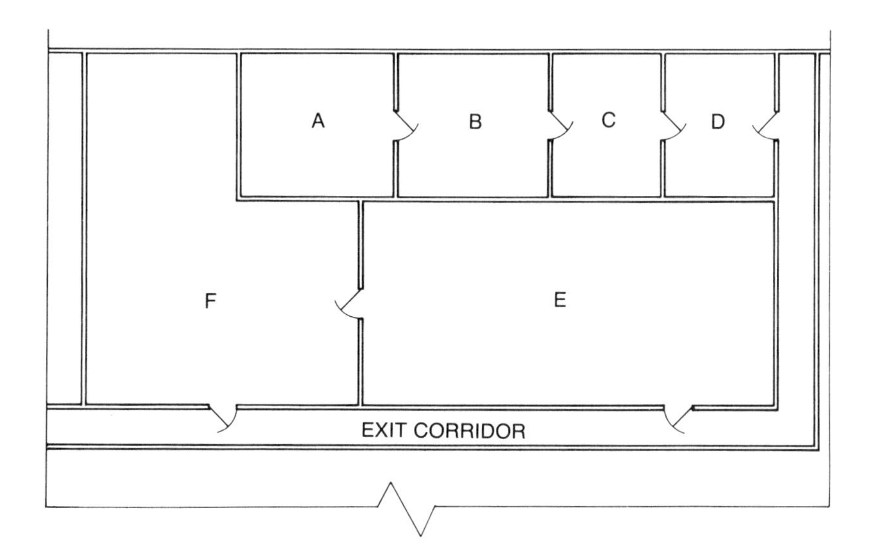

The code permits rooms with a total occupant load of 10 or less to exit through one or more intervening rooms before reaching an exit corridor, enclosure or the exterior. When there are 2 exits required due to the occupant load per Table No. 33-A, one of these exits can go through one intervening room before reaching an exit corridor, enclosure or the exterior; the other exit has to be directly to an exit corridor, enclosure or the exterior.

In the above detail, assuming room A, B, C & D each have occupant loads of two (rooms are less than 200 sq. ft.), A can exit through B, then through C and D and finally to the exit corridor.

If, however, the occupant load in each room were 5, A + B = 10, then the occupant load of rooms A + B can only exit through one intervening room to the corridor. Either A or B would need an exit into E. If A exits into E, then B + C + D can exit into the corridor through D and need not connect with E. B + C = 10 and there would only be one intervening room, D, before the corridor.

If the occupant load in room F were large enough to require two exits per Table No. 33-A, one of the exits could be to room E and the other has to be to exit corridor, enclosure or the exterior.

REFERENCE: SECTION 3303 (e)

FIGURE 7-23 EXITS THROUGH ADJOINING ROOMS

1. The occupant load served by the door is 100 or more.
2. The door is part of a fire assembly.
3. The door is part of a smoke-and draft-control assembly.
4. Panic hardware is required or provided on the door.

EXCEPTIONS: 1. Group I, Division 3 Occupancy used as a place of detention.

2. Doors within or serving an individual dwelling unit.

3. Special door conforming with Subsection (h).

A double-acting door shall be provided with a view panel of not less than 200 square inches.

The swing of an exit door must be in the direction of exit travel when the occupant load served by the door exceeds 50. The direction of door swing is also regulated in areas deemed to be hazardous. The term "hazardous " is not defined specifically in the code, but it has been interpreted by ICBO staff to mean any Group H Occupancy area. With no other clarifying code provision, the ICBO's interpretation will be used in this Guide. Therefore, H Occupancies must have all exit doors swing in the direction of exit travel.

Sec. 3304.

(c) Type of Lock or Latch. Exit doors shall be openable from the inside without the use of a key or any special knowledge or effort.

EXCEPTIONS: 1. In Group B Occupancies, key-locking hardware may be used on the main exit when the main exit consists of a single door or a pair of doors if there is a readily visible, durable sign on or adjacent to the door stating THIS DOOR TO REMAIN UNLOCKED DURING BUSINESS HOURS. The sign shall be in letters not less than 1 inch high on a contrasting background. When unlocked, the single door or both leaves of a pair of doors must be free to swing without operation of any latching device. The use of this exception may be revoked by the building official for due cause.

2. Exit doors from individual dwelling units, Group R, Division 3 congregate housing and guest rooms of Group R Occupancies having an occupant load of 10 or less may be provided with a night latch, dead bolt or security chain, provided such devices are openable from the inside without the use of a key or tool and mounted at a height not to exceed 48 inches above the finished floor.

3. In individual dwelling units, a key which will serve as a thumb turn or knob may be used if the key cannot be removed from the lock when the door is locked from the inside.

Manually operated edge-or surface-mounted flush bolts and surface bolts are prohibited. When exit doors are used in pairs and approved automatic flush bolts are used, the door leaf having the automatic flush bolts shall have no door knob or surface-mounted hardware. The unlatching of any leaf shall not require more than one operation.

This section requires doors to be readily openable without resort to special keys or knowledge. The intent is to facilitate egress in emergency situations. History reveals the tragic results of locked doors in fire or other emergencies. In such situations, an exit door must yield to anyone in need of its use.

The normal method of opening a door without keys is by use of a latchset that does not have a keyway, or by "panic hardware." There is at least one other method by which a locked door can be opened in an emergency. The designer should be aware of this method and, if its use is proposed, should obtain prior approval from the enforcement officials.

The method about to be discussed has been used in many situations where, because of the original arrangement or location of the exits, there are intervening rooms or spaces between an existing exit, such as a fire escape, and the main exit corridor. In such situations, the use of a fire alarm-type pull box door release has often been accepted by the enforcement authority.

This release device operates an electric strike in a manner similar to that used by tenants controlling the entry of persons to their apartment building. The door is required to be openable by either:

- the operation of the fire alarm-type pull box which, when activated, cuts off the electric current that keeps the strike in place or
- a power failure in the building, because power failures usually accompany a fire.

This system must be fail-safe. Whenever a fire door is involved, the electric strike must be approved for fail-safe operation by the listing agency, i.e., ULI. At present there is only one such listing and it requires a mortise lock with two latch bolts to be used in connection with a fire door.

There is another release system, similar to the electric strike operation, that uses an electric lock. As stipulated in the discussion of the electric strike, the installation should:

- provide fail-safe operation,
- be listed for fire door installation,
- be operated by a fire alarm-type pull box.

If one of these release systems is to be used, this author recommends another provision should be considered by the designer. This provision is that, on activating the door release, a signal should be generated indicating that access is being gained into the area. This signal should be a burglar alarm-type relayed to a supervising central station.

The burglar alarm signal feature would prevent entry other than for emergency escape purposes. It would provide the tenant with burglar alarm protection, for the entry door, that otherwise did not exist. This benefit could be used as a selling point by the owner to obtain a tenant's permission to use his space for access to an egress facility.

Section 3304

(e) Special Egress Control Devices. When approved by the building official, exit doors in Group B, Division 2 Occupancies may be equipped with approved listed special egress control devices of the time-delay type, provided the building is protected throughout by an approved automatic sprinkler system and an approved automatic smoke or rate-of-rise detection system. Such devices shall conform to all of the following:

1. Automatically deactivate the egress control device upon activation of the sprinkler system or the detection system.

2. Automatically deactivate the egress control device upon loss of electrical power to any one of the following:

A. The egress control device.

B. The smoke detection system.

C. Exit illumination as required by Section 3313.

3. Be capable of being deactivated by a signal from a switch located in an approved location.

4. Initiate an irreversible process which will deactivate the egress control device whenever a manual force of not more than 15 pounds is applied for two seconds to the panic bar or other door-latching hardware. The egress control device shall deactivate within an approved time period not to exceed a total of 15 seconds. The time-delay established for each egress control device shall not be field adjustable.

5. Actuation of the panic bar or other door-latching hardware shall activate an audible signal at the door.

6. The unlatching shall not require more than one operation. A sign shall be provided on the door located above and within 12 inches of the panic bar or other door-latching hardware reading:

KEEP PUSHING. THIS DOOR WILL OPEN IN SECONDS. ALARM WILL SOUND.

Sign letters shall be at least 1 inch in height and shall have a stroke of not less than 1/8-inch.

Regardless of the means of deactivation, relocking of the egress-control device shall be by manual means only at the door.

This new provision to the code allows exit doors in office buildings and other Group B, Division 2 Occupancies to be locked, using special, approved devices. These devices incorporate a time-delay egress control mechanism. The new section describes the characteristics of such an approved device, which are meant to assure the deactivation of the locking function of the egress control device under any of the following circumstances:

- If a sprinkler system or detection system is activated
- If there is power loss to the control device (fail-safe) or to a detection system
- From a remote switch

When someone pushes with a force of 15 pounds for at least two seconds on the latch-releasing hardware

Although the device will not immediately release the door in the last instance cited, the release must occur within 15 seconds of manual initiation.

The ability of someone to activate the latch-releasing hardware is a security concern. The intent of this new provision, though not stated, is to prevent easy and silent egress from the building. To carry out this security intent fully, a closed-circuit TV monitoring camera should be placed so that the security control facility in the building, the remote location referred to above, can observe the door.

Thus, if someone attempted to leave the building with stolen property, or if an unauthorized person was seen leaving an area, the security people could initiate action before the door release activates. The designer should note this security intent and, further, be aware that the door will require manual relocking by the provisions of the last paragraph.

The designer is further cautioned to advise the owner of the limitations attached to the use of this device.

> In the author's opinion, such notification should be in written form and should contain at least the following information:
>
> The use of this device must be carefully controlled, particularly the limitation of the 15-second maximum time delay for the release of the locking device. If this provision is made inoperative, the door will not open and, because this is an exit doorway, a life-threatening situation could develop.

The designer should clearly indicate in the contract documents that liability for maintenance of the device rests with the owner. In the contract with the owner, there should be a hold-harmless provision protecting the designer from any misuse of this device after the building has been finaled.

The fire service must make special note of these special devices and check its operation during each periodic maintenance inspection. As a recommended alternative to relying on such inspections by its staff, the fire service could require that the owner have independent, periodic inspections made by an approved inspector. A stipulation should require the inspector to send the inspection reports directly to the fire department office.

Corridors and Exterior Exit Balconies

Sec. 3305

(a) General. This section shall apply to every corridor serving as a required exit for an occupant load of 10 or more except Subsection (b) shall apply to all corridors. For the purposes of the section, the term "corridor " shall include "exterior exit balconies " and any covered or enclosed exit passageway, including walkways, tunnels and malls. Partitions, rails, counters and similar space dividers not over 5 feet 9 inches in height above the floor shall not be construed to form corridors. Exit corridors shall not be interrupted by intervening rooms.

EXCEPTION: Foyers, lobbies or reception rooms constructed as required for corridors shall not be construed as intervening rooms.

The analysis of Section 3305 (a) includes a general discussion of the corridor problem, particularly with regard to the requirements of Section 3305 (g). Corridors which are located within an accessible route of travel shall also comply with Chapter 31. The main provisions that apply when a passageway serves as the required exit for 10 or more occupants are:

- the width and height restrictions of the passageway,
- limitation of projections into the passageway, and
- dead end limitations.

For Group I Occupancies see Section 3321 (c).

There are no definitions in the code for the terms "aisle" and "corridor", nor does the dictionary provide much help to aid our understanding of these terms. There is a need for clarification of these terms to assure the proper application of this section. The intent of the code is to impose restrictive requirements on a passageway that:

- confines the movement and view of the user and
- serves 10 or more occupants as their required exit path.

Great latitude is afforded the building official in determining the existence of these characteristics. These characteristics will be reviewed and guidance will be provided to assist in the rational application of the code provisions.

The code's concern with corridors is based on its intent to provide protection whenever an exit passage limits the occupant's choice of action and reduces the occupant's awareness of a hazard. In the traditional open plan of an office, for example, an occupant can readily determine the location of a fire in the office space and can accordingly move away from the fire toward a protected exit passageway. If the aisles within the office space are defined by either tall partitions or full-height walls, the occupant's ability to perceive the danger is substantially reduced or eliminated, thereby increasing the hazard to that occupant. This is the rationale behind the code's corridor requirements.

Unfortunately, conditions found in actual buildings obscure the neat corridor distinctions that the code writers desire. For example, let us examine environments other than the office. All enforcement officials accept high-piled storage racks in warehouses and, in supermarkets, shelves with goods stacked on top of the shelves. In neither instance would these occupancies be required to have their aisles considered as exit corridors.

In a warehouse, it is not unusual to find high-piled storage racks over 20 feet tall lining both sides of aisles over 100 feet long. If the racks were six feet deep, and the aisle eight feet wide to allow for a fork lift truck, the area served by the aisle would be 2,000 square feet. A cross-aisle connecting several of these finger aisles would serve an aggregate area substantially more than 9,000 square feet (300 square feet/occupant x 30). No one would consider requiring the cross-aisle to be of fire-resistive construction with 20-minute fire doors between the aisles and the cross-aisle!

In these uses, compliance with the two concerns stated previously is substantially curtailed and, in fact, ignored by the enforcement officials. The capability for viewing the source of a fire and having a choice of exit passageways probably does not exist in these uses. Most likely, the warehouse and the supermarket occupancies are sprinklered. Therefore, they have a good fire record for occupant safety. As a result, no one is concerned with the failure to apply the corridor provisions to these uses.

Not until the occupant load of the area served reaches 30 do the fire-resistive requirements for the passageway walls, ceiling and doors become effective. Therefore, in a B-2 Occupancy the area served has to be 3,000 square feet or more before the passageway is required to be a fire-resistive exit corridor. The impact of the exception that raises the minimum number of occupants that triggers the fire-resistive requirements to 100 will be discussed later in Section 3305 (g).

A main concern of the designer of an office space is whether fire-rated walls are required for the passageway that serves an area of 3,000 square feet or more, per Section 3305 (g). According to the provisions of this section, if partitions do not exceed 6 feet in height, they do not constitute walls forming a corridor. Therefore, the low partitions are not subject to the fire-resistive requirements that come into play when the passage serves an occupant load of 30 or more (an area of 3,000 square feet or more for an office space). However, if the partitions exceed 6 feet in height, do they form the walls of a corridor? Unfortunately, for an office building the answer is yes. This restrictive determination is inconsistent with the other examples cited. (See Figures 7-24 and 7-25.)

Passage facilities are provided in a large room or area for the movement of either occupants or goods within the space. It is suggested that the designer make certain these aisles are distinguishable from the exit corridor that lies outside the room or area. These aisles are not subject to the corridor requirements so long as they do not form a confining passageway, that is, a passageway that has bounding walls exceeding the 6 feet height permitted in Section 3305 (g).

The national fire experience record for the B-2 Occupancy has been very good, particularly in regard to life safety. The restrictions did not have counterparts in either of the other model codes or the NFPA Pamphlet #101—Life Safety Code.

It is because of this lack of clear definition as to what constitutes a corridor, together with the great variety of configurations of actual constructions, that the ICBO staff has stated in one of their interpretations that, "The final decision as to whether or not such an area is to be

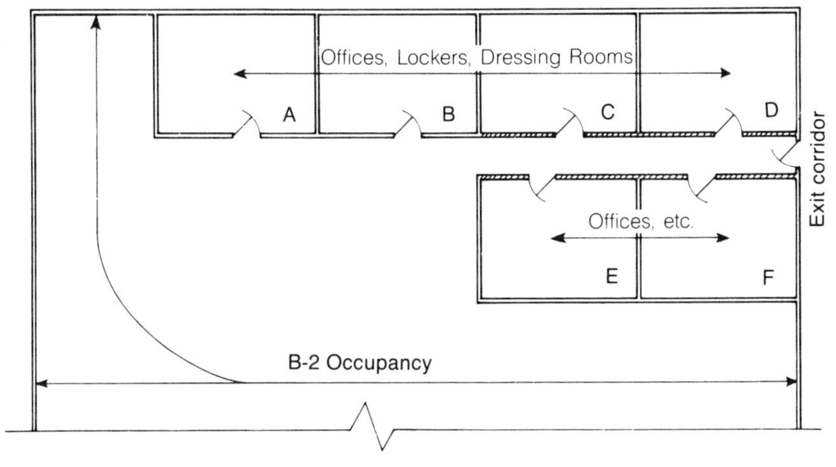

Where the occupant load of an office space exceeds 30, a corridor serving that space has to be of one-hour fire-resistive construction. An Exception to that general requirement, per Section 3305 (g) allows the use of sprinklers for the entire floor in lieu of the rated corridor provided the occupant load does not exceed 100.

Within an office space, only walls exceeding six feet in height define a corridor. When lower partitions are used, the aisle so formed is not subject to the fire-resistive construction provisions of Section 3305 (g). See Exception #7.

B-2 occupant load requiring rated corridor
Unsprinklered floor $\geq$ 30 occupants (3,000 S.F.)
Sprinklered floor $\leq$ 100 occupants (10,000 S.F.)

REFERENCE: SECTION 3305 (g)

FIGURE 7-24 CORRIDOR IN B-2 OFFICE SPACE, ONE-HOUR RATING TRIGGER – FLOOR > 10,000 S.F.

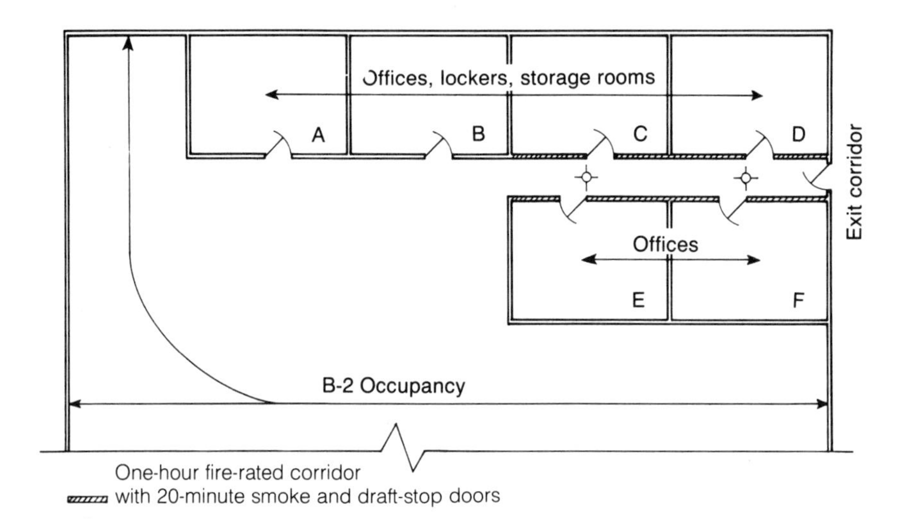

Assume B-2 area ≥ 10,000 square feet, office occupancy

Either: One-hour walls required if corridor serves 30 or more as exit path,
Or: No rated corridors required when:
area served is ≤ 10,000 S.F. and
the entire floor of the building is sprinklered, and
the exit corridor in the B-2 area has a smoke-detector system.

Where the floor area of an office space exceeds 10,000 square feet, the occupant load will exceed 100. Thus, Exception #5 in Section 3305 (g) does not apply; one-hour fire-resistive construction of corridors serving as an exit path are required.

If the space is reduced to under 10,000 s.f. in area, the Exception will apply.

Within an office space, only walls exceeding six feet in height define a corridor. When lower partitions are used, the aisle so formed is not subject to the fire-resistive construction provisions of Section 3305 (g). See Exception #7.

REFERENCE: SECTION 3305 (g) EXCEPTION 5

FIGURE 7-25 CORRIDOR IN B-2 OFFICE SPACE, ONE-HOUR RATING TRIGGER – FLOOR ≤ 10,000 S.F.

classified as an intervening room or as a corridor is judgmental and must be determined by the Building Official."

Because of the problems discussed above, Exception 5 was added to Section 3305 (g) in the 1985 UBC. This provision sidesteps the issue of defining what constitutes a corridor. The exception increased the number of occupants that triggers the one-hour construction requirement from 30 to 100. This is an increase for an office space from a 3,000 square feet area to a 10,000 square feet area. This increase in the controlling occupant load requires that a fire sprinkler system be provided on the entire floor. This full floor sprinklering is mandated even though only a portion of the floor may be involved with the corridor construction issue. Smoke detectors must also be provided in the corridors that are created.

The question of what constitutes a corridor remains unanswered. At least the fire-resistive construction provisions have been waived for B-2 office occupancies when sprinklers and smoke detectors are provided. As a result, the UBC is brought into closer alignment with the other codes on the subject of corridors.

The City and County of San Francisco has adopted a definition that determines when a corridor is subject to either the one-hour or sprinkler requirements. This definition uses the length to width ratio of the passageway in question. When the ratio exceeds three to one (3:1) in a passageway serving 30 or more occupants, the one-hour or sprinkler requirements apply. This San Francisco provision is consistent with the concept expressed in Exception 2 of Section 3305 (g).

The designer may wish to approach local enforcement officials for similar interpretive latitude or may consider advocating such a concept for inclusion in the local ordinances when the 1991 UBC is up for adoption in the jurisdiction.

The exception that raises the number of occupants to 100, when the entire floor is sprinklered, is an important new approach to resolving this ambiguous and restrictive provision. It provides the designer with greater flexibility in space planning.

Low cabinets or storage racks forming a passageway are not considered as defining a corridor: the passageway is an aisle. Similarly, in an office where the desks are arranged to form rows, the circulation passages between the desks are aisles, not corridors.

Notwithstanding the rationale herein presented, it must be understood that in most instances the designer must be prepared to:

- avoid creating corridors that serve occupant loads of 30 or more,
- provide fire sprinklers for the entire floor, if it is a B-2 office area, and thereby raise the occupant load trigger to 100,
- construct the corridors as one-hour fire-resistive assemblies.

As a result of the above discussion, the designer, in reviewing the problem of fire-resistive corridors in existing buildings, should propose to the building owner that the owner consider the installation of sprinklers on each floor when tenant changes or substantial improvements are contemplated. The reasoning is that once these sprinklers have been installed, there will no longer be additional cost attendant to future tenant changes.

The installation will require an initial capital investment by the owner, but after the building becomes fully sprinklered the result will be an added return through reduced fire insurance premiums. The owner will initially have to ensure sufficient water supply capability when connecting to the local water supply system in order that the sprinklers be served on a complete building basis, not just on the initial floor that may be involved.

Because there will generally be more than 100 sprinkler heads in the building, supervision of the system in accordance with Chapter 38, and UBC Standard 38-1, will be necessary. Provision for this supervision will need to be made at the outset.

For new buildings, we recommend that the designer initiate discussion with the enforcement officials for the acceptance of the following alternative to the 100 occupant load criteria (this variation of the 1991 UBC provisions may better serve both the public and the owner). The alternative method is to divide each floor of the building into 10,000 square feet or smaller areas by walls constructed as for one-hour occupancy separations. Once this arrangement is accepted by the enforcement officials, a B-2 office building that is fully sprinklered and divided into the 10,000 square feet compartments on each floor will be clear of any future requirements for one-hour corridors.

In a new low-rise building, this alternative would require that the owner put in the fire sprinkler system as part of the initial construction. The owner would immediately receive the lower insurance premium and would lease space to a tenant with the mutual understanding that the cost of the remodeling for the tenant would be less than that in a comparable building without the sprinklers and compartments. Such advance planning by the owner and designer would increase the flexibility of the designs for the lessees and lessen the burden of the plan check and field inspection requirements by building and fire officials.

> In the author's opinion, the greatest degree of safety to occupants, building owners and fire fighters is afforded when the supervision of the sprinkler system is extended to all shut-off valves on the system.

Tamper switches provide this supervision. They must be connected to the supervisory agency. These systems should also be electrically supervised. As we have indicated elsewhere in this Guide, the reliability of such a system is in the 99.9 percentile.

Corridors and Exit Balconies.

Sec. 3305.

(b) Width. The minimum corridor width shall be determined as specified in Section 3303 (b), but shall not be less than 44 inches, except as specified herein. Corridor serving an occupant load of 49 or less shall not be less than 36 inches in width. For special requirements for Group E and I Occupancies, see Sections 3319 and 3321.

This section and four other sections, Section 3303 (b), 3306 (b), 3307 (b) and 3321 (c), were all changed to use a new method of calculating the width of the required exit. For details of the use of the provisions see Section 3303 (b) discussion.

Sec. 3305

(e) Access to Exits. When more than one exit is required, they shall be so arranged that it is possible to go in either direction from any point in a corridor to a separate exit, except for dead ends not exceeding 20 feet in length.

This section states two basic criteria:

1. **In an exit corridor, one must be able to go in two different directions from any point in the corridor.**
2. **A dead end corridor is permitted provided it does not exceed 20 feet in length.**

The first criterion is consistent with the provisions of Section 3303 (c), where it is stated "they (the exits) shall be arranged that if one becomes blocked the others will be available. " This redundancy is an essential characteristic of exit facilities.

The second criterion is a form of exception usually permitted regarding the primary principle of redundancy. We saw a similar exception in Section 3303 (a), where one exit is permitted when the occupant load is less than 10. In this instance, the ability to go in two different directions in the exit path is waived provided the length of the dead end is limited. The various national codes and standards have lengths for such dead end corridors ranging from 4 to 75 feet. However, although the UBC has arbitrarily selected the 20-foot length, the designer should realize that it is the legally binding dimension. (See Figure 7-26.)

Sec. 3305.

(g) Construction. Walls of corridors serving a Group R, Division 1 or Group 1 Occupancy having an occupant load of 10 or more and walls of corridors serving other occupancies having an occupant load of 30 or more shall be of not less than one-hour fire-resistive construction and the ceilings shall be not less than that required for a one-hour fire-resistive floor or roof system.

EXCEPTIONS: 1. One-story buildings housing Group B, Division 4 Occupancies.

2. Corridors more than 30 feet in width where occupancies served by such corridors have at least one exit independent from the corridor. (See Appendix Chapter 7, Part 1, for covered malls.)

3. Exterior sides of exterior exit balconies.

4. In Group I, Division 3 Occupancies such as jails, prisons, reformatories and similar buildings with open-barred cells forming corridor walls, the corridors and cell doors need not be fire-resistive.

5. Corridor walls and ceilings need not be of fire-resistive construction within office spaces having an occupant load of 100 or less when the entire story in which the tenant space is located is equipped with an automatic sprinkler system throughout and smoke detectors are installed in the corridor in accordance with their listing.

6. In other than Type I or II construction, exterior exit balcony roof assemblies may be of heavy timber construction without concealed spaces.

7. Within offices spaces occupied by a single tenant, partial height partitions which form corridors and which do not exceed 6 feet in height need not be fire resistive, provided they are constructed in accordance with Section 1705 and are not more than 3/4 of the floor to ceiling height.

When the ceiling of the entire story is an element of a one-hour fire-resistive floor or roof system, the corridor walls may terminate at the ceiling. When the room-side fire-resistive membrane of the corridor wall is carried through to the underside of a fire-resistive floor or roof above, the corridor side of the ceiling may be protected by the use of

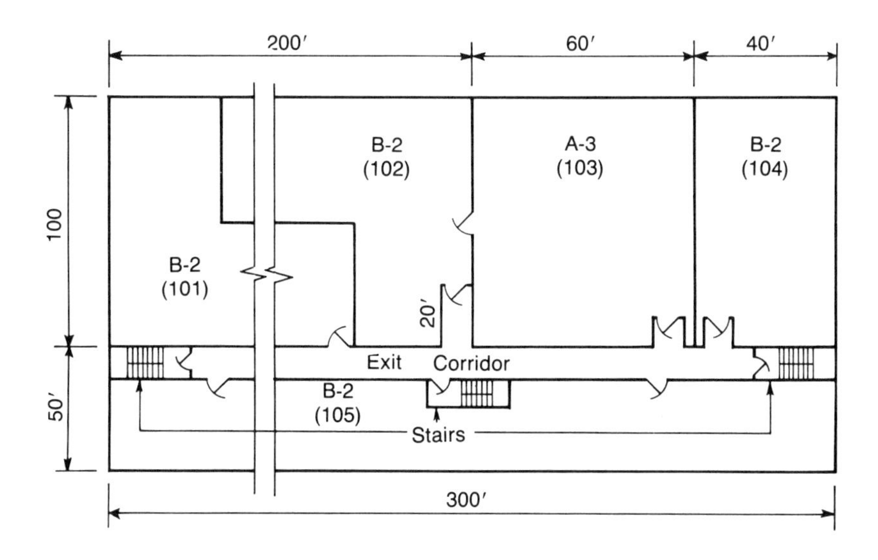

A dead end corridor is an exit corridor in which one can only travel in one direction to reach an exit. The short corridor serving room 102 is such a dead end corridor because there is no second exit once one enters that corridor.

On the other hand, once one enters the main exit corridor there is access to two or three exits.

Although the length of a dead end corridor has been established on an arbitrary basis, it is binding unless other safety provisions are furnished and approved by the enforcement official per Section 105.

Due to occupant load, three exit stairways required:

Room 102 is off a dead end corridor. Maximum length of dead end corridor is 20 feet.

Room 103, public assembly, has occupant load > 50 persons, therefore, door to corridor and room 102 must swing in direction of travel.

REFERENCE: SECTION 3305 (e)

FIGURE 7-26 ACCESS TO EXITS – DEAD END CORRIDOR

ceiling materials as required for one-hour floor or roof system construction or the corridor ceiling may be of the same construction as the corridor walls. Ceilings of noncombustible construction may be suspended below the fire-resistive ceiling.

For wall and ceiling finish requirements, see Table No. 42-B. For restrictions on the use of corridors to convey air, see Chapter 10 of the Mechanical Code.

The fire-resistive construction of the corridor walls and the occupant load that triggers that construction has already been discussed at length in this Article in regard to Section 3305 (a). The designer is urged to review that discussion to obtain a proper understanding of the exit corridor issues.

The second paragraph of this section details the provisions for the construction of the walls and ceiling of a corridor. (See Figure 7-27.)

Exception 6 relates to the permissive use of heavy timber for architectural use over exterior exit balconies. Note the prohibition that the roof of the balcony is at issue. Therefore, Exception 6 is not applicable except on the top level of a tier of balconies. Note further that there is no application of this Exception for the balcony adjacent to an area separation wall. In such a location, the projection of the roof over the exterior balcony is subject to the provisions of Section 505 (e)2, Exception, third paragraph.

The general requirement in buildings required to be of one-hour fire-resistive construction throughout is for the roof assembly to be of one-hour construction. This Exception allows the limited use of heavy timber. This is the recognition that, although the code does not equate heavy timber to one-hour fire-resistive construction, the use has been locally permitted by many enforcement officials and should be recognized if only on a limited basis.

Exception 7 allows an exception to Section 3305 (g), as long as the partition meets Section 1705 (b) requirements within a single Group B, Division 2 Occupancy. This provision increases the height to which a nonfire-resistive partition may extend without being considered as forming a corridor wall requiring one-hour construction. In the standard eight-foot-high ceiling, the partition is limited to six feet in height.

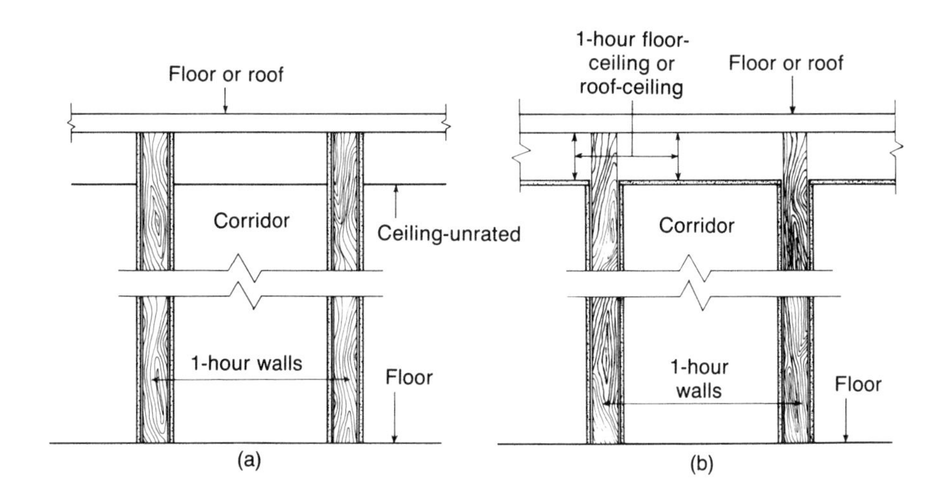

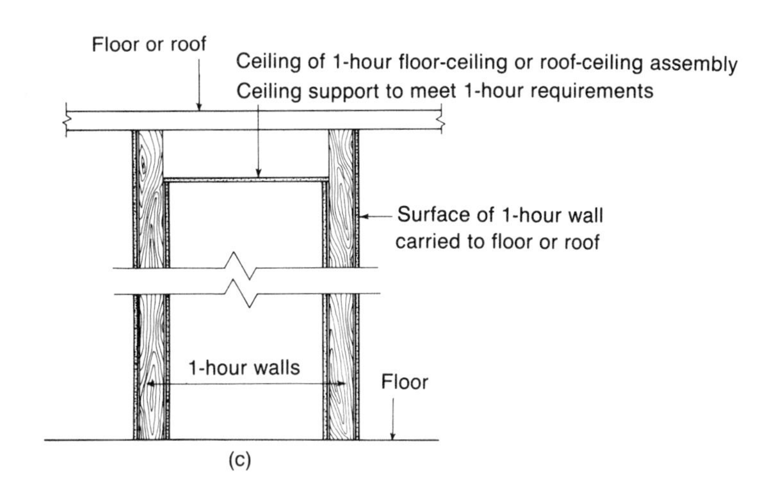

REFERENCE: SECTION 3305 (g)

FIGURE 7-27 ONE-HOUR EXIT CORRIDOR CONSTRUCTION DETAILS

This allowance of six feet for a partition without considering it a corridor wall conflicts with the general limitation of five feet nine inches in Section 3305 (a), first paragraph. However, the greater height is permitted only within a single tenant Group B, Division 2 Occupancy. (See Figure. 7-28.)

The last paragraph emphasizes the prohibition using of corridors as part of the air conveying system. This addresses a frequent and improper use of exit corridors as part of the ventilation air supply system. The reference to the Mechanical Code is to Section 1002 (a), which reads:

> **Corridors shall not be used to convey air to or from rooms if the corridor is required to be of fire-resistive construction by Section 3305 of the Building Code.**

The designer cannot take refuge on the presence of this type of misuse of corridors and the code violation it involves on the basis of precedent. Failing to heed the warnings and prohibitions in both the UBC and UMC will clearly constitute negligence.

Sec. 3305.

(h) Openings. 1. Doors. When corridor walls are required to be of one-hour fire-resistive construction by Section 3305 (g), every interior door opening shall be protected by a tight-fitting smoke- and draft-control assembly having a fire-protection rating of not less than 20 minutes when tested in accordance with U.B.C. Standard No. 43-2. Said doors shall not have louvers. The door and frame shall bear an approved label or other identification showing the rating thereof, the name of the manufacturer and the identification of the service conducting the inspection of materials and workmanship at the factory during fabrication and assembly. Doors shall be maintained self-closing or shall be automatic closing by actuation of a smoke detector in accordance with Section 4306(b). Smoke- and draft-control door assemblies shall be provided with a gasket so installed as to provide a seal where the door meets the stop on both sides and across the top.

EXCEPTIONS:1. Viewports may be installed if they require a hole not larger than 1 inch in diameter through the door, have at least a 1/4-inch-thick glass disc and the holder is of metal which will not melt out when subject to temperatures of 1700°F.

2. Protection of openings in the interior walls of exterior exit balconies is not required where it is possible to exit in two directions.

2. Openings other than doors. Where corridor walls are required to be of one-hour fire-resistive construction by Section 3305 (g), interior openings for other than doors or ducts shall be protected by fixed glazing listed and labeled for a fire protection rating of three-fourths hour in accordance with Section 4306 (i)., approved 1/4-inch-thick wired glass installed in steel frames. The total area of all openings, other than doors, in any portion of an interior corridor shall not

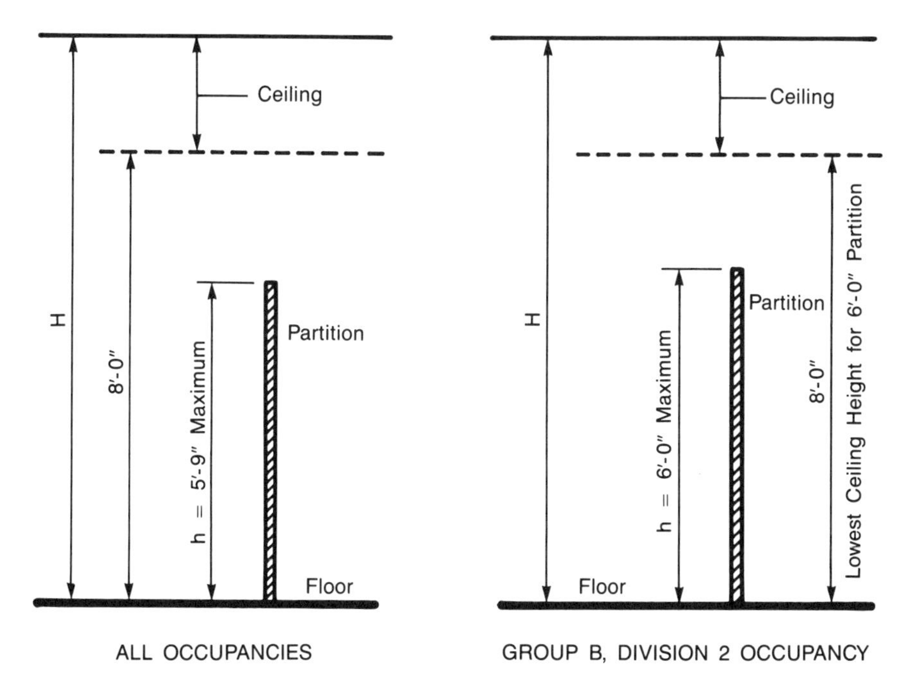

Non-fire-resistive partitions may be 5′-9″ high within any occupancy, regardless of the floor-to-ceiling height of the room or area.

In Group B, Division 2 Occupancy, the non-fire-resistive partition may be 6′-0″ provided that height is ≤ ¾ the height of the floor-to-ceiling height of the room or area.

REFERENCE: SECTION 3305 (a) AND (g)

FIGURE 7-28 HEIGHT OF NON-FIRE-RESISTIVE PARTITIONS FORMING AISLES WITHIN TENANT SPACE

exceed 25 percent of the area of the corridor wall of the room which it is separating from the corridor. For duct openings, see Section 4306.

EXCEPTION: Protection of openings in the interior walls of exterior exit balconies is not required.

The door assembly in an opening of a fire-rated corridor wall must be not less than a 20-minute smoke- and draft-control assembly including its closer. If the door is to be held open, a smoke detector release-type of magnetic hold-open device can be used as described in Section 4306 (b). Any openings, other than doors, into a fire-rated corridor are limited to 25 percent of the corridor wall. This measurement refers to a percentage of each room or space in which the opening is located and not to the length of the corridor in general. These interior openings must be constructed with wired glass in steel frames. There are no approved self-closing or automatic-closing fire windows.

When the openings are in the interior wall of an exterior exit balcony, or when the exterior side of that balcony is not required to have protected openings because of its proximity to a property line, the openings need not be protected.

The designer should note that there is approved fire-resistive clear glass that will permit a greater percentage of glazed openings because this glass has a one-hour fire rating. This new material is in the form of a clear glass sandwich with an intumescent gel between the sheets. The net effect is that of a clear glazing material. When subject to fire, however, the gel foams to form a protective barrier which prevents the fire from entering the other side.

A ULI listing for a one-hour wall assembly with this glazing permits 72 percent of each 100 square feet of wall to be glazed. The new material could be used along with wired glass to lower the overall cost. Because this newly developed glazing is expensive, unless or until the cost is reduced its use will rarely be economically justified. However, the expense may be warranted when the glazing provides a solution to a special situation.

Other possibilities for the designer to consider and discuss with the enforcement officials are:

- doubling up the protection systems in the immediate area. For example, the designer may request an increase in the percentage of wired glass if sprinklers are provided on both sides of the wall.

- if sprinklers are provided for another purpose, the installation of horizontally sliding doors such as the Won-door, which has at least a one-hour UL label, or vertical-rolling fire doors. The horizontally sliding, segmented folding door is being used increasingly for the requirement for elevator separation from corridors in high-rise buildings. Either door's operation should be triggered by a smoke detection system. When the door does not operate by gravity, the operating mechanism would need standby power.

Using Section 105, the enforcement officials could accept either or both of these alternatives, particularly, if in the first alternative, the new fast-response sprinkler heads were used. In both instances, the combination of the wired glass and either the sprinklers or the sliding or rolling door would equal or exceed the one-hour wall rating. In the computation of the allowed percentage of permitted openings, fire doors are not calculated as openings. To obtain the percentage of openings, the total amount of common wall area between the room or space involved and the corridor is computed. The sum of all openings in the corridor wall, other than doors, must not exceed 25 percent.

One means of gaining maximum use from the allowed percentage of the glazed portion of a wall is to use one-hour segments at the floor and ceiling lines and the glazing at mid-height level.

The corridor provision in Section 3305 (g) Exception 5 for accepting the provision of sprinklers for the entire floor provides the designer with considerable flexibility. Using the sprinkler Exception will result in the absence of fire-rated corridor walls in most B-2 office occupancies. Extending the use of this concept to other occupancies and to increase the permitted percentage areas of glazing is a logical approach under the Section 105 provisions.

The second sentence of the first paragraph specifically prohibits louvers in exit corridor doors. This prohibition parallels the comparable provision in NFPA Pamphlet 80. The intent is to assure maintenance of the smoke- and draft-control integrity of the door. This has been the operative requirement for many years because the NFPA provisions regarding corridor were enforced as part of the door provisions.

Sec. 3305.

(i) Location on Property. Exterior exit balconies shall not be located in an area where openings are not permitted or where openings are required to be protected because of location on the property.

Exterior exit balconies are exterior balconies with the outer side open. These balconies cannot be located where protected openings are required for the outside wall of the balcony if it is the exterior wall of the building. (See Figure 7-29.)

If an exterior balcony were constructed in such a location, the outside wall would have to be of one-hour construction with protected openings therein. The balcony would thus become an enclosed corridor with its exterior surface meeting the requirements for protection based on Table No. 5-A and the -03 Sections of Chapters 18, 19, 20 and 21. Being so enclosed, the balcony would not qualify as an exterior exit balcony.

If the balcony is at an angle to the property line in question, and the distance from the exterior side is more than required for unprotected openings, then the balcony exterior opening construction can be unrated and therefore unprotected on that side. At that point the balcony can become an exterior exit balcony. For suggestions on other approaches, refer to the Article 5 discussion of methods for dealing with proximity to property lines. (See Figure 7-29.)

(j) Elevators. Elevators opening into a corridor serving a Group R, Division 1 Occupancy or Group I Occupancy having an occupant load of ten or more, or a corridor serving other occupancies having an occupant load of 30 or more shall be provided with an elevator lobby at each floor containing such a corridor. The lobby shall completely separate the elevators from the corridor construction conforming to Section 3305 (g) and all openings into the lobby wall contiguous with the corridor shall be protected as required by Section 3305 (h).

EXCEPTIONS:1. In office buildings classed as a Group B, Division 2 Occupancy, separations need not be provided from a street floor lobby, provided the entire street floor is protected with an automatic sprinkler system.

2. Elevators not required to meet shaft enclosure requirements of Section 1706.

3. When additional doors are provided in accordance with Section 5106. Elevator lobbies shall comply with Section 5106.

In fully sprinklered office buildings, corridors may lead through enclosed elevator lobbies if all areas of the building have access to at least one required exit without passing through the elevator lobby.

This section combines provisions from other sections in prior codes relating to exits and in particular the separation of the elevator lobby

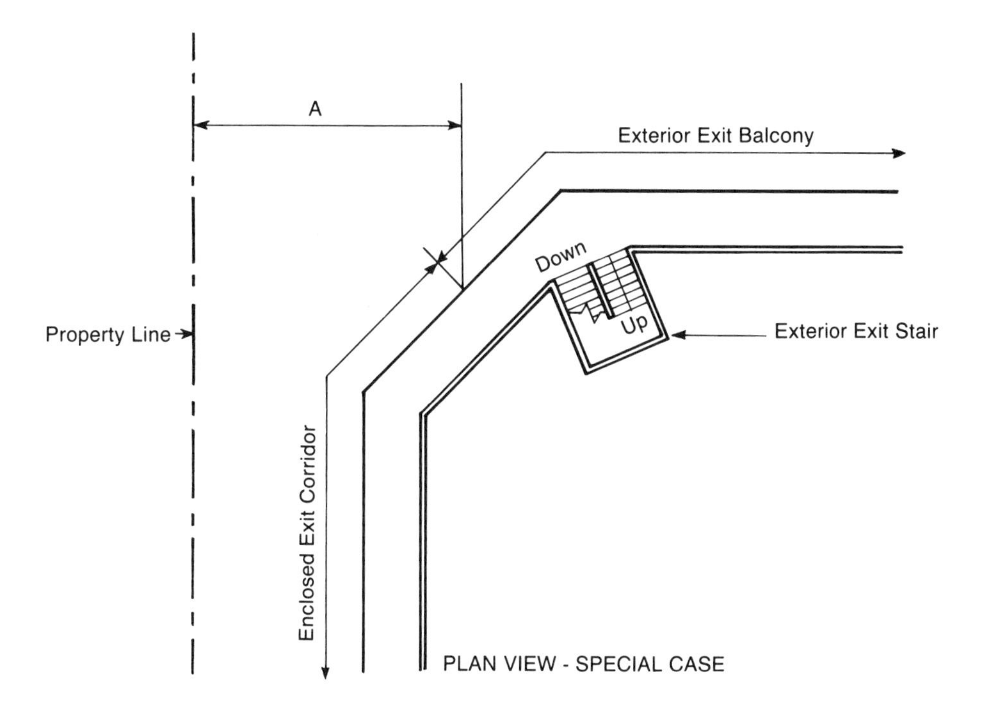

A = Required distance for type of construction and occupancy to permit unprotected openings.

Where an exterior exit balcony extends into the area that protected openings are required by the provisions of Table No. 5-A or the -03 provisions of Chapters 18, 19, 20 or 21, the construction must conform to the fire-resistive exit corridor construction provisions of Section 3305 (g). Openings in the exterior wall of that corridor may have glazing conforming to the requirements of Section 3305 (h).

REFERENCE: SECTION 3305 (i)

FIGURE 7-29 EXTERIOR EXIT BALCONY—PROXIMITY TO PROPERTY LINE

from the exit corridor. The last paragraph is the companion to that of Section 1807 (h), discussed in Article 9 of this Guide.

It is the author's opinion that this provision creates a new requirement where one previously did not exist. Until this section is amended or deleted, we recommend that the second paragraph be considered by enforcement officials as applying only to high-rise buildings, i.e., to buildings for which there is a specific code requirement for the separation of the elevator lobby from the exit corridor.

Our reasoning for this recommendation follows: The high-rise life safety provisions were added to the UBC in the 1973 edition. The elevator requirements were contained in Section 1807 (i) of that edition. It required that the elevators "be separated from the remainder of the building by construction as required for corridors."

In the same edition of the UBC, a new Chapter 51 was added to the code describing the requirements for "Elevators, Dumbwaiters, Escalators and Moving Walks." The only provision in that Chapter relating to fire-resistive requirements was that the shafts for the elevators, dumbwaiters and escalators be of at least the construction cited in Part V, Type of Construction (Chapters 17-22), of the code. The same provisions are contained in the present code.

Thus, prior to the 1973 edition of the UBC, there had been no code requirements for elevators.

This is important code history. Until the time when high-rise requirements were placed in the code, the only corridor opening protection provisions were for doors opening into the corridor, such as doors to dwellings units, offices, and so on. That provision is contained in the first sentence of Section 3305 (h) of the present code in virtually identical language as was in Section 3304 (h) of the 1970 UBC.

At no time before the 1973 UBC were the corridors required to be separated from the elevator lobby.

In 1981, ICBO staff issued an interpretation that the provisions of Section 3305 (h), which was then Section 3304 (h), include the requirement for separating the exit corridor from the elevator lobby for a four-story building. In their interpretation, they indicated the need for elevator doors smoke- and draft-stop capability. That inferred requirement prevented the staff's acceptance of the fire-rated elevator door assembly. The staff's interpretation of that requirement must have stemmed from their concern about the transfer of smoke from floor to floor via the elevator shaft as a result of stack effect. This was a primary concern in the high-rise specific code provision.

However, in low-rise buildings, stack effect is negligible. Therefore, the ICBO staff's concern appears to be based on an extension of the high-rise provision to low-rise structures, even though the circumstances are not comparable.

On examining the circumstance behind the high-rise code change, which was added in the 1973 UBC, and particularly the logic behind the Section 1807 (j) provision in that code, a simple and unequivocal conclusion is reached. Had the ICBO staff's conclusion, that the elevator lobby must have smoke- and draft-stop separations from the exit corridors, been in effect in the pre-1973 period, it would not have been necessary to add the Section 1807 (j) provision to the life safety package!

Section 1807 (j) was obviously added for a reason, which logically could only be that there was no prior code requirement for such elevator/corridor separation! Therefore, Section 1807 (j) was applied only to high-rise buildings. Neither before nor after Section 1807 provisions were placed in the code were separation requirements applicable to low-rise buildings.

Unfortunately, the ICBO interpretation was accepted by many enforcement officials and is now "validated " by the Section 3305 (h) provision. In such situations, one hopes for an evaluation of the code provision's rationale, history and intent, together with a logical determination of whether a negative concept can be used to create a new code requirement.

The designer, in the hope of reaching a reasonable requirement for the building, is urged to discuss this anomaly with the enforcement official, given the above background information.

*The author was the chairman of the subcommittee that developed the UBC high-rise life safety provisions. The subcommittee's members were well aware of the existing code provisions and their applications.

Stairways
Sec. 3306. (a) through (k)

These sections, written in specification language (rise and run, width, etc.), contain the general requirements for stairs.

Stairways
Sec. 3306. (b) Width. The minimum stairway width shall be determined as specified in Section 3303 (b), but shall not be less than 44 inches except as specified herein. Stairways serving an occupant load of 49 or less shall be not less than 36 inches in width.

This section and four other sections, 3303 (b), 3305 (b), 3307 (b) and 3321 (c) were all changed to use a new method of calculating the width of the required exit. For details of the use of the provisions see Section 3303 (b) discussion.

The designer and the enforcement official should note that the requirements of this section were superseded by Section 3104 (b)3 for buildings subject to Chapter 31 provisions. Therefore, in such buildings, the stairway must be designed to provide the 48-inch clear between handrails, and the landings must similarly reflect this width. (See Figure 7-1.)

Similarly, the landings must comply with the handrail extension requirements of Section 3306 (j). This may necessitate a wider landing depending on the width and location of the door opening onto the landing.

NOTE: See the discussion of the provisions of Chapter 31 and the ADA legislation in Article 10. There is a conflict with the handrail extension provisions of Section 3306 (j) and the present federal requirements. In the event the ADA regulations contain similar handrail projection requirements to that in the present federal regulations, the 12 inch handrail projection may be required at both ends of the stair run.

(c) Rise and Run. The rise of every step in a stairway shall be not less than 4 inches nor greater than 7 inches. Except as permitted in Subsections (d) and (f), the run shall be not less than 11 inches as measured horizontally between the vertical planes of the furthermost projection of adjacent treads. Except as

permitted in Subsections (d), (e) and (f), the largest tread run within any flight of stairs shall not exceed the smallest by more than inch. The greatest riser height within any flight of stairs shall not exceed the smallest by more than inch.

EXCEPTIONS: 1. Private stairways serving an occupant load of less than 10 and stairways to unoccupied roofs may be constructed with an 8-inch maximum rise and 9-inch minimum run.

2. Where the bottom or top riser adjoins a sloping public way, walk or driveway having an established grade and serving as a landing, the bottom or top riser may be reduced along the slope to less than 4 inches in height with the variation in height of the bottom or top riser not to exceed 3 inches in every 3 feet of stairway width.

The maximum riser height is 7 inches and the minimum tread width is 11 inches. These dimensions were established in recent editions to reduce the number of accidents occurring on stairs. Based on research into the human response to stair geometry, these new controlling dimensions provide a safer stairway. The UBC conforms with the other model codes and the NFPA Life Safety Code.

Stairs play a major role in slip-and-fall accidents. This section regulates the rise and run of stairways and the tolerances allowed. The designer should be sure that these tolerances are not exceeded. The tolerance of 3/8 inch, which has been permitted because 1979, is the largest allowed variation between any of the risers or runners in the flight; not just between two adjacent steps. Assume there was a 7-inch-high riser, with an adjacent riser of 7 1/4 inches in height and with the next riser 7 1/2 inches in height. That arrangement would violate the 3/8 inch maximum variation in the flight, because the maximum variation in these three risers would be 1/2 inch.

When the stairway involved terminates on a sloping walk or driveway, this 3/8-inch tolerance is inadequate. Exception 2 addresses this situation.

The Exception recognizes the reality of perpendicular building construction on sloping streets, walks, driveways and public ways. The change permits the contact step of an exit stairway, at a walk, driveway or public way that slopes across the width of the stairway, to have a variable riser height. The variation in riser height is not to exceed three inches per three feet of stair width (1:12). See Figure 7-30.

Sec. 3306

(k) Exterior Stairway Protection. Except in Group R, Division 3 Occupancies, all openings in the exterior wall below and within 10 feet, measured horizontally, of an exterior exit stairway serving a building over two stories in height or a floor

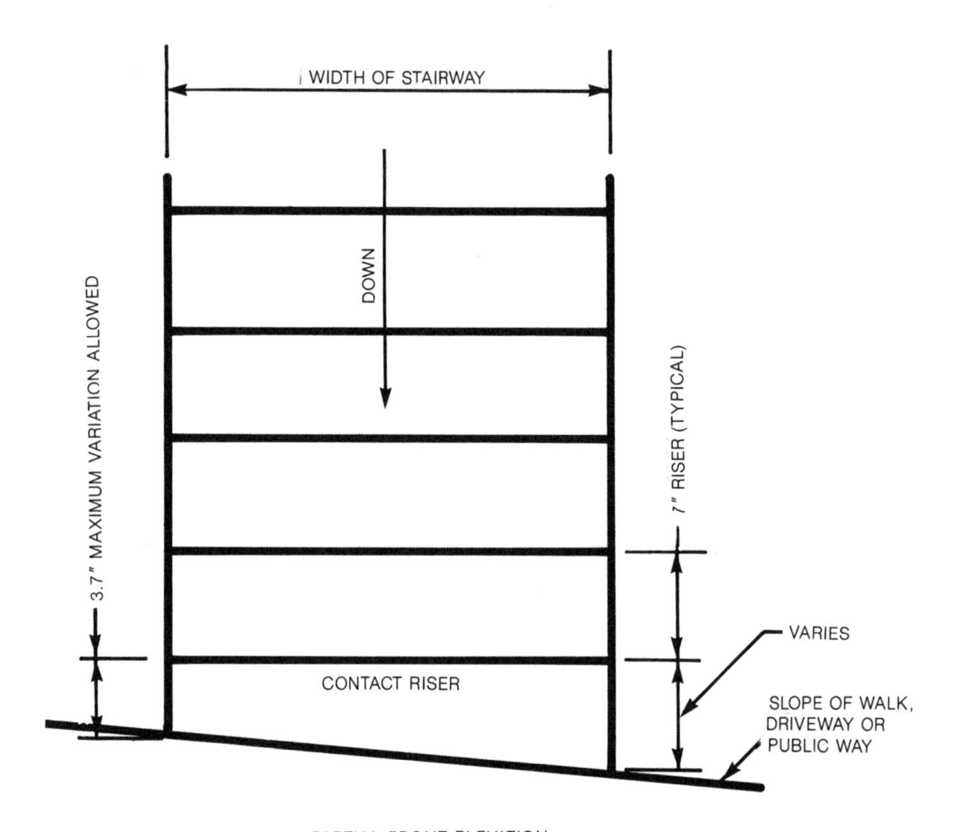

PARTIAL FRONT ELEVATION

ASSUME: Stair width = 44″ Walk, driveway or public way slope = 10% (1″ in 10″) Variation in riser required to match the slope of the walk, driveway or public way 44″ width of stair/10″ = 4.4″ required to parallel the walk, driveway or public way. See Detail "A".

Allowable variation in riser height of contact step 3″:36″ (1″:12″) 44″ width of stair/12 = 3.7″ maximum variation allowed

Therefore the contact step cannot exactly match the walk, driveway or public way slope. They will have to be shaped to conform to the maximum allowable variation of 3.7″ rather than maintain the 10% slope unbroken across the stairway frontage. See Detail "B".)

REFERENCE: SECTION 3306 (a)

FIGURE 7-30 RISER VARIATION PERMITTED FOR STAIRWAYS ON SLOPING WALKS, DRIVEWAYS AND PUBLIC WAYS

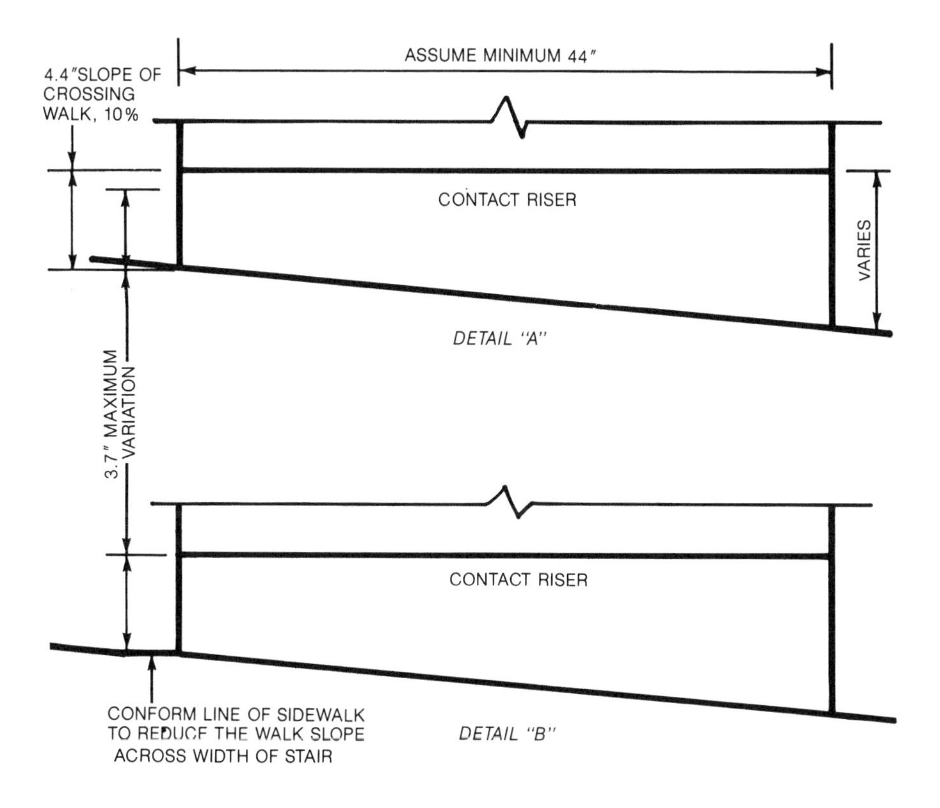
ASSUME MINIMUM 44″
4.4″SLOPE OF CROSSING WALK, 10%
CONTACT RISER
VARIES
DETAIL "A"
3.7″ MAXIMUM VARIATION
CONTACT RISER
CONFORM LINE OF SIDEWALK TO REDUCE THE WALK SLOPE ACROSS WIDTH OF STAIR
DETAIL "B"

level having such openings in two or more floors below shall be protected by self-closing fire assembly having a three-fourths-hour fire-protection rating. Exterior stairways enclosed on three or more sides shall comply with the flame-spread requirements for interior stairways.

EXCEPTION: 1. Openings may be unprotected when two separated exterior stairways serve an exterior exit balcony.

2. Protection of openings is not required for open parking garages conforming to Section 709.

The provisions of this section clarify the intent of the protection requirements for openings in proximity of an exterior stairway. The first sentence specifically indicates that the requirements do not apply to Group R, Division 3 Occupancy (one- or two-family dwelling) buildings. The second provision in the sentence relates to the location of the openings to be protected.

The code provision specifically applies only to openings below the top level platform and within 10 feet of the stair. The openings at the top level platform are not required to be protected.

In Figure 7-31, the doors and openings on the third floor are not required to be protected by this section. Those on the first and second floors to the left side of the stairway require fire assemblies with three-fourths-hour fire-protection ratings. Those on the right side of the stairway on these floors do not require protection, because they are more than 10 feet from the stairway.

(m) Interior Stairway Construction.

Interior stairways shall be constructed as specified in Part IV of this code. Except when enclosed usable space under stairs is prohibited by Section 3309 (f), the walls and soffits of the enclosed space shall be protected on the enclosed side as required for one-hour fire-resistive construction. All required interior stairways which extend to the top floor in any building four or more stories in height shall have, at the highest point of the stair shaft, an approved hatch openable to the exterior not less than 16 square feet in area with a minimum dimension of 2 feet.

EXCEPTION: The hatch need not be provided on smokeproof enclosures or on stairways that extend to the roof with an opening onto that roof.

Stairways exiting directly to the exterior of a building four or more stories in height shall be provided with means of emergency entry for fire department access.

(n) Exterior Stairway Construction. Exterior stairways shall be constructed as specified in Part IV of this code.

Exterior stairways shall not project into yards where openings are not permitted or protection of openings is required.

Enclosed usable space under stairs shall have the walls and soffits protected on the enclosed side as required for one-hour fire-resistive construction.

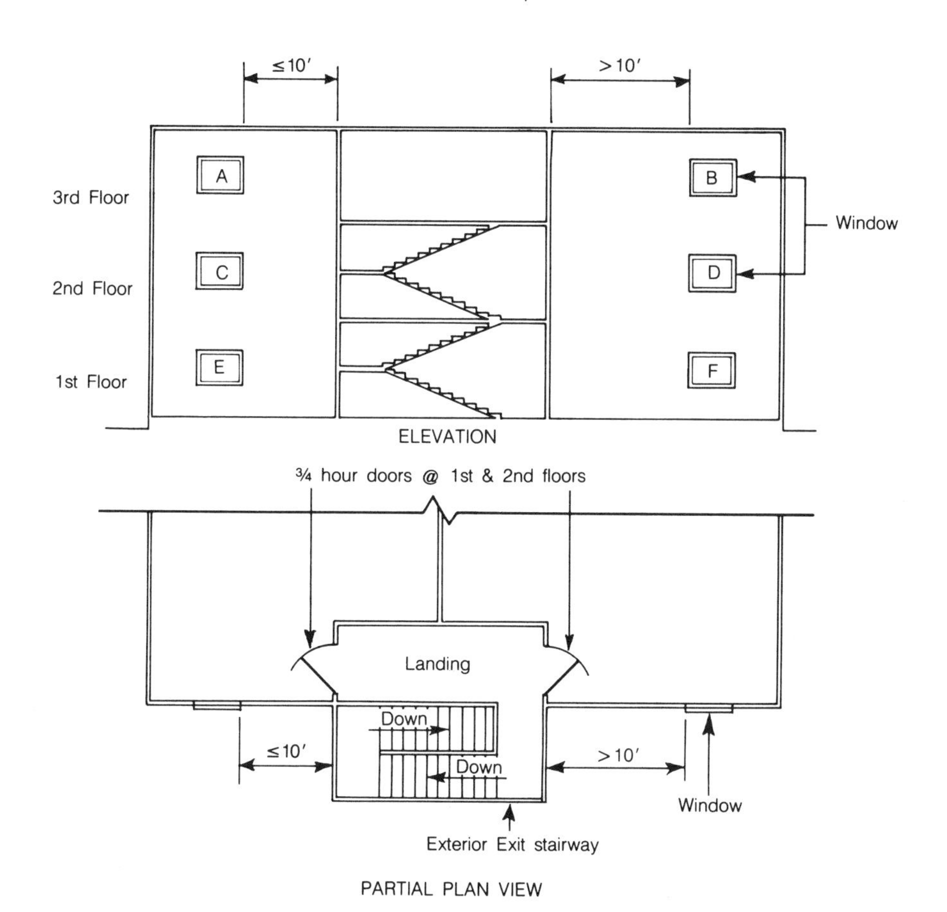

ASSUME: GROUP R-1 OCCUPANCY, 3 STORY TYPE V 1-HOUR BUILDING
EXTERIOR EXIT STAIRWAY @ FRONT, 2ND EXIT NOT SHOWN

Windows A & B and 3rd floor doorways do not require ¾-hour fire assemblies as they are not "below . . . an exterior exit stairway."

Windows D and F do not require ¾-hour fire assemblies as they are more than 10 feet from the exterior exit stairway even though they are below that stairway.

Windows C and E and the doors on the 2nd & 3rd floors require ¾-hour fire assemblies since they are "below and within 10 feet, of an exterior exit stairway."

REFERENCE: SECTION 3306 (k)

FIGURE 7-31 OPENING PROTECTION REQUIREMENTS – EXTERIOR EXIT STAIRWAY

Stairways exiting directly to the exterior of a building four or more stories in height shall be provided with means of emergency entry for fire department access.

These two sections often cause problems for the designer. They describe the construction features of each stairway but fail to define when a stairway changes from an interior to an exterior stairway. The original intent of the last sentence of the first paragraph in Section 3306 (l) was to require that the wall surfaces meet the interior finish requirements of Chapter 42 when the exterior stairway was enclosed on three sides. However, when this text was changed in a prior edition, the added text used the phrase "3 or more sides. "

This change worsens an already muddled situation.

The following analysis shows why an exterior stairway cannot have more than three sides—that is, unless it has more sides than a quadrilateral.

In the NFPA Life Safety Code, an outside (exterior) stairway is defined as a stairway having at least one open side. An enclosed stairway with window openings in the stairway walls is not equivalent to an exterior stairway. Thus, although not stated in the UBC, the intent of the code is that at least one side of an exterior stairway be fully open to the air with only guardrails on that side.

An exterior stairway, therefore, is one that has permanently available ventilation to prohibit smoke accumulation. An interior stairway, on the other hand, is required to have a hatch at the highest point in the stair shaft to permit venting of the stair in the event of fire, as stipulated in the third paragraph of Section 3306 (m).

In the author's opinion, the NFPA concept is the proper one to use in defining the difference between the interior and exterior stairway. The designer should not fully enclose a stairway that is to be constructed according to the provisions of Section 3306 (n). The Section 3306 (l) first paragraph, last sentence, should be interpreted as applying to exterior stairways enclosed on only three sides.

Leaving the roof off the stairway is not sufficient to qualify it as an exterior stairway.

The designer should be aware of the problems that exterior exit stairways can present when designing exit stairways for a multi-family residential project. These exterior stairs usually are not enclosed and frequently serve several floors and dwelling units. The exterior stairs are often located at the ends of an exterior exit balcony. See Figure 7-32.

In the arrangement shown on Figure 7-32, the exterior exit balcony provides exiting for all units on that floor to two exterior exit stairways. The opening "D " and "W" onto the exit balcony may be unprotected, as provided in Section 3305 (h)2 Exception. This concept of exterior exit stairways and balconies is the same that the NFPA Life Safety Code describes. It is the basic concept that unenclosed exterior exit stairways be separated one from the other. The balcony and stairway are both kept smoke free by being directly open to outside air.

Figures 7-33 and 7-34 show two commonly found noncode-complying exit stairway arrangements. In Figure 7-33, the designer intends each exterior stair to serve the dwelling units that directly open onto it and those that open onto the other exterior stairway via the exterior exit balcony. This arrangement does not satisfy the separation of exits requirement of Section 3303 (c), because a fire at point "X" below the floor shown on Figure 7-33—would make both exit paths on the third floor unusable.

Thus, a fire on any floor below the floor in question would affect more than that fire origination floor. This is contrasted with the situation where a double-loaded enclosed exit corridor connects to enclosed stairways. A fire in one stairway would leave the other stairway available to all floors. A fire in a corridor on one floor would leave all the other corridors usable and both stairways available. This level of relative safety must be provided in any use of exterior exit balconies and exterior exit stairways.

In Figure 7-33, the dwelling unit entry doors, D-1 thru D-4, are within 10 feet of the exterior stairway. Those entry doors on the floors below the top floor must have three-fourths hour fire doors per Section 3306 (l).

In Figure 7-34, the designer intends that for this noncode-complying

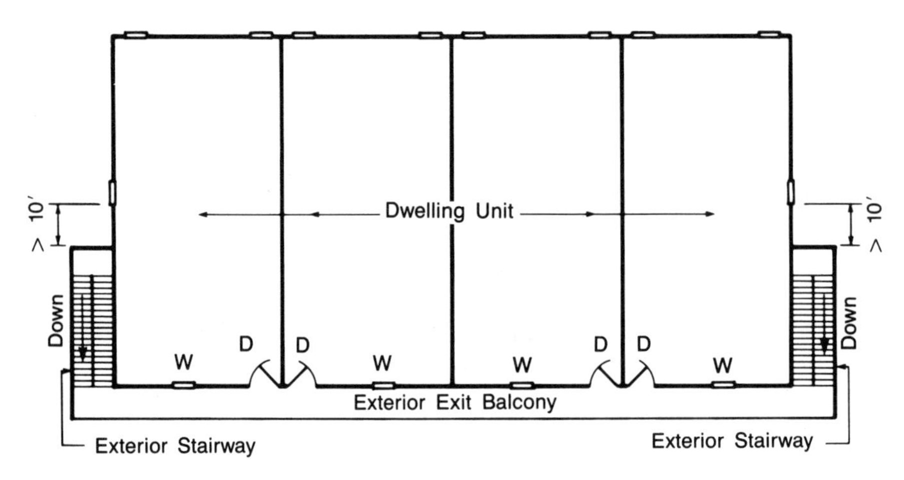

PLAN VIEW - 3rd FLOOR

Exterior exit balconies are permitted to have unprotected openings on either wall provided the balcony is sufficiently set back from adjacent buildings and property lines. The wall construction of the balcony, however, must be of the required construction as for exit corridors per Section 3305 (g).

Openings within proximity of exterior stairways may have to have protection per Section 3306 (k); see Figure 7-31. The exterior stairway may be constructed of any material permitted for that building's type of construction.

GIVEN: Group R, Div. 1 Occupancy
Type V-One Hour Building
Four Dwelling Units per Floor
Three Stories

Two exits are required per Section 3303 (a).
Exterior exit balcony openings "D" and "W" may be unprotected per Section 3305 (h)2.

Openings more than 10 feet and below exterior stairways may be unprotected per Section 3306 (k).

REFERENCE: SECTION 3306 (k)

FIGURE 7-32 EXTERIOR EXIT STAIRWAY—GROUP R, DIVISION 1 OCCUPANCY, TYPICAL CONFORMING DESIGN

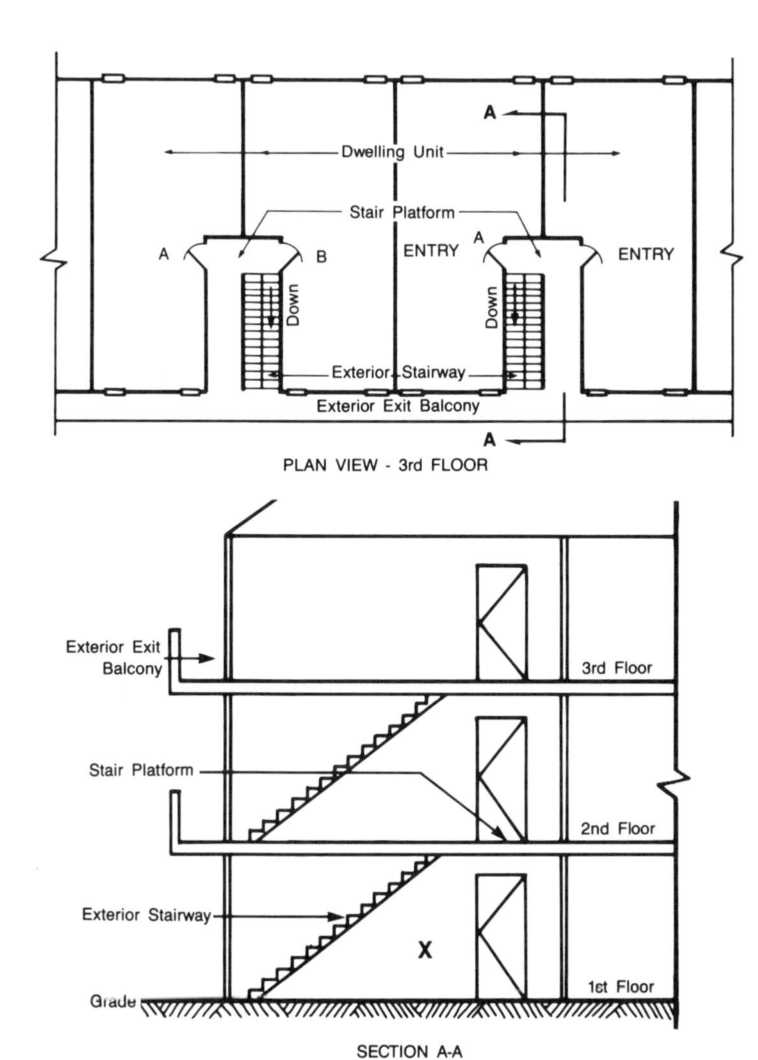

GIVEN: Group R, Div. 1 Occupancy Type V-One Hour Building
Four Dwelling Units per Floor Three Stories

Two exits are required per Section 3303 (a). As designed, the arrangement does not satisfy the separation required for two exits. At Point X, a fire on a floor below will prevent any exiting from this floor or any floor above.

Openings "A" and "B" are required to be protected by one-hour fire assemblies per Section 3306 (k). Opening "W" may be unprotected per Section 3305 (h)2.

REFERENCE: SECTION 3306 (k)

FIGURE 7-33 EXTERIOR EXIT STAIRWAY—GROUP R, DIVISION 1 OCCUPANCY NON-CONFORMING DESIGN, INADEQUATE SEPARATION OF EXITS

NOTES

arrangement, the bridge provides the second exit from this floor. As with Figure 7-34, a fire at Point "X" below the floor in question will make the stairway and the bridge unusable, thereby preventing exiting from the third floor. The separation of exits per Section 3303 (c) is violated.

Furthermore, openings "A" and "B" on the floor below this floor are required to have three-fourths-hour fire assemblies, as they are within 10 feet of the exterior stairway.

The designer must evaluate the potential hazard posed to the occupants of the building by considering the context and intent of the code and not solely the literal readings of selected provisions. Attempting literal code compliance with hazards unresolved does not prevent the design professional's responsibility from being challenged. As with other code intents, such as carrying loads to the ground and carrying fire-rated construction on fire-rated supports, the designer must go past the literal reading of the code in the design.

The enforcement official should review submitted designs in light of the intent of the code and the safety to building occupants. Designs that fail to meet the intent of the separation and protection of exit paths must be changed to assure occupant safety within the code's intent.

Sec. 3306

(q) Stairway Identification. Approved stairway identification signs shall be located at each floor level in all enclosed stairways in buildings four or more stories in height. The sign shall identify stairway, indicate whether there is a roof access, the floor level, the upper and lower terminus of the stairway. The sign shall be located approximately 5 feet above the floor landing in a position which is readily visible when the door is in the open or closed position. Signs shall comply with requirements of U.B.C. Standard No. 33-2.

Stair numbering is one of the life safety provisions added to the code primarily in Section 1807. It identifies the stairway and indicates to the stairway user his relationship to the point of stairway termination.

For high-rise buildings, refer to the Section 1807 (j) provisions. The high-rise provision (j)2 uses the stair identification requirement of Section 3306 (q) for communicating the user's location, by stair and floor, to the central control station.

Ramps

Sec. 3307. (b) Width. The width of ramps shall be determined as specified in Section 3303 (b), but shall not be less than 44 inches, except as specified herein.

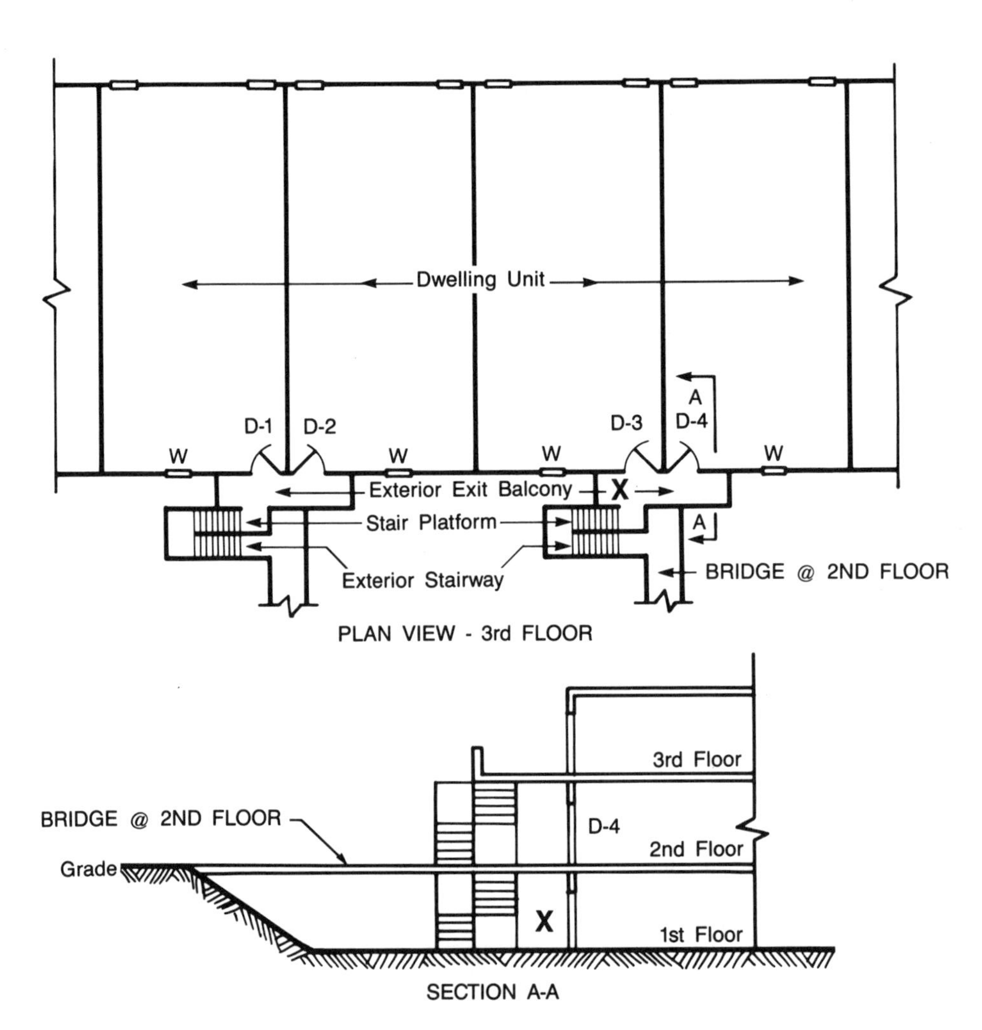

GIVEN: Group R, Div. 1 Occupancy
Type V-One Hour Building
Four Dwelling Units per Floor
Three Stories

Two exits are required per Section 3303 (a). The stair and bridge do not satisfy the separation requirements of the code. At Point "X", a fire on a floor below would prevent either path of exit travel from being available.

Openings "D" and "W" on the first and second floors are required to be protected with 3/4-hour fire assemblies as they are within 10 feet of the exterior stairway per Section 3306 (k).

REFERENCE: SECTION 3306 (k)

FIGURE 7-34 EXTERIOR EXIT STAIRWAY—GROUP R, DIVISION 1 OCCUPANCY, NON-CONFORMING DESIGN, INADEQUATE SEPARATION OF EXITS

Ramps serving an occupant load of 49 or less shall not be less than 36 inches in width. Handrails may project into the required width a distance of 3 1/2 inches from each side of a ramp. Other projections, such as trim and similar decorative features, may project into the required width 1 1/2 inches on each side.

This section and four other sections, Section 3303 (b), 3305 (b), 3306 (b) and 3321 (c) have all been changed to use a new method of calculating the width of the required exit. For details of the use of the provisions see Section 3303 (b) discussion.

The designer should check state and local jurisdiction requirements particularly as they pertain to handicapped access. In all instances, the most restrictive applicable requirements will prevail.

Horizontal Exit

Sec. 3308. (a) Used as a Required Exit. A horizontal exit may be considered as a required exit when conforming to the provisions of this chapter. A horizontal exit shall not serve as the only exit from a portion of a building, and when two or more exits are required, not more than one half of the total number of exits or total exit width may be horizontal exits.

(b) Openings. All openings in the two-hour fire-resistive wall which provides a horizontal exit shall be protected by a fire assembly having a fire-protection rating of not less than one and one-half hours.

(c) Discharge Areas. A horizontal exit shall lead into a floor area having capacity for an occupant load not less than the occupant load served by such exit. The capacity shall be determined by allowing 3 square feet of net clear floor area for each occupant to be accommodated therein, not including areas of stairs, elevators and other shafts or courts. In Group I, Division 1 Occupancies the capacity shall be determined by allowing 15 square feet of net clear floor area per ambulatory occupant and 30 square feet per nonambulatory occupant. The area into which a horizontal exit leads shall be provided with exits adequate to meet the requirements of this chapter but need not include the added capacity imposed by persons entering through the horizontal exits.

The general subject of horizontal exits was discussed under the Section 3301 (b) definition of horizontal exit. Section 3308 provides the details regarding the opening protection and the amount of space required for the refuge or discharge area.

Stairway, Ramp and Escalator Enclosures.

Sec. 3309. (a) General. Every interior stairway, ramp or escalator shall be enclosed as specified in this section.

EXCEPTIONS: 1. In other than Group H and Group I Occupancies, an enclosure will not be required for a stairway, ramp or escalator serving only one adjacent floor and not connected with corridors or stairways serving other floors. For enclosure of escalators serving Group B Occupancies, see Chapter 17.

2. Stairs in Group R, Division 3 Occupancies and stairs within individual

dwelling units in Group R, Division 1 Occupancies need not be enclosed.
3. Stairs in open parking garages, as defined in Section 709, need not be enclosed.

The requirements in this section resemble those of Section 1706 for shaft enclosures. This section also contains Exceptions similar to those in Section 1706. An example of this similarity is Exception 1 from Section 3309 wherein two adjacent floors may have open stairs between them. This is similar to Exception #1 in Section 1706.

Sec. 3309
(b) Enclosure Construction. Enclosure walls shall be of not less than two-hour fire-resistive construction in buildings four or more stories in height or of Types I and II fire-resistive construction and shall be of not less than one-hour fire-resistive construction elsewhere.

EXCEPTION: In sprinkler protected parking garages restricted to the storage of private pleasure motor vehicles, stairway enclosures may be enclosed with glazing meeting the requirements of Section 4306 (g), (h) and (i).

Section 3309 (b) requires two-hour stair enclosures for buildings four or more stories in height. The prior codes invoked the two-hour enclosure provision for stairways more than four stories in height.

The reason behind the prior codes' provision was to permit Type III and V one-hour buildings with full sprinklering to have one-hour stair enclosures, consistent with the rest of the building's construction.

This change was proposed to provide a "safer staging area for fire department operations in four-storied buildings." This rationale could be extended to virtually any lower-height building as well.

> In the opinion of the author, this type of change to the code is unwarranted and adds unnecessary cost without commensurate increased safety.

(c) Openings into Enclosures. Openings into exit enclosures other than permitted exterior openings shall be limited to those necessary for exiting from a normally occupied space into the enclosure and exiting from the enclosure. Other penetrations into and openings through exit enclosure are prohibited except for ductwork and equipment necessary for independent stair pressur-

ization, sprinkler piping, standpipes and electrical conduit serving the stairway and terminating in a listed box not exceeding 16 square inches in area. Penetrations and communicating openings between adjacent exit enclosures are not permitted regardless of whether the opening is protected.

All exit doors in an exit enclosure shall be protected by a fire assembly having a fire-protection rating of not less than one hour where one-hour shaft construction is permitted and one and one-half hours where two-hour shaft construction is required. Doors shall be maintained self-closing or shall be automatic closing by actuation of a smoke detector as provided for in Section 4306(b). The maximum transmitted temperature end point shall not exceed 450°F. above ambient at the end of 30 minutes of the fire exposure specified in U.B.C. Standard No. 43-2.

The general requirements in these sections are:

Enclosure walls

- Buildings 4 stories or more in height construction—2-hour
- Buildings of Type I or II-FR construction —2-hour
- All other buildings construction —1-hour

Opening protection

- Two-hour enclosures—One and one-half hour fire assembly
- One-hour enclosure—One-hour fire assembly

The code contains specific provisions for the types of openings permitted into exit enclosures and those specifically prohibited. These additional specific items should assist the designer and the enforcement official in reviewing a design. The designer should pay careful attention to those limited permissible penetrations and inclusions relating to the stairway pressurization function.

The code text does not indicate the materials allowed for the electrical conduit. The walls of the exit stairways are required to be either one-hour or two-hour fire-rated construction. The materials that penetrate or are included within the walls must maintain the fire integrity of the wall rating. The designer and the enforcement official should pay particular attention to these items to avoid jeopardizing the integrity of the exitway. See Chapter 43 provisions regarding penetrations and the discussion in Article 8 of this Guide.

Sec. 3309

(d) Extent of Enclosure. Stairway and ramp enclosures shall include landings and parts of floors connecting stairway flights and shall also include a corridor

on the ground floor leading from the stairway to the exterior of the building. Enclosed corridors or passageways are not required from unenclosed stairways. Every opening into the corridor shall comply with the requirements of Section 3309 (c).

EXCEPTION: In office buildings classed as a Group B, Division 2 Occupancy, a maximum of 50 percent of the exits may discharge through a street-floor lobby, provided the required exit width is free and unobstructed and the entire street floor is protected with an automatic sprinkler system.

This section reiterates a basic requirement for an exit path: the stairway must connect with an exit passageway to the street. The exit passageway must have the same fire rating requirements as the stairway.

No openings are allowed into the exit path except exit doors from exit corridors or from other areas, such as an open plan office, for which the stair serves as the exitway. Doors into the stairway and exit passageway can be held open by smoke detector-activated hold-open devices. (See Figures 7-2 and 7-35.)

When the stairway run continues down to the basement, there must be a barrier, usually a door, to prevent someone who is using the stair in an emergency situation from continuing past the ground floor level.

Smokeproof Enclosure

Sec. 3310 (a) General. A smokeproof enclosure shall consist of a vestibule and continuous stairway enclosed from the highest point to the lowest point by walls of two-hour fire-resistive construction. There shall be no openings into the stairway portion of the smokeproof enclosure other than those permitted by the first paragraph of Section 3309 (c). The supporting frame shall be protected as set forth in Table No. 17-A.

In buildings with air-conditioning systems or pressure air supply serving more than one story, an approved smoke detector shall be placed in the return-air duct or plenum prior to exhausting from the building or being diluted by outside air. Upon activation, the detector shall cause the return air to exhaust completely from the building without any recirculation through the building. Such devices may be installed in each room or space served by a return-air duct.

(b) When Required. In a building having a floor used for human occupancy which is located more than 75 feet above the lowest level of fire department vehicle access, all of the required exits shall be smokeproof enclosures.

► ■■■ ◄

(c) Outlet. A smokeproof enclosure shall exit into a public way or into an exit passageway leading to a public way. The exit passageway shall be without other openings and shall have walls, floors and ceiling of two-hour fire-resistive construction.

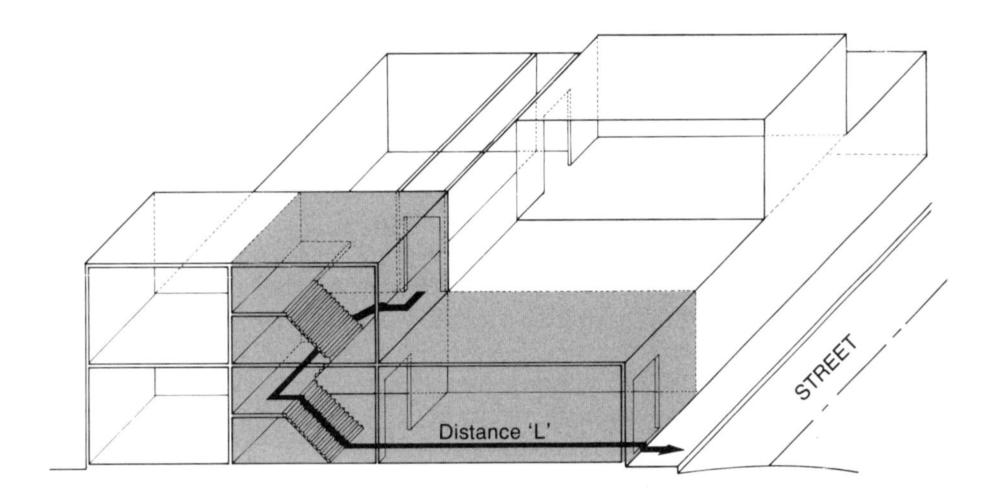

Distance 'L' represents the "extend of the exit enclosure." It includes the stairway enclosure and exit passageway to the exterior of the building on ground level. The enclosure includes parts of floors connecting the stairway flights.

The enclosure may commence at an exit corridor or where an open floor plan is used, at the door to the stairway from the open floor area.

REFERENCE: SECTION 3309 (d)

FIGURE 7-35 EXTENT OF EXIT ENCLOSURE

(d) Barrier. A stairway in a smokeproof enclosure shall not continue below the grade level unless an approved barrier is provided at the ground level to prevent persons from accidentally continuing into the basement.

(e) Access. Access to smokeproof enclosures shall be by way of a vestibule or open exterior exit balcony constructed of noncombustible materials.

A smokeproof enclosure is a stairway into which smoke is either prevented from entering by a naturally ventilated vestibule or from which the smoke is mechanically removed. In the latter case, the pressure relationship is such that the pressure in the stairway is higher than that of the vestibule. Under these conditions, smoke from a corridor is prevented from entering into the stair shaft. (See Figures 7-36 and 7-37.)

Smokeproof enclosures, or smoke towers, as they are usually referred to, are mandatory for all required stairways in buildings more than 75 feet in height, measured to the floor of the highest occupied level. This is the same parameter used to define a high-rise building in the Section 1807 high-rise building requirements. An Exception to this general requirement is contained in Section 3310 (b).

A smoke tower is required to terminate at a public way or at an exit passageway leading to a public way. The passageway must be of two-hour fire-resistive construction and conform to Section 3312. This passageway should be considered the same as the stairway portion of the smoke tower. Any openings into the exit passageway of a smoke tower should have a vestibule conforming to the requirements in Section 3310 (f) or (g), or should be pressurized when the Section 3310 (b) Exception is used.

Only stairways required to be smoke towers need vestibules or pressurization. In low-rise buildings, stairways are not required to have either a vestibule or pressurization.

The requirements for the ventilated vestibule are provided in subsection (f). The requirements for the mechanically ventilated vestibule are provided in subsection (g). A third method of keeping the stairway smoke-free is described in the Exception to subsection (b). That exception offers the alternative of a pressurized stairway. If this option is used, all enclosed stairways must be pressurized. The requirements of subsection (g) 6 and 7 apply to the pressurization because it has to be as reliable as the mechanical ventilation.

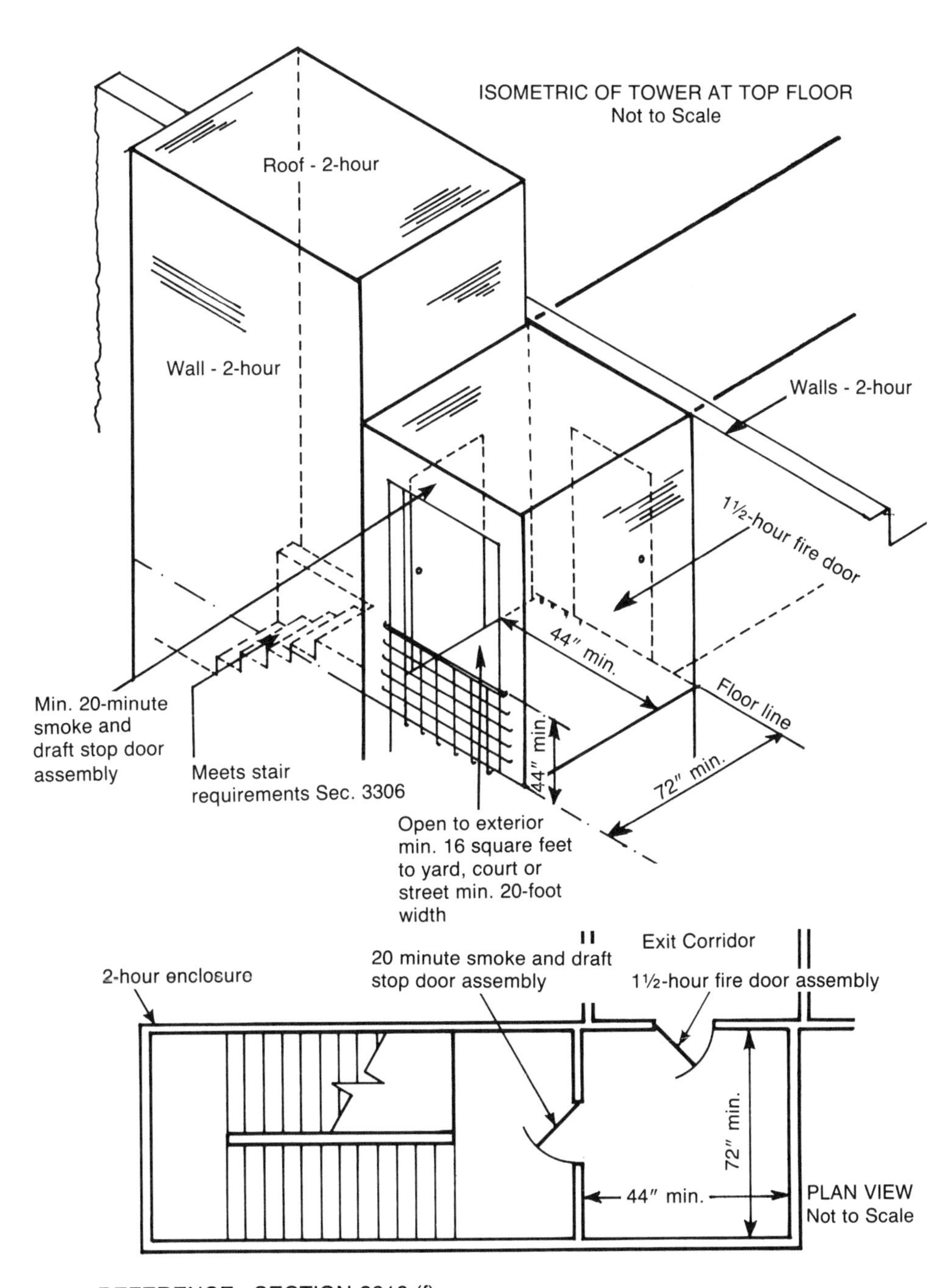

REFERENCE: SECTION 3310 (f)

FIGURE 7-36 SMOKEPROOF TOWER, ENCLOSURE—VESTIBULE OPEN TO EXTERIOR

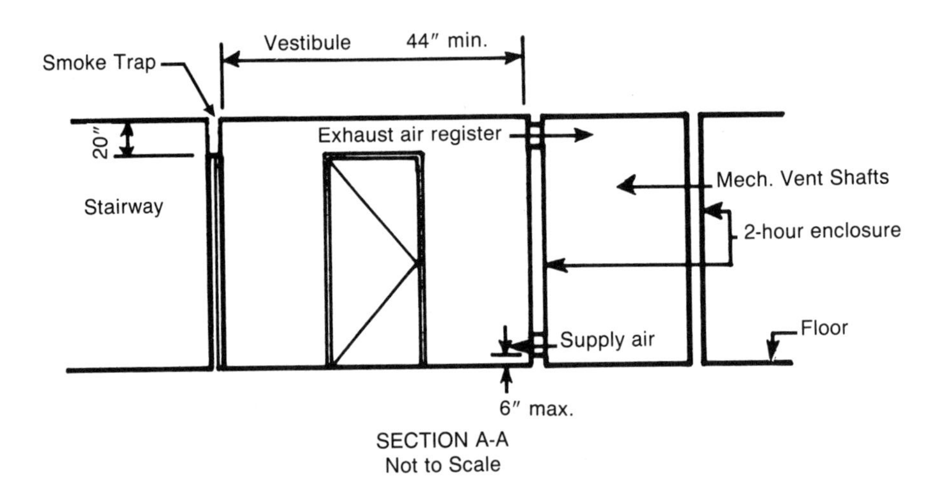

SECTION A-A
Not to Scale

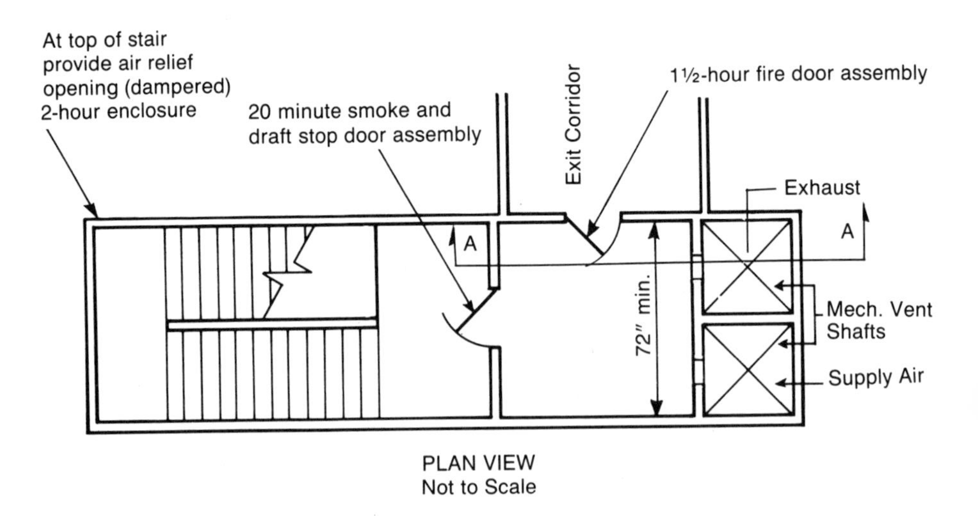

PLAN VIEW
Not to Scale

REFERENCE: SECTION 3310 (g)

FIGURE 7-37 SMOKEPROOF TOWER, ENCLOSURES, MECHANICALLY VENTILATED VESTIBULE

Sec. 3310
(f) Smokeproof Enclosure by Natural Ventilation.
1.Doors. When a vestibule is provided, the door assembly into the vestibule shall have a one and one-half-hour fire-protection rating, and the door assembly from the vestibule to the stairs shall be a smoke- and draft-control assembly having not less than a 20-minute fire-protection rating. Doors shall be maintained self-closing or shall be automatic closing by actuation of a smoke detector. When access to the stairway is by means of an open exterior exit balcony, the door assembly to the stairway shall have a one and one-half-hour fire-protection rating and shall be maintained self-closing or shall be automatic closing by actuation of a smoke detector.
2. Open-air vestibule. The vestibule shall have a minimum dimension of 44 inches in width and 72 inches in direction of exit travel. The vestibule shall have a minimum of 16 square feet of opening in a wall facing an exterior court, yard or public way at least 20 feet in width.

This section contains the construction requirements for a ventilated vestibule. This form of smoke tower uses natural ventilation. The ventilation is provided through one side of the vestibule which is open to the exterior of the building. The vestibule must be on an exterior wall of the building facing a court, yard, or public way. (See Figure 7-36.)

Sec. 3310
(g) Smokeproof Enclosures by Mechanical Ventilation.1. Doors. The door assembly from the building into the vestibule shall have a one-and-one-half-hour fire-protection rating, and the door assembly from the vestibule to the stairway shall be a smoke- and draft-control assembly having not less than a 20-minute fire-protection rating. The door to the stairways shall be provided with a drop-sill or other provision to minimize the air leakage. Doors shall be maintained self-closing or shall be automatic closing by activation of a smoke detector or in the event of a power failure.

► ■■■ ◄

The provisions in Section 3310 (g) relating to the mechanically ventilated smokeproof enclosure are less restrictive than the prior code. The change follows the intent of the code provision, which is to require that a fail-safe smoke-detector-actuated release device be furnished at all smokeproof enclosure doors. The code now permits either:

- self-closing doors or
- automatic closing doors released by activation of a smoke-detector or a power failure.

These alternatives appear to be declared equivalent by the new change. The author reached this conclusion from the text of the code provision. The author's conclusion may be at variance with the intent or original purpose of the Fire & Life Safety Code Development

Committee. However, because the phrase "automatic closing by activation of..." precedes the two means of such actuation, the grammatical sense is that only the automatic closing characteristic is tied to the smoke detector and the power failure.

The proponent of this change tied the operation of the doors in the mechanically ventilated vestibule to the comparable doors in a naturally ventilated vestibule. The proponent's intent was to "provide consistency between Section 3310 (f) and (g)." Unfortunately, this desire for consistency overlooks the considerable difference between natural and mechanical ventilation conditions.

The design of the mechanical system is predicated on all doors being closed, as stated in Section 3310 (g)5.The natural ventilated system provision in Section 3310 (f) uses the same language as is now in Section 3310 (g)1.The code requires the doors in the naturally ventilated systems to close by smoke detector or power failure; does not rely on the doors being closed because the ventilation is naturally provided.

Thus, this provision requires the doors in the mechanically ventilated systems closed—a desirable requirement but not a mandatory one. This is not what Section 3310 (g)5 presumes to occur.

The designer may select the self-closing feature and ignore the automatic closing provisions, with their more costly activation methods. The enforcement agency must accept self-closing doors as complying with the code. The owner must, as throughout the code per Section 104 (d), maintain the self-closing feature, i.e., avoid use of wedges.

The author recommends that the designer maintain the assured closing capability of the doors to the mechanically ventilated smokeproof enclosure, regardless of whether the doors are self-closing or automatic closing. In each case, the closing should be both by a smoke detector and by a power failure. If self-closing is used, there should be a magnetic hold-open device provided to avoid the use of wedges.

After a building is constructed, it is infrequently subject to the building official's inspection. The burden of compliance with Section 104 (d) rests with the owner.

The designer should make a clear, written indication to the owner that choosing the self-closing devices for the doors to a mechanically ventilated smokeproof enclosure will require regular, thorough inspections by the owner's representatives. It may also require lease restrictions and penalties to accomplish the maintenance of the self-closing feature.

The fire service must develop a means for enforcing the maintenance requirements, as the fire code charges the chief with such responsibility.

Sec. 3314.

(e) Floor-level Exit Signs. When exit signs are required by Section 3314 (a), additional approved low-level exit signs which are internally or externally illuminated or self-luminous, shall be provided in all interior exit corridors serving guest rooms of hotels or motels in a Group R, Division 1 Occupancy.

The bottom of the sign shall not be less than 6 inches nor more than 8 inches above the floor level. For exit doors, the sign shall be on the door or adjacent to the door with the closest edge of the sign within 4 inches of the door frame.

Section 3314 (e) is a new subsection that requires low-level exit signs in all interior exit corridors in hotels and motels (Group R, Division 1 Occupancy). These signs may be either internally or externally illuminated or may be self-luminous. They must be placed wherever an exit sign is required in Section 3314 (a). (See Figure 7-38.)

Although exit signs are usually located above the center of a doorway, the location of the low-level exit sign is presently left to the discretion of the designer regarding which side of the door it must be placed. The code requirement does not address the condition when there is a pair of doors, that is, two doors involved. The sign over the door is centered over the opening. The designer should either place such signs on each leaf or verify the local requirements as to the situation. This will be a common occurrence when the exit corridor also serves a large meeting room. In such situations, the occupant load may require a width of corridor greater than four feet, requiring a pair of doors.

If the door is in a horizontal exit, there must be two low-level signs, one on each side of the door.

At present, this provision does not apply to any other occupancy than the Group R, Division 1 hotel and motel occupancies. However, there is a trend to add increased restrictive provisions similar to this for other occupancies. This trend is based on the premise that in a fire, the corridor's upper levels are untenable for breathing and that the exit signs over the exit doors would not be visible because of smoke obscuring the signs and doors.

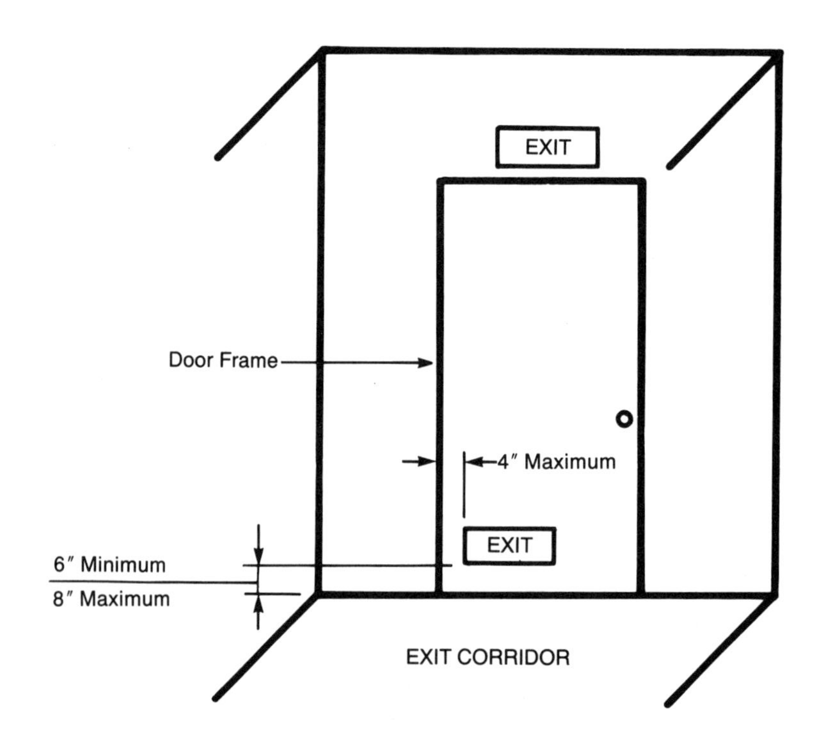

Low-Level exit signs must be provided in Group R, Division 1 hotels and motels wherever exit signs are required in interior exit corridors.

The code provision does not provide guidance for pairs of doors, doors in area separation walls or horizontal exits. See discussion in text. The low-level exit sign may be internally or externally illuminated.

REFERENCE: SECTION 3314 (e)

FIGURE 7-38 LOW-LEVEL EXIT SIGNS IN EXIT CORRIDORS – GROUP R, DIVISION 1 OCCUPANCY, HOTEL OR MOTEL

An even greater restrictive concept proposed but not accepted would have required exit path markings within eight inches of the floor in these corridors. This trend must be watched closely as another of the continuing restrictive provisions being added to the Group R, Division 1 Occupancy. The argument made during the discussion of this change referred to fires of several years ago. These inevitably occurred in buildings that did not meet the current code requirements. The same rationale was used to adopt such changes as that to Section 1209, second paragraph and Section 3802 (h).

In the author's opinion, the continued adding of restrictive provisions not only raises the cost of construction but also weakens the code by not maintaining the code's purpose of setting forth the minimum requirements for public safety and welfare.

Sections 3317 through 3321 relate to Special Requirements based on Occupancy.

These sections provide special exiting requirements for certain occupancies as follows:

Sec. 3317—Assembly Occupancy Division 1
Sec. 3318—All other Assembly Occupancies
Sec. 3319—Schools
Sec. 3320—Hazardous Occupancies
Sec. 3321—Institutional Occupancies

Group I Occupancies

Sec. 3321. (c) Corridors. The minimum clear width of a corridor shall be determined as specified in Section 3303 (b), but shall not be less than 44 inches, except that corridors serving any area housing one or more nonambulatory persons shall not be less than 8 feet in width. Any change in elevation of the floor in a corridor serving nonambulatory persons shall be made by means of a ramp.

This section and four other sections, Section 3303 (b), 3305 (b), 3306 (b) and 3307 (b) have all been changed to use a new method of calculating the width of the required exit. For details of the use of the provisions see Section 3303 (b) discussion.

TABLE NO. 33-A—MINIMUM EGRESS AND ACCESS REQUIREMENTS

USE[1 2]	MINIMUM OF TWO EXITS OTHER THAN ELEVATORS ARE REQUIRED WHERE NUMBER OF OCCUPANTS IS AT LEAST	OCCUPANT LOAD FACTOR[3] (Sq.Ft.)
1. Aircraft Hangers (no repairs)	10	500
2. Auction rooms	30	7
3. Assembly Areas, Concentrated Use (without fixed seats)	50	7
Auditoriums		
Bowling Alleys (Assembly areas)		
Churches and Chapels		
Dance Floors		
Lobby Accessory to Assembly Occupancy		
Lodge Rooms		
Reviewing Stands		
Stadiums Waiting Area		
4. Assembly Areas, Less-concentrated Use	50	15
Conference Rooms		
Dining Rooms		
Drinking Establishments		
Exhibit Rooms		
Gymnasiums		
Lounges		
Stages		
5. Bowling Alley (assume no occupant load for bowling lanes)	50	[5]
6. Children's Homes and Homes for the Aged	6	80
7. Classrooms	50	20
8. Courtrooms	50	40
9. Dormitories	10	50
10. Dwellings	10	300
11. Exercise Rooms	50	50
12. Garages, Parking	30	200
13. Hospitals and Sanitariums-Nursing Homes	6	80
Sleeping Rooms	6	80
Treatment Rooms	10	80
14. Hotels and Apartments	10	200
15. Kitchen – Commercial	30	200
16. Library Reading Room	50	50
17. Locker Rooms	30	50
18. Malls (See Chapter 36)	—	—
19. Manufacturing Areas	30	200
20. Mechanical Equipment Room	30	300
21. Nurseries for Children (Day-care)	7	35
22. Offices	30	100
23. School Shops and Vocational Rooms	50	50

TABLE NO. 33-A—MINIMUM EGRESS AND ACCESS REQUIREMENTS

USE[1 2]	MINIMUM OF TWO EXITS OTHER THAN ELEVATORS ARE REQUIRED WHERE NUMBER OF OCCUPANTS IS AT LEAST	OCCUPANT LOAD FACTOR[3] (Sq.Ft.)
24. Skating Rinks	50	50 on the skating area; 15 on the deck
25. Storage and Stock Rooms	30	300
26. Stores – Retail Sales Rooms	50[4]	30
27. Swimming Pools	50	50 for the pool area; 15 on the deck
28. Warehouses	30	500
29. All others	50	100

[1] Access to, and egress from, buildings for persons with disabilities shall be provided as specified in Chapter 31.

[2] For additional provisions on number of exits from Group H and I Occupancies and from rooms containing fuel-fired equipment or cellulose nitrate, see Sections 3320, 3321 and 3322, respectively.

[3] This table shall not be used to determine working space requirements per person.

[4] See Section 3303 for basement exit requirements.

[5] Occupant load based upon five persons for each alley, including 15 feet of runway.

Though not included in Chapter 33, the designer is reminded that there are also special requirements for Group R Occupancies. These requirements, outlined in Section 1204, relate to escape and rescue windows. They are not exit requirements. See the discussion in Article 9 of this Guide.

In addition, Section 3322 contains requirements for all occupancies that cover the special hazards of areas such as incinerator, boiler and furnace rooms and similar (H) hazardous areas.

NOTE: There are a considerable number of diagrams in the *Life Safety Handbook of NFPA* relating to many items discussed in this Article of the Guide. The reader is cautioned in regard to the *Life Safety Code and Handbook of the NFPA,* because the documents contain some provisions and concepts that are at variance with those of the UBC.

The presence of provisions in another document that may differ in intent or content from the UBC does not affect the UBC intent or content. The other document's views do not prevail unless the rest of the provisions in both the other document and the UBC are the same. When the document expresses a different intent it should not be used by the designer to justify noncompliance with the UBC provisions and intent.

ARTICLE 8
THE INTERIOR FINISH PROVISIONS OF CHAPTER 42 and THE FIRE RESISTIVE PROVISIONS OF CHAPTER 43

Before discussing the next provisions it is necessary to place Chapters 42 and 43 in perspective. Both chapters relate to fire regulations of building construction materials.

The provisions of Chapter 42 regulate the surface burning characteristics of materials used to decorate, sound-deaden or insulate the walls and ceiling of a room or space in a building. The purpose of these regulations is to control the rate of fire spread along the surface of the material.

Chapter 43 regulates the capacity of building elements such as walls, floors, beams and columns, doors and windows to withstand an attack by fire and prevent fire penetration through the element or collapse of the element within a specified time period of up to four hours.

The Chapter 42 provisions go back to the early 1940s when the tragic Boston Coconut Grove fire claimed over 400 lives. A major cause of those deaths was traced to the wall and ceiling coverings. The covering materials permitted the fire to spread rapidly, cutting off access to exits. The subsequent investigations resulted in Underwriters Laboratories Inc. developing a test procedure for surface burning characteristics.

The 1952 UBC contained the first flame-spread regulations. The regulations were and are based on the test procedure, UBC Standard 42-1 (ASTM E-84), commonly called the Tunnel Test.

Materials used for floor coverings are not presently regulated in the UBC. However, under state and federal regulations, certain occupancies such as hospitals are so regulated. It is this author's opinion that within 10 to 15 years such regulations will be included in the UBC for most occupancies. Flooring materials, where they are presently regulated, are tested using an evaluation procedure that differs from the Tunnel Test.

In Tunnel Test, a sample of a material 20 inches wide and 24 feet long is placed at the top surface of a "tunnel" that is 12 inches high, 18 inches wide and 25 feet long. The sample is exposed to a 4 1/2-foot flame tongue at one end with a prescribed air flow, gas supply and pressure. The test period for the burn is 10 minutes. The furnace is initially calibrated with asbestos cement board and red oak samples before testing the particular material.

A row of glass view ports along one side of the furnace allows the flame front's rate of progress for the two calibration samples to be observed and noted during the test period. The rate of flame spread for the asbestos cement board and red oak is rated as 0 and 100, respectively.

The flame front of the red oak sample should reach a point 19 1/2 feet from the end of the ignition flame in 5 1/2 minutes. The asbestos cement board does not produce a spread of flame past the end of the ignition flame tongue. The unknown material is then placed in the Tunnel furnace and exposed to the same flame tongue and test conditions. The time and extent of the flame front is noted and the relative flame-spread value is calculated from the data observed during the test.

Thus, the flame-spread value is a relative number, being compared to the two calibration materials. A material with a flame-spread of 25 can be considered as having a rate of surface burning (flame-spread) one-quarter that of red oak, while one with a 200 value has a flame-spread twice that of red oak.

Two other characteristics are measured in the Tunnel Test:

1. Smoke density.
2. Fuel contributed.

The data for these characteristics are obtained during the same test period from a photo-electric cell and thermocouple placed at the exhaust end of the furnace. The resultant data are compared to that of the red oak standard. The red oak value is set for each of these characteristics at 100.

Knowing the background of the test procedure should assist the reader in understanding the philosophy of the provisions of Chapter 42. We shall provide a similar background discussion later for the Chapter 43 provisions.

General

Sec. 4201. Interior wall and ceiling finish shall mean interior wainscoting, paneling or other finish applied structurally or for decoration, acoustical correction, surface insulation or similar purposes. Requirements for finishes in this chapter shall not apply to trim defined as picture molds, chair rails, baseboards and handrails; to doors and windows or their frames, nor to materials which are less than 1/28 inch in thickness applied directly to the surface of walls or ceilings, if these materials have flame-spread characteristics no greater than paper of this thickness applied directly to a noncombustible backing in the same manner.

Foam plastics shall not be used as interior finish except as provided in Section 1712. For foam plastic trim, see Section 1705 (e).

The types of materials regulated by the code are large expanse covering materials, not the trim and other small or isolated items of decoration. Thin materials essentially made of paper, such as wallpaper, are not subject to regulation. However, vinyl wallcovering is regulated since its burning characteristics, particularly that of smoke generation (smoke density), are considerably greater than those of paper.

The designer is cautioned to avoid materials that could exceed the permissible flame-spread values. Often these fire considerations are overlooked when choosing materials, particularly when a materials representative, in extolling the benefits of a new surfacing product, emphasizes ease of maintenance and glosses over the material's burning characteristics.

Application of Controlled Interior Finish

Sec. 4203. Interior finish materials applied to walls and ceilings shall be tested as specified in Section 4202 and regulated for purposes of limiting surface-burning by the following provisions:

1. When walls and ceilings are required by any provision in this code to be of fire- resistive or noncombustible construction, the finish material shall be applied directly against such fire-resistive or noncombustible construction or to furring strips not exceeding 1 3/4 inches applied directly against such surfaces. The intervening spaces between such furring strips shall be filled with inorganic or Class I material or shall be fire blocked not to exceed 8 feet in any direction. See Section 2516 (f) for fire blocking.

2. Where walls and ceilings are required to be of fire-resistive or noncombustible construction and walls are set out or ceilings are dropped distances greater than specified in paragraph 1 of this section, Class I finish materials shall be used except where the finish materials are protected on both sides by automatic sprinkler systems or are attached to a noncombustible backing or to furring strips installed as specified in paragraph 1. The hangers and assembly members of such dropped ceilings that are below the main ceiling line shall be of noncombustible materials except that in Types III and Type V construction fire-retardant treated wood may be used. The construction of each set-out wall

shall be of fire-resistive construction as required elsewhere in this code. See Section 2516 (f) for fire blocks and draft stops.

3. Wall and ceiling finish materials of all classes as permitted in this chapter may be installed directly against the wood decking or planking of Type IV heavy-timber construction or to wood furring strips applied directly to the wood decking or planking installed and fire-stopped as specified in paragraph 1.

4. All interior wall or ceiling finish that is not more than 1/4 inch thick shall be applied directly against a noncombustible backing.

EXCEPTIONS: 1. Class I materials.

2. Materials where the qualifying tests were made with the material suspended or furred out from the noncombustible backing.

This section regulates the installation of interior finishes. The main concern expressed in the several provisions is the furring out of the finish material because the space behind the finish can cause problems such as the following:

- Fire can spread in the cavity formed by the building surface and finish material.
- The finish material can burn through from the room side of the finish material and burn simultaneously on both sides at a greater rate than as tested, thus spreading the fire faster than permitted in that location.
- The rate of heat release of the finish material may greatly exceed that of the finish as tested.

The designer must be sure that the drawings reflect code-complying filling or fire blocking of any such cavities.

There are two changes in this section; the first is one of several changes made for the previously used term "firestopping," replacing it with fire blocking, as discussed in Section 2516 (f).

Sub-item 4 now allows two types of materials, such as a Class I material, to be unbacked or a material of any thickness provided it was tested in an unbacked condition. Thus, ceiling tile that is usually thicker than 1/4 inch can qualify provided it passes the appropriate fire testing or is a Class I material. Such is the case for tile that is part of a fire-resistive floor-ceiling assembly.

Maximum Allowable Flame Spread

Sec. 4204. (a) General. The maximum flame-spread classification of finish materials used on interior walls and ceilings shall not exceed that set forth in Table No. 42-B.

EXCEPTIONS: 1. Except in Group I Occupancies and in enclosed vertical

exitways, Class III may be used in other exitways and rooms as wainscotting extending not more than 48 inches above the floor and for tack and bulletin boards covering not more than 5 percent of the gross wall area of the room.

2. Where approved sprinkler system protection is provided, the flame-spread classification rating may be reduced one classification, but in no case shall materials having a classification greater than Class III be used.

3. The exposed faces of Type IV-H.T., structural members and Type IV-H.T., decking and planking, where otherwise permissible under this code are excluded from flame-spread requirements.

Table No. 42-B provides the regulatory flame spread values for all occupancies and specific locations within an occupancy. There is a general concept behind this Table: the more important the location is along the exit path from a room or area within the building to the street, the lower the flame spread value (the "safer material") required for the materials forming the wall and ceiling coverings.

The materials permitted within a room or area are generally allowed to have a flame spread of up to 200, double that of red oak. These materials would include most wood products and plywoods. However, a qualifying provision in Section 4203 Item 4, regarding the use of thin materials such as plywood, reads:

4. All interior wall or ceiling finish other than Class I material which is less than 1/4 inch thick shall be applied directly against a noncombustible backing unless the qualifying tests were made with the material suspended from the noncombustible backing.

The reason for this qualifying provision is that thin materials can burn through at a point of weakness in the material. When this occurs in a material that is not solidly backed, the burning will spread very rapidly on both the front and back sides of the material.

In Tunnel tests of backed and unbacked samples, a 3/16 inch thick plywood sample when tested:

- burned for 8 feet of its length in 10 minutes with a backing against it,
- burned for its entire 24-foot length in less than 10 minutes when not backed.

Plywood inner plies are permitted to have a certain amount of "holidays" or unfilled holes. The inner plies are not necessarily laid up with tight butt joints and may have gaps, splits or unfilled knot holes. Thin sheets of plywood usually have only three plies, two face veneers and a core ply. The face veneers of plywood less than 1/4 inch thick are only .083 inch (one-twelfth inch) thick. As a result, thin plywood can burn through very quickly.

> In the author's opinion, backing should be provided for any plywood less than 1/2 inch thick. Use of 1/2 inch gypsum wallboard as the backing is an economical solution. (See Figure 8-1.)

As one progresses along an exit path in the exit corridor the permissible flame-spread drops from 200, allowed in rooms, to 75. Materials meeting this rating include fire-retardant wood and plywood. Few untreated organic materials will have a flame-spread value below 75. Gypsum wallboard has a flame spread value of 25. That low flame-spread is a result of the treated paper covering the gypsum core. Paint or similar finishes on such wallboard generally do not result in a higher flame-spread value.

The most restrictive flame-spread limitation applies to enclosed vertical exitways, i.e., exit stairways, smoke towers and their exit passageways, for the following reasons:

- they serve as the primary path of exiting,
- they provide access for the fire fighting activities for the upper floors of a building and thus must be kept functional,
- they are vertical shafts and thus have a more rapid spread of fire along the wall surfaces due to stack effect, draft and other sources of air movement.

For these reasons the flame-spread of materials in the vertical exitways is limited to 25. (See Figure 8-2.)

One resource for flame-spread values is the Underwriters Laboratories Inc. *"Building Materials Directory"*; another is the ICBO Evaluation Reports. The designer is urged to inquire, in regard to any material considered for wall and ceiling materials, into the flame-spread and smoke density values for the materials.

The manufacturer, and not the designer, has the burden of having

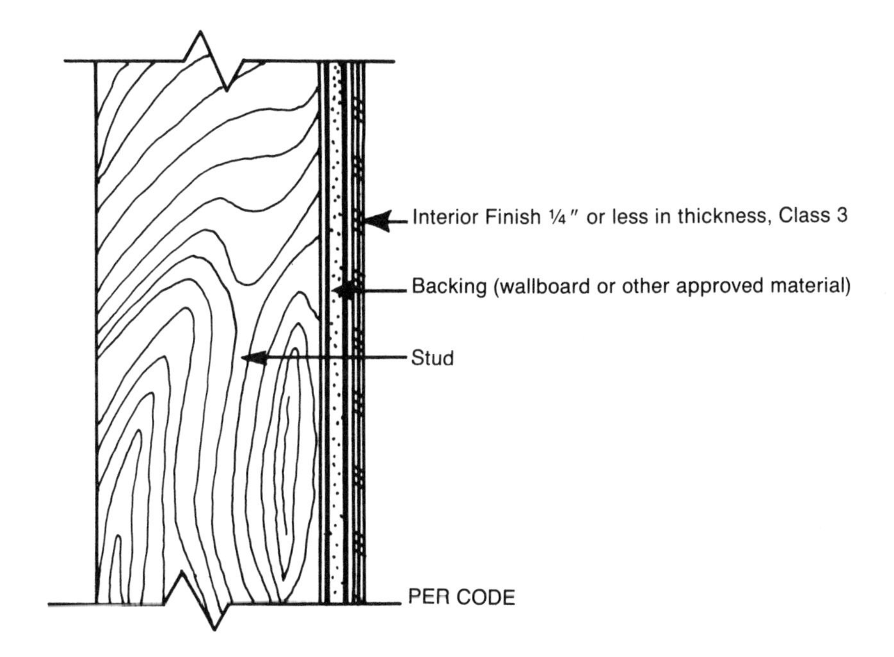

The use of thin combustible finish material requires noncombustible backing per Section 4203. Gypsum wallboard can be used for such backing. Testing has shown that the minimum thickness of combustible finish that should be backed is material less than ½″ thick if a Class 3 finish material.

Recommendation: Use backing behind any Class 3 interior finish material $\leq$ ½″ thickness.

REFERENCE: SECTION 4203 Item 4

FIGURE 8-1 INTERIOR FINISH REQUIREMENT—THIN SURFACE MATERIALS, BACKING

TABLE NO. 42-A—FLAME-SPREAD CLASSIFICATION

MATERIAL QUALIFIED BY:	
Class	Flame-spread Index
I	0- 25
II	26- 75
III	76-200

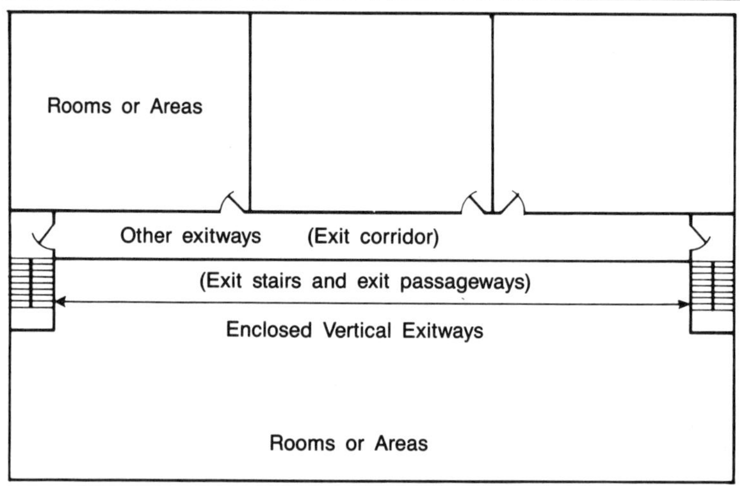

TABLE NO. 42-B—MAXIMUM FLAME-SPREAD CLASS[1]

OCCUPANCY GROUP	VERTICAL EXITWAYS	ENCLOSED OTHER EXITWAYS2	ROOMS OR AREAS
A	I	II	II[3]
E	I	II	III
I	I	II	II[4]
H	I	II	III[5]
B	I	II	III
R-1	I	II	III
R-3	III	III	III[6]
M	NO RESTRICTIONS		

[1]Foam plastics shall comply with the requirements specified in Section 1713.

[2]Finish classification is not applicable to interior walls and ceilings of exterior exit balconies.

[3]In Group A, Division 3 and 4 Occupancies, Class III may be used.

[4]In rooms in which personal liberties of inmates are forcibly restrained, Class I material only shall be used.

[5]Over two stories shall be of Class II.

[6]Flame-spread provisions are not applicable to kitchens and bathrooms of Group R, Division 3 Occupancies.

[7]In Group I, Division 2 and 3 Occupancies, Class II may be used or Class III when the Division 2 or 3 is sprinklered.

REFERENCE: TABLE NO. 42-A, 42-B

FIGURE 8-2 FLAME-SPREAD VALUES BY LOCATION

the listing information available and in a form acceptable to the jurisdiction. As previously indicated in Article 1 of this Guide, if job delays are to be avoided, the designer should avoid specifying a material unless it has been previously submitted by the manufacturer or its representative and accepted by the jurisdiction.

CHAPTER 43
FIRE RESISTIVE STANDARDS

Chapter 43 governs the standards and methods of acceptance of fire-resistive construction materials and assemblies including walls, floors and roofs, beams and girders, columns, doors and windows. These regulations include specific listings of materials and assemblies for particular uses and fire ratings.

Unless the material or assembly has been previously fire tested and listed in an acceptable reference document, a fire test must be conducted to determine the fire-resistive rating of a material or assembly.

Acceptable references include:

UBC Tables No. 43-A,-B and -C

- ICBO Evaluation Reports
- Gypsum Association *"Fire Resistance Design Manual,"*
- many Underwriters Laboratories Inc. listings in their *"Fire Resistance Directory."*

The fire resistance of a material or assembly is determined by a fire test such as the UBC Standard 43-1 (ASTM E-119). This test procedure involves placing a sample of the material or assembly in a furnace and subjecting it to a fire source that exposes the sample to temperatures in accordance with a prescribed time-temperature curve. That curve requires a furnace temperature, five minutes after the start of the test, of 1000°F. At the end of one hour of the test exposure, the furnace temperature reaches 1700°F. (See Figure 8-3.)

For a detailed discussion of the fire testing procedure see Technical Appendix 4.

In the use of Chapter 43, some important common misconceptions arise regarding fire-resistive assemblies. These erroneous concepts need clarification:

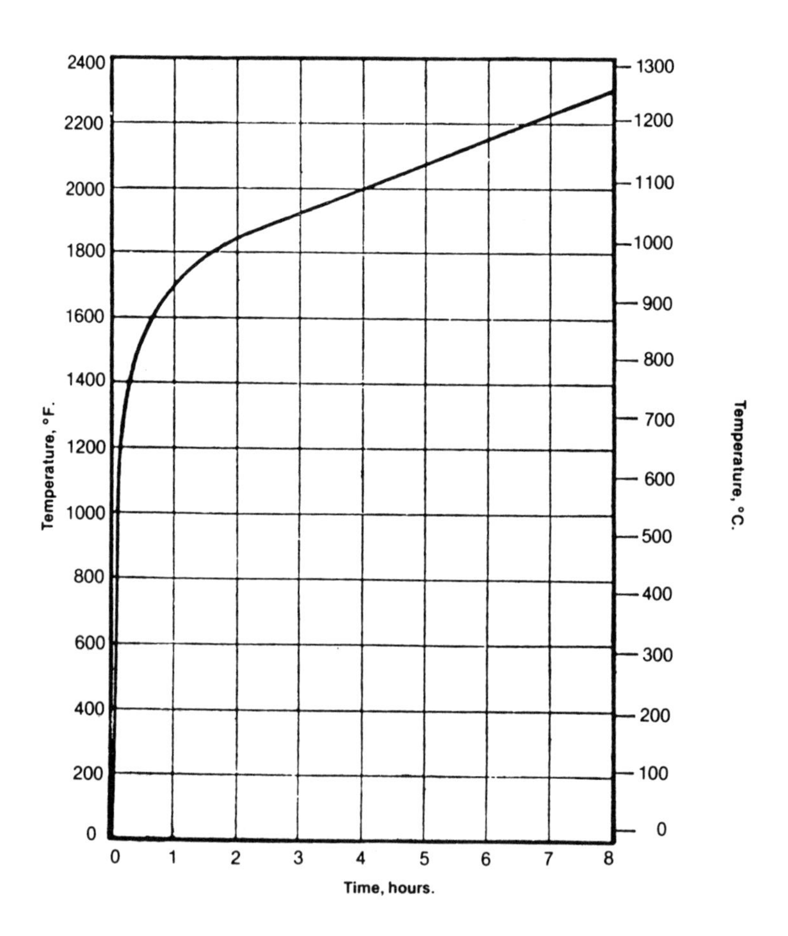

FIGURE NO. 43-1-1

REFERENCE: UBC STANDARD 43-1, FIGURE NO. 43-1-1
ASTM E-119

FIGURE 8-3 STANDARD FIRE TEST TIME-TEMPERATURE CURVE

1. Suspended ceilings.

   The ceiling usually contains steel framing members which are attached by wire or other hangers to the floor assembly above it.

   The tile or board ceilings often used for both acoustical and fire resistance ratings are assumed to be one-hour or two-hour fire rated elements. But it is the assembly, incorporating the ceiling as a part of the fire barrier, that has the rating and not the suspended ceiling by itself. The tiles or boards as well as the framing members bear labels of the inspection agency. These labels are required in order to assure that their fabrication meets the approved fire test criteria.

   In addition to the various components that make up the overall assembly, often the relationship of the elements within the assembly is important in achieving the desired hourly rating. The distance between the floor and the ceiling as well as the clearance between any beams or girders in the cavity and the ceiling protection have bearing on the rating.

   There are no one-hour suspended ceilings: there are only one-hour suspended ceilings as parts of a floor-ceiling assemblies. (See Figure 8-4.)

2. Gypsum wallboard.

   (The trade name that is usually used for this material is Sheetrock, the product of the U.S. Gypsum Company, one of several manufacturers of this generic building material.)

   It is often assumed that 5/8-inch thick wallboard with the designation of Type X, Type XXX, Type C, or a similar label by Underwriters Laboratories Inc., means that the wallboard is one-hour fire rated. The special designation "Type X," or one of the other similar designations, derives from ASTM C-36. In that standard, a wood stud wall assembly, consisting of one layer of 5/8 inch wallboard is placed on each side of a 2x4 wood stud, and tested under the fire test criteria of the code (UBC Standard 43-1 which is based on ASTM E-119). If the assembly can pass a one-hour fire test, the wallboard is given the Type X designation. The manufacturer can use another name for the product and

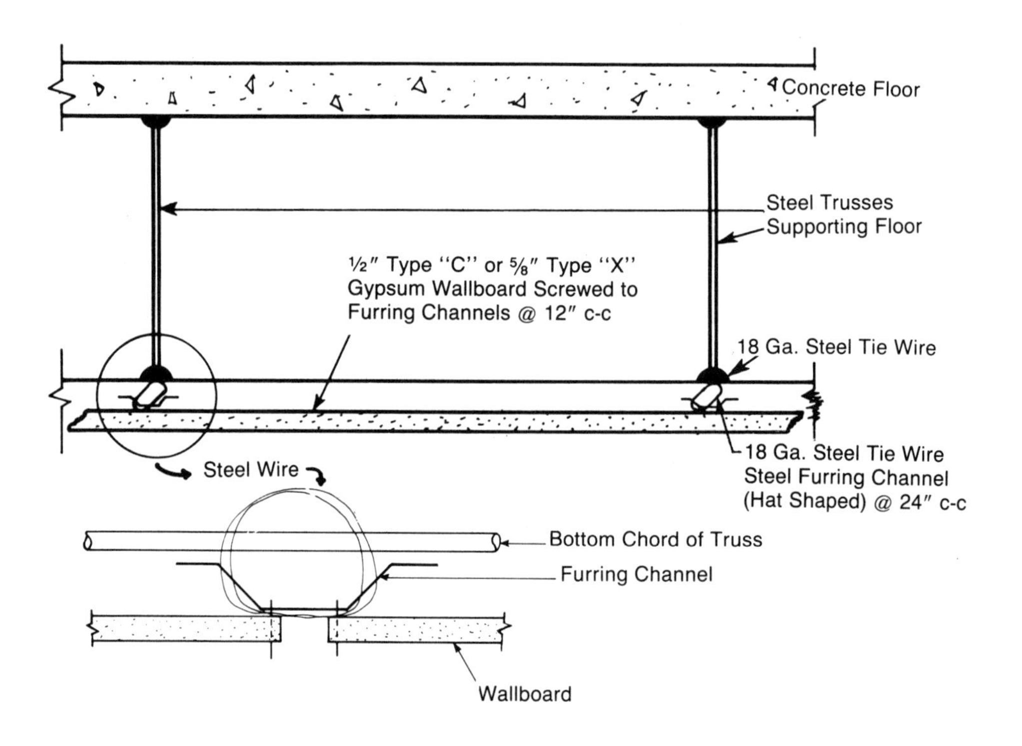

A floor-ceiling assembly consists of several items in most projects, unless the floor is of concrete slab construction that meets the thickness requirements of Table No. 43-C Items 1 through 4. When a suspended ceiling is used as part of the rated floor-ceiling assembly, the elements of that assembly must all be present for the assembly to replicate the approved and tested configuration.

Gypsum wallboard that is customarily used in fire-resistive assemblies is not, by itself, adequate to provide the require hourly rating. Usually there are airspace and attachment requirements and minimum requirements for the floor portion of the assembly. If a tile or lay-in board suspended or directly attached ceiling is part of the floor-ceiling assembly, that ceiling is not, by itself, capable of providing the required fire-resistive rating.

REFERENCE: TABLE NO. 43-C

FIGURE 8-4 FLOOR-CEILING ASSEMBLY

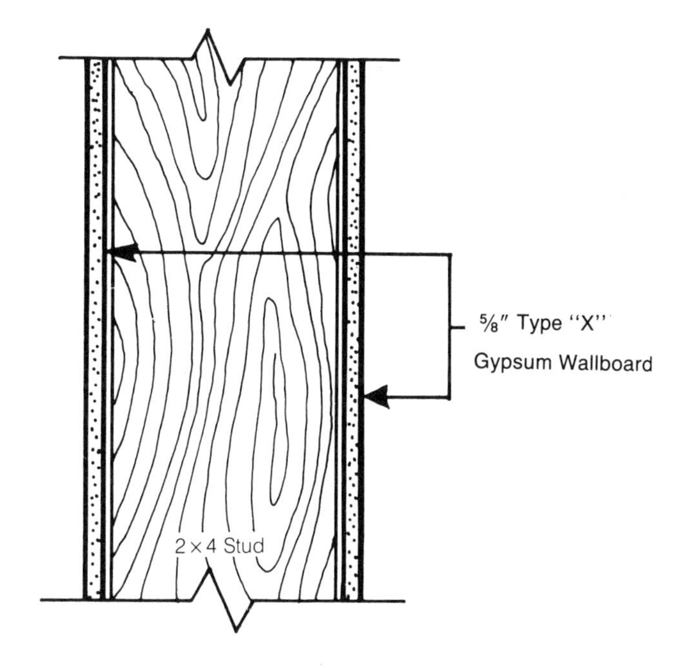

NOTE: Details of attachments and finishes not shown.

The use of gypsum wallboard to provide a one-hour fire-resistive wall assembly, in the configuration shown above, replicates the fire test requirement on which the ASTM Type X conformance is based. That requires a wood stud with wallboard on each side of the stud. The wallboard is not, by itself, adequate to provide the require hourly rating. The airspace and attachment requirements are essential for the fire-resistive rating.

REFERENCE: TABLE NO. 43-B

FIGURE 8-5 GYPSUM WALLBOARD ONE-HOUR WALL ASSEMBLY (ASTM C-36)

still market it for use in one-hour assemblies.

It is the combined assembly of the two layers of Type X wallboard with the stud that achieves the fire rating: there is no such thing as one-hour wallboard by itself. (See Figure 8-5.)

This background discussion has provided a brief overview of a complex subject. It has been abbreviated to avoid getting weighed down in the details of individual tests and passage criteria. If the reader wishes to further study the tests discussed herein, UBC Standards 43-1, 43-2 and 43-4, and the ASTM fire test standards on which they are based are suggested reading. The ASTM standards contain appendices explaining many of the requirements.

Sec. 4301. (a) General. In addition to all other requirements of this code, fire-resistive materials shall meet the requirements for the fire-resistive construction given in this chapter.

(b) Definitions. F RATING is the time period that a through-penetration fire stop limits the spread of fire, flame and hot gases through the fire stop assembly, including penetrating elements, when tested in accordance with the time-temperature curve defined in UBC Standard No. 43-1.

T RATING is the time that a through-penetration fire stop limits temperature rise through the fire stop assembly, including penetrating elements, when tested in accordance with the time-temperature curve defined in UBC Standard No. 43-1.

This section has been expanded to include definitions that directly relate to the test criteria for qualification of a through-penetration fire stop for use in conjunction with Section 4308 and the UBC Standard No. 43-6. To use the material involved with the penetrations of fire-resistive assemblies, refer to the definitions in Chapter 4, particularly Sections 415 and 421 relating to membrane penetration fire stop and through-penetration fire stop, respectively.

The use of membrane penetration fire stops and through-penetration fire stops is shown in Figures 8-6 and 8-7. In the discussion when code provisions relating to penetrations were adopted, an essential installation requirement was dropped to reduce the complexity of the changes. This requirement is contained in Note 2 on both Figures.

All fire tests reviewed when code provisions for penetrations of fire-resistive assemblies were developed contained limitations of the air space around the penetrating item (annular space) to restrict the

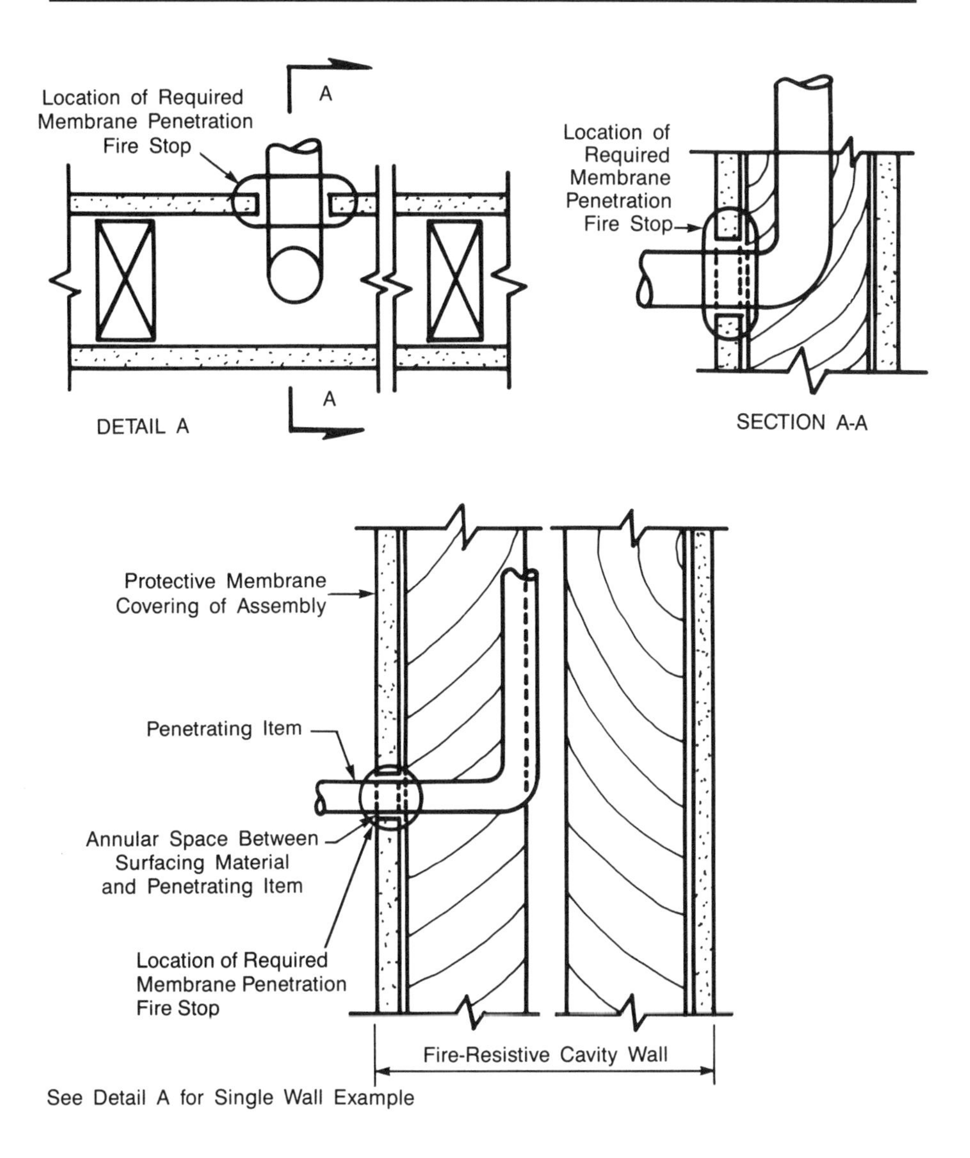

NOTES: 1. See Section 4304 (f) Exception 2.
2. The annular space around the membrane penetrations shall be not more than 1/8-inch wide unless a greater width is permitted by the approved listing.
3. Note #2 also applies to penetrations of plates.

REFERENCE: SECTIONS 414 AND 4304(f)

FIGURE 8-6 ILLUSTRATION OF THE USE OF A MEMBRANE PENETRATION FIRE STOP

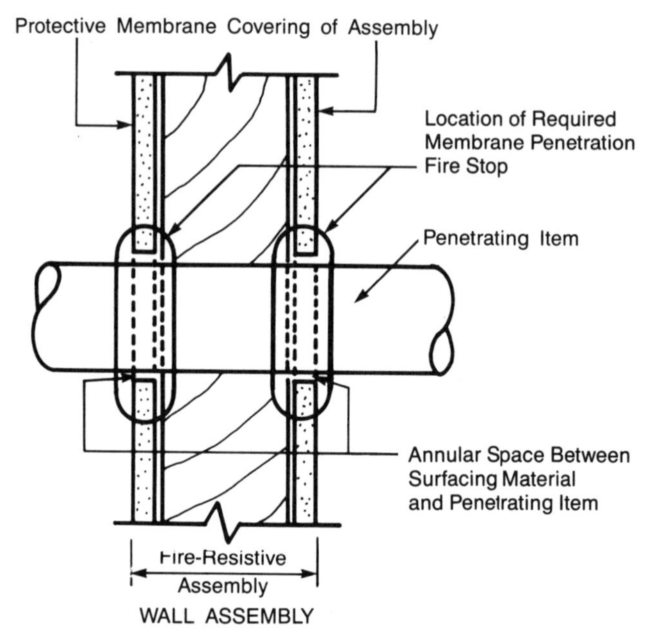

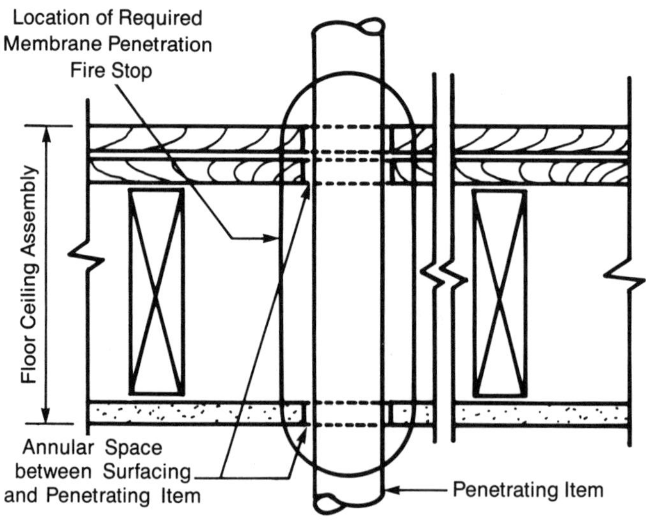

FIRE-RESISTIVE FLOOR-CEILING ASSEMBLY

NOTES: 1. See Section 4304 (e) Exception and 4305 (c) Exception 6.
2. The annular space around the membrane penetrations shall be not more than 1/8-inch wide unless a greater width is permitted by the approved listing.
3. Note #2 also applies to penetrations of plates.

REFERENCE: SECTIONS 421, 4304 (e) AND 4305 (c)

FIGURE 8-7 ILLUSTRATION OF THE USE OF A THROUGH-PENETRATION FIRE STOP

available airflow and thereby reduce the rate of internal burning in the assembly. These reductions in the fire-resistive time period have been shown to be as much as 50 percent of the fire-resistive rating of one-hour wood stud wall assemblies with combustible pipe penetrations.

The designer must provide details of this requirement as part of the design requirements. Building officials must make certain that, particularly when combustible pipings are involved, the annular spaces are limited to the 1/8 inch width.

The references to through-penetration fire stops in Sections 4304 (e) and 4305 (c) Exception 5 require using the definitions in Sections 421 and 4301 (b) and the test criteria in Section 4308. The UBC Standard No. 43-6 is lengthy and complex. The author does not include it in this Guide.

The reader is referred to the ASTM Standard E-814 and the Technical Appendix TA6 in this Guide, which contains a detailed discussion of the technical provisions of UBC Standard No. 43-6 as it relates to the ASTM standard from which it was derived. Examples of the F and T rating determination for Figures 8-8 and 8-9 and the values found in the Underwriters Laboratories, Inc. listings are as follows:

UNDERWRITERS LABORATORIES, INC	F	T
System 1*, Figure 8-8	2 hours	0 hour
System 7*, Figure 8-9	2 & 3 Hours	Rating based on cables used. 1 1/2 hour to 3 hour

* See Underwriters Laboratories, Inc. 1991 Building Materials Directory.

Fire-Resistive Materials

Sec. 4302. (a) General. Materials and systems used for fire-resistive purposes shall be limited to those specified in this chapter unless accepted under the procedure given in Section 4302 (b) or 4302 (c). For standards referred to in this chapter, see Chapter 60.

The materials and details of construction for the fire-resistive systems described in this chapter shall be in accordance with all other provisions of this code except as modified herein.

For the purpose of determining the degree of fire resistance afforded, the materials of construction listed in this chapter shall be assumed to have the fire-resistance rating indicated in Table No. 43-A, 43-B or 43-C.

As an alternate to Tables Nos. 43-A, B and C, fire-resistive construction may

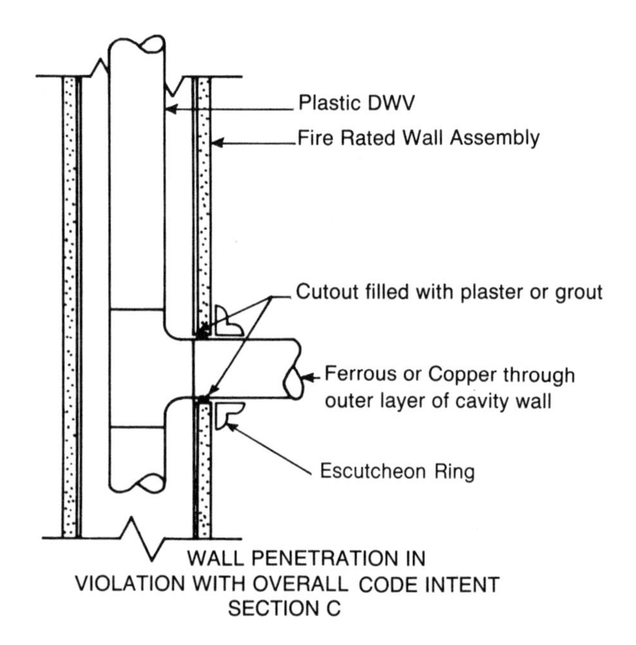

WALL PENETRATION IN
VIOLATION WITH OVERALL CODE INTENT
SECTION C

Unless fire tested mitigation measures are taken for Section C, tests have shown that this construction will not successfully pass a fire test. Underwriters Laboratories, Inc. has an increasing number of assemblies and mitigation devices in their "Building Materials Directory" that should be considered for a particular installation.

An approved mitigation system must be used or the fire-resistive integrity of the wall will be jeopardized.

REFERENCE: SECTION 4302 (b), 4304 (e), UBC STANDARD 43-1

FIGURE 8-8 FIRE-RESISTIVE WALL PENETRATIONS

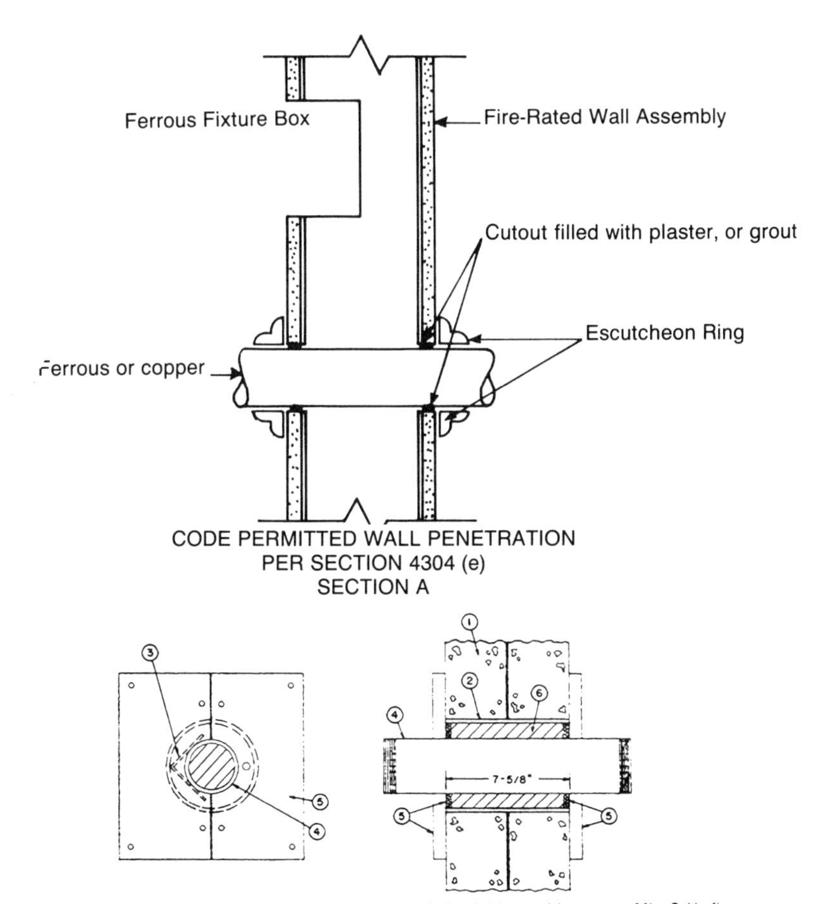

CODE PERMITTED WALL PENETRATION
PER SECTION 4304 (e)
SECTION A

1. **Wall**—Nom 8 in. thick concrete block, or common brick laid up with mortar. Min 2 Hr fire rated wall.
2. **Steel Framing**—Nom 4 in. diam, 0.25 in. thick steel pipe rigidly attached to wall.
3. **Support Angle**—3 by 3 by $\frac{1}{4}$ in. thick steel angle welded to steel framing. For use when steel conduit is used.
4. **Steel Conduit**—Nom $3\frac{1}{2}$ in. diam rigid steel conduit welded to support angle.
5. **Forming Materials**—Materials are used as a form and seal to prevent leakage of the foam sealant when in liquid state.
   A. **Forming Materials***—$\frac{1}{2}$ in. thick units fastened to both sides of wall opening with 2 in. long masonry nails. Units are not removed after foam application.
      See UL "Building Materials Directory"
   B. **Packing Material**—Loose alumina silica fiber packed about form boards, conduit, and cables sufficient to prevent liquid foam leakage.
6. **Fill, Void or Cavity Materials***—Foamed silicone applied as described in application instructions to fill the remaining void in the wall opening to a final thickness shown above. Density 17 pcf min, 20 pcf max.

   See UL "Building Materials Directory"
7. **Cables** (Optional)—(Not Shown)—Placed inside of conduit, aluminum conductor, PVC jacket—10/C, No. 14 AWG. 40 percent max cable fill area.

*Bearing the UL Classification Marking

TYPICAL ULI LISTED
WALL FIRESTOP ASSEMBLY
THRU FIRE-RATED WALL
SECTION B

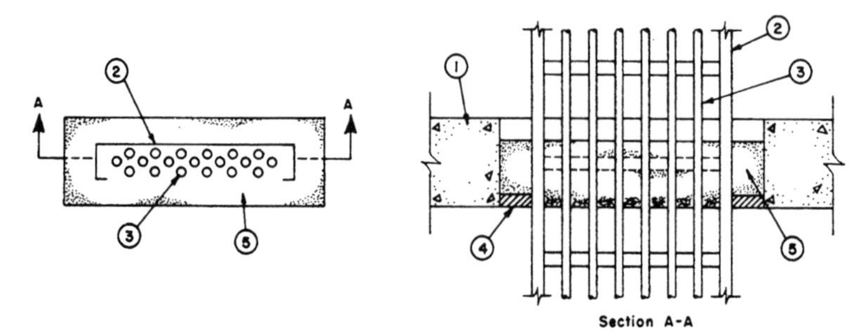

1. **Floor or Wall Assembly**—Min 8 in. thick normal weight concrete. Max area of opening 192 sq in. with max dimension of 24 in. and with min dimension of 8 in.
2. **Cable Tray**—18 in. wide with 3 in. loading depth, open ladder with flattened tube rungs. Side rails min 0.056 in. thick (16 gauge) galvanized steel. Rungs 1 in. diameter galvanized steel tubes spaced 9 in. O.C. Max of one cable tray per opening, centered in opening and reliably supported on both sides of through opening. A min 2 in. clearance shall be maintained between the ends of the cable tray and the concrete.
3. **Cables**—Max 39 percent (max 21 in.^{2} cross-sectional area) fill area per tray. The following types and sizes of copper conductor cables may be used:
   A. 350 MCM; uninsulated PVC jacket or cross-linked polyethylene insulation with PVC jacket (max 5 cables per tray, evenly distributed). When 350 MCM cable is used, Hourly Rating is 2 Hr.
   B. 3/C-No. 2 AWG; PVC insulation with PVC jacket (max 7 cables per tray, evenly distributed).
   C. 7/C-No. 12 AWG; PVC insulation with PVC jacket.
4. **Forming Materials**—Used as a form and sealant to prevent leakage of the fill materials when in a liquid state.
   A. **Forming Materials***—1 in. thick units located at the bottom surface of floor openings and at both surfaces of wall openings. Units tightly fitted into openings to prevent fill material leakage.
      See UL "Building Materials Directory"
   B. **Packing Material**—Loose alumina silica fiber or strips of alumina silica fiber blanket packed between cables to prevent leakage of liquid fill material and to separate adjoining cables permitting full penetration of the fill material.
5. **Fill, Void or Cavity Material***—Silicone material applied as described in the application instructions to fill the remaining void in the opening. Material applied to a min final thickness of 5 in. Density 83 pcf min, 90 pcf max.
   See UL "Building Materials Directory"

*Bearing the UL Classification Marking

TYPICAL ULI LISTED FLOOR FIRESTOP ASSEMBLY THRU FIRE-RATED FLOOR
SECTION A

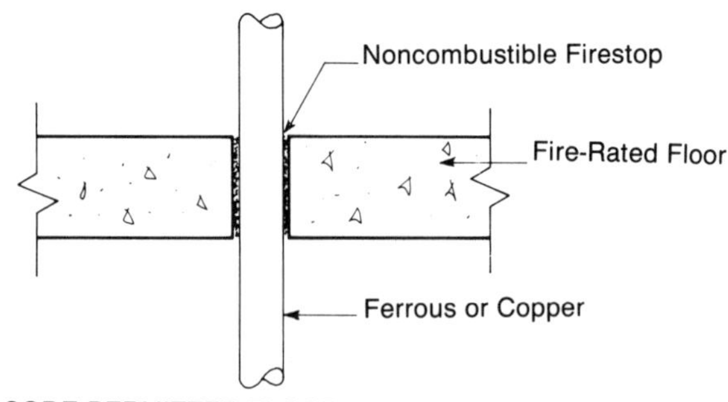

CODE PERMITTED FLOOR PENETRATION
PER SECTION 4305 (b)
SECTION B

REFERENCE: SECTIONS 4302 (b), 4305 (a) AND (b)
UNDERWRITERS LABORATORIES INC. BUILDING MATERIALS DIRECTORY

FIGURE 8-9 FIRE-RESISTIVE FLOOR PENETRATIONS

be approved by the building official on the basis of evidence submitted showing that the construction meets the required fire-resistive classification.

This section stipulates that a fire-resistive assembly is one that is either contained in the Chapter 43 Tables or that has been accepted under the procedures contained in the standards referenced in Chapter 60. The Tables' listings were all derived from fire tests conducted over a period of many years. It is therefore given that a fire-rated assembly must have been tested in accordance with the established test criteria and accepted or approved by a responsible agency.

An assembly must conform not only to the construction details contained in the Tables, but to the general construction requirements of the code as well. For example:

> Plywood installations, when used as diaphragms to resist lateral forces, must meet the provisions of Chapter 25. The nailing of plywood that is part of a fire-resistive floor and that is also being used as a lateral force-resisting diaphragm must meet the nailing requirements of Table No. 25-J and Table No. 43-C, Item 26.

The last paragraph of Section 4302 (a) allows any person to submit the evidence of the equivalent fire-resistive performance to the building official. In the prior code, the requirement was for the person responsible for the structural design to submit the evidence. Although the change applies generally via Section 4302 (a), the specific requirement in Section 4302 (b) remains relating to restrained assemblies; i.e., the structural designer is the only one who can submit the restrained evidence of equivalent performance.

The original intent for adding the criteria for the structural designer was for the restrained assemblies due to the critical nature of the evaluation of these assemblies that may combine structural and thermal restraint.

Sec. 4302.

(b) Qualification by Testing. Material or assembly of materials of construction tested in accordance with the requirements set forth in U.B.C. Standard No. 43-1 shall be rated for fire resistance in accordance with the results and conditions of such tests.

EXCEPTION: The acceptance criteria of U.B.C. Standard No. 43-1 for exterior bearing walls shall not be required to be greater with respect to heat transmission and passage of flame or hot gases than would be required of a nonbearing wall in the same building with the same distance to the

property line. The fire exposure time period, water pressure and duration of application for the hose stream test shall be based upon the fire-resistive rating determined by this exception.

Fire-resistive assemblies tested under U.B.C. Standard No. 43-1 shall not be considered to be restrained unless evidence satisfactory to the building official is furnished by the person responsible for the structural design showing that the construction qualifies for a restrained classification in accordance with U.B.C. Standard No. 43-1. Restrained construction shall be identified on the plans.

This section refers to the UBC Standard No. 43-1, which is based on the national fire test standard ASTM E-119. It further indicates that any assembly submitted to the building official may be accepted if the person responsible for the structural design submits proper evidence that the assembly meets the required fire rating. Considerable responsibility is placed on both the building official and the structural design professional.

In this author's experience there are few structural design professionals knowledgeable in the area of fire testing and qualification of assemblies per UBC Standard No. 43-1 or ASTM E-119.

> We recommend that the design professional who is unfamiliar with the subject of fire-resistant design proceed with caution when planning to undertake the certification required for new assemblies by the second paragraph of this section for new assemblies.

The third paragraph indicates that the preferred method of evaluating a fire-resistive assembly, such as a fire-resistive floor system, is that based on unrestrained conditions. To accept fire test values for an assembly based on the restrained conditions requires evidence approved by the building official and provided by the structural design professional. Furthermore, the restrained constructions must be detailed on the drawings. See discussion in Technical Appendix 3.

> In the author's opinion, unless the designer is confident that both the design and field installations can be satisfied, the unrestrained fire resistance ratings should be used.

It is difficult for the designer to properly control the actual conditions in the field or the personnel responsible for installing the fireproofing. The cost of the additional fireproofing may not be sufficient to warrant the designer taking the responsibility for any design or field deficiencies and the possible resultant liability.

Protection of Structural Members

Sec. 4303. (a) General. Structural members having the fire-resistive protection set forth in Table No. 43-A shall be assumed to have the fire-resistance ratings set forth therein.

Section 4303 (a) refers to the first of the three tables in Chapter 43. Table No. 43-A contains predetermined fire protection thicknesses for individual structural members. These members include beams and columns and similar isolated members rather than systems such as floor- ceiling or wall assemblies.

Table No. 43-B contains the details of fire-resistive wall assemblies of the following types:

- solid
- hollow
- combustible
- noncombustible

Table No. 43-C contains the details of the following fire-resistive assemblies:

- floor
- roof
- floor-ceiling
- roof-ceiling

(b) Protective Coverings. 1. Thickness of protection. The thickness of fire-resistive materials required for protection of structural members shall be no less than set forth in Table No. 43-A, except as modified in this section. The figures shown shall be the net thickness of the protecting materials and shall not include any hollow space back of the protection.

2. Unit masonry protection. Where required, metal ties shall be embedded in transverse joints of unit masonry for protection of steel columns. Such ties shall be as set forth in Table No. 43-A or be equivalent thereto.

3. Reinforcement for cast-in-place concrete column protection. Cast-in-place concrete protection for steel columns shall be reinforced at the edges of such members with wire ties of not less than .18 inch in diameter wound spirally around the columns on a pitch of not more than 8 inches or by equivalent reinforcement.

4. Embedment of pipes. Conduits and pipes shall not be embedded in required fire protection of structural members.

5. Column jacketing. Where the fire-resistive covering on columns is exposed to injury from moving vehicles, the handling of merchandise or other means, it shall be protected in an approved manner.

6. Ceiling membrane protection. When a ceiling forms the protective membrane for fire-resistive assemblies, the constructions and their supporting horizontal structural members need not be individually fire protected except where such members support directly applied loads from more than one floor or roof or more than one floor. The required fire resistance shall be not less than that required for individual protection of members.

Ceilings shall form continuous fire-resistive membranes but may have openings for copper, sheet steel or ferrous plumbing pipes, ducts and electrical outlet boxes, provided the areas of such openings through the ceiling aggregate not more than 100 square inches for any 100 square feet of ceiling area. Regardless of size, duct openings in such ceilings shall be protected by approved ceiling fire dampers. Access doors installed in such ceilings shall be approved horizontal access door assemblies listed for such purpose.

EXCEPTION: 1. Larger openings than permitted above may be installed where such openings and the assemblies in which they are utilized are in accordance with the results of tests pursuant to the provisions of Section 4302 (b).

2. Ceiling fire dampers may be omitted from duct openings where fire-resistive tests have shown that the dampers are not necessary to maintain the fire resistance of the assembly.

Individual electrical outlet boxes shall be of steel and not greater than 16 square inches in area.

7. Plaster application. Plaster protective coatings may be applied with the finish coat omitted when they comply with the design mix and thickness requirements of Tables Nos. 43-A, 43-B and 43-C.

8. Truss protection. Where trusses are used as all or part of the structural frame and protection is required by Table No. 17-A, such protection may be provided by fire-resistive materials enclosing the entire truss assembly on all sides for its entire length and height. The required thickness and construction of fire-resistive assemblies enclosing trusses shall be based upon the results of full-scale tests or combinations of tests on truss components or upon approved calculations based on such tests which satisfactorily demonstrate that the assembly has the required fire resistance.

Section 4303 (b) Item 1 requires the thickness of the materials in Table No. 43-A to be the net thicknesses. Hollow spaces behind the protection are not to be included in the measurement. For example, if two inches of protection are required and there is a furring space between the main member to be protected and its protective coating, only the thickness of the protective coating is to be used for the two-inch measurement; the width of the furring space is not to be considered.

The several cautions and specifications in Items 2 though 8 of this section relate to the Table No. 43-A fire protective coatings. However, some cautions and specifications also have application to materials not in the table, but which are used in a similar manner, such as in spray-applied fireproofing. Items 4 and 5 should be applied by the designer to such materials to obtain proper and long-lasting assemblies.

Item 6 is frequently misunderstood. A ceiling of a floor-ceiling assembly can be used to protect both the flooring and the structural members therein, provided the structural members are not supporting more than one floor or the roof.

> For example, assume there is an intermediate column placed so that a beam on the fourth floor is carrying not only the fourth floor load but also a portion of the fifth floor load via the intermediate column. This beam must have individual fire protection and could not rely on the membrane fireproofing. (See Figure 8-10.)

The second paragraph of Item 6 contains another often-misunderstood provision. Openings are permitted in the ceiling membrane of a floor-ceiling assembly. The openings described in this paragraph are for such things as light fixture outlet boxes.

These openings should not penetrate to the floor above: they are permitted only in the membrane ceiling. For that reason, the phrase "ceilings shall form a continuous membrane" is used in the beginning of the paragraph. If the openings are to be larger than 100 square inches per 100 square feet, tested assemblies must be used to take care of the larger lighting fixtures, ducts and other ceiling penetrations. (See Figure 8-11.)

The last sentence in this paragraph is a clarification of the intent of this Chapter as it relates to openings in ceilings. It requires access doors or hatches where there are openings in a ceiling membrane that is part of a fire-rated assembly. This is a new provision to the code.

Openings in such ceilings require access doors that are either listed by an approved testing agency, such as ULI, or covered by an ICBO Evaluation Report.

The "typical non-conforming sectional detail" shown in Figure 9-15 is, of course, seriously deficient and would violate the new provision.

The term "approved horizontal access door assembly" is not defined

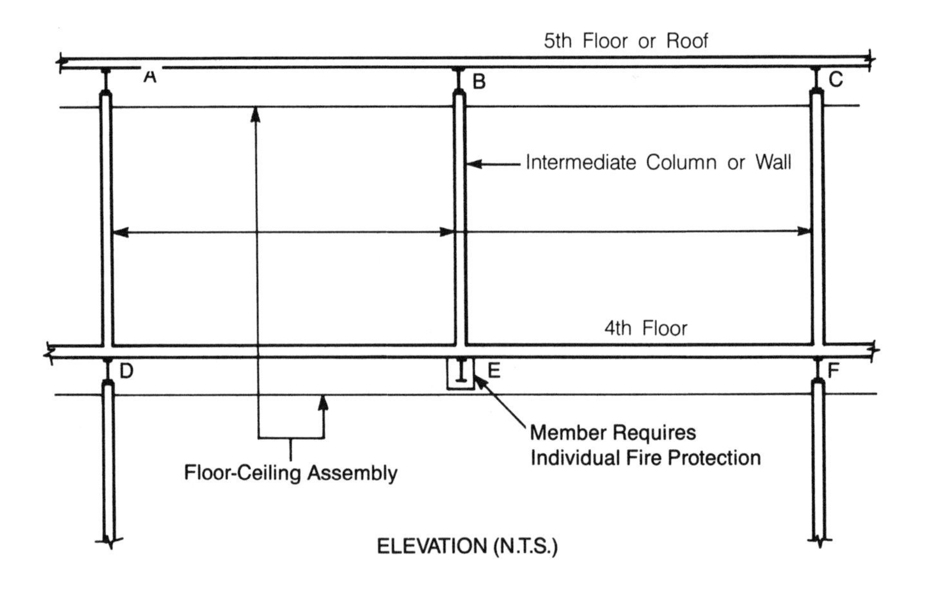

Members A, B, C, D, and F may be fire protected by the fire-rated membrane ceiling of the floor-ceiling assembly.

Member E, which carries its own floor load and that from member B, via the columns, requires individual fire protection.

REFERENCE: SECTION 4303(b)

FIGURE 8-10 INDIVIDUAL BEAM PROTECTION/MEMBRANE PROTECTION

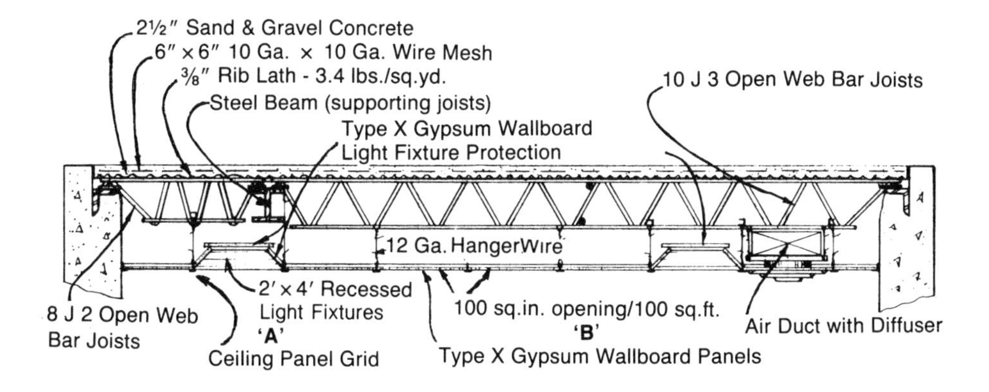

'A'—Openings permitted provided tested successfully per UBC Standard 43-1. Note that, in this test assembly, the ceiling openings for the large light fixtures are covered with Type X wallboard.

'B'—Openings permitted without a fire test verification, per Section 4305 (b).

NOTE: This detail indicates a typical floor-ceiling assembly placed within a fire test furnace prior to loading and testing. The burners would be below the assembly. Not shown are the double steel beams surrounding the top of the concrete walls; with their webs horizontal, providing great restraint to the test assembly.

For the required fire-resistive rating, all of the specific elements shown in the listing or described therewith must be provided. In the above illustration the number or percentage of penetrations of the ceiling portion of the assembly must be strictly met and not exceeded. The grid system and wallboard must be identified as having passed the fire test, usually by a label that correlates with a listing.

Substitution of portions of the assembly with other components should be avoid or only attempted by knowledgeable persons and based on other test data as well as experience.

REFERENCE: SECTION 4302 (b), 4305 (a) & (b), UBC STANDARD 43-1

FIGURE 8-11 OPENINGS PERMITTED IN FIRE-RESISTIVE FLOOR-CEILING ASSEMBLY

in either Chapter 4 or 43 of the code. Section 4306 (b) contains several definitions of doors, windows and dampers used as fire assemblies. Therefore, the ambiguous language used in this provision would appear to be something other than a fire assembly.

Thus, it is necessary to determine what the requirements are for such an assembly to be "approved." The key criteria for a fire-resistive element, such as a door, are that they:

- withstand fire for a period of time,
- stay in place, i.e., remain latched and hinged and
- be closed at time of fire attack.

Another criterion sometimes required of a fire door is that it prevents temperature rise above a stated amount on the back of the door for a period of time, usually 30 minutes. This is not a mandatory criterion.

Therefore, certain and perhaps all of these criteria are not applicable because the code provision does not refer to a "fire-door assembly."

For the access door to be effective, the time period and stay-in-place criteria must apply for the floor-ceiling or roof-ceiling assembly in which the door is located. The closure requirement, therefore must be the criterion that is not satisfied by the term "access door assembly."

> In the author's opinion, a closing device is not required; the access door need not be self-closing or automatic closing. The horizontal access door assembly required by this provision of the code should meet all the fire-door assembly requirements, with the exception of the need for an automatic or self-closing mechanism.

The provisions in Section 3205 (a) do not provide a cross-reference to the Chapter 43 requirements. This has led many designers to overlook the ceiling protection provisions in Chapter 43. With this addition to Section 4303 (b)6, even though the cross-reference in Section 3205 (a) to Chapter 43 is still lacking, a specific code requirement now exists.

To avoid future problems, the author suggests that the designer note in Section 3205 (a) to refer to Section 4303 (b)6 provisions.

(c) Protected Members. 1. Attached metal members. The edges of lugs, brackets, rivets and bolt heads attached to structural members may extend to within 1 inch of the surface of the fire protection.

2. Reinforcing. Thickness of protection for concrete or masonry reinforcement shall be measured to the outside of the reinforcement except that stirrups and spiral reinforcement ties may project not more than 1/2 inch into the protection.

3. Bonded prestressed concrete tendons. For members having a single tendon or more than one tendon installed with equal concrete cover measured from the nearest surface, the cover shall be not less than that set forth in Table No. 43-A.

For members having multiple tendons installed with variable concrete cover, the average tendon cover shall be not less than that set forth in Table No. 43-A, provided:

A. The clearance from each tendon to the nearest exposed surface is used to determine average cover.

B. In no case can the clear cover for individual tendons be less than one half of that set forth in Table No. 43-A. A minimum cover of 3/4 inch for slabs and 1 inch for beams is required for any aggregate concrete.

C. For the purpose of establishing a fire-resistive rating, tendons having a clear covering less than that set forth in Table No. 43-A shall not contribute more than 50 percent of the required ultimate moment capacity for members less than 350 square inches in cross-sectional area and 65 percent for larger members. For structural design purposes, however, tendons having a reduced cover are assumed to be fully effective.

Section 4303 (c) 2 cautions that the protective covering for reinforcement is to be measured to the outside of the reinforcement. To avoid field problems, the designer should include such information in the details of the contract drawings. The steel reinforcement in concrete is subject to loss of load-carrying capability when heated in a fire. To reduce the rate of loss of strength in fire, the proper thickness of coverage of the steel is necessary.

The coverage requirements for prestressed tendons are similarly specified due to the tendon's loss of strength at relatively low temperatures. Prestressed tendons lose strength when their temperature reaches the 800° F range as contrasted to the 1000° F to 1300° F range for carbon steel.

(e) Spray-applied Fireproofing. The density and thickness of spray-applied fireproofing shall be determined following the procedures set forth in U.B.C. Standard No. 43-8.

Section 4303 (e) relates to spray-applied fireproofing. The designer should be aware that the protection afforded by this type of material is a function of:

- the application density and
- its thickness

Unfortunately, when spraying large areas of decking, it is difficult to control the number of hollow spaces or holidays that may occur. It is therefore recommended that the designer consider a minimum thickness of one-half inch for spray-applied fireproofing.

In fire tests, a one-quarter inch fireproofing thickness may be sufficient on a given assembly for a particular fire rating. However, in the field, it is difficult to control the application of fireproofing to that precise degree. The recommendation for a thicker installation will therefore provide a margin of safety for the field installation. With this procedure, any holidays will usually be less than one-quarter inch.

Sec. 4304.

(d) Nonsymmetrical Wall Construction. Walls and partitions of nonsymmetrical construction shall be tested with both faces exposed to the furnace, and the assigned fire-resistive rating will be the shortest duration obtained from the two tests conducted in conformance with U.B.C. Standard No. 43-1. When evidence is furnished to show that the wall was tested with the least fire-resistive side exposed to the furnace, the building official may not require that the wall be subjected to tests from the opposite side.

The designer is urged to avoid the use of this section since it is unlikely that the designer and the building official will agree about the potential source of fire in the proposed building. It will be up to the designer to fully substantiate his position regarding the fire source and, in an obvious manner, convince the official that his design is correct. Unless the designer is sure that this can be done, avoiding use of this section may be the best course of action.

Sec. 4304.

(e) Through-Penetration. Penetrating items passing entirely through both protective membranes of bearing walls required to have a fire-resistance rating and walls requiring protected openings shall be protected with through-penetration fire stops suitable for the method of penetration.

EXCEPTION: Penetrations not larger than a 4-inch nominal pipe or 16 square inches in overall cross-sectional area containing noncombustible penetrating items, where the annular space between the penetrating items and the wall assembly being penetrated is filled with a material which will prevent the passage of flame and hot gases sufficient to ignite cotton waste

when subjected to U.B.C. Standard No. 43-1 time-temperature fire conditions under a positive pressure differential of 0.01-inch water column at the location of the penetration for the time period at least equal to the fire-resistance of the wall assembly. The T rating for through-penetration fire stops in fire-rated walls requiring protected openings shall apply to penetrations in the following locations:

1. Above corridor ceilings which are not part fire-resistive assembly.

2. Below any ceiling.

EXCEPTION: Any through-penetration item not larger than a 4-inch nominal pipe or 16 square inches in overall cross-sectional area need not have a T rating.

(f) Membrane Penetrations. Walls may have openings for steel electrical outlet boxes not exceeding 16 square inches in area, provided the aggregate area of such openings is not more than 100 square inches for any 100 square feet of wall or partition area. Outlet boxes on opposite sides of walls and partitions shall be separated by a horizontal distance of at least 24 inches.

Where wall-protective membranes are penetrated by other materials or where larger openings are required than permitted above, the penetrating items shall be:

1. Protected with membrane penetration fire stops suitable for the penetration, or

2. Installed in accordance with the installation instructions of their listing for such use.

EXCEPTION: Penetrations not larger than a 4-inch nominal pipe or 16 square inches in overall cross-sectional area containing noncombustible penetrating items, where the annular space between the penetrating items and the wall assembly being penetrated is filled with a material which will prevent the passage of flame and hot gases sufficient to ignite cotton waste when subjected to U.B.C. Standard No. 43-1 time-temperature fire conditions under a positive pressure differential of 0.01-inch water column at the location of the penetration for the time period at least equal to the fire-resistance of the wall assembly.

(g) Construction Joints. Construction joints shall comply with the requirements of Section 1707.

Section 4304 (e) has been substantially revised to reflect the concept of penetration fire stops. The prior code provisions appeared to permit penetrations of fire-resistive walls and partitions by steel or copper items without specific need for protection. The only provision relating to protection was the requirement for filling the space between the penetrating item and the wall surface. The present code provisions require a through-penetration fire stop for all such penetrations, except at special cited locations. Note that the noncombustible penetrating item referred to in the Exception applies to any part of the connection between the penetrating item and the internal system, if present, such as a vertical riser.

In the author's opinion, if the interior of the wall contains drain, waste or vent piping (DWV) of combustible piping, the Exceptions do not apply. See Figure 8-6.

Figure 8-8 is for steel and copper pipe up to four-inch nominal pipe size only. Larger sizes require a through-penetration fire stop. The detail entitled "Violation of Overall Code Intent" is still a violation and is in violation of Section 4304 (e) specifically. For examples of through-penetration fire stop and membrane penetration fire stop, see Figures 8-6 and 8-7.

The code provides a performance criteria for the space filler around a penetration. This provision alone does not solve the problems of penetrations or inclusions. It does, however, aid in establishing the physical characteristics essential for such sealant materials, namely that they must prevent passage of flame or hot gases through the seal.

The listed devices referred to in Figure 8-9, as an example, meet both of these criteria.

The use of plastic piping, conduit and ducts in fire-resistive assemblies must require approved penetration devices be provided in accordance with these sections. There are approved penetration devices and installation procedures for PVC electrical raceways and components. It is expected that other devices will be approved for use with other plastic materials and for purposes.

If the designer does not want to provide the penetration devices, these materials should be installed in nonfire-resistive locations instead of within fire-resistive walls.

Floor-Ceilings, or Roof-Ceilings

(a) General

Sec. 4305. (a) General. Fire-resistive floors, floor-ceiling or roof ceiling assemblies shall be assumed to have the fire-resistance ratings set forth in Table No. 43-C. When materials are incorporated into an otherwise fire-resistive assembly which may change the capacity for heat dissipation, fire test results or other substantiating data shall be made available to the building official to show that the required fire-resistive time period is not reduced.

b) Ceiling Membrane Protection. When a ceiling forms the protective membrane for a fire-resistive floor-ceiling or roof-ceiling assembly, the ceiling shall be without openings in order to protect the structural elements.

EXCEPTIONS: 1. Openings for noncombustible sprinkler piping and steel electrical outlet boxes not greater than 16 square inches in area may be installed, provided the aggregate area of such openings through the ceiling is not more than 100 square inches for any 100 square feet of ceiling area.

2. Duct openings protected with approved ceiling fire dampers.

3. Duct openings where tests in accordance with U.B.C. Standard No. 43-1 have shown that the opening protection is not required.

4. Other ceiling openings and penetrations may be installed where such openings and penetrations and the assemblies in which they are utilized are tested in accordance with the provisions of U.B.C. Standard No. 43-1.

5. Openings enclosed in fire-resistance-rated enclosures.

6. Access doors may be installed in such ceilings when they are approved horizontal access door assemblies listed for such purpose.

Where the weight of lay-in ceiling panels as part of fire-resistive floor-ceiling or roof-ceiling assemblies is not adequate to resist an upward force of one pound per square foot, wire holddowns or other approved devices shall be installed above the panels to prevent vertical displacement under such upward force.

(c) Floors. Fire-resistive floors and floors which are part of a floor-ceiling assembly shall be continuous without openings or penetrations in order to completely separate one story or basement from another.

EXCEPTIONS: 1. Openings enclosed in fire-resistance-rated shaft enclosures in accordance with Section 1706 (a).

2. Exit enclosures in accordance with Chapter 33.

3. Openings permitted in accordance with Section 1706 (c).

4. Atria constructed in accordance with Section 1715.

5. Penetrations protected with through-penetration fire stops installed to provide an F rating or a T rating in accordance with Section 4302 (b). The T rating shall apply only to:

A. Penetrations which are not contained within a wall at the point where they penetrate the floor, or

B. Penetrations which are larger than a 4-inch nominal pipe or 16 square inches in overall cross-sectional area.

6. Penetrations not larger than a 4-inch nominal pipe or 16 square inches in overall cross-sectional area containing noncombustible penetrating items, where the annular space between the penetrating items and the wall assembly being penetrated is filled with a material which will prevent the passage of flame and hot gases sufficient to ignite cotton waste when subjected to U.B.C. Standard No. 43-1 time-temperature fire conditions under a positive pressure differential of 0.01-inch water column at the location of the penetration for the time period at least equal to the fire-resistance of the floor assembly.

The intersection of the floor with the exterior wall system shall be constructed to maintain the fire-resistive rating of the floor assembly. Voids between the floor and the wall, or within the wall assembly, shall be filled at the floor line with noncombustible materials to prevent passage of flame and hot gases.

(d) Roofs. Fire-resistive roofs may have unprotected openings. See Chapter 34 for skylight construction.

(e) Wiring in Plenums. Wiring in plenums shall comply with the Mechanical Code.

(f) Construction Joints. Construction joints such as those used to accommodate wind, seismic or expansion movements when located in fire-resistive floors shall comply with the requirements of Section 1707.

The primary use of the through-penetration fire stop and membrane penetration fire stop are for the penetrations of fire-resistive walls and floors. Section 4305 contains the provisions for these penetrations. In prior codes the requirements for walls and floors were contained in two separate code sections; now they are in one section. In addition to the wall and floor regulations in this section, the requirements for roofs, wiring in plenums and the new requirements for construction joints and the exterior wall-floor intersection are also contained herein.

Section 4305 (a) specifically requires that when, in the judgment of the enforcement official, a material is made part of a fire-resistive assembly and may change the assembly's performance, the user must provide substantiation that the fire-resistive time period is not affected.

This provision establishes the authority and responsibility of the enforcement official in assuring proper construction of fire-resistive assemblies. Failure to obtain such valid substantiating data can result in a 50 percent reduction of a fire-resistive assembly's rating, based on full-scale fire tests.

The burden of providing that data for the proposed use rests with the applicant. The enforcement official should obtain these data before permitting a job to proceed, in the same way the official would require structural data for the use of a new truss system.

Section 4305 (b) expands the provisions found in prior codes by cross-referencing to provisions found elsewhere in the code and incorporating, in this section, provisions that were previously in other parts of Chapter 43. None of the provisions in this subsection is truly new.

Section 4305 (c) contains both material that references other parts of the code and new requirements, particularly those relating to through-penetration fire stops.

The two main new provisions are Exception 5, the through-penetration fire stop provision, and Section 4305 (f) construction joints. Note that the through-penetration fire stop must have an F rating for any penetration of a floor, but need only have only a T rating when the item is outside a wall where it penetrates the floor or the item exceeds the minimum allowed sizes for exemption. (See Figure TA6-1.)

The wall-floor intersection, and construction joints in general, have presented serious fire-spread problems over the years. In many high-rise fires, this has been a primary means of fire spread from floor to floor. Although some enforcement officials regulate this area of a building by requiring that the fire-resistive requirement of the floor be maintained, there was not a specific code provision for officials to cite. Prior enforcement was based on the logic of the continuity of fire-resistive construction.

With this section in the code, officials can readily insist that the method for attaining that continuity of fire-resistance rating be demonstrated on the drawings. The designer should provide an adequate number of details to cover the building's various wall-floor and other construction joint conditions. Often at the exterior wall-floor intersection there will be an exterior column and spandrel located in this area. The details should provide for these intersections as well.

> In the author's opinion, three-dimensional representations should be used to assure the closure intended by this provision.

Exception 6 clarifies the permissible noncombustible penetration items that previously were not limited in size. In particular, the space around any such penetration must be filled with noncombustible material meeting specific performance criteria.

A common violation found in the field is a hole drilled through a floor slab to install a new telephone outlet. The cables may be run in the concealed space of the story below. If a fire-resistance rating is required for the floor, an unprotected penetration is not permitted. Such an opening violates that fire rating because it would permit fire, smoke and gases to enter the floor above in less than the rated time period. (See Figure 8-9.)

Intumescent and other materials or devices may be useful in these installations. The ULI Fire Resistance Directory and ICBO Evaluation Reports should be used to determine the best material and arrangement for a particular application. The designer should not rely on the contractor to decide how best to restore the integrity of holes or penetrated areas in floors.

> **Fire-resistive Assemblies for Protection of Openings.**
> **Sec. 4306. (a) General. Where required by this code for the fire protection of openings, fire-resistive assemblies shall meet the requirements of this chapter.**

This section contains the requirements for fire-resistive openings, i.e. doors and windows. When fire doors are installed in corridors, they are often used by designers as part of the air handling system for the corridor or the floor. This has been the case particularly in apartment houses and hotels. This misuse of fire doors is a violation of the integrity of the corridor fire doors.

The basic document on which doors are fire tested and installations controlled is, aside from the ULI standard fire test for doors, the NFPA Standard 80 for fire doors and windows. In that NFPA standard, is the following clear statement:

> **Fire doors equipped with automatic louvers shall be used only where the opening is not in an exit or otherwise located so that products of combustion flowing through the opening could jeopardize the use of exits prior to operation of the louver.**

In the UMC, Sections 706 (b) and 1206 (b) each contain the following prohibition:

> **Corridors shall not be designed nor used as an integral part of a duct system if the corridor is required to be of fire-resistive construction by Section 3305 of the Building Code.**

The prohibition of louvers in corridor fire doors has its corollary in the UMC provisions prohibiting the openings or the undercutting of fire doors to exhaust air from a corridor into a guest room or dwelling unit as part of the corridor air handling system.

The intent is manifest: if the corridor is used as part of the air handling system and smoke is in the corridor, the smoke will be brought into the apartments and the guest rooms. Not only will the corridor be untenable in such a situation, but all dwelling units will also be made untenable. There will be no way for occupants to escape the smoke and gases.

Therefore, the corridor walls are to be maintained as both smoke and fire barriers. In fact, Section 3305 (g) requires a 20-minute door to be "a tight-fitting smoke and draft-control assembly." This smoke and draft-control door should provide protection to the dwelling units and guest rooms in the event the occupants cannot exit through the corridor.

As an extension of this rationale, the designer should avoid specifying excessive undercutting of the corridor fire doors for clearing carpets or other flooring. The designer should note the imposed limitation of three-quarters inch for such undercuts in Section 2-5.4 of the NFPA 80.

Sec. 4306.
(b) Definitions.
FIRE ASSEMBLY is the assembly of a fire door, fire windows or fire damper, including all required hardware, anchorage, frames and sills.
FIRE ASSEMBLY, AUTOMATIC-CLOSING, is a fire assembly which may remain in an open position and which will close automatically when subjected to one or the other of the following:
1. An increase in temperature.
Unless otherwise specified, the closing device shall be one rated at a maximum temperature of 165°F.
2. Actuation of a smoke detector.
The closing device shall operate by the activation of an approved smoke detector set to operate when smoke reduces the intensity of a 1-foot-long beam of white light by 4 percent. Smoke detectors shall meet the approval of the building official as to installation and locations and shall be subject to such periodic tests as may be required by the building official.
FIRE ASSEMBLY, SELF-CLOSING, is a fire assembly which is kept in a normally closed position and is equipped with an approved device to ensure closing and latching after having been opened for use.

These definitions describe two types of fire door closing methods, the automatic-closing and the self-closing.

> In the author's opinion, although both are legal in most locations where fire doors are required, the self-closing door is more reliable.

However, an automatic-closing door activated by a smoke detector release device could be as reliable as the self-closing door.

The reason this author favors the self-closing mode of operation is that automatic-closing doors are all too often accidently, or deliberately, blocked open. These doors normally remain open and are not recognized as providing a necessary closure in emergencies. Furthermore, the automatic door is permitted to have a temperature-activated release device, usually a fusible link. These devices are slow activating and allow considerable quantities of smoke and toxic gases through the opening before activating.

The self-closing door, on the other hand, operates day-to-day in the same way it is expected to operate in an emergency. It is normally in the closed position, thereby preventing the smoke and toxic gases from passing through the opening during the early stages of a fire. The self-closing door is therefore more reliable as a fire assembly.

Sec. 4306.

(f) Hardware. 1. Closing devices. Every fire assembly shall be provided with a closing device as follows:

A. Fire assemblies required to have a three-hour fire-protection rating shall be automatic-closing fire assemblies. Automatic-closing fire assemblies to be activated by an increase in temperature shall have one heat-actuating device installed on each side of the wall at the top of the opening and one on each side of the wall at the ceiling height where the ceiling is more than 3 feet above the top of the opening.

B. Fire assemblies required to have a one and one-half-hour, one-hour or three-fourths-hour fire-protection rating shall be either automatic- or self-closing fire assemblies. Automatic-closing fire assemblies to be activated by an increase in temperature shall have heat-actuating devices located as required in Item A or by a single fusible link in the opening incorporated in the closing device.

C. Fire door assemblies required to have fire-protection rating, which are installed across a corridor, shall be automatic-closing fire assemblies. Such fire assemblies shall be activated by a smoke detector. All hold-open devices shall be listed for the purpose and shall release or close the door in the event of a power failure at the device.

D. Fire assemblies required by provisions of Chapter 33 shall have closing devices as specified in Chapter 33.

Fire doors which are automatically closing by smoke detection shall not have a closing or reclosing delay of more than 10 seconds.

2. Hinges. Swinging doors shall have not less than two hinges, and when such door exceeds 60 inches in height an additional hinge shall be installed for each additional 30 inches of height or fraction thereof. Hinges, except for spring hinges, shall be of the ball-bearing or antifriction type. When spring hinges are used for door-closing purposes not less than one half of the hinges shall be spring hinges.

3. Latch. Unless otherwise specifically permitted, all single doors and both leaves of pairs of side-hinged swinging doors shall be provided with an automatic latch which will secure the door when it is closed.

The designer should consider the installation of the smoke detector-activated hold-open devices of Item 3 for any stairway to be used by the building occupants on a regular basis, such as those in hospitals and schools. Hospital employees often use the stairs when the number of service elevators is inadequate or when they need to rush from floor to floor without delay.

Smoke is the primary hazard in any occupancy. Reliance on fusible links to activate stairway door closure is a poor practice because a substantial amount of smoke could enter before the closer activates. A smoke detector-operated release device is strongly recommended even though they are not mandated for stairway doors in the present code. They afford considerably greater protection at a nominal cost increase.

The designer is also advised to consider the use of smoke detector-activated hold-open devices for all locations where it is believed that a door may constitute a nuisance barrier to the free flow of traffic. In such instances, the occupants tend to wedge the door open. The designer would be exercising good professional judgment if he were to incorporate in the design a reliable method of holding the door open; one which would still afford the desired protection in the event of fire.

Sec. 4306.

(h) Glazed Openings in Fire Windows. Windows required to have a three-fourths-hour fire-resistive rating may have an area not greater than 84 square feet with neither width nor height exceeding 12 feet.

This section establishes the size limitations for three-quarter hour fire windows. The designer is reminded of the glazing materials, discussed in Article 7 in this Guide, which have recently become available. These materials enable the installation of clear glass fire windows - having no internal wires - which have been tested and labeled for one-hour fire resistance. These are expensive at present but in certain locations the cost may be warranted. It is hoped that over time, the costs will decrease. When that time comes, these windows will provide the designer with additional flexibility in design.

Sec. 4306.

(i) Glazing. Glass or glass block assemblies shall be qualified by tests conforming with U.B.C. Standard No. 43-2 (for doors) or Standard No. 43-4 (for windows). Glass or glass block shall be install in accordance with their listing.

This section contains the glazing requirements for glass used in fire doors or windows. The prior codes permitted generic wired glass for such glazing. The code now requires that all glazing be tested, labeled and listed and installed in accordance with the listing. In general, all glazing in fire assemblies must be installed using ferrous frames and retainers. The designer can cover the steel frame of the window with any material desired to make the window more aesthetically acceptable.

(j) Fire Dampers.

Except where fire tests have shown that fire dampers are not necessary to maintain the required fire resistance of the construction, fire dampers complying with the requirements of U.B.C. Standard No. 43-7 shall be installed and be readily accessible for servicing in the following locations:

1. Duct penetrations through area or occupancy separation walls.

2. Duct penetrations through horizontal exit walls.

3. Duct penetrations through shaft enclosures.

EXCEPTIONS; 1. Duct penetrations by steel exhaust air subducts extending vertically upward at least 22 inches in a vented shaft where the air flow is upward.

2. Where not more than one duct penetrates the shaft enclosure between adjacent floor levels, the fire damper at the shaft enclosure may be omitted when the upper adjacent floor opening within the shaft enclosure is protected by horizontal fire dampers.

4. Duct penetrations of the ceiling of fire-resistive floor-ceiling or roof-ceiling assemblies shall be protected in accordance with Section 4305 (b).

5. Duct penetrations through protective elements of fire-rated corridor walls.

EXCEPTION: A minimum of 0.019-inch (26-gauge) steel ducts do not require fire dampers when the ducts have no openings into the corridor.

The requirements for fire dampers can be summarized as follows:

WHERE REQUIRED:

1. Through occupancy separations
2. Through area separation walls
3. Through shaft enclosures
4. Through fire-resistive floor-ceiling assemblies
5. Through fire-resistive elements of corridor walls

WHERE EXCEPTED:

1. Where subducts are used in shafts.
2. Where there are horizontal fire dampers immediately above them in shafts.
3. In corridors where steel ducts without corridor openings are used.

See Figures 8-12 and 8-13 for examples of these conditions.

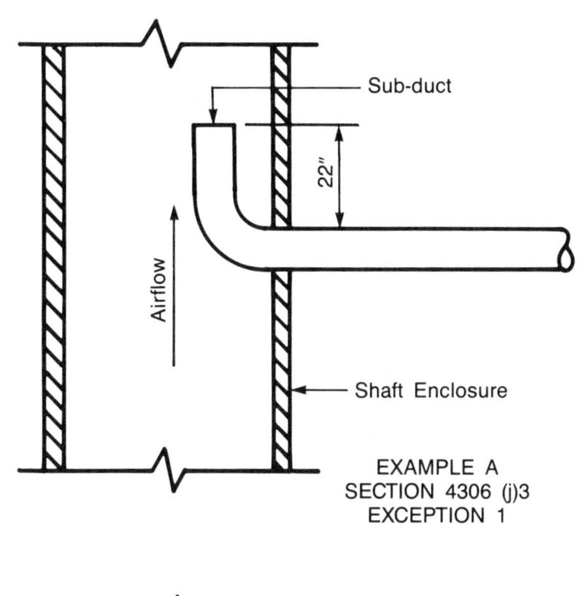

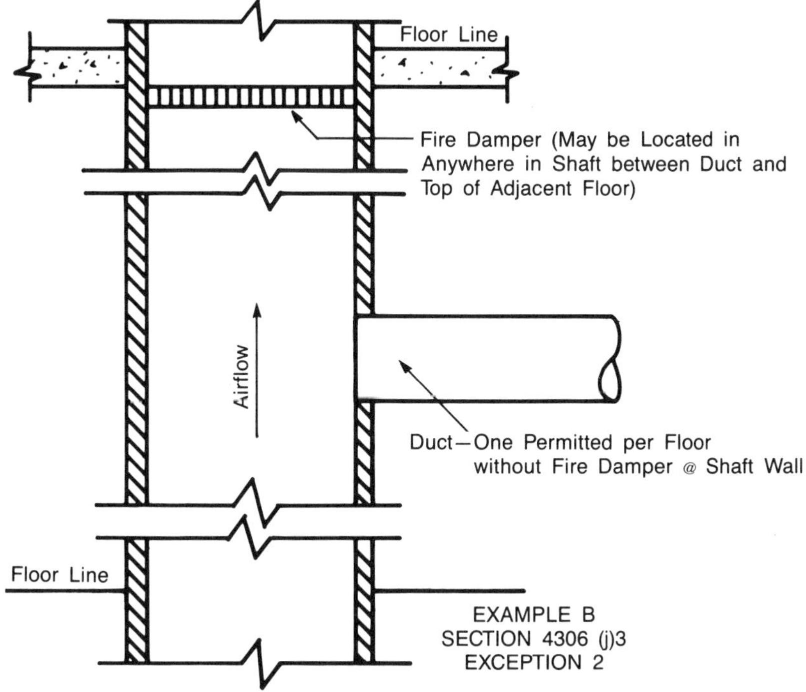

REFERENCE: SECTION 4306 (j)3

FIGURE 8-12 PERMISSIBLE OMISSION OF FIRE DAMPER FOR SHAFTS WITH DUCT PENETRATIONS

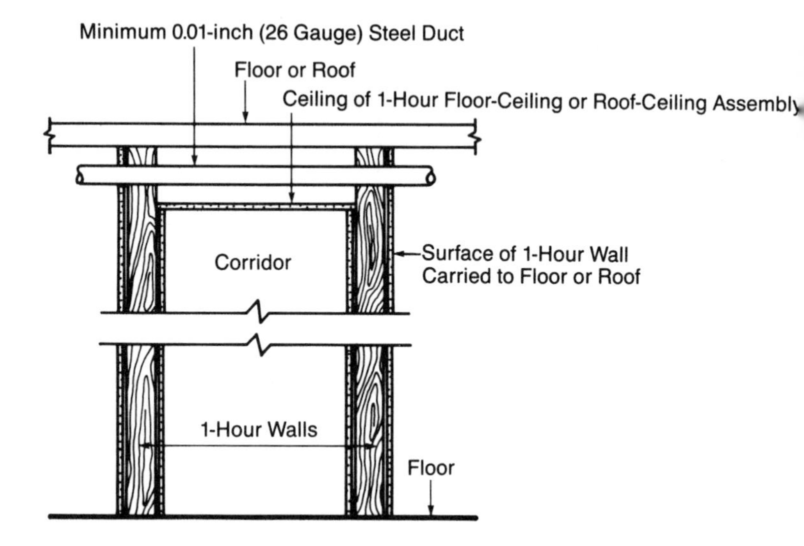

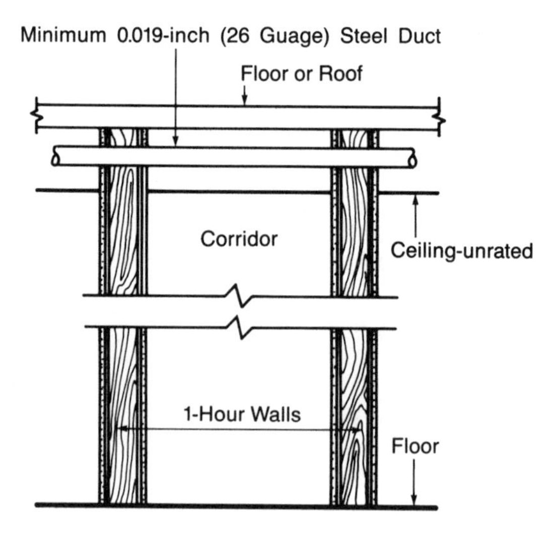

No Openings from Duct into Corridor Permitted
if Fire Dampers are Omitted @ Corridor Walls

REFERENCE: SECTIONS 3305 (g) & 4306 (j)5

FIGURE 8-13 PERMISSIBLE OMISSION OF FIRE DAMPER, ONE-HOUR CORRIDOR WALLS

The substantive changes to this section are:

1. The addition of another Exception to Item 3. This permits the omission of a vertical fire damper on one floor provided there is a horizontal fire damper in the shaft above the location. (See Figure 8-12.)
2. The cross-reference in Item 4 to the revised Section 4305 (b) provisions.
3. The addition of an Exception for 26-gauge steel ducts in Item 5 provided the duct has no openings into the corridor. (See Figure 8-13.)

Through-penetration Fire Stops

Sec. 4308. Through-penetration fire stops required by this code shall have an F or T rating as determined by tests conducted in accordance with U.B.C. Standard No. 43-6.

Through-penetration fire stops may be used for membrane penetrations.

The F rating shall apply to all penetrations and shall be not less than the required fire-resistance rating of the assembly penetrated.

The T rating shall apply to those through-penetration locations required to have T ratings as specified in Sections 4304(e) and 4305(c) and shall be not less than the required fire-resistance rating of the assembly penetrated.

Although this section is located toward the end of Chapter 43, it forms the basis for the through-penetration fire stop performance requirements. The test standard is based on ASTM E-814. For a discussion of the differences between the two standards, see the Technical Appendix TA6.

Presently, there is no test provision for qualifying membrane penetration fire stops. Therefore, for those situations, a through-penetration fire stop can be used.

The common requirement for all penetration fire stops is that they must at least meet the F rating of the assembly penetrated. Thus, if the area separation wall is of two-hour fire-resistive construction, the F rating of the penetration fire stop through that wall must be at least two hours.

Where a T rating is required in Sections 4304 (e) or 4305 (c), that rating must also be not less than the fire-resistive rating of the assembly penetrated. (See Figure TA6-1.)

Smoke Dampers

Sec. 4309. When penetrations of smoke partitions or smoke zone boundaries

by ducts or transfer grilles are requires to be protected, listed smoke dampers conforming to U.B.C. Standard No. 43-12 shall be installed. Where the penetration is also required to have fire dampers, combination fire/smoke dampers conforming to U.B.C. Standard Nos. 43-7 and 43-12 may be used.

Smoke dampers shall have a leakage rating of Class 0, I, II or III.

Smoke dampers or combination fire/smoke dampers shall have a degradation test temperature rating of not less than 250°F.

This is a new provision in Chapter 43. The two citations referred to for smoke dampers are Section 802 (b) and 1002 (b). There are many other situations where smoke-tight compartments are required in the code; however, except for these two specific provisions, the others are not clearly indicated in this code section.

> In the opinion of the author, among these locations are horizontal exits and elevator lobby enclosures in high-rise buildings. The specific location should be listed in this section for ease of use by the designer and enforcement official.

Table No. 43-B Item 71 (Note: This was Item 75 in the 1985 UBC.):

The description of the construction has been changed to delete the reference to "or 3/8 inch exterior type plywood." Also deleted was the last sentence relating to plywood nailing.

The change to this Item in Table No. 43-B resulted from the finding that the original listing of the plywood assembly in the 1967 UBC was not based on actual fire test data. Recent full scale fire tests have proven that the plywood assembly did not meet the one-hour fire test criteria.

Designers desiring to use plywood-surfaced exterior walls can still do so provided the wall assembly complies with an approved one-hour fire-resistive wall. (See Figure 8-14.) One such assembly could be a typical 5/8-inch Type X gypsum wallboard assembly similar to Item 67 in Table No. 43-B.

With the use of water-resistant gypsum wallboard or backing board and the 3/8-inch minimum exterior-type plywood covering, the assembly should satisfy both fire and weather resistance requirements of the code.

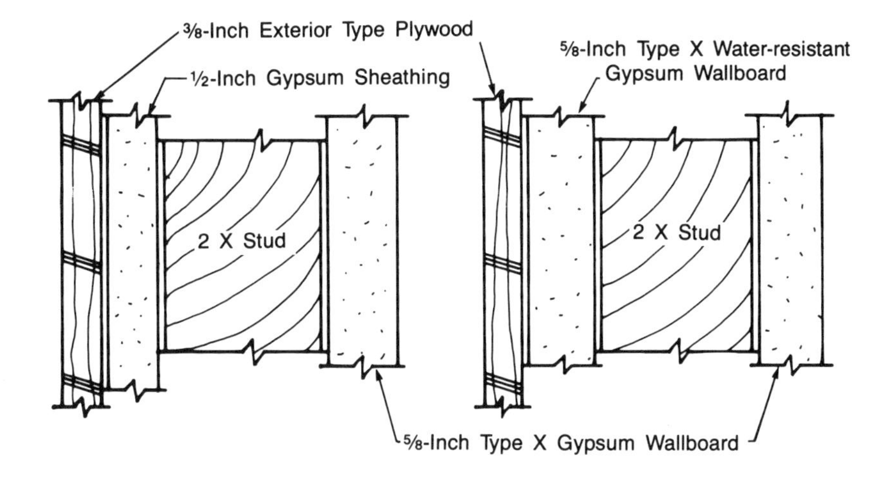

DETAIL "A"

ASSEMBLY DELETED FROM TABLE
FORMERLY PART OF ITEM 75

DETAIL "B"

ACCEPTABLE ASSEMBLY

The plywood assembly with 1⁄2-inch gypsum sheathing, which was contained in Item 75 of prior codes, has been deleted. There are alternative systems that can provide the required one-hour fire resistance ratings. These are one-hour assemblies that are listed in Table No. 43-B for interior use and which, when placed under the plywood weatherboarding can make an acceptable assembly.

One such material to take the place of the 1⁄2-inch gypsum sheathing could be 5⁄8-inch water-resistant Type X gypsum wallboard per Item 67 in Table No. 43-B.

REFERENCE: SECTION 4302 (b), TABLE NO. 43-B

FIGURE 8-14 EXTERIOR PLYWOOD SURFACED ONE-HOUR FIRE-RESISTIVE WALL, TABLE NO. 43-B MATERIALS CHANGE

In Section 4302 (c) of the code, reference is made to the method for calculating the fire resistance of materials or assemblies. These are in UBC Standard 43-9 in the Book of Standards.

In recent years considerable effort has been made to reduce the cost of fire testing by using the existing data, the physical and thermal characteristics of materials, and computers to establish mathematical models of performance. These have been done primarily for steel protected by coverings such as wallboard, concrete and spray-applied fire-protection materials and for concrete walls, floors, roofs, columns and beams.

The provisions for calculating fire ratings for these two basic materials were added to the UBC Book of Standards in 1985. The Book of Standards now includes material to assist in determining fire rating for some wood-based assemblies in Part III of that standard.

UBC Standard 43-9
Methods of Calculating Fire Resistance

Part III
METHODS FOR CALCULATING FIRE RESISTANCE OF WOOD-FRAMED WALLS, FLOORS AND ROOFS
See Section 4302 (c)

Scope

Sec. 43.920. This part establishes acceptable calculation methods for determining the fire-resistive classification of structural parts, walls and partitions and floor- ceiling assemblies. It is intended for use in cases where fire test results specified in U.B.C. Standard No. 43-1 are not available and the specific assembly of materials is not among those listed in Table Nos. 43-A, 43-B and 43-C.

Wood-framed Walls, Floors and Roofs

General

Sec. 43.921. These procedures apply to both load-bearing and nonbearing construction. The calculated fire-resistive ratings shall not exceed one hour. When the wall construction is nonsymmetrical, the provisions of Section 4304 (d) of the Building Code apply.

Procedures

Sec. 43.922. The fire-resistive rating of wood-framed construction is equal to

the sum of the time assigned to the membrane on the fire-exposed side (Table No. 43-9-T), the time assigned to the framing members (Table No. 43-9-V) and the time assigned for other protective measures, such as insulation (Table No. 43-9-W). The membrane on the unexposed side shall not be included in determining the fire resistance of the assembly. When more than one membrane is installed on the wall surface exposed to fire, ratings of each membrane may be added.

Walls and Partitions

Sec. 43.923. Table No. 43-9-T lists the time of fire resistance accredited to the materials used on the fire-exposed side of walls and partitions.

Roof-Ceiling and Floor-Ceiling Assemblies

Sec. 43.924. Table No. 43-9-U specifies the various acceptable membranes and limits the structural frame to wood joists installed on no more than 16-inch spacings. Ratings for roof-ceiling and floor-ceiling assemblies are based on the membranes listed in Table No. 43-9-T being installed on the fire-exposed side in combination with membranes listed in Table No. 43-9-U being installed on the side not exposed to furnace temperatures.

Membrane Fastening

Sec. 43.925. Fastening the membrane to the supporting construction shall be as specified in Table Nos. 43-B, 43-C and 25-Q of the code for corresponding membrane materials.

For brevity, only the opening text of the wood provisions in this standard has been reproduced here. This discussion will relate only to wood assemblies.

The designer desiring to use this method of determining the fire resistance of a system is directed to the complete text of the standard in the 1991 UBC Book of Standards.

An example can best illustrate the procedure used to determine the calculated fire rating for a wood-based assembly. This method of determining the fire resistance is permitted by Section 4302 (c). Table Nos. 43-9-T and 43-9-V are required to determine the times attributed to the various components of an assembly.

Selected items from these tables are reproduced below for the following calculations. The designer is referred to the complete tables for other possible combinations of materials.

Table No. 43-9-T (Partial)
TIME ASSIGNED TO WALLBOARD MEMBRANES

Description of Finish	Time, Min.
1/2-inch fiberboard	5
1/2-inch exterior-glue plywood	10
3/8-inch gypsum wallboard	10*
1/2- + 3/8-inch gypsum wallboard	35

*Membrane rating combined with stud rating is 25.

Table No. 43-9-V (Partial)
TIME ASSIGNED FOR CONTRIBUTION OF WOOD FRAME

Description of Frame	Time Assigned to Frame, Min.
Wood studs 16 inches o.c	20

We have assumed that a one-hour fire rating is required for the wall illustrated in Figure 8-15. Using these tables for the existing wall assembly shown in Figure 8-15, detail (a) provides the following calculated ratings, based on whether the measurement is for the right or left half of the assembly:

For fire exposure on right side:

3/8-inch wallboard	10 minutes /	25 minutes w/stud
1/2-inch fiberboard	5 minutes /	5 minutes w/stud
Wood studs @ 16 inch o.c.	20 minutes /	—
Total	35 minutes	30 minutes w/stud

For fire exposure on left side:

3/8-inch wallboard	10 minutes /	25 minutes w/stud
1/2-inch plywood w/exterior glue	10 minutes /	10 minutes w/stud
Wood studs @ 16 inch centers	20 minutes /	—
Total	40 minutes	35 minutes w/stud

In both instances the wall is deficient in the required one-hour rating. It could be upgraded using the tables as shown below.

The right side is deficient by 30 minutes, based on the combined wallboard and stud time computation; the left side is deficient by 25 minutes. In combination with the other elements on that side of the wall, the following would be the results if one layer of 1/2-inch regular wallboard was placed over the 3/8-inch wallboard presently in place:

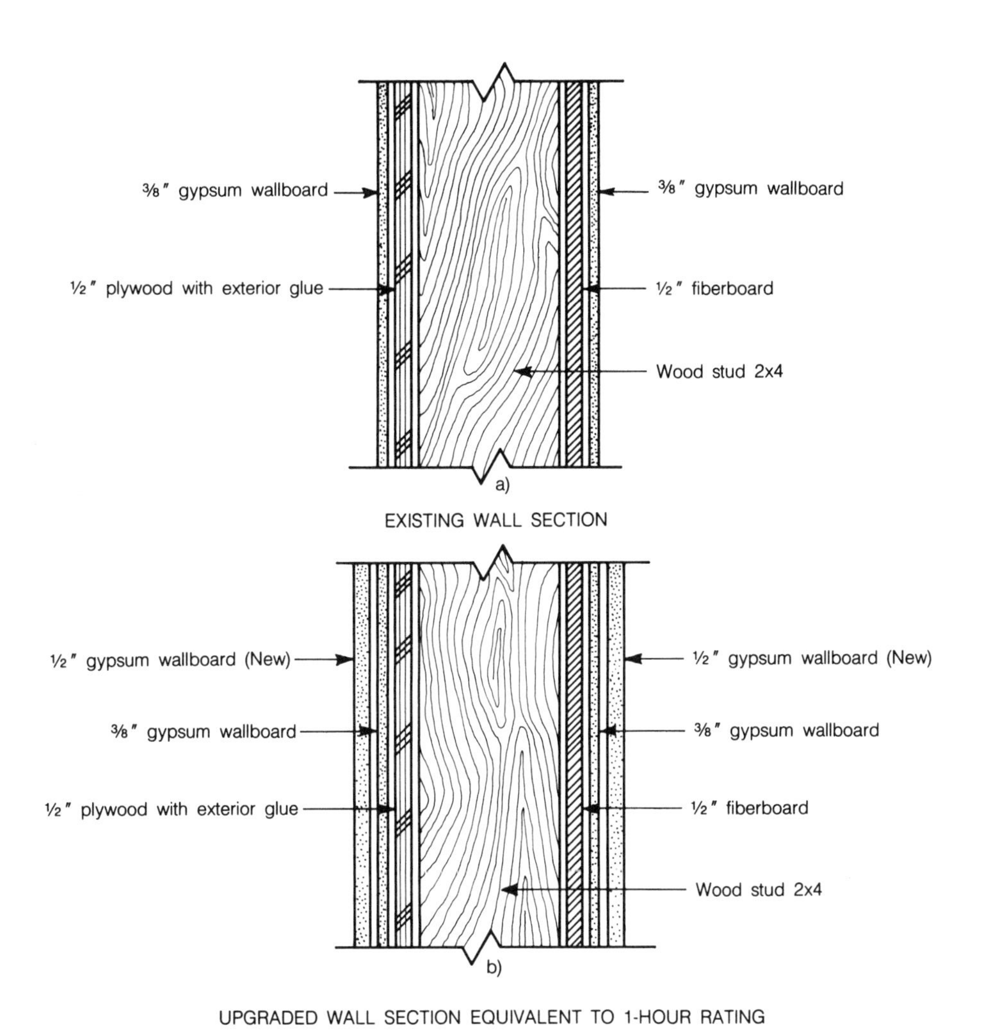

ASSUME: EXISTING WALL REQUIRED TO BE UPGRADED TO MIN. 1-HOUR FIRE RATING

REFERENCE: UBC STANDARD 43-9, UBC SECTION 4302 (c)

FIGURE 8-15 FIRE RATING CALCULATION EXAMPLE, WOOD SAUD ASSEMBLY

For fire exposure on the right side:

1/2-inch + 3/8-inch wallboard	35 minutes
1/2-inch fiberboard	5 minutes
Wood studs @ 16 inch centers	20 minutes
Total	60 minutes

For fire exposure on the left side:

1/2-inch + 3/8-inch wallboard	35 minutes
1/2-inch plywood w/exterior glue	10 minutes
Wood studs @ 16 inch centers	20 minutes
Total	65 minutes

This proposed method of correction — by adding wallboard to each side of the present wall — will thus permit the building official to calculate the wall rating and accept the wall based on Section 4302 (c) of the code.

NOTE: The provisions of Section 43.922 require that the calculation of the fire rating of the assembly be made without "the membrane on the unexposed side included." Earlier in this Article, we pointed out that there was no one-hour wallboard.

This does not mean that one-sided assemblies are permitted by either the Standards or Section 4302 (c) of the code. There must be no confusion generated by the method required for calculating the fire rating of an assembly by the procedure outlined in this standard and our comments in this Guide.

For example, using the Standard for the calculation of the fire rating of 5/8-inch Type X gypsum wallboard on wood studs at 16-inch o.c., a 40-minute rating is assigned to the wallboard and 20 minutes to the stud space, for a total of 60 minutes. This calculation satisfies the one-hour requirement. However, the calculation applies to only one side of the assembly being exposed to a fire. Because the designer does not know the direction of fire exposure of an assembly, the wallboard must be on both faces of the stud. This, however, is not stated in the Standards, and the designer should not be misled.

Our reasons for the above statement are as follows:

For wallboard to be allowed the designation Type X, it must be tested on both sides of a 2x4 stud wall under the ASTM E-119 procedure. The criteria for passing this test are discussed in earlier in this Article, A one-sided assembly would not pass these criteria.

Furthermore, a one-sided assembly with exposed studs would lead to rapid burning of the studs, due to the presence of an unlimited air supply. A failure would occur in considerably less than the one-hour period.

The calculation methods in this standard are useful tools, but as with all tools one must be knowledgeable about how to use them, the limitations of their use and their attendant hazards.

NOTES

ARTICLE 9
MISCELLANEOUS CODE PROVISIONS
CHAPTERS 7, 9, 12, 18, and 20
Including
BUSINESS and RESIDENTIAL OCCUPANCY & HIGH-RISE BUILDING REQUIREMENTS

This article of the Guide reviews certain miscellaneous UBC occupancy provisions that, for a designer, either have frequent application or can cause problems. In Article 10 the provisions in certain additional UBC chapters will be reviewed. The provisions in these two articles are reviewed to supplement those discussed in Articles 3 through 8 herein.

Construction, Height and Allowable Are

Sec. 702. (a) General. Buildings or parts of buildings classed in Group B Occupancy because of the use or character of the occupancy shall be limited to the types of construction set forth in Tables No. 5-C and No. 5-D and shall not exceed, in area or height, the limits specified in Sections 505, 506 and 507.

Other provisions of this code notwithstanding, a basement or first story of a building may be considered as a separate and distinct building for the purposes of area limitations, limitation of number of stories and type of construction when all of the following conditions are met:

1. The basement or first story is of Type I construction and is separated from the building above with a three-hour occupancy separation.
2. The building above the three-hour occupancy separation contains only Group A, Division 3, Group B, Division 2, or Group R, Division 1 Occupancies.
3. The building below the three-hour occupancy separation is used exclusively for the parking and storage of private or pleasure-type motor vehicles.

   EXCEPTION: 1. Entry lobbies, laundry rooms and mechanical rooms and similar uses incidental to the operation of the building.

   2. Group B, Division 2 office and retail occupancies in addition to those incidental to the operation of the building (including storage areas) provided the entire structure below the three-hour occupancy separation is protected throughout by an automatic sprinkler system.
4. The maximum building height in feet shall not exceed the limits set forth in Table No. 5-D for the least type of construction involved.

The provisions in the second paragraph of Section 702 (a) describe a concept that permits one type of construction to support a different and lesser type of construction.

The intent of this concept is that if the base structure can be constructed to simulate the same degree of safety as if it was ground, then separate structures could be built on the base structure. These structures would be considered distinct buildings and could be constructed of any type of construction without the base structure being downgraded to that type of construction.

Thus, a Type I garage could be built with Type V buildings on top of the garage. There is no limit to the size of the base structure or to the number of individual buildings that can be built on top of the base provided the limitations in Section 702 (a) are met. (See Figure 9-1.)

The changes to Section 702 (a) second paragraph from the prior code include adding the Group A, Division 3 Occupancy to those permitted to be above a Type I or II-FR structure housing a Group B, Division 1 Occupancy. In addition, the basement or first story may contain offices or retail stores as well as the garage. These changes increase the flexibility of this concept whereby the lower segment and the upper segment of the building are each considered as separate structures. These identical provisions have been in use in San Francisco in the Embarcadero Center area for more than 20 years without problems. (See Figure 9-1.)

The Group A, Division 3 Occupancy includes restaurants, conference rooms and senior citizen centers. Such Group A, Division 3 Occupancies are commonly needed in conjunction with the Group B, Division 2 Occupancy and Group R, Division 1 Occupancy uses. The new provision will accommodate that need without creating code difficulties.

Proper occupancy separations, per Table No. 5-B, must be provided between the various occupancies.

Shaft and Exit Enclosures

Sec. 706. Exits shall be enclosed as specified in Chapter 33.

Elevator shafts, vent shafts and other openings through floors shall be enclosed, and the enclosure shall be as specified in Section 1706.

EXCEPTION: In Group B, Division 4 Occupancies, exits shall be enclosed as specified in Chapter 33, but other through-floor openings need not be enclosed.

In buildings housing Group B Occupancies equipped with automatic sprinkler systems throughout, enclosures shall not be required for escalators where the top of the escalator opening at each story is provided with a draft curtain and automatic fire sprinklers are installed around the perimeter of the opening within 2 feet of the draft curtain. The draft curtain shall enclose the perimeter of the unenclosed opening and extend from the ceiling downward at least 12 inches on all sides. The spacing between sprinklers shall not exceed 6 feet.

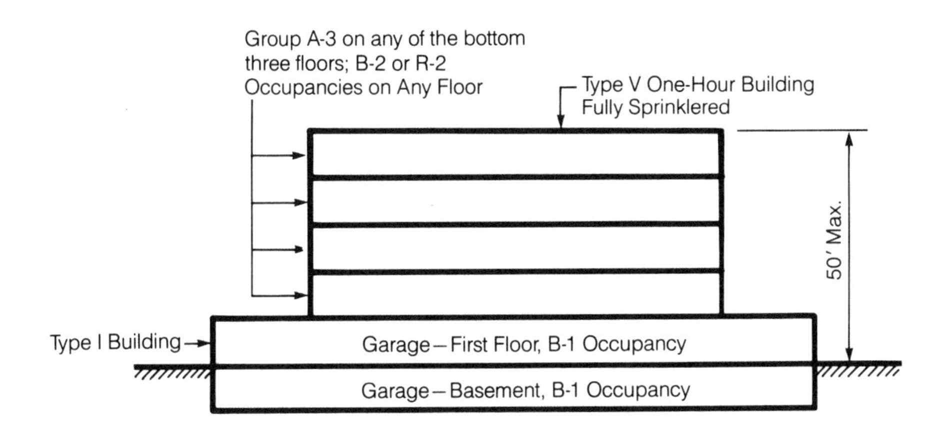

A Type V One-Hour building may be constructed on top of a Type I garage, (Group B, Division 1 Occupancy) building.

The overall height of the Type V building is limited by Table No. 5-D to 50′. If the upper structure were of Type III construction, the height to the top of the upper structure could be 65′ above grade.

The upper building may contain Group A, Division 3, Group B, Division 2 or Group R, Division 1 Occupancies, or a mix of all three occupancies. Table No. 5-D provides the story location limitations for the various occupancies. Thus, the Group A, Division 3 Occupancy in a Type V One-Hour building cannot be above the second floor of the building if the building were not sprinklered or may be on the third floor as it is sprinklered.

REFERENCE: SECTION 702 (a) AND TABLE NO. 5-D

FIGURE 9-1 GROUP A, DIV. 3, B, DIV. 2 AND R, DIV. 1 OCCUPANCIES OVER GARAGE

NOTE: This provision is one part of several code provisions relating to penetrations of fire-resistive wall, floor-ceiling and shaft wall assemblies. See discussions of Section 1706 in Article 6 of this Guide and in Article 8 regarding penetrations in Section 4304 and 4305.

This section has been expanded by adding a new last paragraph. This paragraph transferred material from Section 1706 (a) Exception 2 in prior codes. There were no changes made to the text. This provision permits multi-storied penetrations of floors by escalators provided fire sprinklers are furnished as set forth in the last paragraph.

This unique code latitude addresses a need in Group B, Division 2 Occupancies such as department stores; however, it is inconsistent with the general code provision for shaft enclosures. Fortunately, fire experience in Group B, Division 2 Occupancies has been good and the provision has been used successfully at least since 1949.

Shaft and Exit Enclosures

Sec. 906. Exits shall be enclosed as specified in Chapter 33.

Elevator shafts, vent shafts and other openings through floors shall be enclosed, and the enclosure shall be as specified in Section 1706.

Doors which are part of an automobile ramp enclosure shall be equipped with automatic-closing devices.

In buildings with Group H, Division 6 Occupancies, a fabrication area may have mechanical, duct and piping penetrations which extend through not more than two floors within that fabrication area. The annular space around penetrations for cables, cable trays, tubing, piping, conduit or ducts shall be sealed to restrict the movement of air. The fabrication area, including the areas through which the ductwork and piping extend, shall be considered a single conditioned environment.

NOTE: This provision is one of several code provisions relating to penetrations of fire-resistive wall, floor-ceiling and shaft wall assemblies.

This section was expanded from prior codes by adding a new last paragraph. This paragraph transferred material from Section 1706 (a) Exception 8 of the prior codes. The second sentence of the last paragraph was clarified to refer to the function of a draft-stop material rather than a fire-blocking material.

Group R Occupancies Defined

Sec. 1201 Group R Occupancies shall be:

Division 1. Hotels and apartment houses.

Congregate residences (each accommodating more than 10 persons).

Division 2. Not used.
Division 3. Dwellings and lodging houses.
Congregate residences (each accommodating 10 persons or less).

This occupancy group has been expanded to establish a new category of housing. The new provisions recognize the extreme housing pressures,particularly in urban areas of the country. The new category is referred to as congregate residence.

Congregate residences include such traditional multiple housing as monasteries and convents, but expand into the unconventional or nontraditional housing for students or persons with no binding relationships such as a family. Because there is no family, the prior code definitions would not cover these new forms of house-sharing practices.

Numerous code changes were made for this new concept of housing, essentially deleting the terms for monasteries, convents and dormitories and adding the term congregate residence whenever dwelling unit or similar reference is made to assure application of the requirement to the congregate residence form as well.

Construction Height and Allowable Area.

Sec. 1202. (b) Special Provisions . Walls and floors separating dwelling units in the same building shall be not less than one-hour fire-resistive construction.

Group R, Division 1 Occupancies more than two stories in height or having more than 3000 square feet of floor area above the first story shall be not less than one-hour fire-resistive construction throughout except as provided in Section 1705 (b)2.

Storage or laundry rooms that are within Group R. Division 1 Occupancies that are used in common by tenants shall be separated from the rest of the building by not less than one-hour fire-resistive occupancy separation.

For Group R, Division 1 Occupancies with a Group B, Division 1 parking garage in the basement or first floor, see Section 702 (a).

For attic space partitions and draft stops, see Section 2516 (f).

Section 1202 (b) requires that all dwelling units be separated, one from another, by not less than a one-hour fire-resistive assembly. If there are openings in the separation, the code does not indicate the required fire rating for the opening assembly. This will be discussed later.

Even where the code allows a building to be constructed as a Type II-N, III-N or V-N structure based on floor area, height and occupancy, the dwelling units must be separated by rated construction.

Because of the importance of this provision and the lack of clarifying details, an intensive examination of the implications follows.

DISCUSSION OF THE EFFECT OF THE DWELLING UNIT SEPARATION (DUS) REQUIREMENT

a) **Application to Group R, Division 1 and R, Division 3 Occupancies.**

The code provision is not limited to Group R Division 1 Occupancy. It applies to Group R Division 3, two-dwelling-unit building as well. See Figure 9-2.

b) **Group R, Division 3 Occupancy Buildings**

The provisions also affect the two-family Group R, Division 3 Occupancy. The terminology used in the provision refers only to "walls and floors separating dwelling units in the same building."

Because Section 1202 (a) General refers to the Group R Occupancy in general, and as Section 1202 (b) is not limited to Group R, Division 1 Occupancy, the conclusion that one must reach is that the DUS applies wherever there are adjacent dwelling units. (See Figures 9-2 and 9-5.)

c) **Support of DUS**

The code provision requires that there be a one-hour DUS provided. Note that the type of separation is not specifically designated as either an occupancy separation or an area separation as defined in Chapters 4 and 5.

Therefore, the support provision of Section 503 (b) for an occupancy separation is not directly applicable.

However, the designer is cautioned that it would be poor practice to provide a design such that a rated separation would occur over an unprotected support. Liability may occur if the designer permitted this situation. Therefore, the author believes that whether or not the code requires the separation to be supported by construction of equivalent

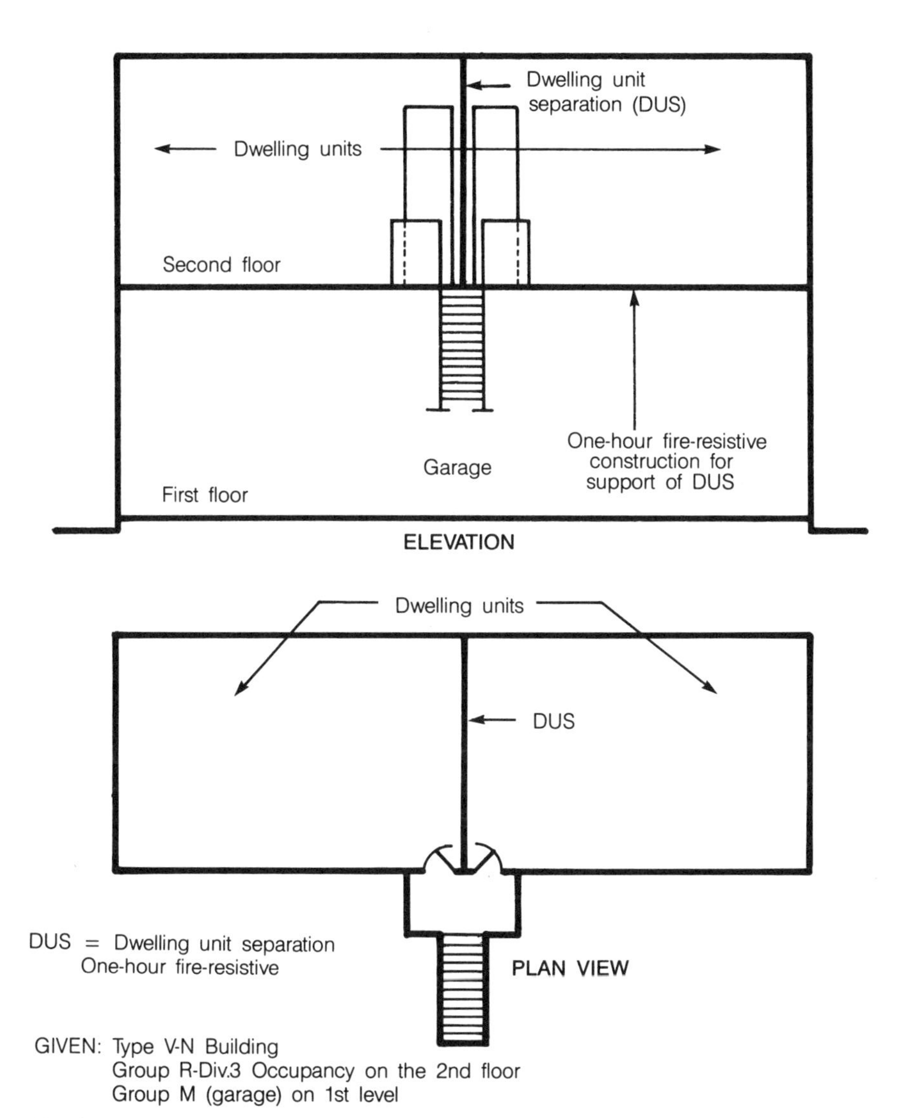

GIVEN: Type V-N Building
Group R-Div.3 Occupancy on the 2nd floor
Group M (garage) on 1st level

Per Section 503(d) Exception 3, the garage/dwelling unit separation need be surfaced only on the garage side as for a one-hour fire resistant floor-ceiling assembly. However, per Section 1202(b), the DUS between the dwelling units must be at least one-hour fire-resistive construction.

Thus, the supports for that DUS, as provided by the floor-ceiling assembly of the second floor over the garage, should be at least a complete one-hour fire-resistive assembly and not simply the surfacing layer of same.

REFERENCES: SECTIONS 503 (d)EXCEPTION 3 AND 1202 (b)

FIGURE 9-2 DWELLING UNIT SEPARATION REQUIREMENTS—TYPE V-N BUILDING, GROUP R, DIVISION 3 OVER GARAGE

fire resistance, this fire rating should be provided in all instances.

d) **Applicability of Type N Construction for Multiple-Dwelling-Unit Buildings**

The designer should recognize that with this code requirement the simple Type V-N construction for a multi-family residential building is no longer permitted. In its place will be a form of hybrid construction.

A considerable portion of the Type V-N building must be of one-hour fire-rated construction, as mandated by this code provision. The author suggests that the designer consider whether it would be best for the entire building to be a Type V one-hour building at the outset. This would provide the benefits of increased area and height and would satisfy the separation requirements. Otherwise, the expenditures required to provide for the DUS will not be compensated by any credits given in the code.

e) **Consideration for Upgrade to One-hour Construction to Satisfy New Requirements**

The impact of this provision should be brought to the attention of the owner/developer in the early stages of the design. If the owner/developer decides on a one-hour building throughout, the benefits of such a building can be readily integrated into that design.

f) **Double-Loaded Corridor and DUS Requirements**

With the new DUS provision, an ambiguous condition occurs in a double-loaded corridor. Although the corridor may be interpreted as providing a form of the required DUS from one dwelling unit to another across the corridor from it, this interpretation is not stated in the code text. Although this is a common type of corridor arrangement, it is not readily evaluated by a reading of the code provision.

The corridor wall must be one-hour fire rated under the provisions of Section 3305 (g)—when the occupant load is 10 or more. The openings therein are permitted to have 20-minute smoke- and draft-control doors per Section 3305 (h).

With this in mind, we can make some general assumptions as to what code provisions would apply for the corridor walls forming the separation between the dwelling units:

1. Occupant Load in Corridor Less Than 10.

When the occupant load is less than 10, the walls of the double-loaded corridor are permitted to be of nonrated construction with the openings therein unprotected, i.e.,nonrated doors. The one-hour DUS requirement is not satisfied, therefore, by this minimal nonrated code-complying construction. Because the doors in such nonrated walls can have only a six-minute fire-resistance rating (a hollow-core door), the net protection from unit to unit across the corridor could be only about 12 to 15 minutes instead of the one-hour separation required by the code. See Figure 9-3.

A. The two nonrated corridor walls would probably provide the equivalence of the one-hour separation. This conclusion is reached by assuming there is 1/2-inch regular gypsum wallboard on both sides of a wood stud. The two layers of wallboard are credited with a 15-minute fire-resistance time period, as noted in Table No. 43-9-A of UBC Standard No. 43-1 (as discussed in Article 8 of this Guide).

The studs are given 20-minute ratings in that standard; thus, each wall assembly will have about a 35-minute rating. The pair of walls on both sides of the corridor can, therefore, be considered equivalent to the one-hour separation, because it can be demonstrated from the UBC Book of Standards that these walls will calculate to a net fire-resistive time period of 70 minutes.

B. The nonrated doors are the problem in the less-than-10-occupant load corridor. They can provide as little as a 12 minute fire rating. Openings in the one-hour separation should have a fire-resistance rating of at least three-quarter hour. This opening-to-barrier ratio is the accepted standard, except where a greater time requirement is specifically cited in the code.

Therefore, in such a double-loaded corridor situation,the author believes that the doors should be not less than 20-minute, self-closing, smoke- and draft-control assemblies. This installation would provide a total of at least 40 minutes for two doors, if located directly opposite each other on the corridor. See Figure 9-4.

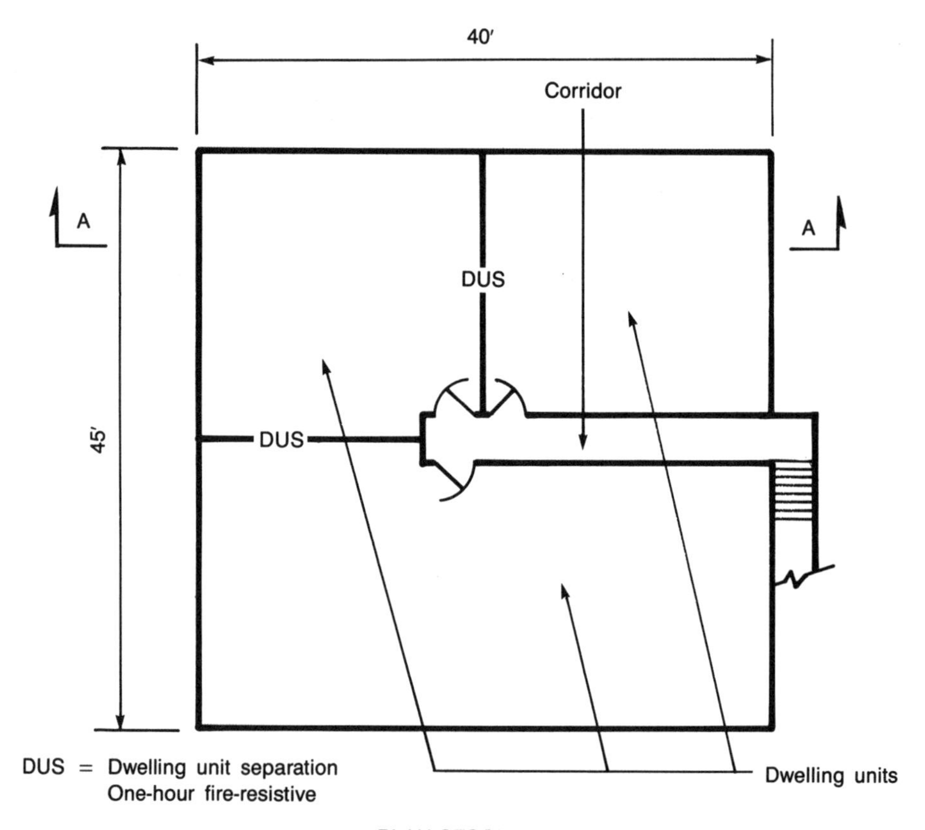

GIVEN: Type V-N Building
Group R Div.1 Occupancy - 2 stories
3 dwelling units on 2nd floor w/double loaded corridor
2 dwelling units on 1st floor

Per Section 3301 (a) the occupant load on the 2nd floor is 1800/200 = 9

Because this occupant load is <10, the corridor is not subject to the Section 3305 requirements for one-hour construction.

However, per Section 1202 (b), a one-hour DUS is required between the dwelling units on the second floor. The corridor is part of that separation. Therefore, the two corridor walls are required to provide the aggregate equivalence of one-hour fire-resistive construction with the openings protected at least with three-quarter hour fire assemblies. The fire assemblies should also meet the smoke- and draft-control requirements of Section 3305 (h).

REFERENCE: SECTIONS 1202 (b), 3301 (a) and 3305 (h) AND TABLE NO. 33-A

FIGURE 9-3 DWELLING UNIT SEPARATION (DUS) REQUIREMENTS – TYPE V-N BUILDING, GROUP R, DIVISION 1

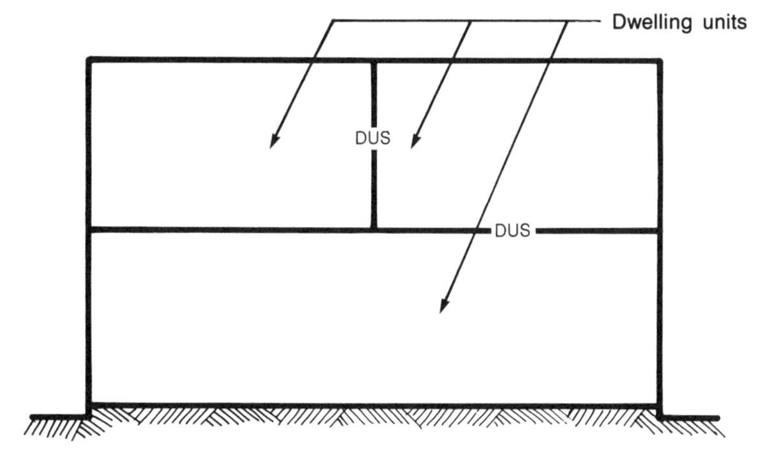

SECTION A-A

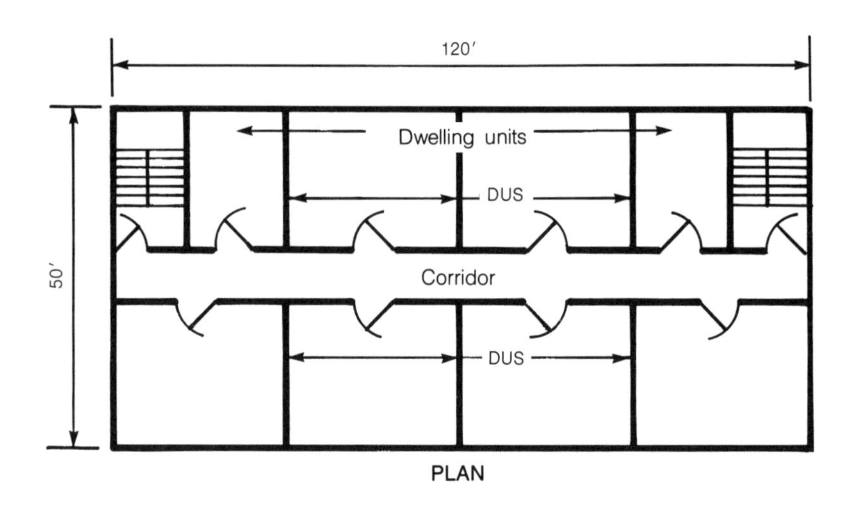

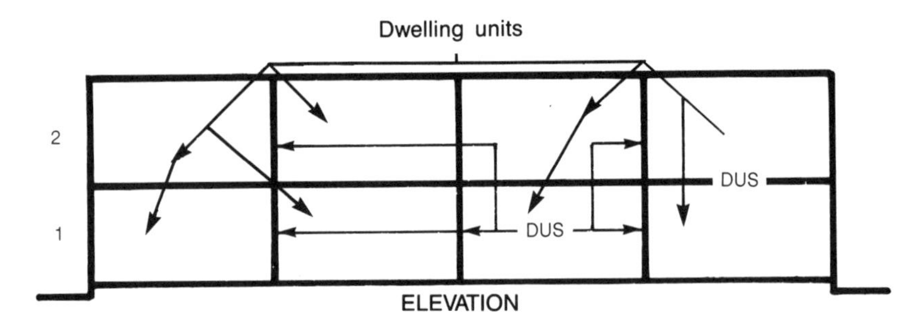

GIVEN: Type V-N Building
Group R Div.1 Occupancy, 4 units per floor
Double loaded exit corridor

DUS = Dwelling unit separation
One-hour fire-resistive

The requirements for the dwelling unit separations (DUS) in subject building require that virtually all elements of the building be of one hour fire resistive construction. The corridor must be of one hour construction per Section 3305(h). The 20 minute smoke and draft control doors can be used to provide the one hour protection of the openings in the DUS across the corridor.

REFERENCE: SECTIONS 1202 (b), 3301 (a) and 3305 (h) AND TABLE NO. 33-A

FIGURE 9-4 DWELLING UNIT SEPARATIONS—TYPE V-N BUILDING, GROUP R, DIVISION 1 OCCUPANCY, DOUBLE-LOADED ONE-HOUR EXIT CORRIDOR

The five minutes needed to reach 45 minutes may reasonably be assumed, when the width of the corridor and the time for a fire to traverse that width to attack the second door are considered. In the opinion of the author, this would be a reasonable interpretation of equivalence, to the extent that the interpretation is limited to the separation requirement due to the newness of same and the need for an interpretive resolution of the ambiguity.

2. Occupant Load in Corridor of 10 or More.

When the occupant load is 10 or more, the corridor walls are required by Section 3305 (g) to be of one-hour fire-resistive construction. The walls, therefore, obviously satisfy the minimal DUS requirement. The doors, which are required by Section 3305 (h) to be 20-minute self-closing smoke- and draft-control doors, are the "weak link." With regard to the less-than-10-occupant-load corridor, by the absence of specific requirements in the DUS provision for this very common condition in most multi-storied multi-family occupancy buildings, we can infer that probably the doors required in Section 3305 (h) would be acceptable. (See Figure 9-5.)

g) **Garage Separation in Group R, Division 3, When Supporting a DUS**

In two-story, two-dwelling-unit Group R, Division 3 buildings with a garage on the ground floor under the residential portion, the separation between the garage and the residential units is usually required to have the ceiling surface of a one-hour floor-ceiling assembly by Section 503 (d)Exception 3. (See Figure 9-2.)

However, that floor-ceiling assembly should be constructed as a full one-hour fire-resistive assembly in most instances, because it provides the support for the required one-hour vertical separation between the dwelling units.

h) **Sprinkler Substitution for DUS, Section 508**

The use of fire sprinklers in lieu of one-hour fire-resistive construction is provided for in Section 508. The code contains a new prohibited Item 4 in the list of items where sprinkler trade-offs are not allowed. Item 4 was added to the code the year after the DUS was ad-

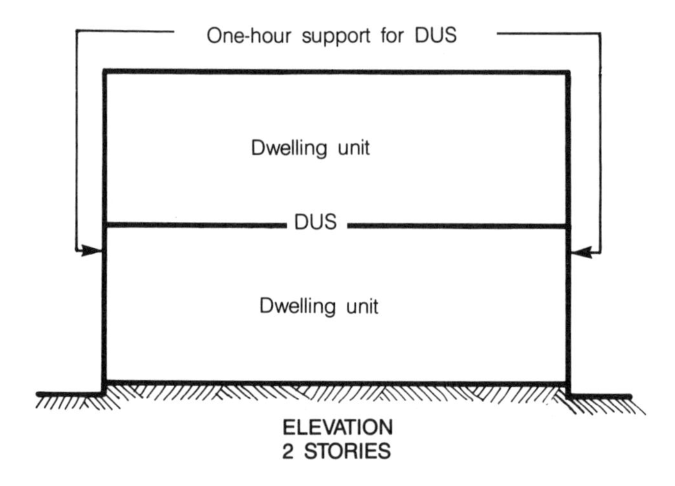

ELEVATION
2 STORIES

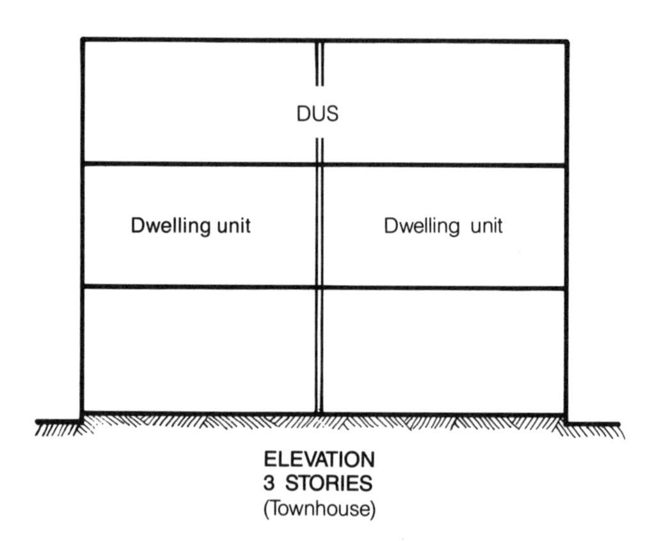

ELEVATION
3 STORIES
(Townhouse)

DUS = Dwelling unit separation
One-hour fire-resistive

GIVEN: Type V-N Building
Group R, Div. 3 Occupancy
Two dwelling units
2 or 3 story

REFERENCE: SECTION 1202 (b)

FIGURE 9-5 DWELLING UNIT SEPARATION REQUIREMENTS—GROUP R, DIVISION 3 OCCUPANCY (TWO FAMILY DWELLING) 2 OR 3 STORIES

ded, even though there had not been time to use the original provision.

Item 4 is "Dwelling unit separations per Section 1202 (b)."

> The author believes that the prohibition in Section 508 for this sprinkler trade-off is unwarranted and overly restrictive; however, it is in force at this time. See the author's overall comments regarding Section 508 in Article 5 of this Guide.

Therefore, the use of a sprinkler trade-off for DUS is not permitted.

i) **Preliminary Plan Check**

In the preliminary plan check, using the DUS provision, the designer should contact the local building official and clear with that office the method and construction to be employed in the project. Make use of the confirmation procedures discussed in this Guide.

j) **Summary of Recommendations**

In summary, therefore, the following are the author's recommendations:

- A designer should consider whether an N-rated type of construction serves the best interests of the client in view of the DUS requirements.
- The code requirements apply to both the vertical and horizontal separations between adjacent dwelling units. A floor-ceiling assembly serving as a DUS must be of at least one-hour fire-resistive construction, in accordance with Table No. 43-C of the code.
- In cases where the one-hour DUS is not supported by fire-rated construction, the designer should provide at least one-hour fire-resistive protection for the support elements. See Figure 9-2.
- All openings into double-loaded exit corridors, regardless of the occupant load served, should be not less than 20-minute

self-closing smoke- and draft-control doors. See Figures 9-3 and 9-4.

- In two-story, two-dwelling-unit Group R Division 3 buildings with a garage on the ground floor level under the residential portion, the separation between the garage and the residential units is usually required to have only the ceiling surface of a one-hour floor-ceiling assembly by Section 503 (d) Exception 3. See Figure 9-2. However, that floor-ceiling assembly should be constructed as a full one-hour fire-resistive assembly in most instances, because it provides the support for the required one-hour vertical separation between the two dwelling units.

This provision, with its considerable effect on the nonrated type of building, will generate both controversy and interpretive problems for all concerned. The author recommends that both the designer and the enforcement official apply conservative and prudent judgments until such time as experience with the provisions develops accepted interpretations. There may well be need for possible modifications of the DUS provisions to clarify the present uncertainties.

Section 1202 (b) relates to dwelling units and guest rooms in Group R, Division 1 Occupancies (apartment houses, hotels and similar multiple unit residential uses). The second paragraph states that an R-1 Occupancy building must be one-hour fire-resistive throughout when either:

- the second floor is greater than 3,000 square feet,
- the building is three or more stories in height.

The floor area measurement must meet the definition of floor area in Chapter 4. That definition requires that all parts of the floor, except vent shafts and courts, be included in the calculation. Thus, stairways, corridors, balconies and landings must be included in the calculation.

> In the author's opinion, where there is a mezzanine in the second floor that does not qualify as a separate story, the area of the mezzanine must also be included in the area of the second floor.

The area criterion that invokes the one-hour fire-resistive requirement should not be confused with the area criterion that invokes the two exit provision of Section 3303 (a); 2,000 square feet for an apartment or hotel occupancy (10 occupants x 200 square feet per occupant). (See Figure 9-6.)

The provisions previously in Section 1204 regarding fire alarms have been transferred to a new Section 1211.

Exits and Emergency Escapes

Sec. 1204. Stairs, exits and smokeproof enclosures shall be as specified in Chapter 33.

Basements in dwelling units and every sleeping room below the fourth story shall have at least one openable window or door approved for emergency escape or rescue which shall open directly onto a street, a public alley, a yard or an exit court. The units shall be openable from the inside to provide a full clear opening without the use of separate tools.

Unfinished basement escape or rescue windows shall be arranged in accordance with Section 3303(c).

All escape or rescue windows shall have a minimum net clear opening of 5.7 square feet. The minimum net clear opening height dimension shall be 24 inches. The minimum net clear openable width dimension shall be 20 inches. Where windows are provided as a means of escape or rescue they shall have a finished sill height not more than 44 inches above the floor.

Bars, grilles, grates or similar devices may be installed on an emergency escape or rescue windows or doors, provided:

1. Such devices are equipped with approved release mechanisms which are openable from the inside without the use of a key or special knowledge or effort; and

2. The building is equipped with smoke detectors installed in accordance with Section 1210.

Article 7 of this Guide, indicates that Section 1202 (b) contains the requirements for the escape and rescue windows in any Group R Occupancy and in all sleeping rooms below the fourth floor of a building with such an occupancy.

There were several changes made to Section 1204 from prior codes. Three changes were made in the escape or rescue window provisions:

1. In the second paragraph, the intent of the escape or rescue window or door is stated. This is an important clarification. These escape or rescue windows or doors must be directly accessible to a public space and by the fire service.

The author has encountered buildings in which bedrooms have

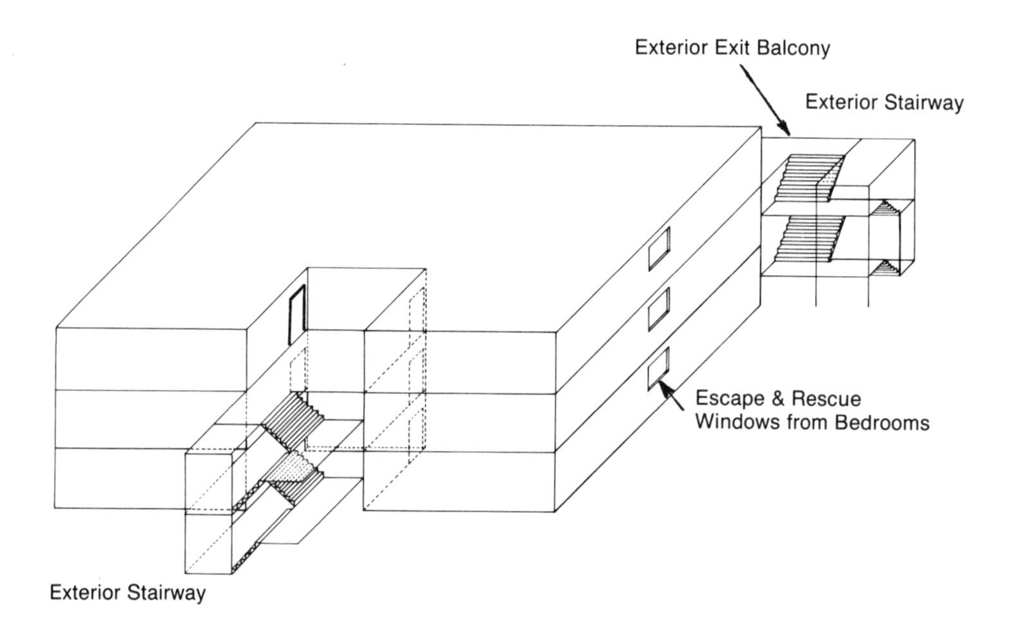

If 2nd floor > 3,000 S.F. - minimum One-hour throughout
If 3 or more stories - minimum One-hour throughout and 2 exits required 3rd floor
If area of 2nd floor + ½ area of 3rd floor ÷ 200 ≥ 10, 2 exits required 2nd floor

Escape and rescue widows are required from every bedroom. These are NOT exits, but are additional openings for building four stories or less in height essentially for fire department rescue. These windows must open onto a street or public alley, yard or exit court.

Escape and rescue windows must be openable and of the minimum size as specified in Section 1204 to facilitate their use.

REFERENCE: SECTIONS 1202 (b), 1204, 3303 (a) AND (c)

FIGURE 9-6 HEIGHT, AREA AND EGRESS RELATIONSHIPS—GROUP R, DIV. 1 OCCUPANCY

had openings, i.e., windows, onto interior stairway landing areas. There were no other accessible openings to the exterior of the building for these bedrooms. (See Figure 9-7.) These bedrooms clearly violate the intent of the code, but due to the lack of clear language in this section at the time of construction, the enforcement official permitted these rooms. They subsequently had to be corrected at considerable cost.

2. In the second and third paragraphs of this section, the term "operable" was corrected to "openable." This change reflects the code intent that these windows must not simply be operable, but openable to facilitate escape or rescue.

3. A requirement added to the second and third paragraphs stating that basements must also have escape or rescue windows. The intent of this provision involves the realization that, in residential buildings, sleeping rooms are often located in basements. To ignore this fact and not provide the escape or rescue windows at the time of construction creates a code enforcement problem. Problems occur when the sleeping room is installed subsequent to the building's construction and is then discovered by the enforcement agency.

By requiring the provision of the windows during the construction phase, regardless of whether the basement is intended for use as a sleeping room at that time, the enforcement problem is obviated. (See Figure 9-8.)

Note that the windows for the unfinished basement may be located anywhere because there is no sleeping room to be served. The reference Section 3303 (c) requires only that if the basement is large enough to require two such windows, the windows be separated from each other.

Escape and rescue windows must provide access to and from a public space such as a street. Windows opening only to the interior of the building and causing one to rely on the interior exits for the escape are not acceptable as escape windows. A fire blocking the exit path from that interior space would also block the escape and rescue path for the window. The escape window must be a separate facility that does not rely on any of the required exits.

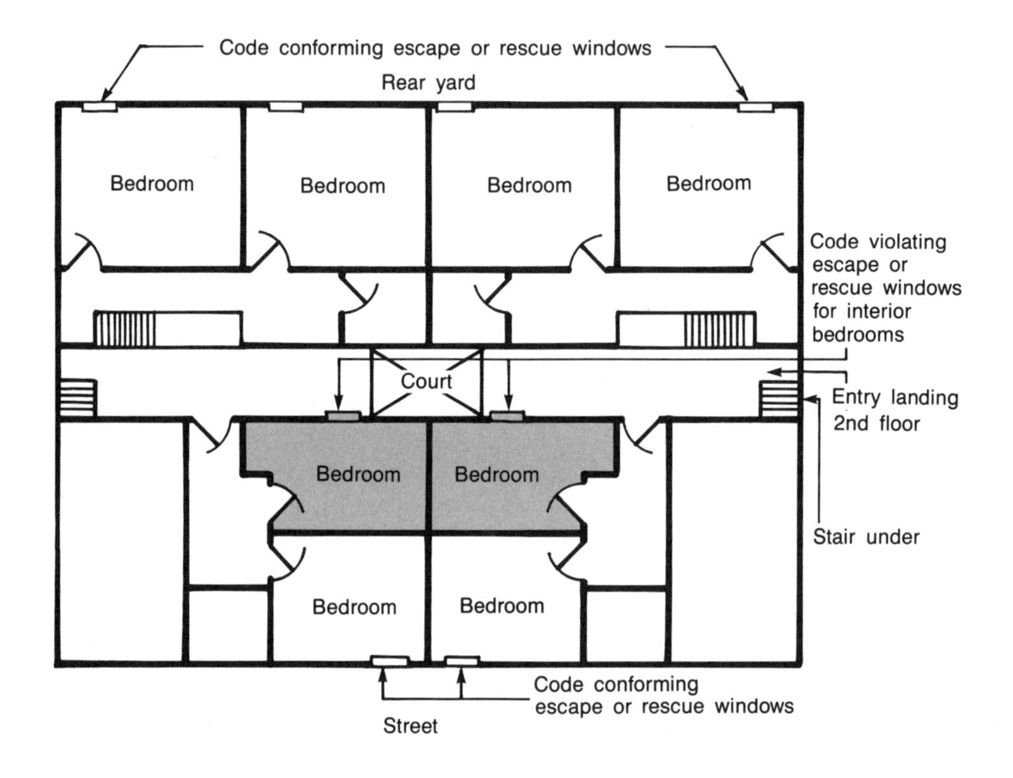

PLAN - 2ND FLOOR

Escape and rescue widows are required from every bedroom. These are NOT exits, but are additional openings for building four stories or less in height essentially for fire department rescue. These windows must open onto a street or public alley, yard or exit court.

Escape and rescue windows must be openable and of the minimum size as specified in Section 1204 to facilitate their use.

The two bedrooms shown shaded which open onto the corridor within the building do NOT meet the requirements for an escape and rescue window.

REFERENCE: SECTION 1204

FIGURE 9-7 ESCAPE OR RESCUE WINDOWS, CODE CONFORMING AND NON-CONFORMING EXAMPLES

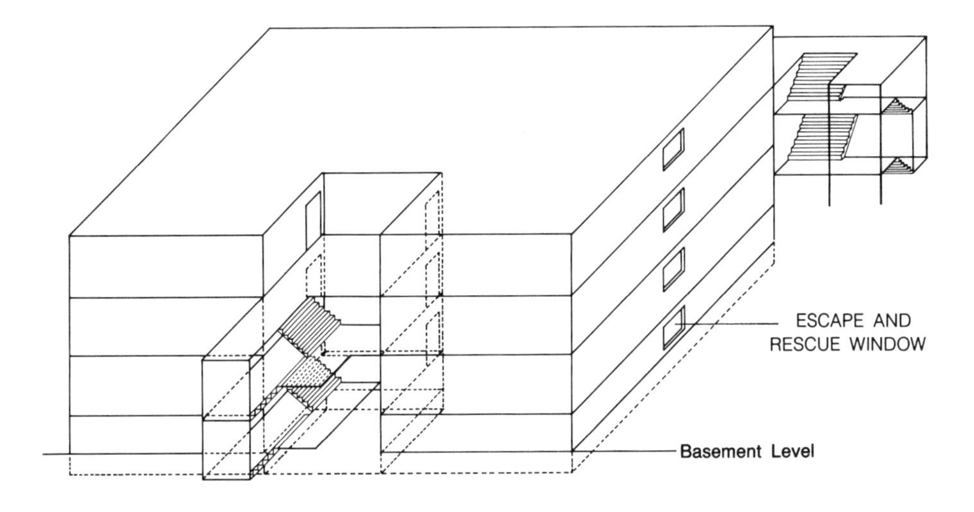

ASSUME:
GROUP R OCCUPANCY BUILDING ≤ 4 STORIES

Escape and rescue widows are required from every bedroom and from basements of dwelling units. These are NOT exits, but are additional openings for building four stories or less in height essentially for fire department rescue. These windows must open onto a street or public alley, yard or exit court.

The requirement for basement is not dependent on whether there is a bedroom located there. The window is required if the basement is in a dwelling unit.

Escape and rescue windows must be openable and of the minimum size as specified in Section 1204 to facilitate their use.

REFERENCE: SECTION 1204, 3RD PARAGRAPH

FIGURE 9-8 ESCAPE OR RESCUE WINDOWS INCLUDING BASEMENT LEVEL

The escape and rescue window is to be provided in addition to all required exits. It cannot be made a substitute for any exit. The escape window must be:

- no smaller than the minimum size,
- no higher than the height above the floor set by the UBC.

This is to facilitate the windows' use in an emergency by firemen or occupants within the bedroom. Each sleeping room must have its own escape window: a window in another sleeping room cannot be used to meet this provision.

The window must open to the required width. Jalousie or louvered-type windows are not permitted. Grilles used over the windows must be openable from inside without special knowledge or tools. All too often, grilles and other devices installed to secure against burglary have trapped occupants who could not open them or have hampered firefighting efforts. (See Figure 9-6.)

Light, Ventilation and Sanitation

Sec. 1205. (a) General. For the purpose of determining the light or ventilation required by this section, any room may be considered as a portion of an adjoining room when one half of the area of the common wall is open and unobstructed and provides an opening of not less than one tenth of the floor area of the interior room or 25 square feet, whichever is greater.

Exterior openings for natural light or ventilation required by this section shall open directly onto a street or public alley or a yard or court located on the same lot as the building.

EXCEPTIONS: 1. Required windows may open into a porch when the porch:

a. Abuts a street, yard or court; and

b. Has a ceiling height of not less than 7 feet; and

c. Has a longer side at least 65 percent open and unobstructed.

2. Skylights.

Residential occupancies require a minimum level of natural light and ventilation. The amount of available openings is arbitrarily set in Section 1205 (b). These amounts have been in effect for many years with only slight variations to develop uniformity with the other model codes.

An alternative means of providing the ventilation is contained in Section 1205 (c), i.e., mechanical systems.

Natural light and ventilation are to be obtained from exterior openings that are directly on a street or other public space. The

Exceptions permit the opening to be onto a roofed porch under specific conditions.

Skylights are another acceptable means for that light. Skylights have been generally accepted by many local jurisdictions for this purpose. Such skylights must comply with Chapter 34 provisions.

When using a skylight for the light requirement, the clear area of the glazing must be used because skylights frequently have heavier supports than wall-mounted glazing.

> In the author's opinion, when the skylight is a domed or other type of skylight that is not in the plane of the roof, the area of the glazing to be used to determine the area being furnished should be the plane area of the skylight.

The required area for light is set forth in Section 1205 (b) as a minimum of 10 square feet. The light requirement can be met by adding the amount of wall and skylight areas furnished.

When it is intended also to use the skylight to provide the required ventilation per Section 1205 (c), the skylight must be operable from a convenient floor-level location. Thus, the operating mechanism should be a readily accessible device that can open the skylight at least to the required minimum area. The need for ready access is to make a skylight, which is otherwise an inaccessible exterior opening, comparable to a wall opening.

The provisions of Sections 1205 (b) and (c) do not state that the openings must be accessible. Logic must be used when a requirement states that the openings must be "operable."

> It is the author's opinion, for example, that clerestory windows can be used for ventilation only when the operating mechanism is extended so that it is operable from the floor level of the room.

Shaft Enclosure

Sec. 1209. Exits shall be enclosed as specified in Chapter 33. Elevator shafts, ventshafts, dumbwaiter shafts, clothes chutes and other vertical openings shall be enclosed and the enclosure shall be as specified in Section 1706.

In nonsprinklered Group R, Division 1 Occupancies, corridors serving an occupant load of 10 or more shall be separated from corridors and other areas on adjacent floors by not less than 20-minute smoke- and draft-control assemblies which are automatic closing by smoke detection or by fixed approved wired glass set in steel frames.

NOTE: Fire sprinklers are required in some Group R, Division 1 buildings. The requirements are in Section 3802 (h) and will be discussed under that provision in this Guide.

Cross-references to particular shaft enclosures are contained in the first two paragraphs of this section.

The last paragraph of this section is important both for its intent and for the change in a basic philosophical provision of the code that it represents.

This provision requires that in a two-story Group R, Division 1 Occupancy building (apartment house, hotel or motel) with corridors serving occupant loads greater than 10 (i.e., floor areas greater than 2,000 square feet), the corridors are to be separated from corridors and other areas of the adjacent floor. This requirement applies only to unsprinklered buildings. Therefore, if the building is sprinklered for any reason, the separation required by this section would not apply.

The separation does not need to be of one-hour fire-resistive construction, but may be a 20-minute smoke- and draft-stop assembly. Thus, a door and equivalent construction for the surrounding wall can be used. (See Figure 9-9.)

In Article 8 of this Guide, our discussion of the provisions of Standard No. 43-9 and Figure 8-14 illustrate methods of achieving fractional wall ratings.

This provision is the result of three fires occurring between 1978 and 1981 that involved two-story motels. Multiple deaths occurred in two of the fires and multiple injuries occurred in the third. In each instance the fire started on the first floor. The code intent is to provide isolation of the individual levels of the building, so that fire or smoke from the lower level will not trap people on the second floor.

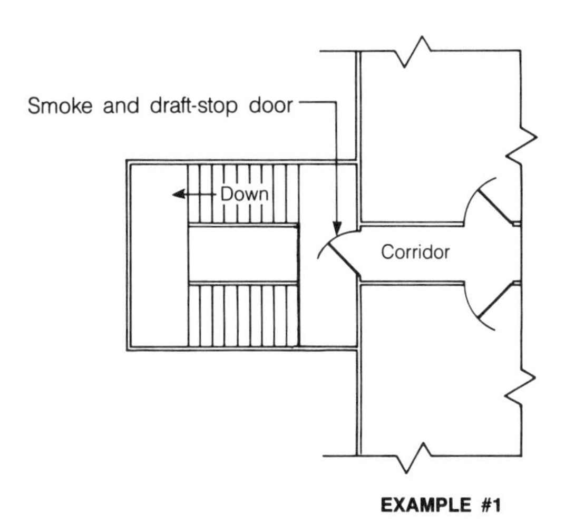

EXAMPLE #1

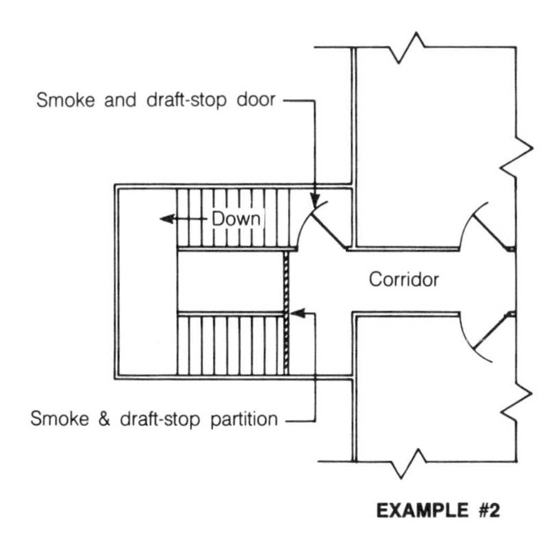

EXAMPLE #2

PARTIAL PLAN VIEWS-2ND FLOOR

REFERENCE: SECTION 1209, 3rd PARAGRAPH

FIGURE 9-9 TWO STORY GROUP R, DIVISION 1 BUILDING, NON-SPRINKLERED, SMOKE STOP BARRIERS

This provision is a major one, because it negates the general provision that two adjacent floors may be unenclosed. [See Section 1706 (c) and Section 3309 (a) Exception 1.] In particular, two-story buildings generally had no requirement for enclosed stairways.

Although this change applies only to Group R, Division 1 Occupancy buildings and does not require fully complying enclosures, it still achieves the effect of enclosures. It will require, where it is the designer's intent to have open railings, walls and the types of aesthetic openness usually found in such buildings, that the separation be provided by some form of smoke- and draft-stop enclosure or separation. The actual method for providing the separation is left to the designer.

Smoke Detectors and Sprinkler Systems
Sec. 1210. (a) Smoke Detectors.

► ■■■ ◄

3. Power source. In new construction, required smoke detectors shall receive their primary power from the building wiring when such wiring is served from a commercial source and shall be equipped with a battery backup. The detector shall emit a signal when batteries are low. Wiring shall be permanent and without a disconnecting switch other than those required for overcurrent protection.Smoke detectors may be solely battery operated when installed in existing buildings, or in buildings without commercial power, or in buildings which undergo alterations, repairs or additions regulated by Subsection 2 of this section.

4. Location within dwelling units. In dwelling units, a detector shall be mounted on the ceiling or wall of each room used for sleeping purposes and at a point centrally located in the corridor or area giving access to each sleeping area.

► ■■■ ◄

Section 1210 provides the requirements for smoke detectors in Group R, Division 1 Occupancy buildings. Over the past several years these devices have proven to be one of the key life-saving tools in residential buildings. The failure of the detector is usually due to battery failure. For this reason, in new buildings the detectors must be hard wired into the building wiring. However, to account for a possible power failure, a battery backup is required together with a warning signal when the battery loses strength.

The change to Section 1210 (a)3 contains two performance criteria for the smoke detector required in existing dwelling units in Group R, Division 1 Occupancy buildings:

1. The detectors must have an integral battery backup
2. The detectors shall have the capability of giving a warning signal when the backup battery runs low.

Smoke detectors with these capabilities are presently available.

There is no requirement that the batteries be rechargeable or that the detector have recharging capability.

The AC-DC type of wired-in detector can use standard carbon zinc, alkaline or other low-cost batteries. The intent of the code provision is to provide a low-cost method of obtaining an emergency backup in the event of a fire-caused power failure in the unit or building.

In Item 4, the detector locations have been increased to include placement of detectors within the sleeping rooms. The purpose is to provide a warning device to room occupants of a fire initiating within the room, e.g., someone smoking in bed and falling asleep. Note that this provision of additional detectors will be triggered in existing buildings when work is done in excess of the Item 2 dollar valuation. These detectors will also be required in some communities where the provisions of Section 1210 are triggered on sale of a property.

Fire Alarm Systems

Sec. 1211. **An approved fire alarm system shall be installed in apartment houses that are three or more stories in height or contain more than 15 dwelling units and in hotels three or more stories in height or containing 20 or more guest rooms, in accordance with the Fire Code.**

EXCEPTIONS: 1. A fire alarm system need not be installed in buildings not over two stories in height when all individual dwelling units and contiguous attic and crawl spaces are separated from each other and from public or common areas by at least one-hour fire-resistive occupancy separations and each individual dwelling unit or guest room has an exit direct to a public way, exit court or yard, exterior stairway or exterior exit balcony.

2. A separate fire alarm system need not be installed in buildings which are protected throughout by an approved automatic fire sprinkler system installed in accordance with U.B.C Standard No. 38-1 and having a local alarm to notify all occupants.

For the purpose of this section, area separation walls shall not define separate buildings.

This section incorporates the fire alarm provisions found in the third paragraph of Section 1204 (b) of prior codes. The last paragraph was added. This paragraph, which relates to the ASW-divided building, for the first time removes a credit provided through the use of an ASW. This provision is more restrictive, because the number of dwelling units or guest rooms will be the aggregate of such units or rooms in the entire structure rather than just the number of such units or rooms in one part of the building as separated by an ASW.

Of greater concern to the designer should be the portent of this type of change.

The concept behind the ASW provision, Section 505 (e), is that it creates separate buildings. That concept is in conflict with this provision. It will require diligence on the part of enforcement officials and designers to avoid enacting more restrictive code changes aimed at removing the credits previously warranted by the ASW-divided building.

Roofs

Sec. 1806. Except in retail sales and storage areas classified as Group B, Division 2 Occupancies and in Group H Occupancies, roofs and their members, other than the structural frame may be of unprotected noncombustible materials when every part of the roof framing, including the structural frame, is 25 feet or more above the floor, balcony or gallery immediately below. Heavy-timber members in accordance with Section 2106 may be used for such unprotected members in one-story buildings.

Roofs

Sec. 2005. Roof coverings shall be as specified in Chapter 32.

Except in retail sales and storage areas classified as Group B, Division 2 Occupancies and in Group H Occupancies, roofs and their members other than the structural frame may be of unprotected noncombustible materials when every part of the roof framing, including the structural frame, is 25 feet or more above the floor, balcony or gallery immediately below. Heavy-timber members in accordance with Section 2106 may be used for such unprotected members in one-story buildings.

The change to Section 1806 prohibits the reduction of the fire resistance of a high roof assembly for retail sales and storage areas classified as Group B, Division 2 Occupancy or Group H Occupancy. The prior code allowed all occupancies to make use of the nonrated roof construction provisions of Section 1806 when there was a minimum height of the roof above the floor. The concern expressed for the change was related to high piled storage and the highly flammable materials in sales and storage areas.

A second change requires that the roof and the structural frame be at least 25 feet above the floor, balcony or gallery. This requirement for the structural frame was added even though the structural frame must have the required fire resistance in accordance with Table No. 17-A. (See Figure 9-10.)

A comparable provision to Section 1806 was added to Section 2005 for the roofs of Type III buildings.

High-Rise Life Safety Requirements
Section 1807

These high-rise life safety provisions apply only to Group B, Division 2 and Group R, Division 1 Occupancies, when they have an occupancy floor more than 75 feet above grade. This provision is not discussed in detail because this section is limited to high-rise buildings, which are a specialized area of design.

The author was requested to clarify some recent changes to these provisions. Areas addressed herein have had recent changes important to the designer and to the enforcement official.

The high-rise life safety requirements include those that provide alternatives for some conventional code requirements and greater safety than the conventional provisions. The items comprising the life safety fire-sprinkler-based package include:

- sprinklers throughout
- elevator recall
- communications
- emergency power
- smoke control
- central control station.

The recent code changes to the high-rise provisions include:

- elimination of the use of compartmentation as an alternative to sprinklering
  the permissive use of the elevator lobby for exit corridor passage and
- changes to use of natural ventilation as an alternative to mechanical smoke control.

ISec. 1807 (a) Scope. This section applies to all Group B, Division 2 office and Group R, Division 1 Occupancies, each having floor used for human occupancy located more than 75 feet above the lowest level of fire department access. Such

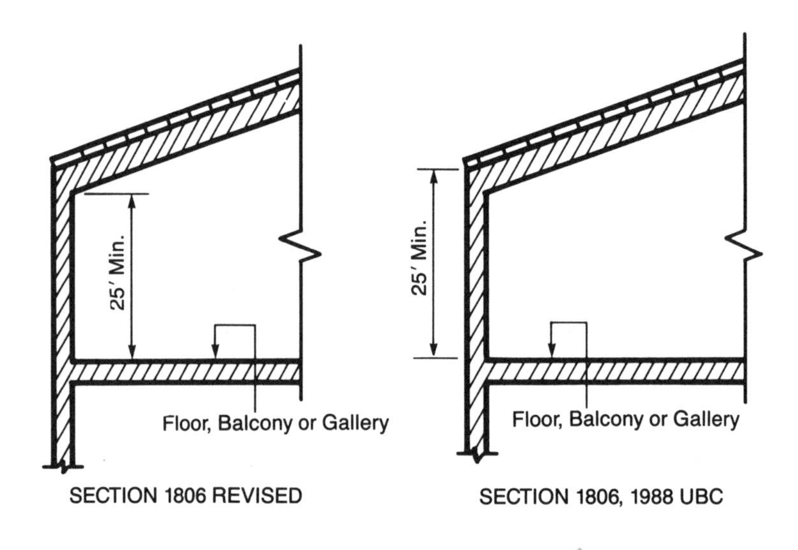

For the permissive use of unprotected noncombustible materials in Type I, II and III buildings. The measurement of the required minimum vertical clearance of 25′ above the floor, balcony or gallery, is applicable to all parts of the roof including the structural frame. This clearance applies even if the frame were fire-protected per Table No. 17-A.

This code provision was previously applicable to all occupancies. The new provision prohibits its application to retail sales and storage areas of Group B, Division 2 Occupancies and for any Group H Occupancy.

REFERENCE: SECTION 1806, 1906 AND 2005

FIGURE 9-10 MEASUREMENT OF HEIGHT FOR UNPROTECTED ROOF TYPE I, II AND III BUILDINGS

buildings shall be provided with an approved automatic sprinkler system in accordance with Section 1807 (c).

► ■■■ ◄

(c) Automatic Sprinkler System. 1. System Design. The automatic sprinkler system required by Section 1807 (g) shall be provided throughout the building. The sprinkler system shall be designed using the parameters set forth in U.B.C. Standard No. 38-1 and the following:

A. Shutoff valves and a water-flow device shall be provided for each floor. The sprinkler riser may be combined with the standpipe riser.

B. In Seismic Zones No. 2, No. 3 and No. 4, in addition to the main water supply, a secondary on-site supply of water equal to the hydraulically calculated sprinkler design demand plus 100 gallons per minute additional for the total standpipe system shall be provided. This supply shall be automatically available if the principal supply fails and shall have a duration of 30 minutes.

2. Modifications. The following modifications of code requirements are permitted:

A. The fire-resistive time periods set forth in Table No. 17-A may be reduced by one hour for interior bearing walls, exterior bearing and nonbearing walls, roofs and the beams supporting roofs, provided they do not frame into columns. Vertical shafts other than stairway enclosures and elevator shafts may be reduced to one hour when sprinklers are installed within shafts at alternate floors. The fire-resistive time period reduction as specified herein shall not apply to exterior bearing and nonbearing walls whose fire-resistive rating has already been reduced under the exceptions contained within Section 1803 (a) or 1903 (a).

B. Except for corridors in Group B, Division 2 and Group R, Division 1 Occupancies and partitions separating dwelling units or guest rooms, all interior nonbearing partitions required to be one-hour fire-resistive construction by Table No. 17-A may be of noncombustible construction without a fire-resistive time period.

C. Fixed tempered glass may be used in lieu of openable panels for smoke-control purposes.

D. Travel distance from the most remote point in the floor area to a horizontal exit or to an enclosed stairway may be 300 feet.

E. Fire dampers, other than those needed to protect floor-ceiling assemblies to maintain the fire resistance of the assembly, are not required except for those which may be necessary to bypass smoke to the outside, those provided to convert from recirculated air to 100 percent outside air, and those which may be required to protect the fresh air supply intake against smoke which may be outside the building.

F. Emergency windows required by Section 1204 are not required.

In the 1988 UBC, the compartmentation option was deleted from the high-rise life safety provisions of Section 1807.

The design problems associated with the compartmentation concept presented formidable and rigorous requirements that had to be met.

In the author's opinion, the concept was a valid one. However, the increasing emphasis on sprinkler solutions to fire problems has resulted in this deletion. For discussion of how one may retain or use the compartmentation option, see Technical Appendix TA-5.

Section 1807

(g) Smoke Control. Natural or mechanical ventilation for the removal of products of combustion shall be provided in every story and shall consist of one of the following:

1. Easily identifiable windows or panels which are manually openable or approved fixed tempered glass shall be provided in the exterior walls. They shall be distributed around the perimeter of the building at not more than 50-foot intervals at the rate of 20 square feet per 50 lineal feet.

EXCEPTION: In Group R, Division 1 Occupancies each guest room or suite having an exterior wall may be provided with a minimum of 2 square feet of venting area.

2. When a complete and approved automatic sprinkler system is installed, the mechanical air-handling equipment may be designed to accomplish smoke removal. Under fire conditions, the return and exhaust air shall be moved directly to the outside without recirculation to other sections of the building. The air-handling system shall provide a minimum of one exhaust air change each 10 minutes for the area involved.

3. Any other approved design which will produce equivalent results.

This section of the high-rise requirements provides the smoke control alternatives, natural or mechanical. The code text for this section is less restrictive than prior codes. It permits a Group R, Division 1 high-rise hotel building to provide only two square feet of venting area, at the exterior wall in each guest room or suite. As written, this provision applies only to hotels and does not apply to dwelling units in apartment houses.

The reason given for this change was that the elimination of the compartmentation alternative to sprinklering, as previously discussed, requires that venting be redefined. Actually, the intent of this provision is to distribute the general venting provision so there is some venting in each guest room. The general venting provision considers that the floor may be undivided as in an office layout. See Figure 9-11 Detail (a).

The prior codes had as their primary venting requirements a means of remotely opening exterior ventilation facilities. When the life safety

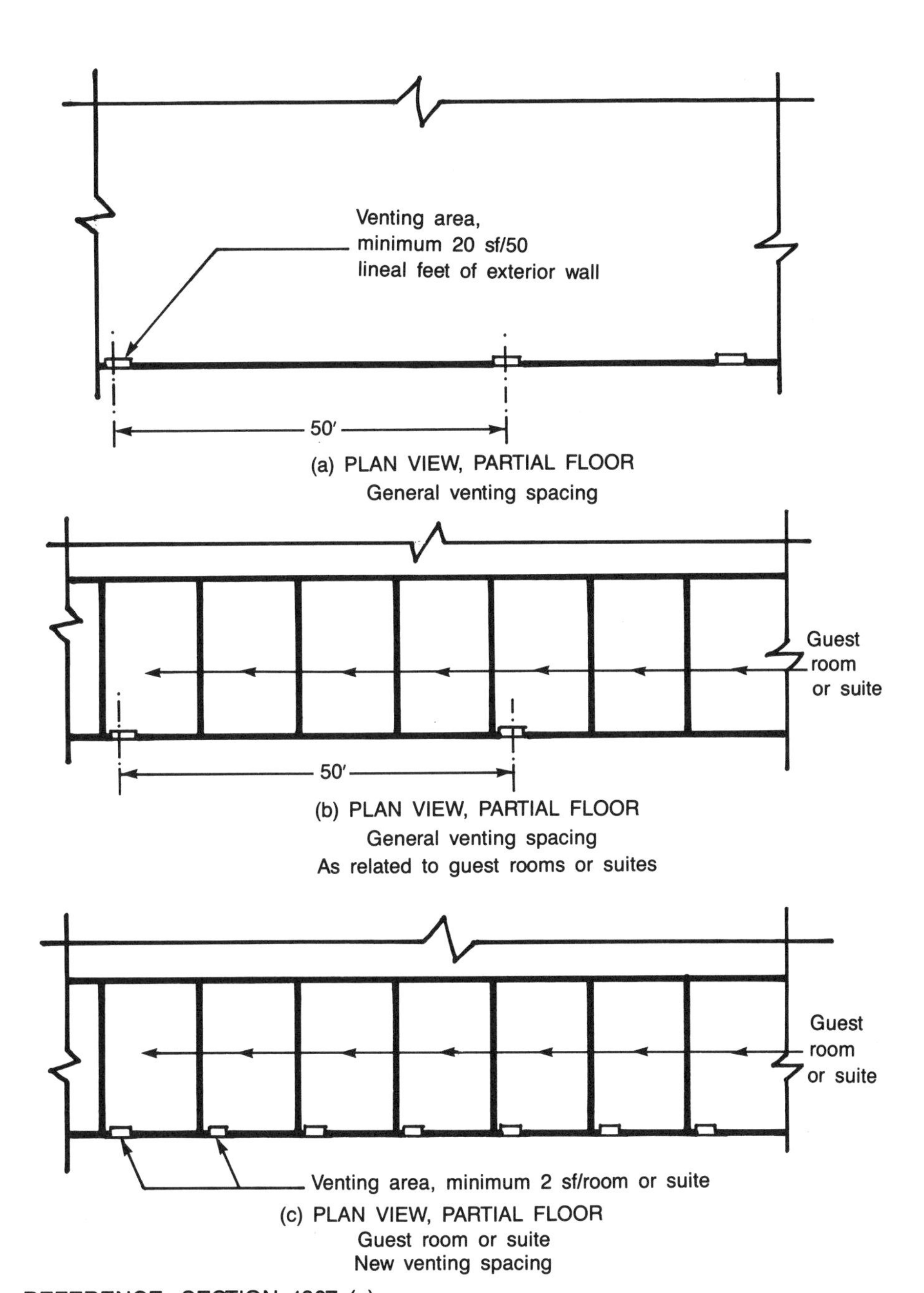

REFERENCE: SECTION 1807 (g)

FIGURE 9-11 GROUP R, DIVISION 1 (HOTEL) HIGH-RISE BUILDING, VENTING REQUIREMENTS FOR GUEST ROOMS

provisions were based on the sprinkler alternative, the Exception allowed the use of manually operated windows or fixed tempered glass windows in lieu of the remote operation. The remote operation was then deleted as part of the dropping of the compartmentation alternative to sprinklering.

The intent is to provide each room's occupants some assurance that they can stay in the room and not be driven out by smoke and toxic gases from a fire on that floor. This concern has been dramatically evident in many hotel fires over the past decade.

The placement of the two-square-foot venting area in each hotel room or suite is preferred because the general venting criteria was essentially based on an open plan Group B, Division 2 Occupancy. In a hotel configuration, the spacing of 20 square feet per 50 lineal feet of exterior wall would result in some guest rooms not having any venting area. See Figure 9-11 Detail (b).

Distributing the venting to each room, with rooms generally less than 300 square feet in total area, causes the venting to be more effective. See Figure 9-11 Detail (c). It is the application to relatively small guest rooms that limits the use of this provision to hotels. Dwelling units usually have larger floor areas per unit. When a larger dwelling unit is involved, two square feet per dwelling unit may not be sufficient.

Thus, the benefit derived from placing the vent area in each hotel room or suite is substantial both to the public and to the owner. If the guest room is assumed to be 12 or 14 feet wide, there would be four-plus such hotel rooms per 50 feet of exterior wall. The gross venting area required to be provided by the Exception is eight-plus square feet versus the 20 square feet of the general venting criteria in the main paragraph.

The two-square-foot venting area has been confirmed as providing adequate ventilation for a suite 14 feet by 20 feet by the Golden Gate Chapter of ASHRAE.

Sec. 1807

(h) Elevators. Elevators and elevator lobbies shall comply with the provisions of Chapter 51 and the following:

NOTE: A bank of elevators is a group of elevators or a single elevator controlled by a common operating system; that is, all those elevators which respond to a single call button constitute a bank of elevators. There is no limit on the number of cars which may be in a bank or group but there may be not

more than four cars within a common hoistway.

1. Elevators on all floors shall open into elevator lobbies which are separated from the remainder of the building, including corridors and other exits, by walls extending from the floor to the underside of the fire-resistive floor or roof above. Such walls shall be of not less than one-hour fire-resistive construction. Openings through such walls shall conform to Section 3305 (h).

EXCEPTIONS: 1. The main entrance level elevator lobby in office buildings.

2. Elevator lobbies located within an atrium complying with the provisions of Section 1715.

3. In fully sprinklered office buildings corridors may lead through enclosed elevator lobbies if all areas of the building have access to at least one required exit without passing through the elevator lobby.

► ■■■ ◄

The primary intent of this section of the high-rise life safety provisions is to prevent smoke migration by stack effect through the elevator shafts onto the upper floors of the building. This is achieved by requiring the upper elevator lobbies to have enclosed lobbies. The enclosures are to be smoke- and draft-tight.

The addition of Exception 3 is an important change involving the exit corridors and elevator lobbies in high-rise life safety buildings.

NOTE: A companion provision to Section 3305 (j) last paragraph is discussed in detail in Article 7 of this Guide.

In the development of the high-rise life safety provisions of Section 1807 in 1973, one of the primary concerns was the smoke migration induced by the stack effect in high-rise buildings, as well as the piston or pumping action of an elevator running in a shaft. For this reason, the requirement for separation of the elevator lobby from the corridors was added in Section 1807 (h).

The 1973 high-rise requirement resulted in a need to redesign the exit corridor arrangements of Group B, Division 2 and Group R, Division 1 high-rise buildings, so that the exit corridors no longer passed through the elevator lobbies. This separation of elevator lobbies from corridors resulted in considerable loss of usable, rentable space. In particular, in a central core-type Group B, Division 2 office building, the redesign usually necessitated a corridor running almost completely around the core.

The present provision permits the exit corridor to use the elevator lobby as part of the exiting path. It allows passage through the one-hour smoke- and draft-stop separation when the specific requirements of Exception 3 are met:

- The building must be sprinklered per Section 1807 (c) of the high-rise requirements. The compartmentation option, which was deleted, would not be acceptable. In the event the locality retains the compartmentation alternative, the elevators still must be separated from the exit corridors.
- The exit passage using the elevator lobby must also provide access to at least one required exit without going through that elevator lobby.

Thus, a corridor with a stair at one end and the other end, traversing the elevator lobby and then leading to another stairway satisfies this requirement.

(See Figures 9-12 and 9-13 for examples of the provisions for a Group B, Division 2 and Group R, Division 1 Occupancy, respectively.)

Figure 9-14 illustrates the conditions in a Group R, Division 1 Occupancy with only two elevators and a small elevator lobby. Floor plan (a) shows a typical arrangement for the present elevator/corridor separation requirements. Note that to provide the separation in floor plan (a) and the separation from the two doors to the units opposite the lobby, the elevator lobby must be set off from the corridor.

Floor plan (b) meets the intent of the new code provisions. The arrangement of cross-corridor smoke- and draft-barrier doors, together with similar doors for the two units opposite the elevators, satisfies the two criteria stated above. This arrangement was the common one found in prehigh-rise buildings and in many low-rise buildings.

The designer should note that when the floor areas involved are large enough to result in occupant loads in the corridor of 50 or more, the requirements of Section 3304 (b) apply, i.e., the exit doors must swing in the direction of exit travel. In such instances, the elevator lobby doors may have to be paired so that one leaf swings in one direction and the other in the opposite direction. (See Figure 9-12 for an example.) This requirement will ensure that occupant loads of 50 or more on either side of the elevator lobby can exit through the lobby by doors swinging in the direction of exit travel.

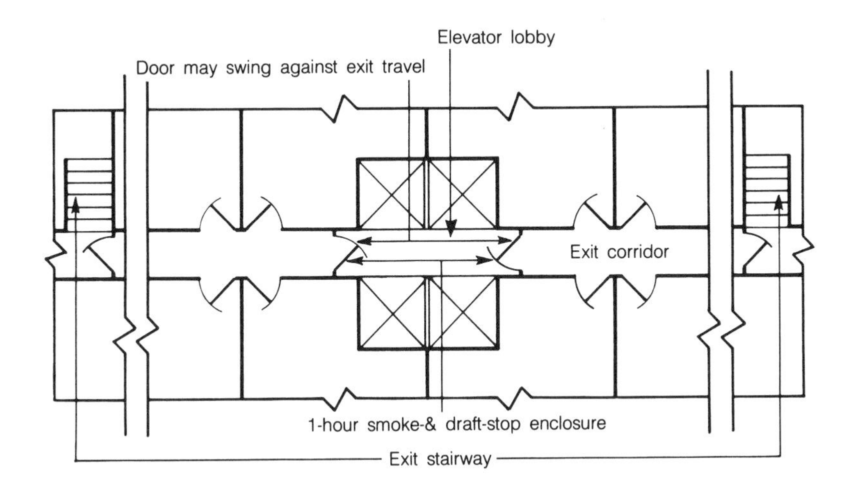

TYPICAL FLOOR WITH OCCUPANT LOAD <50 ON EACH SIDE OF ELEVATOR LOBBY

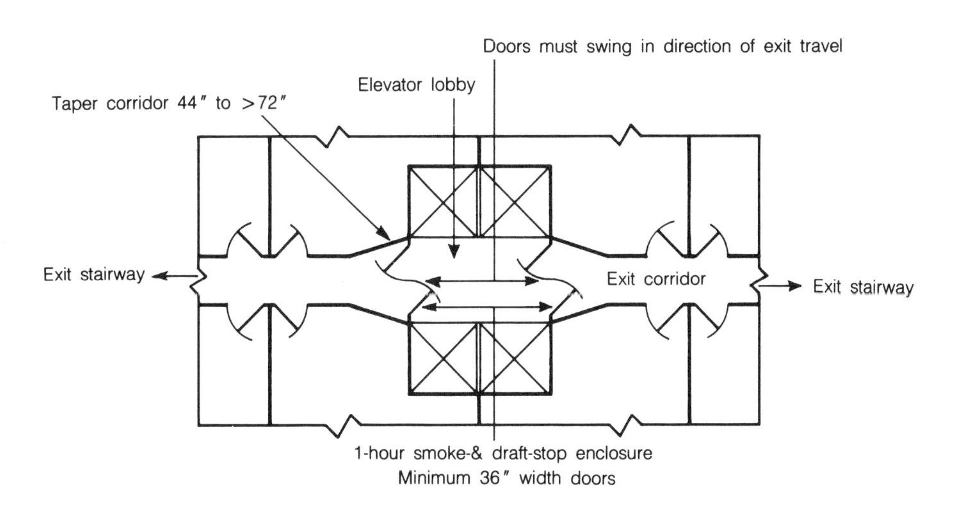

TYPICAL FLOOR WITH OCCUPANT LOAD ≥ 50 ON EACH SIDE OF ELEVATOR LOBBY

REFERENCE: SECTION 1807 (h)

FIGURE 9-12 EXIT CORRIDOR THROUGH ELEVATOR LOBBY, GROUP R, DIVISION 1 OCCUPANCY HIGH RISE BUILDING

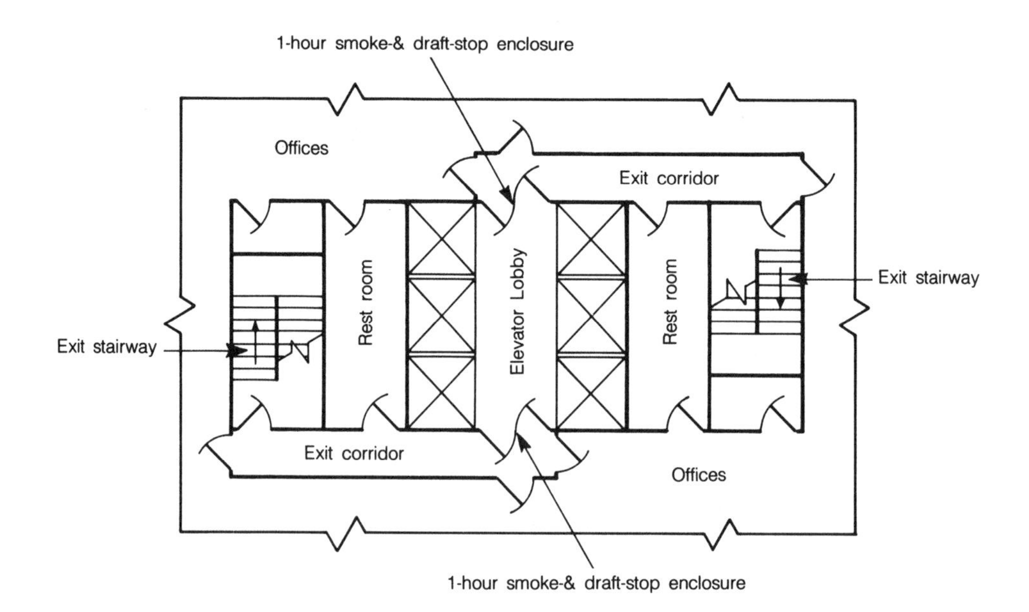

PARTIAL TYPICAL FLOOR PLAN B-2 OCCUPANCY,
HIGH RISE BUILDING W/CENTRAL SERVICE CORE

ASSUME: GROUP B, DIVISION 2 OFFICE OCCUPANCY, HIGH RISE BUILDING
OCCUPANT LOAD >50 ON EACH SIDE OF ELEVATOR LOBBY

NOTE: If 1-hour smoke & draft stop enclosure placed across the exit corridors, the corridors must be of sufficient width to permit two 3′ wide exit doors to be installed, each swinging in a direction of exit travel.

REFERENCE: SECTION 1807 (h)

FIGURE 9-13 EXIT CORRIDOR THROUGH ELEVATOR LOBBY, GROUP B, DIVISION 2 OCCUPANCY HIGH RISE BUILDING

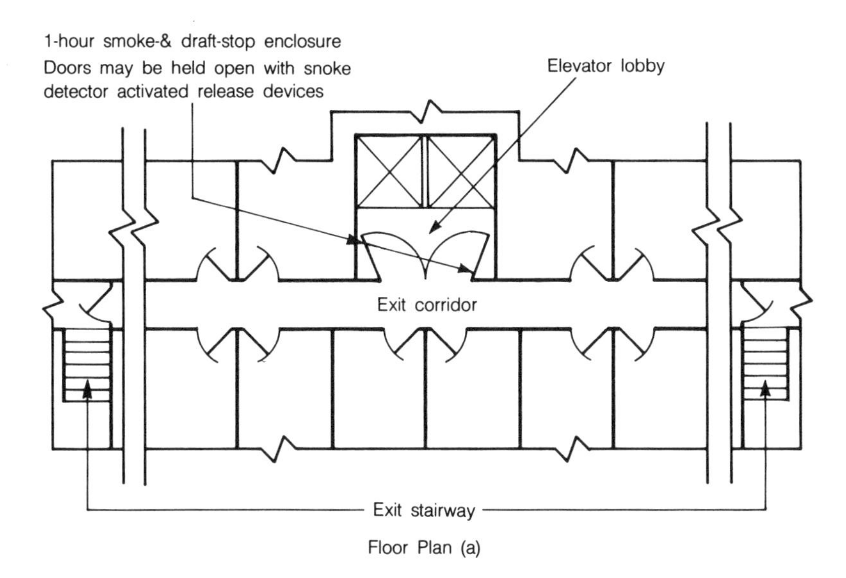

Floor Plan (a)

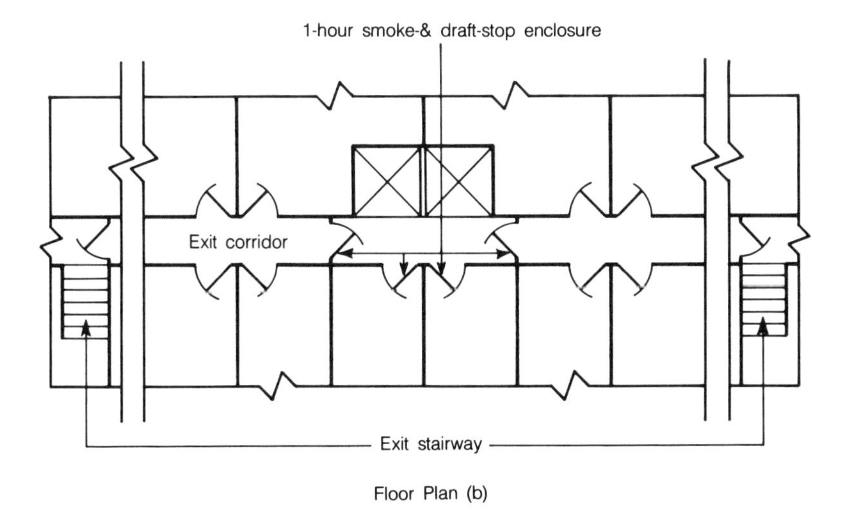

Floor Plan (b)

REFERENCE: SECTION 1807 (h)

FIGURE 9-14 ELEVATOR/CORRIDOR SEPARATION COMPARISON, GROUP R, DIVISION 1 OCCUPANCY WITH & WITHOUT LOBBY

The doors to the elevator lobby may be left in the open position by using smoke-detector-activated release devices. The designer must provide for the required width of the corridor/elevator lobby for the pair of doors in the circumstance described above. A smooth transition should be made between the normal width of the corridor and the widened section. (See Figure 9-12.)

When pairs of doors are required, each swinging in an opposite direction, they should be arranged so that the like-swinging directions are on the same side of the elevator lobby. This is recommended to prevent an occupant from entering the lobby and seeking to enter the other exit corridor, only to find that the door does not swing in the direction of exit travel.

NOTE: As was discussed in regard to Section 3305 (j) last paragraph, the code requirement for separation of the elevator lobby from the exit corridors applies only to high-rise buildings under Section 1807 (h). No prior code provision mandated such separation for any other building prior to the high-rise changes (1973 UBC).

ARTICLE 10
MISCELLANEOUS CODE PROVISIONS
CHAPTERS 25, 31, 32, 38, and 52
And APPENDIX CHAPTER 31
INCLUDING
HANDICAPPED AND SPRINKLER PROVISIONS FOR RESIDENTIAL BUILDINGS

This article of the Guide reviews certain miscellaneous UBC occupancy provisions that, for a designer, either have frequent application or can cause problems. In Article 9, the provisions in certain other UBC chapters were reviewed. The provisions in these two articles are reviewed to supplement those discussed in Articles 3 through 8 herein.

General Construction Requirements
Sec. 2516.
(c) Protection Against Decay and Termites.

8. Wood supporting roofs and floors. Wood structural members supporting moisture permeable floors or roofs which are exposed to the weather such as concrete or masonry slabs shall be approved wood of natural resistance to decay or treated wood unless separated from such floors or roofs by an impervious moisture barrier.

► ■■■ ◄

This section requires that floors and roofs supporting "moisture permeable" surfaces be constructed of:

- decay-resistant wood,
- treated wood,
- wood separated from the permeable surface by an impervious membrane.

Often overlooked is the fact that concrete is a pervious, hygroscopic material, usually containing hairline cracks. Therefore, concrete must be separated from wood by an impervious membrane. This membrane cannot be an impervious material, such as plastic sheeting, simply laid down with lapped, open joints. The joints between adjacent sheets must be sealed to provide a continuity, and the edges or ends of the membrane area must be finished properly to prevent moisture from entering under the membrane. (See Figure 10-1.)

This author has encountered numerous constructions when:

- the membrane was omitted,
- individual sheets of plastic were laid down without regard to the joints other than lapping them,
- the edges permitted water entry under the membrane.

Pervious materials include concrete, deck surfacing materials and lightweight fills used for sound-deadening and fire-resistive purposes.

Sec. 2516. (f) Fire Blocks and Draft Stops. 1. General. In combustible construction, fire blocking and draftstopping shall be installed to cut off all concealed draft openings (both vertical and horizontal) and shall form an effective barrier between floors, between a top story and a roof or attic space, and shall subdivide attic spaces, concealed roof spaces and floor-ceiling assemblies. The integrity of all fire blocks and draft stops shall be maintained.

2. Fire blocks where required. Fire blocking shall be provided in the following locations:

A. In concealed spaces of stud walls and partitions, including furred spaces, at the ceiling and floor levels and at 10-foot intervals both vertical and horizontal. Also, see Section 4203, Item 1.

EXCEPTIONS: Fire blocks may be omitted at floor and ceiling levels when approved smoke-actuated fire dampers are installed at these levels.

B. At all interconnections, between concealed vertical and horizontal spaces such as occur at soffits, drop ceilings and cove ceilings;

C. In concealed spaces between stair stringers at the top and bottom of the run and between studs along and in line with the run of stairs if the walls under the stairs are unfinished;

D. In openings around vents, pipes, ducts, chimneys, fireplaces and similar openings which afford a passage for fire at ceiling and floor levels, with noncombustible materials.

E. At openings between attic spaces and chimney chases for factory-built chimneys.

3. Fire block construction. Except as provided in Item D above, fire blocking shall consist of 2 inches nominal lumber or two thicknesses of 1-inch nominal lumber with broken lap joints or one thickness of 23/32-inch plywood with joints backed by 23/32-inch plywood or one thickness of 3/4-inch Type 2-M particleboard with joints backed by 3/4-inch Type 2-M particleboard.

Fire blocks may also be of gypsum board, cement asbestos board, mineral fiber, glass fiber or other approved materials securely fastened in place.

Walls having parallel or staggered studs for sound-transmission control shall have fire blocks of mineral fiber or glass fiber or other approved nonrigid materials.

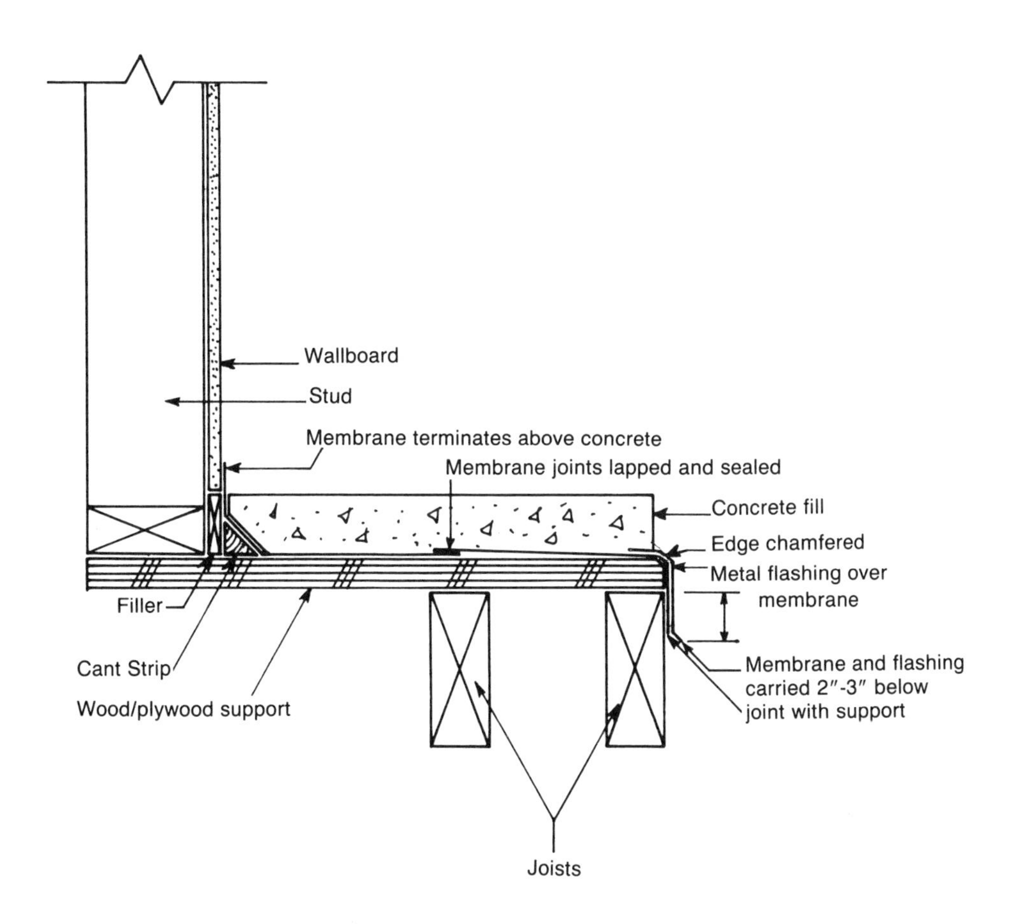

SUGGESTED METHOD OF MEETING SECTION 2516 (c)
AND PREVENTING WIND-DRIVEN WATER ENTRY

REFERENCE: SECTION 2516 (c)

FIGURE 10-1 CONCRETE/MASONRY ON WOOD SUPPORTS

4. Draft stops, where required. Draftstopping shall be provided in the following locations:

A. Floor-ceiling assemblies. (i) Single-family dwellings. When there is usable space above and below the concealed space of a floor-ceiling assembly in a single-family dwelling, draft stops shall be installed so that the area of the concealed space does not exceed 1,000 square feet. Draftstopping shall divide the concealed space into approximately equal areas.

(ii) Draft stops shall be installed in floor- ceiling assemblies of buildings having more than one dwelling unit and in hotels. Such draft stops shall be in line with walls separating individual dwelling units and guest rooms from each other and from other areas.

(iii) Other uses. Draft stops shall be installed in floor-ceiling assemblies of buildings or portions of buildings used for other than dwelling or hotel occupancies so that the area of the concealed space does not exceed 1,000 square feet and so that the horizontal dimension between stops does not exceed 60 feet.

EXCEPTIONS: Where approved automatic sprinklers are installed within the concealed space, the area between draft stops may be 3,000 square feet and the horizontal dimension may be 100 feet.

B. Attics. (i) Single-family dwellings. None required.

(ii) Two or more dwelling units and hotels. Draft stops shall be installed in the attics, mansards, overhangs, false fronts set out from walls and similar concealed spaces of buildings containing more than one dwelling unit and in hotels. Such draft stops shall be above and in line with the walls separating individual dwelling units and guest rooms from each other and from other uses.

EXCEPTIONS: 1. Draft stops may be omitted along one of the corridor walls, provided draft stops at walls separating individual dwelling units and guest rooms from each other and from other uses, extend to the remaining corridor draft stop.

2. Where approved sprinklers are installed, draftstopping may be as specified in the exception to Item (iii) below.

(iii) Other uses. Draft stops shall be installed in attics, mansards, overhangs, false fronts set out from walls and similar concealed spaces of buildings having uses other than dwellings or hotels so that the area between draft stops does not exceed 3,000 square feet and the greatest horizontal dimension does not exceed 60 feet.

5. Draft stop construction. Draftstopping materials shall be not less than 1/2 inch gypsum board, 3/8-inch plywood, 3/8-inch Type 2-M particleboard or other approved materials adequately supported.

Openings in the partitions shall be protected by self-closing doors with automatic latches constructed as required for the partitions.

Ventilation of concealed roof spaces shall be maintained in accordance with Section 3205.

6. Draft or fire blocks in other locations. Fire blocking of veneer on noncombustible walls shall be in accordance with Item 2A above.

For fire blocking of wood floors on masonry or concrete floors, see Sections 1804 and 1904.

For fire blocking ceilings applied against noncombustible construction, see Section 4203, Item 1.

For penetrations of fire-resistive construction, see Chapter 43.

This section provides the mandatory locations for draft stopping and fire blocking in wood framed buildings. The term "draft stopping" refers to the prevention of the free flow of air by means of a barrier material, such as 1/2-inch wallboard or 3/8-inch plywood or particleboard. Fire blocking, on the other hand, must also provide some degree of fire-resistant capability. Thus, the material has to be of more substantial dimension, such as 2-inch thick wood or one of an equivalent built-up assembly of materials.

In both instances, the intent is to slow the spread of fire by blocking the draft or by placing a fire barrier in its path.

The designer should be aware that all too often these hidden elements of construction are frequently left out by the contractor. This is usually the case when double-studded walls are constructed. The designer should provide on the design drawings both the location and the form of the draft stops and fire blocks to use.

The location of draft stops in attics of multi-family buildings is required at the tenant separation walls. In other than residential buildings, there are to be draft stops at not more than 60 foot intervals and creating not more than 3,000 square feet in each subdivided space. These provide draft barriers to fire's rapid spread in attics.

Section 2516 (f)5, last paragraph notes that attics also require ventilation per Section 3205 (c). Thus, each compartment formed by the draft stops must have separate ventilation means without relying on the adjacent space; otherwise the intent of the draft stop is negated.

Where fire sprinklers are provided in the attic the size of the area and the maximum spacing of the draft stops may be increased substantially. Note that this does not require that the entire building be sprinklered.

This section and Sections 1705 (d)2, 1804, 1904, 3707 (m) and 4203 Items 1 and 2 have substituted the terms "fire block," "fire blocks" and "fire blocking" for the terms "firestop" and "firestopping" used in prior codes. These substitutions occur when the intent of the code relates to those uses generally in frame construction using materials comparable in size to the studs or such equivalent acceptable materials as provided for in the various sections.

The new terminology eliminates the conflict in the meaning of the terms in the prior codes, when the intent of the use of firestop and firestopping differed between Section 2516 (f) and Sections 4304 (e) and 4305 (a) and with the new Chapter 43 provisions for penetration fire stops.

Henceforth, the term "firestop" will relate solely to fire-resistive assemblies.

Section 2516 (f)2E adds a new location for fire blocking, namely at any openings between a factory-built chimney and an attic. The concern is with the debris and combustibles found at these locations as well as the need to continue the chimney to the outside.

Section 2516 (f)4Aii and 4Bii have been clarified to require draft stops at walls separating dwelling units and guest rooms and not other tenant spaces such as offices, gift shops and restaurants.

Sec. 2517.

(i) Exit Facilities. In Seismic Zones Nos. 3 and 4, exterior exit balconies, stairs and similar exit facilities shall be positively anchored to the primary structure at not over 8 feet on center or shall be designed for lateral forces. Such attachment shall not be accomplished by use of toenails or nails subject to withdrawal.

The new subsection 2517 (i) reiterates the intent of Chapter 23 that all structures have proper anchorage or design for lateral forces, including those structures built under the "Conventional Construction Provisions" of Section 2517.

The use of Section 2517 does not permit the designer to disregard proper structural design as set forth in Chapter 23, particularly for those essential life safety elements such as exit ways.

In the author's opinion, particularly for Seismic Zones 3 and 4, the use of Conventional Construction is adequate for vertical load-carry considerations. But for seismic force resistance, the design must be in accordance with the provisions of Chapter 23. This recommendation avoids reliance on conventional details when there is a likelihood of severe seismic activity. The modern light-frame building does not have inherent seismic resistance.

CHAPTER 31
ACCESSIBILITY

A. BACKGROUND

This is a new chapter that incorporates provisions previously scattered through the code and adds considerable new material based on ANSI A117.1 provisions. Of major impact to the designer and the building official is the provisions requiring egress and evacuation assistance areas commonly referred to as refuge areas. The latter requirements have no counterpart in either the ANSI provisions or federal regulations and will affect the Chapter 33 exiting provisions because these are more restrictive.

Before discussing the important provisions of the chapter, an overall view of the provisions will be discussed.

Two primary sets of new provisions are in Chapter 31. The first relates to the scoping or application of the accessibility requirements for the various uses and occupancies. These establish the ratio of accessible facilities based on the percentages of the occupant load, seats or rooms involved in the particular use. The scoping provisions are comparable to those in ANSI A117.1, UFAS and other existing regulations, but differ in the actual numbers and percentages that apply.

The second set of provisions are unique to the UBC, although they may eventually be included in the other model codes, the ADA regulations and other existing accessibility regulations. These UBC regulations are based on the premise that once a disabled person has access to a building, the code should provide:

1. locations of areas of evacuation assistance (refuge areas) on a floor. This space must be capable of accepting at least two wheelchair-bound persons and be at least of one-hour fire-resistive construction unless they are within an exit stairway.
2. means of evacuating the disabled person, with the aid of emergency personnel or others, using the exit stairs and a two-person carry of the disabled person. This results in the requirement for wider exit stairs.

The detailed requirements for these second set of regulations will be discussed section-by-section herein.

B. **PHILOSOPHY OF SCOPING PROVISIONS**

The scoping provisions set the stage for the minimum accessibility by using numerical representations of how each facility is to satisfy the presumed real world need of the disabled. The numbers or percentages presumably derive from statistics obtained by unbiased research groups and should be consistent within themselves.

Unfortunately, the disabled lobby has expanded the definition of the term "disabled" to so great a range of the handicapped that it is difficult to reach rational agreement on consistent numbers for each occupancy.

For example, under the ADA committee record are the following disabled characteristics:

Physical or mental impairment including substantial limits of performing manual tasks, walking, seeing, hearing, speaking, breathing, learning, working and participating in community activities.

The claim is that this represents 43 million people or almost 17 percent of the population.

For the purpose of the building codes, where access and egress are to be provided those who cannot traverse areas in the same way as non-disabled, this large ADA listing breaks down to:

- Wheelchair-bound persons
- Persons on crutches on a more or less permanent basis
- Persons requiring use of walkers or similar assisting devices
- Persons with an artificial leg or foot

From statistics garnered by Jake Pauls and Edwina Juillet, these four subgroups represent about 1 percent of the population.

Notwithstanding the above real-world assumptions, the code requires accessibility for population ranges of .3 percent to 50 percent of the seats, tables, rooms or whatever.

> In the author's opinion, the scoping provisions are flawed in this regard with inflated numbers being applied. This will result in higher than justified costs, space demands and warping of the equity concept of the code—whereby all are to be provided equal protection.

C. EGRESS AND AREAS OF EVACUATION ASSISTANCE

These requirements are entirely new to the code and, as of the publication of this edition of the Guide, unique to the model codes of the country and unique to the federal guidelines in effect at the time of publication of this Guide.

In the discussion at the time of the adoption of the Chapter 31 provisions into the UBC, it was stated that a broad range of areas of evacuation assistance facilities was allowed to serve as acceptable methods of meeting the intent of the code. It was anticipated that this list would be amended, added to or deleted as experience provided guidance to their usability.

A detailed discussion of each component will be provided because of the major impact this part of the Chapter 31 provisions will have on future construction and possibly in existing buildings. Our discussions will primarily relate to those provisions in Chapter 31 that affect on the Chapter 33 exiting provisions or that present serious code philosophy problems that warrant pointing out in the hope of stimulating discussion and possible future code clarification or deletion. Appendix Chapter 31, Section II provisions are another critical provision, which will be discussed after the Chapter 31 provisions.

> In the author's opinion, unless the Appendix Chapter 31, Section II provisions are adopted simultaneously with the Chapter 31 provisions, the enforcement official, the designer and the owner of an existing building will be placed in an untenable situation when alterations are to be undertaken.

We will discuss this in greater detail later.

Scope

Sec. 3101. (a) General. Buildings or portions of buildings shall be accessible to persons with disabilities as required by this chapter.

Reference is made to Appendix Chapter 31 for requirements governing the provision of accessible site facilities not regulated by this chapter.

In the second paragraph reference is made to the Appendix Chapter 31. However, in Section 103 of the code, it clearly stated in the third paragraph that the Appendix provisions do not apply unless they are specifically adopted. Thus, the intention was to use the Appendix Chapter 31, but this is not accomplished solely by adding the reference. The jurisdiction must note and adopt the appendix provisions as a specific action simultaneous with the adoption of the 1991 UBC.

Sec. 3101 (b) Design. The design and construction of accessible building elements shall be in accordance with U.B.C. Standard No. 31-1 or other nationally recognized standards as approved by the building official.

Section 3101 (b) is the vehicle for recognizing the ANSI A117.1 provisions and the ADA or other federal regulations and standards. The UBC standard is based on ANSI A117.1-1986 edition.

Definitions

Sec. 3102. For the purpose of the chapter certain terms are defined as follows:

ACCESSIBLE is approachable and usable by persons with disabilities.

ACCESSIBLE ROUTE OF TRAVEL is a continuous unobstructed path connecting all accessible elements and spaces in an accessible building or facility that can be negotiated by a person using a wheelchair and that is usable by persons with other disabilities.

ADAPTABILITY refers to the capability of spaces or facilities to be readily modified and made accessible.

AREA OF EVACUATION ASSISTANCE is an accessible space which is protected from fire and smoke and which facilitates a delay in egress.

PRIMARY ENTRY is the principal entrance through which most people enter the building as designated by the building official.

PRIMARY ENTRY LEVEL is the floor or level of the building on which the primary entry is located.

PERSON WITH DISABILITY is an individual who has a physical impairment, including impaired sensory, manual or speaking abilities, that results in a functional limitation in gaining access to and using a building or facility.

Most of these definitions derive from the ANSI standard. Some, such as "area of evacuation assistance," "primary entry" and "primary entry level," are added because the ANSI provisions have no comparable definitions and Chapter 31 references these terms.

The definition of "person with disability" derives from the ANSI standard and is also in the ADA list.

In the author's opinion, it is excessive insofar as relating to access to and use of a building. There is no functional limitation for a speech- or hearing-impaired person from using stairways or exit corridors in the same fashion as speaking persons. These exit facilities are required to be marked, lighted, provided with flashing lights in many instances, and are in standardized locations for ease of locating.

Building Accessibility

Sec. 3103. (a) Where required. 1. General. Accessibility to buildings or portions of buildings shall be provided for all occupancy classifications except as modified by this chapter. See also Appendix Chapter 31.

► ■■■ ◄

Section 3103 is the scoping section of the accessibility provisions. It contains the ratios, numbers or percentages of the various occupancies and other criteria for determining the access requirement. These will not be discussed in detail because they are specific in nature.

This section is the key to determining whether a building is subject to the accessibility requirements. Each occupancy group has been identified and exceptions cited or ratios of accessibility provided. The designer and the enforcement official should pay careful attention to these provisions because the access requirement triggers the egress provisions that override certain Chapter 33 exit requirements.

Suffice it to say that there is a considerable range of percentages cited in these provisions with no demonstrable rationale for the deviations.

Section 3103 (a), as did Section 3101, makes reference to the Appendix Chapter 31. As stated in regard to Section 3101, such reference is meaningless *unless* the Appendix is adopted simultaneously with the 1991 UBC.

Sec. 3103. (b) Design and Construction. 1. General.When accessibility is required by this chapter, it shall be designed and constructed in accordance with U.B.C. Standard No. 31-1.

► ■■■ ◄

Section 3103 (b) uses the ANSI A117.1 provisions for the detailed accessibility provisions. Those ANSI provisions have been incorporated in virtually all federal, state and national documents and include widths of doorways, turning radii, horizontal and vertical clearances for wheelchairs and other special devices used by disabled persons.

Egress and Areas of Evacuation Assistance

Sec. 3104. (a) General. In buildings or portions of buildings required to be accessible, accessible means of egress shall be provided, in the same number as required for exits by Chapter 33. Where an exit required by Chapter 33 is not accessible, an area of evacuation assistance shall be provided.

Areas of evacuation assistance shall comply with the requirements of this code and shall adjoin an accessible route of travel complying with U.B.C. Standard No. 31-1.

Section 3104 (a) requires that "means of egress" be provided for persons with disabilities in the same number of exits as are required by Chapter 33 calculations of the entire occupant load of the floor of the building.

Thus, if there are 100 occupants on a floor of a building of Group B, Division 2 Occupancy, Section 3303 (a) requires two exits, or two areas of evacuation assistance, each providing space for two wheelchairs. Upper floors. where a direct means of egress is not available for persons with disabilities, will require space for a total of four wheelchairs, divided into two separate locations. This will be the minimum in virtually all but the smallest Group B, Division 2 Occupancy buildings. Note that in this example, using the one percent figure for the number of walking handicapped persons in the country as previously discussed, there may be an average of only one handicapped person on that floor.

These special handicapped provisions are called means of egress although the term is not defined either in the code or in the Chapter 31 provisions.

In the author's opinion, the primary requirement is to provide an accessible means of egress for a person with a disability, such as a horizontal exit or an exit passageway leading directly to the outside. Only if an accessible means of egress cannot be provided may areas of evacuation assistance be used. Thus, the term "means of egress" is used to cover direct exiting while an area of evacuation assistance is used to cover a place for temporary accommodation of a disabled person not capable of self-evacuation.

When an area of evacuation assistance is required, it may be one of seven cited types in Section 3104 (b). These have commonly been referred to as "areas of refuge." It is important to note that there are two elements to this provision:

1. A place to temporarily accommodate a disabled person not capable of self-evacuation, such as a person in a wheelchair .
2. A widened stairway to facilitate the evacuation of the disabled person by carrying that person down the exit stairs. (See Figure 10-2.)

Note that the widened stairway as required in Section 3104 (b)3 applies to all exit stairways in a building subject to the accessibility provisions.

(b) Areas of evacuation assistance. 1. Location and Construction. An area of evacuation assistance shall be one of the following:

A. A portion of a stairway landing within a smokeproof enclosure, complying with Section 3310.

B. A portion of an exterior exit balcony located immediately adjacent to an exit stairway when the exterior exit balcony complies with Section 3305. Openings to the interior of the building located within 20 feet of the area of temporary refuge shall be protected with fire assemblies having a three-fourths hour fire protection rating.

C. A portion of a one-hour fire-resistive corridor complying with Section 3305 (g) and (h) located immediately adjacent to an exit enclosure.

D. A vestibule, located immediately adjacent to an exit enclosure and constructed to the same fire-resistive standards as required by Section 3305 (g) and (h).

E. A portion of a stairway landing within an exit enclosure which is vented to the exterior and is separated from the interior of the building with not less than one-hour fire-resistive doors.

F. When approved by the building official, an area or a room which is separated from other portions of the building by a smoke barrier. Smoke barriers shall have a fire-resistive rating of not less than one hour and shall completely enclose the area or room. Doors in the smoke barrier shall be tight-fitting smoke-and draft-control assemblies having a fire-protection rating of not less than 20 minutes and shall be self-closing or automatic closing. The area or room shall be provided with an exit directly to an exit enclosure. Where the room or area exits into an exit enclosure which is required to be of more than one-hour fire-resistive construction, the room or area shall have the same fire-resistive construction, including the same opening protection, as required for the adjacent exit enclosure.

G. An elevator lobby complying with Section 3104 (d).

Section 3104 (b) lists the description and construction requirements for an area of evacuation assistance. Note that items A and E are

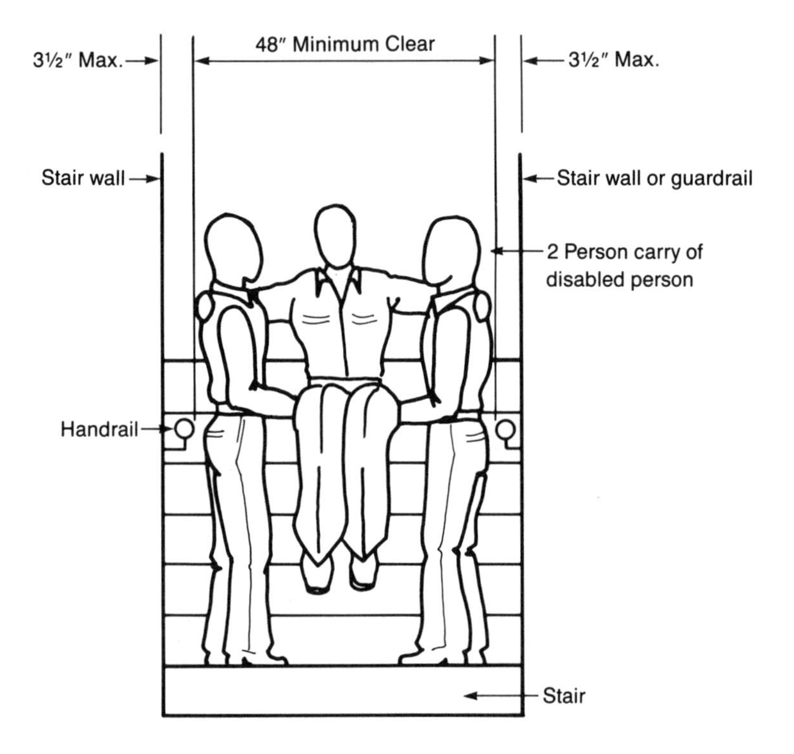

EVACUATION OF DISABLED PERSON DOWN STAIR TWO PERSON CARRY

This illustration shows the basis of the minimum clear width requirement of Section 3104 (b)3. The provisions of Section 3104 (b)3 supersede the minimum provisions of Section 3306 (b) because the minimum requirement in Section 3104 (b)3 are greater than that in Section 3306 (b). The intent of these two sections is also different. Section 3306 (b) was based on the gross width of the stairwell assuming handrails projecting not more than 3½″ from the wall. This would allow a net width between handrails of 37″ and a gross width of stairway of 44″ minimum. Section 3104 (b)3 is based on a net width between the handrails. This will result in a nominal 55″ wide stairway as the minimum.

REFERENCE: SECTION 3104 (b)3

FIGURE 10-2 MINIMUM WIDTH OF STAIRWAY BASED ON TWO PERSONS CARRYING OF DISABLED PERSON DOWN STAIRWAY

actually within the exit stairway; the others must all be adjacent to a stairway. The intent is to have persons with disabilities follow the flow in an emergency and take haven until the fire service can assist in their evacuation. By placing the persons with disabilities in close proximity to the exit stairs it is intended to facilitate their evacuation without requiring a search or blocking of corridors.

Illustrations of the several areas of evacuation assistance are shown in Figure 10-3.

In Item E, the venting requirement is ambiguous in that it does not establish what constitutes "venting" in order to qualify. If this is to be a smokeproof enclosure with natural or mechanical venting, it would be included in Item A. Therefore, it is either a pressurized stairway or some other form of exit stairway with an undefined degree of ventilation.

> In the author's opinion, the designer should avoid this alternative until it is clarified, preferably by a code change. Otherwise, the designer will have no basis for determining on an assured basis that the code intent is met.

Item F is a non-exitway room. It must have a door directly into an exit enclosure. Under Section 3309 (c), such a door qualifies as being permitted into the enclosure provided the fire rating of the door is in accordance with the second paragraph of that section. The door into the room, from a corridor to a tenant space, is to be at a minimum a door conforming to Section 3305 (h).

The room is to be of at least one-hour fire-resistive construction. However, where the exit enclosure into which the area of evacuation assistance exits is required to be of two-hour fire-resistive construction, the room and the other openings into it must conform to the Section 3309 (b) and (c) provisions. (See Figure 10-4.)

Note that although in this section there is no mention of the special outfitting required for this room, Section 3104 (b)4 requires two-way communications be provided.

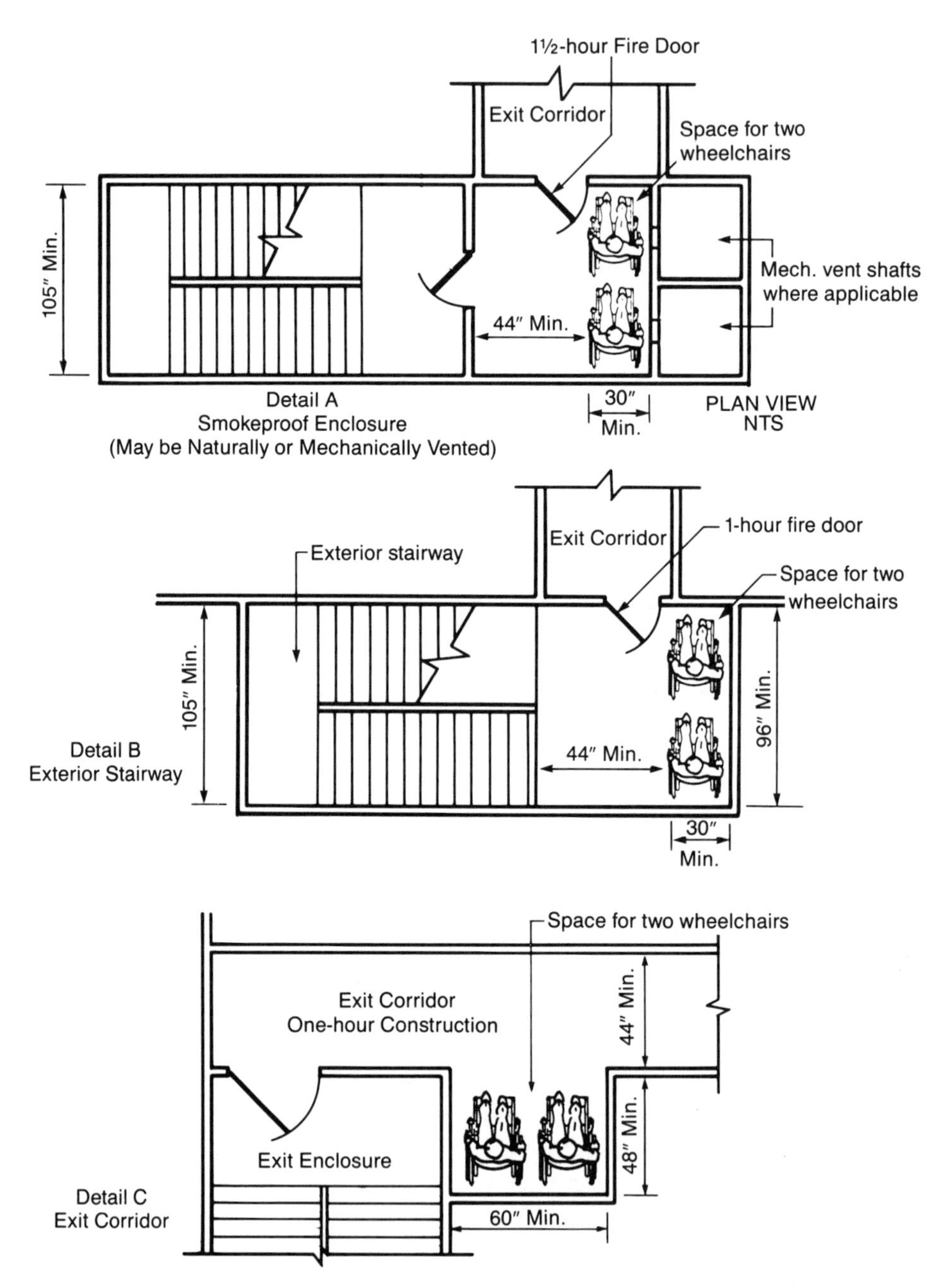

REFERENCE: SECTION 3104 (b)2

FIGURE 10-3 AREAS OF EVACUATION ASSISTANCE – EXAMPLES

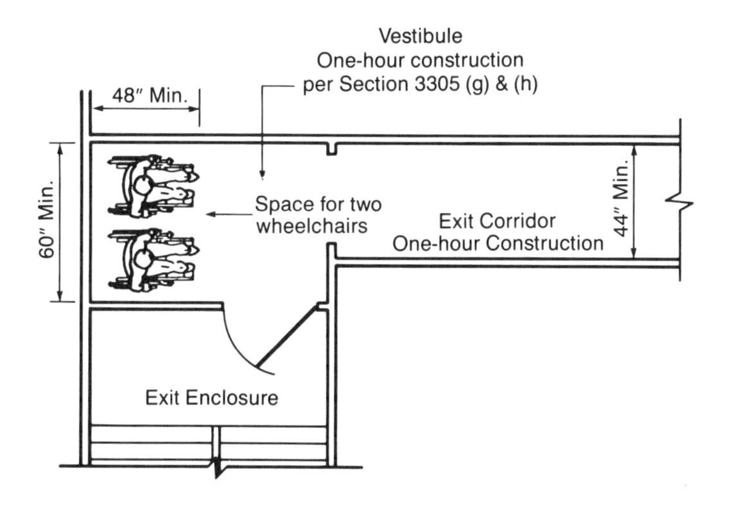

Detail D
Vestibule to Exit Enclosure

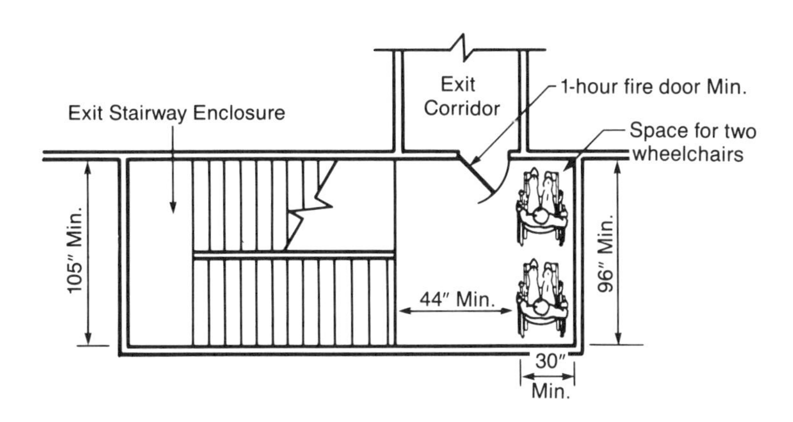

Detail E
Exit Stairway Enclosure

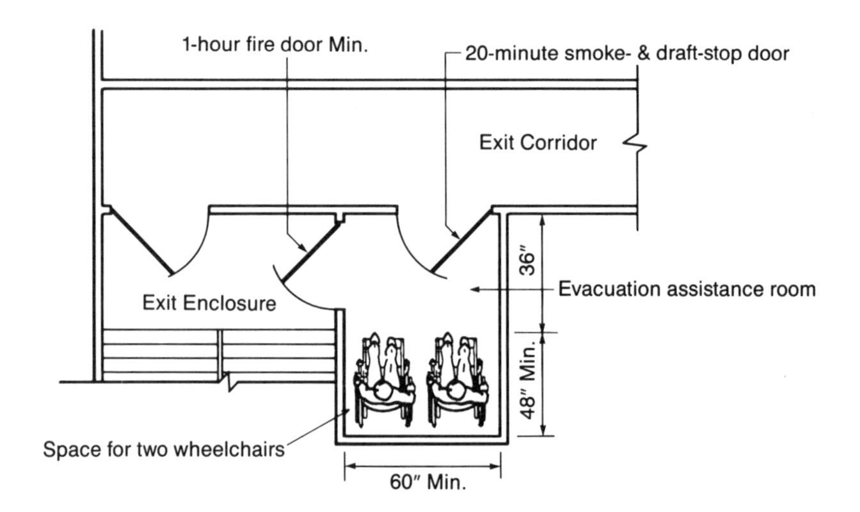

DETAIL F
Evacuation Assistance Room

Evacuation assistance rooms must have fire-resistive construction as for the exit enclosure into which it opens except that the door to the exit corridor may be per Section 3305 (h) i.e., a 20-minute door when the walls are of one-hour construction. The door into the exit enclosure must conform to the requirements of Section 3309 (c) and be at least of one-hour rating.

The room must have a telephone connected to the primary entry area. See Section 3104 (b)4.

The room should have emergency lighting and a security system for entry; see the discussion regarding Section 3104 (b)2.

REFERENCE: SECTION 3104 (b)2 & 4, 3305 (h), 3309 (c)

FIGURE 10-4 AREA OF EVACUATION ASSISTANCE ROOM

In the author's opinion, there should also be emergency lighting and a fire alarm-type opening device to enter the room. This device should be similar to that discussed in Article 7, Section 3304 (c) to prevent persons from using the room except when an emergency exists. The alarm feature would prevent telephone misuse and vandals using the room.

Item G applies only to a building with a complete life safety system in accordance with Section 1807. Using that section's provisions to permit an elevator lobby as a means of egress or area of evacuation assistance is not controlled by the high-rise or occupancy limitations in Section 1807. Thus, where the Section 1807 criteria are met, in a 50-foot-high Group A Occupancy building, the elevator lobby may be used as the means of egress or area of evacuation assistance provided the Section 3104 (d) requirements are met. This requires that the size, two-way communication and identification per Section 3104 (b) are furnished.

In Section 1807 (e) the fire department communication system is required to have a station in the elevator lobby. This could be used, when approved, to meet the Section 3104 (d) requirement.

The elevator lobby pressurization system requirement in Section 3104 (d) could be powered from the standby power system required in Section 1807 (i). The smoke detector activation requirement appears to be in addition to the elevator recall system in Section 1807 (h).

In the author's opinion, unless there are no exit corridors connected directly to the elevator lobby area, the smoke detectors need be placed only in the exit corridors and the elevator lobby. When there are no exit corridors, the detection system must cover the area that would be considered opening into the elevator lobby enclosure.

2. Size. Each area of evacuation assistance shall provide at least two accessible areas each not less than 30 inches by 48 inches. The area of evacuation assistance shall not encroach on any required exit width. The total number of such 30-inch by 48-inch areas per story shall be not less than one for every 200 persons of calculated occupant load served by the area of evacuation assistance.

EXCEPTIONS: The building official may reduce the minimum number of 30-inch by 48-inch areas to one for each area of evacuation assistance on floors where the occupant load is less than 200.

Section 3104 (b)2 establishes the number and size of the spaces required to be provided at each of the locations of a means of egress or area of evacuation assistance. There are four key points contained in this section and the operative Section 3104 (a). These are:

1. There must be at least the same number of means of egress or areas of evacuation assistance as there are required exits per Section 3303.
2. There must be at least two spaces 30 inches by 48 inches at each means of egress or area of evacuation assistance.
3. The total number of spaces shall be based on one space for each 200 occupants calculated in accordance with Section 3302. There will be at least four spaces based on the minimum of two exits required in Section 3303.
4. The Exception permits a reduction in the number of spaces required to one per means of egress or area of evacuation assistance when the occupancy load on a floor is less than 200.

Thus, if we have a three-story office building with a second and third floor area of 15,000 square feet per floor, the occupancy load on each floor is 15,000/100 = 150 persons. There must be two means of egress or area of evacuation assistance based on the Section 3303 (a) provisions with an occupancy load of more than 10. However, because the occupancy load is less than 200, the building official may permit only one space be provided for each means of egress or area of evacuation assistance.

If the floor area in the same building were 45,000 square feet per floor, the occupancy load would be 450 per floor. The calculated minimum number of spaces to be provided at the means of egress or area of evacuation assistance is 450/200 = 2.25 spaces. Because there must be two exit stairways per Section 3303 (a) and because the occupancy load exceeds 200, each means of egress or area of evacuation assistance must have at least two spaces. There will be a total of four spaces provided, thus exceeding the minimum required.

If the floor in the same building were 60,000 square feet per floor, the occupancy load would be 600 per floor. The calculated minimum number of spaces to be provided at the means of egress or area of evacuation assistance is 600/200 = 3 spaces. Because there must be three exit stairways per Section 3303 (a) and because the occupancy load exceeds 200, each means of egress or area of evacuation assistance must have at least two spaces. There will be a total of six spaces provided; thus, exceeding the minimum required.

When the spaces are provided in any portion of the exit way system, corridor, exit stair, exit passageway, horizontal exit, smokeproof tower, or exterior exit balcony, the spaces must not obstruct the required width calculated in accordance with Section 3303 (b). Therefore, as shown in Figures 10-2 and 10-3, there must be either excess general width provided or a recess for the spaces to be located.

3. Stairway width. Each stairway adjacent to an area of evacuation assistance shall have a minimum clear width of 48 inches between handrails.

Section 3104 (b)3 will have the greatest impact on the exit way design because it will supersede the provisions in Section 3306 (b) in buildings requiring accessibility. The requirement establishes a clear width of 48 inches for each stairway adjacent to or serving a means of egress or area of evacuation assistance.

The clear width is a departure from the traditional code consideration of net width as provided for in Section 3306 (b) second paragraph. See Figure 10-5 for an illustration of the difference in concepts between the prior codes and the new requirement.

If an elevator lobby is used as one of the areas of evacuation assistance, and an exit stair is to serve as another area of evacuation assistance or means of egress, the question arises as to whether only one stairway need conform to Section 3104 (b)3.

> In the author's opinion, as of the uncertainty of whether a disabled person can determine the location of the stairway meeting the area of evacuation assistance or means of egress requirements, every required exit must conform to this section.

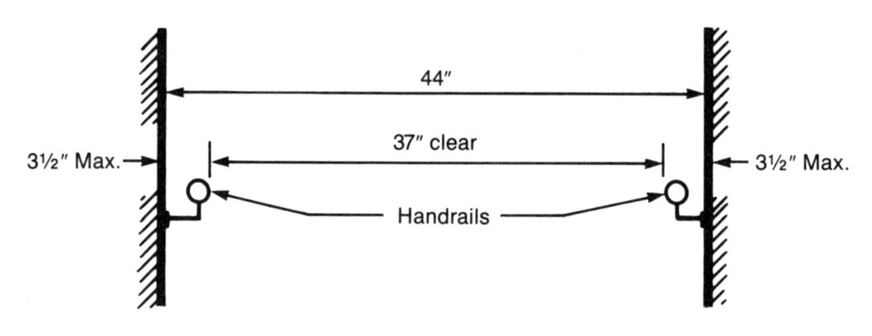

Exit Stair Width Measurement
per Section 3104 (b)3

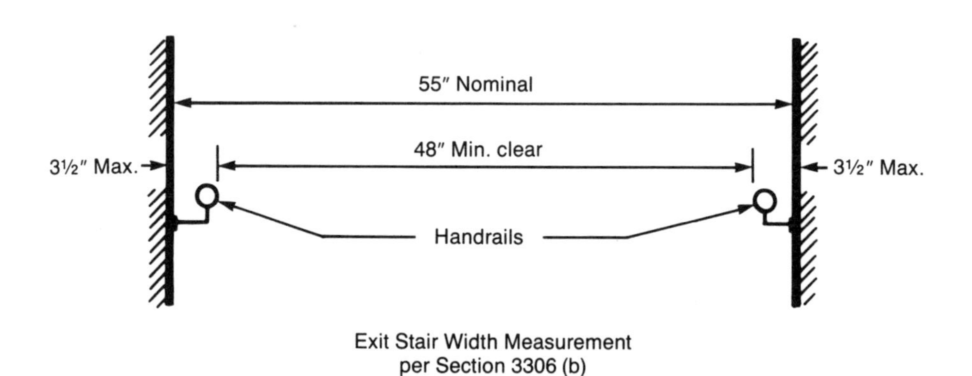

Exit Stair Width Measurement
per Section 3306 (b)

The provisions in Section 3104 (b)3 take precedence over the stair width provisions in Section 3306 (b) where accessibility requirements apply. The key difference is that the minimum widths are measured in different manners. Where the accessibility provisions apply, the width is based on the clear dimension of 48 inches between handrails. Thus, if the handrails project the permitted 3½ inches from the wall of the stairs, the overall width of the stairway must be not less than 55 inches.

The minimum width of 44 inches per Section 3306 (b) is based on the gross dimension for the stair overall, i.e., without considering the handrails. Because the handrails may project 3½ inches into the stairway, the net clear dimension is allowed to be 37 inches.

REFERENCE: SECTION 3104 (b)3, 3306 (b)

FIGURE 10-5 STAIR WIDTH COMPARISON, HANDRAILS GROSS VS NET WIDTH

Thus, the use of an elevator lobby as one of the areas of evacuation assistance may not avoid the increased width requirement for all required exits.

The provisions of this section relate to both the stairway flight as well as any portion of a landing that may have projections into the clear width. The reason for this requirement for a clear width, as previously stated, is to permit the disabled to be carried down by a "two-person-carry" necessitating the greater width.

4. Two-way Communication. A telephone with controlled access to a public telephone system or another method or two-way communication shall be provided between each area of evacuation assistance and the primary entry. The fire department may approve a location other than the primary entry.

Section 3104 (b)4 requires a two-way communication system be provided at any of the seven areas of temporary evacuation. In a high-rise building subject to Section 1807 provisions of the code, this system may already be in place and connected to the central control station. In other buildings, the floor instruments must connect to a location near the primary entry. This will allow the fire department, when responding to an emergency, to communicate with anyone using the area of evacuation assistance.

In the author's opinion, as stated previously, to avoid vandalism there should also be emergency lighting and a fire alarm-type opening device to enter the room. This device should be similar to that discussed in Article 7, Section 3304 (c) to prevent persons from using the room except when an emergency exists. The alarm feature would prevent telephone misuse and vandals using the room.

5. Identification. Each area of evacuation assistance shall be identified by a sign which states "AREA OF EVACUATION ASSISTANCE" and displays the international symbol of accessibility. The sign shall be illuminated when exit sign illumination is required. In each area of evacuation assistance, instructions on the use of the area under emergency conditions shall be posted adjoining the two-way communication system.

Section 3104 (b)5 requires that the area of evacuation assistance be identified in a prescribed manner. For alternative areas of evacuation assistance A, D, and E, this sign must be adjacent to the exit sign required by Section 3314.

Note that the actual location or placement of the sign, the size of the letters and the colors are not detailed. The designer should verify with these details the enforcement officials prior to completing of the contract documents. The ANSI-referenced document provides only ratios of lettering sizes and the need for contrasting colors. There is also no requirement for tactile signs. Therefore, the sign requirements of Section 3314 should be used as the criteria for these signs.

There is no information provided as to the instructions for the occupant of the area of evacuation assistance. This information is to be located adjacent to the two-way communication system. To be able to read the instructions, there must be emergency lighting provided. Such instructions should be protected by a covering material and the text should be provided by the enforcement agency. As a minimum, the text should be in at least in 12-point black type on a white background.

(c) Accessible Exits. All exterior exits which are located adjacent to accessible areas and within 6 inches of adjacent ground level shall be accessible.

Section 3104 (c) expands the prior requirements for accessibility by mandating that all exterior exits within six inches of adjacent ground be made accessible. This provision was made more restrictive due to the addition of the egress provisions and the area of evacuation assistance provisions. Thus, instead of providing only one primary access, when the other exits are near ground level they also must be made accessible.

(d) Area of Evacuation assistance, Highrise Alternative. Within a building, of any height or occupancy constructed in accordance with the requirements of Section 1807 or 1907, an area of evacuation assistance may be located in the elevator lobby when:

1. The area of evacuation assistance complies with the requirements for size, two-way communication and identification as specified in Section 3104 (b); and

2. Elevator shafts and adjacent lobbies are pressurized as required for smokeproof enclosures in Section 3310. Such pressurization system shall be activated by smoke detectors on each floor located in a manner approved by the building official. Pressurization equipment and its duct work within the building shall be separated from other portions of the building by a minimum two-hour fire-resistive construction.

Section 3104 (d) permits the elevator lobby in a high-rise building conforming to Section 1807 or 1907 to serve as one area of evacuation assistance subject to three criteria:

- sufficient size to accommodate the number of wheelchairs based on the occupant load on the floor
- required communications
- pressurized lobby

The elevator lobby is required by Section 1807 to have a fire department communication system. The designer should evaluate with the enforcement officials, the possible use of this system for the Section 3104 (d) provisions.

The intent of these three requirements is to provide a smoke-free location even though the elevator lobby is normally a place where smoke first arrives on a floor from a remote fire source. With positive pressure in the lobby, the smoke in the elevator shaft should not enter the floor with the area of evacuation assistance after the pressurization system is activated on the fire floor.

APPENDIX
Chapter 31
Division II
ACCESSIBILITY FOR EXISTING BUILDINGS

An essential companion set of requirements to Chapter 31 are the provisions of Appendix Chapter 31 relating to existing buildings. Unless these appendix provisions are adopted at the same time as the Chapter 31 provisions, existing buildings must meet the more restrictive Chapter 31 provisions.

Scope

Sec. 3109. The provisions of this appendix apply to renovation, alteration and additions to existing buildings including those identified as historic buildings. This chapter identifies minimum standards for removing architectural barriers, and providing and maintaining accessibility to existing buildings and their related facilities.

Section 3109 of Appendix Chapter 31 establishes the application of the Appendix provisions for existing buildings.

Definitions

Sec. 3110. For the purpose of this chapter certain terms are defined as follows:

ALTERATION is any change, addition or modification in construction or occupancy.

ALTERATION, SUBSTANTIAL is an alteration where the total cost of all alterations (including but not limited to, electrical, mechanical, plumbing and

structural changes) for a building or facility within a twelve-month period amounts to 50 percent or more of the assessed value.

STRUCTURALLY IMPRACTICAL describes alterations that require changes to load bearing structural members other than conventional light frame construction.

Section 3110 of Appendix Chapter 31 adds three definitions relating to existing buildings. The "alteration" definition is identical to that in Section 402 of the code. The two new definitions determine whether the provisions of Chapter 31 and the Appendix Chapter 31 apply to an existing building.

The substantial alteration definition uses a percentage of the assessed valuation as a trigger for the accessibility provisions. This is a return to the concept in effect prior to the 1979 edition of the code.

In the author's opinion, the use of assessed valuation as a trigger is inequitable. In many parts of the country, the assessed valuation is not revised frequently to reflect real values. In California, as a result of Proposition 13, assessed values are the same as they were when the proposition passed, except for an annual 2 percent increase allowed or if the property changes ownership.

A second inequity is that the work exempted by Section 3112 (b)5 involves only related trades, such as electrical or plumbing work. When seismic upgrading or repairs are involved there is no such exemption, and thus the owner will have a substantially increased financial burden resulting from work required to be done beyond the owner's control.

The second new definition, "structurally impractical," applies to additions per Section 3111 and alterations per Section 3112 (a). The term does not apply to Type V buildings because of the use of the term "conventional light frame construction," which is similar to Section 2517 (a) terminology. Whether it will also be applied to some Type II buildings will be the enforcement official's decision.

In the author's opinion, only the Type V buildings should be included as the intent of the term "conventional light frame construction."

The purpose of the "structurally impractical" exemption is to avoid requiring major structural changes in an existing building when the accessibility trigger applies. Thus, if the Chapter 31 provisions were to be invoked for a Type I building built 40 years ago, the stairway width requirements of Chapter 31, Section 3104 (b)4 could not be met unless major structural reframing was done to create a wider shaft.

The reframing would require the removal and replacement of the beams and/or girders framing the stairway. These are load bearing structural members, even though they may only be supporting the wall directly above the member. The term "load bearing" can generate problems for a designer. Therefore, the matter of the definition of the term should be explored with the enforcement authority and the reply documented early in the process of designing an alteration or addition to an existing building.

Additions

Sec. 3111. New additions may be made to existing buildings without making the entire building comply, provided the new additions conform to the provisions of Chapter 31 and applicable sections of U.B.C. Standard No. 31-1. Unless structurally impractical, existing buildings to which additions are attached shall comply with the following:

1. Entrances. When a new addition to a building or facility does not have an accessible entrance, then at least one entrance in the existing building or facility shall be accessible.

2. Accessible Route. When the only accessible entrance to the addition is located in the existing building or facility, at least one accessible route of travel shall be provided through the existing building or facility to all rooms, elements and spaces in the new addition which are required to be accessible.

3. Toilet and Bathing Facilities. Where there are no toilet rooms and bathing facilities in the addition and these facilities are provided in the existing building, at least one toilet and bathing facility in the existing building shall comply with Chapter 31 or with Section 3112 (c) 5 of this appendix.

Section 3111 requires that an addition meet the requirements of Chapter 31 and the Appendix Chapter 31. The rest of the building need not meet these code provisions except for the three items cited relating to entrances, accessible route and toilet and bathing facilities. A further exemption from the imposition of these three items is permitted when the work is structurally impractical.

Although the structurally impractical exemption is provided, designers should be aware that the burden of proof will be theirs. In vertical additions, the entrance and accessible route requirements will affect the existing portion of the building. The designer should be prepared to demonstrate whether in fact the existing entrance or route must be upgraded or cannot be so upgraded.

Alterations

Sec. 3112. (a) General. Unless it is structurally impractical, alterations to existing buildings or facilities shall comply with the following:

1. Where existing elements, spaces, essential features or common areas are altered, then each such altered element, space feature or area shall comply with the applicable provisions of Chapter 31 of this code and applicable provisions of U.B.C. Standard No. 31.1.

2. Where an escalator or new stairway is planned or installed requiring major structural changes, then a means of vertical transportation (e.g. elevator, platform lift) shall be installed in accordance with U.B.C. Standard No. 31-1.

3. Where alterations of single elements, when considered together, provide access to an area of a building or facility, the entire area or space shall be accessible.

4. No alteration of an existing element, space or area of a building shall impose a requirement for greater accessibility than that which would be required for new construction.

5. Where the alteration work is limited solely to the electrical, mechanical or plumbing systems and does not involve the alteration, structural or otherwise, of any elements and spaces required to be accessible under these standards, this appendix and Chapter 31 do not apply.

Section 3112 (a) applies to any alteration as a trigger for accessibility except when structurally impractical. The several items in this section detail what must be done in various circumstances.

Item 1. This requirement invokes the provisions of Chapter 31 for any element, space feature or area involved in the alteration. Thus, wherever the Chapter 31 provisions apply and the alteration work would involve that subject, compliance to Chapter 31 is required.

Item 2. This requirement is very restrictive. It mandates a new elevator when a new stairway or escalator is installed. Thus, if an existing stairway were to be relocated in a building that does not have an elevator, the new stairway triggers the installation of an elevator as well.

The key phrase in this provision is "requiring major structural changes." This phrase is not defined, and one must look to the other concept of structural impracticability for guidance. A major structural change could be the removal, replacement or installation of structural elements as would be necessitated by the new stairway or escalator framing.

In the author's opinion, unless the new stairway is external to the building and therefore does not incur major structural changes, any new stairway or escalator or replacement of same will trigger the installation of an elevator.

Item 3. This requirement is very subjective and places a great responsibility on the enforcement agency to use judgment in its application and not blanket an accessibility requirement for all alterations. The provision is ambiguous and as such can lead to excessive application.

Item 4. This provision places the maximum requirement as that contained in Chapter 31 for new buildings. This is a logical conclusion and is provided to avoid an existing building being subject to greater requirements than would a new building.

Item 5. This provision exempts certain work from being considered in the triggering provisions of the Appendix Chapter 31. If the building alteration work includes walls, floors or ceilings in addition to one or more of these disciplines, then the Section 3110 substantial alteration definition must be evaluated.

(b) Substantial Alterations. Where substantial alteration occurs to a building or facility, each element or space that is altered or added shall comply with the applicable provisions of Chapter 31 of this code and U.B.C. Standard No. 31-1 or this appendix, except where it is structurally impractical. The altered building or facility shall contain:

1. At least one accessible route.

2. At least one accessible entrance, preferably the main entrance. Where additional entrances are altered they shall comply.

3. The following toilet facilities, whichever is greater:

A. At least one toilet facility for each sex in the altered building.

B. At least one toilet facility for each sex on each substantially altered floor, where such facilities are provided.

Section 3112 (b) requires that when the substantial alteration valuation trigger is invoked, all work affected by that alteration must meet Chapter 31. The issue is clouded by the addition of the phrase "or this appendix" after citing that the Chapter 31 provisions are invoked. No criteria are provided regarding to when the Chapter 31 provisions apply and when the Appendix Chapter 31 provisions apply.

In the author's opinion, the designer must be conservative in the approach to making this choice. If the enforcement official accepts the use of the Appendix Chapter 31 provisions, this should be documented and the rationale for such choice included in that documentation.

Because the choice is not dependent on the structural impracticability because this is in effect a third alternative, the rationale must be based on architectural considerations. The only one left, after discarding the structural and specific work covered by the Chapter 31 provisions, is that the architectural work does not encompass most of the Chapter 31 requirements and that the cost of the work that activated the trigger was due to the other disciplines, i.e., electrical, plumbing or mechanical. If this is the case in a project, the documentation must clearly refer to same so that the validity of the choice is understood if subsequentially questioned.

When structurally impractical or when Appendix Chapter 31 is invoked, the three cited provisions are mandated: accessible route, entrance and toilet facilities.

(c) Modifications. The following modifications may be used for compliance when the required standard is structurally impractical or when providing access to historic buildings:

► ■■■ ◄

Section 3112 (c) provides the guidance for historic buildings and the case where structural impracticability applies. These are the minimum requirements in both cases. The modifications apply to ramp slopes, handrail extensions and elevator door reopening devices, minimum size of elevator cab, door clearances and thresholds, toilet rooms and assembly areas. All are substantial lessening of the Chapter 31 and Appendix Chapter 31 provisions.

OVERVIEW OF CHAPTER 31 AND APPENDIX CHAPTER 31 PROVISIONS

In the author's opinion, there are numerous ambiguous provisions, inadequately stated requirements and conflicts with code philosophy in these two chapters. It is hoped that many of these will be resolved through code changes and ICBO code interpretations. Both courses of action should recognize that excessive restrictiveness will require financial and social disruption and are warranted only when cost effectiveness demonstrated. With the imminent application of the ADA regulations and the role of the model codes, judicious code provisions are mandated: not restrictiveness for its own sake.

Attics: Access, Draft Stops and Ventilation

Sec. 3205. (a) Access. An attic access opening shall be provided in the ceiling of the top floor of buildings with combustible ceiling or roof construction. The opening shall be located in a corridor or hallway of buildings of three or more stories in height and readily accessible in buildings of any height.

The opening shall be no less than 22 inches by 30 inches.

Thirty-inch minimum clear head room shall be provided above the access opening.

Attics with a maximum vertical clear height of less than 30 inches need not be provided with access openings.

The attic access provision does not refer to fire-resistive roof-ceiling assemblies. Often, the lack of a code reference to fire-resistive assemblies leads designers to ignore the general requirements set forth in Chapter 43. As was discussed in Article 8 of this Guide with regard to Section 4303 (b)6 second paragraph, the code has a specific requirement that attic access openings through a ceiling portion of a fire-rated assembly must have approved horizontal access door assemblies.

The usual attic access is through a scuttle, made by cutting an opening in the ceiling between two joists. The closure is made with a piece of wallboard supported by thin wood trim. (See Figure 10-6.) This construction does not meet the intent of Section 4303 (b)6.

The installation of an approved access door will require a labeled frame properly attached to the adjacent framing. The essential point is

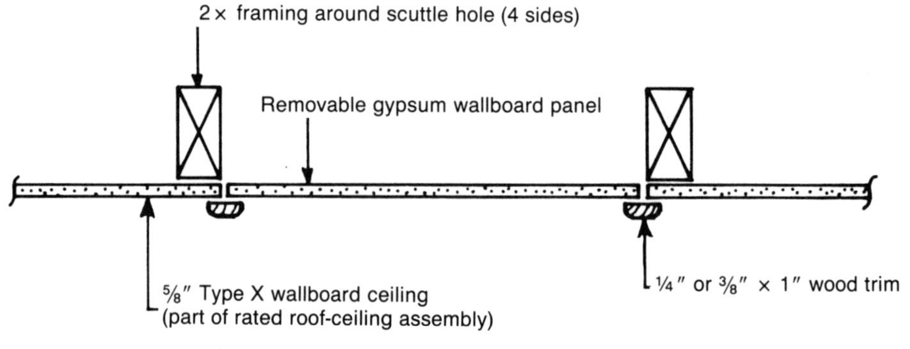

REFERENCE: SECTIONS 3205 (a) and 4302 (b)

FIGURE 10-6 ATTIC ACCESS, NON-CONFORMING DETAIL

that the fire resistivity of the ceiling or other membrane must be maintained.

Automatic Fire-Extinguishing Systems

Sec. 3802 (h) Group R, Division 1 Occupancies. An automatic sprinkler system shall be installed throughout every apartment house three or more stories in height or containing 16 or more dwelling units and every hotel three or more stories in height or containing 20 or more guest rooms. Residential or quick-response standard sprinkler heads shall be used in the dwelling unit and guest room portions of the building.

This sprinkler requirement for Group H, Division 1 apartment houses and hotels is in addition to:

- the one-hour fire-resistive construction required by Section 1202 (b)
- the fire alarm requirements in Section 1211 and
- the smoke detector requirements of Section 1210 (a)

The form of the requirement is identical to the fire alarm requirement, i.e., the sprinklers will be required in the same size building. Therefore, whenever a fire alarm is required, there also must be sprinklers throughout. The sprinkler system must be tied into the fire alarm system, so that a flow in the sprinklers will initiate the fire alarm.

In some buildings the requirement for tying the two systems together may be modified to allow for a “silent alarm,” provided the fire department approves such a system. This will usually require a 24-hour staffed location that will receive the silent alarm and will have the capability of verifying the reason for same before initiating the fire alarm signal.

In buildings that require the sprinkler system throughout, the provisions of Section 508 may not be applicable. That section specifically qualifies the use of sprinklers as a trade-off to situations where the sprinklers are not otherwise required throughout the building.

The code requirement stipulates that either the residential sprinkler head or a quick-response standard sprinkler head be used within the dwelling unit or guest room. The inference, therefore, is that in the “public areas” of the building, which include the corridors, stairways, lobbies, service closets and other rooms not specifically dwelling units or guest rooms, standard heads will be used.

The use of NFPA 13-R, which applies to Group H, Division 1 Occupancy buildings of not more than four stories provides a means for bridging the gap between the NFPA 13 and the 13-D sprinkler requirements. However, for buildings more than four stories, it is unclear whether the NFPA 13-D requirements for residential sprinkler systems may be usable within those dwelling units or guest rooms.

> It is the author's opinion, that such merging of these two sprinkler requirements is reasonable as the fire in a sixth story dwelling unit is no different than a fire in the same unit located on the fourth floor of the building.

There is considerable advantage to the designer to have the use of that set of design criteria because it would substantially reduce water supply and pipe sizes. If the enforcement authorities permit their use within the dwelling units or guest rooms, the officials should require that the UBC Standard 38-1 be used for the public areas. This will result in a hybrid system.

If the quick-response standard heads are used, the system can be designed using only the UBC Standard 38-1 criteria.

The designer should be aware of the considerable difference between the two sprinkler systems and the lack of specific design criteria for the hybrid system. The hybrid system will need the fire department connection and the supervision requirements of UBC Standard 38-1. However, the hybrid system should reduce the overall cost of installation. The author believes that such a system will be commonly accepted as it has for buildings up to four stories. The enforcement officials should give serious consideration to accepting a hybrid system now for taller buildings so that the costs attendant to the new requirements can be reduced.

There has been increasing use of such hybrid NFPA 13-D systems combined with the standard system in public areas. These usually have been in existing buildings either to retrofit them voluntarily or to correct existing code deficiencies. as the code provision now pairs the use of these heads, the designer and the enforcement official must clarify the type and extent of the system to be used, the portions of the two standards that are to apply, the method of determining water demand and the several other aspects of the two systems that either are in conflict or are ambiguous.

In the author's opinion, the following minimum criteria could form the basis of a hybrid system and could be used by the designer and the building official in carrying out the intent of the hybrid requirements:

1. The entire system should be hydraulically designed.
2. The water supply to the building, the fire department connections, risers and public space sprinklering should be per UBC Standard 38-1 conventional design for low hazard, unless the coverage includes other than residential occupancy.
3. Within the dwelling units and guest rooms, the design should permit use of the residential sprinkler system based on NFPA 13-D. The design within the dwelling unit or guest room would have residential quick-response heads. When multiple levels are involved, the design should include up to two heads on each level if they are exposed to a common fire source.
4. The supervisory system should have tamper switches on all shut-off valves.

As can readily be seen by the adoption of this provision, the growing use of sprinkler systems mandated by the code continues unabated. By adding this level of requirement to residential buildings, lives will be saved. However, omitting any cost offsets or trade-offs for the requirements is unfortunate. The reader is directed to Section 1807 (c)2, where the concept of trade-offs, an integral part of the sprinkler requirements in high-rise buildings, is discussed.

Sprinkler System Supervision Alarms

Sec. 3803. All valves controlling the water supply for automatic sprinkler systems and water-flow switches on all sprinkler systems shall be electrically supervised when the number of heads are:

1. Twenty or more in Group I, Division 1 Occupancies.

2. One hundred or more in all other occupancies.

Valve supervision and water-flow alarm and trouble signals shall be distinctly different and shall be automatically transmitted to an approved central station, remote station or propriety supervising station as defined by national

standards, or, when approved by the building official with the concurrence of the chief of the fire department, sound an audible signal at a constantly attended location.

EXCEPTIONS: Underground key or hub valves in roadway boxes provided by the municipality or public utility need not be supervised.

Section 3803 requires that there be complete supervision of water-flow and tamper switches on a sprinkler system. This is a major change from the prior codes, which did not specifically include supervision of valves. The inclusion of the term "All valves controlling water supply ..." refers to a valve on the system.

A further clarification is the requirement for electrical supervision and trouble signals. This covers the electrical continuity of the wiring involved in the supervision of the valves and water-flow alarm. These are improvements to the code and increase the reliability of the sprinkler systems.

> In the author's opinion, the requirement for supervision should be mandated whenever sprinklers are used as an alternative and more than 20 heads are involved because, under Section 105, an alternative must be obviously equal or better. Adding the supervision to the sprinklers helps clarify the obvious nature of equivalence required by assuring that the system will be active when needed.

TABLE NO. 47-I ALLOWABLE SHEAR FOR WIND OR SEISMIC FORCES IN POUNDS PER FOOT FOR VERTICAL DIAPHRAGMS OF LATH AND PLASTER OR GYPSUM BOARD FRAME WALL ASSEMBLIES

Footnote 1 reads:

These vertical diaphragms shall not be used to resist loads imposed by masonry or concrete construction. See Section 4713 (b). Values are for short term loading due to wind. Values must be reduced 25 percent for normal loading. The values for gypsum products must be reduced 50 percent for dynamic loading due to earthquake in Seismic Zones 3 and 4 only.

The addition of the last sentence to footnote 1 is of major importance in Seismic Zones 3 and 4.

This requirement of Table No. 47-I results from testing done in California involving both repetitive loading and full reversals of loads. This approach to the evaluation of shear panels under seismic loading is more realistic than the uni-directional, single push ASTM test standard. The test findings indicated a substantial reduction in the lateral load-carrying capability of gypsum-based panels.

It is the author's opinion that similar reductions must be made to other brittle-type materials used in seismic design.

The designer is cautioned to have designs based on the use of gypsum wallboard as the primary earthquake-resisting material reevaluated in the light of this substantial reduction in allowable loads.

As this provision now represents the "state of the art" in structural design, the designer is urged to consider its application regardless of whether a locality has adopted the 1991 UBC. Failing to utilize the available knowledge can place the designer in jeopardy. This provision was supported by the Structural Engineers Associations of the several western states.

Roof Panels

Sec. 5206. Approved plastic roof panels may be installed in roofs of buildings not required to have a fire-resistive rating, subject to the following limitations:

1. Individual roof panels or units shall be separated from each other by distances of not less than 4 feet measured in a horizontal plane.

2. Roof panels or units shall not be installed within that portion of a roof located within a distance to property line or public way where openings in exterior walls are prohibited or required to be protected, whichever is most restrictive.

Skylights

Sec. 5207. (a) General. Skylight assemblies may be glazed with approved plastic materials in accordance with the following provisions:

6. Skylight units shall be separated from each other by a distance of not less than 4 feet measured in a horizontal plane.

EXCEPTIONS: 1. Except for Groups A, Divisions 1 and 2, I and H, Divisions 1 and 2 Occupancies, the separation is not required where the skylights are:

(i) Serving as a fire venting system complying with this code; or

(ii) Used in a building completely equipped with an approved automatic sprinkler system.

2. Multiple skylights located above the same room or space with a combined area not exceeding the limits set forth in Section 5207 (a), Item 4.

box.eps

7. Skylights shall not be installed within that portion of a roof located within a distance to property line or public way where openings in exterior walls are prohibited or required to be protected, whichever is most restrictive.

These sections provide the regulations for the installation of roof panels and skylights in buildings. The concern is two-fold:

1. The prevention of fire entry into a building from flying brands from an adjacent building, thus preventing the spread of fire, and
2. The prevention of fire spreading from a building to an adjacent structure via an opening in the roof that may be close to the property line.

The intent is to permit unprotected roof openings when they are located the same distance from the property line or public way that would allow unprotected exterior wall openings.

The intent is somewhat clouded as of the negative phrasing used in the two sections. These provisions state that the roof openings are not allowed within the distance that openings in the exterior walls are either prohibited or require protection. (See Figure 10-7.) The converse of the negative statement may be better understood and would read:

Roof openings are permitted when they are located a distance from the property line or public way that would permit unprotected exterior wall openings.

A second Exception was added to Item 6 of Section 5207 (a) that permits multiple skylights in the same room or space, provided the aggregate area does not exceed that allowed in Item 4 of this section. The intent is that so long as the skylights are in the same room or space and meet the area limitations, there is no increase in the hazard if there was a single or multiple skylight involved.

Dependent on the type of plastic used, the area limitations are 100

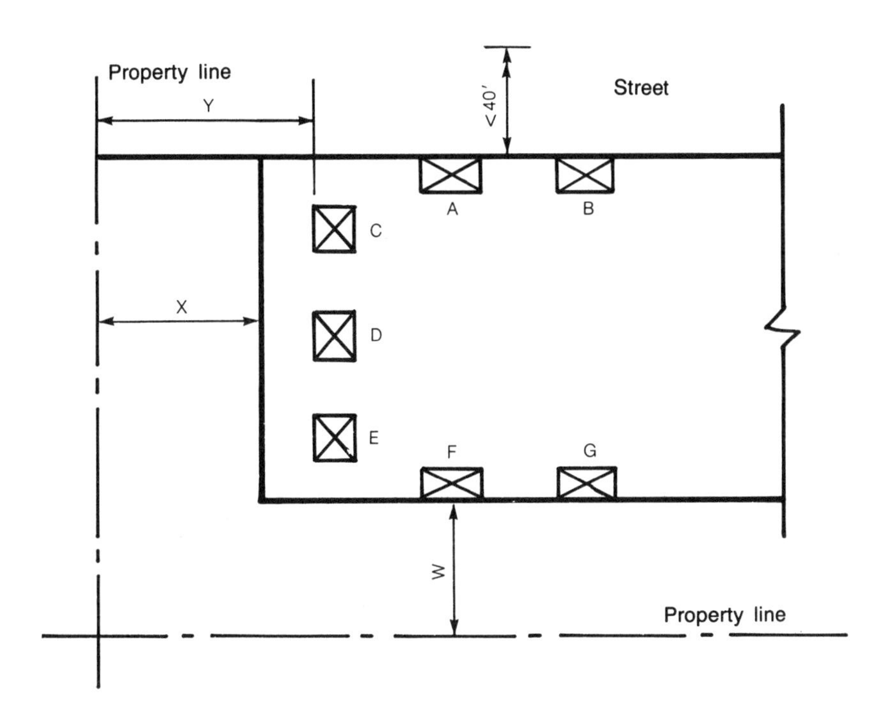

GIVEN: Type III-N building
Group B, Division 2 Occupancy

Per Section 2003 (a) Exception 1 and Section 2003 (b), the exterior wall on the street front may be of unprotected construction and have unprotected openings. Therefore, per the new code change to Section 5206 and 5207 (a)7, roof openings "A" and "B" are permitted without protection.

Per Section 2003 (a) Exception 3 and Section 2003 (b):

a) When X = 5', no openings are permitted in the exterior wall. If Y = 5', no roof openings are permitted.
b) When 5' =< X < 20', protected openings are allowed on the exterior wall. If 5' => Y = < 20', no roof openings are permitted. Roof openings C, D, and E can only be located so that the closest edge of the opening is at least 20 feet from the property line.
c) When X, Y or W > 20', unprotected openings are permitted on the exterior wall. Roof openings are permitted as well; openings F & G are permitted when the closest edge is more than 20' from the property line.

REFERENCES: SECTIONS 2003 (a) & (b), 5206 AND 5207 (a)

FIGURE 10-7 LOCATION CRITERIA FOR ROOF OPENINGS AS RELATED TO EXTERIOR WALL OPENINGS

square feet for CC2 material and 200 square feet for CC1 material. Note that Exception 1 to Item 4 would also apply, allowing unlimited area where that Exception is satisfied.

CHAPTER 60
UNIFORM BUILDING CODE STANDARDS

Chapter 60 contains a listing of all standards referred to in the body of the code. The text of the actual standards is contained in a separate volume that serves as a companion document to the UBC. By listing the standards referred to herein, and by providing the date of the standards volume adopted, one can legally make them a part of the adoptive document in a particular jurisdiction at the time the UBC is adopted.

In addition to the standards listing, a reference to the standard's source document is also provided. The majority of the UBC standards derive from nationally accepted standards promulgated by ASTM, ULI, Federal Specifications, industry design documents as ACI, AISI, AISC, and others. These documents are identified by title and date of issue. With each triennial edition of the UBC, a companion edition of the revised standards is published. Many of these, in turn, are based on updated national standards. The revisions to the national standards are reflected in the new date attached thereto.

ARTICLE 11
LEGAL IMPLICATIONS OF THE CODE

The code is frequently viewed as a hurdle to be surmounted by the designer, the contractor and others involved in the building process. Some can gracefully maneuver over the obstacle; some ignore its presence and try to bulldoze through it; others try to circumvent it.

Unfortunately, we are living in an increasingly litigious society. Because the code is an ordinance or law enacted by a jurisdiction, it is as much the law as any other law on the books. Violation of the code is a violation of the law and can result in financial or personal loss to the individual or firm committing the violation.

The Contractor and the Code

The author has occasionally used, with appropriate modifications, a nationally circulated contract document that indicates that the contractor is not required to know the code but need only follow the drawings that are part of the contract. In many states this is not true. Contractor licensing laws require the contractor to abide by all laws and ordinances. To obtain a contractor's license, the contractor must know the codes in effect in the locality in which the contractor intends to operate.

In fact, the contractor may have a much greater familiarity with the different types of construction and code problems than many designers. It is incumbent on the contractor, in the review and in estimating a job for the materials and methods intended to be used in the project, to pay special attention to those areas found at variance with the locally applicable code. When these areas are encountered, the contractor should notify the designer, in writing, of the findings. The correspondence should state that the contractor will not be liable for what may happen if the suspected violation remains uncorrected.

By writing about these findings to the designer, and by clearly delineating his future noninvolvement with that issue, the contractor may sidestep future liability in that case. The designer must be attentive to those areas of the contract documents the contractor points out.

The Designer and the Code

Under the professional licensing provisions in each state, the designer is also subject to the legal requirement for code compliance.

A substantial number of projects have come to the author's attention where contractors and designers committed code violations either knowingly or unknowingly.

The frequency of these cases indicates that all too often the participants place too great an emphasis on obtaining the permit and consider the building official to be the sole enforcer of the law. They assume that after the permit has been obtained, the code hurdle is successfully negotiated and there need be no further concerns.

Many unusual determinations have come to the author's attention. These involve interpretations by local officials that are totally at variance with the accepted views of the design profession, ICBO and enforcement officials generally and the definitions in the UBC.

The designers had experience in other jurisdictions and should have known better than to follow the misinterpretations of the enforcement officials. In one instance, the designer did what was proper and ignored the ruling of the enforcement official. In the others, the designers followed the bad advice and designed buildings in violation of the UBC. The irony was that the enforcement officials, when the matter was brought to their attention, chose to place themselves above the code, i.e., the law in their own jurisdiction. Such posturing does not serve the public nor the design profession.

The designer should follow the code, when faced with a determination made at the local level that is knowingly contrary to the code and accepted practice in the profession. The choice of a more restrictive reading of the code cannot be overruled by the official. One can always exceed the minimum standards in the code. By so doing, the designer will avoid the trap of taking responsibility for the code violation that the official inadvertently set up. Remember that the code provides an "out" for the official via Section 303 (c); there is no similar one for the designer.

The Building Official's Legal Responsibility and Resources

As indicated in this Guide, many years of statutory liability face the designer, the contractor and others party to the construction. In a paper published in ICBO's Building Standards Monthly, the author indicated concern with the increasing tendency of some building officials to fail to exercise their responsibilities. The locality, in accepting the permit and plan check fees, is obliged to provide the services those fees are meant to procure and to protect the public by means of its checking and inspection functions. In at least one jurisdiction, a suit resulted in the locality paying more than $200,000 to one of the suing parties for the locality's role in failing to prevent faulty construction, the primary issue in that litigation.

Several resources are available to the building official when a design is so complex or unusual that the official's time or level of knowledge may not be adequate to review the design documents properly. The nearest resources are larger jurisdictions or design professionals who have had experience in plan-checking and who may be retained to review the drawings and other design documents for the complex project. This type of assistance can augment the technical capacities of the locality and reduce the possibility of the building official becoming a party to potential code violations.

A second resource is the staff of the International Conference of Building Officials in Whittier, California, and its regional offices. The staff is experienced in plan checking as most are former staff members of building departments. The plan checking services conducted by the Conference can provide the building official with a written review of the permit documents. After a line of communication has been opened with the Conference, questions that occur after the plan check can be resolved with the Conference staff assistance.

The building official can also obtain assistance by making inquiry to the Conference regarding a particular arrangement, configuration or material. The resources of the Conference are available to the building official, and written responses enable the official to arrive at equitable solutions to complex questions.

The enforcement official who chooses to ignore the code, (see "The Designer and the Code" above), places both the jurisdiction and the official in serious jeopardy. Cases have ruled that both the individual and the jurisdiction can sustain liability if the action by the official was knowingly wrong. The official should obtain maximum assistance from the cited sources rather than incur such liability. The public is ill served by officials who choose to ignore the law they are to enforce.

The "Standard of Care"

Another issue that usually arises in litigation is the question of what constitutes the prevailing standard of care in a particular locality, because construction and design practices vary according to the locality.

The acceptance of substandard drawings from several designers does not establish a standard level of acceptance in that locality. If that standard results in drawings that are incomplete for proper construction, in litigation the designer will answer to the courts. It is foolish to hope the courts will rule that the continued presence of inadequate drawings will, over a period of time, establish that level of performance as the professional standard in the locality.

If a building official has made an erroneous interpretation and maintains that misinterpretation when responding to similar inquiries from other design professionals, that repetition of error does not establish a legal basis for violating the code. The designer must know and comply with the code, just as the driver of a car is required to know the speed limits, comply with them and not rely on the traffic cop to verify them.

A court decision in California, (Huang v. Garner) found, among other rulings, that violation of the code was negligence on the part of the designer. It further found the failure of the contractor/developer to comply with the Uniform Building Code, which creates potential risks to future purchasers. Moreover, it indicated that the standard of care required of designers and engineers may, in fact, be the standard for the profession as a whole.

Thus, the local community may not be equivalent to the community at issue. The Huang v. Garner case is having a strong impact on litigation. Its message is clear, and its meaning should warn everyone of the dangers involved in committing code violations.

The Decision-Making Process and Pressures

In the code development process at the committee levels and at the Annual Business Meeting, during which the code changes are finally discussed and voted on, even well-informed individuals differ in their interpretations of provisions. When inexperienced officials attempt to make decisions on complex provisions of the code and do so without the background necessary to formulate those decisions, the day-to-day pressures placed on them by their jobs and by the individuals seeking those decisions increase the likelihood that errors will be made.

It is better for the building official to use the services of the Conference (ICBO). The official can direct an inquiry to the Conference staff, and, after receiving a reply, the official will have a clear-cut understanding of the code's intent. The resultant interpretation will be prepared by personnel impartial yet experienced in code and code development.

If there are doubts about the propriety of a decision, it is best to have the decision evaluated through the Conference or to have the backing of a local chapter of the Conference. These chapters are made up of building officials and others interested in the code. The problem can be brought before the group and discussed, so that the best available expertise in the locality can assist the official.

When a locality adopts a new edition of the code or other ordinances, it provides an opportunity for the design professional and others in the building process to resolve locally recognized code problem areas. This resolution can be accomplished either by adopting a local amendment to the code or by establishing an appeal procedure whereby interpretations or rulings on the code can be made within the locality. As previously stated, if an appeal board for such issues does not exist, one should be established with interested and knowledgeable members of the building industry as active members.

Summary

When errors are made, the public suffers and the individuals involved in the decision are placed in legal jeopardy. Although the code hurdle may apparently have been overcome successfully, one finds, years later, that it was not truly overcome. Instead, it had been simply pushed ahead to a future date at which point it suddenly looms up, much more difficult to conquer and placing much more at stake. Many of the parties originally involved are no longer around, and the circumstances of the original decision-making process are no longer pressing or even known.

In such situations, when dispassionate evaluations can take place, the design professional, the contractor and the building official can find themselves under the scrutiny of the law. The public will want to know why they supported and allowed noncompliance with the laws of the locality.

The author hopes that this Guide will assist the designer and others involved with the building process in avoiding the much tougher legal hurdle by providing methods for avoiding unwitting code violations and by promoting an understanding of the code process and intent.

ARTICLE 12
THE APPLICABILITY OF CODES

An area of code enforcement causing considerable problems for the building official, the designer and the attorney is the determination of what code applies to an existing building. It is important to determine just what codes applied at various times during a building's life. The building may now be the subject of litigation due to alleged defects involving the original construction as well as subsequent alterations.

GENERAL DEFINITIONS, PARAMETERS AND APPROACH

To provide guidance in resolving this type of situation ,we must first establish certain parameters and define terms.

Definition Of Terms

Code at Time of Original Construction. The building code adopted by the jurisdiction prior to the date of the original construction.

Retroactivity. The application of a requirement in a code, ordinance or other regulation to an existing building. The application is not dependent on whether the owner desires to comply or do any work and is mandatory on the owner. Failure of the owner to comply results in the full force of the enforcement process by the local jurisdiction.

Building Code Appendix. As stated in this Guide, the Appendix must be specifically adopted by the local jurisdiction. If not so adopted, it does not apply. Any adopted part of the Appendix has the same force of law as does the rest of the code.

Certain provisions in the Appendix have retroactive intent. In the present code these are Appendix Chapter 1, Division I and Division II. In prior editions of the UBC, the retroactive provisions may have different Chapter designations.

The key terminology is the reference to "existing buildings" in the opening sections of the Appendix provisions. This terminology gives the intent for application of the requirements to all existing buildings. See Section 110 of Appendix Chapter 1, Division I for example.

Prime Criteria

A building must always comply with the code in effect at the time of its original construction.

Building codes are not retroactive.

Retroactive regulations apply only to specific areas of buildings and to buildings that were built either when less-restrictive provisions were in effect or when there was no code in effect in the locality.

Parameters of Application

Retroactive code provisions are aimed at correcting existing conditions that are now deemed to be deficiencies in buildings. The deficiencies were not considered as such under the codes in effect at the time of the original construction. These deficiencies include such conditions as the presence of unenclosed exit stairways or lack of a second exit.

Retroactivity involves constitutional issues as well as economic impacts on the owner and building occupants. The enactment of retroactive provisions requires very careful consideration of the issues involved, the details of the provisions to be invoked and the methods permitted for satisfying them, so that the regulations are not excessive.

It was not until after World War II that enclosed stairways were mandated for all new buildings three or more stories in height. Thus, any building built prior to that period would be subject to retroactive provisions of Appendix Chapter 1, Division I, if such were adopted by the locality.

Sometimes the state adopts retroactive provisions and mandates them for enforcement by the local jurisdiction. Such state action preempts the option of the local jurisdiction to determine whether it wants to have such regulations. The decision is made for the jurisdiction by the state legislature.

When the edition of the building code adopted by a jurisdiction contains provisions of equal or greater restrictiveness than a retroactive requirement, all buildings built after the adoption of that edition must exceed that retroactive provision. The retroactive provisions would apply only to buildings built prior to that edition.

If the original construction did not meet the requirements of the code in effect at the time of the original construction, then under the code in effect at that time there are requirements that apply. These are the provisions in Chapters 1 and 3 requiring that the building must be brought into compliance with the code in effect at the time of original construction. Any permit issued or finaled does not validate noncompliance with that code.

Since before 1950 all editions of the UBC have had provisions similar to those in Sections 104 (i) and 302 (c) of the 1949 UBC. In the 1991 UBC these same provisions are contained in Sections 104 (d) and 302 (c).

Code provisions contained in codes in effect at the time of original construction that exceed the restrictiveness of the retroactive provisions always take precedence over the retroactive provisions. In such buildings, the retroactive provisions of the Appendix do not apply.

Application of the Definitions and Parameters

To provide the reader with a methodology for applying the above definitions and parameters to a variety of conditions, we will assume a broad range of possible situations regarding regulations in effect and evaluate how a given building would be affected in each circumstance. To aid in this evaluation, the conditions and evaluation will be discussed both in text and by several figures.

Main Assumption:

PC = Building built before adoption of local code. See Figure 12-1.

AC = Building built after adoption of local code. See Figure 12-2.

Secondary Assumptions:

Locality adopted Appendix provisions comparable to Chapter 1 Division I.

Locality did not adopt Appendix.

Locality or state adopted UHC or other housing code.

Locality adopted later edition of UBC.

Locality adopted special regulations regarding conversion of condominiums.

Finally, we will examine the effect of one or more of the assumptions on a three story building with multi-family Occupancy Group R, Division 1. See Figure 11-4 for an example of how the assumptions and the evaluations apply to determine the code in effect on the original building at different periods and events in the buildings life.

Rationale in Determining Code in Effect

To determine the code in effect we will progress from the simpler assumptions to the more complex. This technique will enable the reader to use the same rationale for other assumptions that may be applicable to a particular circumstance. In all cases, the evaluation of the condition should parallel the analyses herein.

I. Building "PC" was built in a location where there is no local building code in effect.

1. Building PC: Code in Effect = None. See Bar A in Figure 12-1.

II. Building "AC" was built after the adoption of the local building code.

2. Building AC: Code in Effect = The edition of the UBC adopted by locality prior to construction of the building. See Bar E in Figure 12-2.

Discussion: If there was no code in effect at the time of original construction of building PC, there cannot be any retroactive application of a building code (except for Appendix provisions adopted at some later time). If there is still no code in effect, there is no regulation the locality can apply to the building.

After a building code is adopted in the locality, all buildings, such as building AC, must be built in compliance with that code or a later edition when so adopted. Preexisting buildings, such as building PC, are not subject to the newly adopted code, except for any work done after adoption of the code.

III. Assume locality has adopted UBC with Appendix provision applicable to existing residential buildings.

3. Building PC: Code in Effect = Appendix provisions. See Bar A in Figure 12-1.

4. Building AC: Code in Effect = Appendix provision unless the UBC provisions at the time of original construction exceeded the requirements of the Appendix. The most restrictive provision applies. See Bar E in Figure 12-2.

Discussion: The adoption of the Appendix means the locality has established that all buildings must meet certain minimum standards regardless of whether they were built in conformance to a prior code or built when there was no code in effect in the locality. Those buildings, such as building PC, that do not meet or exceed the requirements in the Appendix for the areas specifically covered therein must be brought up to compliance with the minimum provisions of the Appendix.

Those buildings, such as building AC, that were built when the codes in effect in the locality exceeded the requirements of the Appendix must meet the requirements of the more restrictive UBC editions, because a prime criterion is that a building as a minimum must meet the requirements of the code in effect at the time of original construction.

IV. Assume for both buildings, that the locality has updated its code to a later edition of the UBC.

5. Building PC: Code in Effect = The Appendix. See Row A in Figure 12-1.

6. Building AC: Code in Effect = The prior UBC edition in effect at time of original construction and/or the Appendix, depending on which provisions are more restrictive. See Bar F in Figure 12-2.

Assume that alterations are contemplated in both buildings.

7. Building PC: Code in Effect = Code in effect at the time of the alterations for the work done for the alterations only. If the Appendix was applicable, it also applies. See Row B in Figure 12-1.

8. Building AC: Code in Effect = Code in effect at the time of the alterations for the work done for the alterations only. The rest of the building must still comply with the code in effect at

the time of original construction. If the Appendix is applicable, it also applies. See Column F in Figure 12-2.

Discussion: A locality periodically updates the building code it uses by adopting a more recent edition or latest edition of the UBC. If it had adopted the Appendix in a prior edition, it usually did so as part of the update adoption.

Whenever a later edition of the UBC is adopted, it applies to all work done thereafter whether it is new construction or alterations. If alteration work, only the area subject to the alterations is subject to the new code. As before, the building must always meet the prime criterion of being in compliance with the code in effect at the time of original construction. Where the Appendix provision applies it must also be complied with.

The alteration work must comply with the code in effect at the time the alteration work is done, even if the building was built prior to any code being adopted in the locality.

V. Assume that the locality or the state has adopted the Uni form Housing Code (UHC).

9. Building PC: Code in Effect = Same as #7 plus the UHC. See Figure 12-3.

10. Building AC: Code in Effect = Same as #8 plus the UHC. See Figure 12-3.

Discussion: At times, due to local, state or federal pressures, the state or locality enacts ordinances or adopts the UHC to require that all residential buildings under their jurisdiction be brought up to and maintained to a specified set of standards, including many provisions not found in the building code under which they were originally constructed. Housing codes are retroactive.

UHC provisions include many of the following: freedom from rubbish, vermin and insect infestation; minimum lighting levels in public corridors; minimum electrical requirements; carpeting regulations; painting and wall covering criteria.

These UHC or other similar housing regulations are retroactive to all residential buildings, subject to the jurisdiction of that regulation, regardless of when they were constructed. Failure to comply with the housing code can result in condemnation action against the building and its demolition.

NOTE: We have not covered the following variations of codes in effect:

- those localities that enforce state-adopted building codes,
- those jurisdictions that have local adoption of codes and when either state law preempts certain of the local codes for specific occupancies or
- when state law is retroactive for specific occupancies.

When there are state-mandated codes enforced by the locality, they have the same authority insofar as which code is applicable at different times in a buildings life, as did the locally adopted codes in our discussion. In Figures 12-1 and 12-2, replace chart designation "Local codes in effect" by "State codes in effect."

When their is local adoption of codes *and* state law as well, as in California, both sets of laws must be considered and applied. For that reason, in Figure 12-3 we have noted that the requirements of Figure 12-3 should be superimposed on Figures 12-1 and 12-2 because both sets of requirements apply.

For other states, the designer and enforcement official must check the various applicable laws and create their own charts similar to Figure 12-3.

VI. Assume the locality has adopted regulations applicable to the conversion of existing buildings into condominiums.

11. Building PC: Code in Effect = Appendix plus the UBC in effect for alterations plus UHC and the minimum requirements of the condo minium conversion regulations. See Bar D in Figure 12-1.

12. Building AC: Code in Effect = UBC in effect at time of original construction plus the Appendix, if it

NOTE: The applicablility of a particular ordinance is shown by the heavy vertical line extending from the top of the chart and intersecting the bar representing the life history of the particular building. For example, the adoption of the Appendix intersecting the "A" bar. As of that time, all existing buildings would have had to comply with the Appendix provision of the UBC edition cited as well as any prior UBC edition in effect at the time of original construction.

The UBC in effect at the time the alteration work is done applies only to the specific alteration work, unless the Appendix had also been adopted for the first time.

FIGURE 12-1 CODE/ORDINANCE TIME HISTORY & APPLICATION TO EXISTING BUILDING BUILT PRIOR TO ANY UBC ADOPTION

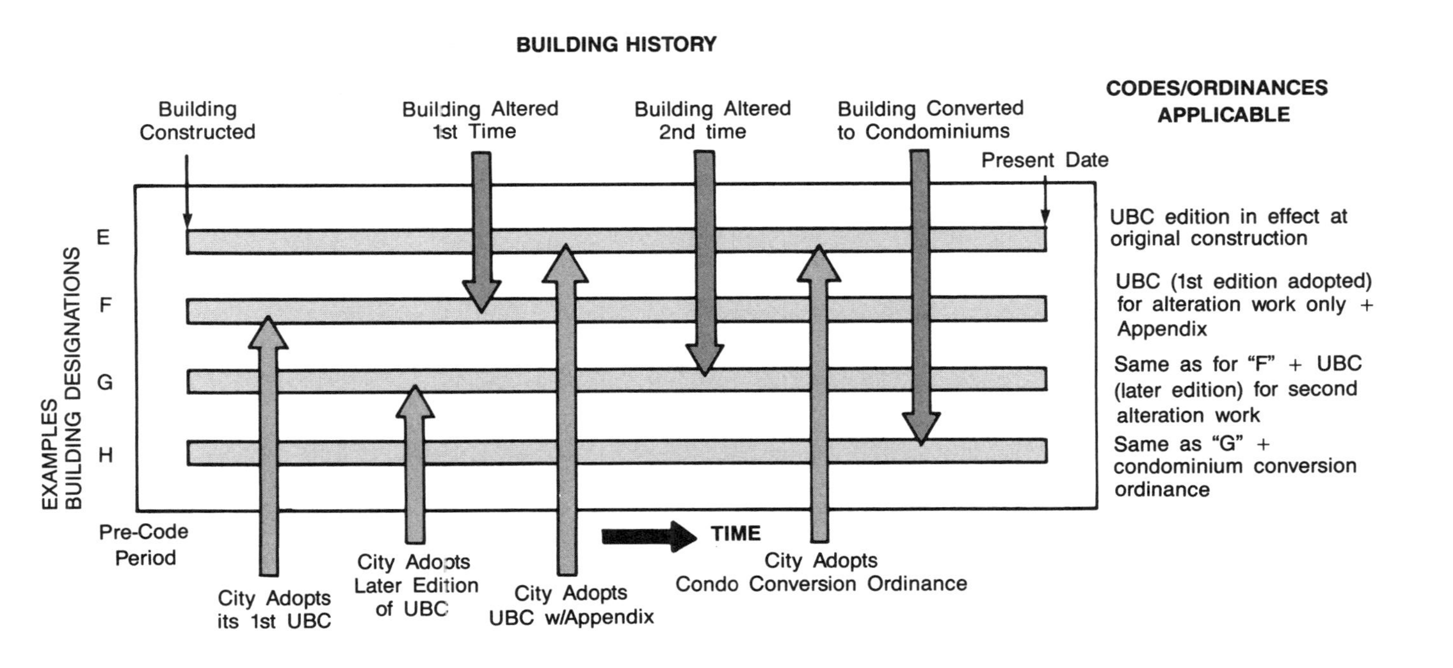
BUILDING HISTORY
Building Constructed
Building Altered 1st Time
Building Altered 2nd time
Building Converted to Condominiums
Present Date
CODES/ORDINANCES APPLICABLE
UBC edition in effect at original construction
UBC (1st edition adopted) for alteration work only + Appendix
Same as for "F" + UBC (later edition) for second alteration work
Same as "G" + condominium conversion ordinance
EXAMPLES BUILDING DESIGNATIONS
E
F
G
H
Pre-Code Period
City Adopts its 1st UBC
City Adopts Later Edition of UBC
City Adopts UBC w/Appendix
TIME
City Adopts Condo Conversion Ordinance
LOCAL ORDINANCES IN EFFECT

NOTE: The applicablility of a particular ordinance is shown by the heavy vertical line extending from the top of the chart and intersecting the bar representing the life history of the particular building. For example, the adoption of the Appendix intersecting the "E" bar. As of that time, all existing buildings would have had to comply with the Appendix provision of the UBC edition cited as well as any prior UBC edition in effect at the time of original construction.

The UBC in effect at the time the alteration work is done applies only to the specific alteration work, unless the Appendix had also been adopted for the first time.

FIGURE 12-2 CODE/ORDINANCE TIME HISTORY & APPLICATION TO EXISTING BUILDING BUILT AFTER A UBC ADOPTION

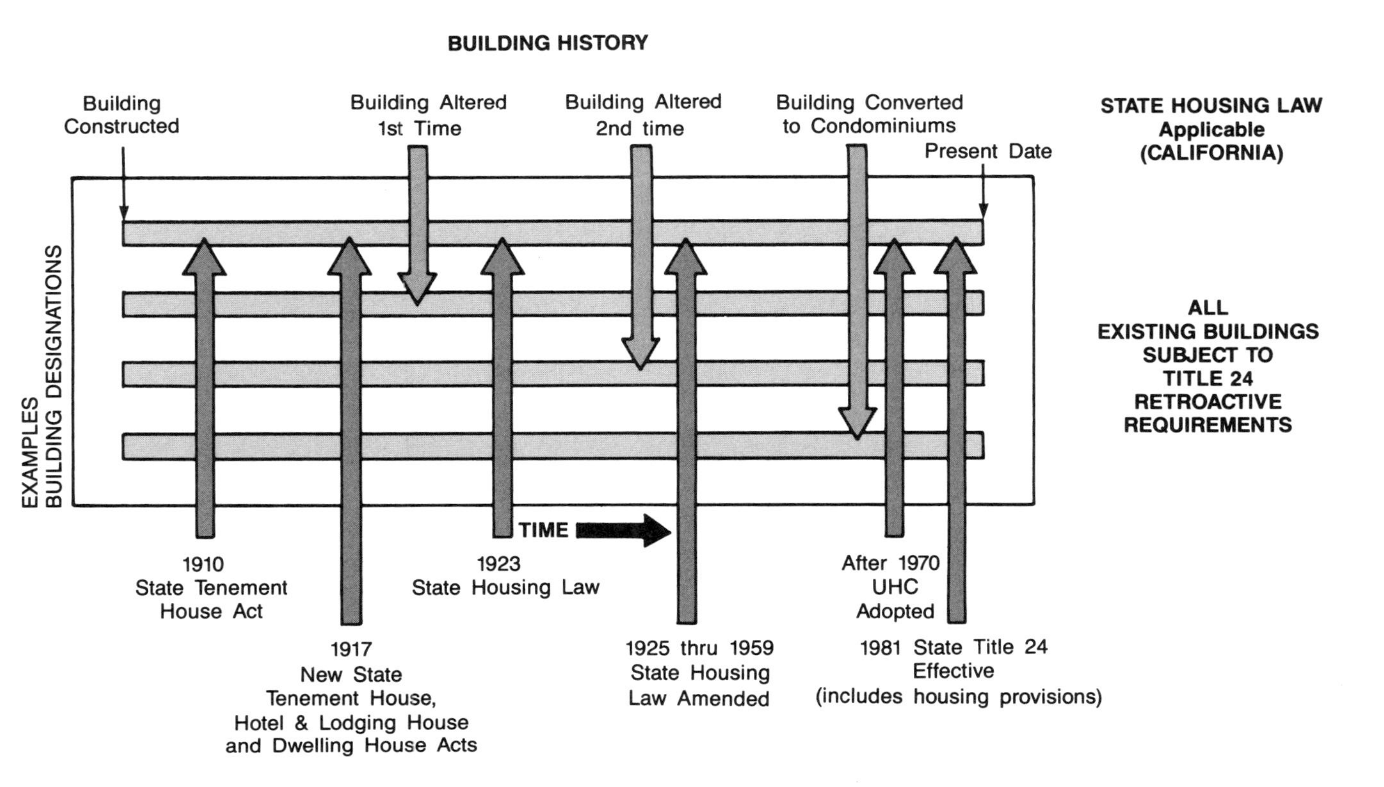
BUILDING HISTORY
Building Constructed
Building Altered 1st Time
Building Altered 2nd time
Building Converted to Condominiums
Present Date
STATE HOUSING LAW Applicable (CALIFORNIA)
EXAMPLES BUILDING DESIGNATIONS
ALL EXISTING BUILDINGS SUBJECT TO TITLE 24 RETROACTIVE REQUIREMENTS
TIME
1910 State Tenement House Act
1917 New State Tenement House, Hotel & Lodging House and Dwelling House Acts
1923 State Housing Law
1925 thru 1959 State Housing Law Amended
After 1970 UHC Adopted
1981 State Title 24 Effective (includes housing provisions)
STATE HOUSING LAW (CALIFORNIA) IN EFFECT

is more restrictive than the UBC at time of original construction, plus the UBC in effect for alterations plus UHC and the minimum requirements of the condo minium conversion regulations. See Bar G in Figure 12-2.

Discussion: The trend in recent years for converting apartment buildings into condominiums has resulted in the enactment of condominium conversion ordinances by local jurisdictions. These ordinances are aimed at protecting the buyer and the locality from the effects of the conversion.

The buyer is purchasing a unit in a building that was built in the past and, therefore, may have unknown defects. The conversion ordinance usually requires that the defects be divulged in public record and be corrected. The ordinance can require that some lower-cost housing, additional parking and so forth, also be provided.

At no time can the conversion ordinance replace or nullify the application of the prior adopted local codes and ordinances of the locality or state. These prior codes and ordinances include the UBC, UHC, Appendix and other enacted regulations. The condominium conversion ordinance is simply *another* requirement to be met *in addition to* all the other requirements.

Illustrative Example

The following simplified example is a composite of conditions in several condominium complexes. The author's purpose is to demonstrate the sort of misinterpretations and misrepresentations that can occur due to faulty understanding of the code intent and the other legal documents that effect a building over its life.

Given: 1. The condominium conversion occurs in 1975 and involves a group of three-story Type V-one hour apartment buildings with Group R, Division 1 Occupancies designed and built between 1963 and 1965.

2. The buildings were originally constructed in a jurisdiction that had the 1961 UBC in effect.

3. In 1968, the state in which these buildings are located adopted the 1967 UBC and the Uniform Housing Code. The

UBC was declared to be the minimum code in effect in that state.

4. In 1969, with the adoption of the 1967 UBC, the Appendix provisions of Chapter 13 of that edition were also adopted. That Appendix Chapter is virtually identical to Chapter 1, Division 1 of the 1988 UBC Appendix.
5. In 1972 the locality adopted a condominium conversion ordinance stipulating that the minimum requirement to be met was the Appendix provision of the local building code.
6. Alterations had been done in 1967 and 1970.
7. The building areas exceed the allowables in the code in effect at the time of original construction and require area separation walls (ASWs). The buildings have exit stairways that exit through garages at the ground level of the building.
8. Investigations disclose that the ASWs were not constructed correctly and the buildings are not one-hour throughout. The required exits are not provided, the exit paths are not properly protected and other violations of the code in effect at the time of original construction exist.

From the details provided for this example, the following are the minimum requirements mandated by the original construction, the subsequent alterations, the state law and the condominium ordinance: (The dates of effective ordinances and the work done on this particular building have been superimposed on Figure 12-1 and are shown on Figure 12-4.)

Evaluation:

Minimum building code: the 1961 UBC, which was the code in effect at the time of original construction.

Alterations should have complied with the edition in effect in 1967 and 1970. Because the state adopted the 1967 UBC in 1968, that would have been minimum code in effect in 1970 for the locality as well.

The Appendix provisions of the 1967 UBC and the provisions of the 1967 UHC are less restrictive than the 1961 UBC requirements. Therefore, *they do not take precedence over the 1961 UBC as the minimum code requirements.*

The requirement invoking of the Appendix in the condominium

Where state law applies in the locality as in California, the chart representing the state laws versus time should be superimposed on the localities chart of ordinance adoption to determine the total legislation applicable to a particular existing building. See Figures 12-1 and 12-2.

The state regulations establish minimum standards for new construction and alterations. The Tenement House Act and Housing laws, the Uniform Housing Code (UHC) and Title 24 (State Building Code) all contain provisions that affect existing buildings and are retrocative; i.e., those provisions are mandatory for all existing buildings as a minimum requirement.

FIGURE 12-3 STATE HOUSING LAW (CALIFORNIA) TIME HISTORY AND APPLICATION TO EXISTING BUILDING

BUILDING HISTORY

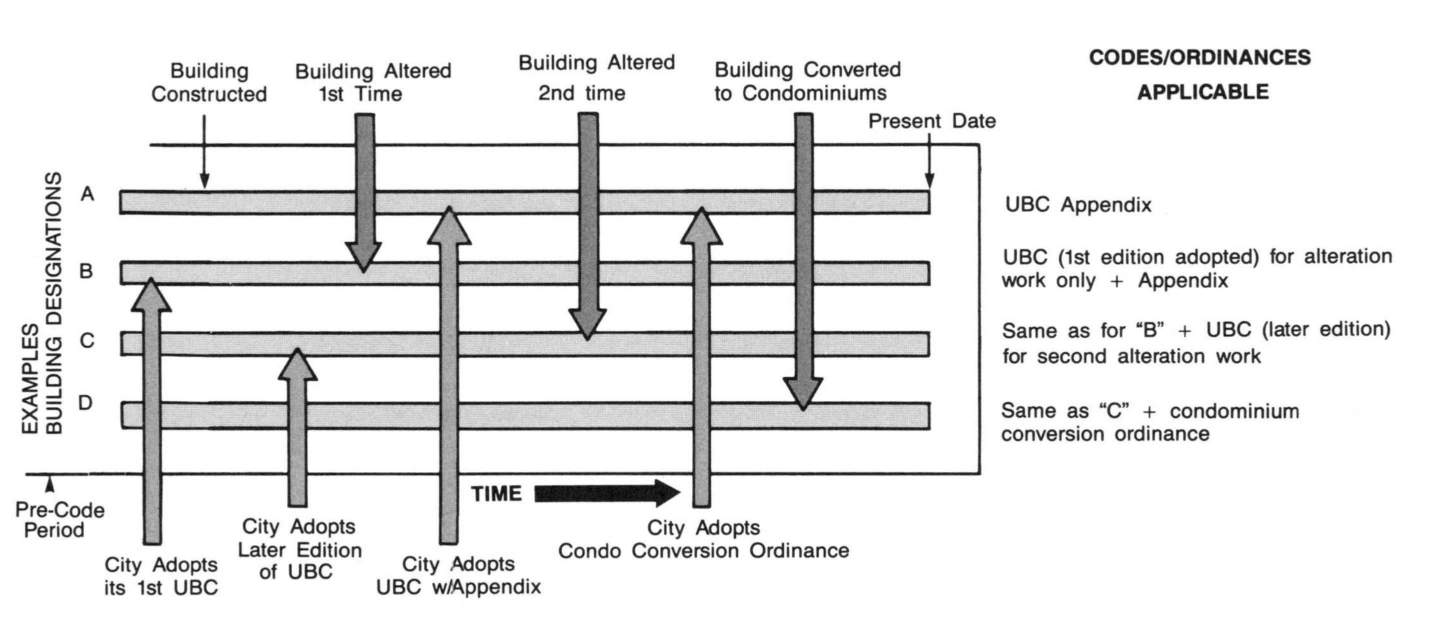
Building Constructed
Building Altered 1st Time
Building Altered 2nd time
Building Converted to Condominiums
Present Date
EXAMPLES BUILDING DESIGNATIONS
A
B
C
D
Pre-Code Period
City Adopts its 1st UBC
City Adopts Later Edition of UBC
City Adopts UBC w/Appendix
TIME
City Adopts Condo Conversion Ordinance
LOCAL ORDINANCES IN EFFECT
CODES/ORDINANCES APPLICABLE
UBC Appendix
UBC (1st edition adopted) for alteration work only + Appendix
Same as for "B" + UBC (later edition) for second alteration work
Same as "C" + condominium conversion ordinance

Minimum building code: The 1961 UBC which was the code in effect at the time of the original construction.

Alterations should have complied with the edition in effect in 1967 and 1970. Since the state had adopted the 1967 UBC in 1968, that would have been the minimum code in effect in 1970 for the locality as well.

The Appendix provisions of the 1967 UBC are less restrictive than the 1961 UBC requirements, therefore the Appendix does not take precedence over the 1961 UBC as the minimum code requirements.

The condominium conversion ordinance invoking the Appendix does not replace the prime criterion. i.e.:

1. The building must conform to the minimim requirements of the code in effect at the time of the original construction.
2. The subsequent alterations must be in compliance with the UBC editions under which that work was done.
3. Any retroactive state requirements are superimposed on the earlier codes. Local conversion ordinance cannot supercede these state requirements or the earlier codes.

FIGURE 12-4 EXAMPLE OF APPLICATION OF CODE/ORDINANCE TIME HISTORY TO A SPECIFIC BUILDING

BUILDING HISTORY

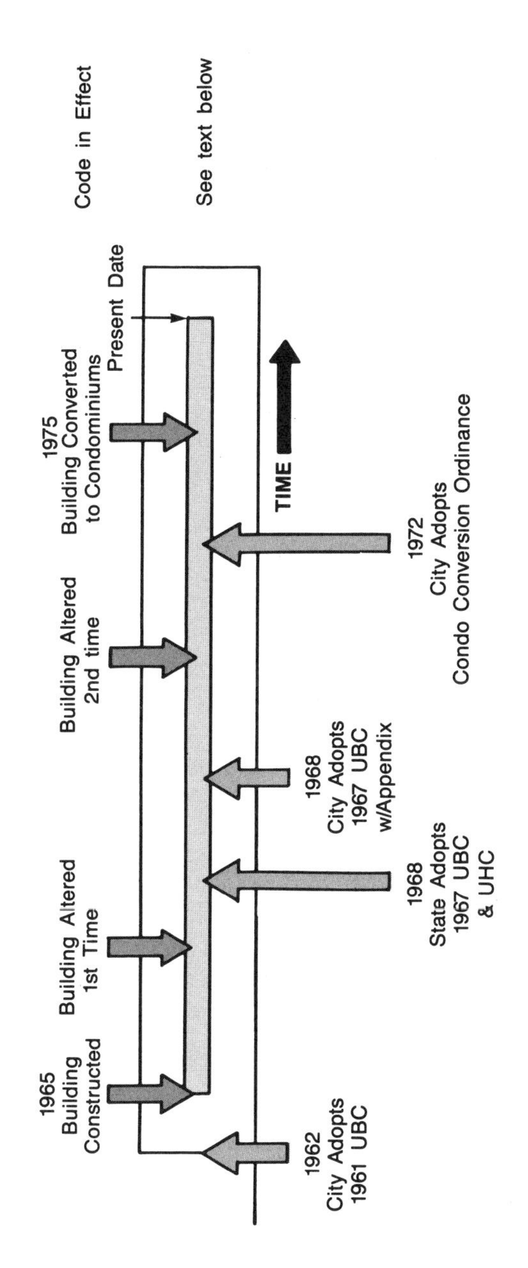
1965
Building
Constructed
Building Altered
1st Time
Building Altered
2nd time
1975
Building Converted
to Condominiums
Present Date
Code in Effect
See text below
TIME
1962
City Adopts
1961 UBC
1968
State Adopts
1967 UBC
& UHC
1968
City Adopts
1967 UBC
w/Appendix
1972
City Adopts
Condo Conversion Ordinance
LOCAL ORDINANCES IN EFFECT

conversion ordinance does not replace the prime criterion; i.e., the building must conform to the minimum requirements of the code in effect at the time of the original construction.

Conclusion:

Unfortunately, given the above circumstances and findings, the locality invoked only the Appendix requirements of the 1967 UBC as part of the condominium conversion considerations. This was done obviously through ignorance of the application of the codes as herein discussed.

The enforcement officials participated in that decision and did not point out that the 1961 UBC should have been the minimum standard applied. The developer who made the conversion came off very well indeed; but occupants of the buildings are denied the minimum safety to which they were entitled.

APPENDIX A1
TYPICAL PERMIT PROCESS

The following description of the permit process is provided for illustration only. It does not represent an actual permit process in any particular city or section of the country and does not define how a jurisdiction should review building permits. The intent of Appendix A-1 is to illustrate:

- the various steps involved in such a process,
- the reason for each step,
- the degree of detail required for a proper review,
- the interaction of the several jurisdictional agencies on a project.

Readers should note that although their local jurisdiction may have a more or less sophisticated process, the essential elements thereof are generally similar.

For this example assume that there exists an industrial park or zone in which a company has some facilities. The company intends to construct a new H-6 facility in a corner of their property.

PRE-PERMIT APPLICATION PHASE

At this stage the facility's general size, schematic layout and building type are known, and the questions of code impact need to be determined before detailed drawings are begun.

A meeting should be scheduled with the planning department for its review of the zoning and planning code provisions including parking, truck loading and traffic patterns.

A separate meeting should be scheduled with the building inspection and fire departments to review the building and fire code general requirements. Since only schematic drawings are available at this time, the items to be discussed will be related to:

- type of construction,
- area of each occupancy,
- height of the building,

- the different occupancies in the building
- the size of overall building,
- the general exit provisions.

As we emphasized in Article 1, all decisions made at these meetings should be confirmed with the jurisdiction to establish mutual concurrence and thus minimize misunderstandings.

There may be several such meetings with the local departments as the plans are refined and completed.

FILING THE BUILDING PERMIT APPLICATION

The jurisdiction will have a building permit application form that must be completed when filing for the permit. This application requires the following minimal information:

1. The address of the proposed building or other identification of location.
2. The names of the owner, contractor and designer.
3. The type of building construction to be used, the floor area of each story and the gross floor area of the building, and the number of stories proposed.
4. The proposed occupancies, by classification, in the building.

Other information may be required, such as sewer size and location, small scale site plan, and location of streets.

The permit application usually comes with two copies. Two sets of drawings and specifications are to be filed with it. At this time, a plan check fee will have to be paid. It is based on the estimated cost of the building as determined by the locality, using standard costs for the type of construction, occupancy, number of stories and various add-ons, such as air conditioning, elevators, etc.

Some jurisdictions also plan check electrical, mechanical and plumbing drawings and require, for these checks, additional fees and possibly additional sets of drawings.

PROCESSING THE PERMIT APPLICATION.

The local jurisdiction's internal review of the permit application usually involves the following minimal steps:

1. The first review checks for conformance with the planning and zoning code. This review could reveal the need for special variances where master plan changes may have imposed new criteria that were not in effect at the time the site was originally obtained.
2. The next review is usually made by the building inspection agency to check for compliance with the building and other codes under its jurisdiction. In some localities the fire service review may be included within the offices of the building department. However, in most jurisdictions the fire review is made as a separate step.
   In this review it is not unusual for additional information or clarifications to be requested by the checker. Many jurisdictions use a plan review check list and will not contact the permit applicant until the completion of the review, at which point, the check list and noted deficiencies are furnished. In some instances, the plan checker will go over the list and discuss the findings.
   The purpose of the check and the deficiencies list is to bring the design documents into code compliance. Any differences in agreement or understanding should be presented, in a meeting, to the person responsible for the checking operation. The meeting's decisions should be documented and confirmed to establish the grounds for either changes in the drawings or possible appeal.
3. The fire department review usually follows that of the building department. A similar procedure should be adhered to with regard to their checker's comments. In some jurisdictions the comments of all the locality's agencies will be accumulated and incorporated into a master list of deficiencies. The designer should carefully evaluate the several concerns shown on that list. Contact is recommended with the various agency checkers whose conclusions differ from those of the designer and from whom clarifications are needed.
4. In many jurisdictions, depending on local and state laws, there may be review of the application by:
   a) An environmental agency responsible for water, sewer, and/or air pollution control.
   b) The health department, which may review the drawings if there is to be a cafeteria in the building.

c) The department of public works or a similar agency charged with the traffic controls, to determine the acceptability of the driveway entrances and exits.
d) Other agencies, or an agency within one previously discussed, which may need to review:
- handicapped access,
- energy conservation,
- sound control,
- hazardous waste disposal,
- security provisions,
- architectural building design,
- landscaping,
- historical building or district requirements.

Once the first review has been completed, it is the responsibility of the submitter to revise the drawings or to otherwise indicate how the deficiencies are to be corrected or eliminated. A revised set of documents should be submitted to the jurisdiction. The review process to validate the resolution of the cited deficiencies will then be a quicker repeat of the original review.

ISSUANCE OF THE BUILDING PERMIT

When a reviewing agency is satisfied that its requirements and codes have been met, a representative of that agency will sign and approve the application. When all required approvals are on the application, the applicant is notified that the permit is ready for issuance.

The issuance of the permit occurs after the various fees levied by the locality are paid. Included may be:

- the building permit fee (to cover the field inspection of the construction),
- the sewer and water connection fees,
- a fee to cut the curb for the driveways, and others.

Some localities require that the plumbing and electrical permits be obtained at the same time as the building permit.

The building permit will be issued and provided to the applicant along with one copy of the approved application, one set of the approved plans and other documents submitted with the application. These documents are of extreme value and importance. Every effort should be made to provide store them safely and, at the completion of the construction, to file them together with a complete record of all correspondence and other communication between the designer and the local agencies. These documents are permanent records of value.

SUMMARY

This outline of the permit process also applies to alterations and additions to existing facilities although the detail and time involved in the review will vary considerably depending on the extent and complexity of the proposed work. However, the legal review requirements pertain regardless of whether the work is new construction or an alteration of an existing facility.

The reader is urged to become familiar with:

- the local jurisdiction's requirements and procedures,
- appeals boards,
- departmental structure of the review agencies,
- other agencies at a regional or state level concerned with proposed construction in that locality.

The responsibility for obtaining such knowledge and for meeting the several agencies; requirements rests with the applicant. Few jurisdictions have the time or staff to provide assistance in guiding the designer through the bureaucratic maze. A little time spent in learning the twists and turns of the permit process in a jurisdiction will be time well spent.

APPENDIX A2
CODE DEVELOPMENT PROCESS

Appendix A-2 discusses the code development process of ICBO for the Uniform Building Code. A similar process is used for the Uniform Fire Code, the Uniform Mechanical Code and the other codes under ICBO's direct or joint jurisdiction. The other model codes, the Basic Building Code and the Southern Standard Building Code have comparable procedures, but ones with different time frames, committees and final adoptive procedures. These codes will not be covered in this Guide.

The various steps in the code development process are:

1. Submission of a proposed code change.
2. Publication of the proposed change and referral to the appropriate code development committee.
3. Open hearing of the proposed code change by the particular code development committee (there are six such committees).
4. Publication of the committee report of action on the proposed code change.
5. Challenges to the committee actions for consideration at the Annual Business Meeting.
6. Action by the membership on the proposed code change challenge.
7. If the proposed change has been voted for "Approval", its publication in the next year's Accumulative Supplement and in the next edition of the UBC.

The details of the above simplified version of the process follow:

1. SUBMISSION OF A PROPOSED CODE CHANGE.

The cut-off date for submitting code changes to ICBO is August 15. For code changes that were carried over from the ABM as a result of Further Study action by the membership, the deadline for submittal of changes to the originally considered code change is around the first week of October.

The reader should check with ICBO for further information on the code change process.

The cut-off date permits sufficient time for publication of the proposed change in the ICBO's bimonthly magazine so that the membership of the conference may read of the upcoming code development hearing on the matter and learn which code development committee will conduct the hearing. The code change should to be forwarded to ICBO at its Whittier, California office.

A proposed code change can be initiated by anyone. The person need not be a member of the conference. The format of the code change must match that of the UBC. The work of preparing the text for the change rests with the proponent. ICBO staff cannot take a general idea from a proponent and put it into code format.

The proposed change should refer to the section of the UBC it affects, and indicate any new, revised or deleted text. The proponent must provide a "Reason" for the proposed change. Any other portions of the code that may be affected by the proposed change should be identified.

2. PUBLICATION OF THE PROPOSED CODE CHANGE AND REFERRAL TO THE APPROPRIATE CODE DEVELOPMENT COMMITTEE.

The proposed code change will be published together with all other changes in the November/December issues of Building Standards Monthly, the ICBO magazine.

Published along with the proposed change will be the "Reason" submitted with it and the code development committee to which it has been referred.

3. HEARING OF THE PROPOSED CODE CHANGE BY THE APPROPRIATE CODE CHANGE COMMITTEE.

There is one hearing session in the latter part of January or in early February of every year by each of the code development committees. An individual committee's session can run from one to four days depending on the workload of the committee. Each committee deals with one subject, such as "Fire and Life Safety," "General Design" or "Seismic Design."

The committees are composed of building officials elected by the general membership and representing the three regions of the code membership: the southern, central and northern segments of the country. Some committees, such as the "Fire and Life Safety Committee", have one member who is not a building official. The Fire and Life Safety Committee has a representative of the Western Fire Chiefs Association, an organization which is responsible for the Uniform Fire Code. We shall hereafter discuss only this particular code development committee since it has primary responsibility for Chapters 5 through 22, 33, 42 and 43. We will assume the proposed change involves one of these chapters of the code.

At the hearing (the agenda of which has been sent to all interested parties), the various code changes are heard in the order of their submission and their relative location in the code sequence. Present at the meeting are "Associate Members" of the committee who are members of the conference but not voting building officials. The associate members are industry representatives, consultants and others who have an interest in the code. A member or associate member may suggest a motion on the proposed change.

The procedures are conducted under Robert's Rules of Order. The proponent, the first speaker on the matter, proposes some course of action on the proposed change so that the discussion of its merits can then proceed.

There are several possible actions that can be taken by the committee:

- Approval
- Approval as Revised
- Disapproval
- Further Study
- Further Study as Revised

If the proposal is "Disapproved," the committee action is complete and the matter can only be reconsidered through a challenge to that decision and taken to the floor of the ABM for vote by the membership. This procedure will be discussed later.

The committee indicated at its January 1985 meeting that it desires to resolve all matters at each meeting and not to continue to "Further Study" most items that are not ready for "Approval." The committee will vote "Further Study" for those items it deems important and on which there is an ICBO chapter willing to work with the proponent and other interested parties. All other items that are not "Approved" or "Approved as Revised" can be revised to resolve the concerns expressed at the hearing and resubmitted in time for the meeting next year.

The hearing provides the opportunity for anyone to speak on the matter, pro or con. The committee and the ICBO staff may ask questions or partake in the deliberations as well. The proponent may respond to questions or opposition to the proposed change, suggest revisions to the text or otherwise react to the deliberations. Anyone may propose revisions to the code change,

The committee will finally close the debate and vote on the motion(s). If successful, that vote will be the final action of the committee. If the vote is not successful, another motion will have to be made. For example: if the first motion is for "Approval" and it fails, a subsequent motion for "Further Study" can be proposed. There are seven members on the committee and a majority vote is needed for an action to be finalized.

As previously indicated, if the matter is held for "Further Study," the committee requires it to be taken on by one of the ICBO Chapters. They also insist on receiving a report, at least six weeks prior to their next meeting, on the status of that study and a copy of the revised submittal. The "Further Study" is intended to provide an opportunity for interested parties to meet, resolve differences and revise the code change so that it may gain acceptance by the committee. Neither the ICBO staff nor the committee provides the "Further Study." The proponent and the volunteer Chapter, together with other interested parties must do the required work.

The revised text, for consideration by the committee, must be sent to the committee before its next scheduled hearing. There is no limit to the number of times that a matter can be carried on the agenda of a committee as long as there is noticeable progress being made with the change.

4. PUBLICATION OF THE COMMITTEE ACTION ON THE PROPOSED CODE CHANGE

All actions of the committee are published in Building Standards Monthly in an April 15 monograph. The recommended action voted on by the committee, together with the reason for their action, is also published. If the text of the change has been revised, the revised text is published.

5. CHALLENGES TO THE COMMITTEE REPORTED ACTION FOR CONSIDERATION AT THE ANNUAL BUSINESS MEETING.

The recommended action by the code development committee, if for "Approval," "Approval as Revised" or "Disapproval," will constitute the final action of the conference on the matter unless that action is "challenged" during the challenge period preceding the Annual Business Meeting. The challenge period lasts from the publication of the April 15 issue of BSM until June 1. The June 1st deadline permits the publication of the challenges by around the August 1st issue of BSM and makes those interested in the particular code change aware of the substance of the challenge that will be discussed on the floor of the ABM.

A recommended action of the committee that is not challenged is automatically endorsed as the conference action.

A challenge, when filed, must identify the change in question and indicate the proposed action suggested by the challenger. The reason for the challenge must accompany the challenge. Only that portion of a change that is challenged can be discussed on the floor of the annual meeting. There may be several challenges to a single code change recommendation, each of which may propose different resolutions. These will be considered at the ABM by the membership.

6. ACTION BY THE MEMBERSHIP ON THE PROPOSED CODE CHANGE.

As previously stated, those actions of the code development committees that are not challenged represent the final action that year on the changes. Those that are challenged are placed on the agenda of the code change sessions of the Annual Business Meeting. These meetings are usually held in mid-September. They are heard according to their sequence in the code, i.e. in numerical section order.

Only Class A members (building officials) can vote at the Annual Business Meeting, although motions can be proposed by any participant in the deliberations, voting or not.

The challengers speak first on each change; the proponent and others then have the opportunity to respond or otherwise partake in the deliberations. Since many items are on the agenda, time constraints are imposed to permit all of them to be heard.

The recommendation of the code development committee, in response to the challenge. is voted on by the membership. Passage of the recommendation requires different majorities for each proposed action on a matter. The following are the several possible voting percentage requirements dependent on the original recommendation of the committee and the proposed action on the floor.

Recommendation of the Development Committee	Proposed ABM Action	Passage Vote
APPROVAL	Approval	Majority
	Approval as Revised	3/4*
	Disapproval	Majority
	Further Study	Majority
APPROVAL AS REVISED	Approval as Revised	Majority
	Approval as Further Revised	3/4*
	Disapproval	Majority
	Further Study	Majority
DISAPPROVAL	Approval	3/4
	Approval as Revised	3/4
	Further Study	Majority
	Disapproval	Majority
FURTHER STUDY	Approval	3/4
	Approval as Revised	3/4
	Disapproval	Majority
	Further Study	Majority

*The three-fourths vote is required only for an amendment which revises the Code Development Committee's recommendation. If an amendment is approved by a three-fourths vote, only a simple majority is necessary to approve the Code Development Committee's recommendation as revised on the floor of the meeting.

7. PUBLICATION OF RESULTS.

The results of the ABM are published in the Accumulated Supplement issued early the following year. If the new edition of the UBC is scheduled that year, the code changes that were approved during the preceding three years are included in the new edition.

A jurisdiction can either adopt the changes from the supplements or wait until the new code is published. In most jurisdictions, a considerable amount of time passes between the availability of the new UBC and the local adoption.

This is due to:

- the necessary local review to be made of the impact of the changes,
- the concerns that may be generated by local individuals and groups,
- the general inertia related to the code adoption process.

Where there are concerned individuals or groups, or where the enforcement agencies recognize the new code as providing needed improvements in the enforcement process, the actions can be speeded up.

SUMMARY

The process described hereinbefore provides ample time for full deliberations and consideration. The procedures are democratically run with all sides to an issue afforded time to debate. It takes time to effect a change; it is rare when such is accomplished within two years from the proposal's initiation to the ABM acceptance. The proponent may desire more expeditious action. Knowing the process involved and actively participating in all the proceedings as well as pressing forward with the "Further Study" activities will serve both the proponent's and the ICBO's interest.

APPENDIX A3
SAMPLE LETTER SUMMING UP MEETING WITH BUILDING OFFICIAL

On the next page is a sample of the type of confirmation letter that should be sent to the local building official after each plan check meeting in which the elements of a project were discussed.

In the sample letter, not only are the main items covered, but the sense of the discussion regarding the question of the setback measurement for the H-2 and H-3 Occupancies per Table No. 5-A is covered as well. Mentioning this discussion item in the letter will establish the time when this matter was brought up and will indicate that, although consideration was given to a different interpretation, the measurement specifically agreed to was from the perimeter walls of the H-2 and H-3 areas. The inclusion of the matter in this confirmation letter should preclude it from being raised as a "new" problem after production drawings are submitted for permit.

This record of the meeting should include as much information as possible to avoid raising issues later and to provide a record of the decision-making process. Copies of the letter should go to all participants at the meeting, even though the final decision rests with the building and fire officials. These courtesy copies will allow others to comment to the officials and to speed up the response.

John J. Jones, Building Official
City of Anywhere
123 Main Street
Anywhere, Any State 00000

Re: Meeting on May 7, 199?
New Building w/H-6 Occupancy
Confirmation of Discussion Items

Dear Mr. Jones:

The purpose of this letter is to confirm the discussion at the meeting held in your office on May 7, 1991 regarding the proposed new building in the Blank Industrial Park, containing the Group H Division 6 occupancy. At that meeting the following persons were also present: Mr. Smith, your plan checker; Fire Marshal Flamb; and Mr. Trace of my office.

We presented the preliminary site plan showing:

- the relationship of the building to the property lines,
- the preliminary arrangement of the different occupancies in the building and
- the type of construction we propose to use.

I am enclosing a copy of these documents for your files.

The 1991 UBC pertains to this project.

We are proposing to use Type III One-Hour construction for the one-story building. The floor area will be 100,000 square feet. The building will be fully sprinklered. The main use will be H-6, although there will also be small areas of A-3, B-2, H-2 and H-3 in the building. The H-2 and H-3 Occupancies exceed 1,500 square feet in area.

You indicated that the proposed construction type and siting was acceptable for the one-story building, with the exception of the setback requirement for the H-2 and 3 Occupancies, which are required to be not less than 30 feet from adjacent property lines per Table No. 5-A. To meet this requirement you will note that we have relocated the building to provide the 30-foot setback from both exterior walls of the H-2 and H-3 areas.

Fire Marshal Flamb was concerned with the interpretation of Table No. 5-A for the H-2 and H-3 Occupancies and whether the entire building should have the 30-foot setback. It was your opinion that the provisions of Table No. 5-A are met by the measurement of the required setback distances from the perimeter walls of the H-2 and H-3 areas. This was our position as well and your concurrence is appreciated.

We will provide the occupancy separations between the several occupancies as required in Table No. 5-B.

You indicated that, in the event we decide to construct a two-story structure with these same occupancies, at least one area separation wall must be provided to bring the areas within the code allowables. We will consider this matter further and, if the two story concept is to be used, will return to discuss this item. In the meantime we will proceed with the schematic drawings for the interior arrangement of the occupancies, exitways and service corridors. We will contact your office to arrange another meeting when we have completed this preliminary interior design to be sure we are in code compliance before we commence production drawings.

Please confirm in writing this summary of the May 7th discussions. In the event you find that your understanding of the conclusions differ, please advise me as to the particulars. Your earliest response will assist me in moving forward with this project.

Very truly yours,

John Doe

Attachments: 3
cc: Fire Marshall Flamb
Plan Checker Smith

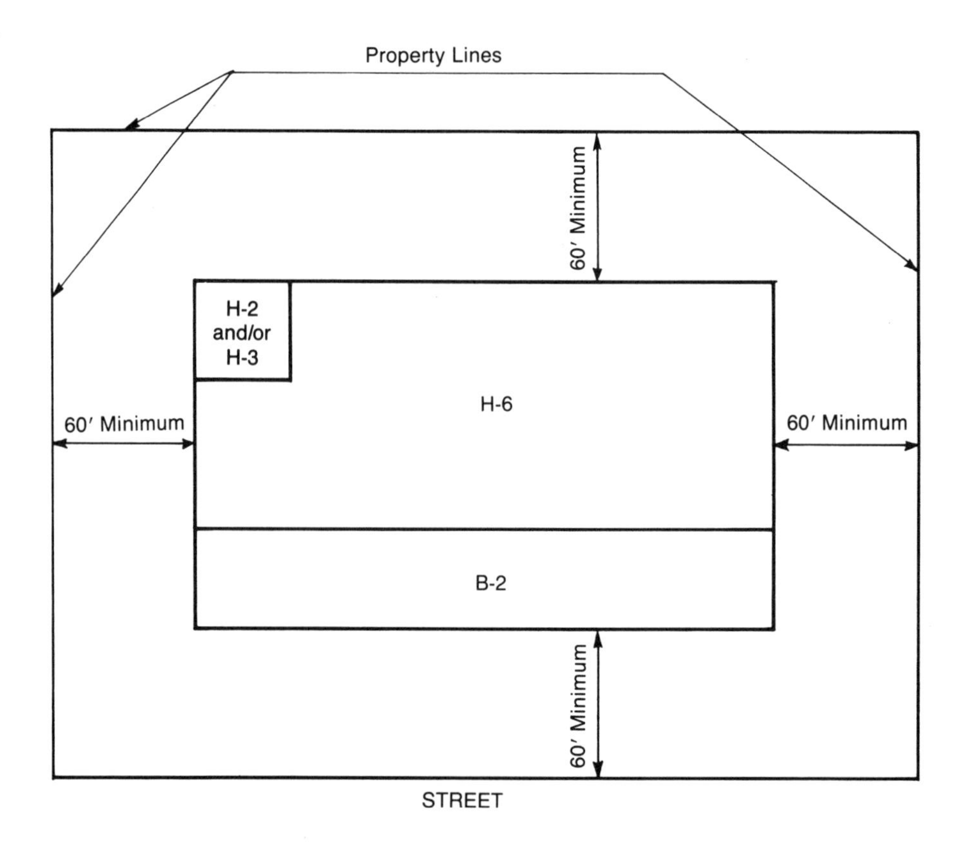

An H-2 or H-3 building or a mixed occupancy building (as shown) with H-2 or H-3 as one of the occupancies is required to be 30 feet from all property lines and streets or public ways, when the area of the H-2 or H-3 exceeds 1,500 square feet.

The method for measuring the setback as shown above assumes that the building cannot be closer than 30 feet to these lines. In the author's opinion, the measurements for the H-2 and H-3 Occupancies to the property line should be made from the boundary lines of these H Occupancies and not from the exterior walls of the overall building. See Figure A3-2.

REFERENCE: SECTION 505 (c)

FIGURE A3-1 SITE REQUIREMENT—GROUP H DIV. 2 OCCUPANCY

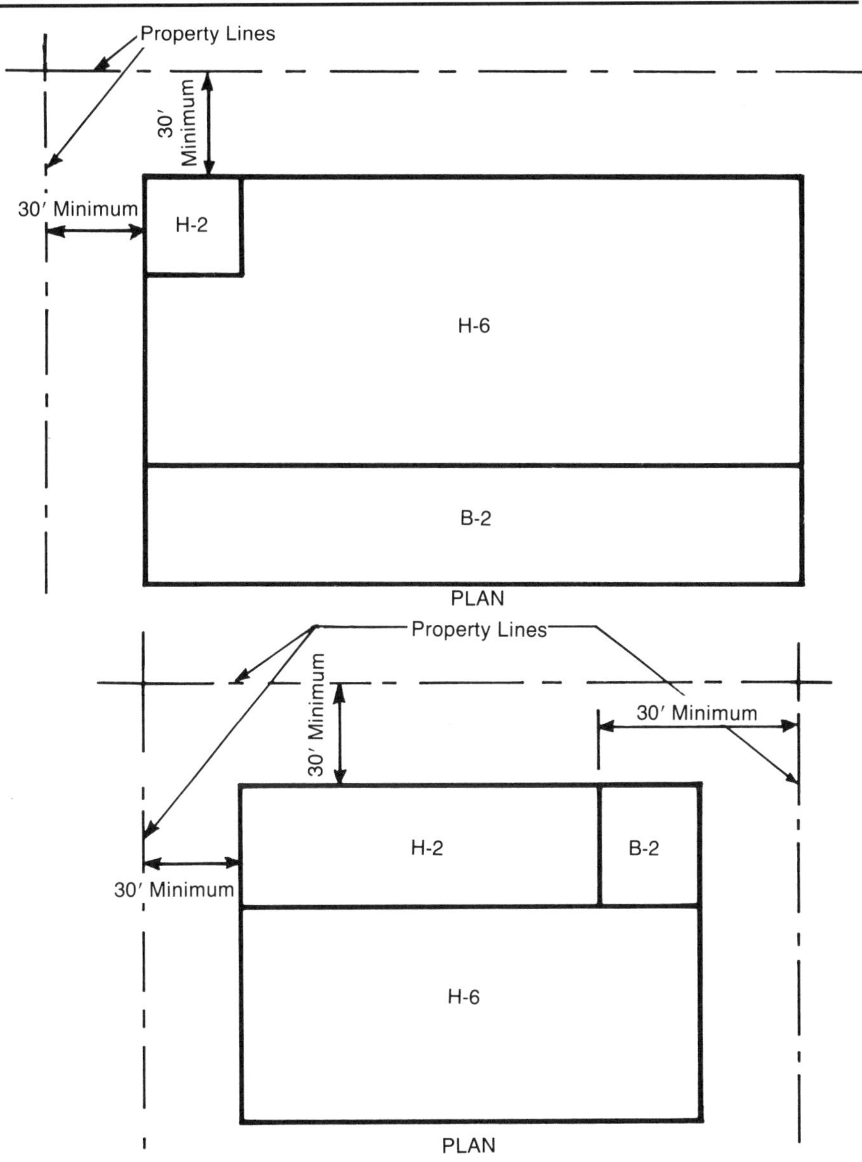

An H-2 or H-3 Occupancy building or a mixed occupancy building containing an H-2 or H-3 occupancy (as shown) requires that all walls of the H-2 or H-3 Occupancy be at least 30 feet from property lines, streets and public ways when the area of the H-2 or H-3 Occupancy exceeds 1,500 square feet.

The H and B-2 Occupancy provisions are based on the Table No. 5-A and the -03 Sections of Chapters 18-21.

REFERENCE: SECTION 503 AND 903, TABLE NO. 5-A

FIGURE A3-2 SITE REQUIREMENT—GROUP H DIV. 3 AND DIV. 6 OCCUPANCIES

APPENDIX A-4
COMMON DESIGNER OMISSIONS OR INADEQUACIES IN DESIGNS

The author has been requested to provide a checklist of the areas often overlooked or improperly understood by designers. Over the years these areas have formed a common thread in many litigation cases.

The purpose of such a checklist is to assist the designer and the enforcement official by providing a review source of key items for use on a job-by-job basis and a cross-reference to the detailed discussion within this Guide. If one of the subjects is not discussed elsewhere in this Guide, it will be discussed in this Appendix.

Each of the listed items below will be discussed and referenced to the appropriate Article in this Guide.

1. Measurement of Floor Area
2. Area Separation Walls
   a. Inadequate details for project conditions
   b. Improper fire-rating determination
   c. Interchanging terminology with "party walls"
   d. Improper termination at roof in lieu of parapet
3. Complex Designations of Wall/Ceiling Construction
4. Multiple Lengths of Fasteners in Multiple Layer Fire-Rated Assemblies
5. Protection of Openings Below and Adjacent to Exterior Exit Stairways

1. Measurement of Floor Area. See Article 4.

Areas to be included in the floor area computation include covered balconies, decks, entry landings and stairways. Mechanical areas, shafts and similar nonhabitable spaces are also to be included.

2. Area Separation Walls (ASW). See Article 5.

a. Inadequate details for project conditions

This subject includes the innumerable variations that a particular project may present to the designer. When deciding to use an ASW, it is important for the designer to understand exactly how the project's unique conditions may affect the construction and extent of the ASW. The designer must not rely on the plan check to find deficiencies that may exist.

b. Improper fire-rating determination

The minimum fire rating of an ASW per Section 505 (e) is two hours, not one hour.

c. Interchanging terminology with "party walls"

Whenever terms are used without careful discrimination, confusion and inappropriate design may occur. Frequently tenant party walls are referred to instead of either a true property line wall or an area separation wall. Tenant separation walls are also confused with both property line and area separation walls. The designer must understand the specific code terminology and whenever possible use that terminology on the contract documents.

Tenant separation walls, the new dwelling unit separation or ASWs will be within a building. It is very unlikely that there would be a property line wall. Regardless of how condominium units may have been sold, property line walls would not be within a building.

d. Improper termination at roof in lieu of parapet

The provisions of Section 505 (c)3 must be followed whenever the ASW will not have a parapet. The designer must not go by local tradition of construction, particularly in this regard. In most instances, local tradition may be no more than the continuation of misinterpretations by designers and contractors.

A good example of this misguided approach is the use of sheetmetal over the roof sheathing or the placement of wallboard directly under the roof sheathing in lieu of the one-hour roof-ceiling assembly required by the code.

3. Complex Designations of Wall/Ceiling Construction.
See Article 8.

The designer's concern with meeting the minimum code requirements can result in the contract documents generating an almost assured field deficiency. In some projects, the wallboard required by the drawings, were:

- 1/2-inch regular gypsum wallboard for walls and ceiling coverage of nonrated construction
- 1/2-inch Type C gypsum wallboard for the ceiling coverage within five feet of an ASW to provide that portion of a one-hour roof-ceiling assembly.
- 5/8-inch Type X gypsum wallboard for the ASW construction.

The designer should be aware that such complex requirements on a drawing do not reflect the field problems faced by the contractor in trying to carry them out. It is unrealistic to expect three types of wallboard either to be on hand or to be properly located and installed. To obtain the desired result, careful field observation by the designer's personnel is required.

Inevitably an error will occur in this situation. In one project, all surfaces were found to be covered by 1/2-inch regular wallboard including the two layers on the ASW.

4. Multiple Lengths of Fasteners in Multiple Layer Fire-Rated Assemblies

Frequently the designer cites, as part of the description of the minimum construction for multiple layer fire-rated assemblies, the description from the code or from an Evaluation Report. Such an assembly will usually describe two different lengths of fasteners. For example, a two-hour wall assembly would have two layers of 5/8-inch Type X gypsum wallboard on each side of a stud. The inner layer, per Item 69 of Table No. 43-B, is required to have 6d nails, and the outer layer, 8d nails. The longer, outer layer nails are required to assure that the wallboard is fastened to the studs and not just to the inner layer of wallboard.

If the outer layer was nailed with the shorter, inner layer nails, there would be only 3/4-inch penetration into the stud instead of the required

1 and 1/4-inch minimum required. Such inadequate embedment would cause the assembly to be disqualified as a two-hour wall; the wall would fail in less time due to the pullout of the outer layer nails shortly after the start of the fire test, as the wallboard undergoes dimensional changes.

In the construction of real buildings and not simply of test samples, a carpenter usually does not carry nails with minor differences in their in the work apron. If the carpenter has only one size nail—the size commonly to be used that day—it usually is the 6d nail, because most wallboard the carpenter installs is in a single layer application. The result, therefore, of having only one length of nail is that the second or outer layer of a two layer assembly may be fastened only with the 6d nails. Unfortunately, this occurs in many projects.

The author recommends that where a project has multiple layer fire-rated assemblies, the designer should specify only one nail length to be used for any installation, including single layer installations. That nail should be the larger of the two nails required for the multiple layer installation, i.e., the 8d nail in the example cited.

Furthermore, the designer should place emphasis on this change from the standard length nail either on the drawings or in the specifications. This will alert the contractor that special care need be taken for the wall installations.

5. Protection of Openings Below and Adjacent to Exterior Exit Stairways. See Article 7.

Included in the range of openings to be protected are the entry door, windows, vents, air inlets and exhausts and any other opening to the interior normally found near a stairway.

NOTES

TECHNICAL APPENDIX TA-1

Chapter 5 UBC
Mixed Occupancy Analysis and Rationale

This Technical Appendix is provided to aid in understanding the mixed occupancy provisions of Section 505 (c) for allowable floor area determination. The two criteria or rules contained in Section 505 (c) are:

1. The unity rule
2. The 10 percent rule

To facilitate the explanation of these mixed occupancy provisions the following examples will be used:

Building:
- Type II-N one story
- Sprinklered throughout
- 60' separations all around.

CASE A Occupancies	• Group B, Div. 1	100,000 sq.ft.
	• Group A, Div. 3	5,000 sq.ft.
	• Group H, Div. 3	3,000 sq.ft.
CASE B Occupancies	• Group B, Div. 1	65,000 sq.ft.
	• Group A, Div. 3	3,000 sq.ft.
	• Group H, Div. 3	2,000 sq.ft.
CASE C Occupancies	• Group B, Div. 1	45,000 sq.ft.
	• Group A, Div. 3	1,000 sq.ft.
	• Group H, Div. 3	4,000 sq.ft.

Several questions are usually raised by the mixed occupancy provisions. Some occur because of the presentation order of the code requirements; others occur because of the wording of the provisions.

The first requirement is stated in the second paragraph: the unity rule. Because the unity rule precedes the presentation of the other provisions, it represents the primary requirement for mixed occupancies.

The other rule together with its key stipulation is in the third paragraph: the 10 percent rule and the basic allowable area limitation. In the author's opinion, this third paragraph is really an exception to the unity rule in the second paragraph. For instance, the use of the 10 percent rule, limited only by the basic allowable area in Table No. 5-C, can result in minor use areas that will not satisfy the unity rule.

In the Case B example an illustration of this can be seen, because the aggregate minor use area is 5,000 sq.ft. This is less than 10 percent of the floor area of the building. If the unity rule is also applied, the following would be the calculations:

$$\frac{\overset{\text{B-2}}{65{,}000}}{12{,}000 \times 6} + \frac{\overset{\text{H-3}}{2{,}000}}{7{,}500 \times 2} + \frac{\overset{\text{A-3}}{3{,}000}}{9{,}100 \times 6} = .90 + .13 + .05 = 1.08 \text{ Not OK}$$

As the Group B, Division 2 area increases to near the maximum allowed by Table No. 5-C including the increases for sprinklers and separations, the allowable areas for the minor uses are substantially reduced. This would be contrary to the intent of the 10 percent rule, because that provision considers a small minor use as presenting no unusual hazard to the major use.

Finally, the code considers that when the minor uses are less than 10 percent of the floor area, the major use will determine the occupancy classification of that floor. This provision runs counter to the second paragraph, where the first sentence states that each portion of the building must conform to the occupancy requirements therein.

Thus, the conclusion reached by the author is that when the 10 percent rule and the basic allowable area stipulation are both satisfied the unity rule does not apply. This makes the second paragraph of Section 505 (c) an exception to the first paragraph. This determination is important to the designer and to the enforcement official.

Specific Questions of the Intent of the Provisions

Questions are raised that need to be addressed regarding the mixed occupancy provisions. For example:

a) Should the area increases permitted in Sections 506 (a) and 506

(c) apply to the basic allowable areas referred to in the third paragraph? Both the unity and 10 percent rules? Why?

b) Do both rules apply to each building situation?

c) How do the rules apply when the unlimited area permitted in Section 506 (b) is involved?

d) How are the allowable areas for an unlimited area building to be calculated when a mixed occupancy is involved?

e) How are the relative hazards assessed when the minor use is of a greater hazard than the major use?

The following discussion of the answers is provided both to resolve the questions and to stimulate debate, which possibly will lead to clarification of the mixed occupancy provisions presently in the code. Answers will be presented in the same order as the five questions were posed.

a) For the calculation of the 10 percent rule and the related stipulation, the Section 506 increases for separations and sprinklers are not to be added to the Table No. 5-C basic allowable areas. The intent of this code provision is to keep the minor uses to a small percentage of the total floor area.

If the Section 506 (a) and (c) increases were to be permitted for the calculation of the basic allowable area in the stipulation attendant to the 10 percent rule, that basic allowable area could then be as large as 54,600 sq.ft. for the Group A, Division 3 Occupancy, as in our CASE A example. This size is achieved by adding the sprinkler credits for a one-story building and the credit for four separations to the basic allowable area.

The area of the Group B, Division 2 Occupancy is 100,000 sq.ft. This large a "minor-use" basic allowable area would not be in keeping with the intent of the code regarding a minor use. Only the 9,100 sq.ft. basic allowable area in Table No. 5-C should be used.

If the Section 506 (b) provisions for unlimited area (infinite size) were allowed to be used for the major use in the calculation of the 10 percent rule, the minor areas would also be allowed to be "infinite" as well, because 10 percent of infinity is still infinity. This interpretation would be grossly in conflict with the intent of limiting the size of the minor uses. Using only the 10 percent rule is obviously inadequate in limiting the size of the minor use. Some absolute limit to the size of the minor use is needed. That limit is the basic allowable area stipulation based on Table No. 5-C.

The second paragraph with the unity rule does not refer to the basic allowable area, whereas the third paragraph does refer to basic allowable area when referring to allowable areas. Instead, the second paragraph refers to the total allowable area. The total allowable area includes the Table No. 5-C areas and the increases allowed by Section 506.

> In the author's opinion, for these reasons only the unity rule should be calculated based on the Table No. 5-C areas plus the applicable increases of Section 506.

b) Whether both the unity and 10 percent rules apply to all buildings involves the order of consideration of the code provisions, as discussed earlier. The 10 percent rule should always be checked first to determine whether it can be met.

If the 10 percent rule is applied and satisfied, the code requirements in the second paragraph of Section 505 (c) are met. With the basic allowable area also satisfied, it is the author's opinion that the unity rule need not be applied. As stated earlier, the third paragraph is considered by the author to be an exception to the second paragraph, which contains the unity rule. Therefore, the unity rule in the second paragraph should not be used in this case.

If, however, the 10 percent rule is not met, i.e., the sum of minor use areas exceeds 10 percent of that floor of the building, or if the area for the minor uses is greater than the basic allowable area permitted by Table No. 5-C, then the unity rule must be applied because the "exception" of the third paragraph does not apply.

The code does not provide the necessary guidance to lead to the order in which the second and third paragraphs are to be evaluated. Just as we found that it is necessary to avoid using the infinite area for the Group B, Division 2 Occupancy determination in applying the 10 percent rule, the order of consideration is an unstated criteria; that is, when the 10 percent rule is not met, the unity rule must apply.

For the CASE A example, the basic allowable areas from Table No. 5-C are:

Group A, Division 3 = 9,100 sq.ft.
Group H, Division 3 = 7,500 sq.ft.

Because the actual areas proposed for our CASE A example are less than these basic allowable areas, and because the 8,000 sq.ft. aggregate area of the two minor uses is less than 10 percent of the floor area of the building, the 10 percent rule is satisfied. Thus, the unity rule does not apply.

In summary, the 10 percent rule and the basic allowable area provision should always be applied as a first trial. If the 10 percent rule is also satisfied, there is no need to meet the unity rule. If the 10 percent rule is not satisfied, i.e., the aggregate areas of the minor uses exceed 10 percent of the floor area of the building, then the unity rule must be used and satisfied.

c) For the unlimited area building permitted by Section 506 (b) with a mixed occupancy (for example, the building described in CASE A of this discussion), it would not be reasonable to use only the infinite allowable area to determine whether the 10 percent rule is satisfied. As previously stated, 10 percent of infinity is still infinity and, thus, of no assistance in determining whether the 10 percent rule is met. In these buildings the controlling finite limitation is the basic allowable area provision in the third paragraph.

When there is more than one minor use or occupancy in an unlimited area building, it is not obvious how to determine whether the basic allowable areas are exceeded. It is not sufficient simply to take each such minor use and compare it to its Table No. 5-C basic allowable area. If this was done and there were several different minor uses, the aggregate of these minor uses would quickly mount up and not be a controlling factor.

In the author's opinion, the method of handling multiple minor uses in determining whether the aggregate exceeds the intent of the code for the basic allowable area limitation is similar to that of the unity rule calculation. If there was only one use involved, the basic allowable area and the actual allowable area permitted would be the same, or the ratio of the actual over the allowable would be unity.

Thus, for the evaluation of whether the minor use areas meet the basic allowable area intent of the code, where there is more than one minor use the sum of the ratios of the various actual floor areas for each use, divided by the basic allowable area for that use, cannot exceed one (1).

In CASE A example:

$$\underset{\text{A-3}}{\frac{5{,}000}{9{,}100}} + \underset{\text{H-3}}{\frac{3{,}000}{7{,}500}} = .55 + .4 = .95 < 1.0 \text{ OK}$$

Because the basic allowable area limitation is met, the 10 percent rule is satisfied and the unity rule does not apply.

d) In the application of the unity rule, the unlimited allowable area for the Group B, Division 2 Occupancy from Section 506 (b) is used. For the minor uses, the total allowable areas are used. The reason for using the Section 506 (b) provisions in the unity rule calculation only is as follows:

If the building contained only the B-2 Occupancy, the application of the Unity rule would be

$$\frac{\text{Actual Area (B-2)}}{\text{Total allowable area (B-2)}} =< 1.0$$

Per Section 506 (b), the total allowable area for the B-2 Occupancy may be infinite. That denominator is, therefore, unlimited or infinite; no matter what the numerator is, the equation will always be satisfied, even if the numerator was infinite.

If any other denominator was used, i.e., assuming Section 506 (b) was not allowed to apply as the denominator for the allowable area, then the numerator, which is permitted to be infinite by Section 506 (b), would result in a fraction greater than 1.0 and the unity rule would not be satisfied. The fraction would be:

$$\frac{\text{Infinity}}{\text{Any finite number}} = \text{Infinity} > 1.0 \quad \text{Not OK}$$

Therefore, the only logical denominator for the unity rule application to the major area where Section 506 (b) applies is infinity. Because the denominator of the ratio calculation is to be the total allowable area, each minor occupancy area is to be calculated with the allowable increases of Sections 506 (a) and 506 (c) added.

Thus, in the unlimited area building the unity equation (5-1) becomes:

$$\frac{a_1}{A_1} + \frac{a_2}{A_2} + \ldots \frac{a_n}{A_n} =< 1.0 \qquad (5.2)$$

Where: a_1 = Area of one use
a_2 = Area of a second use
a_n = Area of any other use
A_1 = Maximum allowable area of first use per Table No. 5-C and allowable increases
A_2 = Maximum allowable area of second use per Table No. 5-C or infinity if Section 506 (b) applies
A_n = Maximum allowable area of any other use per Table No. 5-C and allowable increases

For CASE A this becomes:

$$\frac{\text{Actual (A-3)}}{\text{Total Allowable (A-3)}} + \frac{\text{Actual (H-3)}}{\text{Total Allowable (H-3)}} + \frac{\text{Actual (B-2)}}{\text{Infinity (B-2)}} = <1.0$$

$$\frac{5{,}000}{9{,}100 \times 6} + \frac{3{,}000}{7{,}500 \times 2} + \frac{100{,}000}{\text{Infinity}} =< 1.0$$

$$.09 \qquad\qquad .20 \qquad\qquad 0 \qquad = .29 \text{ OK}$$

As has been shown, the control for CASE A is the 10 percent rule stipulation regarding basic allowable area limitation. The unity rule does not control and need not apply.

We can see this rule applies by examining this equation and the equation for determining the basic allowable areas criteria for multiple minor uses. They are identical in regard to the minor uses, with the exception of the added divisor in the denominator when the unity rule is calculated. In the unlimited area building, most occupancies will have increased allowable areas for the separations—in many uses the sprinkler increases as well. Thus, the denominators will have a multiplier of 2 or more times the basic allowable area from Table No. 5-C.

If the basic allowable area calculations and the 10 percent rule are satisfied, the unity rule need not be tested; it will undoubtedly also be satisfied.

NOTE: As shown in Figure TA1-1, if the other use is located on an exterior wall of the unlimited area building, the requirement of Section 506 (b) for the Group B, Division 2 Occupancy to have 60 foot separation all around is violated.

> In the author's opinion, an unlimited area building must meet the Section 506 (b) criteria as stated. There is no latitude on the part of the enforcement official to waive adherence with those criteria.

e) When a minor use is more hazardous than the major use, i.e., the relative hazard of an H-3 Occupancy exceeds that of the B-2, the question arises of whether that greater hazard affects the use of the two rules for mixed occupancies.

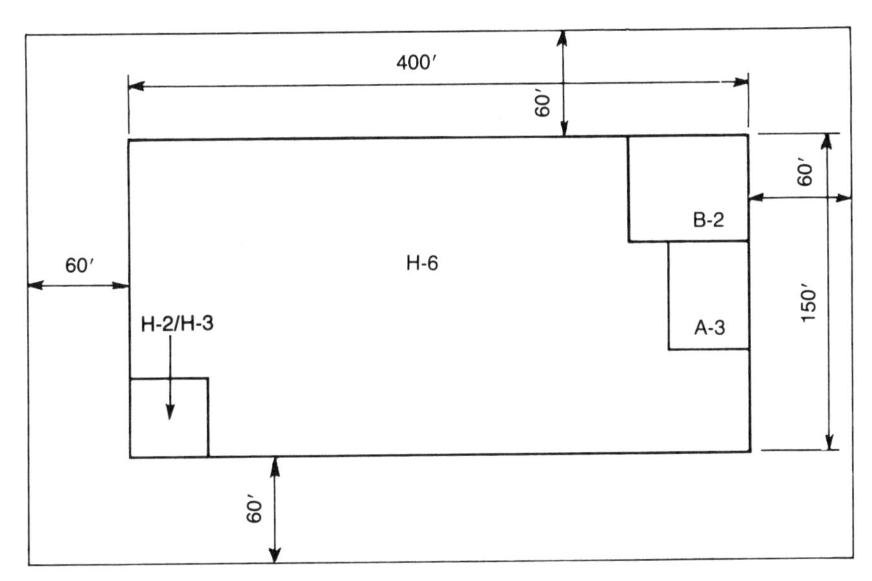

Given:
Type II 1-Hour, 2 Story Building – 60,000 s.f. overall
Fully Sprinklered; 60′ clear all around building (4 separations)

Group H-6 space	=	50,000 s.f.
Group H-2/H-3 space	=	1,500 s.f.
Group B-2 space	=	5,500 s.f.
Group A-3 space	=	3,000 s.f.
		60,000 s.f.

(Note: Arrangement of Occupancies within building shown schematically only.)

Allowable Areas

	Basic Allowable (Table No. 5-C)		Sprinkler Increase		Separation Increase*		Gross Allowable Area
H-6	18,000	×	2	×	2	=	72,000
H-2/H-3	5,600	×	-	×	2	=	11,200
B-2	18,000	×	2	×	2	=	72,000
A-3	13,500	×	2	×	2	=	54,000

*Separation increase for 60′ all around = (60 – 20) × 2.5% = 100%

Mixed Occupancy Calculation Per Sec. 503 (a)

$$\frac{\text{Actual Area}}{\text{Allowable Area}} \leq 1.0$$

$$\underset{\text{H-6}}{\frac{50{,}000}{72{,}000}} + \underset{\text{H-2/H-3}}{\frac{1{,}500}{11{,}200}} + \underset{\text{B-2}}{\frac{5{,}500}{72{,}000}} + \underset{\text{A-3}}{\frac{3{,}000}{54{,}000}} \leq 1.0$$

$$0.69 + 0.13 + 0.08 + 0.06 = 0.96 < 1.0 \quad \text{O.K.}$$

REFERENCE: SECTION 505 (c)

FIGURE TA1-1 MIXED OCCUPANCY EXAMPLE

As the higher-hazard actual areas increase in a building, the ratio for that occupancy's contribution to the basic allowable area evaluation increases as well. This will effectively limit the increase of the high-hazard minor use area. For example, consider the H-3 ratio in the example shown in Item (c) above:

Assume H-3 = 3,000 sq.ft $\frac{3,000}{7,500} = .40$

and if = 5,000 sq.ft. $\frac{5,000}{7,500} = .67$

By checking the calculations for the basic allowable area limitation, we see that a small increase in the H-3 area would result in this limit being exceeded, because the sum of the ratios was already at 0.95 as calculated in Item (c) above, without being the maximum basic allowable area allowed.

As was shown in Item (a) above, even if there was only one minor use in the building, for instance, an H-3 Occupancy in the CASE A example without the A-3 Occupancy, the maximum area allowed for the H-3 Occupancy would be its basic allowable area from Table No. 5-C and not the area resulting from the use of the 10 percent rule.

If the building was smaller in the overall area than the CASE A example, for instance, with an aggregate area of 45,000 sq.ft., and if the H-3 Occupancy was more than 10 percent of that area, 5,000 sq.ft., the unity rule could be applied without consideration of the relative hazards. On the other hand, in an unlimited area building, the unity rule would not control the higher hazard. Thus, there must another controlling requirement. The code provides no guide to this controlling criteria in such buildings.

> In the author's opinion, the direct means of dealing with this unlimited area condition in a manner consistent with the overall intent of this section of the code is to require that the unlimited area building unity equation (5-2) not use infinity for the denominator of the major use.

Therefore, when the Section 506 (b) provisions are used for a mixed occupancy building that does not exceed the total allowable area for the major use, the unity equation should be calculated using the total allowable area in determining the ratio of that major use and not the unlimited or infinite total allowable area.

By doing this, the relative hazard as well as the relative sizes of the spaces would be reflected in the evaluation, and excessively large hazardous uses would be avoided.

In the CASE C example, the basic allowable area calculation for the minor areas is:

$$\overset{\text{A-3}}{\frac{1{,}000}{9{,}100}} + \overset{\text{H-3}}{\frac{4{,}000}{7{,}500}} = .1 + .53 = .63 \text{ OK}$$

The unity rule calculation is:

$$\frac{1{,}000}{54{,}600} + \frac{4{,}000}{15{,}000} + \frac{45{,}000}{72{,}000} = .02 + .27 + .62 = .91 \text{ OK}$$

The unity rule is satisfied. Note that even small increases in the size of either minor-use area would have a considerable effect and possibly lead to the unity requirement being exceeded. (See Figure TA1-2)

iii. Summary of the mixed occupancies provisions and rules

1. Check for whether the aggregate area of the minor uses is less than 10 percent of that floor area of the building.

2. Check whether the basic allowable areas meet the Table No. 5-C allowables. Use the sum of the ratios when there is more than one minor use involved, this must be equal or less than 1.0.

3. If Items 1 and 2 above are satisfied, there is no need to go further except in unlimited area buildings.

4. If the aggregate area of the minor uses exceeds 10 percent, check the unity rule, equation 5-1.

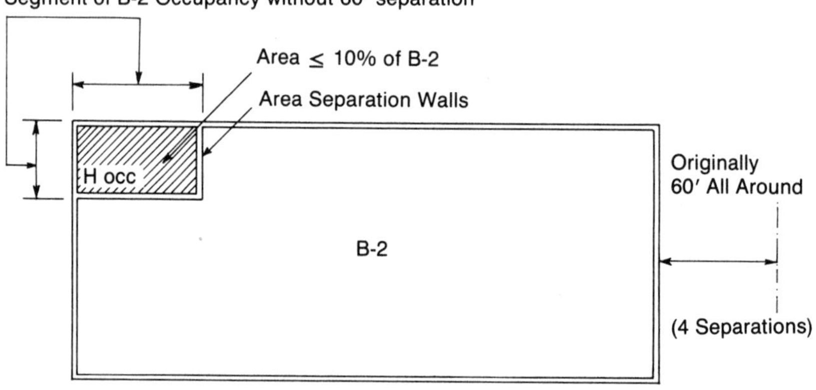

The addition of the small H Occupancy, into an unlimited area B-2 Occupancy building, results in the revocation of the "unlimited" area permitted under Section 506 (b) since the B-2 Occupancy no longer has 60-foot separation all around it.

REFERENCE: SECTION 506 (b)

FIGURE TA1-2 UNLIMITED AREA BUILDING WITH H OCCUPANCY ADDED

5. If the building design uses the unlimited area provisions of Section 506 (b), use equation 5-2 to check the unity rule.

6. If the building design uses the unlimited area provisions of Section 506 (b) and the aggregate area of the building is less than the total allowable area of the major use, use the unity rule equation 5-2 with, as the denominator of the major use, the total allowable area of that major use amd not infinity.

TECHNICAL APPENDIX TA-2
TYPE OF CONSTRUCTION ANALYSIS
TABLE NO. 17-A

This Technical Appendix discusses the provisions of Table No. 17-A regarding the types of construction and the relationship of the provisions therein.

TYPE V CONSTRUCTION

Starting with the least fire-resistive type of building construction, the Type V-N building in Table No. 17-A, no building elements other than shaft enclosures require hourly fire ratings. A check of the referenced Section 1706 reveals that, in fact, the Type V building's shaft enclosures need not be fire rated because:

- in a two-story building the shafts need no protection (Exception Nos. 1, 5 and 6)
- in a three-story building, either a shaft needs no protection or a sheet metal lining for a partial enclosure will suffice (Exception Nos. 3 and 6).

In the review of the concepts of Table No. 17-A, we will address only the major requirements and not those special items whose exceptions are cross-referenced to other portions of the code, as with the Type V shaft enclosures.

The Type V-N building is assigned the lowest allowable area in Table No. 5-C and the lowest allowable number of stories and overall height in Table No. 5-D for each occupancy group. Thus, the least fire-resistive building has the smallest allowable areas and the lowest allowable heights. These limitations mean that a fire in such a building would affect only a limited number of stories and occupants.

TYPE II-N and III-N CONSTRUCTION

Presumably, the other two nonfire-rated building types, Types II-N and III-N, would have similar restrictive heights and areas per Chapter 5. This, however, is not the case. The Table No. 17-A requirements — and the character of the buildings these two types of construction represent—will be discussed in light of the two main fire spread criteria of the code concept.

All Type II buildings are required to be constructed of noncombustible materials; i.e., the structure will not provide fuel to a fire. With this noncombustible requirement satisfied, the allowable area, but not the number of stories of the Type II-N building is permitted to be increased. A comparison of these two types of construction with the Type V-N building, using Tables No. 5-C and 5-D, shows the greater allowable area afforded to Type II buildings as a result of their noncombustible construction materials.

The noncombustible characteristic theoretically will limit the intensity of the fire and thus reduce the overall conflagration potential. Therefore, the allowable area for the Type II-N building is increased over that allowed for the Type V-N building. However, the lack of fire separations and protection for building support members within the building permits fire spread from floor to floor or collapse, if a bearing member were attacked by a fire. Thus, the number of allowable stories remains the same in the Type II-N building as in the Type V-N building.

The Type III-N building, however, has fire-resistive requirements for the exterior walls of the building. Although this type of building can be constructed internally of any type of material, combustible or noncombustible, the exterior wall has to be noncombustible.

The fire-resistive rating of the exterior wall elements will assist considerably in limiting conflagration potential from a fire either within the structure or from another building. Accordingly, the Type III-N building is considered on a par with the Type II-N building for allowable area. However, the exterior wall protection does not provide any additional safety within the building from either fire spread or internal collapse if interior support members are attacked by a fire. The number of stories for the Type III-N building is therefore the same as the Type II-N and V-N buildings.

TYPE II ONE-HOUR, III ONE-HOUR and V ONE-HOUR CONSTRUCTION

The three building types having at least a minimum one-hour fire-resistive requirement, Types II One-hour, III One-hour and V One-hour, are substantially more fire-resistive than the nonfire-rated types.

The Table No. 17-A provisions indicate that both the conflagration hazard and the internal fire spread or collapse hazard are mitigated by the one-hour construction requirement.

Accordingly, their allowable areas are greater than for the comparable nonfire-rated buildings. The three types of one-hour buildings are not considered equal to one another in their limitation of the conflagration hazard. The Type V one-hour building has neither the degree of exterior wall protection required for the Type III One-hour building nor the limitation of combustibility for the materials used to construct the Type II One-hour building. Therefore, the Type V One-hour building is permitted a lesser allowable floor area than the other two one-hour building types.

TYPE I and II-FR CONSTRUCTION

The component of the Type I and II-FR buildings are required to have substantially greater fire-resistive ratings than those of the one-hour buildings. Except for the roof and the interior nonbearing partitions, all the fire-resistive ratings for the Type II-FR building are for the most part double those of the one-hour structures. The allowable area is generally at least double those allowed for the one-hour buildings.

The hazard of interior fire spread or collapse is sharply reduced due to the minimum two-hour requirement for the floors, structural frame and interior bearing walls. As a result, for many of the occupancies the allowable number of stories in the Type II-FR building is greatly increased over that allowed for the one-hour buildings. The danger to the occupants and fire fighters in such a building is reduced because more time is available for evacuation and fire fighting.

The Type I building represents the highest type of fire-resistive construction because the fire rating for the entire structural support system is raised to three or four hours. The resultant reduction of the building collapse hazard is considerable. The code allows unlimited area and height of the Type I building for almost all occupancies because of the substantial fire resistance of the building.

The only exception to this unlimited allowable area applies to the Group H-1 and H-2 Occupancies. The code considers that the hazards associated with the H-1 and H-2 Occupancies could be such that even the fire-resistive requirements of the Type I building are insufficient to permit more than a 15,000 square-foot basic allowable area.

TYPE IV CONSTRUCTION

The remaining type of construction, Type IV, is an anomaly insofar as our prior rationale is concerned. This building type is also known as a Heavy Timber or HT type. It represents a construction type common for factories at the turn of the century: the mill building. This was a structure built with exterior walls of masonry and exterior openings protected by steel shutters. The interior was all wood of very heavy and substantial dimensions. The columns, beams and girders were massive timbers. The floors, because they had to support a heavy load of equipment or storage, were of heavy planking usually at least three inches thick and tightly joined.

The fire experience with these buildings indicated that a fire was usually contained within the structure. In most instances the heavy floor members helped slow the fire's spread from floor to floor and allowed evacuation and fire fighting to proceed. The massive columns and beams were slow to burn through and cause collapse. For these reasons, the Type IV or HT building is permitted the same allowable areas and stories as the Type II and III One-hour buildings.

However, the system of establishing fire-resistive ratings using the ASTM standard E-119 fire test procedure does not equate HT with one-hour construction, nor does the code. In this instance we are guided by experience rather than scientific rationale.

TA3
TECHNICAL APPENDIX 3
RESTRAINED VS UNRESTRAINED ASSEMBLIES
CHAPTER 43

The concept of restraint as it applies to fire-resistive assemblies will be discussed in this Technical Appendix. The code citations are in Section 4302 (b).

In the general discussion in Article 8 of Chapter 43, it was indicated that the temperature of the structural elements such as columns, beams and girders is used to determine the endpoint of the test. This became a generally required condition for horizontal structural elements after it was noted that several tests had been deemed successful even though they had "structurally" failed. An evaluation of the many fire tests conducted in the 1950s and 1960s clearly indicates that the main structural members in these tests had expanded under the heat from the furnace and were subjected to very high compressive thermal restraint from the test furnace.

The horizontal fire test furnace has two heavy steel beams enclosing the top of the furnace, which form a box-shaped ring that resists the forces that occur when a floor system expands during a test. These heavy furnace beams are capable of exerting sufficient reaction to the expansion of the test assembly to cause, shortly after the start of the fire test, what originally was to be a simple beam, i.e., a pin-ended member, to become a fixed-ended member. The fire test protocol requires that the member must be loaded to produce stresses comparable to the field conditions. When the end support and fixity conditions of the structural member change, the loading condition no longer meets that test criteria. The change from pin-end to fixed-ended conditions substantially reduces the test loading condition, particularly the maximum bending moment.

The solution to this fire test problem was to establish a two-track system of rating an assembly based on one fire test.

1. The first method uses the endpoint temperatures of 1100-1300°F as previously discussed. This method and the resultant test value is called the unrestrained value for the assembly. It

is a conservative value, independent of how the assembly is installed in the field.

2. The second method allows a restrained or higher hourly rating to apply, but requires that the method of providing the thermal restraint of the assembly in the actual building be certified by the structural designer as meeting the conditions attendant to such assemblies in the standard.

One further comment is necessary regarding the latter test condition of passage. The restraint that develops in the fire test and for which the structural design must provide evidence is not the restraint associated with continuous members or similar standard structural restraint. The fire test restraint is thermally induced and therefore will exist in addition to any structural design values that result from the normal design calculations. The structural designer should be aware of this difference and how to deal with it.

In the author's opinion, unless the designer is confident that both the design and field installations can be satisfied, the unrestrained fire resistance ratings should be used.

TECHNICAL APPENDIX 4
CHAPTER 43
FIRE TESTING PROCEDURES

This Technical Appendix will discuss the fire test procedures cited in Chapter 43 that form the basis of acceptance of fire-resistive assemblies.

The standard fire test is a severe performance requirement. It provides a means of comparing different configurations of materials and constructions under standardized test conditions. The ASTM E-119 test has its counterparts in other countries. They use similar fire exposure time-temperature curves. The test requires a minimum 100 square-foot sample for walls and 180 square-foot sample for floor and roof.

The fire test procedure originated in the early 1900s. Early tests consisted of measuring the amount, by weight, of the usual combustibles found in various occupancies. Duplicates of furnishings and other combustible loadings were placed in instrumented rooms that were then ignited. The time-temperature curves in these burn-outs were plotted, with repeated testing for confirmation. (See Figure TA4-1.)

Eventually, the replicas of the furnishings and other combustibles were replaced by wooden pallets that contained fuel loads equivalent to the materials found in real rooms. A wood pallet loading equivalent to 10 pounds of fuel per square foot was comparable to the furnishings in a room that would provide a one-hour fire exposure as measured by the time-temperature curve: 20 pounds per square foot for two hours.

To avoid needing a large room in which to make these tests, and to provide better control of the test procedure, the wood pallets were later replaced by gas burners. In the present tests, thermocouples are positioned in the furnace so that the time-temperature curve can be accurately duplicated by varying the rate of gas being consumed at a given moment.

The test sample is placed in close proximity to the burners with an orientation either horizontal or vertical, depending on whether it is material for a wall, floor, beam or column. Separate furnaces are used

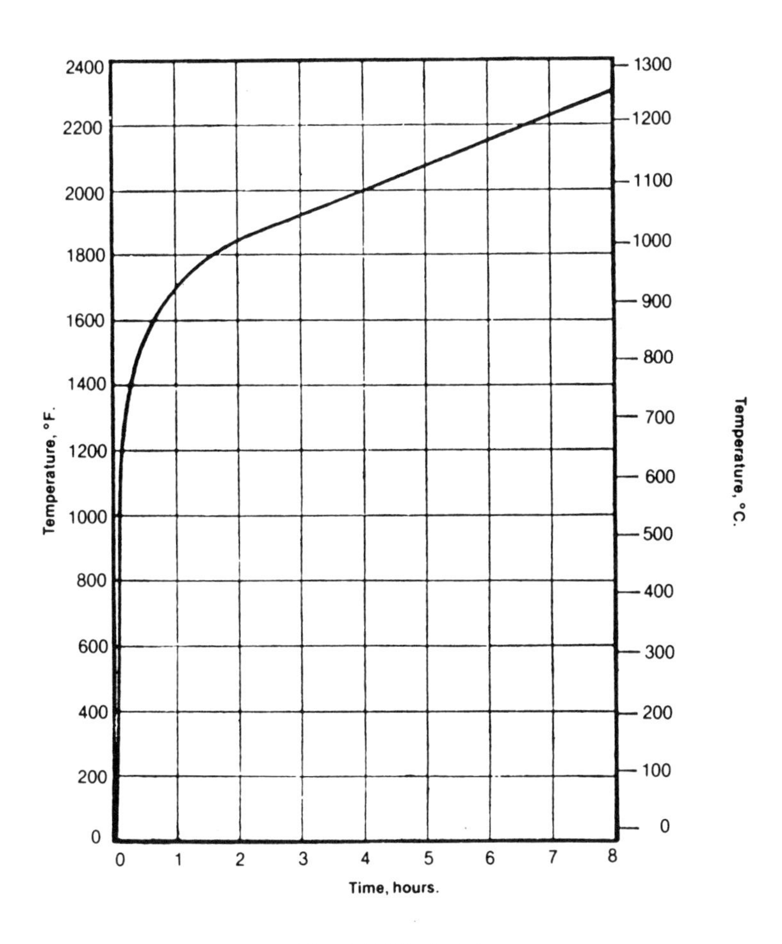

FIGURE NO. 43-1-1

REFERENCE: UBC STANDARD 43-1, FIGURE NO. 43-1-1
ASTM E-119

FIGURE TA4-1 STANDARD FIRE TEST TIME-TEMPERATURE CURVE

for floor-ceiling and roof-ceiling assemblies including beams and trusses.

In the vertical tests, the furnace burners are arranged vertically facing the test assembly. (See Figure TA4-2.) In the horizontal tests, the burners are situated below the test sample. Columns are subjected to fire from burners placed on all four sides.

The purpose of the test procedures is to evaluate the ability of the assembly to withstand exposure to the fire and to prevent the fire from breaching the barrier the assembly presents or to cause a collapse if the sample is a load-bearing member. To standardize these criteria, conditions of passage have been set up as part of the test protocol. These conditions establish the time or point in the fire test that an assembly "fails." These test endpoints are:

1. **For wall and floor systems**
   (See Figures TA4-3, TA4-4 and TA4-5.)

   - There should be no flame penetration.
   - The temperature of all thermocouples on the side away from the fire shall not exceed an average of 250°F above the initial room temperature (ambient).
   - The temperature on a single thermocouple shall not exceed 325°F above ambient within the time period sought for the assembly.
   - Cotton waste applied to any point on the unexposed surface should not ignite.
   - If the assembly is loadbearing, the load must be carried for the rating time period.

2. **For columns**, the endpoint is based on the critical surface temperatures at any cross-section, dependent on the materials used. (See the general discussion hereafter.)

3. **For beams and girders**, the critical temperatures are dependent on the end restraint of the members. This subject will be covered in detail in the following general discussion.

When the fire-resistive assembly involved in a proposed fire test is loadbearing, it is often considered too dangerous to subject the member to load during the test because a collapse could damage the test facility. It is also impractical to attempt to load large members, such as heavy

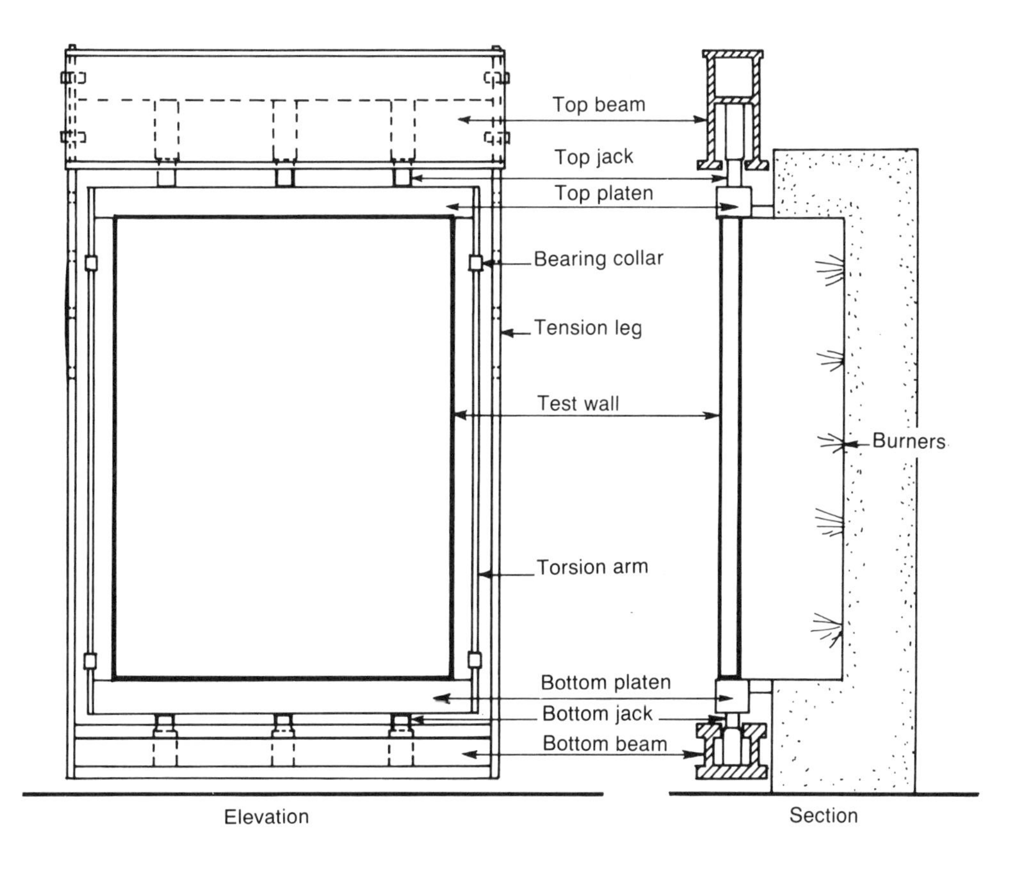

Specimen size must be minimum 100 S.F. The test can be either load-bearing or non-load bearing. Thermocouples are located within the furnace space, within the wall (if hollow) and on the non-fire side.

REFERENCE: SECTION 4302 (b), UBC STANDARD 43-1
FIRE TECHNOLOGY MAY 1979, PAGE 109

FIGURE TA4-2 STANDARD WALL FIRE TEST FURNACE

period, the fireproofing of the steel must be effective in preventing the steel from reaching temperatures above 1000 °F. (See Figure 8-8.)

The test conditions for columns are explicit. A failure condition is reached when there is an average temperature of 1000 °F on any cross-section of the member being tested or when any individual thermocouple reaches 1200 °F.

Beams and girders are rated by one of two methods, either:

- by use of endpoint temperatures as described for columns but with 1100 °F and 1300 °F as the respective temperature limits, or

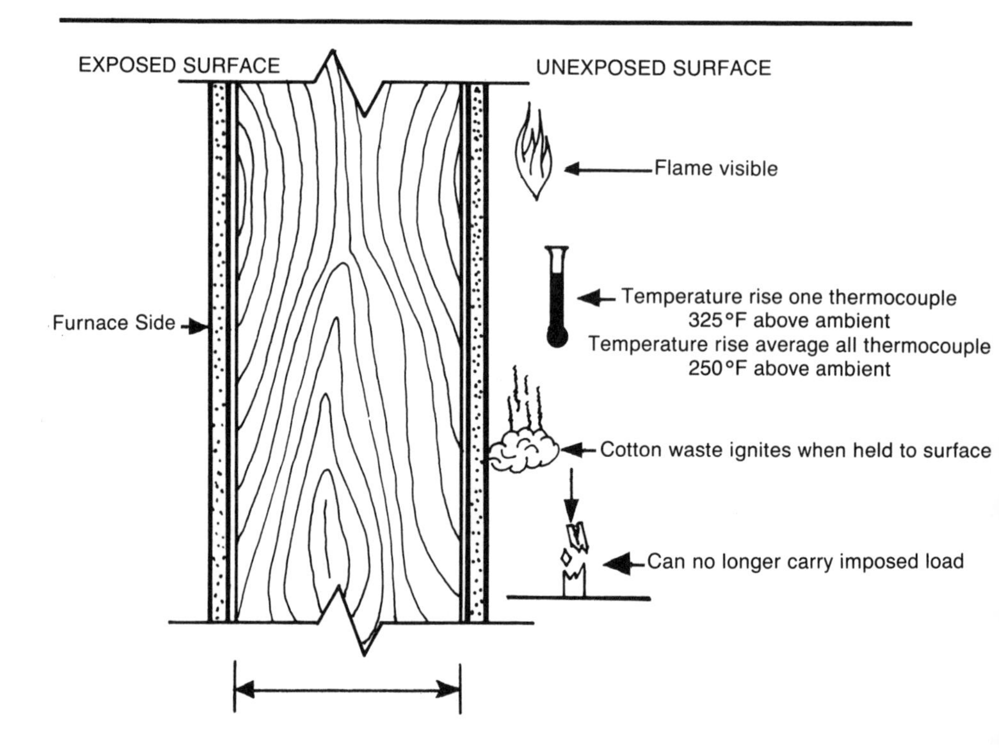

REFERENCE: UBC STANDARD 43-1

FIGURE TA4-3 WALL FIRE TEST—CONDITIONS OF PASSAGE

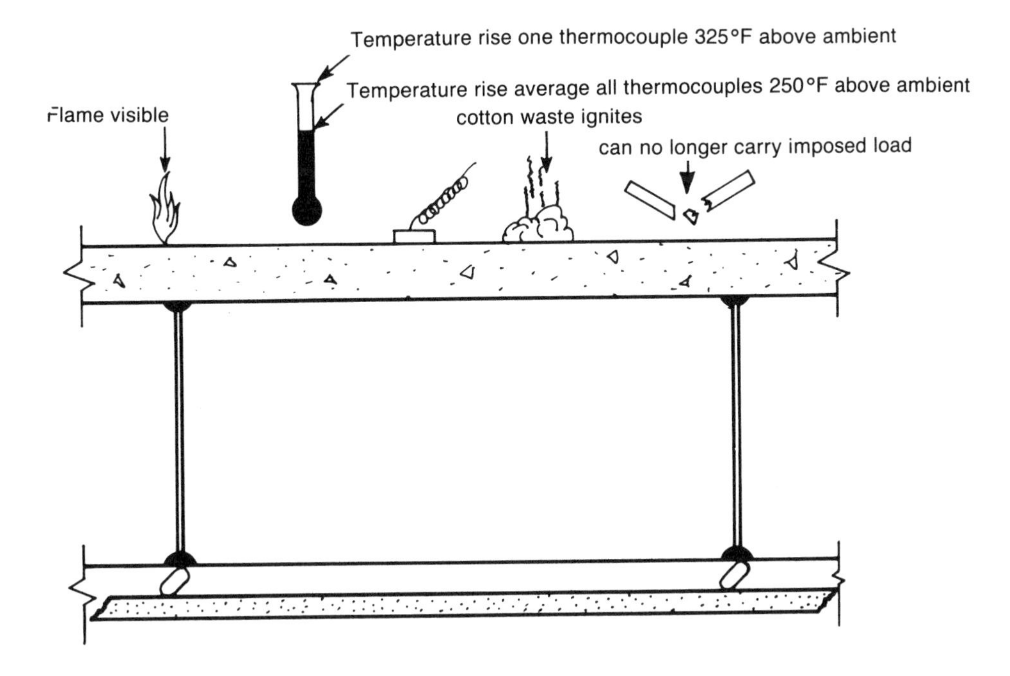

REFERENCE: UBC STANDARD 43-1

FIGURE TA4-4 FLOOR OR ROOF FIRE TEST—CONDITIONS OF PASSAGE

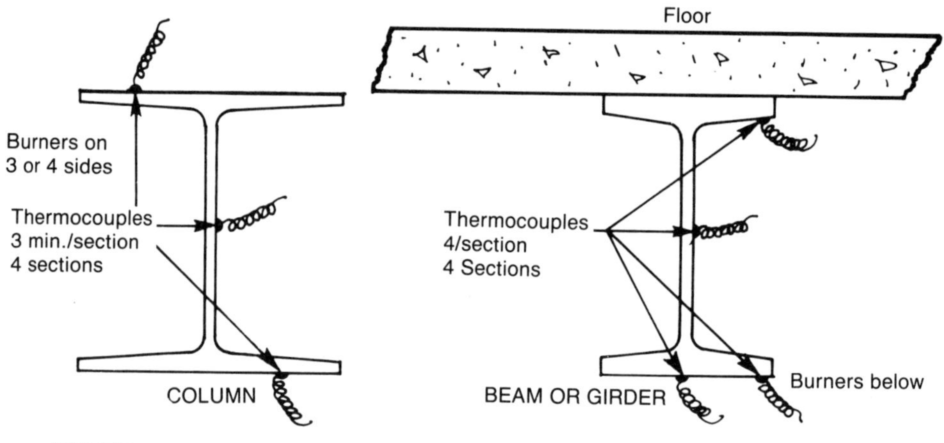

EITHER:
1. Carry applied load for rating period, or
2. a) Maximum temperature at any one thermocouple < 1200 °F
   b) Average temperature at any level of 4 sets of thermocouples < 1000 °F

UNRESTRAINED BEAM/GIRDER
1. The specimen shall have sustained the applied load during the classification period.
2. For steel beams the temperature of the steel shall not have exceeded 1300 °F at any location during the classification period nor shall the average temperature recorded by four thermocouples at any section have exceeded 1100 °F during this period.
3. For conventionally designed concrete beams, the average temperature of the tension steel at any section shall not have exceeded 800 °F for cold-drawn prestressing steel or 1100 °F for reinforcing steel during the classification period.

RESTRAINED BEAM/GIRDER
1. The specimen shall have sustained the applied load during the classification period.
2. The specimen shall have achieved a fire-endurance classification on the basis of the temperature criteria specified below of one half the classification of the assembly or one hour, whichever is the greater.
3. For specimens employing steel structural members (beams, open-web steel joists, etc.) spaced more than 4 feet on centers, the temperature of the steel shall not have exceeded 1300 °F at any location during the classification period nor shall the average temperature recorded by four themocouples at any section have exceeded 1100 °F during the classification period.
4. For specimens employing steel structural members (beams, open-web steel joists, etc.), spaced 4 feet or less on center, the average temperature recorded by all joist or beam thermocouples shall not have exceeded 1100 °F during the classification period.

REFERENCE: UBC STANDARD 43-1

FIGURE TA4-5 COLUMN, BEAM OR GIRDER FIRE TEST, CONDITIONS OF PASSAGE

columns and girder sections, because their design condition may involve hundreds of tons. Therefore, for these building elements, a set of conditions of passage takes into account the effect of elevated temperatures on the material being tested.

For example, structural steel's ultimate strength at temperatures above 1000°F is substantially reduced to the range of its yield and design stresses. At these elevated temperatures the load-carrying capacity of a steel member may no longer be able to support the load for which it was designed without serious distortion or collapse. Because the furnace temperature for a one-hour rating will reach 1700°F at the end of that time period, the fireproofing of the steel must be effective in preventing the steel from reaching temperatures above 1000°F. (See Figure TA4-6.)

The test conditions for columns are explicit. A failure condition is reached when there is an average temperature of 1000°F on any cross-section of the member being tested or when any individual thermocouple reaches 1200°F.

Beams and girders are rated by one of two methods, either:

- by use of endpoint temperatures as described for columns but with 1100°F and 1300°F as the respective temperature limits, or
- by using a variation that takes into account the thermal restraint provided for the member:

In the restrained test condition, the conditions of passage require the temperature limits be used only for one-half the desired hourly rating period, or one hour, whichever is the lesser time.

> In the author's and others opinion, the restrained values are difficult to regulate or control in practical application. The designer is therefore urged to consider using only unrestrained values in any design for a building.

For a further detailed discussion of the restrained/unrestrained test values, see Technical Appendix 3.

Ferrous materials other than structural steel have comparable endpoint temperatures:

- For prestressed steel, the value is 800°F.
- For reinforcing steel, the value is 1100°F.

Fire doors and windows are subjected to fire tests similar to those for walls. However, their conditions of passage are not as stringent as those for the fire-resistive assemblies, because endpoint temperature limitations are either not applicable or apply to certain fire doors and then only for the first 30 minutes of the test.

Fire doors and windows are subject to fire tests similar to those for walls. However, their conditions of passage are both more severe and less stringent in certain regards. The doors and windows are mandatorily subject to a fire hose stream impact test immediately after the fire test. In the ASTM E-119 fire tests when hose streams are required, they can be imposed either on the test sample after the full time period of the test or to a replica of the sample tested for one-half the test period.

On the other hand, the door and window test conditions of passage are not as restrictive, in that openings are allowed in the plane at right angles to the plane of the door or window. Thus, from a direct view of the sample there is no visible flame, but there can be openings due to bowing at right angles to that plane. In addition, endpoint temperature limitations are either not applicable or apply to certain fire doors and then only for the first 30 minutes of the test.

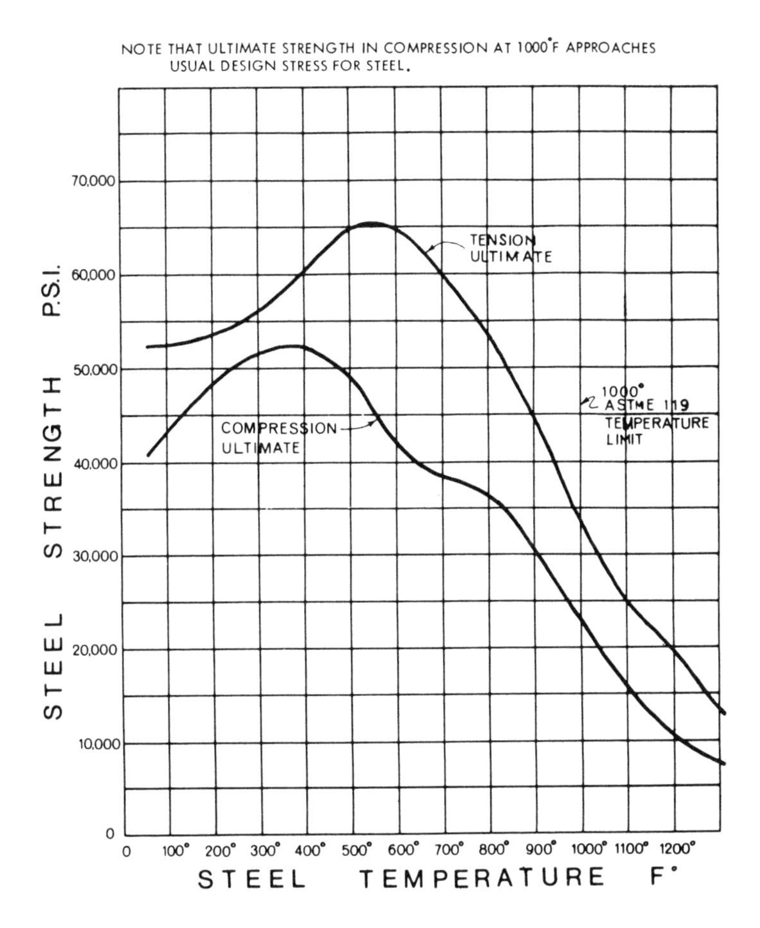

The graph indicates the values for A-36 structural steel. Other steels have similar relationships.

REFERENCE: SECTION 4302 (b), UBC STANDARD 43-1
CARBOLINE "SPECIFIERS GUIDE"

FIGURE TA4-6 STRENGTH VS. TEMPERATURE—STRUCTURAL STEEL

NOTES

TECHNICAL APPENDIX TA-5
SUGGESTIONS FOR RETENTION OF THE COMPARTITION OPTION FOR HIGH-RISE BUILDINGS

This Technical Appendix is directed to those jurisdictions and designers who wish to retain the code flexibility through use of the compartition concept. It represents the author's opinion on how this might be done in a local jurisdiction while avoiding possible legal exposure for the jurisdiction or the designer.

The committee that developed the high-rise safety provisions for the UBC conceived of safety being provided either by the sprinkler-based package or by having, in effect, two buildings side by side. In the latter instance, the connecting openings at each floor between the two buildings permitted a relatively simple way of leaving the endangered portion of the structure and reaching a safe haven.

In addition, the safe haven provided an excellent fire-fighting platform, easily accessible for the fire service by its elevator. This could be reached without the problems associated with accessing the involved portion of the building, either from the floor above or below the fire floor.

In the reason given for the code change, the cost of the sprinkler-based solution versus the compartition approach was cited as cheaper. Although this may be true, in the author's opinion it is not a valid reason for deleting a code-permitted alternative method of construction. Economic considerations regarding how to meet the code are the province of the owner and designer. It should not be a factor in setting minimal code requirements. The marketplace will determine the economic feasibility of the alternative.

Those jurisdictions wanting to retain code flexibility for compartition should consider doing so via a code amendment, in conjunction with the adoption of the 1991 UBC. Amending the code in this regard would be going against the action of this particular code change. Therefore, it would be prudent to require more than just the retention of the prior UBC text for compartition. This would avoid the argument that compartition was, by the present code, considered to be a less-than-equivalent level of safety.

The following list considers some of the additional items that would add to the level of safety for a compartmented building. (See Figure TA5-1.)

1. Reduce the area of a compartment from 15,000 sq. ft. to 10,000 sq.ft.
2. Require all stairways to be smokeproof enclosures.
3. Require that there be no unprotected openings within 10 feet of the compartition wall.
4. Require only ferrous or copper piping for either penetrations or inclusions in or through the compartition wall (pipe or conduit runs within the wall or shafts at the wall).
5. Require two-hour fire-resistive vestibules for the horizontal exit, with all openings protected with one-and-one-half hour fire assemblies that are automatic closing by action of not less than two smoke detectors on the same floor. The action of the detectors should also send an alarm through the fire alarm system to the central control station and to an outside supervisory station.
6. Require manual fire alarm pull boxes be tied to an outside central station.

In the deliberations attendant to any amendment to retain the compartment concept, at least one of the cited examples of the additional safeguards should be selected.

> In the author's opinion, in no instance are all items required for this amendment. Such an amended compartition provision would provide a higher level of safety for the overall proposed amendment than in the prior codes.

By increasing the regulatory requirements attendant to the compartition concept, the jurisdiction would avoid legal challenges to the adequacy of the level of safety. Retention of the concept provides the designer with flexibility in design that is often overlooked when code changes are deliberated.

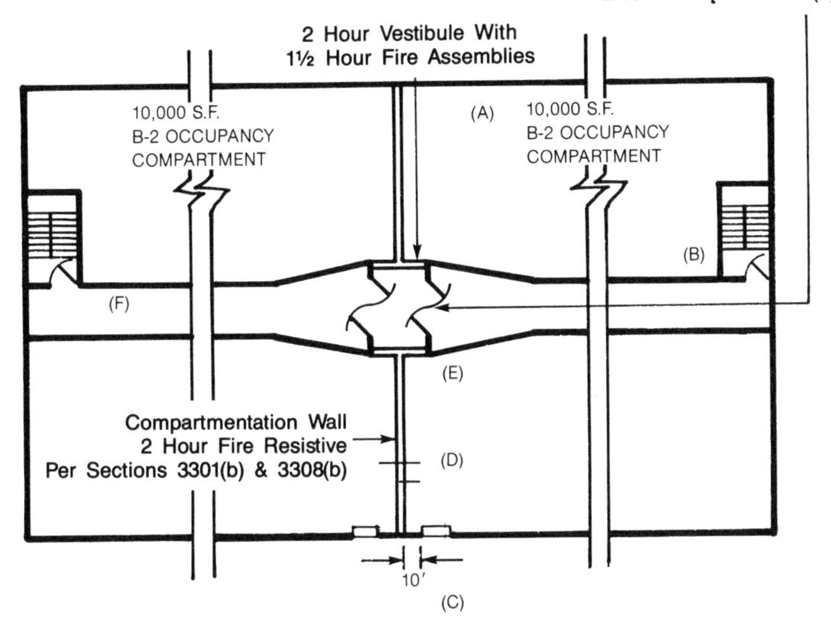

PLAN VIEW

GIVEN: HIGH RISE BUILDING - GROUP B, DIVISION 2 OCCUPANCY
10,000 S.F. / FLOOR MAXIMUM BETWEEN COMPARTMENTATION WALLS

INTENT: TO RETAIN, VIA CODE AMENDMENT, THE COMPARTMENTATION
ALTERNATIVE IN SECTION 1807(b)

Possible changes to UBC Section 1807(l) to raise level of safety of compartmentation concept. One or more to be selected as part of amendment consideration to retain compartmentation if desired by local jurisdiction. See plan view for location of referenced items.

A) Change maximum size of compartment from 15,000 sf to 10,000 sf
B) All stairways to be smokeproof enclosures.
C) Openings in exterior wall within 10′ of compartmentation wall shall be protected.
D) All pipe or conduit through, in or into the compartmentation wall shall be ferrous or copper.
E) At horizontal exit through compartmentation wall, provide two hour vestibule with one and one-half hour fire assemblies.
F) Fire alarm shall be connected to outside central station and central control station.

REFERENCES: SECTIONS 1807, 3301(b), 3304(b) & 3308(b)

FIGURE TA5-1 TYPES OF ADDITIONAL REQUIREMENTS FOR RETENTION OF COMPARTITION CONCEPT ALTERNATIVE IN HIGH-RISE BUILDINGS

TECHNICAL APPENDIX TA-6
CHAPTER 43
Penetration Fire Stops

This Technical Appendix provides some background to the penetraton fire stops used for sealing holes in fire-resistive assemblies for the installation of various pipes, conduit and other devices anbd materials.

The fire stops referred to herein and in the text of Article 8 use F and T ratings as the criteria of acceptability. The F and T ratings are not entirely new concepts to the code. They are comparable to the fire-resistive time periods commonly used in conjunction with fire-resistive assemblies based on UBC Standard No. 43-1. However,these ratings derive from a fire test usually conducted on a much smaller test sample using UBC Standard No. 43-6. The test is with the same time-temperature curve as is used in the UBC Standard No. 43-1. The new ratings are time values in hours and minutes as are fire-resistive ratings.

The test sample of UBC Standard No. 43-6 need only be large enough to provide a minimum of one-foot clearance between the penetration fire stop device and the furnace-enclosing frame. Thus, a three-foot-square sample would usually suffice.

Essentially, the F rating is comparable to the standard fire test criteria of passage discussed in Technical Appendix TA4 and in Article 8 of this Guide. That is, there should be no passage of flame through the entire test sample including the penetration device; no water should penetrate to the unexposed side during the hose stream portion of the test; and the temperature on the added thermocouple on the enclosure surrounding the penetration device should not exceed 325^0 above the initial surface temperature.

The F rating derives from the flame criterion of the ASTM standard.

The T rating is the time at which the temperature:

- on any portion of the penetrating item,
- the penetration device or

- any portion of the test assembly containing the penetrating item or penetration device exceeds the 325 ° rise above the initial temperature.

Examples of the F and T rating determination for Figures 8-13 and 8-14 of this Guide and the values found in the Underwriters Laboratories, Inc. listings are as follows:

UNDERWRITERS LABORATORIES, INC	F	T
System 1, Figure 8-13	2 hours	0 hour
System 7, Figure 8-14	2 & 3 Hours	Rating based on cables used. 1 1/2 hour to 3 hour

* See Underwriters Laboratories, Inc. *1991 Building Materials Directory*.

The UBC Standard No. 43-6 is based on ASTM E 814-83, with the addition of two required temperature measurements that are not in the ASTM standard. These added locations are noted in the figures that accompany the new standard. They are located on the nonfire side of the test assembly. One measures the temperature on the penetrating item, and the other, that of the surface penetrated adjacent to the fire stop.

The addition details and thermocouple locations added are shown in Figure TA6-1 and are contained in Figure No. 43-6-1 of the UBC standard.

Other important differences from the ASTM E 814 standard, aside from format, are:

- The omission of an Appendix.
- The requirement that the test be conducted with a positive pressure differential between the fire side and nonfire side of the assembly of at least 0.10 inch of water.
- Separating the through-penetration fire stop provisions from the preparation and conduct of the test. This was done to facilitate the introduction at some later date of membrane penetration fire stop provisions.
- The addition of a third criteria of passage, for the F rating, using the added thermocouple on the wall adjacent to the through-penetration fire stop assembly.

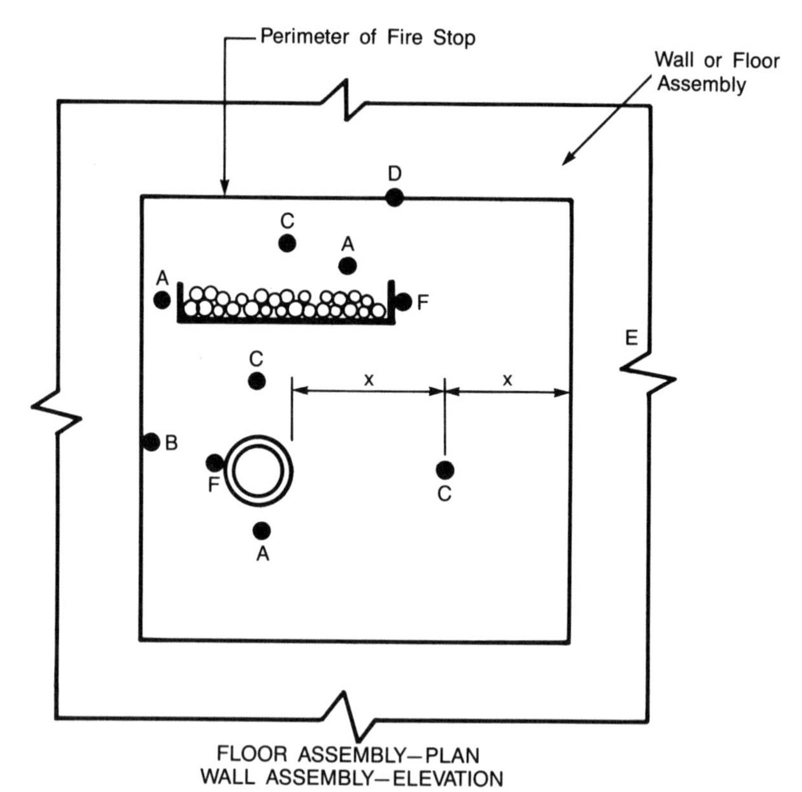

FLOOR ASSEMBLY–PLAN
WALL ASSEMBLY–ELEVATION

Legend:
A– At point on surface of the fire stop 1 in. from one through-penetration item for each type of penetrating item employed in the field of the fire stop. If the grouping of penetrating items through the test sample prohibits placement of the thermocouple pad, the thermocouple shall not be required.
B– At a point on the fire stop surface at the periphery of the fire stop.
C– At a minimum of three points on the fire stop surface approximately equidistant from a penetrating item or group of penetrating items in the field of the fire stop and the periphery.
D– At one point on any frame that is installed about the perimeter of the opening.
*E– At one point on the unexposed surface of the wall or floor that is a maximum of 12 inches from any opening.
*F– At one point on each type of through-penetrating item, 1-inch beyond thermal protection.
*G– At surface of thermal protection assembly, 1-inch beyond test sample.

*Thermocouples added or relocated from ASTM E-814 locations.

TEMPERATURE MEASUREMENT LOCATIONS
(FROM FIGURE NO. 43-6-1, U.B.C. STANDARD NO. 43-6)

REFERENCE: U.B.C. Standard No. 43-6, ASTM E814

FIGURE TA6-1 PENETRATION FIRE STOP FIRE TEST CONFIGURATION THERMOCOUPLE LOCATIONS

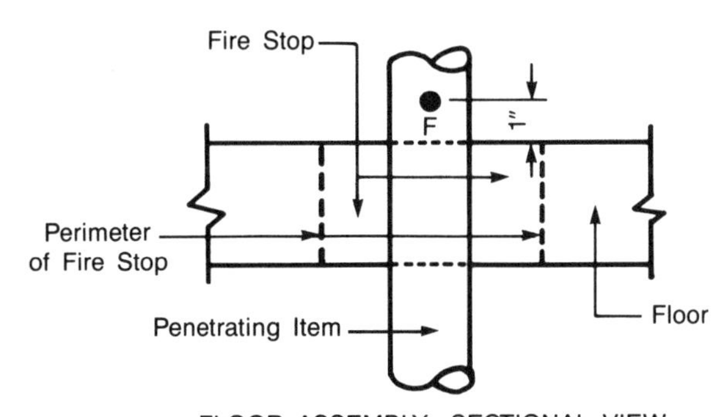

FLOOR ASSEMBLY—SECTIONAL VIEW

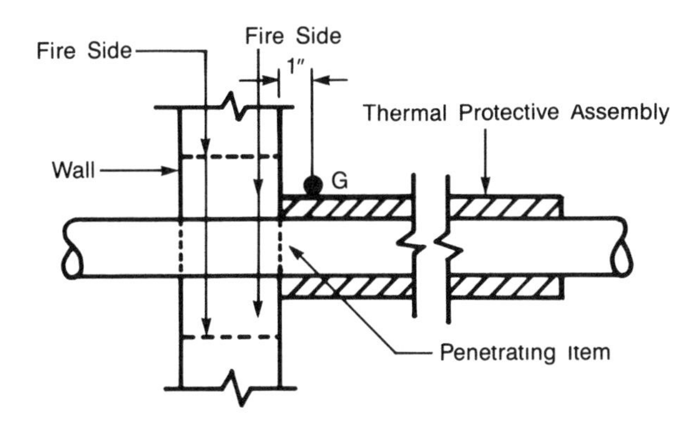

WALL ASSEMBLY—ELEVATION

NOTES

BIBLIOGRAPHY

Code, General

1991 edition of the Uniform Building Code published by ICBO[1]

UBC Code Application/Interpretation Manual published by ICBO[1]

Plan Review Manual published by ICBO[1]

Handbook to the Uniform Building Code by Vincent R. Bush published by ICBO[1]

Area Separation Walls Revisited by Paul Sheedy published in Building Standards Monthly Sept./Oct. 1982 by ICBO[1]

Wood—Detailing for Performance published by GRDA[4]

H-6 Design Guide to the Uniform Codes for High Tech Facilities published by GRDA[4]

Sprinkler Systems

NFPA Pamphlets 13, 13D and 13R Installation of Sprinkler Systems, Sprinkler Systems One- and Two-Family Dwellings and Mobile Homes published by NFPA[2]

Automatic Sprinkler Handbook published by NFPA[2]

Exits

NFPA Pamphlet 101 Life Safety Code published by NFPA[2]

Life Safety Handbook published by NFPA[2]

Fire Resistance

Fire Resistance & Sound Control Design Manual published by Gypsum Association 1603 Orrington Avenue, Evanston, IL 60201

Building Materials Directory published by ULI[3]

Fire Resistance Directory published by ULI[3]

Accessibility

American National Standard for Buildings and Facilities Providing Accessibility and Usability for Physically Handicapped People published by American National Standards Institute, Inc. 1430 Broadway, New York, NY 10018

Access for the Handicapped, The Barrier-Free Regulations for Design and Construction in all 50 States by Peter S. Hopf and John A. Raeber published by BNI[5]

California Architectural Barriers Laws and Interpretative Manual for Barrier-Free Design by John A. Raeber published by BNI[5]

Uniform Federal Accessibility Standards published by jointly by General Services Administration, Department of Defense, U.S. Postal Service and the Department of Housing and Urban Development of the Federal Government

Recent Social and Technical Development Influencing the Life Safety of People with Disabilities by Jake Pauls and Edwina Juillet in Building Standards Monthly May-June 1990 published by ICBO[1]

[1] International Conference of Building Officials, 5360 South Workman Mill Road, Whittier, CA 90601

[2] National Fire Protection Association, Batterymarch Park, Quincy, MA 02169

[3] Underwriters Laboratories, Inc., 333 Pfingsten Road, Northbrook, IL 60062-2096

[4] GRDA Publications, P.O. Box 1407, Mill Valley, CA 94941

[5] BNI Books, 3055 Overland Avenue, Los Angeles, CA 90034

INDEX

Page notation preceeded by letter A are in the Appendix.
Page notation preceeded by letter TA are in a Technical Appendix.

A